UNIVERSITY OF NORTH CAROLINA AT CHAPEL HILL

DEPARTMENT OF ROMANCE LANGUAGES

NORTH CAROLINA STUDIES
IN THE ROMANCE LANGUAGES AND LITERATURES

ESSAYS; TEXTS, TEXTUAL STUDIES AND TRANSLATIONS; SYMPOSIA

Founder: URBAN TIGNER HOLMES

Distributed by:

UNIVERSITY OF NORTH CAROLINA PRESS

CHAPEL HILL

North Carolina 27514

U.S.A.

NORTH CAROLINA STUDIES IN THE
ROMANCE LANGUAGES AND LITERATURES
Number 180

A QUANTITATIVE AND COMPARATIVE STUDY OF THE VOCALISM OF THE LATIN INSCRIPTIONS OF NORTH AFRICA, BRITAIN, DALMATIA, AND THE BALKANS

A QUANTITATIVE AND COMPARATIVE STUDY OF THE VOCALISM OF THE LATIN INSCRIPTIONS OF NORTH AFRICA, BRITAIN, DALMATIA, AND THE BALKANS

BY

STEPHEN WILLIAM OMELTCHENKO

CHAPEL HILL

NORTH CAROLINA STUDIES IN THE
ROMANCE LANGUAGES AND LITERATURES
U.N.C. DEPARTMENT OF ROMANCE LANGUAGES

1977

Library of Congress Cataloging in Publication Data

Omeltchenko, Stephen William.
 A quantitative and comparative study of the vocalism of the Latin inscriptions of North Africa, Britain, Dalmatia, and the Balkans.

 (North Carolina studies in the Romance languages and literatures; 180)
 Bibliography: p.
 1. Inscriptions, Latin. 2. Latin language — Vowels. I. Title: A quantitative and comparative study of the vocalism of the Latin inscriptions ...
II. Series.

PA3391.04   471'.7   77-1893
ISBN 0-8078-9180-0

I. S. B. N. 0-8078-9180-0

IMPRESO EN ESPAÑA

PRINTED IN SPAIN

DEPÓSITO LEGAL: V. 705 - 1977   I. S. B. N. 84-399-6388-2

ARTES GRÁFICAS SOLER, S. A. - JÁVEA, 28 - VALENCIA (8) - 1977

To my beloved father whose inspiration and memory have been the source of my love for learning since my tenderest years.

ACKNOWLEDGMENTS

My sincerest gratitude and appreciation go to Professor Mario A. Pei for his unselfish guidance and counsel, both during his tenure at Columbia University and after his retirement. My indebtedness to him goes back two decades when I was his student in Romance Philology and he first opened my eyes to the beauty and fascination of this wonderful discipline, a field to which I have since devoted my professional energies and avocational pursuits. For his knowledge, inspiration, and humaneness, I affectionately proffer these few words of debt to a gentleman, to "zio Mario."

Many thanks are also due Professor Lawton P. G. Peckham for his continual encouragement, for having read the entire manuscript, and for graciously lending me books from his personal library. Knowing him has been an awarding experience.

I thank Professor Charles W. Ferris, Jr., head of the Department of Humanities at the United States Merchant Marine Academy for persuading me to undertake my doctoral studies, and for his unstinting cooperation in questions of leave and classroom assignments.

And finally, my thanks and love to my wife, Maria, and our children, Bill Jr., Alexis, Chris, and Vicky, for their understanding of the problems inherent in the writing of "Poppy's book."

TABLE OF CONTENTS

Page

PRELIMINARY NOTE

CRITICAL SIGNS AND SYMBOLS

Almost all of the signs, symbols, and abbreviations found in the present work are readily available in most of the standard manuals dealing with General and Romance Linguistics. For a clear understanding of the few epigraphical notations used in the body of this study, we offer the following explanations:

(a) Letters enclosed in parentheses ( ) have been added by the particular editor to facilitate the reading of an abbreviation. The letters did not appear in the original inscription. Compare, for example, the formula *I(ovi) O(ptimo) M(aximo)*, where only *I. O. M.* appear on the inscription.

(b) Letters enclosed in square brackets [ ] have been supplied by the editor to facilitate a reading of letters which are missing or partially understandable because of weathering or damage, but which can be restored with certainty. Compare the word *[p]a[ce]*, for example, where the original inscription had four letters, but only one letter was clearly delineated, the other three being added by the editor with certainty because of the language of the inscription or a partial remains of a line or curve.

(c) Letters enclosed in a diamond < > have been used by the editor to show that the original inscription had a mistake, probably an oversight on the part of the stonemason. Compare the word *<p>erit*, where the original had *ierit.*

(d) A vertical line / is used to show that a division took place between lines on the original inscription.

(e) A word in parentheses after a particularly difficult spelling found in an inscription has been offered by us so as to show the reader the intended form. Compare, for example, the proper name *Quiriace* (=*Cyriacae*), where the epigraphical orthography may be confusing.

Letters enclosed in square brackets, parentheses, or diamonds, have not been included for tabulation.

An inscription from the collection *Inscriptiones Latinae Christianae Veteres*, edited by Ernst Diehl, with the additional designation of the letter N, signifies that the inscription in question comes from Diehl's notes and not from the numbered inscriptions in the corpus. Although there are 5,000 numbered inscriptions in Diehl's compendium, there are other pertinent inscriptions that are given for the informative knowledge they offer the reader. Compare, for example, the inscription given as *D.* 4323N, where the N means that the inscription is found in the Notes given by Diehl for inscription number 4323.

When a particular inscription is also found in the *Corpus Inscriptionum Latinarum*, this information is added to apprise the reader of this fact. An item such as *cives, RIB* 108, *CIL* VII 66, means that the word is found in our primary sources, in this case *The Roman Inscriptions of Britain*, as well as the seventh volume of the *Corpus Inscriptionum Latinarum*.

PART I
INTRODUCTION

Background and Nature of This Study

Of the multiple theories concerning Vulgar Latin,[1] two have emerged as the dominant themes. A summation of these two types is aptly given by Ernst Pulgram when he writes the following:

> First, there are theories which propose that there was, especially during the Empire and early Middle Ages, a linguistic unity of popular speech throughout the Roman and Romanized world; according to some scholars this unity dissolved in the 5th or 6th century of our era; according to others not before the end of the 8th or 9th century. Second, there are theories which insist on early dialectalization of Latin, or indeed maintain that there never was, outside of early Latium, a single unified Latin, or anything but a number of local dialects especially in the Romania outside of Italy.[2]

Between the most avid adherent of early dialectalization, F. George Mohl,[3] and the foremost proponent of Latin unity, Henri F. Muller,[4]

---

[1] Louis F. Sas, in *The Noun Declension System in Merovingian Latin* (Paris: Pierre André, 1937), p. 491, counts 19 definitions of Vulgar Latin.

[2] Ernst Pulgram, "Spoken and Written Latin," *Language*, 26 (1950), 458. This summary is repeated almost verbatim in Pulgram's later work, *The Tongues of Italy* (Cambridge, Mass.: Harvard University Press, 1958), pp. 312-13.

[3] Mohl's extreme view can best be summarized by his own words in his *Introduction à la chronologie du latin vulgaire* (Paris: E. Bouillon, 1899), p. 16, when he says that "Pour notre part, nous n'hésitons pas à considérer le latin provincial d'Italie comme la source presque exclusive de toutes les manifestations linguistiques attribuables au latin vulgaire de l'Empire romain; c'est là, c'est dans la prononciation sabine, volsque, hernique, pélignienne, osque, marse, picénienne, falisque qu'il faut chercher la cause première des langues romanes, et c'est dans ces dialectes qu'il faut rechercher les premiers germes de cette forme nouvelle de la latinité."

[4] H. F. Muller's statement in "A Chronology of Vulgar Latin," *Zeitschrift für romanische Philologie*, Beiheft 78 (Halle: Max Miemeyer, 1929), p. 50,

so many scholars have interspersed their thoughts that the modern researcher encounters a plethora of interpretations and contradictions which seem to indicate a chaotic situation. This multiplicity of opinions seems to be generated by the various sources used (inscriptions, documents, Classical Latin writers, late Latin authors, Latin grammarians, the Romance Languages, et al.) and the different methodologies utilized (searching of popular elements in the Latin writings themselves, reconstructions from the modern Romance languages, geographical dialectology, etc.). [5] The idea of a Vulgar Latin unity derived from the reconstruction of the modern Romance languages and dialects with the concomitant disregard for the importance of inscriptions and documents was couched in strong wording by W. Meyer-Lübke in his "Die lateinische Sprache in den romanischen Ländern," in Gröber's *Grundriss der romanischen Philologie* (Strassburg: Karl J. Trübner, 1888), I, 359. His view was modified in the second edition of Gröber's *Grundriss* but the influence of Meyer-Lübke and his neo-grammarian reconstructionist views were a powerful force for the ensuing decades. [6] Although many scholars have considered the reconstructionists' emphasis of a unitary Latin as being too abstract and monolithic, others have considered it as a basic premise in the understanding of the development of the Romance languages. [7]

---

that "We do not find before the IXth century the background apparently necessary for the dialectalization that effectively took place in the Romance Languages of the three important western regions" was probably meant to apply only to Spanish, French, and Italian and was not intended to cover all of Romania.

[5] Cf. Helmut Schmeck, *Aufgaben und Methoden der modernen vulgärlateinischen Forschung* (Heidelberg: Carl Winter, 1955), p. 7, and B. E. Vidos, *Manuale di linguistica romanza* (Geneva: Olschki, 1959), pp. 3, 5.

[6] It is interesting to note that Silva Neto in his *História do latim vulgar* (Rio de Janeiro, 1957), p. 57, considers the prestige of Meyer-Lübke as one of the main reasons for the eclipse of Mohl's theory. The influence of Meyer-Lübke on other scholars is also mentioned by Tovar in his "A Research Report on Vulgar Latin and Its Local Variations," *Kratylos*, 9 (1964), 113.

[7] Mohl, p. 269; A. Rosetti, *Istoria limbii romîne*, 4th ed. (Bucharest: Editura Ştiinţifică, 1964), p. 56. It must also be remembered that Schuchardt, whose epoch-making work *Der Vokalismus des Vulgärlateins* issued in the period of Vulgar Latin studies, stood aloof from comparative reconstructions and availed himself of Latin documents, inscriptions, and modern Romance material. For this same anti-reconstructionist view, cf. also Vidos, p. 209, and C. Tagliavini, *Le origini delle lingue neolatine*, 3rd ed. (Bologna: Patròn, 1962), p. 293. On the other side of the ledger, in addition to the influential Meyer-Lübke, we also have a strong adherent in T. Maurer, *O problema*

The American linguist, Robert A. Hall, although an avowed re-constructionist, attempts to modify the stigma attached to the neo-grammarian, reconstruction concept of a unitary Vulgar Latin by stating in a very important article entitled "The Reconstruction of Proto-Romance," in *Language*, 26 (1950), 7, that:

> It must be emphasized that our reconstruction does not lead us to set up a completely "unified" or "unitary" Proto-Romance, as is often assumed. We do not have to suppose absolute uniformity for proto-languages, any more than for any actually observed language. Our Proto-Romance was un-doubtedly a composite of several dialects of the Latin spoken at the end of the Republican period.

In the same article, Hall calls for (p. 26) a conciliatory attitude on the part of the proponents of the conflicting methodologies saying, "We must emphasize especially that synchronic analysis, comparative reconstruction, and the direct study of historical data such as do-cuments and texts are by no means mutually exclusive. They are but different angles from which the same material — human speech and its history — can be approached, and all are equally essential." [8]

In recent decades Romance scholars have been more inclined to accept the theory of local varieties. [9] One of the most important de-velopments in the breakdown of the unitary theory has been the work of Heinrich Lausberg in his distinctions of the various vocalic systems that exist in the Romance world. He explains four distinct vocalic

---

do latim vulgar (Rio de Janeiro: Livraria Acadêmica, 1961), p. 55. Bloom-field's equating in his *Language* (New York: Holt, Rinehart and Winston, 1933), p. 302, of reconstructed Primitive Romance with "Vulgar Latin" is termed (p. 7) a "misconception" by Hall in his same article "Reconstruction." Väänänen, in his *Introduction au latin vulgaire* (Paris: Klincksieck, 1967), p. 6, rightly distinguishes Vulgar Latin from "roman commun" or "proto-roman" (primitive Romance) when he writes that "ils s'appliquent, en prin-cipe, à une forme de langue reconstituée d'une part, et d'autre part ils ex-cluent l'étude des phénomènes qui faisaient partie du fond populaire du latin, mais n'ont pas survécu en roman." Like other scholars in the field, we prefer to replace "Vulgar Latin" with the terms "spoken Latin" or "Um-gangsprache" but like them, too, we will maintain the misleading term "Vulgar Latin" for the sake of convenience.

[8] For a similar view of the importance of comparing and coordinating the results of the different methods, see Sofer, *Zur Problematik des Vulgär-lateins: Ergebnisse und Anregungen* (Vienna: Gerold, 1963), p. 40.

[9] Tovar, p. 116.

systems that are the basis of the various primitive qualitative systems of Romance. We will briefly describe these distinct vocalic systems in accordance with Lausberg's views. [10]

A. *The so-called "Vulgar Latin" or Italic qualitative system:*

Quantity in Classical Latin: ī ĭ ē ĕ ā ă ŏ ō ŭ ū

Quality in Vulgar Latin: i ẹ ę a ǫ ọ u

As to the extent of this Italic qualitative system, Lausberg says (p. 210):

> Esta pronunciación de las vocales se impuso también en la pronunciación vulgar de la ciudad de Roma y se extendió sobre una vasta zona del occidente del Imperio. El 'sistema cualitativo itálico' alcanza la siguiente extensión en el románico: Italia central, parte norte del sur de Italia (Campania, Abruzzos, norte y centro de Apulia hasta Brindis, norte de Lucania), norte de Italia, Dalmacia, Istria, Retorromania, Galorromania, Iberorromania.

We now come to the equating of this vocalic system with the misunderstanding of what the Vulgar Latin vocalic system was, an equation that has been an extremely important factor in the underestimation of Vulgar Latin differences. Lausberg writes in strong terms about the excessive adherence to this one particular vocalic system, almost to the exclusion of the other systems, when he writes (p. 210):

> Como —prescindiendo del rumano— todas las lenguas literarias románicas se basan en este sistema (sistema cualitativo itálico), éste desempeña un papel fundamental en la enseñanza actual de las lenguas romances. Por ello, con frecuencia se le designa, abusivamente, como *el* [11] sistema vocálico 'del latín vulgar' sin más, aunque consta que jamás hubo un

---

[10] In the following discussion and hereafter, we will use the Spanish translation *Lingüística románica*, 2 vols. (Madrid: Editorial Gredos, 1966) of the original *Romanische Sprachwissenschaft*, 3 vols. (Berlin: Walter de Gruyter, 1956-63).

[11] The underlining is mine to give the force of the original German: "Es wird deshalb missbräuchlich oft als das schlechthin 'vulgärlateinische' Vokalsystem bezeichnet," ... (p. 145).

sistema vocálico unitario en el latín vulgar, teniendo, por tanto, los sistemas que a continuación vamos a presentar igual derecho al calificativo de 'latino-vulgares.' [12]

B. *The archaic system in Sardinia, Lucania, and Africa*:

The archaic system, characterized by the maintenance of the Latin quantities, is schematized as follows (p. 212):

Classical Latin Quantity: ī ĭ ē ĕ ā ŏ ō ŭ ū

Archaic System: i e a o u

The extent of this quantitative system is interesting since, although it is found in Campidanese and Logudorese (as well as in Nuorese), Gallurese and southern Corsican, it is also found in areas not geographically joined to Sardinia. [13]

Este sistema vocálico arcaico se conservó —sin unión geográfica con Cerdeña— incluso en una zona retirada de la Península italiana (franja norte de Calabria, sur de Lucania), y en una faja montañosa (Monte Papa, Monte Pollino) que va desde el Golfo de Policastro hasta el mar Jónico (desembocadura del Agri). También el latín africano tenía vocalismo 'sardo,' como prueban los gramáticos (San Agustín, Consencio) y las palabras que han quedado en berberisco (*akiker* < *cicer, ulmu* < *ulmu*. Asimismo, los préstamos latinos del vascuence (*pike* < *pice, urka* < *furca*) revelan un vocalismo 'sardoafricano.' [14]

---

[12] Hall gives a very similar point of view when he writes (p. 7): "But it [Vulgar Latin or Proto-Italo-Western Romance] will not work for Eastern (Balkan) Romance or for Southern Romance (Sardinian, Sicilian, Calabrian, Lucanian), which are in general conveniently neglected, or passed over with the remark that they show divergent developments from 'Vulgar Latin.'"

[13] Lausberg, *Lingüística*, I, 212-13.

[14] Since the present work is particularly concerned with African Latin, British Latin, Balkan Latin, and Dalmatian Latin, it may be well to mention the fact that the examples given for the maintenance of Latin *i* and *u* (*akiker* < *cicer* and *ulmu* < *ulmu*) in Berber as proof of African Latin representing the archaic system are probably taken from Hugo Schuchardt's pioneering article "Die romanischen Lehnwörter im Berberischen," *Akademie der Wissenschaften in Wien*, Sitzungsberichte, 188 (1918), 1-82. Although the examples adduced are adequate, there are others which do not show this development. Compare, for example, the following Latin words in Berber which do not fit into this convenient scheme: *ae* to *ĕ* to *i*: *aesculus* >

C. *The compromise system of eastern Lucano and Balkan Romance (pp. 213-14):*

Ambos sistemas vocálicos [the Italic qualitative system and the archaic quantitative system] entraron en contacto en el sur de Italia. En el sudeste de Italia se llegó a la formación de un sistema de compromiso, consistente en adoptar el ʿsistema itálicoʾ para las vocales palatales, mientras que en las vocales velares se mantuvieron, al parecer, durante más tiempo las cantidades del latín clásico, acabando finalmente por fundirse sin diferencia cualitativa como en el ʿsistema arcaico.ʾ

Classical Latin Quantity: ī ĭ ē ĕ ā ă ŏ ō ŭ ū

Compromise System: i ẹ   ę   a   o   u

Este sistema de compromiso se ha conservado hasta el día de hoy en una zona-reducto de la montaña del este de Lucania (en torno a Castelmezzano, al oeste de Matera). Hay que suponer que antiguamente abarcaba una zona mucho más vasta y que llegaba a la costa del Adriático, pues con-

---

isker; ĭ > *e: pirus* > *tiferest* (with the Berber feminine article *te-* or *ti-* prefixed; *a-* is the masculine article); *e* > *i: celsa* > *tkilsit; ŏ* > *u: hortus* > *urthu, pŏrta* > *tabburt.* Since Schuchardt himself did not consider his article as definitive ("Für das Berberische fehlte es mir an Vorarbeiten verschiedener und sehr wesentlicher Art und so wäre der Vorwurf der Verfrühtheit nicht unangebrache") (p. 4), and since he did not take into consideration the chronological factor ("Die Bezeichnungen Romanisch und Berberisch, wie sie im Titel dieser Schrift miteinander verbunden sind, gebrauche ich im weitesten Sinne") (p. 5), it would be hazardous to consider the examples brought forth from Berber as proof of African Latin having the archaic vocalic system. Wartburg in his *Die Ausgliederung der romanischen Sprachraume* (Bern: A. Francke, 1950), p. 31, says with respect to final -*s,* that "über das Latein Nordafrikas haben wir, mit Bezug auf das -*s*, keine eindeutigen Nachrichten, und aus den lateinischen Elementen in den Berbermundarten sind, soviel ich sehe, keine sichern Rückschlusse zu gewinnen" and this scepticism may also be extended to vowels of Berber loanwords for an understanding of the vocalic system of the Latin of North Africa. Karl Sittl in his *Die lokalen Verschiedenheiten der lateinischen Sprache mit besonderer Berücksichtigung des afrikanischen Lateins* (Erlangen: Andreas Deichert, 1882), p. 67, had, however, pointed to the keeping apart in African inscriptions of the *ŭ* and *ō*: "Bei genauer Betrachtung unterscheidet sich [Africa] wesentlich von der anderer Ländern: so ist der sonst überall so häufige Wechsel von U and O sehr selten, zumal in Flexion, wo U für O nie und O für U nur zweimal und blos in Numidien eintritt." Vidos likewise accepted (p. 195) the separation of *ĭ, ē* and *ŭ, ō*. The problem definitely needs to be investigated more thoroughly before a final verdict can be given.

tinúa al otro lado del Adriático en el románico de los Balcanes, y aun hoy constituye la base del vocalismo rumano.

D. *The Sicilian System (p. 216):*

En Sicilia, en Calabria [except in the extreme northern strip], en el sur de Apulia (al sur de Brindis), esto es, principalmente en una región de fuerte adstrato o sustrato griego, la reducción del vocalismo cuantitativo del latín clásico se realizó de manera que primeramente latín clásico ē ō coincidieron con latín clásico ĭ ŭ en las cualidades *i̯ *u̯; después *i̯ *u se confundieron con latín clásico ī ū (> i u̯) en las uniformes *i u*:

Classical Latin Quantity: ī ĭ ē ĕ ă ŏ ō ŭ ū
Sicilian Qualities: i ẹ a ọ u

Aside from the linguistic reasons adduced by Lausberg, we have another analysis, likewise essentially linguistic in its outlook, of early differentiation of Latin by Georges Straka [15] and Elise Richter, [16] strong proponents of a relative chronology. On the basis of his analysis, Straka comes to the conclusion that "la différenciation du latin parlé selon les régions et, en conséquence, les débuts de l'individualisation et de la formation des divers idiomes romans remontent jusqu'au IIe siècle de notre ère, sinon encore plus haut." [17]

Other than the linguistic reasonings for differentiation on the basis of the various vocalic systems and relative chronology, most other

---

[15] Straka's contributions to the theory of relative chronology are presented in his articles "La Dislocation linguistique de la Romania et la formation des langues romanes à la lumière de la chronologie relative des changements phonétiques," *Revue de Linguistique Romane*, XX (1956), 249-67, and "Observations sur la chronologie et les dates de quelques modifications phonétiques en roman et en français prélittéraire," *Revue des Langues Romanes*, LXXI (1953), 247-307.

[16] Richter's ideas are incorporated in her work, "Beiträge zur Geschichte der Romanismen: I. Chronologische Phonetik des Französischen bis zum Ende des 8. Jahrhunderts," *Zeitschrift für romanische Philologie*, Beiheft 82 (Halle: Max Niemeyer, 1934). Of importance to our work is her statement (p. 4): "Die chronologische Darstellung erweist, dass viele Veränderungen früher eingetreten sind, als im allgemeinen angenommen wird. Sie zerstört die Vorstellung einer einheitlichen lateinischen Sprache, einer lateinischen κοινή, die viele Gelehrte als Ausgangspunkt der romanischen Sprachen voraussetzen."

[17] Straka, "Dislocation," p. 254.

scholars have to resort to logical, geographical, ethnical, cultural, historical, or social bases for their interpretations. A typical example of a non-linguistic, logical basis for differentiation is given by Palmer: [18]

---

[18] L. R. Palmer, *The Latin Language* (London: Faber and Faber, 1954), p. 174. A similar view is expressed by Gerhard Rohlfs, *Vom Vulgärlatein zum Altfranzösischen* (Tübingen: Max Niemeyer, 1960), p. 21. Alwin Kuhn, *Die romanischen Sprachen* (Bern: A. Francke, 1951), I, 80, gives an exhaustive summary of the various factors causing differentiation. For further discussion of differentiation on the basis of various influences see, among others, Väänänen, *Introduction*, p. 22; for the importance of the cultural factor, see Rohlfs, *Romanische Philologie*, 2nd ed. (Heidelberg: Carl Winter, 1966), I, 181; Wartburg emphasizes the social differences in *Ausgliederung*, pp. 21-22, *Les origines des peuples romans* (Paris: Presses Universitaires de France, 1941), p. 56, *Problèmes et méthodes de la linguistique*, 2nd ed. (Paris: Presses Universitaires de France, 1963), p. 28, the substratum in *Ausgliederung*, p. 82, *Origines*, p. 63, the importance of the Germanic invasions in *Ausgliederung*, pp. 85, 187, 191, *Problèmes*, pp. 177, 238. Meillet stresses the Gaulish influence on the innovations of the Latin of Gaul in *La Méthode comparative en linguistique historique* (Paris: Honoré Champion, 1966), p. 80; Sofer in his article "Die Differenzierung der romanischen Sprachen," *Die Sprache*, II (1950-52), 24, 36, mentions the ethnic and historical aspects; for a cultural and political interpretation of the importance of the third century, see Puşcariu, *Études de linguistique roumaine* (Cluj-Bucharest: Imprimeria Naţională, 1937), p. 100; see Pulgram, *Tongues*, p. 260, for a socioeconomic approach; Densusianu in his *Histoire de la langue roumaine* (Paris: Ernest Leroux, 1901), I, 51, 234, 240-41, attributes great importance to the lack of schools in the Balkan Peninsula, the substratum, the Slavic invasions; Löfstedt, *Late Latin* (p. 39), conjectures on the basis of the geographical extent of the Roman Empire; for innovations on the basis of areal considerations, see Bàrtoli, *Introduzione alla neolinguistica* (Geneva: Olschki, 1925); see Stolz and Debrunner, *Geschichte der lateinischen Sprache*, 4th ed. (Berlin: Walter de Gruyter, 1966), p. 126, for their insistence on the influence of the substratum, chronology of Romanization and later historical development; for a logical interpretation of the need for dialectalization on the basis of chronological and geographical factors, see Sittl, pp. 1, 43; Migliorini, *The Italian Language* (London: Faber and Faber, 1966), pp. 18, 20, 31, points out the loss of prestige and the breaking up of communications in the third century as instrumental in the creation of innovations; Mohrmann, *Études*, II, 146, points out the general and special tendencies in the process of differentiation: the substratum, the date of the Roman colonization, the social position of the colonizers, the isolation of the area, the existence of bilingualism, the influence of the superstratum, the decrease of Rome's centralizing power; Silva Neto expresses the "common sense" attitude of differentiation: "O bom senso deixa-nos fora de dúvidas que nas várias províncias o latim tomava aspecto próprio, colorido peculiar," (p. 29) and "O latim provincial que, sem dúvida, havia de apresentar colorido dialectal." (p. 46). Although the opinions of scholars on this intricate problem of differentiation of Latin can be traced almost indefinitely, we will finish our list of references with the words of Pulgram, *Tongues*, when he says (p. 407):

Latin, like all languages, had continued to evolve, and it is certain that the Latin of the settlers of the third century B.C. differed from that of the legionaries of Caesar in the first century B.C. and of Trajan in the second century A.D. If we add to this the immense variety in race, language, and culture among the subjugated peoples and the notable differences in Roman policy towards them, the philologist would confidently expect to observe considerable differences of dialect in a language spread over so vast an area and acquired as a foreign language by peoples of such differing backgrounds.

The proponents of a late dialectalization or of a relative unity of Latin also have to use non-linguistic reasonings in their interpretation of the various factors. For the most part, these scholars are governed by the relative political stability of Roman administration in the various parts of the Empire, the open communications and constant interchanges between Rome and the outlying provinces, and the unifying influence of the Church which replaced Roman military power after the downfall of the Western Empire in the year A.D. 476.

With all the acrimonious writings, contradictions, and recantations, [19] it is striking to find the conciliatory view as expressed by Väänänen (*Introduction*, p. 26):

"No wonder, then, that those who consider only what is written marvel at the uniformity and the lack of dialectalization of the language through the Empire down to the eighth century — a uniformity which contradicts all sensible expectations and all that we know of the ways of human speech, whose outstanding quality is change, notably that of disintegration of an idiom through the agencies of longevity, expansion, and superimposition upon multiple linguistic substrata."

[19] It is interesting to note that Mohl, a very strong advocate of early dialectalization, has to admit (p. 23) even in his seminal work *Introduction à la chronologie du latin vulgaire* that "sans doute le principe de l'unité du latin vulgaire ... est en soi-même un principe juste et excellent et qui, croyons-nous, doit rester l'axiome fondamental de toute étude sérieuse sur les origines des langues neo-latines." Sittl, who formulated his theory of early dialectalization of Latin at the age of twenty, and who expressed (p. iii) the hope that "eine erschöpfende Behandlung des Themas [of local variations] wird frühestens in zehn Jahren, wenn das grosse Inschriftenwerk, fertig vorliegt und eine hundert neue Monographieen unsere Kenntnis des Lateinischen noch mehr erweitert haben, möglich sein" later recanted this view in *Bursian-Müller*, 68 (1892), 226 ff. Kroll, in his article "Das afrikanische Latein," *Rheinisches Museum für Philologie*, 52 (1897), 569-90, on learning of Sittl's recantation, had hopes that the latter's original theory would be abandoned and that no other scholar would bring up the subject.

En fait, les deux thèses, la thèse unitaire et celle qui veut
que le latin ait commencé à se différencier selon les régions
de très bonne heure, voire dès son introduction dans les provinces conquises, ne sont pas aussi opposées et inconciliables
qu'elles semblent l'être à première vue. L'unité du latin postclassique et tardif dans ses grandes lignes, du moins dans sa
forme écrite, est un fait indéniable, puisque il est démontré
par l'analyse des textes. Certes, les faits que les romanistes
ont établis et dont ils supposent l'existence dans la langue
parlée de telle ou telle région dès le IIIe ou le IIe siècle,
sans que la langue des documents écrits les ait encore adop-
tés, parlent en faveur d'une tendance ancienne et toute na-
turelle à différencier localement le latin vulgaire. Mais cette
différenciation ne devait pas aller très loin, du moins, au
début, à l'époque dont il s'agit. Les faits allégués sont en
effet encore assez limités en nombre et ils pouvaient ne pas
être très avancés au point de vue de leur évolution, surtout
physiologique, mais aussi morphologique, sémantique, syn-
taxique, etc., de sorte qu'entre les différentes régions attein-
tes par ces changements locaux, l'aspect général de la langue
parlée, malgré ces amorces de différenciation, ne devait pas
être à cette époque très varié.

Although there is a welter of controversial writings on the vexing
problem of the differentiation of Latin among the various schools
of thought, there is a paradoxical unanimity in the opinion of most
scholars on the role played by inscriptions in this process. The con-
sensus of investigators in the field is negative; inscriptions play almost
no part in the determination of local dialects of Latin. This is not
to say that scholars deny the importance of inscriptions in historical,
anthropological, and linguistic research. On the contrary, inscriptions
may be the sole or major source for the basis of our knowledge in
some areas of study, [20] but the contention remains that inscriptions
shed little, if any, light on the problem of local differentiation of
Latin in Romania. It should be emphasized that many scholars also
consider inscriptions as one of the main sources for our understanding

---

He jocularly writes (p. 571) that "nichts konnte irriger sein als diese Hoff-
nung."

[20] Compare the statement made by Peter H. Blair in his *Roman Britain
and Early England* (New York: Morton, 1963), p. 22, that "the most
important single source of information about the history and organisation of
Roman Britain is of a kind which in its form is written, but in its context
is archaeological — namely inscriptions."

of the spoken Latin for all periods of the Roman Empire, but again, according to these same scholars, inscriptions are almost valueless for a chronological or geographical determination of local variations. Pirson in his study of the inscriptions of Gaul concludes with these words about the general and specific characteristics of inscriptions in the study of dialectalization:

> Nous avons également étudié les inscriptions au point de vue des différences locales, mais nous sommes forcé d'avouer . . . que les résultats obtenus en ce point sont peu importants. L'existence de différences locales dans le latin de l'Empire est incontestable et incontestée, mais on peut se demander si les documents latins que nous possédons nous permettront jamais d'approfondir cette question. On peut en douter lorsqu'on les compare entre eux : on constate qu'une foule de particularités qu'on serait tout d'abord tenté de considérer comme spéciales à une province, se retrouvent dans les textes provenant d'autres régions. D'autre part, les traits qui restent isolés après la comparaison, trahissent des altérations d'un caractère si général qu'il serait très hasardeux d'y reconnaître des différences locales. [21]

Writing about the inscriptions of Spain, Entwistle [22] concludes that :

> The inscriptions of Spain from the first to the eighth century have been examined with a view to throwing light on the phonetic changes which presumably took place within that period. They offer the guarantees of precise dating and location, together with the centainty of being still in their original form, unmutilated by the scribal tradition which diminishes the authority of written documents. But they have proved surprisingly uninstructive. The masons of Baetica, in particular, show few local peculiarities, and may have been foreigners in some instances. It is only in Lusitania that vulgarisms are numerous. These vulgarisms are typically those of all Romania rather than Spain in particular, and not infrequently run contrary to later Peninsular speech-habits.

---

[21] Jules Pirson, *La Langue des inscriptions latines de la Gaule* (Bruxelles, 1901), pp. 324-25.

[22] William J. Entwistle, *The Spanish Language*, 2nd ed. (London : Faber and Faber, 1962), p. 51.

Densusianu likewise denigrates the value of inscriptions in the attempt to discover local variations when he states (p. 53):

Il serait chimérique de chercher dans les inscriptions d'une province quelconque, du moins jusqu'à une certaine époque, des faits linguistiques propres à cette province et qui n'auraient jamais existé dans les autres pays de l'Empire. Tout ce qu'on peut demander aux inscriptions, ce n'est guère la découverte d'un latin provincial, mais la confirmation de certaines particularités du latin vulgaire que nous devons placer à la base de toutes les langues romanes.

Speaking about inscriptions which pertain to those areas that are important for the development of Rumanian, Densusianu states (p. 63) that "(les particularités) ne nous offrent en général que des faits communs et qui se retrouvent plus ou moins souvent dans les inscriptions des autres provinces romaines. On n'y voit rien qui soit spécialement roumain, et tout ce que nous avons relevé au latin caractérise les monuments épigraphiques de tous les pays de la Romanie." [23]

In all these critiques against epigraphical evidence as a means of discovering variations, there is a basic common denominator: the equating of linguistic phenomena found in various areas of the Empire with proof that dialectalization of Latin did not occur; there is hardly any consideration of the frequency of occurrence. [24] It is

---

[23] Among the other scholars who have considered inscriptions as a poor source for dialectalization, we can mention Richter, p. 5; Stolz and Debrunner, p. 106; Mohrmann, Études, II, 142; R. Posner, The Romance Languages: A Linguistic Introduction (New York: Doubleday, 1966), p. 43; W. Elcòck, The Romance Languages (London: Faber and Faber, 1960), p. 28; Löfstedt, Late Latin, p. 39; Kroll, p. 573; Palmer, p. 174; Schmeck, p. 22; Schuchardt, Vokalismus, I, 44, 92; Mohl, p. 20; Rosetti, I, 53; J. Loth, Les Mots latins dans les langues brittoniques (Paris: Émile Bouillon, 1892), p. 48; B. Kübler, "Die lateinische Sprache auf afrikanische Inschriften," Archiv für lateinische Lexikographie und Grammatik, 8 (1893), 165; Pulgram, Tongues, pp. 321, 324; Väänänen, Introduction, p. 22; Muller, pp. 88-89. In fact, Schuchardt's comments in his Vokalismus, I, 92, that examples of deviations are found "in den Denkmälern aller Gegenden und aller Jahrhunderte n. Chr." or that "Dieses (rustike Latein) erscheint nämlich auf den Denkmälern aller Gegenden eigentlich immer als ein und dasselbe. Eigenthümlichkeiten einer einzigen romanischen Sprache oder Mundart entdecken wir schon in den ältersten Schreibungen; selten aber sind diese lokal genau oder ausschliesslich entsprechende." may have been a decisive negative indicator for subsequent study of elements of dialectalization in inscriptions.
[24] There have been, of course, a few scholars who considered inscriptions as a medium to show local variations, but they have been relatively few.

sufficient for a single deviation from Classical Latin to be found in one area, compared to numerous finds in another, for a scholar to claim that it is a widespread practice in both regions. [25] There seems to be an inherent need for scholars to find an innovation in one area,

---

Mohl, in his underestimated work, *Introduction,* makes an interesting comparison between the value of inscriptions of the Empire and the archaic inscriptions of Italy in the searching of dialectal particularities when he says (p. 46) that "en effet, tandis que les inscriptions tant italiennes que provinciales de l'époque impériale montrent une unité de langage surprenante et qui, comme nous l'avons vu, constitue depuis longtemps l'un des problèmes les plus obscurs de la philologie latine, les inscriptions archaïques de l'Italie fourmillent au contraire de particularités dialectales, d'idiotismes locaux d'un caractère tout à fait transparent, et qui, pour la plupart, correspondent précisément à des particularités identiques de la langue ou du dialecte italique de la région." Tovar says (p. 132) that "there is no doubt that in the first or at least in the second century A.D. the local differences were so considerable, as to occasionally show the 'accent' in the epigraphical misspellings." Herman, in his "Aspects de la différenciation territoriale du latin sous l'Empire," *Bulletin de la Société de la Linguistique de Paris,* 60 (1965), reminds us (p. 55) that "l'influence de la langue parlée une fois admise, il est inimaginable que cette influence se soit limitée aux seuls phénomènes communs à toute la Romanie, à l'exclusion des éventuels traits particuliers à tel ou tel territoire. Force est donc de considérer le témoignage des inscriptions comme un témoignage valable et qui... peut être utilisé pour la reconstruction de quelques particularités de la langue parlée."

[25] Mario Pei, in his article "Accusative or Oblique?", *Romanic Review,* 28 (1937), is likewise very critical of the exaggerated importance of a single occurrence when he criticizes (p. 243) those scholars who believe that "a single sporadic occurrence of a Romance feature in the midst of hundreds of classical forms is... conclusive evidence that the Romance feature in question held undisputed sway in the spoken tongue, instead of being accepted as evidence of the fact that the language was *beginning* to change." We are, however, not ignoring the importance of a single occurrence in our concept of dialectalization on the basis of frequency. Any bit of information may be helpful in our understanding of complex linguistic matters. Sittl, in his *Verschiedenheit* states (p. 60): "Dennoch glaube ich vorläufig folgende Resultate mit einger Sicherheit aufstellen zu können: nur gallische inschriften und Urkunden ziehen in lateinischen Wörten OE zu I zusammen, wodurch Formen wie *cipit* (= *coepit*) und *opidiencia* (= *oboedientia*) entstehen." This remark is completely shattered by the form *ciperunt* (= *coeperunt*) which is found in *Diehl* 2426, *CIL* III, 10, 190, in Podgorica near Doclea in Dalmatia at some unknown date. Pușcariu, *Études,* p. 28, likewise speaks of the importance of individual words in the expansion of a phonological change. According to Löfstedt, *Late Latin,* p. 166, "with our fragmentary knowledge of spoken Latin even one isolated example may be of great value." Kroll warns of an exaggeration of a single use when he says (p. 572) that "Für eine starke Überschätzung des Werthes sprachlicher Argumente halte ich es auch, wenn man aus einem einzigen Sprachgebrauche einen Beweis für die Herkunft eines Werkes zieht."

with its total exclusion in another. There is little concern for tendencies. According to Guiraud [26] "les linguistes ont été les seuls à ignorer que la fréquence constitue un des caractères du langage." In almost all of the research that has been done in inscriptions, up to the present time, investigators have looked for exclusiveness of innovations to the overlooking of tendencies. We feel that conclusions reached on the basis of a superficial comparison may have to be reevaluated.

It should be noted, in passing, that most of the important works done in the field of inscriptions have been devoted to specific regions, as exemplified by the works of Pirson, Carnoy, Väänänen, Skok, Maccarrone, among others. [27] The few epigraphic studies that have been of a comparative nature have delved mainly into specific problems without giving an overall picture of the areas under consideration. [28] Scholars have been aware of this lack of a "synthesis" on the part of researchers and this need is aptly expressed by Silva Neto when he says (p. 102) that "agora seria possível, e desejável, aproveitando-se os materiais já carreados e acrescentando-se outros, das numerosas inscrições recentemente publicadas, levar a cabo um estudo de síntese." [29]

---

[26] P. Guiraud, *Problèmes et méthodes de la statistique linguistique* (Paris: Presses Universitaires de France, 1960), p. 29. Discussing the vulgarisms in the sources of spoken Latin, Pulgram, *Tongues,* also complains (p. 317) that "nothing is said, of course, about the frequency of these 'errors' at any given time. This subtracts considerably from their value as evidence for speech." Sittl was one of the first to realize the importance of frequency when he wrote (p. 47) that "gewisse Lautveränderungen sind vielleicht allen Dialekten einer Sprache gemeinsam, aber der Unterschied besteht dann darin, dass sie in einem äusserst selten, in einem anderen fast regelmässig vorkommen."

[27] Jules Pirson, *La Langue des inscriptions latines de la Gaule* (Bruxelles, 1901); Albert J. Carnoy, *Le Latin d'Espagne d'après les inscriptions,* 2nd ed. (Louvain: J. B. Istas, 1906); Veikko Väänänen, *Le Latin vulgaire des inscriptions pompéiennes,* 2nd ed. (Berlin: Akademie-Verlag, 1959); Petar Skok, *Pojave vulgarno-latinskoga jezika na natpisima rimske provincije Dalmacije* (Zagreb: Hartman, 1915); Nunzio Maccarrone, "Il latino delle iscrizioni di Sicilia," *Studi romanzi,* 7 (1911), 75-116.

[28] E. Diehl, *De m Finali Epigraphica* (Leipzig: B. C. Teubner, 1899); C. Proskauer, *Das auslautened s auf den lateinischen Inschriften* (Strassburg: Karl J. Trübner, 1909); O. Prinz, *De O et U Vocalibus inter se Permutatis in Lingua Latina* (Halle: Éduard Klinz, 1932); E. Cross, *Syncope and Kindred Phenomena in Latin Inscriptions* (New York: Institute of French Studies, 1930).

[29] This lack of synthesis was acknowledged as far back as 1916 by Ettmayer. Silva Neto cites (p. 6) the foresight of Ettmayer with the following

This deficiency has been partly overcome by the most important inscriptional work of synthesis in the past few decades, with the publication in 1960 of *Limba latină în provinciile dunărene ale imperiului român* by H. Mihăescu. [30] Sorin Stati, [31] in an extensive review of the work, stresses its uniqueness with the following words:

> Cartea lui H. Mihăescu este o sinteză întemeiată pe o analiză minuțioasă și competentă. Este pînă ora actuală singura lucrare de cest gen; celelalte monografii care tratează limba inscriptiilor se limitează la cîte o singură provincie și uneori la un singur aspect (fonetic, morfologic) al textelor dintr-o provincie. Este, de asemenea, singura lucrare în care se dă o atentie egală tuturor compartimentelor limbii. (pp. 962-63)

The purpose and results of Mihăescu's study can be judged by his own words: [32]

> ...am cercetat înscripțiile și textele din primele șase veacuri ale erei noastre din provinciile romane Dalmația, Noricum, Pannonia superioară și inferioară, Moesia superioară și inferioară și Dacia. (p. 5)

words: "Em 1916, no seu conspecto bibliográfico acerca do latim vulgar, von Ettmayer acentua a riqueza das investigações de fatos e pormenores, em contraste con a pobreza de sínteses, de visões de conjunto." Cf. Herman (p. 56: "Les recherches faites jusqu'à ce jour ne comportent aucune comparaison systématique des données recueillies dans les diverses provinces, elles ne soumettent à aucune analyse détaillée la répartition statistique des phénomènes rencontrés."

[30] H. Mihăescu, *Limba latină în provinciile dunărene ale imperiului român* (Bucharest: Editura Academiei Republica Populare Romîne, 1960). The work is not entirely based upon inscriptional evidence, but the textual material must be considered secondary on the basis of the more than 21,000 inscriptions that were studied.

[31] Sorin Stati, Review of *Limba latină în provinciile dunărene ale imperiului român*, by H. Mihăescu, *Studii și Cercetări Lingvistice*, 4 (1960), 957-63. Translation of the Rumanian: "H. Mihăescu's book is a synthesis based on a detailed and competent analysis. It is up to now the only work of this kind; the other monographs which deal with the language of inscriptions limit themselves to a single province and at times to a single aspect (phonetic, morphological) of the texts in a province. It is, likewise, the only work in which equal attention is given to all aspects of the language."

[32] Translation of the Rumanian: "...I have investigated the inscriptions and texts of the first six centuries of our era of the Roman provinces of Dalmatia, Noricum, Pannonia Superior and Inferior, Moesia Superior and Inferior, and Dacia." (p. 5)

Faptele linguistice păstrate în înscriptiile și textele din provinciile dunărene sînt numeroase și variate, dar nu sînt nici
specifice acestor ținuturi și nici unice. Pentru fiecare din ele
m-am străduit să culeg fenomene analogice din apus și am
reușit aproape pretutindeni. Aceasta înseamnă că ele erau
fenomene sau inovații răspîndite pe un spațiu mai larg.
Resultă, prin urmare, că provinciile dunărene nu formau
un domeniu lingvistic izolat independent. (p. 279)

This extremely important conclusion concerning the Latin of the
Danubian provinces, namely, that they do not show any distinctive
dialectal traits, is likewise based on the assumption that linguistic
variants found in Eastern Romance are neither unique nor specific
to the area, but are found in general Romance, and thus it appears
that the inscriptions prove that Balkan Latin is the same as that of
other regions of Romania. Although Mihăescu's conclusion is for the
most part accepted by scholars,[33] there have been a few criticisms
questioning his findings precisely on the basis of his having overlooked the frequency of forms in his analysis. Messing remarks that
"if one were to reason from the frequency of forms in the Danube
provinces or their absence, one might reach conclusions decidedly at
variance with Mihăescu's."[34] Stati (Review, p. 959) likewise mentions
the lack of a comparison between the frequency and extent of some
phonetic phenomena in the noun and verbal flexion. Straka (Review,
p. 404) contends that "quand on aura rendu la valeur exacte aux
graphies relevées, ces différences apparaîtront tout de même plus
grandes que l'auteur ne semble vouloir l'admettre." The key to the

---

"The linguistic facts observed in inscriptions and texts from the Danubian
provinces are numerous and varied, but they are neither peculiar to these
areas nor are they unique. For each of them I have endeavored to collect
similar phenomena from the west and I have succeeded in almost every case.
This means that they were phenomena or innovations spread over a wider
area. The result is therefore that the Danubian provinces did not form an
isolated or independent linguistic zone." (p. 279).

[33] Rudolf Hanslik, in his review of Mihăescu's work in Kratylos, 10 (1965),
says (p. 213) that "Die Schlussfolgerung von M(ihăescu) aus dem Gesamtma-
terial ist absolut richtig." Väänänen in his review in Neuphilologische Mitteilungen, LXII (1961), 228, likewise concurs. Straka states in his review, Revue
de Linguistique Romane, XXIV (1960), p. 404, that "l'auteur en conclut
avec raison, qu'il n'y avait pas de différences sensibles entre le latin des
Balkans et celui des autres régions de l'Empire."
[34] Gordon M. Messing, Language, 39 (1963), 675.

interpretation of inscriptional material in the study of dialectal differences in the various parts of the Roman Empire seems to lie in a quantitative and comparative analysis.

The main comparative, quantitative study of Latin inscriptions in the search for local variations is, as far as this writer knows, the work entitled *An Inquiry into Local Variations in Vulgar Latin as Reflected in the Vocalism of Christian Inscriptions* by Paul A. Gaeng.[35] Gaeng studies (p. 17) quantitatively the inscriptions of the Iberian Peninsula, further subdivided into Baetica, Lusitania, and Tarraconensis; Gaul, comprising Gallia Narbonensis and Gallia Lugdunensis; Italy, divided into Northern, Central, and Southern Italy, and Rome. Gaeng concludes (pp. 349-50) that:

> ... despite the strongly formulaic nature of our inscriptional material and the fact that deviations from the Classical Latin norm do appear to be more or less identical in all areas, it *is* possible to cull information as to the language in which Christian inscriptions are written, by means of the kind of statistical analysis that we have attempted to undertake. Unsatisfactory as this method may be in relation to other documentary material which offers more abundant language, it, nevertheless, does seem to enable us to detect certain features that occur more frequently in one area as against another, thus pointing to regional differentiations in the Vulgar Latin period covered by this material, i.e., roughly the fourth, fifth and sixth centuries.

---

[35] Paul A. Gaeng, *An Inquiry into Local Variations in Vulgar Latin as Reflected in the Vocalism of Christian Inscriptions* (Chapel Hill: University of North Carolina Press, 1968). Herman's article "Différenciation" is also a quantitative analysis comparing the fifth and sixth century inscriptions of the Iberian Peninsula, Gaul, northern Italy, Rome, southern Italy, and Dalmatia. His figures, however, are derived quite differently from Gaeng's. Herman prefers to take the total number of deviations from the classical norm without any consideration of the correct number of occurrences. He is, in fact, against any mention of correctness in the figures: "Même si nous mettions en relation le nombre des graphies (= graphie contraire à la norme classique et susceptible de révéler des caractéristiques phonétiques de la langue parlée) avec l'étendue des textes, nous n'obtiendrions rien de linguistiquement valable: la proportion 'graphie fautive/étendue de texte' ne révèle directement que le niveau de la correction orthographique et non pas les caractéristiques de la langue parlée" (p. 61). We consider Herman's view only partially valid and believe that important information can be obtained from a consideration of both the correctness and deviations in inscriptional material. We are following Gaeng's format.

The present work is an extension of Gaeng's, but in areas not studied by him. It is, therefore, a comparative, quantitative study of the vocalism of the inscriptions of Britain, North Africa, Dalmatia, and the Balkans to determine whether the epigraphic material available is capable of shedding light on the controversial problem of the dialectalization of Latin. [36]

To give some idea of the methodology employed, we will provide a few examples of this quantitative approach to show the value attached to the principle of frequency of occurrence. Although this study is primarily concerned with vocalic phenomena, the confusion of Latin *b* and *v* is an admirable example of the efficacy of the methodology. This *b* and *v* confusion is well known and attested to in Vulgar Latin inscriptions. [37] In *The Roman Inscriptions of Britain*, Vol. I, edited by Collingwood and Wright, we find just two examples of an initial *v* and *b* confusion (*bagis, bitam* in inscription No. 1), and only one example of an intervocalic *b* to *v* confusion (*Vivio* in inscription No. 17); it is extremely strange to find in this collection which is, in the opinion of the present writer, probably the best compendium of inscriptions as yet edited, the explanation (p. 1) of the initial *b* and *v* confusion with the words: "As in many inscriptions of the later centuries, the letter *b* is used instead of *v* for *vagis vitam*." In their explanation of *Vivio*, we find (p. 9): "*Vivius*, a variant spelling of *Vibius*. This substitution of letters occurs even on early inscrip-

---

[36] We are not presuming the necessary competence to call this work a statistical analysis which would require a basic understanding of a specialized discipline. Speaking of the specific requirements needed by a statistician, Guiraud says (p. 8) that "le statisticien, lui, a besoin d'un index qui puisse lui donner rapidement le nombre total de mots d'un texte, le nombre de mots différents, le nombre de formes différentes, le nombre de formes pour chaque catégorie grammaticale (substantifs, adjectifs, singuliers, futurs, etc...), le nombre de formes pour chaque catégorie sémantique (couleurs, sons, etc...), enfin la distribution des mots et des formes dans le texte, le nombre de ceux qui sont employés 1, 2, 3 fois etc..." Wherever possible, we will try to explain our figures with some of the above data that may help in the interpretation of the cold numbers.

[37] See C. H. Grandgent, *An Introduction to Vulgar Latin* (1907; reprint New York: Hafner, 1962); Richter, pp. 60-63; Edgar H. Sturtevant, *The Pronunciation of Greek and Latin*, 2nd ed. (Philadelphia: Linguistic Society of America, 1940), pp. 142-43, 174; Max Niedermann, *Précis de phonétique historique du latin*, 4th ed. (Paris: Klincksieck, 1953), pp. 87-88. R. Politzer, in his article "On *b* and *v* in Latin and Romance," *Word*, 8 (1952), 211-15, gives the previous bibliography on the subject.

tions." We encounter two other examples of an intervocalic confusion of *v* and *b* in British Latin inscriptions in *Corpus Inscriptionum Insularum Celticarum*, Vol. II, edited by Macalister, in the words *prope[ra]bit* (= *praeparavit*) (Inscription 1011) and *proparabit* (= *praeparavit*) (Inscription 1015). Although we have not counted the incidence of confusion of *b* and *v* initially and medially in the other regions under consideration, the confusion is so common that a comparison of the five examples in Britain with the innumerable examples elsewhere gives a glaring picture of a differentiation of the Vulgar Latin in Britain. Jackson, in his brilliant book *Language and History in Early Britain,* in his analysis of the problem, writes (pp. 89-90):

> Latin *v* and intervocalic *b* remained rigidly distinct in British, clearly because they were pronounced in Britain as [u̯] and [b] respectively. It is significant that neither in the Latin inscriptions of Roman Britain nor in the later inscriptions of the Dark Ages ... are there any examples of confusion of *v* and *b*; ... We can be reasonably sure, then, that *v* and intervocalic *b* retained their earlier values in British Latin; and it is to be noted that this seems to agree with the pronunciation of the more educated among the Continental speakers of VL. by contrast with that of the mass of population. [38]

This uniqueness of the Latin in Britain, in this respect, would have been misinterpreted and completely lost if the inscriptions in Britain had been analyzed in the usual manner without the frequency of occurrence having been taken into consideration. It should also be noted that the inscriptions agree with the Latin loanwords into British in this problem of the *b* and *v* confusion. Speaking of the nature of the loanwords, Jackson states (p. 80) "that the great mass [of Latin words], if not practically the whole, were borrowed from

---

[38] To explain the few examples of *b* and *v* confusion in British Latin, it may suffice to say that a Gaulish stonemason, speaking the continental variety of Vulgar Latin, cut the inscriptions under consideration. Cf. Jackson, *Language,* p. 111: "It is not easy to say why a good number of Latin words should not also have entered British from the normal Vulgar Latin speech of the towns, the army, and the rest. In one or two cases apparently they did so, or may have; but these are quite exceptional." At any rate Carnoy's remark (p. 14) that "il n'y a pas de province où *b* pour *v* soit aussi peu repandu qu'en Espagne" is definitely erroneous.

spoken Latin is a point which needs to be stressed. These are for the most part not 'learned' loans from book Latin and written sources, but popular borrowings from the living Latin tongue used in Roman Britain."

The two formulae *vixit annos* and *vixit annis* give another example of the importance of the frequency of occurrence in our methodology. The accusative of duration of time is the classical usage, although the ablative is not unknown in this function.[39] This use of the ablative takes hold in prose writers in the first century A.D. and spreads gradually.[40] Both forms are found in the inscriptions of all regions of the Empire and their distribution may be more important than a casual glance may indicate.

Pirson, although not giving any figures for their respective frequency, states (p. 183) that "dans les inscriptions de la Gaule, à quelque époque qu'elles appartiennent, l'ablatif se rencontre aussi souvent que l'accusatif." Speaking of the complete freedom of choice in the use of the contending forms, Pirson says (p. 183) that "l'ablatif a été complétement assimilé à l'accusatif pour exprimer la durée, comme le prouve à l'évidence la présence simultanée de ces deux cas avec la même valeur dans la même proposition." Mihăescu reports (*Limba*, p. 157) that in a study of approximately 31,000 inscriptions of Rome, there were 2,483 cases of the ablative and only 539 cases of the accusative of time. In the Danubian provinces (excluding Dalmatia) there were 84 cases of the ablative to 31 times for the accusative. He then derives from these figures the important conclusion that "această predilecţie pentru 'annis' în loc de 'annos' în Italia şi în provinciile dunărene ne este întîmplătoare, ci arată că în limba vorbită pluralul substantivelor masculine tendea spre forma unică în ī, din care a rezultat în romîneşte *ani*, în italiană *anni*."[41]

---

[39] William G. Hale and Carl Darling Buck, *A Latin Grammar* (1903; reprint Alabama: University of Alabama Press, 1966), pp. 204, 231; Allen and Greenough's *New Latin Grammar*, ed. J. B. Greenough, G. L. Kettredge, A. A. Howard, and Benj. L. D'Ooge, rev. ed. (Boston: Ginn and Company, 1916), p. 266.
[40] Mihăescu, *Limba*, p. 158.
[41] H. Mihăescu "Cîteva observaţii asupra limbii latine din provinciile dunărene ale imperiului român," *Studii şi Cercetări Lingvistice*, 10 (1959), 89. Translation of the Rumanian: "this predilection for 'annis' instead of 'annos' in Italy and in the Danubian provinces is not fortuitous, but shows that in the spoken language the plural of masculine nouns tended to the

Taking our figures for the inscriptions of North Africa, we see, without taking into consideration the chronology of this particular linguistic particularity, that the ablative of time *annis* is used 357 times compared to the accusative *annos* that is used 67 times. These figures show conclusively that the situation is similar to that of Rome and the Balkans. Since Italian and Rumanian lost final -*s* in their development, the form *annis*, as previously mentioned, shows that in the spoken Latin of Eastern Romance the masculine plural of second declension nouns tended to an -*i* rather than to the -*os* form which later became the basis of masculine plural nouns in Spanish, Rheto-Romance, Portuguese, Catalan, Sardinian, Provençal, and French. [42] If African inscriptions point to the *annis* form rather than to the *annos* type, the Latin of North Africa may, in this respect, conform with Eastern rather than with Western Romance. Since scholars have maintained that the final -*s* did remain in the Latin of North Africa, [43] the numerical superiority of the *annis* form and its corollary that the loss of -*s* was instrumental in the formation of the second declension masculine plural nouns may require a reevaluation of the placing of

---

single form in -*i*, the result of which was the Rumanian *ani*, the Italian *anni*."

[42] Lausberg, *Lingüística*, II, 31.

[43] It is interesting to note that Wartburg has equivocal feelings about final -*s* in the Latin of North Africa. In his review of M. L. Wagner's book *Restos de latinidad en el Norte de Africa*, in *Zeitschrift für romanische Philologie*, LVII (1937), 653, he writes that "besonders wertvoll ist auch, dass Wagner an die Erhaltung des -*s* der lat. Nominative erinnert, womit sich die Zuteilung des lateinischen Nordafrikas zur Westromania bestätigt." In his own *Ausgleiderung*, he writes (p. 31) that "Über das Latein Nordafrikas haben wir, mit Bezug auf das -*s*, keine eindeutigen Nachrichten." Lausberg affirms (*Lingüística*, I, 428) that "el latín mantenía también la -*s*." Nothing certain can be said of the fate of -*s* on the basis of the lists of Latin words in Berber in Schuchardt's "Lehnwörter." Mohl's comment (p. 120) that "celui qui étudie avec quelque attention le VIIIe volume du *Corpus* . . . se persuade facilement que les dialectes de l'Italie méridionale y ont laissé des traces numéreuses" may indicate that the southern Italian's tendency to drop -*s* may have an echo in the Latin of North Africa. The problem of final -*s* in African Latin, as well as other phenomena, such as the outcome of intervocalic unvoiced consonants and the place of African Latin in the division of West and East Romania, is delicate and the last word has yet to be written on the subject. Cf. Pei's concise summary of the loss of final -*s* and its implication in the debated question of "East" and "West" Romance in his article "Intervocalic Occlusives in 'East' and 'West' Romance," *Romanic Review*, XXXIV (1943), 235-47.

African Latin in the dichotomy of the East-West division of the Romance languages.

As a verification that the form *annis* is not just a whimsical choice on the part of the speakers of African Latin, but is the result of a definite cause, we will bring forth the figures of other nouns used in the same construction. It happens quite often that in inscriptions the life span of the person buried is given in years, months, days, and even hours. Although the ablative *annis* was the overwhelming choice in the African inscriptions, it turns out that the accusative is even more widespread in the other divisions of time. We have 39 cases of the accusative of time for the word "month" (*menses*, 38 times and *mensis*, 1 time) and just one case of the ablative *mensibus*. *Dies* is used 37 times to four cases of *diebus*; there are thirteen examples of *horas* to just one example of *horis*. The use of the ablative in *annis* cannot, therefore, be considered as fortuitous, but must be the result of a definite underlying cause. We are inclined to consider the morphological process of reducing the Classical Latin multi-case declensional system to a one-case system as the basic reason. Although the accusative *menses* and *dies* may be preferred to the ablative *mensibus* and *diebus* for reasons of harmony,[44] the accusative *horas* would

---

[44] Väänänen, *Introduction*, p. 119; Einar Löfstedt, *Syntactica* (Lund: C. W. K. Gleerup, 1933), II, 61-62. Löfstedt's comments are particularly interesting, but do not answer the question to our complete satisfaction: "Wie ist diese eigentümliche Vorliebe für den Abl. *annis* neben den Akk. *menses* und *dies* in der Vulgärsprache ... zu erklären? Da sowohl syntaktische wie logisch-psychologische Gründe ausgeschlossen sind, muss die Erscheinung durch rein äusserliche, formale Momente bedingt sein. Offenbar hatte man ... das Gefühl, durch die Endungen -is, -es (-is), -es werde eine bessere äussere Harmonie gebildet als durch -is, -ibus, -ebus, sei es, dass man diese Harmonie vorzugsweise in der Zweisilbigkeit der Formen *annis, menses, dies* (im Gengensatz zu dem zweisilbigen *annis* neben den dreisilbigen *mensibus, diebus*)." This idea of "harmony" may be repudiated precisely because of the last member of the time series: *horas*. Wouldn't the ablative *horis* fit more "harmoniously" into the scheme with its -*is* ending, rather than the accusative -*as*? Although the examples are limited, as we have seen, there are still thirteen cases of *horas* to a single example of *horis*, which casts aside any doubt as to the possibility of a fortuitous cause. We are led to believe that each division of time (*annis, menses, dies, horas*) must be explained by its involvement in the declensional system. *Annis* with its loss of final -*s* merged with the nominative to form the single plural form ending in -*i*; *menses* and *dies* were both preferred over their longer forms because of the general tendency to drop the ablative and dative -*bus* endings as well as to equate the accusative plural with the nominative. Löfstedt does mention the loss of -*bus* as a possible reason

probably show the tendency to a single-case system in the first declension.

The use of frequency of occurrence thus shows that a downright error can be avoided, as in the case of the *b* and *v* confusion, and that important insights can be gotten from a careful scrutiny of tendencies, as is the case in the use of the ablative and accusative of time. In the bulk of the present work, we will devote a major portion to phonology, but those phonetic phenomena impinging on morphology, especially in final vowels, will also be treated.

Although we are following, for the most part, the format set down by Gaeng in his treatment of vocalism in the Latin of inscriptions, there are two essential points where we differ: the evaluation of pagan inscriptions as contrasted with Christian inscriptions, and the inclusion in the tables of figures derived from non-dated inscriptions.

Pagan Inscriptions Versus Christian Inscriptions

Gaeng, as the title of his dissertation indicates, is interested only in the study of Christian inscriptions without considering pagan inscriptions at all. Because of the paucity of Christian inscriptions, especially in Britain, and of theoretical reservations as to the feasibility of excluding pagan inscriptions, we are including them in our study, although pagan inscriptions are kept apart, precisely to see whether any generalizations can be made on the basis of information derived from our investigation as to the possible differences inherent in the two kinds of inscriptions. In discussing the inscriptions of Gaul, Pirson differentiates the two as to chronology and difference in language:

(p. 61): "Vielleicht ist ausserdem in der späteren Vulgärsprache überhaupt mit einer gewissen Abneigung gegen die im Romanischen ausgestorbene und also sicher nicht volkstümlich beliebte Endung -*bus* zu rechnen." *Horas* was preferred because of the one-case ending -*as* assuming nominative functions as well as accusative. Väänänen mentions (*Introduction*, p. 115) that "la forme en -*as*, plutôt que celle en -*ae*, semble être à la base du pl. it. en -*e*, et sans doute aussi de celui du roumain." See also R. Politzer, "On the Origin of the Italian Plurals," *Romanic Review*, XLIII (1952), 272-81. We can only agree with Löfstedt when he says (p. 62) that "diese Frage würde übrigens eine besondere Untersuchung verdienen, die sich allerdings auf ein sehr grosses, kritisch-statistich gesichtetes Material stützen müsste."

On doit, en outre, distinguer les inscriptions paiennes des inscriptions chrétiennes. Les premières disparaissent généralement dès le IVe siècle, tandis que les dernières ne commencent à se répandre en Gaule qu'à partir de la même époque, se multiplient surtout pendant les Ve et VIe siècles, et se prolongent jusqu'au VIIe, parfois jusqu'au VIIIe siècle... (p. IX)

La langue des documents paiens n'est certainement plus du latin classique, mais la langue des textes chrétiens est encore bien plus altérée, ce qui s'explique par les deux siécles d'intervalle qui séparent ces deux catégories de monumonts. Les inscriptions chrétiennes, comme tous les documents de l'époque mérovingienne, à cause de leur date relativement récente, doivent donc être étudiées principalement au point de vue de la transformation du latin en roman. Elles ont encore sur les marbres paiens l'avantage d'être fréquemment datées et de fournir ainsi des points de repère d'une certitude absolue. (p. X)

It is obviously true that the bulk of pagan inscriptions are earlier in date than the Christian ones. However, it should also be realized that the influence of Christianity in Latin literature is early. In the second half of the second century, the first Christian texts written in Latin make their appearance: in North Africa, the *Acta Martyrum Scillitanorum* and the *Passio Felicitatis et Perpetuae*; in Rome, the Latin version of Saint Clement's epistle; it is also during the second century that there is begun the translation of the Bible into Latin. [45] There is certainly no impassible line of demarcation between pagan and Christian inscriptions. [46] We find both types of inscriptions in the third century. It has been also noted that, notwithstanding the rapid advance of Christianity in the third century in North Africa, it is certain that most town councils, and even some whole towns were still almost entirely pagan. [47] The African town of Thibilis, when excavated, showed no Christian inscriptions before the sixth century. [48]

---

[45] Mohrmann, *Études*, I, 53, 96; J. Schrijnen, *Charackteristik des altchristlichen Latein* (Nijmegen: Dekker & van de Vegt, 1932), p. 24.

[46] Migliorini, in his *The Italian Language*, accepts (p. 15) the Edict of Milan (A.D. 313) as a convenient line of demarcation.

[47] Warmington, *The North African Provinces from Diocletian to the Vandal Conquest* (Cambridge, 1954), p. 36.

[48] *Ibid.*

It is also well known that paganism was still strong in other cities of North Africa in the time of Augustine.[49]

It is most interesting to note that Pirson, as we have seen, differentiates Christian and pagan inscriptions in theory. However, in his listing of the various examples of deviations from Classical Latin, he includes pagan inscriptions as well as Christian, placing a cross (+) after the number of the inscription to show its Christian origin. Mihǎescu, in his comparative study, states (p. 5) that his material includes inscriptions of the first six centuries of our era which would, of necessity, have to include both pagan and Christian inscriptions. Skok (*Pojave*) and Carnoy likewise give examples from both, in their studies of the Latin inscriptions of Dalmatia and Spain, respectively. The monumental *Corpus Inscriptionum Latinarum* likewise includes pagan and Christian inscriptions in its collection.[50]

Diehl in his *Inscriptiones Latinae Christianae Veteres*, also has reservations as to the strictly Christian origins of some of the inscriptions which he has incorporated into his collection.[51] We see in some of his editorial comments such phrases as "*num christianus sit titulus, non constat*" (*D.* 814); "*de origine christiana non constat*" (*D.* 3609, *D.* 3621, *D.* 3932, *D.* 3952, *D.* 4318A, *D.* 4502); "*nescio an sit christiana*" (*D.* 3095D); "*titulus si christianus est*" (*D.* 3631A); "*num christianus est?*" (*D.* 3722, *D.* 3952A, *D.* 4038, *D.* 1853A); "*titulus christianus videtur esse*" (*D.* 4156C); "*am titulus est ethnicus iudaicus?*" (*D.* 3457); "*vereor ut christianus sit titulus*" (*D.* 746); "*christianam esse nequaquam certum est*" (*D.* 1610N).

Christian symbols, except for the Chrisma, a good indication of the origin of some inscriptions, are for the most part absent in the British Christian inscriptions.[52] Some crosses were even added at a

---

[49] *Ibid.*

[50] It is incredible that Vossler, a scholar of universal reputation, could write the completely erroneous remark in his *Einführung in Vulgärlatein* (Munich: Max Hueber, 1953), p. 62: "Das Corpus (*CIL*) enthält keine christlichen Inschriften."

[51] Diehl even gives admittedly pagan inscriptions for comparative purposes in his comments: cf. the phrases "*adde ethnicum: ... in titulo ethnico*"; in reference to his inscription 3314 and others.

[52] Cf. *Inscriptiones Britanniae Christianae*, ed. Emil Hübner (Berlin: Georg Reimer, 1876), p. xvii: "Reliqua symbola in aliarum regionum titulis christianis obvia, palma, aves pisces simila, in titulis Britannicis prorsus deficiunt."

later date. [53] Even formulae which are considered typically pagan or Christian are no sure indication. Knott [54] reminds us that "Christians did not completely abandon all the old pagan terms. For the most part, they continued to compose inscriptions after the old formulaic pattern, including not only neutral inherited terms, but definitely pagan ones, such as the dedication *D.M.* or *D.M.S.*" She likewise makes the important observation (p. 75) that "in many inscriptions the only linguistic sign of Christian origin is the addition of the Christian phrase *In Pace*; in the case of others it is practically impossible to tell whether we have to do with a Christian or pagan inscription." In the *Roman Inscriptions of Britain*, we see (p. 587) that the phrase "*sine ulla macula* has a Christian flavour ... The pagan use of the phrase, however, is not unknown."

This discussion of the fine distinction between pagan and Christian inscriptions brings up the general problem of Christian Latin. The Dutch linguists, Joseph Schrijnen and his disciple and colleague, Christine Mohrmann, are staunch believers in Christian Latin as a *Sondersprache* or special language. A general statement of this movement is given (p. 8) by Schrijnen in his book, *Charackteristik des altchristlichen Latein*, which is generally considered as the first work to attempt to formulate this school of thought:

> Es wäre zwar ganz und gar undenkbar, wenn eine so gewaltige Kulturerscheinung wie die des weltreformierenden Christentums auf die Sprache der Länder, in denen sie geboren wurde und heranreifte, keinen tieffurchenden Eindruck hinterlassen hätte. Es handelt sich infolgedessen auch nicht um einige gereinfügige Differenzierung und um den Nachweis von einigen Bedeutungsverschiebungen und Lehnwörtern. Denn die christliche Welle ergoss sich auf das gesamte Sprachgebiet, die Differenzierung ist also semantlischer, lexikologischer, morphologischer, syntaktischer, ja sogar phonetischer Art.

---

[53] Cf. Hübner, p. xvii: "alias (cruces) in titulis antiquioribus posteriore denum tempore additas esse diserte traditur." Kenneth Jackson, *Language and History in Early Britain* (Edinburgh: Edinburgh University Press, 1953), footnote 3, p. 165, also writes: "But Nash Williams seems now to have shown that, at any rate in some instances, crosses *were* [italicized in original] added much later to monuments which previously bore only inscriptions of the fifth to sixth century."

[54] Betty Knott, "The Christian 'Special Language' in the Inscriptions," *Vigiliae Christianae*, X (1956), 75.

Although the claims of this school are extended to include phonology, morphology, syntax, vocabulary, and semantics, they seem to be questioned by various scholars.[55] Palmer, although admitting (p. 183) the unquestionable importance of Christian Latin for the history of the Latin language and indeed of Western civilization, has definite reservations as to the uniqueness of this Christian Latin. He remarks (p. 194) that "the existence of a special Christian vocabulary is thus established beyond reasonable doubt. The attempts to isolate corresponding facts of morphology and syntax have been less convincing: the separate phenomena adduced, such as the *quia* and *quod* construction for the accusative and infinite, the indicative in indirect questions, the infinitive of purpose, the nominativus pendens, etc., can all be paralleled from contemporary texts." Knott also concludes (p. 66) that "the existence in the speech of the general lay community of a differentiation affecting lexicology, semantics, morphology, and syntax, has yet to be demonstrated." Sofer rejects the Schrijnen thesis and Schmeck disagrees with it.[56] Morhmann herself admits the traditional processes in the development of Christian Latin, stating that "le latin des chrétiens est très révolutionnaire et en même temps il est très fidèle à la tradition latine. Il est révolutionnaire en tant qu'il introduit beaucoup d'éléments nouveaux, et il est traditionnel en ce sens que ces éléments nouveaux sont tout à fait conformes aux tendances générales qui réglaient la vie de la langue latine dès ses origines."[57] Löfstedt gives the following evaluation of Mohrmann and Schrijnen when he writes (*Late Latin*, p. 69) that "her work is distinguished by depth of learning and clarity of exposition, although she seems to me to fall, as Schrijnen does, into the error of exaggerating the peculiarities of Christian Latin and its claim to be a separate language ('eine Sondersprache'). Wartburg, in generalizing

---

[55] Migliorini seems to accept the Schrijnen view when he acknowledges (p. 19) that "Christian Latin developed into a special language belonging to a particular social and religious group."

[56] Sofer, *Problematik*, p. 23: "Die Ansicht [about special language] ist durch die genannten vielfach gründlichen Untersuchungen als widerlegt anzusehen." Schmeck, p. 11: "Die starke Orientierung auf das Sondersprachliche, wie sie von J. Schrijnen vorbereitet und von Chr. Mohrmann, zwei Exponenten der holländischen altchristl. Philologie, vertreten wird, vermag ich nicht mitzumachen."

[57] Christine Mohrmann, *Latin vulgaire, latin des chrétiens, latin médiéval* (Paris: Klincksieck, 1955), p. 22.

on French argot and its relationship to the French language in general (*Problèmes*, p. 117) maintains that "le cas le plus extrème d'une langue de groupe est l'argot" and, on page 121, that "une chose frappe avant tout, c'est que l'argot ne se distingue du français ni phonétiquement ni morphologiquement ni syntactiquement. . . . La différenciation se limite entièrement au lexique." On the basis of the aforesaid comments of various scholars, it may be said that although the influence of Christian Latin on the lexicological development of the Latin language was undeniable, to consider Christian Latin as a special language and the corollary that Christian inscriptions differ unmistakably from pagan inscriptions would be an extremely hazardous assumption.

Non-Dated Inscriptions

Pirson's other remark referring to the advantage of Christian inscriptions over pagan inscriptions because of the greater number of dated inscriptions of the former and consequently inferring a more accurate chronology on the basis of the linguistic phenomena studied is easily refuted by a consideration of some figures. Gaeng gives the following percentages for the areas studied by him:

		Dated	*Non-Dated*	*% Of Dated*
1.	*Iberian Peninsula* (p. 30)			
	a) Baetica	90	22	80.3 %
	b) Lusitania	93	11	89.4
	c) Tarraconensis	114	32	78.0
2.	*Gaul* (p. 31)			
	a) Narbonensis	104	110	48.5 %
	b) Lugdunensis	84	182	31.3
3.	*Italy* (p. 32)			
	a) Northern	190	228	45.4 %
	b) Central	127	153	45.3
	c) Southern	155	330	31.8
4.	*Rome* (p. 33)	744	1074	42.0 %

It is clearly seen that the figures for dated inscriptions vary remarkably between 89.4 % and 31.3 %. It must also be noted that in the percentages given by Gaeng many inscriptions are not specifically dated by reference to a consul, an emperor, or to an *era* of a specific area, but are approximately dated by scholars, either by Diehl or by a previous editor who had placed the inscription in a certain century.[58] Hübner's criteria in determining the date of an undated inscriptions on the basis of its historical content, language, and lettering still seem valid.[59] However, further epigraphical studies could easily change the percentage figures of dates for collections of inscriptions, especially when the degree of accuracy requires only a century as the approximate dating. Our own figures show how one scholar's delving into the approximate dating of non-dated inscriptions can alter percentages considerably:

	Pagan Inscriptions			Christian Inscriptions		
Area	No. Dated	No. Undated	% Dated	No. Dated	No. Undated	% Dated
1. Britain	180	306	37.0	62	15	80.5
2. Balkans	24	75	24.2	10	73	12.0
3. Africa	—	—	—	175	580	23.2
4. Dalmatia	—	—	—	45	167	21.2

Since it is well known that Christian inscriptions of Britain were normally undated,[60] it may be surprising to see the percentage of 80.5 % given for dated Christian inscriptions in Britain. We are simply accepting the date established by Jackson from his comparative study of the form of the letters of the individual inscriptions. Jackson himself states (*Language*, p. 160):

> It is not easy to lay down any precise principles; the dates assigned throughout this book have been reached ... by comparing all of them one with another and constructing a relative typological sequence which makes it possible to say, for instance, roughly, "late fifth century" or "mid sixth century," etc., of any given monument. I believe that few epigraphers would be disposed to assert positively that in any one example these datings are inaccurate by more than half a century. This would seem to be about as much as can be hoped for in the present state of knowledge.

---

[58] Gaeng, p. 26, footnote 14.

[59] Hübner, p. VIII: "Tria sunt, unde talis quaestio ordiri potest: res in titulis memoratae, sermo eorum, litterarum formae."

[60] Hübner, on discussing dating in Christian inscriptions in Britain, writes (p. VIII): "Temporum autem notas, quas cum maximo desideramus, si titulis recte uti volumus, statim fatendum est deesse in eis paene omnibus." Jackson also speaks (p. 163) of the "practically universal absence of dates in Britain."

It is also striking to find that in Britain and Africa the areas where we analyze the greatest number of inscriptions, pagan inscriptions are dated 37.0 % in Britain while only 23.2 % of Christian inscriptions in Africa are dated. Although the number of inscriptions in the Balkans is limited, it is interesting to find in this region that 24.2 % of the pagan inscriptions are dated, but only 12.0 % of the Christian inscriptions are dated. Among the pagan inscriptions of Britain, we have 96 milestones (numbered in *Roman Inscriptions of Britain* from 2219-2314), of which 86 % are specifically dated because of the dedication to one or more emperors. This figure would be almost 100 % if some inscriptions had not been mutilated. It would seem that Pirson's statement that Christian inscriptions are dated more often than pagan ones would have to be reevaluated on the basis of our findings.

In the present quantitative study we have also undertaken a numerical analysis of linguistic deviations from Classical Latin, even for non-dated inscriptions. This is contrary to the methodology of Gaeng who made a count only for dated inscriptions and simply gave examples of deviations from non-dated inscriptions for the purpose of illustrating further a particular phenomenon observed in dated material and to supplement it without giving any numerical analysis. [61] It is obvious that both areal and chronological data are of the utmost importance in determining the differentiation of Latin in Romania, but to omit a numerical analysis of the linguistic phenomena encountered in non-dated inscriptions would be tantamount to ignoring a critical factor in a study of this nature. The detailed information gotten from the non-dated inscriptions indeed serves as a check on our results obtained from dated inscriptions. Mihăescu stresses the two-part areal and chronological purpose of his work by saying that "am urmărit deci pe de o parte repartitia geografică a fenomenenlor și pe de alta succesiunea lor în timp." [62] Bàrtoli states (*Neolinguistica*, p. 99) that what the neolinguists have added to the methodology of the neogrammarians is precisely "un maggiore rispetto alle esigenze del tempo e dello spazio nella storia dei linguaggi." Sittl criticizes (p. 45) Schuchardt with the words that "Freilich konnte Schuchardt

---

[61] Gaeng, p. 27.
[62] Mihăescu, *Limba*, p. 6. Translation of the Rumanian: "I have followed therefore on the one hand the geographical distribution of the phenomena and on the other hand their succession in time."

in der Aussprache keine Unterschiede herausfinden, weil er die Beispiele nicht geographisch ordnete." Sofer summarizes some needs of Vulgar Latin studies by emphasizing (*Problematik*, p. 41) that "unbedingt notwendig sind aber auch die Hinweise, dass der Beginn mancher Spracherscheinungen noch in frühere Zeit zu setzen ist und dass die Lautentwicklungnen nicht überall zu gleicher Zeit eingesetzt haben." Since the geographical aspect as well as the chronological factor are so indispensable to the study of dialectalization of the Latin language, we feel that any insights derived from non-dated inscriptions should be gladly acknowledged.

Primary Sources

The following primary sources were used in our quantitative and comparative study of the vocalism of Latin inscriptions from Africa, Britain, Dalmatia, and the Balkans:

1. Ernst Diehl's *Inscriptiones Latinae Christianae Veteres (ILCV)* was our main sources for all of our Christian African inscriptions (755 inscriptions), Dalmatian material (212 inscriptions), and Christian Balkan inscriptions (83 inscriptions — about 46 % of the Balkan inscriptions considered), and for just two Christian inscriptions from Britain.

This work likewise was the main source material for Gaeng in his work, but it had to be supplemented (Gaeng, p. 25) by D. José Vives, *Inscripciones cristianas de la España Romana y Visigoda,* for his Iberian epigraphical material because of its more up-to-date and more voluminous material. The paucity of material for both the Balkan and Britain areas forced us to turn to other sources for inscriptional matter.

2. *The Roman Inscriptions of Britain (RIB)* by R. G. Collingwood and R. P. Wright served as our source material for all of the 486 pagan inscriptions of Britain. This collection is by far the most comprehensive, up-to-date (the closing date for the inscriptions included 31 December, 1954) and scholarly work ever produced for the Roman inscriptions of Britain and should be emulated in other regions as a model for epigraphical scholarship. This supersedes the first comprehensive collection of Roman inscriptions found in the British Isles, published in 1873 by Emil Hübner as Volume VII of the *Corpus Inscriptionum Latinarum.*

3. For the 77 Christian inscriptions of Britain, we turned to R. A. S. Macalister's *Corpus Inscriptionum Insularum Celticarum*, published in 1945, as our almost exclusive source material. Although Diehl does include approximately 30 Christian inscriptions from Britain and although Hübner's *Inscriptiones Britanniae Christianae*, published in 1876, does contain all of the inscriptions found in *CIIC*, we have consistently accepted Macalister's reading. On those extremely rare occasions (twice) where an inscription was missing from the *CIIC* and was given by both Diehl and Hübner, we chose the Diehl variant. We have, however, consulted both Diehl and Hübner for any information that we felt might be useful. Hübner's introduction was particularly informative.

4. The Latin inscriptions of the *Antike Denkmäler in Bulgarien*, edited by Ernst Kalinka in 1906, were our source for the pagan inscriptions of the Balkans. These inscriptions are from Thracia, Moesia Superior, and Moesia Inferior. It is interesting to note that three inscriptions incorporated into the collection are also recorded in Diehl's corpus of Christian inscriptions.

The fact that a certain inscription is recorded in more than one collection may, at times, lead to a confusing situation because of the variant readings offered. We will give just one example of how an investigator of epigraphical material has to cope with problems of interpretation of several scholars. In Diehl, we have inscription No. 782 recorded as: ☩ / *te [do]minu* / *laudamu. Latinus* / *annorum XXXV et* / *filia sua* / *anni VI* [...] / *iclinum* / *fecerut* / *in opus* / *Barrova* / *di*. Diehl also states (Vol. I, 147) that "hic titulus antiquissimus Britanniae christianus esse videtur." Macalister, on the other hand, gives (p. 499) the following reading for the same inscription (*CIIC*, 520): *TE DOMINVM LAVDAMVS LATINVS ANNORVM XXXV ET FILIA SVA ANNI V IC SINVM FE-CERVTN* [sic] *NEPVS BARROVADI*. Macalister does not assign any date to the inscription. In Diehl's reading, besides the loss of final *m* in *dominu*, the loss of the final *s* in *laudamu*, the different age given to the young daughter, the complete misinterpretation of the key words *ic sinum*, the misreading of the ligatured *n* in the verb form *fecerutn* (according to Macalister, p. 499, the engraver "omitted the *n* and had to insert it afterwards, ligatured to the upright bar of the *t* and on the wrong side of it."), the reading *opus* for *nepus*, we have the statement that this inscription is probably the oldest Christian inscription in Britain. Jackson, in his chapter discussing the early Christian inscriptions and the VL *ō* and *ŭ* writes (*Language,* p. 191) that "we have the spelling *V* in Latin words in no. 520 [of Macalister's *CIIC*], beginning in the sixth century, *NEPVS.*" Jackson thus accepts Macalister's reading for the word *nepus,* which is an important example of a VL *ō* to *ŭ* confusion, since Jackson adds (p. 191) "in British Latin such a pronunciation was apparently not regular but did occur." Jackson's attributing this inscription to the early sixth century renders Diehl's dating of the inscription completely useless. [63] We accept Macalister's reading as previously mentioned, but wonder, however, how many linguistic errors have been written because of poor epigraphical readings.

Method of Analysis

Our method of analyzing the vocalism encountered in the inscriptions was to count all the occurrences of the individual phenomena to be studied which were according to Classical Latin orthography as well as the deviations thereof. In this way, we get the overall picture of the Latin of the various areas without being unduly swayed by the more striking deviations from the Classical Latin norm. It is hoped that an overemphasis of a particular variation will thus be avoided. We agree with Sas when he states (p. 5) that "the argument that only the 'errors' are interesting, that only the 'diseased' portions of the ... system are significant leaves us unconvinced. ... The 'errors' or deviations from the norm become significant only when related to the entire ... system." Schmeck also warns against this tendency to overemphasize the deviations when he says (p. 24) that "wir müssen die vlt. Forschung davor bewahren, sich lediglich der 'Kuriositäten' anzunehmen."

---

[63] See Macalister, *Corpus Inscriptionum Insularum Celticarum,* I (Dublin: Stationery Office, 1945), 499-501, for a brilliant interpretation of this inscription. It should be brought out that Diehl's *ILCV* as well as the multivolume *CIL* do not have any drawings of the inscriptions contained in them. Macalister's *CIIC* and the *RIB* have the great advantage of having excellent drawings or photographs of every inscription. Kalinka's *Antike Denkmäler in Bulgarien,* likewise, has drawings or photographs of the individual inscriptions.

In the present work, we have made a count of the correct stressed and unstressed vowels and diphthongs and the deviations from the Classical Latin norm. A percentage of the deviation is then calculated for each region and a comparative idea is then gotten by comparing the extent of the deviation among the various areas. We have also used Gaeng's figures for the areas studied by him so as to get the fullest picture possible of the individual vocalic phenomena as found in the inscriptions of almost all of Romania. [64] We will also comment on the chronology of the linguistic changes whenever the figures warrant it. In our numerical analysis, we have been somewhat selective in our choice of inscriptions (as we have not analyzed numerically all inscriptions) when we felt the particular inscription was too poetical or too close to the Classical Latin model. A comparison of two extreme examples of Latin epigraphy will quickly show the tremendous difference inherent in the quality of the workmanship of stonemasons. The possibility of a linguistic error (and thus evidence of the popular speech) is evidently more probable on the part of the slovenly, almost unlettered stonemason than of the more cultured, language-conscious, careful, and better-paid artisan. [65]

---

[64] Raetia and Asia Minor are the two main areas not included in this study.

[65] The two examples are from *Roman Inscriptions of Britain*. The first is a *defixio, RIB* 7, from London, no date. The reading, given by Collingwood, is as follows: "Tretia(m) Maria(m) deficio et / illeus vita(m) et me(n)tem / et memoriam [e]t iocine/ra pulmones interm<x>ix<i>/ta fata cogitata menor/iam sci (= sic) no(n) possitt loqui / (quae) sicreta si(n)t neque SINITA / MERE possit neque [. / ...] CLVDO." The second is part of a commemorative tablet, *RIB* 665, from York, dated A.D. 107-A.D. 108.

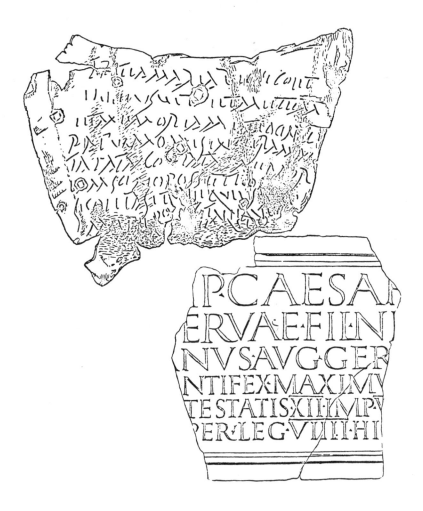

Areas

The areas studied in the present work are Africa, Britain, Dalmatia, and the Balkans. These regions are, for the most part, either peripheral and/or areas where Latin died out without leaving a Romance language heritage. Linguists have recognized, however, the importance of relic words for a better understanding of the development and character of Latin even in those areas which were subsequently lost to Romania. Tagliavini has coined the term "Romània

perduta" for those areas which, once having spoken Latin, relinquished
it and took on another language. The importance of those lost territories is aptly expressed by Tagliavini with the words (*Origini,*
p. 130): "... Romània perduta, nella quale è però possibile nella
maggior parte di casi, studiare gli stadi della spenta latinità attraverso
la toponomastica, i relitti latini rimasti nelle lingue che riuscirono a
soffocare il latino stesso." A more specific value of this "Romània
perduta," particularly important for a phonological study of spoken
Latin, is the fact as Tagliavini states (p. 133) that it can furnish
us with "sicuri indizi cronologici sull'evoluzione fonetica nel campo
romanzo." [66] It is also important to note the complementary relationship between studies of "Romània perduta" and inscriptions. Tagliavini again pointedly brings out the mutual value of both types of
investigation when, on referring to the specific case of Latin words
borrowed by the Berber languages, he states (p. 136) that "è appunto
examinando le voci latine penetrate nei dialetti berberi e fino ad oggi
conservate che possiamo farci un'idea del carattere della latinità dell'
Africa, che integra e completa quella fornitaci dall'analisi delle iscrizioni." A general characteristic of the Latin of this "Romània perduta"
seems to be its archaic nature. [67]

Africa. Of the various regions lost to Romania, Africa and its
Latinity have been by far the most studied by scholars. As Kübler
wrote (p. 162), "es musste unwilkürlich locken, als man nach den
provinziellen Färbungen der lateinischen Sprache zu forschen begann,
mit Afrika den Anfang zu machen ... Lag doch hier das reichste und,
wie der erste Blick zeigte, ergiebigste Beobachtungsmaterial vor."
Africa has been a prime target of researchers because of its vital
economic importance, its eminent place in Roman history with its
name so closely linked to Carthage, the Vandals, the Byzantines, and
the Arabs, its primacy in the early stages of Christianity with out-

---

[66] Väänänen, *Introduction,* p. 20, expresses the worth of "Romània perduta" in the particular problem of palatalization with the words: "Les
langues non romanes de la 'Romania perdue' et des régions limitrophes
fournissent, elles aussi, diverses données intéressant le latin vulgaire, notam-
ment le lexique et la phonétique. Ainsi, les emprunts latins du basque, du
berbère, du celtique, et du germanique confirment que la palatalisation de
$k^{e, i}$, $g^{e, i}$, est relativement tardive, n'ayant pas atteint les régions périphéri-
ques." Cf. also Tagliavini, *Origini,* p. 136.

[67] Tagliavini, *Origini,* p. 146; Sofer, "Differenzierung," p. 32; Mohl,
p. 243; Sittl, p. 81.

standing names like Augustine, Tertullian, Arnobius, and Cyprian, its pagan writers like Apuleius and Terence who contributed to popular Roman literature, and even its material wealth and claim to scholarship.

With the final downfall of Carthage in 146 B.C., Rome was able to cross into Africa. [68] The increased importance of Africa can be inferred from the words of Budinszky who states that "in der Kaiserzeit gehörte Afrika nicht nur zu den wohlhabendsten, sondern auch zu den geistig regsamsten Provinzen und darf, was intellectuelle Kultur betriff, unbedenklich in eine Linie mit Spanien und Gallien gestellt werden." [69] Carthage itself was by far the most important city in Roman Africa, its importance as a center of Roman studies likewise having been emphasized. [70]

The extent of the Romanization of North Africa was decidedly curtailed in the east by the hegemony of Greek civilization. The region from Cyrenaica to Egypt was Greek-speaking. [71] With the death of Theodosius in A.D. 395, the inheritance was divided between his two sons, Honorius ruling in the west, and Arcadius becoming the first Emperor of the east. The line of territorial division was drawn from Sirmium on the River Save, southwards through Illyricum to the Adriatic, all of Greece proper thus coming within the eastern sphere; in Africa, Cyrenaica was allotted to the east, while Tripolitana remained with Rome. [72] It can be said that the coastal strip from the Atlantic to Leptis Magna was almost completely romanized. [73] Of the various Roman provinces of North Africa, Tripolitana, Byzacena, Proconsular (these three originally the ancient Province of Africa), Numidia, Mauretania Sitifensis, and Mauretania Caesariensis, the Proconsular province with Carthage as its main center was decidedly the most romanized. These six provinces formed the diocesis of Africa which, in turn, was part of the praefecture comprising Illyria, Italy, and Africa under the administrative division of the Roman Empire,

---

[68] Wartburg, Origines, p. 137.
[69] Alexander Budinszky, Die Ausbreitung der lateinischen Sprache (Berlin: Hertz, 1881), p. 257.
[70] Warmington, p. 104; Tagliavini, Origini, p. 137.
[71] Tagliavini, Origini, p. 134.
[72] Elcock, p. 203.
[73] Tagliavini, Origini, p. 135.

established by Diocletian and brought to its fruition by Constantine. [74]
The final province of North Africa, Mauretania Tingitana, was included in the diocesis of Spain because of the difficulty of communication between it and the rest of Roman North Africa, and its
natural connection with Spain across the Straits of Gibraltar. [75]

Although the Roman sway over North Africa lasted until the
invasion of the Asding Vandals under Gaiseric in A.D. 429, with
the subsequent recognition of the Vandal kingdom in North Africa,
it should be remembered that native populations were always important in the outlying areas and in the isolated mountainous regions.
The Punic-speaking natives formed an important non-Latin language
group and their importance in the linguistic development of North
Africa is highlighted by a theory of Lot who maintains (p. 124) that
"le punique ne disparut pas des campagnes. C'est ce qui explique
qu'aucune langue romane ne s'est constituée, que l'on sache, même
dans la Proconsulaire ou la Numidie." [76] The historic sucession of
Roman, Vandal, Byzantine, and Arabic powers with their relations
with the surviving indigenous tribes and the resultant demise of the
Roman Empire in North Africa are admirably described by Gaston
Paris when he writes:

> En Afrique, ce ne furent pas les Vandales qui mirent fin
> du romanisme; il paraît au contraire probable que là comme
> en Espagne et en Gaule les Germains finirent par se fondre
> avec les vaincus et il se serait sans doute formé dans le ro-
> yaume de Genseric une langue romane particulière, si l'éta-

---

[74] Warmington, p. 3; J. B. Bury, *The Invasion of Europe by the Bar-
barians* (New York: Norton & Company, 1967), p. 29.

[75] Warmington, p. 3; Budinszky mentions (p. 250) that Mauretania
Tingitana had already been formed out of Mauretania by Emperor Claudius
in A.D. 42.

[76] For the importance and duration of Punic speech in North Africa,
cf. Sittl, p. 92 "Die punische Sprache erhielt sich mit einer ungewöhnlichen
Zähigkeit bis in die Zeit Augustins, sie war dessen Muttersprache und in
den besseren Ständen so verbreitet, dass der Kaiser im dritten Jahrhundert
den Gebrauch der punischen Sprache bei Testamenten gestatten mussten."
Compare also the well known example of Septimus Severus' sister who still
spoke Punic and scarcely knew Latin. Mohl reminds us (p. 58) that "il ne
faut pas oublier qu'en Afrique . . . , le punique, protégé par une civilisation
séculaire et des traditions illustres, dut opposer à la langue de Rome une
très longue et très tenace résistance." Sofer says ("Differenzierung," p. 37)
that "In Afrika erhielt sich das Punische und Libysche bis in die Zeit der
Vandalenherrschaft, wie u.a. Prokopios bezeugt."

blissement vandale n'avait pas été détruit par les Grecs, et surtout si la funeste invasion des Musulmans n'avait arraché ces belles contrées au monde chrétien. Il est vraisemblable que quand les Arabes arrivèrent il restait encore de nombreux Romains dans le pays; toutefois l'élément indigène n'avait jamais disparu même du temps de la domination romaine et dans le cœur des provinces, qu'il entourait de tous côtés; il s'allia étroitement avec les Arabes, et les derniers vestiges du romanisme disparurent bien vite de l'Afrique. [77]

Because of the significant number and outstanding quality of early Christian writers originating from North Africa, and because of the fact that the oldest extant official act of the martyrs, the *Acta Martyrum Scillitanorum* (A.D. 180), relating to the Christians of the town of Scilli, was written first in Latin, the view has been held that the birthplace of Christian Latin was in North Africa. This opinion has been questioned by Christine Mohrmann because of the early date of the epistle of St. Clement, written in Rome also in the second century. "Il devient de plus en plus clair que déjà vers le milieu du IIe siècle le processus de la latinisation de l'Eglise de Rome était en cours; on a donc affaire à une évolution contemporaine en Afrique et à Rome." [78] Whatever view is taken, the outstanding influence of North Africa in the early Christian church is undeniable. Sittl's words on the importance of Africa in church affairs still ring true when he writes (p. 84) that "im allgemeinen hat . . . die lateinische Kirche ihre geistvollsten Vertreter in unserer Provinz [Africa] gefunden, wodurch

---

[77] Gaston Paris, "Romani, Romani, lingua romana, romanicum," *Mélanges Linguistiques Gaston Paris*, publiés par Mario Roques (Paris, 1909), pp. 25-26. Wartburg, *Origines*, p. 90, also remarks that North Africa and the islands of Sardinia, Corsica, the Baleares, and western Sicily were politically detached from the Empire with their inclusion in the Vandal Empire after the Vandal invasion of A.D. 455. Wartburg concurs with the view that the Arabic invasion of North Africa put an end to Roman influence in the area. He writes (pp. 188-89) that "la langue et la culture romanes ne furent balayées que par la vague des Arabes. En 670 ceux-ci apparurent dans le Sud de la Tunisie, en 698 la conquête du Maghrab fut terminée par la prise de Carthage." Rohlfs, *Vulgärlatein*, pp. 20-21, states that "in dem von den Vandalen besetzten nordafrikanischen Küstenstreifen scheint die lateinische Sprache sich bis zum Zeitalter der arabischen Expansion (7. Jahrundert) erhalten zu haben."

[78] Mohrmann, *Latin vulgaire*, p. 28; Palmer agrees (p. 199) with this view.

es sich leicht erklärt, dass noch in der ersten Periode des Christentums die Afrikaner entschieden die Fürherstelle einnahmen."

Linguistically speaking, Sittl's attempts to show an African dialectal
form of Latin were abortive, but even though he himself retracted his
view in a famous palinode (see *supra*, footnote 19, p. 15), scholars
have continued to investigate African Latin for its particularities and
deviations from Classical Latin. [79] Although Kroll, one of Sittl's
strongest adversaries, discounted the latter's attempts to show dialectalization in the Latin spoken in North Africa, basing his opposition
mainly on the fact that peculiarities propounded for Africa were also
found in other regions of the Empire, [80] he nevertheless concludes
(p. 590) with the words: "Es wäre Unrecht zu leugnen, dass in der
Zeit des Apuleius und Tertullian die Ansätze zu einer Sonderentwicklung des in Afrika gesprochenen Lateins vorhanden gewesen sein
können. Aber das uns überkommene sprachliche Material ist nicht
der Art, dass es uns gestattet, über diese Dialekticismen mehr zu
erfahren als einige unsichere Einzelheiten." Kübler, in his study of
North African inscriptions, likewise has a generally negative view of
the distinctiveness of African Latin on the basis of his research,
although his work did not include phonology. He himself writes
(p. 201): "Die Untersuchung der lautlichen Erscheinungen haben wir
vermieden." He summarizes his findings with the statement (p. 201)
that "die Ausbeute für Flexion und Syntax war, wie nicht anders
zu erwarten, gering. Nicht einmal im Einzelnen finden sich Unterschiede von den grammatischen Sünden des Vulgärlateins anderer
Provinzen ... und geradezu vermessen wäre es, aus den wenigen Verstössen gegen die Schulgrammatik, die sich in unserm inschriftlichen
Material finden, ein System herauskonstruieren zu wollen." He does
admit (p. 201), however, that "reicher ist der Gewinn für Wortbildung,

---

[79] Cf. Kroll, pp. 569-70: "Obwohl er selbst [referring to Sittl] nachdem
bald starke Zweifel an seinen Aufstellungen laut geworden waren, in eine
sehr beachtenswerthen Palinode seine früheren Behauptungen zurückgenommen hat, ist doch gerade seine zusammenfassende Darstellung des afrikanischen Dialektes der Grund geblieben, auf dem Gelehrte wie Wölfflin, Landgraf, Thielmann und Andere gebaut haben und noch bauen."

[80] *Ibid.*, p. 571: "Recht fatal war es freilich, auch bei Angehörigen
anderer Provinzen viele der sichersten Eigentümlichkeiten des afrikanischen
Lateins anzutreten." Cf. Löfstedt, *Late Latin*, p. 40: "The so-called 'Africitas' was soon shown to be a figment. Its alleged peculiarities are in fact
much the common features of Late Latin rhetorical prose."

Stilistik und Wortschaft." Although scholars have been sceptical about the uniqueness of African Latin, its archaic qualities, its extensive Greek borrowings, its debt to Hebrew tradition, and its baroque ornateness have been repeatedly pointed out.[81]

The placing of African Latin in the archaic vocalic system on the basis of Latin grammarians and Berber loanwords and the discussion of the validity of this judgment, on the basis of the criteria available, have already been discussed. (See *supra*, footnote 14, p. 8.) A problem tangential to the linguistic question is the mutual relationship of North Africa to Sardinia, southern Italy, and the Iberian Peninsula and the resulting influences. During the Vandal domination of North Africa, and later under the Byzantine hegemony, Sardinia was administratively bound to Africa. This could not fail but influence, from the linguistic viewpoint, the Latinity of Sardinian which shows many contacts with the Latin of North Africa.[82] It has also been pointed out that the Latin of Africa presented special points of contact with that of Hispania and that a continuous migratory movement favored the extension of isoglosses and innovations of African origin in the Iberian Peninsula.[83] Budinszky likewise states (p. 262) that "Die lingua rustica Afrikas mag sich somit einerseits mit der Volkssprache Unteritaliens, anderseits mit derjenigen Hispaniens berührt haben, was auch vom geographischen Standpunkt alle Wahrscheinlichkeit für sich hat, da sich eben mit diesen Gegenden ein Bevölkerungsaustausch am häufigsten vollzogen haben wird." Mohl, on explaining the Latin of Carthage, even gives an historical reason for the influence of southern Italy on North Africa when he speaks (p. 120) of the "nombreux colons de l'Italie méridionale qui émigrèrent, après les Guerres Puniques, dans la nouvelle colonie. Peut-être même pourrait-on préciser la date, en se rappelant que C. Gracchus fut chargé de conduire comme triumvir, peu avant la Guerre Sociale, six mille Italiotes, particulièrement des Samnites, dans la nouvelle colonie de Junonia, fondée précisément sur les ruines mêmes de Carthage." The importance of the Latin of Africa and its relations with the Latin of Spain, southern Italy, and Sardinia have been touched upon, as we

---

[81] See Kroll, pp. 569, 578, 580-81; Kübler, pp. 162, 187, 201-2; Mohl, pp. 81, 243; Tagliavini, *Origini*, p. 136; Sittl, pp. 81, 112, 120, 125.

[82] Tagliavini, *Origini*, p. 85.

[83] *Ibid.*, pp. 136-37; Rohlfs, *Review*, p. 301; Sittl, p. 94; Sofer, "Differenzierung," p. 37.

have seen, but since North Africa lacks the modern Romance languages
for a viable comparison, it has been said that the data available to us
shed little light on our attempts to classify African Latin on a precise,
phonological basis. [84] Although scholars have expressed the opinion
that the problem of African Latin has been solved and now has
nothing more than an historical interest, [85] we consider Mohl's opinion
(p. 81) that "ce fameux latin d'Afrique sur lequel on a déjà tant écrit
et sur lequel il reste tant à dire" to be still valid.

Britain. Although scholars have written voluminously on the problem of the Latin language and literature [86] of North Africa, Romance
linguists have almost completely ignored the Latin as spoken in Britain. The void has been, of necessity, filled mainly by Celtologists
who, in their main pursuit of the history of Celtic, have delved into
the problems of the Roman occupation of Britain and the nature of
Latin spoken there, but their attention to Latin linguistic problems
has been of a secondary order, subservient to their prime interest of
getting information from whatever source available in their attempts
to elucidate the chronological development of the British languages. [87]

---

[84] Wartburg, *Ausgliederung*, p. 63.

[85] Löfstedt, *Late Latin*, p. 42; Sofer, *Problematik*, p. 40.

[86] Speaking about the lack of any great contribution of Latin writers
from Britain to early Roman literature, Budinszky notes (p. 133) that "über
die Betheiligung der Briten an der römischen Literatur liegt keine Kunde
vor und die Reihe mehr oder minder klangvoller Namer, durch welche die
romanisierten Provinzen des Westens wie Spanien, Gallien oder Afrika vertreten sind, erfuhr von der nordischen Insel her keine Bereicherung."
Although the intellectual and spiritual life of Roman Britain does not appear
to be on the same high level as elsewhere in the Empire, Jackson remarks
(p. 144): "As for the intellectual and religious life in Britain at the end of
the fourth century and in the first half of the fifth, religious thought was
active enough to foster one of the great early Christian heresiarchs, Pe-
lagius, who left the country about 380." This is not to deny the later
importance of Anglo-Latin literature with its most outstanding representative, the Venerable Bede (C.A.D. 670-735), the contribution of the Irish
monks of Iona to the return of Christian and Latin tradition to the north
of England, and the importance of Alcuin (A.D. 735-804) in the Carolingian
Renaissance. In our study we will not include the Latin of Ireland as
Hibernia was never colonized by the Romans and those Latin loanwords
found in Irish are, for the most part, transmitted through Welsh borrowings.
See Budinszky, p. 125; Loth, p. 21; Hübner, p. V; Tagliavini, *Origini*,
p. 142.

[87] Cf. Jackson's acknowledged purpose of his book *Language and History
in Early Britain*, pp. v, vi: "...this is a chronological history of the sound-
system of the British language and its descendants during the Roman period

The extent and importance of the Latin element in the Brittonic lexicon have been forcefully expressed (p. 76) by Jackson:

Approximately eight hundred of these Latin words have survived among the three Brittonic languages (Welsh, Cornish, and Breton); so that if a Romance language is one which has developed by the ordinary processes of linguistic growth from the colloquial Latin of a province of the Roman Empire, a small but not negligible part of the Brittonic vocabulary may be said to form a fragment of a Romance language; a fact which has been almost entirely ignored by Romance scholars.

Those Romance linguists who do touch on British Latin normally limit themselves to a slight discussion of the Latin relic-words in the Brittonic languages, with hardly a mention of any phonological, morphological, or syntactical element worthy of note.[88] The Latin of Britain has been equated to that of Gaul. In fact, Pogatscher, in his study of the Latin element in Anglo-Saxon, goes so far as to say that "im Allgemeinen mag hier bemerkt werden, dass die grammatische Form des AE. Lehnworte für das britannische Volkslatein ein so enges

---

and the subsequent Dark Ages. In the course of working out these problems, a number of questions of a historical nature entered in, are examined here for the information they give on the development of British languages. A certain amount of light appears to the writer to be reflected back into some of the darker corners of early British history. For instance, the lingua franca of the Roman Empire, Vulgar Latin, was widely spoken in the Roman province of Britain; some conclusions are offered here about the special character of Vulgar Latin in Britain, of a kind ignored by previous writers, and about the extent of the spoken Latin language there, and the people who used it." Cf. Loth, p. 1: "Les mots latins passées dans les langues brittoniques sont trop importants, tant par leur nombre et leur caractère, qu'en raison des circonstances exceptionelles dans lesquelles ils ont été empruntés, pour qu'ils n'aient pas appelé l'attention des celtisants."

[88] It is noteworthy that Vidos gives (p. 76) the important relic-word "plebs" with its meaning "parocchia" as an example of the former extension of a Latin word, subsequently lost in French, but with its original meaning kept in the Brittonic languages; Tagliavini gives (p. 131) the same example of "plebs." Elcock mentions briefly the historical background of the Romans in Britain (p. 229) and gives a partial list of Latin words now found in modern Welsh (p. 298). Bourciez and Lausberg have nothing to say about the Latin in Britain. The subject of the Celtic influence on the Romance languages, especially on French, is a different subject and has, of course, been treated in detail, although the substratum question has been hotly debated.

Zusammengehen mit dem gallischen erweist, dass wenn die Angelsa-
chesen nicht nach Britannien gekommen wären, England wohl eine
dem Französischen sehr nahestehende Sprache erhalten hätte." [89]
Although the Gaulish tribes on both sides of the English Channel
were extremely similar in their religious beliefs, customs, tribal or-
ganization, language, superstitions, and other facets of their lives, [90]
the belief that the Latin spoken in Britain was only a continuation
of the Latin spoken in Gaul has to be clarified. Although it can
hardly be said that there was a special dialect of Vulgar Latin, used
in Britain by the great mass of the Latin-speaking population, unlike
the speech of the rest of the Empire, the Latin of Britain did present
some particularities that did show marked differences from the Latin
spoken in the western Empire in general and of Gaul in particular. [91]
We will summarize the differences between British Latin and the
western variety of Vulgar Latin in accordance with the views of
Jackson (*Language*, pp. 80-94) on the basis of his study of Latin
loanwords found in the Brittonic languages.

a)   Short stressed Classical Latin /ĭ/ and /ŭ/ became, respectively, ẹ and ọ in western Vulgar Latin in contrast to British Latin
where they remained. This is reminiscent of the archaic vocalic
system.

b)   The breakdown of the Classical Latin system of vowel quantity into a qualitative system has been assumed for almost all of
Romania. There is no certain trace of this in British Latin; with one
or two possible exceptions, the loanwords show that the classical
quantity system was preserved, even with unstressed vowels, in the
Latin of Roman Britain. [92] The collapse of the Latin quantity system

---

[89] Alois Pogatscher, *Zur Lautlehre der griechischen, lateinischen, romanischen Lehnworte im Altenglischen* (Strassburg: Karl J. Trübner, 1888), p. 13.
The idea of British Latin as an extension of Gaulish Latin is also expressed
by Vidos, p. 76; Tagliavini, *Origini*, p. 131.

[90] Budinszky, pp. 119-20.

[91] See Kenneth Jackson, "On the Vulgar Latin of Roman Britain," in
Mediaeval Studies in Honor of Jeremiah Denis Matthias Ford, ed. Urban
T. Holmes, Jr., and Alex J. Denomy, C.S.B. (Cambridge, Mass.: Harvard
University Press, 1948), pp. 83-103, for a summary of the similarities and
differences of the British Latin with the Continental variety. In his book
Language and History in Early Britain, Jackson gives a detailed study of all
aspects of the problem.

[92] This persistence of the Classical Latin quantitative system has also
been noted by Lot, p. 118; Carnoy, p. 27; Loth, pp. 4, 64, 74.

with its important consequences has been interpreted as the "Vorgang der romanischen Sprachgeschichte, der als eine der folgenschwersten Umgestaltungen des lateinischen Lautsystems zugleich eine entscheidender Schritt auf dem Wege der Ausgliederung der romanischen Sprachräume war." [93]

c) The Latin loanwords in British show no sign of a prosthetic vowel before impure *s*.

d) Latin *v* and *b* were kept distinct in British Latin.

e) There is an absence of palatalization and assibilation in *ti̯, di̯, ci̯, ce, ci, gi̯, ge,* and *gi* in the Latin of Britain. This is in strong contrast with the development of Latin in Gaul.

f) There is almost no trace of voicing of intervocalic *p, t, k*.

g) Latin *li̯, ni̯* apparently did not become palatalized in Britain.

h) The insertion of a consonant glide *u*, such as in *puteus >
puteuus*, although not unknown in other parts of the Empire, seems to be more prevalent in British Latin.

These differences from western Vulgar Latin seem to be an indication that the many Latin loanwords in Brittonic came ultimately from the upper class, educated speakers in the Lowlands of rather stilted school Latin, and not from the standard Vulgar Latin of the middle and lower classes in the Roman Empire. The Latin of the loanwords was, therefore, for the most part, aristocratic.

Another problem that has been hotly debated by scholars in the field of Roman Britain has been the extent of the Romanization of the country. [94] On the basis of the Latin inscriptions collected by Hübner, Pogatscher came to the conclusion (p. 2) that the Latin language was the "Verkehrssprache in Britannien für längere Zeit nach dem Abzug der Römer" and that there was also a "weitgehende Romanisierung wenigstens gewisser Teile des Landes." Loth was vehemently opposed to this concept of a thorough Romanization of Britain (except for the Celtic population living in the more rugged, isolated Highlands of the west) and maintained (p. 11) that "le latin a disparu avec les troupes qui l'avaient apporté." He concludes (p. 16) that "les inscriptions, la numismatique, l'archéologie sont d'accord sur

---

[93] H. Weinrich, *Phonologische Studien zur romanischen Sprachgeschichte* (Münster, Westfalen: Aschendorffsche, 1958), p. 14.

[94] The best book on the whole question of Roman Britain is *Roman Britain and the English Settlements,* 2nd ed. (Oxford: Clarendon Press, 1963), written by R. G. Collingwood and J. N. L. Myres.

les conséquences de l'occupation: avec le départ des troupes romaines coincide une brusque et complète interruption de la vie romaine en Bretagne." Jackson considers (p. 248) the controversy between Pogatscher and Loth out-of-date in many ways, and gives the more conciliatory view (p. 248) that "Latin was spoken in Roman Britain much more widely than merely among the army; but also that immediately before and during the course of the English invasion the Roman military and civil governments were disrupted, organized town life disappeared, the rural upper classes of the villa system ceased to exist; and, in short, that all those elements in the population of the Lowland Zone which were the strength of the Latin language melted away with the decay and eventually the collapse of the Roman way of life before the onset of the English, leaving little but a British-speaking peasantry behind. This is not to say that the invaders can have had no contact whatever with Latin speakers in the Lowland Zone; so rigid a hypothesis would be absurd." [95]

The present study will try to see whether the conclusions concerning British Latin, reached on the basis of loanwords, can be corroborated by the language of Latin inscriptions.

Dalmatia. Geographically speaking, Dalmatia is a natural region constituted by the narrow, coastal strip of the eastern Adriatic and its islands, with its northern boundary limited by the Gulf of Quarnaro and its southern boundary extending as far south as Cattaro or possibly Antivari. It is effectively isolated from the Balkan Peninsula by the Velebit Mountains and the Dinaric Alps. Because of its geographical, climatic, and biological characteristics, Dalmatia is set off from the rest of the Balkan Peninsula. [96] The northernmost island of Dalmatia is Veglia (Krk). It is the speech of the last Vegliote-speaking subject, Antonio Udina Burbur, who died in 1898, that formed the basis of Bàrtoli's monumental work *Das Dalmatische: Altromanische Sprachreste von Veglia bis Ragusa und ihre Stellung in der Apennino-Balkanischen Romania,* published in 1906, but still a fundamental work in the field. Although we can define the Dalmatian language

---

[95] Cf. Collingwood-Myres, p. 313: "The 'Departure of the Romans' contributed very little to the cessation of Roman life in Britain. Nor was it ruinous either to the political fabric or to the well-being of the country."
[96] See Antonio Renato Toniolo's article entitled "Dalmazia," *Enciclopedia Italiana* (Rome: Istituto Giovanni Treccani, 1931), p. 245.

as the "idioma neolatino preveneto, oggi estinto, formatosi lungo la costa dalmata, dalla spontanea e diretta continuazione del Latino," [97] our knowledge is unfortunately limited and, by forfeit, we consider Vegliote as Dalmatian per se. Romance linguists usually consider two main dialects of Dalmatian: a northern type embodied in Vegliote and a southern variant in Ragusa. [98] An attempt has also been made to divide Dalmatian into three dialect areas, mainly on the basis of the development of stressed *a*. [99] The extinction of Dalmatian was mainly due to the pressures of Venetian: the stronger the influence of Venetian, the quicker the smothering of Dalmatian. In Zara, the Dalmatian language died out quickly; in Ragusa, not until the end of the fifteen century, and in Veglia, in the last years of the nineteenth century.

One of the serious problems about Dalmatian has been its classification among the Romance languages. Bàrtoli placed it in his Apennino-Balkan grouping, but this was bitterly debated by his contemporary Merlo, who saw in Dalmatian a link which joined Ladin to Rumanian. A precise determination of Dalmatia's place in Romania has always been precarious. Tagliavini placed it in Italo-Romance, but with hesitation. He acknowledged that his division was inevitably defective. Tagliavini writes (*Origini*, p. 298) that although "il Dalmatico ... viene posto nel grupo Italo-romanzo ... ora è indubbio ... che il Dalmatico presenta molti punti di contatto, reali o apparenti, coll'Italiano, ma è sicuro che il Dalmatico representa piuttosto una continuazione della romanità orientale e, pur essendo nettamente distinto dal Rumeno," he is forced to conclude (p. 298), that "il Dal-

---

[97] Tagliavini, *Origini*, p. 316. It should be realized that Diez in his classification of the Romance languages in 1836, did not know of the existence of Dalmatian. In Budinszky's work *Die Ausbreitung der lateinischen Sprache*, published in 1881, still useful for its informative historical aspect, we can still see a lack of perspective in the case of Dalmatia, when he writes (p. 190): "Der Umstand aber, dass aus der hierher verpflanzten Sprache Latiums nicht ein besonderes romanisches Idiom erwuchs, sondern dass sich dieselbe hier ungefähr so wie auf der appeninischen Halbinsel entwickelte, dieser Umstand wird einerseits in dem nie unterbrochenen regen Verkehr, den die dalmatischen Seeplätze mit Italien unterhielten, seine Erklärung finden."

[98] Kristian Sandfeld, *Linguistique balkanique* (Paris: E. Champion, 1930), p. 51; Wartburg, *Origines*, p. 64, and *Ausgliederung*, p. 13.

[99] Bernhard Rosenkranz, "Die Gliederung des Dalmatischen," *Zeitschrift für romanische Philologie*, 71 (1955), 269-79.

matico quindi può essere considerato come il ponte di passaggio fra il Balcano-romanzo e l'Italo-romanzo." This intermediate position of Dalmatian between Italo-Romance and Balkan Romance has been also mentioned by other scholars. [100] A revision of Dalmatian's place in East Romance has been recently made by Hadlich who considers that "we must revise Bàrtoli's placing of Vegliote in the East Romance group, and consider Vegliote rather a linguistic system in which according to the normal criteria, the East-West division of Romance languages does not apply." [101] Hadlich, on the basis of his findings that the Latin vocalic system of Veglia by the beginning of the seventh century was the same as that postulated for the early period of all of the West Romance languages, concluded (p. 87) that "if a division of Romance languages were to be made on the basis of vowel development, Vegliote would have to be considered a West Romance language." [102] It should be mentioned that the subsequent development of the Dalmatian vowel system showed a plethora of diphthongization and a general innovating tendency. The consonantal system of Dalmatian, however, is extremely conservative. There is no evidence of voicing of intervocalic occlusives, a phenomenon which is important in any attempt to distinguish Dalmatian elements in Serbo-Croatian from the voiced Venetian counterpart. Hadlich observes (p. 87) that "consideration of the development of the Vegliote consonant system leads one to the exactly opposite conclusion that Vegliote is an East Romance language." Hadlich accounts for the dichotomy of the Dalmatian systems by saying (p. 88):

> Thus the Vegliote vowel system developed like those of the West Romance languages and the consonant system developed like those of the East Romance languages. This situation resulted from the chronology of the changes which characterize the West Romance languages. That is, the

---

[100] Densusianu, p. 232; Vidos, p. 282; Elcock, p. 18; Bourciez, *Éléments de linguistique romane*, 5th ed. (Paris: Klincksieck, 1967), p. 137; Puşcariu, *Études*, p. 27.

[101] Roger L. Hadlich, *The Phonological History of Vegliote* (Chapel Hill: University of North Carolina Press, 1965), p. 88.

[102] Lausberg, *Lingüística*, p. 84, had already maintained that Dalmatian belonged to the Italic qualitative vocalic system; Mihăescu, *Limba*, p. 32, mentions that Dalmatian had the parallelism of ĭ > é and ŭ > ó in contrast to Rumanian and the Latin loanwords in Albanian where only ĭ > é took place.

changes characteristic of the West Romance vowel system had already taken place (including Vegliote Latin) by the time that Veglia was isolated from the West by the Slavs. However, the Western consonant changes took place considerably after this isolation, so that West Romance influence on changes in Veglia was impossible. [103]

Although Dalmatian has a definite place in any study of Balkan Romance, it has been noted that the Latin spoken in Dalmatian was different in some important respects from the Latin of other parts of the Balkan Peninsula. [104] It was precisely Rumanian's treatment of Lat. $\bar{\imath} > e$ and not the parallel development of $\bar{\imath} > e$ and $\bar{u} > o$ as found in Western Romance in general and Dalmatian in particular that caused Skok to write that "wir müssen daher zwei Typen der Balkan-Latinität annehmen." [105] Skok also mentions (p. 454) the decisive significance of the placing of the definite article in the division of Balkan Latin: "Der wichtigste Unterscheid zwischen der Balkanlatinität des Adria-Typus und derjenigen des Festland-Typus bildet die Vorsetzung bzw. die Nachstellung des Artikels. Den post-positiven Artikel kennt die Adrialatinität nicht, nur den praepositiven wie die ganze West Romania."

Most scholars agree that the two historical events that were instrumental in causing the Latin of Dalmatia to develop differently from that of the inland Balkan Peninsula were the Diocletian division

---

[103] Hadlich's conclusion on the position of Dalmatian among the Romance languages was endorsed by Vihman in her review of his book in *Romance Philology*, XXII (1969), 621-26, when she writes (p. 626): "Hadlich's lucid reassessment of Vegliote's position among the Romance languages appears to be valid; this is a major contribution for which the scholarly world may be grateful."

[104] Cf. Rudolf Hanslik's assertion in his review of *Limba latină în provinciile dunărene ale imperiului român*, by H. Mihăescu, in *Kratylos*, 10 (1965), 212: "Am eigenartigsten hat sich das Latein im dalmatischen Raum entwickelt"; Elcock, p. 483: "Sharing many features with the Italian dialects, Old Dalmatian seems to have possessed an invididuality which marked it off from the inland Romance of Illyricum and Moesia"; Vidos, p. 282: "...il dalmatoromanzo (fondamento del dalmatico) si distingue dal balcanoromanzo..."; Mihăescu, *Limba*, p. 32: "...limba latină a evolutat altfel in Dalmatia decît în provinciile dunărene din părtile răsăritene." (Translation of the Rumanian: "...the Latin language evolved in Dalmatia differently than in the Danubian provinces of the eastern parts.")

[105] Petar Skok, "Zum Balkanlatein," *Zeitschrift für romanische Philologie*, 54 (1934), 182.

towards the end of the third century, whereby the southern part of Dalmatia, with the cities of Lissus, Scodra, and Doclea, was separated from the rest of the province and formed into a new province named Dalmatia Praevalitana, thus included in Illyricum oriental, and the official division in A.D. 395 of the Roman Empire into the eastern and western parts, Dalmatia remaining with Rome and Praevalitana (modern Montenegro and northern Albania) going with Constantinople. Since most of Dalmatia remained under the influence of Rome, it could thus take part in those linguistic evolutions which affected Western Romance, innovations which the Latin of the Eastern Empire did not undergo. [106] In the present study, we will investigate whether the vocalism of Dalmatia differs from that of the inland Balkan Peninsula on the basis of inscriptional material.

Balkans. Our last region to be studied is extremely vast, encompassing the Latin provinces of Noricum, Pannonia, Moesia, Macedonia, Thracia, and Dacia. Since Dacia is north of the Danube, it should technically not be included in a strict classification of the Balkans, but for the obvious reason that the Latin spoken in Dacia evolved into the only modern Romance language in the area (outside of the now defunct Dalmatian), any serious discussion of Balkan Latin must, of necessity, include Dacia. It should be noted that scholars have insisted on an extensive area as the cradle of Rumania, a specifically well-defined, limited area being discarded because of the nomadic nature of the Rumanian people in the course of their evolution. [107] Balkan Latin is limited in the south by Greek, a culturally richer language whose sphere of influence thwarted the advance of Latin in that part of the Roman Empire. Although isolated in a sea of disparate languages, Rumanian has tenaciously survived in spite of the waves of marauding tribes that have overwhelmed its territory. Dacia, as is well known, was conquered by the Romans in A.D. 107 under Trajan and officially abandoned by Aurelius in A.D. 271. Since Roman

---

[106] Cf. Budinszky, p. 188; Vidos, pp. 282-83; I. Şiadbei, "Sur l'élément latin de l'Albanais," in *Mélanges Linguistiques,* publiés à l'occasion du VIIIe Congrès international des linguistes à Oslo, du 5 au 9 août 1957 (Bucharest: Academia Republicii Populare Romîne, 1957), p. 63; Bàrtoli, *Das Dalmatische,* p. 124; Mihăescu, *Limba,* pp. 24-25, 32.

[107] Rosetti, I, 39-40; Densusianu, p. 48; Kuhn, p. 124; Sextil Puşcariu, *Die rumänische Sprache: Ihr Wesen und ihre volkliche Prägung,* trans. Heinrich Kuen (Leipzig: Otto Harrassowitz, 1943), p. 411.

troops and administration left Dacia after only a century and a half of occupation and resettled south of the Danube, the mere existence of a Romance language in southeastern Europe is an unparalleled event in the history of Romance-speaking peoples. [108] This potpourri of distinct languages in the Balkans has given rise to a Balkan mentality not only in a community of civilization and beliefs but in the development of common linguistic traits to form "une unité linguistique remarquable." [109]

For an understanding of Balkan Latin, it is necessary to study the Latin elements that have survived in the Balkan languages. A study of the Latin influence in Albanian is particularly worthwhile because of the deep penetration of the Latin layer in a language that has undergone a strong influence of Balkan Latin. [110] The distinctive Rumanian vocalic system is also found in the Latin of Albanian. [111] Albanian poses an interesting problem, as of the two fairly divergent dialects, a northern Gegue and a southern Tosk, Rumanian has similarities mainly with Tosk. [112] The fact that the Latin elements in Albanian also differ from the interior Balkan Latin likewise has historical significance, as stated by Şiadbei ("Albanais," p. 63): "... beaucoup d'éléments latins n'existent que dans l'une des deux langues en question, l'albanais et le roumain; ils constituent des aires lexicales différentes. Ces aires prouvent l'interruption du contact entre les deux territoires où se sont dévéloppés l'albanais et le roumain."

The Latin loanwords in the south Slavic languages (Serbo-Croatian and to a lesser degree, Bulgarian) and in modern Greek have

---

[108] For a discussion of the embittered, politically-motivated problem of modern Rumanian as a survival of the Latin spoken north of the Danube or as a language carried northward in the Middle Ages, see Matthias Friedwagner, "Über die Sprache und Heimat der Rumänen," *Zeitschrift für romanische Philologie*, 54 (1934), 641-715. See also Lausberg, *Lingüística*, p. 82; Puşcariu, *Rumänische Sprache*, pp. 250-51; and *Études*, pp. 61-64.

[109] For a detailed study of the Balkan languages and their interpretation, see Sandfeld, *Linguistique balkanique*. Cf. also Puşcariu, *Rumänische Sprache*, p. 197 ff.; Rosetti, II, 34.

[110] Sandfeld, p. 51; Kuhn, p. 143; Tagliavini, *Origini*, p. 307.

[111] See Bidwell, "The Chronology of Certain Sound Changes in Common Slavic," *Word*, 17 (1969), 114; Tagliavini, *Origini*, p. 191; Skok, "Balkanlatein," 54 (1934), 182.

[112] Cf. Rosetti, II, 42, 99; Wartburg, *Problèmes*, p. 108; Puşcariu, *Rumänische Sprache*, p. 336; Sandfeld, p. 66. Both Puşcariu and Sandfeld consider the change of intervocalic -n- to -r- in Tosk, no rhotacism in Gegue, as the most important difference between these two dialects.

also been studied with a view to determining the nature of Balkan Latin. In a general appraisal of the Slavic influence on the Balkan Peninsula, Skok, in a series of articles dedicated to the study of Balkan Latin, [113] considers the place of Rumanian within the Romance languages on the basis of mainly two distinctive features: a) the already mentioned change of Latin $ĭ > e$, but the retention of short $ŭ$, contrary to the Dalmatian vocalism, and thus an important division of Balkan Latin into two areas, with the main centers on the Adriatic coast and in the Justinian Praefecture, and b) the Rumanian diphthongization of Latin $ĕ$, but not of $ŏ$. Skok attributes this lack of parallelism precisely to the Slavic incursion of the Balkan Peninsula:

> Die romanische Dipthongierung ist aus dem Westen gekommen. Sie kannte ursprünglich, wie das Rumänisch-Albanische zeigt, keinen Parallelismus in der Vokalreihe *e o*. Dieser älteste Zustand hat sich in der justinianischen Praefektur deshalb treu erhalten können, weil dieses Gebiet, von den Slaven schon anfangs des 6. Jrs. überflutet, von dem adriatischen Typus der Latinität vollständig losgerissen wurde. Der letzte Typus blieb sowieso nur auf die Küstenstädte beschränkt, konnte daher keine Irradiation mehr auf die Balkan-latinität des festländischen Typus ausüben. [114]

In his discussion of the Slavic influence on Rumanian, Densusianu considers it a decisive step in the evolution of the Rumanian language.

> C'est, en effet, à partir de l'invasion slave que le roman balkanique est devenu le roumain... Jusqu'alors, le parler qui était résulté du latin transplanté sur les deux rives du Danube ne pouvait être considéré que comme une variante dialectale... de l'italien. C'est le contact avec les Slaves qui transforme ce parler en une langue spéciale, toujours romane sans doute dans sa constitution interne, mais sensiblement différente de celles qui sont sorties de la même souche. [115]

Puşcariu, in a more sober discussion of the influence of the Slavic superstratum on the development of Rumanian, acknowledges its im-

---

[113] Petar Skok, "Zum Balkanlatein," *Zeitschrift für romanische Philologie*, 48 (1928), 398-403; 50 (1930), 484-532; 54 (1934), 175-215, 424-99.
[114] Skok, "Balkanlatein," 54 (1934), 183.
[115] Densusianu, pp. 240-41.

portance on vocabulary, but maintains (*Rumänische Sprache*, p. 356) that "die hauptsächlichsten Lautveränderungen im Rumänischen schon abgeschlossen waren und die Ordnung der Sprache in ihren Hauptzügen schon festlag."

The Romanization of Dacia was also instrumental in determining the type of Latin that was to evolve in the area. Because of the destruction of the region as a result of the Dacian Wars (A.D. 101 and A.D. 106-107), colonists were forced to immigrate into this part of the Roman Empire. These Romans were, for the most part, of a lower social class, and their rustic imprint on the future development of Rumanian was considerable. It has been advanced that the loss of the final -s in Rumanian, a phonetic change with important morphological consequences, was the result of the low social stratum of the speakers of Dacian Latin. This social-linguistic differentiation was transformed into a geographical differentiation. [116] A similar influence of the social layer of the Latin speaker in the future development of Rumanian was expressed by Puşcariu (*Rumänische Sprache*, p. 445) when he writes that "unter den Erscheinungen sozialer Nature, die einen entscheidenden Einfluss auf die Entwicklung der rumänischen Sprache gehabt haben, muss vor allem die Verbäuerlichung der lateinischen Sprache in Südosteuropa genannt werden." Closely related to the type of Latin spoken in Dacia because of the influence of the lower social classes is the lack of schools and literary centers. The consequence was that the Latin continued to evolve apart from literary preoccupations and that the speech of the people was less influenced by a learned literary tradition as was the case in the more aristocratically romanized provinces of Gaul and Spain. [117]

It has been said by a non-Rumanian that "le latin vulgaire de la Dacia ... nous offre l'image la plus pure et la plus exacte de ce qu'était au IIème siècle de notre ère l'idiome généralement parlé par les légionnaires de l'Empire Romain. La conservation de la langue roumaine est en ce sens le plus grand bienfait dont la philologie romane soit redevable au hasard des événements politiques." [118] It has

---

[116] Wartburg, *Origines*, p. 56; *Ausgliederung*, pp. 21-22; *Problèmes*, p. 28.

[117] Densusianu, p. 51; Rosetti, I, 184; Budinszky, p. 220; Mohl, p. 258; Elcock, p. 272.

[118] Mohl, p. 259.

also been said by a proud Rumanian that "la conscience de cette origine illustre [Latin origin] nous a donné... la force de renaître comme peuple latin; elle nous a empli de fierté nationale et de puissance spirituelle... Notre rôle entre les peuples du monde ne peut être que celui que nous indique notre langue elle-même: représenter la civilisation et l'âme latine au cœur de l'Europe orientale." [119] We will see what the inscriptions have to say about the development of Latin in this part of the Roman Empire.

[119] Puşcariu, *Études*, p. 54.

PART II
PHONOLOGY

CHAPTER I

THE ACCENTED VOWEL

Latin /ā/ and /ă/, Represented by the Letter a

Although there is no indication in the inscriptions of any distinction in the vocalic length of /ā/ and /ă/, there is good evidence in the Latin loanwords in the Brittonic languages to show that the quantitative difference in Latin was maintained until relatively late, even for the long and short *a*, which usually merged in the Romance languages. In Brittonic, Latin stressed /ă/ was kept intact, while stressed /ā/ became an open /ō/.[1] This change of /ā/ to /ō/ shows that the long vowel /ā/ probably had somewhat of a back position rather than the low-central position that is usually posited for the Latin /ā/.[2] This is in direct contrast to the reflex of stressed /ā/ in open syllables in French where it is palatalized to an *e*.[3] The velarization of Latin /ā/ also took place in Vegliote, giving /u/ in an open syllable and /wa/ in a closed syllable.[4]

In the inscriptions from Britain, we do have Celtic proper names with an *o* for an original /ā/: *Conetoci* (*CIIC* 477, 7th. cent.), *Bodvoci* (*CIIC* 408, 6th. cent.), *Catuoconi* (*CIIC* 427, 8th. cent.), *Cunomori* (*CIIC* 487, 5th. cent.). It should be stated that the vowel /ā/

---

[1] Jackson, *Language*, pp. 271, 287; Loth, pp. 107, 110.
[2] Sturtevant, p. 106.
[3] Lausberg, I, 229; Grandgent, p. 82; Sturtevant, p. 107.
[4] Matteo G. Bàrtoli, *Das Dalmatische: Altromanische Sprachreste von Veglia bis Ragusa und ihre Stellung in der apenninobalkanischen Romania* (Vienna: Alfred Hölder, 1906), II, 329-31; Hadlich, p. 73; Lausberg, I, 228.

is usually kept. [5] The only Latin noun showing this change of /ā/ to *o* is in the proper noun *Iuliona* (*RIB* 1252, no date).

The ablative of the number *duobus* for *duabus* (*RIB* 1322, A.D. 155-59) and *aeror(um)* for *aerarum* (*RIB* 201, no date) are simply masculine forms for the feminine, a common morphological change. The noun *peace* (= *pace*) (*D.* 2513H, Carthage, [Proconsularis], Africa, no date), is probably a stonemason's mistake. The correct form *pace* is an extremely common form in Christian inscriptions. *Trhaec(um)* (= *Thracum*) (*RIB* 109, Cirencester, about A.D. 103), with the diphthong *ae*, is a variant form of the more common *Thrax*. *Thracum* is also found in *RIB* 291, Wroxeter, no date. The noun *cuviculurio* (= *cubiculario*) (*D.* 359, Carthage, Byzantine Age) either shows a change of suffix or an assimilation caused by the preceding vowel.

The Germanic deities *Unseni Fersomari* are represented in *RIB* 926, Old Penrith, no date, as *Unsenis Fersomeris* (dat. plur.), showing the change of *a* to *e*.

The extension of the use of the masculine form of the relative pronoun *quem* for the feminine *quam* is common, although the examples are limited.

			Correct Use Of *quam*:		Masculine *quem* For Feminine:	
A.	*Africa*	4th. cent.	1	(*D.* 2442)	2	(*D.* 2071, 3686)
		no date	1	(*D.* 2285)	0	
B.	*Britain*	No Examples	—		No Examples	
C.	*Dalmatia*	4th. cent.	1	(*D.* 821)	0	
		6th. cent.	0		1	(*D.* 3791A)
		no date	0		5	(*D.* 405, 832, 3750, 3791, 4288)
D.	*Balkans*	4th. cent.	0		2	(*D.* 1336 bis)
		Totals:	3		10	

It appears that the use of the masculine *quem* is widespread and has already usurped the function of the feminine relative pronoun. Gaeng also mentions (p. 41) that the masculine *quem* is found in all his areas under investigation. The popular language had already ex-

---

[5] Jackson, *Language,* p. 291. This scholar distinguishes /ā/ and /ă/ on the basis of Indo-European and Celtic linguistics.

tended the masculine forms of the relative to the feminine in the inscriptions of Pompei. [6] The ablative singular *quo* is also used once for *qua* (*D*. 3644B, Africa, no date).

Latin /ĕ/, Represented by the Letter e

Latin /ĕ/ does not undergo any appreciable change in the inscriptions under consideration, but several sporadic changes do occur which merit our attention.

Although Weinrich considered that the diphthongization of Latin /ĕ/ and /ŏ/ took place between the third and ninth centuries and that the diphthongization first took place in open syllables with the generalization of the diphthong in the closed syllable as a secondary development, [7] our material shows no true diphthongization of /ĕ/ in either open or closed syllables. The sporadic occurrences of diphthongization found in open and closed syllables are so minimal or questionable compared to the bulk of the material in which /ĕ/ remains that we must conclude that diphthongization did not take place in the inscriptions under consideration. This is in complete agreement with the findings of Gaeng who found no example of diphthongization of /ĕ/ in open syllables, and a single, very questionable case in closed syllables. [8]

Another important vocalic change is the closing of /ĕ/ to an *i*. It has been noted that the Romance languages which confuse /ē/ and /ĭ/, distinguish the /ī/ and /ĕ/, at least when stressed. [9] Any change of /ĕ/ to *i*, then, should be carefully scrutinized in inscriptions to see whether this closing is contrary to later Romance developments.

An *i* for /ĕ/ has been occasionally found in other works dealing with inscriptions. [10] This change has been explained, however, on the basis of the phonetic environment which caused the closing of the preceding vowel. [11]

---

[6] Väänänen, *Introduction*, p. 133.
[7] Weinrich, p. 40; cf. also Lausberg, I, 226.
[8] Gaeng, pp. 41-46.
[9] Carnoy, p. 27.
[10] Carnoy, p. 28 ff.; Pirson, pp. 6-7; Skok, *Pojave*, p. 14; Maccarrone, p. 79.
[11] Carnoy, pp. 28-31; Pirson, p. 6.

The evidence for both diphthongization and closing of /ĕ/ to *i*, as found in our inscriptional material, is as follows:

Open Syllable

Area:	Century	/ĕ/ > e	/ĕ/ > ie	/ĕ/ > i
Africa	3rd.	1	0	0
	4th.	18	0	0
	5th.	12	0	0
	6th.	11	0	0
	7th.	3	0	0
	n.d.	99	0	0
	Totals:	144	0	0

There is no example of the reverse spelling *ae* for /ĕ/ in African inscriptions, although *ae* for /ĕ/ occurs in the unstressed positions.

Britain	Century	/ĕ/ > e	/ĕ/ > ie	/ĕ/ > i
(Pagan)	1st	7	0	0
	2nd.	11	0	0
	3rd.	18	0	0
	4th.	2	0	0
	n.d.	65	0	0
	Totals:	103	0	0
(Christ.)	5th.	1	0	0
	6th.	4	0	0
	Totals:	5	0	0

The only example of a reverse spelling *ae* for stressed /ĕ/ in Britain is in the word *aeques* in the undated pagan inscription no. 356 of the *RIB*, found at Isca Silurum.

Dalmatia	Century	/ĕ/ > e	/ĕ/ > ie	/ĕ/ > i
	4th.	6	0	0
	5th.	15	0	0
	6th.	3	0	0
	n.d.	58	0	0
	Totals:	82	0	0

There is no example of a reverse spelling of *ae* for stressed /ĕ/ in Dalmatia, although there are examples in the unstressed position.

Balkans	Century	/ĕ/ > e	/ĕ/ > ie	/ĕ/ > i
(Pagan)	3rd.	3	0	0
	n.d.	39	1	0
	Totals:	42	1	0

The one example of diphthongization of /ĕ/ in pagan inscriptions of the Balkans is in the word *Ziepyr(um)* (= *Zephyrum*), *Kalinka* 109, Moesia Inferior, no date. Kalinka considers "das i nach Z anaptyktisch."[12] Since the Greek aspirated *ph* is given as a *p* in the word, this inscription is undoubtedly old, probably before the second century, A.D.[13] This early date and the rarity of diphthongization in all inscriptions make this case of diphthongization of /ĕ/ to *ie* very suspect.

Balkans	Century	/ĕ/ > e	/ĕ/ > ie	/ĕ/ > i
(Christ.)	4th.	3	0	0
	5th.	2	0	0
	n.d.	19	0	0
	Totals:	24	0	0

There are no cases of reverse spellings in Balkan inscriptions in open syllables, although *ae* is found for /ĕ/ in closed, stressed position.

Closed Syllable

Area:	Century	/ĕ/ > e	/ĕ/ > ie	/ĕ/ > i	% Of Dev.	/ĕ/ > a
Africa	3rd.	10	0	0		0
	4th.	53	0	0		0
	5th.	79	0	1	1.3	0
	6th.	35	0	0		0
	7th.	5	0	0		0
	n.d.	246	0	1	0.4	0
	Totals:	428	0	2	0.5	0

---

[12] *Antike Denkmäler in Bulgarien,* ed. Ernst Kalinka (Vienna: Alfred Hölder, 1906), p. 104.
[13] Niedermann, p. 86.

The closing of /ĕ/ in a closed syllable is found in *Vincincius* (= *Vincentius*), *D.* 2751, Hadrumetum (Byzacena), no date, and in <*q*>*uiscin*<*ti*> (probably for *quiescenti*), *D.* 2850, Orléansville, A.D. 468. It would seem that the following nasal plus consonant causes the closing of /ĕ/ to *i*.[14]

An example of the reverse spelling *ae* for /ĕ/ in Africa is *Aennia* in *D.* 3272B, Albulae, (Mauretania Caesariensis), A.D. 519.

Britain	Century	/ĕ/ > e	/ĕ/ > ie	% Of Dev.	/ĕ/ > i	% Of Dev.	/ĕ/ > a	% Of Dev.
(Pagan)	1st.	8	1	11.1	0		0	
	2nd.	20	0		0		0	
	3rd.	22	0		0		0	
	4th.	1	0		1	50.0	0	
	n.d.	92	0		1	1.1	2	2.1
	Totals:	143	1	0.7	2	1.4	2	1.4

The one example of apparent diphthongization in pagan Britain is in the word *fabriciesis* (= *fabricensis*), *RIB* 156, Aquae Sulis (Bath), late first or early second century. It is best to consider this case as a change of suffix rather than a true diphthongization. The correct form *fabricensis* is found in Dalmatia, *D.* 530A, no date. Its very early date would make diphthongization implausible and the very important reason that Latin *ĕns* had already become ē̦s in Vulgar Latin and was treated like British e̦ would invalidate any possibility of the diphthongization of /ĕ/.[15] The examples of /ĕ/ closing to *i* are found in *simper*, *RIB* 2311, on the Military Way, A.D. 305-06 (considered by the editors as an error on p. 726), and *mintla* (= *mentula*, 'membrum virile'), *RIB* 631, Adel, no date, although the correct form *mentula* is found in *RIB* 983, Castra Exploratorum (Netherby), no date.

---

[14] Pirson, p. 6; Carnoy, p. 28; W. M. Lindsay, *The Latin Language* (Oxford: Clarendon Press, 1894), p. 23.

[15] See Jackson, *Language,* p. 278. It is improbable that the *i* in *fabriciesis* indicates early palatalization or incipient assibilation since, as Jackson reminds us (p. 402), "None of these changes is apparent in Brit., where all Latin *c* of whatever kind and origin is treated as [k], exactly the same as native *c*; so that the assibilated or voiced VL. sounds could hardly have been present in the Latin from which the loanwords were borrowed in Roman Britain."

The change of /ĕ/ to *a* is found in two examples in pagan inscriptions: in the words *Vian(na)* (= *Vienna*, a *colonia* in Gallia Narbonensis on the River Rhône), *RIB* 1826, Hadrian's Wall, no date, although the correct form *Vienn(a)* is found in *RIB* 525, Deva (Chester), no date, and *Sardi(ca)*, the modern Sofia, *RIB* 201, Camulodunum (Colchester), no date. Pirson gives the forms *Vianna*, *Viana* and its derivative *Viannensis* and considers (p. 8) that "ces formes . . . trahissent un caractère propre au latin du midi de la Gaule, car le dialecte narbonnais de nos jours se distingue par une tendance fortement marquée à changer en *a* l'*e* tonique, atone, entravé ou libre, isolé ou dans une diphthongue." This use of the *a* for /ĕ/ in Britain may show contact with southern Gaul. [16]

Although the use of *a* for /ĕ/ in *Sardi(ca)* may not be a true vocalic as *Serdica* is accepted as a variant form, Jackson does remark (p. 281) that "possibly *er* > *ar* was especially characteristic of the VL. of Roman Britain; it is rare in regular VL., at least in that of Gaul, though commoner in southern Italy and Spain." [17] This may show a tendency in British Latin to prefer an *a* before an *r* in a closed syllable.

---

[16] Jackson, *Language*, specifically mentions (p. 163) that "at the end of the fourth and beginning of the fifth century the Christian Church [of Britain] was in close contact with that of southern Gaul, especially with that primary home of Gallic Christianity, the Lyon-Vienna area."

[17] Lindsay states (p. 15) that "varieties in the spelling of foreign names like Sardica and Serdica . . . prove nothing for Latin *a*." Pirson and Carnoy give no examples of the change of stressed /ĕ/ to *a* in their works. It is true that the *Appendix Probi* gives the recommendation (item 168) *noverca non novarca*, (the only example of stressed /ĕ/ in a closed syllable going to *a*, inasmuch as the other admonitions refer to unstressed syllables, i.e., *camera non cammara* (item 84), *carcer non car<car>* (item 43), *anser non ansar* (items 129, 164) and *passer non passar* (item 163). Compare, however, the Welsh forms given by Jackson on page 280: *tafarn, Padarn, ystarn, sarff*, and colloquial *yffarn*, which require an *a* in the Latin: *taberna, Paternus, sternere, serpens, inferna*. This Vulgar Latin tendency for /ĕ/ to change to *a* in instrussed syllables is reflected also in the French *dauphin, marché*, and *marchand*. Pei in his *The language of the Eighth-Century Texts in Northern France* (New York, 1932), p. 42, records this change in unstressed syllables in *Dalfinus, marcado, marcadantes, marcatum, marcato*. Politzer in his *A Study of the Language of Eighth-Century Lombardic Documents* (New York: privately printed, 1949) does not give any examples of either stressed or unstressed /ĕ/ to *a* in his investigation.

There are no examples of a reverse spelling of *ae* for /ĕ/ in Latin inscriptions in Britain, although it does occur in unstressed position.

There is one pagan example of /ĕ/ changing to *u* in the gerundive *faciundum*, *RIB* 688, Eboracum (York), no date, although the more usual form is found in *RIB* 356, Isca Silurum (Caerleon), no date, and in *RIB* 1026, Piercebridge, no date. The form *-undum* is considered a legal and archaic type. [18]

Britain	Century	/ĕ/ > e	/ĕ/ > ie	/ĕ/ > i	% Of Dev.	/ĕ/ > a
(Christ.)	6th.	3	0	1	25.0	0
	7th.	1	0	0		0
	8th.	1	0	0		0
	9th.	1	0	0		0
	n.d.	1	0	0		0
	Totals:	7	0	1	12.5	0

The only example of /ĕ/ > *i* in Christian inscriptions is found in the Celtic proper name *Catotigirni*, *CIIC* 408, Glamorgan (Wales), 6th. cent. [19]

Dalmatia	Century	/ĕ/ > e	/ĕ/ > ie	/ĕ/ > i	/ĕ/ > a
	4th.	16	0	0	0
	5th.	17	0	0	0
	6th.	10	0	0	0
	n.d.	111	0	0	0
	Totals:	154	0	0	0

There are no reverse spellings of *ae* for stressed /ĕ/ in closed position, although there are examples of *ae* for /ĕ/ in unstressed syllables.

In closed syllables, our findings are very similar to Gaeng's. There is no clear case of diphthongization.

---

[18] Lindsay, p. 544; Alfred Ernout, *Morphologie historique du latin*, 3rd ed. (Paris: Klincksieck, 1953), p. 173.

[19] See Jackson, *Language*, p. 279 ff., for a discussion of /ĕ/ before *rn*.

Balkans	*Century*	/ĕ/ > e	/ĕ/ > ie	/ĕ/ > i	/ĕ/ > a
(Pagan)	1st.	1	0	0	0
	2nd.	3	0	0	0
	3rd.	3	0	0	0
	n.d.	22	0	0	0
	Totals:	29	0	0	0
(Christ.)	4th.	14	0	0	0
	n.d.	25	0	0	0
	Totals:	39	0	0	0

The closing of /ĕ/ to *i* is very sporadic in all areas studied by both Gaeng and this investigator, although Rome would appear to show this closing tendency more than other areas, with ten examples from dated and non-dated inscriptions. A following nasal is the main cause for this phenomenon, although an *s* followed by a consonant may also produce this change.

Latin /ĕ/ in Monosyllables

There are just three cases of /ĕ/ changing to *i* in monosyllabic words. We find *it* (= *et*) twice: once in Britain, *RIB* 108, Corinium Dobunnorum (Cirencester), no date, and once in Africa, *D.* 2068, Toqueville, A.D. 359. There is one questionable case of *ix* for *ex* in the phrase *ixtabu[l]a[ri]* (=*ex tabulari*) in an undated inscription from Dalmatia, *D.* 376. There are no cases of a reverse spelling of *ae* for /ĕ/.

This lack of change of /ĕ/ to *i* is somewhat in disagreement with Gaeng's findings. Although there is doubtless no systematic closing of /ĕ/ to *i* in the Iberian Peninsula, Gaul, Italy, and Rome, Gaeng did find some cases of the change in the words *quim, quin, cuin* (all for *quem*), *ist*, in addition to more numerous examples of *it*. In Rome, for example, Gaeng gives five examples of *it* and 197 cases of *et* in the third and fourth centuries, for a percentage of 2.5 %. Just taking Africa as a basis for comparison, we find in our inscriptions only one case of *it* with 281 cases of *et* for both dated and undated inscriptions. We are giving below the complete picture of the conjunction *et* in our areas.

Africa	Century	et	it	% Of Dev.
	4th.	34	1	2.9
	5th.	56	0	
	6th.	24	0	
	7th.	2	0	
	n.d.	165	0	
	Totals:	281	1	0.4
Britain (Pagan)	1st.	6	0	
	2nd.	29	0	
	3rd.	61	0	
	4th.	2	0	
	n.d.	87	1	1.1
	Totals:	185	1	0.5
(Christ.)	5th.	1	0	
	6th.	5	0	
	8th.	1	0	
	9th.	1	0	
	n.d.	2	0	
	Totals:	10	0	
Dalmatia	4th.	12	0	
	5th.	21	0	
	6th.	2	0	
	n.d.	76	0	
	Totals:	111	0	
Balkans (Pagan)	1st.	1	0	
	2nd.	3	0	
	3rd.	5	0	
	4th.	2	0	
	n.d.	21	0	
	Totals:	32	0	
(Christ.)	4th.	4	0	
	5th.	2	0	
	n.d.	50	0	
	Totals:	56	0	

Gaeng considers (p. 48) that this closing of /ĕ/ to *i* may be due
to the proclitic position of the monosyllabic word and that the word
may change in accordance with the general confusion of these vowels
in unstressed syllables. Our data would indicate that monosyllabic

words having /ĕ/ are extremely stable in Africa, Britain, Dalmatia, and the Balkans, and that the vowels are probably not subject to change on the basis of proclitic position. [20]

Latin /ĕ/ in Hiatus

The change of /ĕ/ in hiatus to *i* is found in our inscriptions as follows:

Area	Century	/ĕ/ > e	/ĕ/ > i	% Dev.
Africa	4th.	10	0	
	5th.	3	0	
	6th.	3	0	
	n.d.	93	2	2.1
	Totals:	109	2	1.8
Britain	1st.	1	0	
(Pagan)	2nd.	10	0	
	3rd.	11	0	
	4th.	1	0	
	n.d.	50	3	5.7
	Totals:	73	3	3.9
(Christ.)	No Date	2	0	
Dalmatia	4th.	2	0	
	5th.	3	0	
	6th.	1	0	
	n.d.	22	0	
	Totals:	28	0	
Balkans (Pagan)	No Date	1	0	
(Christ.)	No Date	12	0	

---

[20] It is not uncommon for monosyllables to be stressed in the Romance languages and even diphthongize: cf. /ĕ/ > *ie* in *quien* < *quem* (Sp.), *et* > *ye* (Leonese and primitive Spanish), *est* > *get* or *yet* (Navarro-Aragonese). See Entwistle, p. 226; Elcock, p. 406; Menéndez-Pidal, *Manual de gramática histórica española*, 9th ed. (Madrid: Espasa-Calpe, 1952), p. 339, for diphthongization of these monosyllables. This is not to deny the importance of proclisis in consonantal development. Cf. Lausberg, I, 439: "En rumano se conserva también la forma plena *este* (< *est*) (cuya -*t* persistió en la proclisis ante vocal, pudiendo la forma generalizarse después y recibir una *e* paragógica.)"

The two examples of the closing of /ĕ/ to *i* in hiatus in the undated inscriptions of Africa are *mios, D.* 1618, Byzacena, and *dio* (dat. of *deus*), *D.* 1702, Theveste (Proconsularis). The three examples in the undated pagan inscriptions of Britain are surprisingly enough all the dative singular form *die* (= *deae*), *RIB* 1525, Hadrian's Wall at Brocolitis (Carrawburgh), *RIB* 1543, likewise at Brocolitis, and *RIB* 1897, Hadrian's Wall at Camboglanna (Birdoswald).

Our findings are slightly different from those of Gaeng who found (p. 48) only a single instance of /ĕ/ in hiatus closing to *i*: the neuter plural form *ia* for *ea* in a fourth / fifth century inscription from the northern Italian area. He found 48 correct occurrences in the same area and even the form *ea* (= *eam*) in the same inscription.

Sturtevant mentions (p. 113 ff.) the close quality of /ĕ/ in hiatus. A possible British pronunciation of the Latin /ĕ/ in hiatus may explain the /ĕ/ > *i* in Britain since the British /ĕ/ "was probably closer than Lat. e." [21]

Latin /ē/, Represented by the Letter e

The development of the Latin /ē/ as seen in our inscriptions differs in some areas markedly from the results found in Gaeng's work. Since the merger of /ē/ and /ĭ/ is common in most of the Romance languages, except in Sardinian, a careful scrutiny of inscriptional material should reveal some tendencies that may appear subsequently in different areas of Romania. The finding of *i* for /ē/ in inscriptions is usually interpreted as proof of their similar pronunciation. [22] Inasmuch as Sardinian follows the archaic vocalic system in which /ē/ and /ĕ/ merge, a system which African Latin supposedly follows, as against the Italic qualitative vocalic system in which there is a merger of /ē/ and /ĭ/, adhered to by Dalmatian as well as the languages of Western Romance, and likewise valid for the compromise system of inner Balkan Romance, it should be interesting to see whether the inscriptions can corroborate these various vocalic systems. Since British Latin is not included in any vocalic system by Lausberg, but is considered by Jackson as maintaining

---

[21] Jackson, *Language,* p. 278.
[22] Carnoy, p. 22; Pirson, p. 2; Lindsay, p. 29; Grandgent, p. 83; Rosetti, I, 78.

the classical quantity system on the basis of the Latin loanwords into the Brittonic languages, it is hoped that the inscriptions can furnish us with information as to the placing of British Latin. One of the important keys to the above-mentioned vocalic systems (and thus to a differentiation of Latin) is precisely the treatment of /ē/ and /ĭ/ (the treatment of /ŭ/ and /ō/ will be given later) and if the inscriptions themselves afford any contribution to the solving of the problem, the importance of inscriptions in the study of Vulgar Latin and its differentiation are greatly enhanced. Here are the results of our investigations:

Open Syllable

Area	Century	/ē/ > e	/ē/ > i	% Of Dev.	-ērunt	-irunt
Africa	3rd.	8	0		1	0
	4th.	42	0		7	0
	5th.	46	1	2.1	12	0
	6th.	17	0		3	0
	7th.	1	0		0	0
	n.d.	315	3	0.9	22	0
	Totals:	429	4	0.9	45	0

The examples of deviation are as follows:

fidilis, D. 1402N, *CIL* VIII 14,326, Utica (Proconsularis), n.d.
Eufimie (= *Euphemiae*), D. 2069, Kherbet-el-Ma-el-Abiad, A.D. 474.
ri[b] (= *rebus*), D. 512, Simitthus (Proconsularis), n.d.
ius (= *eius*), D. 2118, near Theveste (Proconsularis), n.d. 23.

---

[23] We are considering the *e* of *eius* as long because it is written long in *Harper's Latin Dictionary*. Mihăescu and Gaeng likewise consider the vowel as long although Väänänen in his review of Mihăescu's *Limba latină în provinciile dunărene în imperiului român* in *Neuphilologische Mitteilungen*, LXII (1961), 229, questions this as a change of long *e* to *i*, considering it as short *e* to *i*. The probably correct pronunciation *eiius* is also found in D. 403, Arbal (Africa), A. D. 372, and *RIB* 601, Lancaster, no date. It is interesting to note that other forms also show this transitional *i* in the words *Maiias*, D. 2791, Sufasar (Africa), A. D. 318, D. 2858, Altava (Africa), A.D. 361, D. 3052A, Mauretania Caesariensis, no date, *muliier*, *CIIC* 356, Cardigan (Wales, no date, *Maiiorica*, D. 4360A, Mauretania Caesariensis, A.D. 366, and *ipsiius*, D. 3622N, Sitifis (Africa), no date. All the above

There are no examples of reverse spelling *ae* for /ē/ although it is found in unstressed syllables.

All third person plurals of the perfect indicative end in *-erunt*, without any change to *i*. Gaeng reported a few changes of *-ērunt* to *-irunt* and considered this phenomenon as a result of the change of stress in these verb forms, the closing of /ē/ to *i* being thus due to a general merger of Latin /ē/ and /ĭ/ in unstressed position. [24] It is interesting to note that the original third person plural ending in *-ēre* is also found five times in African inscriptions: *peperere, D.* 229, 4th. cent.; *defuere, D.* 1103, no date; *ingemuere, D.* 1641, no date; *meruere, D.* 1911, no date; *posuere, D.* 2285, no date, but always in a poetical inscription. We will summarize our findings for the third person plural of the perfect indicative after all areas have been surveyed.

Area	Century	/ē/ > e	/ē/ > i	-erunt	-irunt
Britain	1st.	5	0	1	0
(Pagan)	2nd.	16	0	2	0
	3rd.	42	0	6	0
	4th.	3	0	0	0
	n.d.	118	0	9	0
	Totals:	184	0	18	0
Britain	5th.	3	0	0	0
(Christ.)	6th.	3	0	1	0
	7th.	3	0	0	0
	n.d.	4	0	0	0
	Totals:	13	0	1	0

There are no cases of reverse spelling in stressed open syllable in Britain, but the *ae* for /ē/ does appear in unstressed vowels.

---

forms with the transitional *i* are found in Africa and Britain, where the vocalic systems seem to be of the archaic type, with the keeping of the Classical Latin quantities. See Lindsay, p. 439; Ernout, *Morphologie*, p. 82; Grandgent, p. 73; Palmer, p. 255; and Roland G. Kent, *The Forms of Latin* (Baltimore: Linguistic Society of America, 1946), p. 66. The first syllable of *eius* is pronounced both long and short by some poets and the word is even monosyllabic at times in poetry.

[24] For a discussion of the third person plural of the perfect indicative, see Ernout, *Morphologie*, p. 213 ff.; Väänänen, *Introduction*, p. 151; Kent, p. 126. Ernout, Väänänen, and Kent, however, all state that the *-ĕrunt* form gives the Romance language reflexes (true for Catalan, Italian, and Old French), but fail to mention the Spanish forms in *-ieron* or *-eron* (*comieron, fueron*) which would require the Latin *-ērunt*.

Dalmatia	Century	/ē/ > e	/ē/ > i	% Of Dev.	-erunt	-irunt
	4th.	13	0		1	0
	5th.	8	1	11.1	0	0
	6th.	3	0		0	0
	n.d.	99	4	3.9	12	0
	Totals:	123	5	3.9	13	0

The following are deviations for this area:

[ec]clisiae, D. 1289, CIL III 13,142, Salona, no date.
Eclisio, D. 3638A, CIL III 6402, Salona, no date.
eclisiae, D. 3835, CIL III 9585, Salona, no date.
Agapit[o], D. 3842N, CIL III, 9526, Salona, no date.
eclisie, D. 3870, CIL III 13,124, Salona, A.D. 426.

There are no examples of reverse spelling although ae does appear in unaccented syllables.

Area	Century	/ē/ > e	/ē/ > i	% Of Dev.	-erunt	-irunt
Balkans	2nd.	4	0		0	0
(Pagan)	3rd.	11	0		0	0
	n.d.	46	0		7	0
	Totals:	61	0	0.0	7	0
Balkans (Christ.)	4th.	6	0		1	0
	5th.	3	0		1	0
	n.d.	39	2	4.9	9	0
	Totals:	48	2	4.0	11	0

The examples of the closing of /ē/ to i are as follows:

Aurilia, D. 3659, Purbach (Pannonia), no date.
Aurilius, D. 3659, Purbach (Pannonia), no date.

There are no examples of reverse spelling.

When we compare our results with Gaeng's, we find some interesting contrasts. Gaeng found the change of /ē/ to i in open syllables in Gaul to a degree that is entirely absent in the areas investigated by us. Gaeng reports (p. 50) that in Gallia Narbonensis in the 6th./7th. centuries, there is a 12.5 % incidence of the closing of /ē/. In Gallia

Lugdunensis in the 4th./5th. centuries, there is a 15.3 % change and in the 6th./7th. centuries, we find the change of /ē/ to *i* to be 27.2 %. This change of /ē/ to *i* was already mentioned by Pirson who considered (p. 2) this assimilation as especially rich in the inscriptions of Gaul. The number of examples of this deviation for the Iberian Peninsula, Italy, and Rome[25] is not as great as that for Gaul, but these areas show enough changes of this type to show that there was a tendency for /ē/ to be written as *i*. In our areas, we find that there are 429 examples of unchanged /ē/ and only four examples of *i* in all inscriptions (dated and undated combined) from Africa, which would give us an incidence of less than 1 %. We could interpret this minimal change as proof that the /ē/ in African Latin remained and did not merge with /ĭ/, an indication that African Latin in this respect retained the Latin archaic quantitative system. This same conclusion is reached with respect to British Latin where we find not a single case of *i* for /ē/ in either pagan or Christian inscriptions, although we have a total of 184 cases of /ē/ in all pagan inscriptions and 13 in Christian inscriptions. The area that shows a relatively high incidence of change is Dalmatia, with a total incidence of 3.9 % for all dated and undated inscriptions (123 examples of unchanged /ē/ and five examples of *i*). This would seem to show that Dalmatian Latin tended to merge the /ē/ and /ĭ/, which would indicate that inscriptions corroborated the conclusion that Dalmatian Latin fitted

---

[25] Taking the figures on a global, areal basis without consideration of chronology, we find that the Iberian Peninsula shows a 3.7 % deviation (130 cases of /ē/ to 5 cases of *i*), Italy a 3.1 % incidence (123 cases of /ē/ to 4 of *i*), Rome a 2.7 % deviation (183 cases of /ē/ to 5 of *i*), while Gaul shows a 17.4 % incidence (52 cases of /ē/ to 11 of *i*). On the basis of our investigation of inscriptional material we find the following results for /ē/ in open syllables: Africa with a 0.9 % (432 cases of /ē/ to 4 of *i*), Britain 0.0 % (with 184 cases of /ē/ in pagan inscriptions and 13 cases in Christian inscriptions), Dalmatia 3.9 % (123 cases of /ē/ and 5 of *i*), and Balkans 1.8 % (in pagan inscriptions 61 cases of /ē/ and no examples of *i* and in Christian 48 cases of /ē/ and 2 of *i*; if we separate the inscriptions, we find 0.0 % for pagan compared to 4 % Christian). The change of /ē/ to *i* is very common in the language of the eighth-century texts of Gaul as evidenced by the conclusion arrived at by Pei, *Texts*, who states (p. 20): "The change of accented long *e* to *i* in the spelling of the Eighth-Century documents ... is one of the most noteworthy characteristics of these texts." It would appear that this change was already visible in the Vulgar Latin inscriptions of Gaul at a much earlier date.

into the Italic quantitative vocalic system. [26] We do not have any examples of *i* for /ē/ in the pagan inscriptions of the inner Balkans, but there are two cases of *i* in undated Christian inscriptions in the Balkans. Although the Christian inscriptions in the Balkans show a 4 % incidence of *i* for /ē/ (48 examples of /ē/ to 2 examples of *i*), compared with the 61 cases of /ē/ retained in pagan inscriptions without any change to *i*, it may be possible to say that there was an increasing tendency in the inner Balkans to merge /ē/ with /ĭ/, but since both examples of *i* appear in the same inscription, it would be hazardous to make any bold assertions. What may be said with more certainty is that in the extreme cases of African and British Latin on the one hand and Gaul on the other, the inscriptions seem to show that Latin /ē/ was quite different in its pronunciation.

Gaeng found sporadic cases of *-irunt* in the third person plural of the perfect indicative for the regular *-erunt* in Southern Italy and in Rome, although surprisingly enough not in Gaul (nor in the Iberian Peninsula, but this lack of change here would be expected), but the lack of examples of *-irunt* in Gaul would not be conclusive because of the paucity of any forms of the third person plural of the perfect indicative (only three correct cases of *-erunt*). As previously mentioned (p. 88), this change of *-erunt* to *-irunt* was explained by Gaeng as the result of a change of the stress, the *-ērunt* becoming *-ĕrunt,* the resulting /ē/ to *i* change then being considered as a change in unstressed position. Since Italian and Old French forms do require an /ĕ/, the inscriptions may be indicating this shift of stress. What it clearly brought out in the inscriptions of our areas is the presence of the *e* in all areas studied, at all times, both pagan and Christian, without a single example of the form *-irunt*. We found the third person plural of the perfect indicative quite frequently in our inscriptions, as evidenced by the 45 examples of *-erunt* in Africa, 19 times in Britain, 13 cases in Dalmatia, and 18 times in the Balkans. Although the lack of change from /ē/ to *i* in our inscriptions is no irrefutable proof that the stress remained on the penult, it may be

---

[26] Skok in his *Pojave* points out (p. 13) an /ē/ to *i* change in early Latin loanwords in Serbian: *tikula* < *tegula, golida* < *galeta, bandima* < *vindemia,* and concludes (p. 13) that the *i* approximates the Latin speech in the province of Dalmatia.

very likely that the peripheral areas did maintain the -*ērunt* form
rather than adopt the more popular -*ĕrunt* type. [27]

Closed Syllable

Africa	Century	/ē/ > e	/ē/ > i	% of Dev.
	3rd.	4	0	
	4th.	6	0	
	5th.	11	0	
	6th.	5	0	
	n.d.	71	2	2.7
	Totals:	97	2	2.0

The two examples of deviation are as follows:

> *quiiscit, D.* 3106D, *CIL* VIII 21,424, Caesarea Maurorum,
> no date.
> *minses, D.* 3263, *CIL* VIII 11,099, Byzacena, no date.

There are no examples of reverse spelling of *ae* for /ē/ in closed
syllables in either stressed or unstressed position.

Britain	Century	/ē/ > e	/ē/ > i	% of Dev.
(Pagan)	1st.	1	0	
	2nd.	1	0	
	3rd.	2	0	
	4th.	2	0	
	n.d.	17	2	10.5
	Totals:	23	2	8.0

The two examples of deviation in the pagan inscriptions are:

> *collign(io)* (= *collegio*), *RIB* 2102, *CIL* VII 1069, Blatobul-
> gium (Birrens), Scotland, no date. [28]
> *colligni* (= *collegii*), *RIB* 2103, *CIL* VII 1070, Scotland, no
> date.

---

[27] See Kent, p. 125, for the popular nature of the -*ĕrunt* form.

[28] Since both examples *collign(io)* and *colligni* stand for forms of *collegium*,
it may be questionable to include these rare forms which would tend to
distort the figures for the area, which are based on a small number of total
examples.

Britain	Century	/ē/ > e	/ē/ > i	% of Dev.
(Christ.)	7th.	1	0	

Dalmatia	Century	/ē/ > e	/ē/ > i	% of Dev.
	4th.	1	0	
	5th.	4	1	20.0
	6th.	2	0	
	n.d.	11	1	8.3
	Totals:	18	2	10.0

The examples of deviation in this area are:

requiiscet (= *requiescit*), D. 307, *CIL* III 2657, Salona, A.D. 435.
vindedit (= *vendidit*), D. 3791A, *CIL* III 14,305, Salona, n.d. [29]

Balkans	Century	/ē/ > e	/ē/ > i	% of Dev.
(Pagan)	3rd.	1	0	
	n.d.	5	0	
	Totals:	6	0	0.0
(Christ.)	4th.	1	0	
	5th.	1	0	
	n.d.	13	0	
	Totals:	15	0	0.0

Although our figures do not enable us to come to any definite conclusions in most areas because of the lack of examples and uncertainty of some forms of /ē/ in closed syllables compared to the abundance of forms in open syllables, a comparison with Gaeng's figures can be made for African Latin. Gaeng found an incidence of 2.7 % in the Iberian Peninsula (36 examples of /ē/ to one of *i* in all dated inscriptions), 33.3 % for Gaul (96 examples of /ē/ to 48

---

[29] The change of /ē/ to *i* in *vindedit* may be in an initial syllable rather than in a stressed syllable since many compound verbs with the second element derived from *dare* reconstruct the perfect indicative with the stress on the perfect *dedi* on the basis of analogy with the simple form. This would, of course, change our figures considerably because of the scantiness of examples.

of *i*), 7.1 % for Italy (209 examples of /ē/ to 16 of *i*), and 6.2 %
for Rome (182 examples of /ē/ for 12 of *i*). Our figure of 2.0 % for
African Latin (97 examples of /ē/ and two for *i*) sharply contrasts
with the 33.3 % for Gaul and deviates considerably from the 7.1 %
for Italy and the 6.2 % for Rome. Gaeng's Iberian tabulation likewise suffers from a relative lack of examples.

   It is interesting to note that the /ē/ changes to *i* fairly often in
closed syllables under the influence of the following consonant or
consonant cluster in Italy, Rome, and especially Gaul. The Iberian
Peninsula is the only area where the closing of the /ē/ to *i* takes
place only once. It has been observed that an *n* plus consonant, or
-sc-, may cause this closing. [30] Gaeng also considers (p. 57) that the
-ct- group may also exert a closing influence on the preceding /ē/.
Although Pirson mentions (p. 3) the form *requiiscet* as the most
common word representing the change of /ē/ to *i* and its contraction
requiscet as the normal form in the Latin inscriptions in Gaul, and
Gaeng likewise considers (p. 55) the form *requiiscit* as the most
frequent in which Latin /ē/ is represented by *i*, our inscriptional
material gives only two cases which show *requiiscet* (Dalmatia) and
quiiscit (Africa) with the *i* for /ē/. The correct form with the /ē/
is by far the most common type encountered. In our Christian inscriptions, where the word is common, we find ten correct examples
of *requiescit, quiescit,* or derivatives thereof in Africa, eight in the
inner Balkans, seven in Dalmatia, and one in Britain. The closing
effect of *n* plus consonant is likewise very sporadic, just one example
having been recorded in Africa (*minses*). We have 37 examples of
the Latin word *menses* or its derivatives with /ē/ in Africa, nine
examples in pagan Britain, six in Dalmatia, and six in the Balkans
(both pagan and Christian). As a corollary of the statement that the
Latin in Africa and Britain seems to show the maintenance of the
quantitative vocalic system, it may be said that in these areas the
/ē/ seemed to be unaffected by the following consonants or consonant
clusters.

Latin /ē/ in Hiatus

   There are very few examples of stressed /ē/ in hiatus found in
inscriptions. We find the Hebrew name *Bartolomius* found in D. 2436,

---

[30] Väänänen, *Introduction,* p. 36; Pirson, p. 5.

CIL III 12,877, Salona (Dalmatia) no date, although the correct form *Bartholomeus* is found in other parts of the Roman Empire (2 cases in Ravenna [Italy] *D.* 1961B and *D.* 1962D, and 1 case in Mérida [Spain] *D.* 1964). *Apamia* in *D.* 1346, *CIL* VIII 11,106 in Byzacena, no date, is given by Diehl for the correct form with /ē/, but *Harper's Latin Dictionary* considers both forms as possible from the Greek Ἀπάμεια. On the basis of these few examples, nothing certain can be said of the stressed /ē/ in hiatus.

Latin /ē/ in Monosyllables

The /ē/ is very stable in monosyllables. Although Gaeng does find (p. 58) *si* for *se* in inscriptions from Rome (4 examples of *se* and 3 of *si* in the 6th./7th. cent.), our inscriptions regularly show the correct *se*. We found *se* three times in Africa (1 in 5th. cent. and 2 undated), eleven times in pagan Britain (1 in 2nd., 5 in 3rd., and 5 undated), seven times in Dalmatia (all 7 undated), and one in Christian Balkans (4th. cent.).

Although Maccarrone states (p. 81) that the form *tris* is very frequent in Latin inscriptions, this is not true in the case of our inscriptions. We found only two cases of *tris* in *D.* 2426, *CIL* III 10,190, near Doclea (Dalmatia), no date, in the nominative, and *CIIC* 461, Cornwall (Britain), 6th. cent., also in the nominative, [31] but nine cases of *tres* (3 cases in the accusative in undated Christian inscriptions in the Balkans, and 6 cases in Africa, 2 in the nominative in undated inscriptions, 4 in the accusative, 3 of which were undated and 1 from A.D. 377). Gaeng found six cases of *tris,* all accusatives, two from Gaul, one from Sicily, and three from Rome.

Latin /ĭ/ Represented by the Letter i

The importance of the merger of Latin /ē/ and Latin /ĭ/ in the Romance languages has already been explained (see p. 86 ff.). Since we found examples of an *i* for Latin /ē/, it is only natural

---

[31] Lindsay states (p. 412 ff.) that the grammarians prescribe *tres* in the nominative and *tris* in the accusative, although *tris* nominative is found on late inscriptions. The form *tris,* found in Dalmatia, is undated according to Diehl, but Skok, *Pojave,* considers (p. 12) it as dating from the 4th or 5th century.

that we should expect to find a corresponding reading of an *e* for
/ĭ/. If the inscriptions are to prove the merger of these two vowels,
it is imperative that the change of Latin /ĭ/ to *e* be found in those
areas where the Romance languages subsequently posit this merger.
The most important areas in this problem of the merger of /ē/ and
/ĭ/ are Africa and Britain which run counter to the general merger
of these two phonemes. Below are the results of our findings for /ĭ/
in open and closed syllables:

Open Syllable

Area	Century	/ĭ/ > *i*	/ĭ/ > *e*	% of Dev.
Africa	3rd.	4	0	
	4th.	28	0	
	5th.	27	1	3.6
	6th.	21	0	
	7th.	4	0	
	n.d.	123	0	
	Totals:	207	1	0.5

The single example of an *e* for /ĭ/ is in the word *menus,* D.
3691A, *CIL* VIII 9984, Numerus Syrorum (Mauretania Caesariensis),
A.D. 429. This almost complete maintenance of Latin /ĭ/ in open
syllables is indicative of a lack of merger of /ĭ/ and /ē/ in the
Latin of Africa.

Area	Century	/ĭ/ > *i*	/ĭ/ > *e*	% of Dev.
Britain	1st.	2	0	
	2nd.	22	0	
(Pagan)	3rd.	33	1	2.9
	4th.	3	0	
	n.d.	72	1	1.4
	Totals:	132	2	1.5

The two examples of deviation found in pagan Britain are:

> *demediam* (= *dimidiam*), *RIB* 306, *CIL* VII 140, Lydney
> Park, no date.
> *baselicam, RIB* 978, *CIL* 965, Netherby (Castra Exploratum),
> A.D. 222.

Jackson states (p. 191) that "Latin *i* and *u* are commonly written *e* and *o* in Continental Christian inscriptions, because the sounds had actually become *e* and *o*, though apparently it did not happen in Britain." He explains (p. 191) this writing of *e* for /ĭ/ as "spelling habits introduced from Gaul without having any real phonetic bearing on British Latin pronunciation." Since the changes above are found in pagan inscriptions, and since one is specifically dated to A.D. 222, it seems that this change may be dated in Britain earlier than Jackson had imagined. [32]

Britain	Century	/ĭ/ > i	/ĭ/ > e	% of Dev.
	4th.	3	0	
(Christ.)	6th.	2	0	
	7th.	1	0	
	8th.	1	0	
	n.d.	1	0	
	Totals:	8	0	0.0

Dalmatia	Century	/ĭ/ > i	/ĭ/ > e	% of Dev.
	4th.	14	0	
	5th.	13	0	
	6th.	2	0	
	n.d.	75	6	7.5
	Totals:	104	6	5.5

The examples of the /ĭ/ and *e* confusion are as follows:

ve[de] (= *vide*, imperative), D. 2389, CIL III p. 961, Tragurium, no date.
ignefera, D. 2389, CIL III p. 961, Tragurium, no date.
semilem, D. 3363, CIL III 9623, Salona, no date.
sene, D. 3835A, Salona, no date.
Tegri[s], D. 3837A, CIL III 9569, Salona, no date.
[depo]setio, D. 4455, CIL III 9567, Salona, no date.

The 5.5 % deviation of Latin /ĭ/ would seem to indicate a tendency in the Latin of Dalmatia to merge the /ĭ/ with /ē/. This assimilation is strongly corroborated by Skok who asserts (p. 14 ff.) in his *Pojave* that the inscriptions from Salona show *e* instead of

---

[32] For a discussion of the early occurrence of this change of /ĭ/ to *e*, see Richter, p. 51; Väänänen, *Introduction*, p. 36; Grandgent, p. 84.

i very often in pagan inscriptions, and particularly in Christian inscriptions. The difference in speech between ē and ĭ therefore had disappeared.

Balkans	Century	/ĭ/ > i	/ĭ/ > e	% of Dev.
(Pagan)	2nd.	3	0	
	3rd.	5	0	
	n.d.	26	0	
	Totals:	34	0	0.0
(Christ.)	4th.	9	0	
	6th.	1	0	
	n.d.	27	1	3.6
	Totals:	37	1	2.6

The single occurrence of the deviation of Latin /ĭ/ is in the word *artefices*, D. 1613A, Viminacium (Moesia Superior), no date. Although Mihăescu states (p. 63) in his *Limba Latină* that this change is "atestată în mod copios în secolul al treilea în toate provinciile imperiului român," [33] our figures seem to question this statement. Since Mihăescu investigates the Danubian provinces, with Dalmatia included, his assertion may be more valid for Dalmatia than for the other Balkan provinces.

Closed Syllable

Area	Century	/ĭ/ > i	/ĭ/ > e	% of Dev.
Africa	3rd.	6	0	
	4th.	28	2	6.7
	5th.	23	0	
	6th.	22	0	
	7th.	2	0	
	n.d.	161	1	0.6
	Totals:	242	3	1.2

The examples of deviation are:

Cresti, D. 1470, Tingi (Mauretania Tingitana), A.D. 345.
sexagenta, D. 3085AN, *CIL* VIII 11,899, Maktar (Byzacena), no date.

---

[33] Translation from the Rumanian: "attested copiously in the third century in all provinces of the Roman Empire."

kres[s]ume (= *carissimae*), D. 4192A, *CIL* VIII 12,805, Numerus Syrorum (Mauretania Caesariensis), A.D. 359.

The total percentage of 1.2 % is likewise compatible with the overall picture of a lack of merger of /ĭ/ and /ē/.

Britain	Century	/ĭ/ > i	/ĭ/ > e	% of Dev.
(Pagan)	1st.	3	0	
	2nd.	4	0	
	3rd.	19	1	5.0
	4th.	1	0	
	n.d.	58	1	1.7
	Totals:	85	2	2.3

The two examples of confusion between /ĭ/ and /ē/ in pagan Britain [34] are:

Felicessemus [proper name], *RIB* 988, *CIL* VII 974, Bewcastle (Banna), 3rd century.
ell[a], *RIB* 154, Bath (Aquae Sulis), no date.

Britain	Century	/ĭ/ > i	/ĭ/ > e	% of Dev.
(Christ.)	8th.	2	0	
	9th.	1	0	
	n.d.	2	0	
	Totals:	5	0	0.0

Dalmatia	Century	/ĭ/ > i	/ĭ/ > e	% of Dev.
	4th.	7	0	
	5th.	8	0	
	6th.	2	0	
	n.d.	66	2	2.9
	Totals:	83	2	2.4

[34] The orthography of the Celtic deity *Vitiris* is variable with several spellings being found: *Vetri, Veteribus, Votri, Hviteribus, Hveteri, Hvitri, Vetiri, Viteri, Hvetiri*; confusion with the Latin *vetus, veteris* (gen.) probably caused several of the above spellings. The aspirate may be caused by Germanic influence. For a discussion of the importance of the divinity and the various spellings, see Collingwood-Myres, pp. 269-70. We have not included any of these *i* and *e* confusions in our tabulations since the original spelling is doubtful.

The examples of deviation for this area are:

caresseme, **D.** 3044A, Salona, no date.
derelecto, **D.** 3381, *CIL* III 14,306, Salona, no date.

Balkans	*Century*	/ĭ/ > *i*	/ĭ/ > *e*	% of Dev.
(Pagan)	1st.	1	0	
	2nd.	1	0	
	3rd.	2	0	
	n.d.	20	0	
	Totals:	24	0	0.0

Balkans	*Century*	/ĭ/ > *i*	/ĭ/ > *e*	% of Dev.
(Christ.)	4th.	6	0	
	5th.	1	0	
	n.d.	31	0	
	Totals:	38	0	0.0

Although the figures are numerically low, and a definite assertion with respect to the merger of Latin /ĭ/ and /ē/ would be precarious on the basis of our tabulation, it appears, however, that the inscriptional material concerning a confusion of /ĭ/ and /ē/ in closed syllables would seem to indicate that Balkan Latin inscriptions, both pagan and Christian, do not show a tendency to merge these two phonemes.

Latin /ĭ/ in Monosyllables

The Latin /ĭ/ in monosyllables is extremely stable on the basis of our investigation.

Although the preposition *in* is overwhelmingly used in all of our inscriptions, we do find one example when it is written *en*: D. 1403, *CIL* VIII 8651, Sitifis (Mauretania Sitifensis), no date. We also find *bis* written as *bes* in D. 3870, *CIL* III 13,124, Salona (Dalmatia), no date. Compare, however, the comparative figures for the correct forms and the deviations:

Area	Century	in	en	% Dev.	bis	bes	% Dev.
Africa	3rd.	2	0				
	4th.	12	0				
	5th.	24	0				
	6th.	10	0				
	7th.	1	0				
	n.d.	407	1	0.3	4	0	
	Totals:	456	1	0.2	4	0	0.0

Area	Century	in	en	% Dev.	bis	bes	% Dev.
Britain	1st.	2	0				
(Pagan)	2nd.	2	0				
	3rd.	2	0				
	n.d.	1	0				
	Totals:	7	0				
(Christ.)	5th.	3	0				
	6th.	3	0				
	8th.	1	0				
	9th.	2	0				
	n.d.	4	0				
	Totals:	13	0				
Dalmatia	4th.	1	0				
	5th.	5	0				
	6th.	1	0				
	n.d.	23	0		2	1	33.3
	Totals:	30	0		2	1	33.3
Balkans	3rd.	0	0		1	0	
(Pagan)	n.d.	1	0				
	Totals:	1	0		1	0	
(Christ.)	4th.	1	0				
	5th.	1	0				
	n.d.	19	0				
	Totals:	21	0				

Latin /ĭ/ Represented as y

There are sporadic cases of this orthographic change in our inscriptions both in open as well as closed syllables and in pagan as well as Christian inscriptions. The following are the words where this change occurs:

relyquie, D. 2089, CIL VIII 23,921, Africa, no date.
byrgo (= virgo), D. 2934, Salona (Dalmatia), no date.

Mytrae (= Mithrae, the Persian God), *RIB* 1395, *CIL* VII 541, Rudchester (Vindovala), no date.
Mytrae, *RIB* 1599, *CIL* VII 645, Hadrian's Wall (Housesteads, Vercovicium), 3rd. century.

These are probably reverse spellings which would indicate that the Greek *upsilon* had already assumed the sound of Latin /ĭ/. [35]

On comparing our findings with those of Gaeng, we find some important differences in the treatment of Latin /ĭ/ in open and closed syllables. By far the most striking is the inscriptional evidence for the merger of Latin /ē/ and /ĭ/ in Gaul with the almost complete lack of confusion of these two phonemes in Africa. Taking the liberty of interpolating Gaeng's figures for each individual area without taking into consideration the chronological breakdown into centuries, we find that Gaul showed an incidence of deviation of 35.8 % in open syllables (61 cases of /ĭ/ to *i* and 34 of /ĭ/ to *e*). This is in strong contrast to the Latin of North Africa where we have a deviation of only 0.5 % in open syllables (207 cases of /ĭ/ to *i* and only one case of /ĭ/ to *e*) and 1.2 % in closed syllables (242 cases of /ĭ/ to *i* and 3 cases of /ĭ/ to *e*). This minimal confusion of /ĭ/ and /ē/ in Africa seems to indicate that African Latin indeed followed the archaic scheme of the Sardinian vocalic system, in contrast to other parts of

---

[35] There exists the possibility that this *y*-spelling represents the sound of /y/, and is not merely a reverse spelling. There was a tendency in Latin for the /ĭ/ to become /y/ after ṷ and labials in general. Cf. Ferdinand Sommer, *Handbuch der lateinischen Laut- und Formenlehre*, 2nd. and 3rd. ed. (Heidelberg: Carl Winter, 1948), p. 63: "Nach Berichten der Nationalgrammatiker nahm hinter ṷ- das *i* eine dem *y*, gr. υ ähnliche labialisierte Färbung an. ... Auf jüngeren Inschriften scheint auch sonst ein (gräzisierendes) *y* für *i* vorzugsweise nach Labialen zu stehen." On the basis of the corrections in the *Appendix Probi* (*vir non vyr, virgo non vyrgo, virga non vyrga*), Lindsay states (p. 29) that "the existence of this tendency to pronounce accented *i* as *ü* after *v* can hardly be doubted." It must be pointed out that in the *Appendix Probi* we also have the admonition, *crista non crysta*, which shows the change of /ĭ/ to *y* when a labial does not precede. The Persian sun-god Mithras is transmitted to Latin via the Greek, and although a labial precedes, a reverse spelling seems more probable. The *y* in *byrgo* and *relyquie* is a single occurrence and the innumerable times that the correct form is encountered in both words and their derivatives would militate against any /y/ sound. The possibility that the *y*-spelling in *byrgo* and *relyquie* is an indication of the alleged "intermediate" vowel between /ĭ/ and /ŭ/ is dispelled, since, as Sturtevant reminds (p. 120) us, it is "an unstable phoneme, short in quantity and confined to unaccented syllables."

Romania where we have to posit a merger of /ĭ/ and /ē/.[36] An interpretation for British Latin is more difficult. In open syllables British Latin shows a 1.5 % deviation (132 cases of /ĭ/ to i and 2 of /ĭ/ to e), in pagan Britain and 0.0 % in Christian Britain (8 cases of /ĭ/ to i and none for /ĭ/ to e). In closed syllables we have 2.3 % deviation (85 cases of /ĭ/ to i and 2 cases of /ĭ/ to e), in pagan Britain and 0.0 % in Christian Britain (just five cases of /ĭ/ to i). On the basis of higher percentages of deviation for this confusion of /ĭ/ and /ē/ in the other areas of the Roman Empire, we are tempted to consider that the Latin of Britain likewise tended to maintain /ĭ/ and /ē/ separately, although the picture is not as clear for Britain as it is for Gaul and Africa. The confusion of /ĭ/ and /ē/ in Dalmatia is seen with an incidence of 5.5 % in open syllables (104 cases of /ĭ/ to i and 6 cases of /ĭ/ to e), and 2.4 % in closed syllables (83 cases of /ĭ/ to i and 2 cases of /ĭ/ to e). The inner Balkans show 0.0 % for pagan inscriptions (34 cases of /ĭ/) and 2.6 % in Christian inscriptions (37 cases of /ĭ/ to i and 1 case of /ĭ/ to e), in open syllables, but 0.0 % in closed syllables for both pagan and Christian inscriptions (24 cases and 38 cases of /ĭ/ respectively). To get the full areal picture of this critical problem of Latin /ĭ/ and /ē/, we are summarizing in tabular form the results of our findings and those of Gaeng, once again interpolating his figures for each entire area without the chronological breakdown into centuries. [37]

---

36 See Lausberg, I, 221 ff.

37 For Gaeng's interpretation of the merger of /ĭ/ and /ē/ according to centuries and his general conclusions, see his pages 66-68. His main conclusion which concerns us most here is his statement (p. 68) that "The complete merger of Latin /ē/ and /ĭ/ in both areas of Gaul seems to be rather clearly established by the fourth/fifth centuries."

Area	Open Syllable		% Of Dev.	Closed Syllable		% Of Dev.	Total Dev.
	/ē/ > e	/ē/ > i		/ē/ < e	/ē/ > i		
Iber. Pen.	130	5	3.7	36	1	2.7	3.5
Gaul	52	11	17.5	96	48	33.3	28.5
North. Italy	47	1	2.1	81	7	8.0	5.9
Central & South. Italy	76	3	3.8	128	9	6.6	5.6
Rome	183	5	2.7	182	12	6.2	4.5
Africa	429	4	0.9	97	2	2.0	1.1
Britain (pagan)	184	0	0.0	23	2	8.0	1.0
(Christian)	13	0	0.0	1	0	0.0	0.0
Dalmatia	124	5	3.9	18	2	10.0	4.7
Balkans (pagan)	61	0	0.0	6	0	0.0	0.0
(Christian)	48	2	4.0	15	0	0.0	3.1

Area	Open Syllable		% Of Dev.	Closed Syllable		% Of Dev.	Total Dev.
	/ĭ/ > i	/ĭ/ > e		/ĭ/ > i	/ĭ/ > e		
Iber. Pen.	65	5	7.1	55	2	3.5	5.5
Gaul	61	34	35.8	34	8	19.0	30.7
North. Italy	72	7	8.9	39	1	2.5	6.7
Central & South. Italy	138	3	2.1	65	4	5.8	3.3
Rome	182	3	1.6	171	5	2.8	2.2
Africa	207	1	0.5	242	3	1.2	0.9
Britain (pagan)	132	2	1.5	85	2	2.3	1.8
(Christian)	8	0	0.0	5	0	0.0	0.0
Dalmatia	104	6	5.5	83	2	2.4	4.1
Balkans (pagan)	34	0	0.0	24	0	0.0	0.0
(Christian)	37	1	2.6	38	0	0.0	1.3

In addition to the conclusion that the Latin of Gaul showed a definite trend to merge /ĭ/ and /ē/ compared to the absence of this phenomenon in Africa and probably in Britain, we also have other points that have to be explained. In the Latin of Gaul, Northern Italy, Central and Southern Italy, and Rome the change of /ē/ to i is greater in closed syllables than in open syllables. There is little difference in the Latin of the Iberian Peninsula. In African Latin this change is negligible in both open and closed syllables. British pagan Latin shows no change of /ē/ to i in open syllables, but does have an 8 % deviation in closed syllables, although the figures are low and may not be conclusive. The total deviation of 1 % in both open and closed syllables in the pagan inscriptions of Britain is probably a more accurate figure on the basis of a more quantitative sampling. The /ē/ to i is also changed more in the closed syllable than in the open in Dalmatian Latin. In closed syllables it would appear that the consonantal environment was the principle cause of the closing of /ē/ to *i*. In open syllables, most cases of /ē/ to *i* are probably the result of an umlaut effect.

Since the Vulgar Latin /ē/ evolved in a closed syllable differently from the way it developed in an open syllable in French, Franco-Provençal, Rheto-Romance, Northern Italian dialects, southeast Italy, and Vegliote, [38] the inscriptional material may show this incipient divergent development in a quantitative analysis. Unfortunately the greater degree of change in closed syllables in inscriptions is, at times, contrary to later Romance development where the /ē/ develops more radically in open syllables. [39] At the outset of Romance vocalic development, there is no divergent evolution of vowels according to their open or closed position, and this situation is maintained in Sardinian, Iberian Romance, Provençal, southwestern Italian dialects, and Balkan Romance (except for Vegliote). [40] If we consider that African Latin does show the same archaic vocalic system as Sardinian, our findings on the different syllabic make-up in the various areas of the Roman Empire are surprisingly close to the future development of the Romance languages.

The position of Northern Italian Latin with respect to the Latin of Gaul and the other Italian areas has to be commented upon. The merger of /ē/ and /ĭ/ is well established in Gaul by virtue of the exceedingly high percentage of deviation for both /ē/ to *i* and /ĭ/ to *e* (28.5 % and 30.7 % respectively). A comparison with the frequency of occurrence for Northern Italy shows that this area is far behind Gaul in the important merger of these two vowels. The 5.9 % percentage of deviation for /ē/ to *i* and the 6.7 % for /ĭ/ to *e* would probably indicate that the merger was going on. However, when we compare Northern Italy with the Central and Southern areas, we find that the /ē/ to *i* change has a total deviation of 5.9 % in Northern Italy against a 5.6 % for Central and Southern Italy. This would seem to indicate that Northern Italy merged to ap-

---

[38] Lausberg, I, 223.

[39] This is not to preclude any possibility of vowels developing more in closed syllables than in open ones. Weinrich does, in fact, give examples (p. 177) in Italian dialects where vowels evolve further in closed syllables than in open syllables, but this is not the general rule.

[40] Lausberg, I, 217.

proximately the same degree as Central and Southern Italy. When
we consider the /ē/ to *i* change in open syllables, we find that
Northern Italy even has a lower percentage of deviation (2.1 %)
than Central and Southern Italy (3.8 %). In closed syllables Northern
Italy has a slightly higher percentage of deviation (8.0 %) than
Central and Southern Italy (6.6 %), but the difference is too slight
to warrant Gaeng's assertion (p. 68) that "the almost 10 % deviation
in No. Italy, i.e. a 5 % or so differential with respect to the other
Italian areas during a comparable period, would point, it would
seem, to somewhat earlier merger of these two Latin vowel phonemes
in this region." [41] In the change of /ĭ/ to *e*, Northern Italy does
show a marked incidence of deviation with an 8.9 % in open syllables, compared to a 2.1 % for Central and Southern Italy; it
must be remembered, however, that Sicilian and some southern
Italian dialects do have an /ĭ/ to *i* reflex in addition to the /ē/
to *i* change in the vocalic system. [42] Surprisingly enough the picture
is blurred in closed syllables where Central and Southern Italy have
a 5.8 % deviation compared to the 2.5 % for Northern Italy. If
inscriptions have value in a study of differentiation in the Latin of
the various areas of Romania, it may be necessary to consider the
syllabic structure in which the vowel is found much more than has
been the case in previous studies of this type. [43]

Although Gaul is unsurprisingly the most evolutionary of the
areas in the Roman Empire, far outstripping the other areas in
the confusion of /ĭ/ and /ē/, it is striking to find that the Latin
of the inscriptions of the city of Rome is relatively equal to that of
other regions. It may be said that the Latin schools and general
culture of Rome were superior to that of other regions, and that the
scribes consequently wrote a better Latin. If this is the explanation
for the difference in the treatment of vocalic phenomena in Rome

---

[41] Gaeng's claim for an earlier merger of /ē/ and /ĭ/ in Northern Italy
is somewhat vitiated because of a mistake in arithmetic. In his table on p. 67,
he inadvertently gives the total of 147 cases of the correct occurrences and
15 for total deviation. It should be 177 correct cases, a figure which gives
us a percentage of deviation of 7.8 % rather than his 9.2 %.

[42] See *supra*, p. 25 of our Introduction for the Sicilian vocalic scheme;
cf. also Grandgent, p. 85.

[43] Weinrich has, precisely, a chapter entitled "Vokaldifferenzierung nach
freier und gedeckter Stellung" (pp. 177-193) in his *Phonologische Studien
zur romanischen Sprachgeschichte.*

compared to that of Gaul, it may be then inferred that the Latin education in Gaul was faulty and that the scribes were fairly untutored. Although Latin traditions were undeniably strong in Rome, it would appear erroneous to attribute confusion in Latin inscriptions in Gaul to untutored Latin scribes there. In fact it has been maintained that "the conservation of the final -s in Gaul, for instance, was due to the fact that Latin was first learned there by an aristocracy anxious to assimilate Roman culture." [44] It would seem to be inconsistent to consider a socially better-educated, higher élite in Gaul as the reason for the conservation of final -s, but to blame the confusion of /ĭ/ and /ē/ on poorly educated Gaulish scribes. It may be truer to the actual state of affairs to consider the Latin of non-official inscriptions as representative of the speech of the populace. We agree with Herman when he says (p. 54) that

> ...il est... généralement connu que les inscriptions pri-
> vées, surtout les inscriptions tardives, s'écartent d'innombra-
> bles fois de la norme orthographique et grammaticale et que
> plusieurs types d'écarts sont de toute évidence déterminés
> par des processus qui préparent de futures évolutions ro-
> manes, donc par des processus propres à la langue parlée
> (p.e. les confusions entre I et E, V et O). L'influence de la
> langue parlée une fois admise, il est inimaginable que cette
> influence se soit limitée aux seuls phénomènes communs à
> toute la Romania, à l'exclusion des éventuels traits particu-
> liers à tel ou tel territoire. Force est donc de considérer le
> témoignage des inscriptions comme un témoignage valable.

A quantitative comparative analysis of Latin inscriptions in the various parts of Romania does seem to show that there was a differentiation in the Latin of the Roman Empire.

Latin /ī/ Represented by the Letter i

Latin /ī/ is generally kept as i, but a few sporadic changes to e do occur. Since the spelling e for /ī/ has been the subject of

---

[44] Migliorini, p. 20; Densusianu, p. 50; cf. also Wartburg, Ausgliederung, p. 22: "Anders ist die Latinisierung Galliens und Iberiens erfolgt. Hier ist sie vielmehr von den Städten und von den höhern Schichten der Gesellschaft ausgegangen. Schule und Verwaltung verbreiteten die mehr literarische Form des Lateins unter der einheimischen Bevölkerung."

[45] Lindsay, pp. 29-30; Sturtevant, pp. 114-15; Sommer, pp. 63-64, 73-74.

some discussion on the part of scholars, [45] we will give a full tabulation of our findings. The *e*-spelling is usually considered as an
early dialectal development which evolved from a diphthong *ei*, this
e being the regular development in Umbrian and in other parts of
Italy. This rustic sound *e*, cited by the Latin grammarian Varro,
seemingly maintained itself in some country districts at least down
to the Ciceronian period. [46] Below are the findings of our inscriptions
in open and closed syllables:

Open Syllable

Area	Century	/ī/ > i	/ī/ > e	
Africa	3rd.	11	0	
	4th.	49	0	
	5th.	38	0	
	6th.	35	0	
	7th.	2	0	
	n.d.	281	0	
	Totals:	416	0	
Britain	Century	/ī/ > i	/ī/ > e	% of Dev.
(Pagan)	1st.	27	0	
	2nd.	29	1	3.3
	3rd.	56	0	
	4th.	32	0	
	n.d.	205	0	
	Totals:	349	1	0.3

The only example found in open syllables in this region was
the proper name *Septimenus*, *RIB* 903, *CIL* VII 353, Old Carlisle
(Olerica), A.D. 185. This change of /ī/ to *e* may be, however, a
simple change of suffix, inasmuch as other scholars have pointed
out the fairly common confusion between the *-inus* and *-enus* suf-
fixes in vulgar texts. [47]

It is possible, however, that this suffix *-enus* for *-inus* does show
a dialectal trait. [48] Lindsay does mention (p. 29) that "ī is rarely

---

[46] Sturtevant, p. 115; this scholar also gives the chronology of this diphthong *ei* and its changes to *e* and *i*. See also Väänänen, *Le Latin vulgaire
des inscriptions pompéiennes*, 2nd ed. (Berlin: Akadamie-Verlag, 1959), p. 22;
Niedermann, pp. 58-59.

[47] Pirson, pp. 5, 10; Carnoy, pp. 44-45; Lindsay, p. 29; cf. also *Appendix Probi* where we find *Byzacenus non Bizacinus* (item 48).

[48] Carnoy, p. 44.

written *e* except in Gaul and Britain." Jackson states (p. 304) that Latin /ī/ remains as /ī/ in the Brittonic languages, but "in a few cases Latin /ī/ behaves like Lat. *ē*; e.g. *paradīsus* > W. *paradwys; sentīre* > W. *synnwyr; papīrus* > W. *pabwyr*. These are presumably cases where VL., at least in Britain, had *ẹ̄*." Since the percentage of deviation is only 0.3 %, it would seem more probable to consider this isolated case of /ī/ to *e* as an interchange of suffix.

Area	Century	/ī/ > i	/ī/ > e	% of Dev.
Britain	4th.	1	0	
(Christ.)	5th.	7	0	
	6th.	29	0	
	7th.	6	0	
	9th.	0	1	100.0
	n.d.	9	1	10.0
	Totals:	52	2	3.7

The following are the two examples of /ī/ to *e* in Christian Britain:

speretus (gen.), *CIIC* 1011, Glamorgan, Wales, A.D. 870.
speritus (gen.), *CIIC* 1022, Glamorgan, Wales, no date.

It is interesting to note that both Jackson and Loth discuss this particular word because of its peculiar development in the Brittonic languages. The Welsh *ysbryd* would require a change in the stress of the Latin *spiritus* from the antepenult to the penult. Jackson considers (p. 304) the history of this word unclear, but accepts in principle Loth's suggestion (p. 108) that "les formes obliques comme *spiritui* y ont sans doute beaucoup contribué." Richter, on explaining the French *esprit*, points out the fact (p. 28) that "seit der karolingischen Renaissance, ... werden im allgemeinen lateinische Wörter als Paroxytona gelesen. Alle proparoxytonen Buchwörter, die seitdem in die Umgangssprache kommen, sind durch Akzentverschiebung gekennzeichnet. Wohl das älteste und bekannteste ist *spiritus*." Since both examples are found in very late inscriptions (A.D. 870 and even the undated inscription probably is not before the later part of the eighth century, if it falls within the Old Welsh period), they may show this general change of stress with a concomitant shortening of the initial vowel *i*. Jackson, however, considers (p. 304) this explanation as "too late to have been the source of the Brittonic development." The problem of the evolution of the Latin *spiritus* in the Brittonic languages apparently remains.

Area	Century	/ī/ > i	/ī/ > e	% of Dev.
Dalmatia	4th.	20	0	0.0
	5th.	19	0	0.0
	6th.	5	0	0.0
	n.d.	122	1	0.8
	Totals:	166	1	0.6

The single example of this change of /ī/ to *e* is in the word *cremine*, D. 2426, CIL III 10,190, Podgorica (near Doclea), no date. Skok, *Pojave*, considers (p. 14) this example as being dated between the fourth and fifth centuries and as a scribal mistake. It should be remembered, however, that in Vegliote the Latin /ī/ in an open syllable diphthongizes to /aj/, and opens to an /e/ in closed syllables, but the intermediate stage was an *e* in open syllables also before diphthongizing. This intermediate stage, however, was of a relatively late development. [49] On the basis of this single occurrence and the early date, it would be hazardous to attribute too much importance to this /ī/ to *e* change.

Area	Century	/ī/ > i	/ī/ > e	% of Dev.
Balkans	1st.	2	0	0.0
(Pagan)	2nd.	10	0	0.0
	3rd.	11	0	0.0
	n.d.	60	0	0.0
	Totals:	83	0	0.0
(Christ.)	4th.	8	0	0.0
	5th.	2	0	0.0
	n.d.	64	0	0.0
	Totals:	74	0	0.0

Mention must be made of the fact that the only form of *idus* or its derivatives is with /ī/ in all of our inscriptions, although the archaic spelling with *e* or *ei* is found in numerous inscriptions from

---

[49] Lausberg, I, 220; Hadlich, p. 73; Bàrtoli, *Dalmatische*, writes (II, 337) with respect to VL /ĭ/: "Veglia. In freier Silbe ai̯; in gedeckter *e*. Zwischenstufen: i̯ wohl zu ẹ, das in freier Silbe ... zu ei̯ ai̯ diphthongiert.... Selbst de Zwischenstufe *e* ist verhältnismässig jung."

Pompei, Spain, Gaul, and Italy. [50] One is led to believe that the scribes of the peripheral areas of Britain, Dalmatia, the Balkans, and even Africa were not inclined to this archaic or possibly dialectal spelling of the word. Gaeng, however, does not find in Rome any case of *idus* spelled other than in the classical manner.

Closed Syllables

Area	Century	/ī/ > i	/ī/ > e	% of Dev.
Africa	3rd.	3	0	0.0
	4th.	35	0	0.0
	5th.	61	0	0.0
	6th.	10	0	0.0
	n.d.	278	2	0.7
	Totals:	387	2	0.5

The two examples of an /ī/ > e change in this region are:

vexssit (= *vixit*), D. 2648, Thabraca (Proconsularis), n.d.
ceqe (= *quinque*), D. 2679, *CIL* 12,200, Hr. Sidi Amara (Byzacena), n.d.

In view of the overwhelming number of correct cases with *i* (the form *vixit* or other stressed variants such as *vixsit, bixit, vicsit,* etc., are found 324 times compared to this single occurrence of *vexssit*), this isolated case of an /ī/ to e change must be viewed with extreme caution. [51] The e of *ceqe* is difficult to explain. Its popular nature is proven by the dissimilation of *qu-* to *c-* and the loss of *n* before a consonant, but there is no apparent reason for this *e* rather than the expected *i*. [52] The *i* is found twice in *cinqe* (D. 1383, no date), and *quinque* (D. 3947, no date).

---

[50] Väänänen, *Pompéiennes*, p. 22; Carnoy, p. 44; Gaeng, pp. 70-71.

[51] This is not to deny the possibility of a "rustic" pronunciation found in African Latin. The form *vexit* or a variant thereof has been encountered in inscriptions in various parts of the Empire. Gaeng found four examples of the *e* spelling in undated examples from Rome and one case in an undated inscription from Gaul. Cf. Pirson, p. 13; Maccarrone, p. 82, considered this *e* as "forse per affettazione d'arcaismo."

[52] The Latin *i* from the Indo-European e in **pĕnqwĕ* before a velar nasal took place centuries before. For the development of I.E. **pĕnqwĕ* to its Latin form *quinque*, see Palmer, pp. 215-225; Ernout, *Morphologie*, p. 108; Lindsay, pp. 229, 414; Sommer, p. 57. The form *ceqe* may have

We have an isolated case of an *ii* orthography for the stressed /ī/ in *viixit*, *D.* 3681, *CIL* VIII 9910, Pomaria, no date. Since *ii* is used in the Pompeian *graffiti* for *e*, this may be another example of an *e* for /ī/ change. [53] This assumption is substantiated by the form *feciit* found in the same inscription, where *ii* could stand for an *e* > ĭ. It is strange, however, to find this archaic or dialectal spelling in a Christian inscription.

Area	Century	/ī/ > i	/ī/ > e	% of Dev.
Britain	1st.	2	0	0.0
	2nd.	6	0	0.0
(Pagan)	3rd.	19	0	0.0
	4th.	5	0	0.0
	n.d.	108	0	0.0
	Totals:	140	0	0.0

Area	Century	/ī/ > i	/ī/ > e	% of Dev.
Britain	4th.	1	0	0.0
	5th.	1	0	0.0
(Christ.)	6th.	3	0	0.0
	8th.	1	0	0.0
	n.d.	0	0	0.0
	Totals:	6	0	0.0
Dalmatia	4th.	14	0	0.0
	5th.	6	0	0.0
	6th.	6	0	0.0
	n.d.	56	1	1.8
	Totals:	82	1	1.2

The single occurrence of this /ī/ to *e* is in *ecne* (= *igne*), *D.* 2426, *CIL* III 10,190, Podgorica, no date. [54] In Dalmatian the Latin /ī/ in closed syllable opens to *e*. [55]

---

been influenced by the Greek πέντε, since the Greek influence in Northern Africa was strong in Christian times.

[53] See Väänänen, *Pompéiennes*, p. 20 ff.; Lindsay, p. 10, considers *II* as a "common symbol for *E*."

[54] We are considering the stressed vowel of *ignis* as long on the authority of the *New Latin Grammar* by Allen and Greenough, although Skok, *Pojave*, considers (p. 15) the *e* in *ecne* as a change of /ĭ/ to *e*. Lindsay considers (p. 229) the *i* as short. Lewis' *Elementary Dictionary of Latin* considers it long. If this change is indeed a case of /ĭ/ to *e*, it would be another example of this /ĭ/ and /ē/ confusion in Dalmatia. See *supra*, p. 97 ff.

[55] See footnote 49, p. 110.

Area	Century	/ī/ > i	/ī/ > e	% of Dev.
Balkans	3rd.	2	0	0.0
	4th.	4	0	0.0
(Pagan)	n.d.	38	0	0.0
	Totals:	44	0	0.0
(Christ.)	4th.	1	0	0.0
	n.d.	34	0	0.0
	Totals:	35	0	0.0

It is interesting to note that in all our areas the forms *dignus,*
signus, benignus, and *lignum* occur with an *i* spelling. Pirson reports
(p. 12) a form *benegnus* from Gaul as did Gaeng (p. 72). The Romance languages waver on the quality of the *i* before the consonant
cluster *gn* (cf. It. *degno, segno, legno*; Rum. *semn, lemn*; Span.
desdén, seña, leño; Fr. *dédain*; but Sp. *digno* [learned]; Fr. *bénin*;
It. *benigno*).

Latin /ī/ in Monosyllables

We have a single example of *que* (for the masculine relative pronoun) in *D.* 3297, *CIL* VIII 27,917, Theveste (Proconsularis), Africa,
no date. The feminine *quae* replaces the masculine *qui* in *D.* 2755,
CIL VIII 21,337a, Caesarea Maurorum, no date: *Ulpi Valeriani, fili*
rarissimi, corpus hic sepultum est. quae bis binos annos et dies
XXVIIII hic fuit in seculo. The correct form *qui* is, of course, very
common. In fact the masculine relative pronoun *qui* usurped the function of the feminine *quae* or *que* as can be seen from the following
table: [56]

Area	Century	Correct Fem. *quae*	Monophthong. *que*	Masc. *qui* For Fem.	% of Dev.
Africa	4th.	1	0	10	90.0
	5th.	3	0	12	80.0
	n.d.	4	5	1	10.0
	Totals:	8	5	23	63.9

---

[56] Lausberg, II, 218, discusses the relative pronoun *qui,* but does not give
any chronology as to the time when it assumes the function of the feminine
quae: Elcock mentions (p. 95) "the extension of the masculine forms to
include the feminine" and says that the "inscriptions of the third and fourth
century bear ample witness to this change." Bourciez considers (p. 95) that
"au IIIe et au IVe siècle, le relatif fem, *quae* a été supplanté par le masc.
qui dans l'usage parlé."

The oldest dated case of the use of the masculine *qui* for the feminine *quae* in our corpus of African inscriptions is A.D. 302.

Area	Century	Correct Fem. *quae*	Monophthong. *que*	Masc. *qui* For Fem.	% of Dev.
Britain	3rd.	1	0	0	0.0
	n.d.	2	1	1	25.0
(Pagan)	Totals:	3	1	1	20.0
(Christ.)	4th.	2	0	0	0.0
	5th.	2	0	0	0.0
	6th.	0	0	1	100.0
	n.d.	11	1	7	36.8
	Totals:	15	1	8	33.3
Dalmatia	4th.	1	0	0	0.0
	5th.	2	0	0	0.0
	n.d.	11	1	6	33.3
	Totals:	14	1	6	28.6
Balkans (Pagan)	n.d.	2	0	2	50.0
(Christ.)	4th.	0	0	1	100.0
	n.d.	4	2	5	45.5
	Totals:	4	2	6	50.0

The *CIL* assigns the single dated Christian inscriptions of the Balkans to the general period of the fourth century, but does not give any more specific time.

Our results show that the masculine *qui* had replaced the feminine *quae* in all our areas, although Africa is the region where this extension is most evident with a 63.9 % use of *qui*. The earliest example we found in our inscriptions of the use of *qui* for *quae* was in A.D. 302 in Altava (Africa), which is in general agreement with what has been said on the subject by other scholars. [57]

Latin /ī/ in Hiatus

The only important change of /ī/ to *e* found in hiatus is the single example of *illeus* (= *illius*) found in a pagan *defixio* inscription written in cursive script: *RIB* 7, London, no date. This may be an

---

[57] See footnote 56, p. 113 for references.

analogical feminine form with an -e- from -ae-.[58] Since the *defixio* in which *illeus* is found is of a popular nature, this /ī/ to *e* may show a popular development.[59] There is, of course, nothing to prevent this isolated form from being a simple scribal mistake.

Latin /ŏ/, Represented by the Letter o

Latin /ŏ/ has been generally considered as remaining unchanged in Latin throughout the Empire.[60] Those cases where Latin /ŏ/ changed to *u* were considered by Pirson (p. 14) as the result of the influence of the "phonèmes environnants, du jod ou d'une nasale." Lausberg gives (I, 230-32) the development of Latin /ŏ/ in the Romance languages. He mentions (I, 230) that Latin /ŏ/ merges in Sardinian and Rumanian with Latin /ō/; that in those languages of the Italic qualitative system /ŏ/ goes to open *o*, which is kept in Portuguese, Catalan, Provençal, and Surselvan but diphthongizes to *uo* and then to *ue* in Spanish. In Vegliote, /ŏ/ generally diphthongizes to *uo* and subsequently develops into *u* in open syllables and *ua* in closed syllables. In French, Franco-Provençal, sporadically in Rheto-Romance (Central Ladin), and Northern Italian dialects, in addition to Tuscan, Latin /ŏ/ undergoes a different treatment according to the syllabic structure: in closed syllables it is kept, but it diphthongizes to *uo* in open syllables.

In our findings, Latin /ŏ/ is extremely stable, not influenced by any following nasal or yods and not diphthongized. Its stability is found in both open and closed syllables. Below are the results of our investigations:

---

[58] Sommer reports (p. 430) the feminine form *illeius* found in *CIL* VI 14,484; cf. Väänänen, *Introduction*, p. 130; Kent, p. 70.

[59] See p. 109 for a discussion of /ī/ to /ē/ in Britain.

[60] Grandgent, p. 86; Jackson, *Language*, p. 272; Sommer, p. 64. A contrary position is expressed by Prinz, *De O et U Vocalibus inter se Permutatis in Lingua Latina* (Halle: Eduard Klinz, 1932), p. 91, who states that "apparet et in titulis ethnicis et in titulis christianis non raro U pro O brevi occurrere." This opinion was based, however, on the confusion of /ŏ/ and *u* in all positions in all areas, and without any consideration of chronology. Prinz does not give, of course, any percentage of deviation. Our findings are at complete variance with those of Prinz for what concerns stressed position.

Open Syllables

Africa	Century	/ŏ/ > o	/ŏ/ > u	% of Dev.
	3rd.	5	0	
	4th.	46	0	
	5th.	51	0	
	6th.	19	0	
	7th.	3	0	
	n.d.	244	0	
	Totals:	368	0	0.0
Britain	1st.	5	0	
	2nd.	10	0	
(Pagan)	3rd.	38	0	
	4th.	1	0	
	n.d.	80	0	
	Totals:	134	0	0.0
(Christ.)	4th.	1	0	
	6th.	7	1	12.5
	8th.	1	0	
	n.d.	5	0	
	Totals:	14	1	6.7

The single occurrence of this change of /ŏ/ to *u* is found in the Greek word *apustoli, CIIC* 519, Wigtown (Scotland), sixth century. [61]

Dalmatia [62]	Century	/ŏ/ > o	/ŏ/ > u	% of Dev.
	4th.	9	0	
	5th.	23	0	
	6th.	2	0	
	n.d.	78	0	
	Totals:	112	0	0.0

---

[61] Prinz (*De O et U*, p. 90) explains this change with the words: "fortasse U ad analogiam praepositionis 'post > pus' orta est; sed etiam dissimilatione vocalis mutation effecta esse potest." Since the preposition *pus* from *post* is not found in Britain either in Prinz' own work or in our inscriptions, its influence on *apustoli* is hardly probable. Vocalic dissimilation is, of course, always possible, but at times seems to be too facile an explanation. Gaeng considers (p. 79) *pus* as a result of its proclitic position. It would be unlikely for *pus*, having lost its stress, to have influenced the stressed vowel of *apustoli*. The closing effect of the consonant cluster *st* may have influenced the change.

[62] It is significant that Skok does not even mention any change in /ŏ/ in his *Pojave*, thus implying a stability of /ŏ/ in stressed position.

Balkans	Century	/ŏ/ > o	/ŏ/ > u	% of Dev.
(Pagan)	1st.	1	0	
	2nd.	3	0	
	3rd.	5	0	
	4th.	2	0	
	n.d.	27	0	
	Totals:	38	0	0.0
(Christ.)	4th.	3	0	
	n.d.	58	0	
	Totals:	61	0	0.0

Closed Syllable

Africa	Century	/ŏ/ > o	/ŏ/ > u	% of Dev.
	3rd.	2	0	
	4th.	16	0	
	5th.	12	0	
	6th.	5	0	
	7th.	2	0	
	n.d.	94	0	
	Totals:	131	0	0.0
Britain	1st.	1	0	
	2nd.	5	0	
(Pagan)	3rd.	17	0	
	n.d.	69	0	
	Totals:	92	0	0.0
(Christ.)	6th.	1	0	
	7th.	2	0	
	8th.	1	0	
	n.d.	1	0	
	Totals:	5	0	0.0
Dalmatia	4th.	19	0	
	5th.	4	0	
	6th.	5	0	
	n.d.	75	1	1.3
	Totals:	103	1	1.0

The only example of a u for /ŏ/ is seen in the word *urbem* (= *orbem*), in D. 3363, *CIL* III 9623, Salona, no date. Rather than a vocalic confusion, *urbem* is more likely interchanged with *orbem* because of their similarity in meaning. [63]

Balkans	Century	/ŏ/ > o	/ŏ/ > u	% of Dev.
(Pagan)	1st.	1	0	
	3rd.	3	0	
	n.d.	25	0	
	Totals:	29	0	0.0

Balkans	Century	/ŏ/ > o	/ŏ/ > u	% of Dev.
(Christ.)	4th.	4	0	
	5th.	1	0	
	n.d.	22	1	4.3
	Totals:	27	1	3.6

The single change of /ŏ/ to *u* is represented by the word *cumpare* (= *compare*, dative), in *D*. 3611, *CIL* III 10,237, Sirmium (Pannonia Inferior), no date. This change is probably an example of reconstruction with the prefix *cum-* rather than a true change of /ŏ/ to *u*. [64]

Latin /ŏ/ in Monosyllables

There are no examples in our inscriptions of any change of /ŏ/ to *u* in monosyllables. Gaeng reports (p. 79) two cases of *pus* for *post* in Gaul and Central Italy. Prinz brings out the fact that in these Christian inscriptions *pus* is found without the final *t*. [65] In our inscriptions an *o* is always written, even when the final *t* is dropped: cf. *pos*, *D*. 1593, Madauros (Proconsularis), attributed to the fourth century.

Our findings definitely point to an extremely stable /ŏ/ in the peripheral areas even more so than the results obtained by Gaeng for the more central areas of Romania. Gaeng's comment (p. 79) that "in open syllables Latin /ŏ/ remained stable throughout the centuries

---

[63] Cf. Prinz, *De O et U*, pp. 31, 76. On speaking about the words *urbs* and *orbis*, Prinz says (p. 31) that "Haec confusio ea re facilior reddita est, quod significationes harum vocum non multum diversae erant."

[64] Cf. Prinz, *De O et U*, p. 82.

[65] *Ibid.*, p. 90: "Nota in ambobus exemplis T finalem omissam esse."

covered by our inscriptions" reflects our situation, but we are at variance when he concludes (p. 79) that "in closed syllable, on the other hand, Latin /ŏ/ ... occasionally appears transcribed with *u* possibly indicating, with due allowances made for cases where etymological reconstruction may have been at work, that the checked position favored the merger of /ŏ/ and /u/, especially before a nasal consonant."

Latin /ō/, Represented by the Letter o

Since stressed Latin /ō/ and /ŭ/ merged in those languages belonging to the Italic qualitative vocalic system (see *supra*, p. 22) and were kept separate in the archaic vocalic system (see *supra*, p. 23), it should be interesting to see whether our inscriptions corroborate these various vocalic schemes and thus point to a vocalic differentiation of Latin in the various areas of Romania or whether the inscriptions are of little import in the determination of local differences in Latin. The investigation of the problem of the merger of /ō/ and /ŭ/ complements our previous study of the merger of /ē/ and /ĭ/ (see *supra*, p. 86 ff.) and taken together, both studies must be considered crucial if inscriptions are to play any part in the problem of the differentiation of Latin. Since African Latin is supposedly of the archaic vocalic system, while British Latin is presumably to have maintained the Classical Latin quantitative system, and Balkan Latin is considered to be part of the compromise system, but Dalmatian Latin belongs to the Italic qualitative system, we expect to find few or no inscriptional deviations of /ō/ and /ŭ/ in the Latin of Africa, Britain, and the Balkans, but confusion of /ō/ and /ŭ/ in Dalmatian Latin.

Our findings are as follows:

Open Syllable

Africa	Century	/ō/ > o	/ō/ > u	% of Dev.
	3rd.	9	0	
	4th.	56	0	
	5th.	38	0	
	6th.	47	0	
	7th.	2	0	
	n.d.	299	1	0.3
	Totals:	451	1	0.2

The one example of deviation in this area is the word *nu[mine]*, *D.* 2104N, *CIL* VIII 23,040, Uppena, no date. This confusion of /ō/ and /ŭ/ is probably caused by analogy with *numen* because of the similarity in meaning [66] rather than a true case of /ō/ and /ŭ/ merger. Since the percentage of deviation (0.2 %) is so insignificant in comparison with the overwhelming number of examples where /ō/ remains, we can safely say that the Latin of Africa is characterized by its conservative nature and does not partake in the merger of /ō/ and /ŭ/ in open syllables. [67]

Britain	Century	/ō/ > o	/ō/ > u	% of Dev.
(Pagan)	1st.	16	0	
	2nd.	35	0	
	3rd.	49	0	
	4th.	2	0	
	n.d.	131	0	
	Totals:	233	0	0.0

Britain	Century	/ō/ > o	/ō/ > u	% of Dev.
(Christ.)	6th.	3	0	
	7th.	2	0	
	8th.	1	0	
	9th.	2	0	
	n.d.	3	0	
	Totals:	11	0	0.0

The lack of any deviation of /ō/ for Britain would appear to prove that British Latin maintained the Classical Latin quantity system. This is especially true for pagan inscriptions where the material is abundant and probably so for Christian inscriptions although the epigraphical material is too scanty for any definitive statement.

Dalmatia	Century	/ō/ > o	/ō/ > u	% of Dev.
	4th.	19	0	
	5th.	14	1	6.6
	6th.	6	0	
	n.d.	85	5	5.6
	Totals:	124	6	4.6

---

[66] Cf. Prinz, p. 61: "Accedit huc, quod 'nomen' et 'numen' significatione haud multum distabant."

[67] Prinz, without giving any percentages, agrees (p. 75) with this conclusion: "Etiam in Africam hanc vocalium permutationem non transisse ex exiguitate exemplorum epigraphicorum concludam."

Deviations are found in the following examples:

Victuri, D. 745A, *CIL* 9516, Salona, A.D. 431.
sarturi, D. 646, *CIL* 9614, Salona, no date.
Octub. (= *Octobres*), D. 1225a, *CIL* III 14,893, Salona, no date.
Diunan (= *Ionas*), D. 2426, *CIL* III 10,190, Podgorica, no date.
[f]usuri (= *fossori*), D. 3634A, *CIL* III 9062, Salona, no date.
punere, D. 3835, *CIL* III 9585, Salona, no date.

In addition to the inscriptional evidence for proof of merger of /ō/ and /ŭ/, Skok points out in his *Pojave* (p. 16) this change of /ō/ to /ŭ/ in Latin loanwords into Serbian: *neput* < *nepotem*, *krpatur* < *coopertorium* and concludes that this *u* in loanwords probably represented the Latin speech of the province of Dalmatia. This conclusion closely parallels Skok's statement concerning the confusion of /ē/ and /ĭ/ in Dalmatia. (See *supra*, footnote 26, p. 91.)

Balkans	Century	/ō/ > o	/ō/ > u	% of Dev.
(Pagan)	1st.	1	0	
	2nd.	4	0	
	3rd.	10	0	
	n.d.	20	0	
	Totals:	35	0	0.0
(Christ.)	4th.	5	0	
	5th.	2	0	
	n.d.	35	0	
	Totals:	42	0	0.0

Although the figures are low, it would appear that no merger took place in either pagan or Christian inscriptions of the Balkans.

Closed Syllable

There are, unfortunately, very few cases of /ō/ in our inscriptional material. We found no case of *u* for /ō/.

Africa	Century	/ō/ > o	/ō/ > u	% of Dev.
	4th.	1	0	
	6th.	4	0	
	n.d.	6	0	
	Totals:	11	0	0.0

Britain	2nd.	1	0	
(Pagan)	3rd.	3	0	
	n.d.	3	0	
	Totals:	7	0	0.0
(Christ.)	No Examples	—	—	

Dalmatia	Century	/ō/ > o	/ō/ > u	% of Dev.
	4th.	2	0	
	5th.	2	0	
	6th.	2	0	
	n.d.	2	0	
	Totals:	8	0	0.0

Although our figures are too low to draw any firm conclusions for the treatment of /ō/ in closed syllables, Prinz, basing himself on a larger corpus, remarks (p. 73) that "lingua Dalmatica o et u vocales Latinas in syllabis in consonantem exeuntibus nondum confudisse videtur." This difference in treatment of /ō/ in Dalmatian Latin inscriptions according to the nature of the syllable may forecast a subsequent development in Vegliote, where /ō/ in open syllable evolves to /aw/ and in closed syllable to /u/. [68]

---

[68] Lausberg, I, 232; Hadlich, p. 72. Bàrtoli gives the correspondences of Latin /ō/ in open and closed syllables as au and a respectively in Dalmatische, II, 334-35. Bàrtoli does admit (p. 335) that the reflexes of Latin /ō/ in closed syllables are "spärliche und unsichere Belege." Bàrtoli's two examples of /ō/ in closed syllable, samno < somnium and stal, equivalent to the Italian stollo, are inconclusive, the o in somnium in some Romance languages being /ŏ/ (cf. Spanish sueño) and stal itself being "fremd" according to Bàrtoli himself (p. 335). Hadlich gives (p. 83) the examples of Latin forma > Vegliote /furm/ and soricem > Vegliote /surko/, which would show that Latin /ō/ did evolve to Vegliote /u/. Bàrtoli's attempt to show that Latin /ō/ and /ŭ/ in closed syllable evolved differently is corrected by Hadlich who convincingly shows that Latin /ŭ/ and /ō/ were represented by one phoneme.

Balkans	Century	/ō/ > o	/ō/ > u	% of Dev.
(Pagan)	3rd.	3	0	
	4th.	2	0	
	n.d.	2	0	
	Totals:	7	0	0.0
(Christ.)	No Date	3	0	0.0

The figures are too scanty for us to draw any conclusions.

Latin /ō/ in Monosyllables

Although Gaeng found (p. 86) sporadic examples of /ō/ > u in monosyllables (vus, nus, and huc, although the latter may be simply the accusative hunc with a loss of the n rather than a true case of /ō/ > u in the ablative hoc), we found no case of a closing of /ō/ to u in our inscriptional material. This is reminiscent of the treatment of /ŏ/ in monosyllables where Gaeng occasionally found /ŏ/ to u, but which was absent in our findings. (See supra, pp. 118-19.) Once again it seems that peripheral areas of Romania are more conservative than the more central areas.

Inasmuch as the reverse change of /ŭ/ to o is an integral part of the problem of the merger of /ō/ and /ŭ/, we will withhold further comment until we have disclosed the incidence of occurrence for this change.

Latin /ŭ/, Represented by the Letter u

The Latin /ŭ/ was maintained in Sardinian, Rumanian, and the Latin loanwords borrowed by Albanian, but merged with Latin /ō/ in those languages adhering to the Italic qualitative vocalic system.[69] Latin /ŭ/ also remained in British Latin.[70] If inscriptions are valid in the discernment of differentiation in Latin, they must point to this distinctive development in the various areas of Romania. We should, therefore, expect to find little or no deviation in the Latin of Africa, Britain, and the Balkans, but a definite trend of a confusion of /ŭ/ with /ō/ in Dalmatian Latin. This is the complement of the

---

[69] Lausberg, I, 234; Vossler, p. 86; Sturtevant, p. 116; Rosetti, I, 81; Grandgent, p. 87; Lindsay, p. 34; Väänänen, Introduction, p. 37.
[70] Jackson, Language, p. 274; Loth, p. 106.

picture found for /ō/ and both vowels are inextricably linked in our survey of stressed vowels. (See *supra*, p. 119 ff. for the figures concerning /ō/.) The following are the results of our investigation for /ŭ/:

Open Syllable

Africa	Century	/ŭ/ > u	/ŭ/ > o	% of Dev.
	4th.	4	1	20.0
	5th.	2	0	
	6th.	2	0	
	n.d.	25	0	
	Totals:	33	1	2.9

The single occurrence found in Africa was the word *consolibus*, D. 1470, Tingi (Mauretania Tingitana), A.D. 345.

Britain	Century	/ŭ/ > u	/ŭ/ > o	% of Dev.
(Pagan)	1st.	2	0	
	2nd.	3	0	
	3rd.	7	0	
	n.d.	19	0	
	Totals:	31	0	—
(Christ.)	5th.	3	0	
	6th.	5	0	
	8th.	1	0	
	9th.	1	0	
	n.d.	4	0	
	Totals:	14	0	0.0

Dalmatia	Century	/ŭ/ > u	/ŭ/ > o	% of Dev.
	4th.	3	0	
	5th.	2	0	
	6th.	2	0	
	n.d.	21	0	
	Totals:	28	0	0.0

Balkans	Century	/ŭ/ > u	/ŭ/ > o	% of Dev.
(Pagan)	3rd.	1	0	
	n.d.	1	0	
	Totals:	2	0	0.0
(Christ.)	4th.	4	0	
	n.d.	3	0	
	Totals:	7	0	0.0

It is unfortunate that the total figures in open syllables for all four areas are too scanty to permit any conclusion to be drawn. In closed syllables, however, Latin /ŭ/ is more often encountered and does afford an insight into the problem of the maintenance of /ŭ/ or the merger of /ŭ/ with /ō/.

Closed Syllable

Africa	Century	/ŭ/ > u	/ŭ/ > o	% of Dev.
	3rd.	6	0	
	4th.	16	0	
	5th.	24	0	
	6th.	14	0	
	7th.	1	0	
	n.d.	84	1	1.2
	Totals:	145	1	0.7

The only case of deviation found in this area was the proper name *Saecondus* (= *Secundus*), D. 3950, *CIL* VIII 12,197, Hr. Sidi Amara (Byzacena), no date. The correct form is found quite often (*Secundus*, D. 82, 6th cent.; *Secundo*, D. 403, 4th cent.; *Secundulae* (bis), D. 1570, 3rd cent.; [*Se*]*cundus*, D. 1848, no date; [*Secu*]*ndulus*, D. 2041, no date; *Secunda*, D. 2042, no date; *Secundae*, D. 2043, 6th cent.; *Secundi*, D. 2090, no date; *Secundi*, D. 2095, no date; *Secunda*, D. 2648, no date; *Secunda*, D. 2865A, no date; *Secundi*, D. 2866A, 5th cent.; *Secu*[*nda*], D. 3138A, no date; *Secundi*, D. 3268, 5th cent.; *Secunda*, D. 3297, no date; *Secunda*, D. 3319, 3rd cent.). The low percentage of deviation (0.7 %) on the basis of 145 correct forms versus one case of deviation would seem to prove that African Latin maintained Latin /ŭ/ intact.

Britain	Century	/ŭ/ > u	/ŭ/ > o	% of Dev.
(Pagan)	1st.	5	0	
	2nd.	13	0	
	3rd.	14	0	
	4th.	3	0	
	n.d.	45	0	
	Totals:	80	0	0.0
(Christ.)	5th.	1	0	
	6th.	2	0	
	9th.	1	0	
	n.d.	3	0	
	Totals:	7	0	0.0

The lack of any example of /ŭ/ > *o* in either pagan or Christian inscriptions, in open as well as closed syllables, would seem to corroborate the opinion that Latin /ŭ/ remained in British Latin. (See footnote 70 for references.)

Dalmatia	Century	/ŭ/ > *u*	/ŭ/ > *o*	% of Dev.
	4th.	6	0	
	5th.	4	0	
	6th.	3	0	
	n.d.	40	7	14.9
	Totals:	53	7	11.7

Deviations of /ŭ/ in this area are as follows:

> *ubiconqua* (= *ubicumque*), found twice in D. 2389 *CIL*
> p. 961, Tragurium, no date.
> *corret*, D. 2389, *CIL* III p. 961, Tragurium, n.d.
> *quorere* (= *currere*), D. 3835, *CIL* III 9585, Salona, no date.
> *oxor*, D. 3835, *CIL* III 9585, Salona, no date.
> *oxsor*, D. 4115, *CIL* III 9605, Salona, no date.
> *perquodset* (= *percussit*), D. 2426, *CIL* III 10,190, Podgorica, no date. [71]

The high percentage of deviation of Latin /ŭ/ in this area appears to show that the merger of /ŭ/ and /ō/ was taking place. Since the examples of this confusion are found in undated inscriptions, we have no way to determine the chronology of this important merger on the basis of inscriptional material.

Balkans	Century	/ŭ/ > *u*	/ŭ/ > *o*	% of Dev.
(Pagan)	1st.	1	0	
	2nd.	1	0	
	3rd.	4	0	
	4th.	11	0	
	n.d.	16	0	
	Totals:	33	0	0.0
(Christ.)	5th.	2	0	
	n.d.	12	0	
	Totals:	14	0	0.0

---

[71] Skok, *Pojave*, p. 16, considers this word to be from a fourth or fifth century inscription. There is another reading for this word according to Prinz, *De O et U*, p. 59, and *Diehl* 2426: *perquouset*. Prinz considers this *ou* as "fortasse vocalis inter o et u media."

The numerical sampling is low, but the complete lack of any deviation would seem to indicate that the /ŭ/ was stable in the Balkans.

Latin /ŭ/ in Monosyllables

Although the preposition *cum* is written in various ways in some parts of Romania (*con, com, co*), only the correct form is found in our inscriptions. This is in relative agreement with Prinz who states (p. 30) that " 'com, con, co' Romae et in reliqua Italia creberrime, in Dalmatia et Pannonia saepe, in ceteris autem regionibus rarissime occurrunt." Prinz does give (p. 30) one example of *com*, ten of *con*, and two of *co*, in Dalmatia and Pannonia but these are all in pagan inscriptions. For Christian inscriptions, Prinz surprisingly mentions *ubiconqua* as an example of *con* for prepositional *cum* and admits that the other example *con* [. . .] *conio[g]en suam* is of "incertae interpretationis." Our Christian inscriptions for Dalmatia thus do agree.

Gaeng, on discussing the forms of *cum*, concludes (p. 93) that "in any event the absence of the forms *com* and *con* in the area of Gaul may be insofar interesting to note, as this preposition in the form of *con* has survived in Spanish and Italian only." Unfortunately Prinz found (p. 30) no examples of deviation in pagan Spain and only one example of *com* in Christian inscriptions. It is difficult to understand the lack of more examples of *con, com,* and *co* in the Iberian Peninsula compared to the abundant reference to them in Rome and other parts of Italy.

Although we did not find any examples of deviation for the /ŭ/ in *cum* in African inscriptions, Prinz did find one (p. 30) in a pagan inscription. Since we found *cum* 40 times and *cun* twice in our corpus, it appears that the /ŭ/ was very stable in African Latin. Once again it appears that the Latin of North Africa was conservative with respect to its vowel system.

Latin /ŭ/ in Hiatus

The only deviation in our inscriptions is in the possessive adjective *soi* (= *suae*, dat.), found in D. 3659, Purbach (Pannonia), no date. This isolated case assumes importance when we consider that the Rumanian possessive *său* is derived from **sous* which shows dissimilation from the classical *suus*. The form *său* shows the development of the vowel in unstressed position. [72]

In order to discuss fully the significance of our findings for the Latin stressed vowels /ō/ and /ŭ/, we will summarize our results in tabular form.

Area	Open Syllable		% Of Dev.	Closed Syllable		% Of Dev.	Total Dev.
	/ō/ > o	/ō/ > u		/ō/ > o	/ō/ > u		
Africa	451	1	0.2	11	0	0.0	0.2
Brit. (Pagan)	233	0	0.0	7	0	0.0	0.0
(Christian)	11	0	0.0	0	0	0.0	0.0
Dalmatia	124	6	4.6	8	0	0.0	4.3
Balkans (Pagan)	35	0	0.0	7	0	0.0	0.0
(Christian)	42	0	0.0	3	0	0.0	0.0
	/ŭ/ > u	/ŭ/ > o		/ŭ/ > u	/ŭ/ > o		
Africa	33	1	2.9	145	1	0.7	1.1
Brit. (Pagan)	31	0	0.0	80	0	0.0	0.0
(Christian)	14	0	0.0	7	0	0.0	0.0
Dalmatia	28	0	0.0	53	7	11.7	8.0
Balkans (Pagan)	2	0	0.0	23	0	0.0	0.0
(Christian)	7	0	0.0	14	0	0.0	0.0

When we consider the percentages of deviation for the above areas, we are immediately struck by the stability of the Latin /ō/ and /ŭ/ in Africa, Britain, and the Balkans, both in open and closed syllables as well as for pagan or Christian inscriptions. It is also evident that Dalmatia is the only area that shows a tendency to confuse /ō/ and /ŭ/. When we compare our epigraphical results with Lausberg's breakdown of the vocalic systems (Sardinian archaic, Italic qualitative, and Balkan compromise systems) for Romania, we find a striking conformity: African Latin and British Latin, belonging to the archaic system, do distinguish the /ō/ and /ŭ/, as does Balkan Latin, a follower of the compromise system, while Dalmatian Latin, included in the Italic qualitative system, does show a tendency to merge /ō/ and /ŭ/. The inscriptions may even go further and point to a divergent development of the /ō/ and /ŭ/ in Dalmatian Latin according to whether they are found in open or closed syllables. This agrees with the subsequent vocalic evolution of Vegliote, where the

---

[72] Lausberg, II, 229, 234.

vowels do show different reflexes according to the syllabic nature.[73] Since our epigraphical corpus must, of necessity, contain only a limited number of inscriptions, there is no reason why a further search should not turn up a few cases where /ō/ and /ŭ/ do merge in Africa, Britain, and the Balkans. However, the percentages would probably not change to an appreciable degree. Other investigators have, in fact, mentioned cases of confusion of /ō/ and /ŭ/ in Balkan Latin.[74] This sporadic occurrence of a merger of /ō/ and /ŭ/ is mirrored in Rumanian where the word *toamnă* shows that the /ŭ/ changed to /ō/ in *autumnus*.[75] Mihăescu's inference (*Limba*, p. 70), however: "Trecerea lui ŭ scurt accentuat în *o* a avut loc în secolul al treilea sau chiar mai înainte și s-a extins pe tot cuprinsul imperiului roman. Ea ne este atestată în toate provinciile dunărene..."[76] must be seriously questioned on the basis of the minimal percentage of deviation found for Africa, Britain, and the Balkans. Dalmatian Latin undoubtedly showed this merger of /ō/ and /ŭ/ to a greater degree in contrast to other parts of the Balkans where the confusion was, for all intent, absent and the merger abortive at best. That inscriptions can tell us about the differentiation of Latin in the various parts of Romania is likewise substantiated by a comparison of our figures for the incidence of occurrences with the findings of Gaeng for the Iberian Peninsula, Gaul, Italy, and Rome. Taking the liberty of interpolating Gaeng's figures for an areal study of each region without considering the chronological aspect, we derive the following figures:[77]

---

[73] Lausberg, I, 232; Hadlich, p. 72; Bàrtoli, *Dalmatische*, II, 334.

[74] Mihăescu, *Limba*, p. 70; Rosetti, I, 81; Prinz, *De O et U*, p. 55; Vidos, pp. 194-95; Pușcariu, *Études*, p. 28; Lausberg, I, 214; Tagliavini, *Origini*, p. 147.

[75] According to Rosetti, I, 81, *toamnă* is the only Rumanian word showing this change of /ŭ/ to /ō/. Other apparent cases of this change can be explained away because of other factors. This sporadic change of /ŭ/ to /ō/ is usually explained as a Western innovation that did not take root because of the breakdown of communications between the Balkans and the West. See the previous footnote for references.

[76] Translation: "The change of short stressed *u* to *o* took place in the third century or even before and spread throughout the entire territory of the Roman Empire. It is attested for us in all of the Danubian provinces..."

[77] For a chronological interpretation of the percentage of deviation for the Latin /ō/ and /ŭ/ in the Iberian Peninsula, Gaul, Italy, and Rome, see Gaeng, pp. 96-99.

Area	Open Syllable		% Of Dev.	Closed Syllable		% Of Dev.	Total Dev.
	/ō/ > o	/ō/ > u		/ō/ > o	/ō/ > u		
Iber. Penin.	55	2	3.5	3	0	0.0	3.3
Gaul	123	9	6.8	12	0	0.0	6.3
North. Italy	77	4	4.9	50	0	0.0	3.1
Centr. Italy	63	7	10.0	8	1	11.0	10.1
South. Italy	79	1	1.3	8	0	0.0	1.1
Rome	317	10	3.1	14	0	0.0	3.0

Area	/ŭ/ > u	/ŭ/ > o		/ŭ/ > u	/ŭ/ > o		
Iber. Penin.	11	4	26.7	35	1	2.8	9.8
Gaul	37	23	38.3	28	1	3.2	27.0
North. Italy	25	1	3.8	45	0	0.0	1.4
Centr. Italy	4	1	20.0	16	0	0.0	4.8
South. Italy	14	0	0.0	30	0	0.0	0.0
Rome	38	0	0.0	116	2	1.7	1.3

It is important to note that in those areas studied by Gaeng the merger of /ō/ and /ŭ/ is supposed to take place in all according to the Lausberg scheme, except for Southern Italy (of which Sardinia is a part). Gaeng's figures likewise point to the tendency for /ō/ and /ŭ/ to merge in all areas except Southern Italy. Once again Gaul shows such a high numerical incidence of occurrence (especially for /ŭ/ to /ō/ in open syllables) that the inscriptions are remarkably accurate in their portrayal of this most important point of the merger of stressed /ō/ and /ŭ/. Sturtevant had previously acknowledged the validity of conclusions based on epigraphical evidence when he stated (p. 116) that "the misspellings [of /ō/ and /ŭ/] of inscriptions confirm the evidence of the Romance languages."

Several scholars have written precisely on the confusion of /ō/ and /ŭ/ in inscriptions and it may be appropriate to quote some of them in view of our findings of a different treatment according to the various parts of Romania. Pirson describes the situation in Gaul by saying that (p. 13) "les inscriptions de la Gaule, et surtout les inscriptions chrétiennes, se distinguent encore par la permutation fréquente de l'ō et de l'ŭ toniques . . ." Lindsay maintains (p. 37) that "the coincidence of Latin ō and ŭ in the Romance languages makes it natural that we should find o written for ŭ on late inscriptions, and in plebeian forms." Lindsay also wrote (pp. 33-34) that "in late Latin inscriptions the expression of ō by u is very common." Although Pirson is certainly correct in his analysis of the merger of

/ō/ and /ŭ/ in the Latin inscriptions of Gaul, Lindsay is much too vague and even misleading when he fails to mention the areas where the merger of /ọ/ and /ŭ/ is "very common." In fact, African Latin is characterized by its remarkable conservatism in the matter of stressed vowels.

On summarizing our figures for the vowels /ē/ and /ĭ/ (see *supra*, p. 104) as well as for /ō/ and /ŭ/, we conclude that inscriptional material does show a clear tendency for /ē/ and /ĭ/ to be kept separate in Africa and Britain, but to merge in Dalmatia and probably so in the Balkans, while /ō/ and /ŭ/ are kept separate in Africa, Britain, the Balkans, but do merge in Dalmatia. A comparison of our figures with those of Gaeng shows that inscriptions are capable of showing differentiation in the Latin of the various regions of Romania, especially in the evolutive Latin of Gaul as compared to the conservative Latin of Africa and Britain. Since our areas of Africa and Britain do not show a merger of /ē/ and /ĭ/, and since Africa, Britain, and the Balkans keep separate the vowels /ō/ and /ŭ/, we cannot, of course, discuss the problem of chronology. Our epigraphical evidence does, however, corroborate the distinctive vocalic systems as set forth by Lausberg.

Latin /ū/, Represented by the Letter u

Although the development of /ū/ in the Romance languages is varied and controversial,[78] epigraphical evidence pointing to its palatalization, diphthongization, or an influence of a substratum appears to be lacking.[79] This is even more surprising when we realize that the palatalization of /ū/ to /y/ is relatively old because of its independence of the nature of the syllable in which it is found.[80] A change of /ū/ to *o* is sporadically encountered in inscriptions.[81] The results of our investigations are as follows:

---

[78] For the development of /ū/ in Romania, see Lausberg, I, 235-37.
[79] Grandgent, p. 86; Carnoy, p. 62; Sommer, p. 70.
[80] Although Lausberg mentions (I, 236) the "gran antigüedad del cambio u > ü," he is unfortunately not more specific.
[81] Pirson, p. 16; Carnoy, p. 62; Sommer, p. 70; for a thorough study of this change of /ū/ to *o*, see Prinz, *De O et U*, pp. 91-98.

Open Syllable

Area	Century	/ū/ > u	/ū/ > o	% of Dev.
Africa	3rd.	5	0	
	4th.	21	0	
	5th.	32	0	
	6th.	7	0	
	7th.	2	0	
	n.d.	136	0	
	Totals:	203	0	0.0
Britain	1st.	8	0	
	2nd.	28	0	
(Pagan)	3rd.	32	0	
	4th.	2	0	
	n.d.	102	0	
	Totals:	172	0	0.0
(Christ.)	6th.	1	0	
	n.d.	1	0	
	Totals:	2	0	0.0
Dalmatia	4th.	7	0	
	5th.	4	0	
	6th.	2	0	
	n.d.	0	0	
	Totals:	13	0	0.0
Balkans	4th.	2	0	
(Pagan)	n.d.	32	0	
	Totals:	34	0	0.0
(Christ.)	4th.	4	0	
	n.d.	15	0	
	Totals:	19	0	0.0

Closed Syllable

Africa	Century	/ū/ > u	/ū/ > o	% of Dev.
	4th.	2	0	
	5th.	1	0	
	6th.	2	0	
	7th.	1	0	
	n.d.	37	0	
	Totals:	43	0	0.0

Britain	Century	/ū/ > u	/ū/ > o	% of Dev.
(Pagan)	2nd.	3	0	
	3rd.	5	0	
	n.d.	9	0	
	Totals:	17	0	0.0
(Christ.) [82]	6th.	1	0	
	n.d.	1	0	
	Totals:	2	0	0.0
Dalmatia	5th.	1	0	
	6th.	1	0	
	n.d.	11	2	15.4
	Totals:	13	2	13.3

The form *denontio* is found twice in *D.* 2389, *CIL* III, p. 961, Tragurium, no date. Lindsay mentions (p. 250) that the simple verb *nontio* became *nuntio* at the close of the Republican period. The spelling *denontio* is probably an archaic spelling for the more modern form *denuntio,* although Prinz offers the opinion (p. 97) that "factum esse potest, ut in ea regione, ubi haec tabula reperta est, U ante nasales vulgo ad O inclinaverit." Diehl likewise considers the form as archaic when he writes (I, p. 463) that "denontio est forma vetustissima tabulae Bentinae." Skok surprisingly considers (*Pojave,* p. 16) this *o* as a /ŭ/ to *o* change.

----

[82] Jackson, *Language,* mentions (p. 191) that the proper name *R[o]stece* (= *Rusticae*) appears as an example of an *o*-spelling for a *u.* He apparently had /ŭ/ in mind since he states that "Latin *i* and *u* are commonly written *e* and *o* in Continental Christian inscriptions, because the sounds had actually become *e* and *o,* though apparently it did not happen in Britain. This appears very rarely in Britain." Since this name is given as *R[a]stace* by Macalister (*CIIC* 421) and *R[e]stece* by Hübner, no. 125, we have considered it best not to accept this word as an indication of a /ū/ to *o* change. *Diehl* 3573 does give the form as *Rostece* and Prinz accepts (p. 98) this reading but does say that "de O vocali in hac voce non satis constat."

Area	Century	/ū/ > u	/ū/ > o	% of Dev.
Balkans	1st.	1	0	
(Pagan)	n.d.	4	0	
	Totals:	5	0	0.0
(Christ.)	4th.	3	0	
	n.d.	0	0	
	Totals:	3	0	0.0

On the basis of our findings we see that /ū/ remained stable in both open and closed syllables in our epigraphical material.

CHAPTER II

THE UNACCENTED VOWELS

In our treatment of unaccented vowels, we will keep to Gaeng's general format of dividing the material into five categories: (a) initial; (b) pretonic (non-initial); (c) in hiatus (with its subsequent subdivisions into initial, pretonic, posttonic); (d) posttonic (non-final), and (e) final.

In any discussion of unaccented vowels, mention must be made of the stress accent. As a result of the less intensive stress accent on the unaccented vowels three main vocalic phenomena usually take place: (a) a loss of the qualitative distinctions; (b) a tendency to omit syllabic function (the question of hiatus), and (c) a tendency for the vowels to be weakened and possibly to disappear (syncope). [1] The difference of the stress accent between the accented and unaccented vowels was emphasized in some parts of Romania more than others with a resultant distinctive development in the evolving Romance languages and dialects. [2]

---

[1] Lausberg, I, 281; cf. also Niedermann, pp. 10-17; Sturtevant, p. 176 ff.

[2] Richter is most forceful in her insistence on the importance of the stress accent, when she maintains (p. 7) that "das wichtigste Charakteristikum der einzelnen romanischen Sprachen und der einschneidenste Unterschied zwischen ihren Entwicklungen liegt im stärkeren oder schwächeren Anwachsen des Hervorhebungsdruckes." An important exception to this increasing stress accent is Sardinian which according to Richter (p. 100) is the only language that does not partake in this process: "Nur das Sardische nimmt fast nicht daran Teil." A contrary opinion to this overwhelming influence of the stress accent has been taken by Jungemann who maintains in his *La teoría del sustrato y los dialectos hispano-romances y gascones* (Madrid: Editorial Gredos, 1955), pp. 310-14, that the slurring of unaccented vowels may not be caused by the havoc wrought by the stress accent, but because lexical, mor-

As we have previously seen with stressed vowels, the Latin vocalic system was divergent with respect to unaccented vowels in the various parts of Romania. (See *supra*, pp. 22-25, for the schematic synopses of the qualitative Italic, the Sardinian archaic, the Balkan compromise, and the Sicilian accented vocalic systems.) Although the qualitative Italic vocalic system is reduced to five vowels for unaccented vowels, the seven vowels of the qualitative system in stressed position having lost Latin /ĕ/ and /ŏ/ in the unaccented position, this Italic or common "Vulgar Latin" scheme, admittedly the most important in the development of the Romance languages, is not the sole system to have evolved. In fact, it is precisely the existence of other systems that destroys the concept of a unified Vulgar Latin. We are giving below a synopsis of the various qualitative systems of primitive Romance for unaccented vowels. [3]

Classical Latin	ī	ĭ	ē	ĕ	ă̄	ŏ	ō	ŭ	ū
"Vulgar Latin" (Italic Qualitative)	i		e		a		o		u
Sardinian	i			e	a	o		u	
Balkan	i		e		a		u		
Sicilian			i		a		u		

It is interesting to note that although the Sardinian system likewise has five vowels, it is in striking contrast to the Italic qualitative five vowels inasmuch as the latter has an *e* which shows a loss of distinction of Classical Latin /ĭ/, /ē/, and /ĕ/, and an *o* for the merger of /ŏ/, /ō/, and /ŭ/. The Sardinian system shows an *e* and *o* but for a merger of /ĕ/ and /ē/, and /ŏ/ and /ō/ respectively.

---

phological, and syntactical developments were making redundant the distinctions between the unaccented vowels concerned. It is most surprising, then, to find Richter explaining the shortening of final vowels on the basis of syntactical periphrases: "Durch das Überhandnehmen der periphrastischen Ausdrucksweise sank die auslautende Länge als Kasuszeichen zur Tautologie herab: de filiā, cum palliō war überflüssig, daher die Kürzung dieser Längen belanglos" (p. 101).

[3] We are following Lausberg, I, 282, for this survey of unaccented vowels. Bourciez and Elcock, while allowing for different schemes for accented vowels, mention only the five vowel scheme for unaccented vowels. See Bourciez, p. 43, and Elcock, p. 44.

The Balkan four vowel system and the Sicilian three vowels are, of course, quite different in their development from Classical Latin. Although Lausberg does not mention British Latin in the various vocalic schemes, other scholars have pointed out that the Classical Latin quantity system is preserved intact both in stressed and unstressed syllables. [4] Our investigation of inscriptional material seems to show that accented vowels in British Latin were indeed kept separate.

It is unfortunate, however, that an important Latin vocalic development cannot be discerned in inscriptions: a shortening of Vulgar Latin pretonic long vowels. According to Jackson (*Language*, p. 269), there must have been a clear tendency in VL. to shorten long vowels before the accent, definitely before the time when the Latin quantitative system was undergoing its transformation to a qualitative scheme. Jackson makes the pertinent remark (p. 269) that this shortening of the Vulgar Latin pretonic long vowels "does not seem to have received very clear recognition from Romance scholars presumably because of the nature of the evidence to which they mostly confine themselves." On the basis of Latin loanwords in Brittonic this VL. shortening of pretonic long vowels happened very generally with ā, occasionally with ō and ē, very rarely with ī, and apparently not at all with ū. Jackson gives the following examples of this phenomenon: *creātūra* > W. *creădur, peccātōrem* > W. *pechădur; scrīptūra* > VL. *scrĭttūra* > W. *ysgrythur; ōcĕănus* > **ŏcęănus* > W. *eigion; sēcūrus* > VL. **sĕcūrus* > W. *segur.* That this shortening of pretonic long vowels is a Latin development and not Brittonic is proved by the fact that native Brittonic pretonic long vowels are not affected. [5]

We will now offer the results of our investigations on unaccented vowels for Africa, Britain, Dalmatia, and the Balkans.

Latin /ā/ and /ă/, Represented by the Letter a

Initial. Probably the most interesting phenomenon of Latin /ă̆/ in initial syllables is the change of *ia-* to *ie-* in some parts of the

---

[4] Jackson, *Language*, p. 270; Loth likewise mentions (p. 65) the conservation of Latin quantities in unaccented syllables, especially in posttonic position, when they have not undergone syncope.

[5] Jackson, *Language*, pp. 269, 289-90, 303-4, 308, 331.

Roman Empire. Lausberg states (I, p. 289) that "en lat. es visible la tendencia a inflexionar ia- en ie-. En román. pervive preferentemente la pronunciación ie-; sin embargo, la antigua articulación ia- también ha dejado vestigios." [6] Although Lindsay maintains (p. 17) that "the Vulg. Lat. name of the month was *Jenuarius*," it appears that this statement is too sweeping a pronouncement on the basis of a quantitative analysis. It is, of course, true that the reflex of *ianuarius* in the Romance languages does presuppose *ie-* in many cases: cf. It. *gennaio*, Sic. *yinnaru*, Friul. *dzenar*, Old Picard *jenvier*, Prov. *genvier*, Cat. *gener*, Sp. *enero* compared to Fr. *janvier* (although Old French *jenvier*), and Pg. *janeiro*. Gaeng, although not giving any percentages of deviation for *ia-* to *ie-*, does list (pp. 103-04) 13 cases of *ie-*, *ge-* or *ze-*, and even one case of *gi-* (*Ginnoarius*) from Gaul, Italy (exclusive of the Southern area), and Rome. He did not find any example of this change in the Iberian Peninsula. Below are our findings for the *ia-* to *ie-* change in the areas which we studied:

Area	Century	*Ianuarius* (Or Derivatives)	*Ienuarius* (Or Derivatives)
Africa	4th.	3	0
	5th.	9	0
	6th.	1	0
	n.d.	17	1
	Totals:	30	1

The one example of *ie-* was found in *Ie*[*nuarius*], D. 3723N, *CIL* VIII 20,411, Sitifis (Mauretania Sitifensis), no date. There are two other forms in African inscriptions, *Eanuria*, D. 4192, *CIL* VIII 21,804 (Mauretania Caesariensis), no date, and *Aianuarias*, D. 1408AN, Carthage, no date, but they probably refer to initial consonantal development rather than the vocalic change of *a* to *e* due to a preceding palatal. It is interesting to note that Sardinian shows reflexes of both *ia-* and *ie-* in its various dialects: Logudorese *bennárdzu*, Nuorese *ĝennáryu*, Campidanese *ĝennárĝu*, but Bitti *ĝannarĝu*. [7]

---

[6] See also Grandgent, p. 96; Väänänen, *Introduction*, p. 36; W. Meyer-Lübke, *Einführung in das Studium der romanischen Sprachwissenschaft*, 3rd. ed. (Heidelberg: Carl Winter, 1920), pp. 157-58.

[7] Max L. Wagner, "Historische Lautlehre des Sardischen," *Zeitschrift für romanische Philologie*, Beiheft 93 (Halle: Max Niemeyer, 1941), p. 90, and "Lautlehreder südsardischen Mundarten," *Zeitschrift für romanische Philologie*, Beiheft 12 (Halle: Max Niemeyer, 1907), p. 19.

Britain	Century	Ianuarius	Ienuarius
(Pagan)	2nd.	1	0
	3rd.	1	0
	n.d.	3	0
	Totals:	5	0

Although all examples show the correct form *ia-*, the total number of five examples would forbid any definite conclusion to be made. The conjecture, however, that British Latin did maintain the Classical Latin form is corroborated by the Latin loanword into the Brittonic languages. The Welsh *Ionor* or *Ionawr* would require the Latin *Ianarius*.[8] The loss of *u* in hiatus would indicate the popular nature of the word.

Dalmatia	Century	Ianuarius	Ienuarius
	4th.	1	0
	5th.	1	0
	n.d.	3	0
	Totals:	5	0

Although we did not find any examples of this *ia-* to *ie-* change in Dalmatia, other scholars have encountered sporadic cases of this phenomenon.[9] The Dalmatian *jenér* (Bàrtoli, *Dalmatische*, II, 189) would posit a Latin *ie-*.

Balkans	Century	Ianuarius	Ienuarius
(Christ.)	4th.	1	0
	n.d.	11	0
	Totals:	12	0

The inscriptional material would seem to agree with the modern Rumanian reflex, *Januarie*, to the effect that the *ia-* form was preferred. Schuchardt informs us that "dieses Wort [*ianuarius*] behielt sein

---

[8] Jackson, *Language*, p. 290; Loth, p. 115.
[9] Skok, *Pojave*, p. 26; it is interesting to note that Mihăescu, *Limba*, p. 78, gives the same three examples as Skok, all coming from Dalmatia, none from the inscriptions of the inner Balkans. It must be remembered, however, that Mihăescu was interested in showing that the Latin of the Balkans was the same as that of other areas of the Roman Empire.

a in den drei entferntesten romanischen Sprachen: *Janeiro* [Port.], *Janvier* [Fr.], *Januarie* [Rum.]." [10] Mihăescu gives three examples of the change to *ie-* in the Balkans, but all three come from Dalmatia. [11] It would appear, then, that the *ie-* innovation did not reach the inner Balkans. Besides the inner Balkans the Classical Latin *ia-* was taken over by Latin loanwords into Welsh.

Another interesting vocalic phenomenon is the change of initial *a* to *e* in *Delmatia* and its derivatives. Although Lindsay (p. 15) says that "varieties in the spelling of foreign names like . . . *Delmatia* and *Dalmatia* prove nothing for Latin *a*," inscriptional material may prove enlightening in respect to British Latin. The other regions apparently preferred the initial syllable *Dal-* as this is the only form found in our corpus for Africa, Dalmatia, and the Balkans (although admittedly of a rare occurrence: Africa: 1 example; Dalmatia: 2 examples, and the Balkans: 2 examples). In the inscriptions of Britain, however, we have two examples of *Dal-* but five with *Del-*, all cases being found in pagan inscriptions. This preference for *e* rather than *a* seems to be contrary to what was found for stressed vowels where *er* > *ar* was considered characteristic of British Latin. (See *supra*, p. 81.)

There is one case of initial *a* going to *o* in *Tro[iano]*, *RIB* 2263, *CIL* VII 1163, Caernarvon (Wales), A.D. 249-51. We find the correct form *Traianus* five times in the second century and once in the third century in other Latin inscriptions of Britain. Although the editors of the *RIB* state (p. 708) that "Trojanus is an error for Trajanus," we do have examples of initial *o* for *a* in Brittonic: *Ionor* (Mod. Welsh) < *Ianarius*, *ystrodur* (Mod. Welsh) < *strātūra*, *Nodolyc* (Middle Welsh) < *nātālicia*. [12]

Intertonic. There is seemingly a weakening of /a/ to *e* or *i* in the name of the Celtic deity Belatucadrus. We find *Belleticauro* in *RIB* 1521, *CIL* VII 620, Carrawburgh (Broccolitia), Hadrian's Wall, no date, and *Baliticauro* in *RIB* 1775, Carvoran (Magnis), Hadrian's Wall, no date. The correct form with pretonic *a* is encountered, however, 21

---

[10] Hugo Schuchardt, *Der Vokalismus des Vulgärlateins* (Leipzig: B. G. Teubner, 1866-68), I, 187.

[11] See *supra*, footnote 9, for reference to Mihăescu.

[12] See Jackson, *Language*, pp. 289-90, and Loth, p. 115, for further examples. It should be remembered that Latin /ā/ in stressed position also changed to *o* in the proper name *Iuliona* in *RIB* 1252. (See *supra*, p. 76.)

times in the Latin inscriptions of Britain.[13] This weakening of the intertonic /a/ is quite irregular as "vowels following the secondary and preceding the primary stress in Vulgar Latin became indistinct and sometimes disappeared, but *a* was generally retained."[14] Since this weakening of intertonic /a/ took place only sporadically in a non-Latin proper name, not much significance can be attached to this vocalic change.

Posttonic. We have one example of a weakening of /a/ to an *i* in the German proper name *Geilimer* found in *D.* 43N, *CIL* VIII 10,862, Saddar (Numidia), A. D. 530-33. The correct form *Geilamir* is seen in *D.* 43, *CIL* VIII 17,412, Hippo Regius (Proconsularis), A.D. 530-33. Since this weakening of a posttonic /a/ is found in a single German proper name, it is of limited importance for a study of Vulgar Latin vocalism.

There are no deviations of /a/ in hiatus, a rare phenomenon even in Classical Latin.

Final. The final *ā* in the ablative singular of first declension nouns is changed to *e* in the proper name *Peregrine, D.* 883, *CIL* VIII 21,553 in Mauretania Caesariensis, A.D. 434. The nominative singular form of first declension nouns is written *ae* in *ancillae,* used as a noun in apposition, in *D.* 1471, *CIL* VIII 21,816, Tingi (Mauretania Tingitana), no date, and *sobriae, D.* 1570, *CIL* VIII 20,277, Satafi (Mauretania Sitifensis), A. D. 299. These are probably confusion of cases, which will be discussed more fully when we analyze the final vowels of the more numerical cases of confusion involving masculine nouns. The *ae* form used for the nominative *a* in *ancillae* is interesting as it is probably a reverse spelling for a noun in apposition. The more common phenomenon of a feminine singular noun in apposition having a genitive or dative ending in *a* will be discussed under the heading of final *ae*.

We seem to have a rare occurrence of a first declension feminine noun becoming fifth declension in the proper noun *Casthe, D.* 1683, *CIL* VIII 10,689, Theveste (Proconsularis), no date. On the basis of the incorrect use of the *h,* apparently intended to show Greek as-

---

[13] For a discussion of the Celtic deity Belatucadrus in general, see Collingwood-Myres, pp. 262, 265, 269.

[14] Jackson, *Language*, p. 268; see also Grandgent, p. 98.

piration, *Casthe* may also be in imitation of Greek first declension feminine nouns. We also have two other examples of a final *a* becoming *e* in African inscriptions: *alogies* (= *cena funeraticia*), D. 1573, *CIL* VIII 20,334, near Satafi (Mauretania Sitifensis), no date, and *Felicie*, D. 2966, *CIL* VIII 8708a, near Sitifis (Mauretania Sitifensis), A.D. 448. The word *alogies*, however, is found in a mutilated inscription and it cannot be determined whether the *-es* ending is a shift to the fifth declension nominative or whether it is a vulgar genitive formation of the first declension with the addition of an *-s*. A full discussion of the vulgar genitive formations will be given under the heading of final *ae*. A sporadic change of *a* to *e* in the accusative singular of feminine nouns is seen in *Romule* in D. 3688A, *CIL* VIII 9971, Numerus Syrorum (Mauretania Caesariensis), A.D. 399. This change is found in the common phrase ... *domu Romule instituerunt* ..., and is isolated since the correct form *domum Romulam* or its variant without final *m* is a common formula in Christian inscriptions of Africa. [15] There is no apparent reason for this change.

It is interesting to note that the above phenomena dealing with the changes taking place in final /a/ all occur in the Latin inscriptions of Africa, but this may be due to the greater number of inscriptions in Africa as compared to other areas which we are investigating. A more complete analysis will be given when we treat masculine forms.

What is decidedly a characteristic of British Latin is the use of the genitive for normative and vice versa as the most common confusion of cases. [16] Since Celtic feminines are handled always in Latin as first declension nouns, with nominative in *-a* and genitive in *e*, [17] we find several examples of this confusion of cases with a genitive in *-e* used for a first declension feminine nominative ending in *-a:* *R[o]stece*, *CIIC* 421, Llanerfyl (Wales), fifth century, and *Cunaide*, *CIIC* 479, Cornwall, fifth century. This confusion of cases is much more obvious for masculine nouns because of their numerical preponderance. The ultimate reason for this confusion of cases is the fact that the spoken Brittonic of the time had undergone a loss of

---

[15] See Diehl *ILCV*, inscriptions 3682-3691D, all from Africa.

[16] Jackson, *Language*, p. 193; R. A. S. Macalister, *Corpus Inscriptionum Insularum Celticarum* (Dublin: Stationery Office, 1945), I, xiv.

[17] Jackson, *Language*, p. 188.

case-endings and the established custom of using the Latinizing genitive termination would consequently be wrongly applied to nouns in
Latin inscriptions. [18] Jackson considers (p. 631) the completion of the
loss of final syllables as "later than the late fifth to early sixth century,
and probably already by the second half of the sixth century." The
importance of the loss of British final syllables, with the concomitant
changes wrought on the morphological and syntactical systems of the
language, can be readily understood by the fact that this process
may be regarded as the starting-point of Welsh, Cornish, and Breton. [19]

We have an example of an *ad sensum* use of the masculine nominative plural rather than the feminine singular in the adjective
con[t]r[i]buti, in the pagan British Latin of *RIB* 1322, Newcastle
upon Tyne (Pons Aelius), Hadrian's Wall, A.D. 155-59, in the phrase:
vexilatio . . . con[t]r[i]buti ex Ger[maniis] duobus, where the collective
force of the noun *vexillatio* is evident.

Latin /ĕ/, Represented by the Letter e

In the analysis of initial /ĕ/ and /ē/, we will keep both vowels
separate on the basis of the different unaccented vocalic systems that
prevail in the Romance world. (See *supra*, p. 136 for a synopsis of
the various systems.) This is contrary to the methodology followed
by Pirson who considered both vowels together because of the belief
that they had lost their quantitative differences and had merged into
a close *e*. Pirson's words (p. 30) that "le latin vulgaire avait déjà,
comme plus tard les langues romanes, la tendance à fusionner l'ĕ et
l'ē atones en un même son fermé," do hold true for those Romance
languages and dialects that follow the Italic qualitative system, but
are inaccurate for other unaccented vocalic systems. Loth, on speaking
of the Latin vowels /ē/, /ĕ/, and /ĭ/ in initial position in loanwords
in Brittonic, states (p. 114) that "tous ces sons sont parfaitement
distincts les uns des autres: gall. *ynyd* < *initium; estron* < *extra-
neus*." [20] Loth gives as proof (p. 114) that "ē initial non accentué . . .
a évidemment conservé d'abord sa quantité et son timbre différent

---

[18] *Ibid.*, pp. 623-24; Macalister, *CIIC*, p. xiv.

[19] Jackson, *Language*, p. 618.

[20] Jackson, *Language*, p. 270, is more general when he says that "the
Classical quantity system is preserved intact both in stressed and unstressed
syllables."

d'ĕ initial prétonique" the fact that "c'est ... ē et non ĕ [qui] est arrivé à ī sous l'influence de ī suivant conservé dans le corpus du mot: gall. *ciniaw* < *ceniare*, à côté de *cwyn* dans *cwynos*." It appears that the Latin loanwords in Brittonic are a rich source for proof of a differentiation of the Latin language in the various parts of Romania, in the case of British Latin, a proof of an extreme conservatism.

It is the tendency of initial /ĕ/ to become *i* that has been a great concern of scholars. Lindsay explains this change by saying (p. 19) that the "probable history of the change of ĕ to ĭ in unaccented syllables is that the open e first became close e, and then passed into ĭ." [21] This closing of /ĕ/ to *i* is characteristic of Italian, especially in open syllables. [22]

Because of the possible importance of a distinctive treatment of initial /ĕ/ in open and closed syllables, we will give our figures for initial /ĕ/ in both types of syllables, contrary to Gaeng who studies initial /ĕ/ and /ē/ separately, but who does not take the syllabic nature into consideration. We will then combine our figures for open and closed syllables, to get a total percentage of deviation which can then be compared with the percentages obtained by Gaeng.

Initial

Africa	Century	Open Syllable		% Of Dev.	Closed Syllable		% Of Dev.	Totals		% Of Dev.
		/ĕ/ > e	/ĕ/ > i		/ĕ/ > e	/ĕ/ > i				
	3rd.	9	0		2	0		11	0	
	4th.	55	0		10	0		65	0	
	5th.	72	0		14	0		86	0	
	6th.	31	0		16	1	5.9	47	1	2.1
	7th.	0	0		1	0		1	0	
	n.d.	243	0		94	1	1.1	337	1	0.3
	Totals:	410	0	0.0	137	2	1.4	547	2	0.4

The two examples of an initial /ĕ/ > *i* change in closed syllables are:

---

[21] See also Carnoy, p. 32; Pirson, p. 30.
[22] Lausberg, I, 287; Väänänen, *Introduction*, p. 37; Mario Pei, *The Italian Language*, 2nd ed. (New York: S. F. Vanni, 1954), p. 36.

[t]*imporib.*, D. 793, CIL VIII 12,035, Limasa (Byzacena), between A.D. 582-602.
Sirvata (proper name), D. 2670, CIL VIII 14,125 add. p. 2459, Carthage, no date.

On the basis of the high number of correct occurrences compared to just two cases of /ĕ/ > *i*, it appears that initial /ĕ/ was extremely stable in African Latin and did not merge with /ĭ/.

Britain	*Century*	Open Syllable		% Of Dev.	Closed Syllable		% Of Dev.	Totals		% Of Dev.
		/ĕ/ > *e*	/ĕ/ > *i*		/ĕ/ > *e*	/ĕ/ > *i*				
(Pagan)	1st.	15	0		4	0		19	0	
	2nd.	31	0		17	0		48	0	
	3rd.	44	0		20	0		64	0	
	4th.	4	0		1	0		5	0	
	n.d.	152	0		46	0		198	0	
	Totals:	246	0		88	0	0.0	334	0	0.0
(Christ.)	4th.	1	0		1	0		2	0	
	5th.	3	0		0	0		3	0	
	6th.	3	0		2	0		5	0	
	7th.	0	0		1	0		1	0	
	8th.	0	0		1	0		1	0	
	n.d.	6	0		0	0		6	0	
	Totals:	13	0	0.0	5	0	0.0	18	0	0.0

There is no case of /ĕ/ > *i* in initial syllables, open or closed, in British Latin.

Dalmatia	*Century*	Open Syllable		% Of Dev.	Closed Syllable		% Of Dev.	Totals		% Of Dev.
		/ĕ/ > *e*	/ĕ/ > *i*		/ĕ/ > *e*	/ĕ/ > *i*				
	4th.	9	0		4	0		13	0	
	5th.	14	0		6	0		20	0	
	6th.	3	0		3	0		6	0	
	n.d.	58	1	1.7	36	1	2.7	94	2	2.1
	Totals:	84	1	1.2	49	1	2.0	133	2	1.5

The two examples of deviation in this area are:

binefacta, D. 3363, CIL III 9623, add. p. 2141, Salona, no date.
Virgilianus, D. 3835, CIL III 9585, Salona, no date.

On the basis of just two deviations and a total percentage of deviation of 1.5 %, it would appear that initial /ĕ/ was relatively stable in the Latin of Dalmatia.

Balkans	Century	Open Syllable		% Of Dev.	Closed Syllable		% Of Dev.	Totals		% Of Dev.
		/ĕ/ > e	/ĕ/ > i		/ĕ/ > e	/ĕ/ > i				
(Pagan)	1st.	0	0		2	0		2	0	
	2nd.	1	0		2	0		3	0	
	3rd.	9	0		5	0		14	0	
	4th.	3	0		1	0		4	0	
	n.d.	56	0		10	0		66	0	
	Totals:	69	0	0.0	20	0	0.0	89	0	0.0
(Christ.)	4th.	4	0		0	0		4	0	
	5th.	1	0		0	0		1	0	
	n.d.	41	2		9	0		50	2	3.8
	Totals:	46	2	0.0	9	0	0.0	55	2	3.5

The two examples of initial /ĕ/ > i in Christian inscriptions are:

> *mimoriae*, D. 3659, Purbach (Pannonia), no date.
> *sipurclu* (= *sepulcrum*), D. 3659, Purbach (Pannonia), no date.

Since there are only two occurrences of deviation, and both are found in the same inscription, the percentage of deviation (3.5 %) of initial /ĕ/ in the Christian inscriptions of the Balkans must be considered as suspect.

When we consider the figures obtained by Gaeng for the Iberian Peninsula, Gaul, Italy, and Rome, we see that most areas show sporadic changes of initial /ĕ/ to i at best, except for Southern Italy and Rome, where the percentages are somewhat higher. Rome in the sixth and seventh centuries has the highest percentage of change with 4.3 % (88 correct occurrences to 4 deviations) and several examples in undated inscriptions. The total number of nine cases of /ĕ/ > i in Rome for all inscriptions, dated and undated, is well above anything found in our areas. Southern Italy had six examples of i in initial syllables, in dated and undated inscriptions. On the basis of extremely sporadic cases of /ĕ/ > i in Africa, Dalmatia, and the Balkans, and none in Britain, compared to a relatively higher percentage of deviation in Rome and Southern Italy, it may be that the latter two areas were a focal point for this innovation, but nothing more positive can be asserted because of the inconclusiveness of the evidence. It appears that Grandgent's words (p. 96): "E, long or short, is very often replaced by *i* in Gallic inscriptions" must be questioned, at least for short e.

Intertonic

The retention, weakening, and loss of the intertonic vowels are all dependent on the intensity of the stress accent, which varied in the different parts of Romania, and which was therefore an important factor in the development of the Romance languages and dialects. (See *supra*, p. 135 ff.) Lausberg, on discussing this relative intensity of the stress accent and its consequences, states (I, 305), with respect to the intertonic vowels, that "en sar. e it. (especialmente en el centro de Italia) las vocales se conservan casi todas. Son menos conservadores el rum., el port., el esp. (precisamente en el orden citado). - En los restantes dominios (cat., prov., fr., retorrom., norteit.) se nota una fuerte tendencia a suprimir las vocales intertónicas, lo que está en relación con una intensificación de la gradación intensiva." We will give our figures for the maintenance and weakening of intertonic /ĕ/ to *i*, but these findings will have relevance only when taken with the complementary phenomenon of syncope, which will be given later. If inscriptions have value in a study of the differentiation of Latin in the various parts of Romania, the ratio of the total number of correct occurrences of intertonic vowels (posttonic vowels are also pertinent in this study of local differences of Latin) to the number of cases of weakening or syncope should be significantly different in the several areas under consideration.

Africa	*Century*	Open Syllable		% Of Dev.	Closed Syllable		% Of Dev.	Totals		% Of Dev.
		/ĕ/ > e	/ĕ/ > i		/ĕ/ > e	/ĕ/ > i				
	3rd.	2	0		1	0		3	0	
	4th.	10	0		5	0		15	0	
	5th.	5	0		3	0		8	0	
	6th.	1	0		10	0		11	0	
	7th.	0	0		4	0		4	0	
	n.d.	44	1	2.2	25	3	10.7	69	4	5.5
	Totals:	62	1	1.6	48	3	5.9	110	4	3.5

The examples of this deviation are as follows:

univir[sorum], D. 1003, CIL VIII 25,045, Carthage, no date.
apir[tiorem], D. 1003, CIL VIII 25,045, Carthage, no date.
Gemilians (= Gemellianus), D. 2443, CIL VIII 18,705, Numidia, no date.
angiloru, D. 2090, CIL VIII 20,619, Mauretania Sitifensis, no date.

Britain	Century	Open Syllable		% Of Dev.	Closed Syllable		% Of Dev.	Totals		% Of Dev.
		/ĕ/ > e	/ĕ/ > i		/ĕ/ > e	/ĕ/ > i				
(Pagan)	1st.	1	0		5	0		6	0	
	2nd.	7	0		6	0		13	0	
	3rd.	13	0		20	0		33	0	
	4th.	0	0		1	0		1	0	
	n.d.	22	1	4.3	31	0		53	1	1.9
	Totals:	43	1	2.3	63	0	0.0	106	1	0.9

The one case of intertonic /ĕ/ > i is in the word Macid[onicae], RIB 509, Chester (Deva), no date.

Britain	Century	Open Syllable		% Of Dev.	Closed Syllable		% Of Dev.	Totals		% Of Dev.
		/ĕ/ > e	/ĕ/ > i		/ĕ/ > e	/ĕ/ > i				
(Christ.)	5th.	0	0		1	0		1	0	
	6th.	2	0		3	0		5	0	
	7th.	0	0		1	0		1	0	
	n.d.	1	1	50.0	0	0		1	1	50.0
	Totals:	33	1	25.0	5	0	0.0	8	1	11.1

The single occurrence of /ĕ/ > i is in Bonemimori, CIIC 476, Cornwall, no date.

Dalmatia	Century	Open Syllable		% Of Dev.	Closed Syllable		% Of Dev.	Totals		% Of Dev.
		/ĕ/ > e	/ĕ/ > i		/ĕ/ > e	/ĕ/ > i				
	4th.	4	0		3	0		7	0	
	5th.	2	1	33.3	5	0		7	1	12.5
	6th.	1	0		2	0		3	0	
	n.d.	16	0		17	0		33	0	
	Totals:	23	1	4.2	27	0	0.0	50	1	2.0

The only example of this change is in *derilict[is]*, *D*. 185, *CIL* III 9515, Salona, A.D. 425.

Balkans	Century	Open Syllable		% Of Dev.	Closed Syllable		% Of Dev.	Totals		% Of Dev.
		/ĕ/ > e	/ĕ/ > i		/ĕ/ > e	/ĕ/ > i				
(Pagan)	3rd.	0	0		3	0		3	0	
	4th.	3	0		1	0		4	0	
	n.d.	3	0		14	0		17	0	
	Totals:	6	0	0.0	18	0	0.0	24	0	0.0

Balkans	Century	Open Syllable		% Of Dev.	Closed Syllable		% Of Dev.	Totals		% Of Dev.
		/ĕ/ > e	/ĕ/ > i		/ĕ/ > e	/ĕ/ > i				
(Christ.)	4th.	3	0		1	0		4	0	
	n.d.	9	0		11	0		20	0	
	Totals:	12	0	0.0	12	0	0.0	24	0	0.0

We will withhold comment until all other intertonic vowels have been analyzed so as to get a composite figure for each area.

Besides the change of /ĕ/ > *i*, there are sporadic cases of a change of /ĕ/ to *a*, normally before the consonants, *n, r, l*. In the Latin inscriptions of Britain, where there may be a tendency for the /ĕ/ to open to an *a* (see *supra*, p. 81, for the change of stressed /ĕ/ to *a* in British Latin), we have *piantissime* (adverb), *RIB* 1064, South Shields (Arbeia), no date, the German deity *Vagdavarcustus*, *RIB* 926, Old Penrith (Voreda), no date (the spelling *Vagdavercustis* is found in *CIL* XIII 8662, 8702, 8805, 12,057), the chief Belgic tribe *Catauallauna*, *RIB* 1065, South Shields (Arbeia), no date (the correct form *Catuvellaunorum* is found in *RIB* 1962, *CIL* VII 863, Hadrian's Wall, Cumberland, A.D. 369). [23] In the Balkans we find *Alaman(ico)*, Kalinka 76, *CIL* III 12,333, Sofia (Serdica), Thrace,

---

[23] Loth, on speaking of Old Celtic vocalism, considers (p. 67) that "vers la IIe siècle après Jésus-Christ, en Bretagne, le vocalisme du vieux celtique avait subi, en brittonique, d'importantes modifications" and mentions that "ĕ atone devant les liquides paraît avoir passé à ă ou pris un son voisin de l'a"; Loth specifically cites the tribe Catuallauna, but waters down any definite conclusion by stating that "ce phénomène étant aussi latin vulgaire, on ne peut tirer ... aucune conclusion certaine."

A.D. 361-62, although the spelling with *e* is also accepted in *Harper's Latin Dictionary*, and *Ipa[r]atori* (= *Imperatoris*, gen. sing.), *Kalinka* 125, *CIL* III 14,207, Thrace, A.D. 246-47, explained by Kalinka in the following way (p. 118): "Übergang von *er* in *ar*, gefördert durch das benachbarte *a*."

We have isolated cases of intertonic /ĕ/ going to *o*, probably influenced by preceding labial consonants, in British Latin: *Numoriano*, *RIB* 2250, *CIL* VII 1165, Kenchester (Magnis), A.D. 283-84, in a milestone dedicated to Emperor Marcus Aurelius Numerianus. The correct vowel, but with a consonant change of *m* to *b*, is found in *Nuberiano*, *RIB* 2307, in a milestone found near Cawfields, dated A.D. 282-83. The local Celtic deity *Conventina* is written *Covontine* in *RIB* 1533, although altars dedicated to her near Hadrian's Wall at Carrawburgh (Broccolitia) usually appear with *e* (*RIB* 1522, 1523, 1524, 1525, 1526, 1527, 1528, 1529, 1531, 1532, 1534, 1535).

Posttonic

The retention, weakening, and loss of the posttonic vowels are likewise intricately tied to the increased stress accent. Since the treatment of the posttonic vowels was inconsistent in Vulgar Latin and the conditions differed widely in different regions, [24] we should expect the inscriptions of the various regions to reflect this variegated picture to some degree. Lausberg considers (I, 302) that "el sar. y el román. oriental (it. y rum.) conservan los proparoxítonos en gran escala. En cambio, en la Romania occidental sucumben las más veces a la reducción, siendo el port. el más conservador dentro de la Romania occidental. En esp. la reducción alcanza ya proporciones considerables; el cat., el galorrom., el retorrom. y el norteit. muestran fenómenos de reducción creciente." Once again our findings for the retention or weakening of posttonic vowels must be coordinated with its loss (syncope) so as to get a true picture of the stress accent in the various parts of Romania.

---

[24] Lausberg, I, 302; Grandgent, p. 99.

Area	Century	/ĕ/ > e	/ĕ/ > i	% of Dev.
Africa	3rd.	2	0	
	4th.	9	0	
	5th.	6	0	
	6th.	5	0	
	n.d.	53	0	
	Totals:	75	0	0.0
Britain	2nd.	2	0	
(Pagan)	3rd.	1	0	
	n.d.	10	0	
	Totals:	13	0	0.0
(Christ.)	6th.	1	0	
	n.d.	0	0	
	Totals:	1	0	0.0
Dalmatia	4th.	9	0	
	5th.	5	0	
	6th.	6	0	
	n.d.	48	0	
	Totals:	68	0	0.0
Balkans	3rd.	1	0	
(Pagan)	n.d.	5	0	
	Totals:	6	0	0.0
(Christ.)	4th.	3	0	
	5th.	1	0	
	n.d.	9	0	
	Totals:	13	0	0.0

It is seen that posttonic /ĕ/ was not weakened to *i* in any of the areas which we studied. We must consider Grandgent's comment (p. 99) that "we find in late Latin much confusion of *e* and *i* [in this position]" a very questionable statement, although posttonic /ĭ/ does appear as *e* in our inscriptions. It would seem that posttonic /ĭ/ changed to *e* in the Latin inscriptions much more than the reverse change of /ĕ/ > *i*.

Hiatus

Since unaccented /ĕ/ and /ĭ/ in hiatus became the semivowel i̯ with a loss of their syllabic value in the first century A.D., we can expect to find a confusion of these two vowels in hiatus in all of the Roman Empire as a general Romance tendency.[25] To get a clear picture of the evolution of the unaccented vowels in hiatus we will give a breakdown according to their initial, pretonic, and posttonic positions. We will then give a final figure for all confusion of each individual vowel in hiatus throughout Romania.

Africa	Century	Initial		Pretonic		Posttonic		Totals		% Of Dev
		/ĕ/ > e	/ĕ/ > i	/ĕ/ > e	/ĕ/ > i	/ĕ/ > e	/ĕ/ > i			
	3rd.	0	0	0	0	2	0	2	0	
	4th.	3	0	0	0	7	0	10	0	
	5th.	3	0	0	1	1	0	4	1	20.0
	6th.	5	0	0	0	1	0	6	0	
	7th.	1	0	0	0	0	0	1	0	
	n.d.	28	0	11	0	15	1	54	1	1.8
	Totals:	40	0	11	1	26	1	77	2	2.5

The two examples of /ĕ/ in hiatus changed to *i* are:

Cerialis, D. 2054, CIL VIII 9866, add. p. 975, Altava (Mauretania Caesariensis), not before A.D. 449.
tidiat (= taedeat), D. 2388A, Carthage, no date.

Britain (Pagan)	Century	Initial		Pretonic		Posttonic		Totals		% Of Dev.
		/ĕ/ > e	/ĕ/ > i	/ĕ/ > e	/ĕ/ > i	/ĕ/ > e	/ĕ/ > i			
	1st.	0	0	0	0	1	0	1	0	
	2nd.	1	0	0	1	1	1	2	2	50.0
	3rd.	4	0	0	0	6	0	10	0	
	4th.	0	0	0	0	0	0	0	0	
	n.d.	11	0	0	0	8	0	19	0	
	Totals:	16	0	0	1	16	1	32	2	5.9

---

[25] Cf. Lausberg, I, 283; Grandgent, p. 93; Väänänen, *Introduction*, pp. 46-47. The confusion between /ĕ/ and /ĭ/ in hiatus does not necessary mean a loss of syllabic value as evidenced by the Provençal *ordi* < *hordeum* (see Carnoy, p. 34, and Lausberg, I, 389). The confusion between /ĕ/ and /ĭ/ in hiatus has been considered dialectal in archaic inscriptions (see Sommer, p. 111; Väänänen, *Introduction*, p. 46). The *Appendix Probi* censures many cases of the /ĕ/, /ĭ/ confusion in hiatus: *toloneum, laneo, dolium, vinia, osteum, cavia, brattia, coclia, cocliarium, paliarium, lancia, solia, calcius, aleum, lileum, tinia, baltius, lintium, noxeus*. For examples of /ĕ/ to *i* in hiatus at Pompei, see Väänänen, *Pompéiennes*, p. 36 ff.

The two examples of /ĕ/ > i in hiatus in this area are:

Ociano, RIB 1320, Newcastle upon Tyne (Pons Aelius),
Hadrian's Wall, not before A.D. 122.
adpertiniat, RIB 659, York (Eboracum), before A.D. 120.

itain (hrist.)

Century	Initial /ĕ/ > e	Initial /ĕ/ > i	Pretonic /ĕ/ > e	Pretonic /ĕ/ > i	Posttonic /ĕ/ > e	Posttonic /ĕ/ > i	Totals	Totals	% Of. Dev.
5th.	0	0	0	0	1	0	1	0	
6th.	1	0	0	0	1	0	2	0	
n.d.	0	0	0	0	0	0	0	0	
Totals:	1	0	0	0	2	0	3	0	0.0

almatia

Century	Initial /ĕ/ > e	Initial /ĕ/ > i	Pretonic /ĕ/ > e	Pretonic /ĕ/ > i	Posttonic /ĕ/ > e	Posttonic /ĕ/ > i	Totals	Totals	% Of. Dev.
4th.	2	1	1	0	6	0	9	1	10.0
5th.	6	0	0	0	3	0	9	0	
6th.	0	0	0	0	1	0	1	0	
n.d.	10	0	3	0	24	1	37	1	2.6
Totals:	18	1	4	0	34	1	56	2	3.4

The two examples from this area are:

[n]iofita (= neophyta), D. 1505, CIL III 9595, Salona,
A.D. 359.
habias, D. 2389, CIL III p. 961, Tragurium, no date.

alkans (agan)

Century	Initial /ĕ/ > e	Initial /ĕ/ > i	Pretonic /ĕ/ > e	Pretonic /ĕ/ > i	Posttonic /ĕ/ > e	Posttonic /ĕ/ > i	Totals	Totals	% Of. Dev.
1st.	0	0	0	0	1	0	1	0	
4th.	1	0	0	0	0	0	1	0	
n.d.	2	0	0	0	4	0	6	0	
Totals:	3	0	0	0	5	0	8	0	0.0
(hrist.) 4th.	2	0	0	0	0	0	2	0	
6th.	1	0	0	0	0	0	1	0	
n.d.	14	0	1	0	2	0	17	0	
Totals:	17	0	1	0	2	0	20	0	0.0

We will reserve comment on the treatment of this vowel in hiatus until the other vowels, especially /ĭ/, have been analyzed.

Final

With the intensification of the stress accent, final vowels were weakened, slurred, and at times dropped. This pattern developed differently in the various parts of the Romance-speaking areas as can be seen by a glance at the Romance languages. In Sardinian and Italian (central and southern) final vowels are almost entirely maintained. In Rumanian they are also kept, but to a slighter degree. Spanish and Portuguese reduce final vowels more. In the remaining areas of Provençal, Catalan, Rheto-Romance, and Gallo-Italian dialects, there was a strong tendency to reduce final vowels. [26] On the basis of the modern Romance reflexes, it would seem that some dialectal differences did appear in the Latin of the different parts of Romania, although Grandgent remarks (p. 102) that ". . . [final] vowels regularly remained through the Vulgar Latin period. Later, about the eighth century, they generally fell, except *a* and *ī*, in Celtic, Aquitanian, and Ligurian territory." The time element is therefore problematical, but a careful scrutiny of Latin inscriptions may show greater tendencies in some areas to weaken final vowels than in others, thus presaging a later, clearer delineation. Since the increased stress accent effected pretonic and posttonic vowels, it is only reasonable to assume that final vowels also underwent some changes. A desired end-product of epigraphical research is a picture of an emerging pattern in the various areas. With specific reference to the fate of final *e* in the Iberian Peninsula, Lausberg claims (I, 299) that "se puede comprobar cómo la tendencia a la desaparición se acrecienta progresivamente de occidente a oriente . . ." although he does not go into the problem more deeply. It is interesting to note that Pirson, after studying the change of final *e* to *i* in Gaul, states (p. 32) that "il n'y a certes pas lieu de chercher . . . des traces de différences locales." We will try to determine whether Pirson's dim view of inscriptions as a means to detect local differences is accurate or not.

A problem inherent in the weakening or slurring of final vowels is the difficulty in deciding whether the main factor in the change is

---

[26] Lausberg, I, 294.

phonetic or morphological or possibly a combination of both. Pirson gives a phonetic explanation for all changes of unaccented /ē/ and /ĕ/ to *i* when he writes (p. 30) that "on peut donc en conclure que le latin vulgaire avait déjà, comme plus tard les langues romanes, la tendance à fusionner l'ē et l'ĕ atones en un même son fermé qui pouvait s'exprimer au moyen de *i*." Discussing the change of final /ĭ/ to *e* in third declension dative and ablative forms in the Latin inscriptions of Spain, Carnoy considers (p. 45) that "il y a lieu de croire que des actions morphologiques ont eu part à ce phénomène." When we take a look at the 227 items censured in the *Appendix Probi*, it is interesting to note that between one-fourth and one-fifth of all the items refers to final vowels, some clearly morphological, others probably more phonetical in nature than morphological, and some with an admixture of both to a degree that would make it difficult to ascertain which was the prevailing cause. Examples such as *acre non acrum, tristis non tristus, palumbes non palumbus, teter non tetrus, aper non aprus, nurus non nura, socrus non socra,* et al. are obviously analogical in nature because of a morphological leveling. Other cases such as *carcer non car <car>, anser non ansar, passer non passar* are probably phonetic because of the opening effect of the following *r* or because of assimilation with the stressed vowel, but analogy with the morphological ending -*ar*, such as *Caesar,* cannot be discounted. The rather long list of examples of -*ĕs* to *is* as in *ales non <alis>, cautes non cautis, plebes non plevis, vates non vatis, tabes non tavis, suboles non subolis, vulpes non vulpis, lues non luis, deses non desis, reses non resis, vepres non vepris, fames non famis, clades non cladis, Syrtes non Syrtis, sedes non sedis, proles non prolis,* etc., is probably a proof of the influence of the morphological third declension ending -*is*, which is numerically greater than the -*es* ending, those nouns having -*is* in both the nominative and the genitive likewise being an important factor, although a final /ē/ closing to *i* for purely phonetic reasons cannot be excluded. Taking our findings for the Latin inscriptions of Africa as an example, we see that the third declension nominative, endings in -*ēs* and *ĕs* are found sixteen times, while the third declension nominative ending -*is* is found 128 times. This great discrepancy in frequency is to a large degree the result of the one common form *fidelis,* but when we consider that many third declension nouns and adjectives have the -*is* ending in both nominative and genitive singular forms (in African inscriptions alone, we have the genitive singular -*is* 134 times), the morphological factor looms overpowering.

Since the main categories where this final /ĕ/ to *i* change is found are non-morphological words as well as the morphological categories embodied in the third person singular of second conjugation verbs, the nominative singular of third declension nouns and adjectives ending in -*ĕs*, the passive imperative singular, the ablative singular of third declension nouns and adjectives, and the third person singular of third and fourth conjugation verbs in the future indicative, we will devote most of our efforts to these areas to see whether any conclusions can be reached as to an areal differentiation.

Final /ĕ/ in Non-Morphological Words

Africa	Century	/ĕ/ > e	/ĕ/ > i	/ĕ/ > a
	3rd.	3	0	0
	4th.	21	0	0
	5th.	7	0	0
	6th.	9	0	0
	n.d.	67	0	0
	Totals:	107	0	0

Britain	Century	/ĕ/ > e	/ĕ/ > i	% Of Dev.	/ĕ/ > a	% Of Dev.
(Pagan)	2nd.	4	0		0	
	3rd.	9	0		0	
	4th.	1	0		0	
	n.d.	12	0		0	
	Totals:	26	0	0.0	0	0.0
(Christ.)	6th.	2	0		0	
	7th.	1	0		0	
	n.d.	1	0		0	
	Totals:	4	0	0.0	0	0.0
Dalmatia	4th.	7	0		0	
	5th.	2	0		0	
	6th.	1	0		0	
	n.d.	48	2		2	
	Totals:	58	2	3.3	2	3.3

The two examples of final /ĕ/ changing to *i* in non-morphological words in Dalmatia are in the words [e]cci, D, 2436, CIL III 9625, Salona, no date, and [conc]orditir, D. 3842, Salona, no date. The two examples of final /ĕ/ > *a* are both in the same word, found in the same inscription: *ubiconqua* (bis), D. 2389, CIL III p. 961, Tragurium, no date. The *a* is probably used in analogy with other adverbs where final *a* is correct.

Balkans	Century	/ĕ/ > e	/ĕ/ > i	/ĕ/ > a
(Pagan)	2nd.	1	0	0
	4th.	1	0	0
	n.d.	9	0	0
	Totals:	11	0	0
(Christ.)	4th.	3	0	0
	6th.	1	0	0
	n.d.	8	0	0
	Totals:	12	0	0

Our figures coincide almost perfectly with those of Gaeng for his dated inscriptions. However, Gaeng does give several cases of /ĕ/ > *i* in Gaul for undated inscriptions: *decim, septim, quinqui,* and *sempir.* Gaeng considers (p. 118) that these forms do tend to support Grandgent's claim that "final vowels were especially obscure in Gaul in the sixth and seventh centuries." [27] Since our figures show that non-morphological final *e* is very stable in our areas, corroborated by Gaeng's findings for all areas except Gaul in his investigation, the inscriptions may show that Gaul was the one area where the merging of /ĕ/ and /ĭ/ did take place to a greater degree than in other parts of Romania. Before this hypothesis can be asserted more vigorously, it would be well to consider the outcome of final /ĕ/ in morphological endings, both nominal and verbal.

Although final /ĕ/ is relatively stable, there are enough examples of a change to *i* to warrant an explanation.

A. *Africa.* We have the following examples of final /ĕ/ > *i*:

The nominative singular of the third declension ending in -*ex* > *is*: We find the form *senis* (= *senex*), D. 1418A, CIL VIII 25,347,

---

[27] Grandgent, p. 103.

FINAL /Ē/ IN MORPHOLOGICAL ENDINGS

The Results of Our Findings for the Change of /ĕ/ > i
In Noun-Adjective Endings are as Follows:[28]

Area	Century	A er	ir	B es	is	%	C ex	ix	%	D em	im	E e	i[29]	%	F e	i	G en	in	H eps	ips
Africa	3rd.	0	0	0	0		0	0		0	0	2	0		0	0	0	0	0	0
	4th.	8	0	0	0		0	0		7	0	29	1		1	0	5	0	0	0
	5th.	8	0	1	0		0	0		3	0	35	0	3.3	0	0	0	0	0	0
	6th.	3	0	1	0		0	0		6	0	21	5	19.2	0	0	0	0	0	0
	n.d.	19	0	7	0		1	1	50.0	29	0	380	11	2.8	8	0	9	0	0	0
	Totals:	38	0	9	0		1	1	50.0	45	0	467	17	3.5	9	0	14	0	0	0
Britain (Pagan)	1st.	1	0	0	0		0	0		0	0	3	0		0	0	0	0	0	0
	2nd.	0	0	1	0		1	0		1	0	14	1	6.7	0	0	0	0	0	0
	3rd.	2	0	1	0		0	0		5	0	26	1	3.7	0	0	0	0	0	0
	4th.	0	0	0	0		0	0		1	0	1	0		0	0	2	0	0	0
	n.d.	12	0	10	2	16.7	3	0		9	0	20	2	9.1	0	0	2	0	0	0
	Totals:	15	0	12	2	14.3	4	0		16	0	64	4	5.9	0	0	2	0	0	0
(Christ.)	5th.	1	0	0	0		0	0		0	0	0	0		0	0	0	0	0	0
	6th.	3	0	0	0		0	0		0	0	0	0		0	0	0	0	0	0
	7th.	0	0	0	0		0	0		0	0	1	0		0	0	0	0	0	0
	9th.	0	0	0	0		0	0		1	0	2	0		0	0	0	0	0	0
	n.d.	0	0	0	0		0	0		3	0	3	0		0	0	0	0	0	0
	Totals:	4	0	0	0		0	0		4	0	6	0		0	0	0	0	0	0

		A	B	D (acc.)	E (abl. -e)	E (abl. -i)	F	Totals
Dalmatia	4th	1		4	9	1		
	5th	0		2	5	0		
	6th	1	1	3	7	0		100.0
	n.d.	10		9	35	4	1	
	Totals:	12	1	18	56	5	1	50.0
Balkans (Pagan)	2nd	0		0	4	0		
	3rd	2		0	5	0		
	n.d.	8		2	2	0	1	
	Totals:	10		2	11	0	1	
(Christ.)	4th	1		2	4	0		
	5th	0		1	0	0		
	6th	0		0	1	0	1	
	n.d.	6		9	7	0		
	Totals:	7		12	12	0	1	

---

28 The letters A, B, C, D, E, F, G, H stand for the following declensional endings: A = nom. sing. -er of second/ third decl.; B = nom. sing. of third decl.; C = nom. sing. of third decl.; D = acc. sing. of third=fifth decl.; E = abl. sing. of third decl.; F = nom. sing. of third decl.; G = nom. sing. of third decl.; H = nom. sing. of third decl.

29 We are giving all ablatives ending in -i, although pure i-stems have -i in the ablative as a usual termination. Some forms in the -i column, therefore, are perfectly correct and are in no way a deviation, but to show the ratio between the -e and -i ablative endings we are giving the -i form as a separate item. For a detailed analysis of the ablative endings for both nouns and adjectives, see Allen and Greenough, *New Latin Grammar*, pp. 28 ff., 49 ff.

Carthage, no date. Since the genitive singular of this particular word is precisely *senis* and since there are many third declension nouns having the ending *-is* for both nominative and genitive, our deviation is probably the result of an analogical levelling and would, therefore, be morphological rather than phonetic.

The ablative singular of third declension nouns and adjectives in *-e*: The ablative singular ending of consonant stems of third declension nouns was regularly *-e*. The ablative singular ending of i-stems was *-i*.[30] This clear distinction was blurred, however, from early times with a subsequent confusion in the endings of the ablative singular. Kent reminds us (pp. 40, 45) that "not infrequently the *-īd* of -i- stems was taken over" for consonant stems and "in many words this *-ī* was replaced by the *-e* of consonant-stems, either optionally or regularly" for i-stems. Ernout mentions (p. 35) that "la 3e déclinaison est la plus compliquée de toutes ... et des actions analogiques et phonétiques de toutes sortes sont venues troubler l'état ancien, si bien que les deux flexions, consonantique et sonantique, ont réagi l'une sur l'autre." Of the seventeen third declension ablative singulars ending in *-i*, seven are adjectives and have the correct *-i* ending: *omni*, D. 779, 4th. cent.; *sp[lendent]i*, D. 787, 6th. cent.,[31] *simplici*, D. 1583, no date; *perenni*, D. 1641, no date; *fideli*, D. 1697, no date; *perenni*, D. 3443C, no date; *simili*, D. 3938, no date; the monosyllable noun *vi* in the ablative is also correct: D. 1903, no date; the place name *Tigisi*, D. 1832, no date, is likewise probably correct since with names of towns, the ablative singular ending usually ends in *-i*.[32] This leaves eight ablatives in *-i* which show a true change of *-e* to *-i*: the proper name *Masgivini*, D. 42, 6th. cent.; *operi*, D. 787, 6th. cent.; *Ioanni*, D. 793, 6th. cent.; *duci*, D. 795, 6th. cent.; *menti*, D. 2331, no date; three cases of *-i* in *paci*, D. 1247, no date; *paci*, D. 2648AN, no date, and *baci*, D. 3232N, no date. The correct form *pace* is overwhelmingly used in African inscriptions, however, as can be seen by the following table:

---

[30] Kent, pp. 40, 45; Ernout, *Morphologie*, pp. 41, 52-53.

[31] Participles in *-ns* used as such (especially in the ablative absolute), or as nouns, regularly have *-e*; but participles used as adjectives have regularly *-i*. See Allen and Greenough, *New Latin Grammar*, p. 53; Hale and Buck, *A Latin Grammar*, p. 57.

[32] Hale and Buck mention (p. 44) that names of rivers, cities, and months always or usually have the ablative singular in *-i*, although there are exceptions, such as the place-name *Praeneste*.

In African inscriptions:

Century	pace	paci	% Dev.
4th.	8	0	
5th.	25	0	
6th.	7	0	
n.d.	304	3	1.0
Totals:	344	3	0.9

The three sporadic cases of -*i*, therefore, lose their force in the midst of 344 right occurrences. Since there are so few cases of -*i* in the ablative singular (all nouns), the final -*e* seems to have definitely assumed the ending of third declension ablative singular nouns. The -*i* ending for ablative singular adjectives, although few in number, is therefore correctly maintained. It would therefore appear that the sporadic confusion in the ablative singular form of nouns is mainly due to a hesitancy that is morphological in nature.

B. *Britain*. In pagan Britain, of the six forms that show a final *i* for /ĕ/, two are perfectly correct: the ablative *vi*, *RIB* 730, 2nd. century, and the ablative *caelesti*, *RIB* 1791, 3rd century.

The incorrect ablatives ending -*i* are *veteri*, *RIB* 798, no date, and *principi*, *RIB* 1981, no date. The correct form *principe* is found, however, in *RIB* 2042, 3rd century. This confusion in the ablative singular ending of third declension forms is most likely due to morphological uncertainty rather than a phonetic change, especially in the case of *veteri* which, as a third declension adjective of one termination, would normally end in -*i*, but as an exception ends in -*e*.[33]

The final two forms with a final *i* for /ĕ/ are third declension nominative nouns: *equi*[s], *RIB* 907, *CIL* VII 353, no date, and *Superstis* (a proper noun), *RIB* 1586, *CIL* VII 640, no date. Taking into consideration the numerical superiority of third declension nouns ending in -*is* over those ending in -*ēs*, the genitive singular of many imparisyllabic nouns having the stem vowel weakened from -*e*- to -*i*- (as in the above cases: *eques*, *equitis* (gen.), *superstes*, *superstitis*), and the many cases of censure in the *Appendix Probi* of third declension nominatives incorrectly ending in -*is* (see *supra*, pp. 154-56), we feel that the change of -*es* to *is* is mainly morphological in nature.

There is no case of confusion of final /ĕ/ in our corpus of Christian inscriptions of Britain.

---

[33] Allen and Greenough, p. 50 ff.; Hale and Buck, p. 57 ff.

C. *Dalmatia.* The single occurrence of a change of /ĕ/ to *i* in final position is found in the third declension nominative *obsis, D. 79a, CIL* III 9527, Salona, A.D. 599. This would seem to be one more case of a morphological confusion because of the more common *-is* third declension ending for nouns. The fact that there are 56 correct cases of the ablative singular *-e* without a single example of a change to *-i* would also seem to indicate that a phonetic reason for the change is unlikely.

D. *Balkans.* There are no examples in our corpus of a change of final /ĕ/ to *i.* On the basis of our findings we see that those cases involving a change of final /ĕ/ to *i* are encountered in certain noun-adjective categories, i.e. ablative singular of third declension nouns and adjectives. In both types the analogical factor seems to be prevalent, a morphological confusion being more probable than a phonetic change. Let us now investigate the final /ĕ/ to *i* change in the conjugation.

Final /ĕ/ in Conjugational Endings

The three categories where the inscriptions in our corpus show a change of final /ĕ/ to *i* in verbal forms are: (a) the third person singular of second conjugation verbs; (b) the passive imperative singular, and (c) the third person singular of the future indicative of third and fourth conjugation verbs. We will first give the verbal categories where the correct forms appear so as to give a general idea of the treatment of final /ĕ/ in each area, and then the deviations and, if possible, an explanation of the changes.

A. *Africa*

Century	A [34]	B₁	B₂	C	D	E	F	G	H	
	-et	-sset	-ssent	-re	-sse	-re	-ēre	-et	sing. -e	pl. -te
4th.	1	0	2	3	1	1	1	0	0	0
5th.	0	0	0	3	0	0	0	0	1	0
6th.	0	0	0	1	0	0	0	0	1	0
n.d.	2	3	0	27	0	0	4	1	9	7
Totals:	3	3	2	34	1	1	5	1	11	7

---

[34] The following is the explanation of the symbols: A: 3rd pers. sing. of first conj. verbs in pres. subjunctive; B1: 3rd pers. sing. of pluperfect

We are giving below in tabular form the results of those categories where deviations were encountered in any of our areas. Since the verb forms *iacet* and its deviation *iacit* are especially important in the Christian inscriptions of Britain, we are giving them a special category to see how they fare in comparison with other second conjugation verbs.

Africa

Century.	iacet	iacit	iacent	Other 2nd. Conj.			Pass. Imp. Sing.		Future Ind.		
				-et	-it	-ent	-re	-ri	-et	-it	-ent
4th.	0	0	0	1	0	0	0	0	1	0	0
5th.	6	0	0	2	0	1	0	1	0	0	1
6th.	0	0	0	1	0	0	0	0	0	0	0
n.d.	6	0	1	13	0	4	2	1	4	0	0
Totals:	12	0	1	17	0	5	2	2	5	0	1

It is most interesting to note that the third person singular and plural of second conjugation verbs are extremely stable without a single deviation. This is in contrast with the findings of Gaeng who states (p. 127) that "the spelling *it* for *et* appears in most areas where this particular verb form occurs." Although our corpus for African inscriptions is, of necessity, limited, the combined figures of twelve cases of *iacet* and seventeen cases of other third person singular forms of the second conjugation (in addition to the 1 case of *iacent* and 5 cases of other third person plurals of the second conjugation) would seem to indicate that the final /ĕ/ in second conjugation present indicative forms was very stable. It will be enlightening to see whether final /ĭ/ is as stable as final /ĕ/ or whether it did tend to weaken to *e*. If final /ĭ/ goes to *e*, this would show a one-directional movement and final *e* would be the outcome for all /ĕ/ and /ĭ/ verb forms.

The only two verbal forms that do show the change of final /ĕ/ to *i* are the passive imperative singular forms: *doleri*, D. 883, *CIL* VIII 21,553, Mecharasfa (Mauretania Caesariensis), A.D. 434, and

---

subjunctive; B2: plural of pluperfect subjunctive; C: present active infinitive; D: perfect active infinitive; E: 2nd per. sing. of future passive; F: 3rd pers. plural of present perfect ind. ending in *-ēre*; G: 3rd pers. sing. of imperfect subjunctive; H: singular and plural of active imperative of 3rd conjugation.

orari, D. 2339, Utica (Proconsularis), no date. It is a good possibility that these forms are influenced by analogy with the present passive or middle infinitive. Since final /ĕ/ is stable in all other verb forms, the change to *i* appears morphological in nature.

In pagan British inscriptions we have the following figures for those verbal categories where final /ĕ/ is stable:

B. *Britain* (Pagan)

Century	Pres. Act. inf.: -re	Perf. Act. inf.: -sse	3rd Pers. Pl. Pres. perf.: -ere	Imp. Subj. -et	Active Imp. -e	Active Imp. -te	Compounds Of *sum*: -est
1st.	0	0	0	0	0	2	0
2nd.	0	0	0	0	0	0	3
3rd.	0	1	0	0	0	0	1
n.d.	2	0	1	1	0	1	16
Totals:	2	1	1	1	0	3	20

In those three verbal categories where final /ĕ/ does change to *i* in any area which we are investigating, we have the following results:

Britain (Pagan)

Century	iacet	iacit	iacent	Other 2nd Conj. -et	Other 2nd Conj. -it	Other 2nd Conj. -ent	Pass. Imp. Sing. -re	Pass. Imp. Sing. -ri
1st.	0	0	0	0	0	1	0	0
3rd.	0	0	0	1	0	0	0	0
n.d.	0	1	0	0	0	0	1	0
Totals:	0	1	0	1	0	1	1	0

The only example found in verbal categories in the pagan inscriptions of Britain where final /ĕ/ changed to *i* is in the form *iacit*, *RIB* 1722, *CIL* VII 724a, Hadrian's Wall, Chesterholm (Vindolanda), no date. The importance of this form will be discussed under the following heading of Christian inscriptions of Britain.

The following are the verbal categories in Christian inscriptions of Britain where final /ĕ/ remains:

Britain	Century	Pres. Subj. -ent	Perf. Inf. -sse
(Christian)	8th.	1	0
	n.d.	0	1
	Totals:	1	1

In the three important categories where final /ĕ/ does change to *i*, we have the following results:

Britain (Christian)

Century	iacet	iacit	iacent	Other 2nd Conj.			Pass. Imp. Sing.	
				-et	-it	-ent	-re	-ri
5th.	0	8	0	0	0	0	0	0
6th.	2	19	2	0	0	0	0	0
7th.	1	3	0	0	0	0	0	0
n.d.	2	3	0	1	0	0	0	0
Totals:	5	33	2	1	0	0	0	0

It is seen that the only deviations of verbal forms are the overwhelming cases of *iacit* (86.8 %).[35] All other verbal forms do end in the correct *-e*. It is also noteworthy to find that the only deviation encountered in pagan inscriptions of Britain was also the single verb form *iacit*. Taking into consideration both pagan and Christian inscriptions of Britain as regarding verbal forms, we are led to believe that the final conjugational /ĕ/ was very stable except for the single verb form *iacit* where the morphological change from the second conjugation to the third probably took place. The phonetic factor, if involved, would be minimal in its importance. The agreement between pagan and Christian inscriptions in having this unique deviation (albeit a single case in pagan inscriptions) shows that there was no sudden break in continuity in the Latin of Britain, but rather a continuation of the Latin that had been implanted there, even in the case of incorrect forms.

On the basis of our findings for final /ĕ/ in both pagan and Christian inscriptions of Britain it appears that the vowel is stable in non-morphological and morphological (both nominal and conjugational) endings, and that those sporadic deviations to an *i* are due to morphological rather than to phonetic reasons.

For the Christian inscriptions of Dalmatia, the following are the verbal categories where final /ĕ/ does not change:

---

[35] Jackson, *Language*, mentions (p. 158) that "the correct *iacet* is very rare" although he does not say anything about other 2nd conjugation verbs.

C. Dalmatia

Century	Pres. Subj.	Pres. Act.	3rd. Pers. Pl. Pres.	Imp. Subj.	Active Imp.		Compounds Of *sum*:
	-et [36]	inf.: -re	perf.: -ere	-et	-e	-te	-est
4th.	0	4	0	0	0	0	0
5th.	1	1	0	0	0	0	0
6th.	0	2	0	0	0	0	0
n.d.	4	26	2	3	3	0	1
Totals:	5	33	2	3	3	0	1

In the three important categories where there is a change of final /ĕ/ to *i*, we have the following results:

Dalmatia

Century	iacet	iacit	iacent	Other 2nd Conj.			Future Ind. Of [37] 3rd & 4th Conj.	
				-et	-it	-ent	-et	-it
4th.	0	0	0	1	0	0	1	0
6th.	0	1	0	0	0	0	1	0
n.d.	4	1	0	2	0	1	3	2
Totals:	4	2	0	3	0	1	5	2

The examples of deviation from /ĕ/ to *i* are in this area two cases of *iacit*, D. 79a, CIL III 9527, Salona, A.D. 599, and D. 117, CIL III 9534, Salona, no date, and two examples of the third person singular of the future indicative *inferit*, D. 3836A, CIL III 9528, Salona, no date, and D. 830N, CIL III 9667, Salona, no date. It should be noted that the confusion in the third person singular of second conjugation verbs is limited to *iacit* since other second conjugation verbs have the correct ending -et. With respect to the future indicative of third and fourth conjugation verbs, it must be remembered that the ending -et was not very distinctive, being confused with the present indicative where the -it and -et endings were phonetically merged. The Latin future itself (except for *ero*) did not survive in Romance, and was replaced by the present indicative with an adverbial modifier or by a periphrastic construction. [38] Since Dal-

---

[36] All the examples of the present subjunctive of 1st conj. verbs are *det*.
[37] All future indicatives ending in both -et and -it are *inferet* and *inferit*.
[38] Cf. Lausberg, II, 310-11.

matian is a member of the "Italic qualitative vocalic system," the change of /ĕ/ to *i* may be phonetic in nature, but since the majority of verbal forms does maintain the final /ĕ/, the two cases of *inferit* may be the present tense used for a future indicative. Lausberg considers this use of a present indicative for a future as an example of catachresis and mentions (II, 311) that "en algunos dialectos suditalianos el presente, que no choca en su función tradicional, se utiliza como sustituto del futuro." We thus see that the change of final /ĕ/ to *i* is found in non-morphological endings (*[e]cci*, *[conc]orditir*: see *supra*, p. 157), nominal morphological endings (*obsis*: see *supra*, p. 162), and verbal morphological endings (*iacit* and *inferit*: see *supra*, p. 166), although the change of /ĕ/ to *i* is sporadic in all three categories. It is difficult to judge whether the phonetic or morphological factor is more prevalent.

The results of final /ĕ/ in the Balkans are given below, although there are very few examples of verbal forms ending in this vowel.

D. Balkans (Pagan)

Century	Pres. Subj.	Pres. Act.	Imp. Subj.	Act. Imp. Pl.	& Of Dev.
	-et	inf.: -re	-et	-te -tis	
n.d.	1	5	1	0 1	100.0

The one change of final *e* to *i* is in the form *havetis*, *Kalinka* 379, *CIL* III, 756, Steklen (Novae) Moesia Inferior, but this is really the use of the indicative for the imperative.

There are no examples in our corpus of pagan inscriptions of the three categories where we found a change of final /ĕ/ to *i*.

Our findings for Christian inscriptions of the Balkans are only slightly more numerous than for their pagan counterparts.

Balkans	Century	Pres. Act.	Perf. Act.	Imp. Subj.	Compounds Of *sum*
		inf.: -re	inf.: -se	-et	-est
(Christ.)					
	4th.	1	0	0	0
	n.d.	0	1	1	1
	Totals:	1	1	1	1

We did not find any inscriptions in our corpus having the verb *iacet* or its variant. We found just two cases of verb forms ending in /ĕ/ of the second conjugation.

Balkans (Christ.)	Century	Other Second Conj. Verbs		
		-et	-it	-ent
	4th.	0	0	1
	n.d.	1	0	0
	Totals:	1	0	1

Although our data are too few for us to come to any conclusion, Mihăescu, without distinguishing /ĕ/ and /ē/ or Dalmatia from the rest of the Balkans, states (*Limba,* p. 61) that "foarte des apare *i* neaccentuat în loc de *e* neaccentuat, în silabă închisă sau deschisă." [39] Since he does not specifically mention the treatment of final /ĕ/ in verbal endings, his statement is much too vague for our purposes. More epigraphical material is needed for a better understanding of the development of final /ĕ/ in verbal forms. In non-morphological endings (see *supra,* pp. 157, 162) final /ĕ/ is stable, but the paucity of examples likewise invalidates any definite conclusion.

Latin /ē/, Represented by the Letter e

Initial

A.　*Africa*

Century	Open Syllable		% Of Dev.	Closed Syllable		% Of Dev.	Totals		% Of Dev.
	/ē/ > e	/ē/ > i		/ē/ > e	/ē/ > i				
3rd.	4	0		0	0		4	0	
4th.	17	1	5.6	3	0		20	1	4.8
5th.	18	0		1	0		19	0	
6th.	13	0		1	0		14	0	
7th.	5	0		0	0		5	0	
n.d.	98	1	1.0	18	0		116	1	0.9
Totals:	155	2	1.3	23	0		178	2	1.1

The two examples of deviation in this area, both in open syllable, are:

didikuiu (= *dedicavi*), D. 3715A, *CIL* VIII 20,474, near Sitifis (Mauretania Sitifensis), A.D. 331.

---

[39] Translation of the Rumanian: "Unaccented *i* appears very often instead of unaccented *e,* in open or closed syllable."

ficerunt, D. 3709, near Orléansville (Mauretania Caesariensis), no date.

On the basis of the small total percentages of deviation (1.1 %) for the area, and the fact that the correct form *fecerunt* is encountered nineteen times to the single occurrence of *ficerunt*, we may conclude that the initial /ē/ is stable in the Latin of Africa.

B. Britain (Pagan)

Century	Open Syllable		% Of Dev.	Closed Syllable		% Of Dev.	Totals		% Of Dev.
	/ē/ > e	/ē/ > i		/ē/ > e	/ē/ > i				
1st.	5	0		0	0		5	0	
2nd.	18	0		3	0		21	0	
3rd.	37	0		6	0		43	0	
4th.	2	0		0	0		2	0	
n.d.	42	1	2.3	9	0		51	1	1.9
Totals:	104	1	1.0	18	0		122	1	0.8

The single occurrence of deviation from initial /ē/ to *i* in the pagan inscriptions of Britain is found in the word *sicreta, RIB* 7, London, no date. This particular inscription is a *defixio,* written in a very garbled cursive script, and the initial *i* for /ē/ may be a simple scribal error. Under any circumstances, however, initial /ē/ is very stable in the British Latin of pagan inscriptions.

The Latin of Christian inscriptions in Britain does not show many examples of initial /ē/, and nothing definite can be stated.

Britain (Christian)

Century	Open Syllable		% Of Dev.	Closed Syllable		% Of Dev.	Totals		% Of Dev.
	/ē/ > e	/ē/ > i		/ē/ > e	/ē/ > i				
6th.	2	0		0	0		2	0	
7th.	2	0		0	0		2	0	
n.d.	0	0		0	0		0	0	
Totals:	4	0		0	0		4	0	0.0

C. Dalmatia

Century	Open Syllable		% Of Dev.	Closed Syllable		% Of Dev.	Totals		% Of Dev.
4th.	10	0		0	0		10	0	
5th.	19	0		0	1	100.0	19	1	5.0
6th.	1	0		0	0		1	0	
n.d.	58	2	3.3	2	1	33.3	60	3	4.8
Totals:	88	2	2.2	2	2	50.0	90	4	4.3

The four examples of an initial change of /ē/ to *i* in this area are:

vinist[*i*], *D.* 2389, *CIL* III p. 961, Tragurium, (Troghir), no date.
Filiciano, D. 3634A, *CIL* III 9062, Salona, no date.
Criscentiani, D. 1225a, *CIL* III 14,893, Salona, no date.
Criscenti, D. 1245, *CIL* III 9520, Salona, A.D. 443.

The total percentage of deviation of 4.3 %, derived from 90 correct cases to four deviations, is certainly higher than the figures for Africa (1.1 %) and pagan Britain (0.8 %), and may show that there was a tendency to merge initial /ē/ and /ĭ/. Basing himself on the number of instances in which initial /ē/ is represented by *i* in non-dated inscriptions of Southern Italy, Gaeng states (pp. 131-32) that this confusion "would seem to point in the direction of a development which, eventually, resulted in the merger of these vowels." Our findings, although not conclusive, would seem to show that on the eastern coast of the Adriatic Sea the merger of initial /ē/ and /ĭ/ was likewise probably developing. We will have to wait for the section on initial /ĭ/ to see whether there was a confusion of initial /ĭ/ and /ē/ in Dalmatia and, consequently, a merger of these two vowels in initial position.

D. Balkans (Pagan)

Century	Open Syllable		% Of Dev.	Closed Syllable		% Of Dev.	Totals		% Of Dev.
	/ē/ > e	/ē/ > i		/ē/ > e	/ē/ > i				
2nd.	4	0		0	0		4	0	
3rd.	11	0		0	0		11	0	
n.d.	9	0		2	0		11	0	
Totals:	24	0		2	0		26	0	0.0

Balkans (Christian)

Century	Open Syllable		% Of Dev.	Closed Syllable		% Of Dev.	Totals		% Of Dev.
	/ē/ > e	/ē/ > i		/ē/ > e	/ē/ > i				
5th.	1	0		0	0		1	0	
n.d.	17	1	5.6	1	1	50.0	18	2	10.0
Totals:	18	1	5.3	1	1	50.0	19	2	9.5

The two examples of deviation in Christian inscriptions of the Balkans are:

Disiderium (proper name), D. 2181, CIL 10,223, Sirmium (Pannonia Inferior), no date.
Ciriscentina (Crescentina), D. 3659, Purbach (Pannonia), no date.

Although the final percentage of deviation is high (9.5 %), it cannot be taken at face value because of the limited number of examples. It is interesting to note, however, that while there are no deviations in pagan inscriptions, there are some in Christian inscriptions, which may show that a merger was developing in the later centuries in the area.

When we compare our findings with those of Gaeng, we get some startling insights into the treatment of initial /ē/ in the Latin inscriptions of Romania. We have seen that initial /ē/ in the Latin inscriptions of Africa (1.1 % total deviation on the basis of 178 correct occurrences to two deviations) and pagan Britain (0.8 % total deviation from 122 correct occurrences and just one deviation) is stable, whereas the inscriptions of Dalmatia and the Balkans may show a merger of initial /ē/ and /ĭ/ because of higher total deviations, but positing a merger for Dalmatia and the Balkans is risky because of the low, total number of examples. While Gaeng's figures for the Iberian Peninsula, Gaul, and Italy are inconclusive because of the sporadic occurrences of deviations, his findings for Rome are both numerous and clear. We are reproducing his figures in tabular form to give an accurate picture of the treatment of initial /ē/ in Rome:[40]

Rome	Century	/ē/ > e	/ē/ > i	% Of Dev.
	3rd./4th.	162	10	5.8
	5th.	95	10	9.4
	6th./7th.	38	6	13.6
	Totals:	295	26	8.1

We thus see that Rome is undoubtedly the area where initial /ē/ and /ĭ/ merged to the greatest extent and Gaeng's conclusion (p. 132)

---

[40] Gaeng, pp. 129-30.

that "the merger of Latin /ē/ and /ĭ/ is well underway by the third/ fourth centuries and that this area can, indeed, be considered the focal point of this phenomenon" appears fully justified by a comparative study of the various areas of Romania. It must also be brought out that the dichotomy of the Sardinian archaic system with its conservation of Classical Latin /ē/, /ĕ/, and /ĭ/ in initial position, as represented by African and British Latin, and the Italic qualitative system with its merger of these three phonemes, as represented by the Latin of Rome (and possibly of Dalmatia and the Balkans) is substantiated by a comparative study of inscriptions. The lack of more data for some areas is regrettable.

The inscriptions also seem to show that the tendency in Italian to have an *i* initially where the other Romance languages and dialects prefer an *e* was characteristic as far back as the third century A.D. [41]

Intertonic

The results of intertonic /ē/, infrequent in this position, are as follows:

A. *Africa*

Century	Open Syllable		% Of Dev.	Closed Syllable		% Of Dev.	Totals		% Of Dev.
	/ē/ > e	/ē/ > i		/ē/ > e	/ē/ > i				
4th.	1	0		0	0		1	0	
6th.	2	1	33.3	0	0		2	1	33.3
n.d.	16	0		2	0		18	0	
Totals:	19	1	5.0	2	0		21	1	4.8

The one example of change is in the place name *Mauritanie*, D. 1109, *CIL* VIII 23,035, Uppena, ascribed to the time of Justinian (A.D. 527-565).

---

[41] For the characteristic *i* initially in Italian, see Lausberg, I, 287; Bourciez, p. 157; Väänänen, *Introduction*, p. 37; Pei, *Italian Language*, p. 36; Gerhard Rohlfs, *Historische Grammatik der italienische Sprache und ihrer Mundarten* (Bern: A. Francke, 1949), I, 216.

B. *Britain* (Pagan)

Century	Open Syllable		% Of Dev.	Closed Syllable		% Of Dev.	Totals		% Of Dev.
	/ē/ > e	/ē/ > i		/ē/ > e	/ē/ > i				
1st.	2	0		0	0		2	0	
2nd.	1	0		1	0		2	0	
3rd.	5	0		0	0		5	0	
4th.	1	0		0	0		1	0	
n.d.	11	0		0	0		11	0	
Totals:	20	0		1	0		21	0	0.0
(Christ.) n.d.	1	0		0	0		1	0	

C. *Dalmatia*

Century	Open Syllable		% Of Dev.	Closed Syllable		% Of Dev.	Totals		% Of Dev.
	/ē/ > e	/ē/ > i		/ē/ > e	/ē/ > i				
4th.	1	0		0	0		1	0	
5th.	1	0		0	0		1	0	
n.d.	5	1	16.7	1	0		6	0	14.3
Totals:	7	1	12.5	1	0		8	0	11.1

The single case of deviation is in the word *centinarius*, D. 507, Salona, no date.

D. *Balkans* (Pagan)

Century	Open Syllable		% Of Dev.	Closed Syllable		% Of Dev.	Totals		% Of Dev.
	/ē/ > e	/ē/ > i		/ē/ > e	/ē/ > i				
2nd.	0	0		0	0		1	0	
3rd.	1	0		0	0		1	0	
n.d.	4	0		0	0		4	0	
Totals:	5	0		0	0		6	0	0.0
(Christ.) n.d.	1	0		2	0		3	0	0.0

There are too few examples for any definite conclusion to be made with respect to intertonic /ē/ in our areas. It can be said, however, that the /ē/ to *i* change was sporadic at best, without any clear pattern. Comparing our results with those of Gaeng, we find that the /ē/ change to *i* in this position appears more widespread in Southern Italy and Rome, but the figures are too scanty for any true comparative evaluation.

Final (Non-Morphological)

Final /ē/ is quite stable in those areas where we have examples of this infrequent vowel in this position.

A. *Africa*

Century	/ē/ > e	/ē/ > i	% Of Dev.
4th.	1	0	
5th.	1	0	
6th.	1	0	
n.d.	10	0	0.0
Totals:	13	0	

B. *Britain* (Pagan)

	/ē/ > e	/ē/ > i	% Of Dev.
1st.	1	0	
2nd.	1	0	
n.d.	2	0	0.0
Totals:	4	0	
(Christian) *NO EXAMPLES*			

C. *Dalmatia*

	/ē/ > e	/ē/ > i	% Of Dev.
4th.	1	0	
5th.	2	0	
n.d.	2	1	33.3
Totals:	5	1	16.7

The one example of deviation is *decis* (= *decies*), D. 3836A, *CIL* III 9582, Salona, no date.

D. *Balkans.* No Examples for either pagan or Christian inscriptions.

Although we have only one example of an /ē/ to *i* change, Gaeng does report four cases of this change in the province of Narbonnensis in sixth century inscriptions: *pridi* (= *pridie); pridii; decis* (= *de-*

cies), and *oxciis* (= *octies*) and on the basis of his percentage of deviation (33.3 % by virtue of 8 correct occurrences and 4 deviations) concludes (p. 134) that "the area of Gaul is once again ahead of other areas in the matter of the apparent vowel confusion in this position [final]." It may be, as Grandgent reminds us (p. 103) that "final vowels were especially obscure in Gaul in the sixth and seventh centuries."

Morphological Endings: Declensional (Nouns and Adjectives)

The most important declensional categories where the final /ē/ is found in this position are the third declension nominative and accusative plurals, the third declension nominative singular endings (-ēs, ēl, etc.), the present participles ending in -ens and -iens, the fifth declension nominative singular and plural endings -es, and the fifth declension accusative plural ending -es. Of these declensional endings the third declension nominative and accusative plural termination -es and the variant in -is are by far the most pertinent because of their possible importance in the development of the third declension plural formations in Italian and Rumanian. We will therefore concentrate our attention on the comparative distribution of these forms in order to see whether they may shed some light on this most argued of morphological and phonological problems.

A. *Africa*

éntury	3rd Decl. Nom. Plur. -es	-is	% Of Dev.	3rd Decl. Acc. Plur. -es	-is	% Of Dev.	3rd Decl. -es	-is	%	Nom. Sing. -el	-il	%
3rd.	3	0		1	0		0	0		0	0	
4th.	6	0		10	0		0	0		0	0	
5th.	6	0		10	1	9.1	0	0		0	0	
6th.	3	0		7	0		1	0		1	0	
7th.	0	0		1	0		0	0		0	0	
n.d.	34	1	2.9	75	4	5.1	6	0		8	0	
otals:	52	1	1.9	104	5	4.6	7	0		9	0	

The one example of the nominative plural ending in -is is in the word *fidelis*, D. 1416, *CIL* VIII 13,545, Carthage, no date. This single deviation must be questioned as it is found in the phrase: *Caritosa fidelis in pace. / Natalica et Clarissima ff. fidelis in pa[ce],* where the first *fidelis* is rightly the nominative singular and may have influenced the stonemason who may have mistakenly repeated it for the expected plural form. The second *fidelis* may also be a singular adjective modifying the second noun of the compound subject. [42] At any rate, in the Latin of African inscriptions the nominative plural of third declension nouns and adjectives is overwhelmingly -*es*.

The third declension accusative plural forms are numerous and, for the most part, end in -*es*. The sporadic deviations are found in both adjectives and nouns.

> *sedis*, D. 1101, *CIL* VIII 8634, Sitifis (Mauretania Sitifensis), A.D. 440.
> *mensis*, D. 2681, *CIL* VIII 23,578, Maktar (Byzacena), no date.
> *omnis*, D. 1641, *CIL* VIII 9519, Caesarea Mauroum, no date.
> *Aprilis*, D. 2061, near Sitifis (Mauretania Sitifensis), no date.
> *Aprilis*, D. 2816CN, *CIL* VIII 1393a, Bisica (Proconsularis), no date.

One can get a good idea of the preference for the -*es* ending in the third declension accusative plurals by a comparison of the accusative of the expressions *menses* and *mensis*. There are 39 cases of *menses* (or its variants *meses* and *minses*) to only one case of *mensis*. Although the -*is* ending is the reflex of i-stems in Latin in the accusative plural and was normal through Republican times, the -*es* of consonantal stems began quite early to pass into i-stems and became generalized in imperial times. [43] The Latin of North Africa apparently preferred the accusative plural ending -*es* (104 cases of -*es* to only 5 cases for -*is* for a percentage of deviation of 4.6), but did allow for a few cases of -*is*, contrary to the nominative plural where the -*es* ending is almost exclusively used (only 1 questionable case of -*is* compared to 52 cases of -*es*). [44]

---

[42] Alfred Arnout and François Thomas, *Syntaxe latine*, 2nd ed. (Paris: Klincksieck, 1953), pp. 128-30.

[43] Kent, p. 46; Ernout, *Morphologie*, pp. 41-42, 53-54.

[44] There is a form *marturas* (= *martyres*, acc. plur.), D. 2044, *CIL* VIII 9692, Cartenna (Africa), which is probably formed on the analogical singular *martyra* (a change from a third declension noun to the first declension) with the accusative used as a nominative.

Africa

ntury Pres. Part.	% Of Dev.	5th Decl. Nom. Sing. and Plur.			5th Abl. Sing.	% Of Dev.	5th Decl. Acc. Plur.		% Of Dev.
-(i)ens -ins		-es	-is	% Dev.	-e -i		-es	-is	
3rd. 1 0		0	0		1 0		0	0	
4th. 4 0		1	0		4 0		2	0	
5th. 4 0		1	0		21 0		0	0	
6th. 2 0		0	0		8 0		1	0	
7th. 0 0		0	0		1 0		0	0	
n.d. 22 0		12	0		34 0		34	1	2.9
otals: 33 0		14	0		69 0		37	1	2.6

The single occurrence of an /ē/ to *i* change in the fifth declension accusative plural is found in *dis* (= *dies*), *D.* 2682, *CIL* VIII 23,570, Maktar (Byzacena), no date. This form may possibly be an abbreviation as abbreviated forms do abound in this inscription. It is interesting to note that all 37 correct occurrences are the one form *dies*.

B. Britain (Pagan)

Century	3rd Decl. Nom. Plur.		% Of Dev.	3rd Decl. Acc. Plur.		% Of Dev.	3rd Decl. Nom. Sing.		% Of Dev.
	-es	-is		-es	-is		-es	-is	
1st.	2	0		0	0		0	0	
2nd.	1	0		0	0		1	0	
3rd.	3	0		1	0		0	0	
n.d.	23	0		8	0		8	0	
Totals:	29	0		9	0		9	0	0.0

We see that the Latin of pagan inscriptions of Britain favors final -es for both nominative and accusative plurals. The accusative of time offers six examples of *menses* without any case of *mensis*.

Britain (Pagan)

Century Pres. Part.	% Of Dev.	5th Decl. Nom. Sing.		% Of Dev.	5th Decl. Acc. Plur.		% Of Dev.	5th Dec. Abl. Sin.		% Of Dev.
-(i)ens -ins		-es	-is		-es	-is		-e	-i	
1st. 2 0		0	0		0	0		0	0	
2nd. 2 0		0	0		1	0		0	0	
3rd. 2 0		1	0		0	0		0	0	
n.d. 12 0		1	0		3	0		1	0	
Totals: 18 0		2	0		4	0		1	0	0.0

Britain (Christian)

Century	3rd Decl. Nom. Pl.		% Of Dev.	5th Decl.Abl. Sing.		% Of Dev.
	-es	-is		-e	-i	
5th.	0	0		1	0	
6th.	1	1	50.0	0	0	
Totals:	1	1	50.0	1	0	0.0

The one example of a nominative plural in *is* is in the number *tris, CIIC* 461, Cornwall, sixth century. [45]

C. *Dalmatia*

Century	3rd Decl. Nom. Plur.		% Of Dev.	3rd. Decl. Acc. Plur.		% Of Dev.	3rd Decl. Nom. Sing.				% Of Dev.
	-es	-is		-es	-is		-es	-is	-el	-il	
4th.	1	0		6	1	14.3	0	0	0	0	
5th.	0	0		3	1	25.0	0	0	0	0	
6th.	0	0		1	0		1	1	0	0	50.0
n.d.	9	1	10.0	9	5	35.7	0	1	2	0	100.0
Totals:	10	1	9.1	19	7	26.9	1	2	2	0	66.7

The one example of a nominative plural ending in -*is* is in the number *tris,* D. 2426, *CIL* III 10,190, near Doclea, no date.

The seven examples of an accusative plural ending in *is* are as follows:

> *De(c)enbris,* D. 3835C, *CIL* III 9508, Salona, A.D. 382.
> *Octobris,* D. 151, *CIL* III 13,127, Salona, A.D. 428.
> [*Oc*]*tobris,* D. 376, Sebenicum, no date.
> *Octobris,* D. 3042B, *CIL* III 2664, Salona, no date.
> *mensis,* D. 3044, *CIL* III 14,915, Salona, no date.
> *Novembris,* D. 3363, *CIL* III 9623, Salona, no date.
> *mensis,* D. 3633, *CIL* III 9623, Salona, no date.

On the five accusatives of time there are two forms *mensis*. Since the percentage of deviation is high (26.9 % calculated for 19 correct occurrences and 7 deviations), it appears that the -*is* ending for accusative plurals of the third declension was a common termination.

---

[45] For a comparative picture of the number *tris,* see *supra,* p. 95.

The two cases of the nominative singular ending -es changed to is are:

Johannis, D. 79b, *CIL* III 9527, Salona, A.D. 599.
Ioannis, D. 2436, *CIL* III 12,877, Salona, no date.

These two cases of change of -es to -is in the nominative singular of third declension nouns are most likely morphological in nature because of the analogical influence of the more numerous third declension nouns and adjectives ending in -is. A phonological explanation, nevertheless, cannot be discounted.

Dalmatia

Century	Pres. Part.		% Of Dev.	5th Decl. Nom. Sing.		% Of Dev.	5th Decl. Acc. Plur.		% Of Dev.	5th Dec. Abl. Sin.		% Of Dev.
	-(i)ens	-ins		-es	-is		-es	-is		-e	-i	
4th.	1	0		2	0		0	0		9	0	
5th.	0	0		1	0		0	0		10	0	
6th.	0	0		0	0		0	0		1	0	
n.d.	3	0		0	0		6	1	14.3	19	0	
Totals:	4	0		3	0		6	1	14.3	39	0[46]	

The single occurrence of change of /ē/ to *i* in the fifth declension accusative plural is found in *diis*, D. 3837C, near Heraclea Lyncestis, no date.

D. Balkans (Pagan)

Century	3rd Decl. Nom. Plur.		% Of Dev.	3rd Decl. Acc. Plur.		% Of Dev.	5th Decl. Abl. Sing.		% Of Dev.	Pres. Part.		% Of Dev.
	-es	-is		-es	-is		-e	-i		-ens	-ins	
1st.	0	0		1	0		0	0		0	0	
2nd.	0	0		0	0		0	0		0	0	
3rd.	0	0		2	0		0	0		2	0	
4th.	0	0		0	0		1	0		0	0	
n.d.	1	1	50.0	0	0		0	0		7	0	
Totals:	1	1	50.0	3	0		1	0		9	0	0.0

---

[46] We do have an ablative singular in *dia*, D. 376, Sebenicum (Dalmatia), no date, but this is, of course, a case of a declensional change, the fifth declension noun *dies* changing to the first declension.

The one case of an *-is* ending in the nominative plural of third declension nouns is the form *viatoris* (really a vocative), *Kalinka* 379, *CIL* III 756, Steklen (Nova), Moesia Inferior, no date. Although our percentage of deviation of nominative plurals is extremely high (50.0 %), nothing really conclusive can be stated because of the limited number of examples (1 case of *-es* and 1 example of *-is*).

Balkans (Christian)

Century	3rd Decl. Nom. Plur.		% Of Dev.	3rd Decl. Acc. Plur.		% Of Dev.	3rd Decl. %			Nom. Sing. %		
	-es	*-is*		*-es*	*-is*		*-es*	*-is*		*-el*	*-il*	
4th.	1	1	50.0	0	1	100.0	0	0		0	0	
n.d.	8	0		7	0		2	0		3	0	
Totals:	9	1	10.0	7	1	12.5	2	0		3	0	

The one case of an *-is* ending in the nominative plural of third declension nouns is *amantis*, *D.* 1336, Wels (Ovilava), Noricum, fourth century.

The single example of an *is* in the accusative plural of third declension nouns is *dulcis*, *D.* 1336, Wels (Ovilava), Noricum, fourth century.

Although our figures are once again scanty (10 % deviation for nominative plural and 12.5 % for accusative plural on the basis of nine correct occurrences and one deviation and seven correct cases and one deviation respectively), when we consider both pagan and Christian inscriptions, it appears that the *-is* ending was at least present throughout the Latin of the inner Balkans. A lack of sufficient data, however, makes it impossible to state unequivocally that the *-is* ending was firmly entrenched in the Latin of the Balkans.

Balkans (Christ.)	Century	Pres. Part.		5th Decl. Acc. Plur.		% Of Dev.	5th Decl. Abl. Sing.		% Of Dev.
		-ens	*-ins*	*-es*	*-is*		*-e*	*-i*	
	n.d.	2 [47]	0	3	0		1	0	0.0

---

[47] There is an example of a change in conjugation in *dolies* (= *dolens*), *D.* 3611, *CIL* III 10,237, Sirmium (Pannonia Inferior), no date.

Final /ē/: Conjugational Endings

Although a final /ē/ is found in several verb terminations (the second person singular of second conjugation verbs in the indicative; the second person singular in first conjugation subjunctive; the second conjugation singular imperatives; the second person singular of third and fourth conjugation future indicatives; the second person singular of imperfect subjunctives, and the second person singular of past perfect subjunctives), Romance philologists have been mainly concerned with the change of -es to -i in the second conjugation second person singular of the present indicative and first conjugation second person singular of the present subjunctive in Italian and Rumanian. [48] Bourciez goes so far as to say (p. 214) that "l'unification de 2 sg. en -ī(s) est un des traits les plus caractéristiques qui sépare les langues de l'Est du reste de la Romania." Unfortunately, the Latin inscriptions of our areas do not furnish us with many examples of a final -es in verb forms. We will give below our findings for conjugational endings in /ē/ although nothing conclusive can be stated because of the paucity of quantitative material.

A. Africa

Century	2nd Conj. Pres. Ind. -es	-is	% Of Dev.	1st Conj. Pres. Subj. -es	-is	% Of Dev.	3rd Conj. Fut. Ind. -es	-is	% Of Dev.	2nd Conj. Imp. Sing. -e	-i	% Of Dev.
3rd.	1	0		0	0		0	0		0	0	
4th.	1	0		0	0		0	0		2	0	
5th.	0	0		1	0		0	0		0	0	
6th.	0	0		0	0		0	0		1	0	
n.d.	4	0		2	0		1	1	50.0	7	0	
Totals:	6	0		3	0		1	1	50.0	10	0	

The change from -es to -is in the future indicative of third conjugation verbs was found in dilicis (= diliges), D. 2439, CIL VIII 8620, Sitifis (Mauretania Sitifensis), no date.

---

[48] See Pei, Italian Language, pp. 94, 105; Lausberg, I, 431-33; Bourciez, p. 214.

B. *Britain* (pagan and Christian). No conjugational forms ending in -es were found in either pagan or Christian inscriptions of Britain.

C. *Dalmatia*

Century	2nd Conjugation Imperative Sing.		% Of Dev.	Imperfect Subjunctive		% Of Dev.
	-e	-i		-res	-ris	
5th.	1	0		0	0	
n.d.	3	0		0	1	100.0
Totals:	4	0		0	1	100.0

The examples of final -es going to -is in the imperfect subjunctive is found in the verb form *opteneris* (= *obtineres*), D. 2389, *CIL* p. 961, Tragurium, no date.

D. *Balkans* (Pagan). There are no examples in our corpus of final -es in conjugational forms in the pagan inscriptions of the Balkans.

Balkans	Century	2nd Conj. Imp. Sing.		% Of Dev.
		-e	-i	
(Christ.)	n.d.	2	0	

Summary of Distribution of Latin Third Declension Nominative and Accusative Plurals Ending in -ēs And -īs in Their Relationship to the Formation of Romance Third Declension Plurals Ending in -i

Various theories have been proposed to explain the Italian and Rumanian third declension plural nouns ending in -i developing from a Latin -ēs (or -īs). The main theories advanced can be summarized as (a) a phonetical interpretation, with the final -s causing a closing of final /ē/ to i; (b) an analogical borrowing of the final -i from the second declension, since with the loss of final -s, a need was felt to distinguish the singular from the plural; (c) the continuation of the archaic accusative ending -īs, also found, to a lesser degree, in the nominative plural, with the subsequent loss of final -s; (d) the normal phonetic outcome of /ē/ to i in Italian and Rumanian with a loss of -s; (e) the influence of the adjectival second declension ending -i on the nouns ending in -ēs when both nouns and adjective are found closely bound; (f) the influence of the definite article (the Latin *illi*) in conjunction with the plural of the adjective of the second declension (with *-i* endings) on third declension nouns ending in *-ēs: illi canes sunt boni* changed to *illi cani sunt boni*; (g) the influence of the dative singular of third declension nouns and adjectives ending in *-i* on the third declension plurals on the basis of the proportion: first declension genitive and dative feminine singular: first declension nominative plural = third declension dative singular: third declension nominative plural. [49] Arguments for and against these theories have been adduced, although it is most probable that the solution to the problem lies in a combination of several factors. In all of the discussions concerning the development of the third declension plurals ending in *-i* in Italian and Rumanian, inscriptions have been, for the most part, only cursorily referred to. The value of inscriptions has been acknowledged mainly for the documentation of *-īs* endings in Latin third declension accusative and nominative plurals, but no systematic study of inscriptions has ever been made to see whether they can afford any clue to the solving of a problem that has been termed "the crux of a controversy that still persists among scholars." [50] A comparative and quantitative analysis of the Latin third declension

---

[49] The bibliography on the particular problem of the formation of the Italian and Rumanian third declension plurals in *-i* is exceedingly long and we will give only a few referrences pertinent to this question: W. Meyer-Lübke, *Grammaire des langues romanes* (Paris: Stechert, 1890-1906), I, 890; II, 33; Rohlfs, *Grammatik*, II, 42, 49; Grandgent, p. 154; Puşcariu, *Études*, pp. 291-96; Pei, *Italian Language*, p. 73 (for a summary of four theories); Densusianu, II, 166; Rosetti, I, 117; Lausberg, II, 53; Bourciez, p. 229; Sorin Stati, "Din problemele istoriei declinării romîneşti," *Studii şi cercetări lingvistice*, X (1959), 63-75, summarizes seven theories and gives his own (not convincing) of the analogy on the basis of the similarity in forms of the genitive singular and nominative plural in the first declension (VL. *case*), second declension (*lupi*), fourth declension (*manu*, with loss of *-s*), influencing the third declension where, after final *-s* was lost, the *ī* of the third declension merged with the *ī* of the second genitive, thus bringing the third declension genitive singular and nominative plural in line with the other declensions. For a historical interpretation of the Latin third declension plurals, see Sommer, pp. 382, 385-86; Ernout, *Morphologie*, pp. 41-42, 53-54; Kent, pp. 40-41, 45-46. The loss of final *-s* which is at the root of the formation of third declension plurals (as well as, of course, other morphological changes) has been called by Wartburg, *Ausgliederung*, p. 20: "Die einschneidendste, bedeutsamste und folgenschwerste aller lautlichen Differenzierungen innerhalb der Romania."
[50] Pei, *Italian Language*, p. 73.

nominative and accusative endings may aid in the resolution of this thorny problem, as well as dispelling some vague ideas that have been proposed up to the present time. The table below lists the findings of Gaeng for his areas of Iberia, Gaul, Italy, and Rome, and our results for the areas of Africa, Britain, Dalmatia, and the Balkans.

Area	Century	3rd Decl. Nom. Plur.		% Of Dev.	3rd Decl. Acc. Plur.		% Of Dev.
		-es	*-is*		*-es*	*-is*	
Baetica	4th to 6th	0	0		8	0	
	7th	0	0		7	0	
	Totals:	0	0		15	0	
Lusitania	4th to 6th	0	0		2	0	
	7th	0	0		0	0	
	Totals:	0	0		2	0	
Tarraconensis	4th to 6th	0	0		2	2	50.0
	7th	0	0		0	0	
	Totals:	0	0		2	2	50.0
Narbonensis	4th to 5th	0	0		2	1	33.3
	6th to 7th	0	0		7	5	41.6
	Totals:	0	0		9	6	40.0
Lugdunensis	4th to 5th	0	0		4	3	42.8
	6th to 7th	0	0		1	3	75.0
	Totals:	0	0		5	6	54.5
Northern Italy	4th to 5th	1	0		6	3	33.3
	6th	1	0		4	2	33.3
	Totals:	2	0		10	5	33.3
Central Italy	3rd to 4th	9	0		16	1	5.9
	5th	0	0		4	0	
	6th to 7th	0	0		3	2	40.0
	Totals:	9	0		23	3	11.5
Southern Italy	3rd to 4th	5	0		2	2	50.0
	5th	0	0		3	1	25.0
	6th to 7th	3	0		7	3	30.0
	Totals:	8	0		12	6	33.3

Area	Century	3rd Decl. Nom. Plur. -es	-is	% Of Dev.	3rd Decl. Acc. Plur. -es	-is	% Of Dev.
Rome	3rd to 4th	12	3	20.0	37	19	33.9
	5th	1	1	50.0	20	3	13.0
	6th to 7th	1	1	50.0	2	2	50.0
	Totals:	14	5	26.3	59	24	28.9
Africa	3rd	3	0		1	0	
	4th	6	0		10	0	
	5th	6	0		10	0	9.1
	6th	3	0		7	0	
	7th	0	0		1	0	
	no date	34	1	2.9	75	5	5.1
	Totals:	52	1	1.9	104	5	4.6
Britain (Pagan)	1st	2	0		0	0	
	2nd	1	0		0	0	
	3rd	3	0		1	0	
	no date	23	0		8	0	
	Totals:	29	0		9	0	
(Christ.)	5th	0	0		0	0	
	6th	1	1	50.0	0	0	
	Totals:	1	1	50.0	0	0	
Dalmatia	4th	1	0		6	1	14.3
	5th	0	0		3	1	25.0
	6th	0	0		1	0	
	no date	9	1	10.0	9	5	35.7
	Totals:	10	1	10.0	19	7	26.9
Balkans	1st	0	0		1	0	
	2nd	0	0		0	0	
(Pagan)	3rd	0	0		2	0	
	4th	0	0		0	0	
	no date	1	1	50.0	0	0	
	Totals:	1	1	50.0	3	0	
(Christ.)	4th	1	1	50.0	0	1	100.0
	no date	8	0		7	0	
	Totals:	9	1	10.0	7	1	12.5

When we compare the results of the percentages of deviation for the accusative plurals of third declension Latin nouns (and to a lesser degree for nominative plurals), we see that some areas are particularly favorable to the -is form, while others are overwhelmingly in favor of the -es ending. Leaving out those areas where the figures are too low for any definitive conclusion, we may safely say that the Latin of Africa showed a marked tendency to prefer the -es endings in the plural accusative (and especially the nominative) as did the Latin inscriptions of pagan Britain. The Latin of Iberia probably favored the -es endings. [51] On the other hand, the Latin of Gaul, Italy, Rome, and Dalmatia shows a strikingly high percentage of deviations in the use of -is with respect to the -es ending of the accusative plurals. When we consider that the educational level of the average stonemason must have been considerably higher than that of the average person in these particular areas, we can surmise that the use of the -is ending must have been even more widespread among the general populace. In the Balkans we find examples of the -is ending in both nominative as well as accusative endings, in both pagan and Christian inscriptions, which would appear to show that the -is termination was frequent in Balkan Latin, although unfortunately the figures are too low to show this conclusively.

Analyzing the distribution of the -is ending in accusative plurals of the third declension (and to a certain extent the nominative plurals), we find that inscriptions are instrumental in their portrayal of a differentiation of the Latin in the various parts of the Romance Empire with respect to the crucial problem of the treatment of the -is ending and its connection with the formation of the third declension plural endings in Italian, Dalmatian, and Rumanian. The -is ending was also strongly represented in inscriptions of Gaul, but since the final vowels e and i were both lost in French, the development of the French plurals of the third declension was not influenced by the existence of the -is ending. In French it is the maintenance of final -s in the accusative plural which is decisive in the development of the plural formation of the third declension, not the preceding vowel i or e. In those areas, however, where final -s was lost, Italian, Dalmatian, and Rumanian, the final vowel becomes critical. Since the -is ending was commonly used in these areas alongside of the -es

---

[51] Cf. Carnoy, p. 219: "...l'accusatif en -is n'apparaît en Espagne que dans les inscriptions officielles d'un latin rigoureusement classique." He stresses the preponderance of the -es accusative ending over the -is when he adds that the -is ending "n'a jamais eu de racines bien profondes dans la langue populaire." This, of course, cannot be said for all parts of Romania.

terminations, the final -*i* after the loss of -*s* was thus able to fill the pertinent need to distinguish the plural from the singular. If the -*e* had been selected, there would have been an equality of singular and plural forms. The analogical extension of the masculine endings -*i* of the second declension could have helped in the determination of final -*i* as the third declension plural marker, after the loss of -*s*, but it is primarily the frequency of the -*is* accusative ending that is the prime factor in the formation of the third declension plurals. In our entire corpus we did not find a single case of a second declension masculine plural nominative ending -*i* that replaced third declension nouns and adjectives. It is also interesting to note that the final -*s* is always used in the -*is* third declension plural ending, although the -*s* is occasionally lost in the dative and ablative second declension plural endings (cf. *anni* = *annis*). Even the -*es* ending which is so characteristic of African Latin (only 4.6 % deviation in accusative plurals on the basis of 104 correct occurrences of -*es* compared to 5 examples of -*is* and a 1.9 % deviation in nominative plurals from 52 correct examples and 1 questionable case of -*is*) agrees with the subsequent development of Sardinian where the -*es* ending is decisive in the plural formation. [53]

When we consider the chronological factor of the existence of the -*is* ending in some areas of Romania and its relationship with the Romance formation of the plurals of third declension nouns and adjectives in Italian, Dalmatian, and Rumanian, we see that the -*is* accusative plural ending was frequent in some areas from at least the third century A.D. to the seventh (cf. the city of Rome where there was a 33.9 % deviation in the third and fourth centuries on the basis of 37 cases of -*es* and 19 cases of -*is*). It is precisely in those areas where a Romance plural in -*i* evolved (Italian and Rumanian) that there was *no* break in continuity of the accusative plural in -*is*. The continuity of the -*is* accusative plural completely demolishes the objection raised by some scholars that the archaic Latin -*is* ending is too far removed in time to be considered as a valid explanation of the Italian and Rumanian -*i* plurals. [54] The complete lack of any ex-

---

[52] See Pei, *Texts*, p. 45; Bourciez, p. 229; Meyer-Lübke, *Grammaire*, II, 63.

[53] Lausberg, II, 58 ff.

[54] Sorin Stati, "Problemele," on summarizing the possible theories to account for the Italian and Rumanian plurals in -*i* states (p. 64) that "distanţa

ample in our inscriptional material of an analogical extension of the
-*i* plurals of the second declension to the third declension likewise
diminishes the impact of this theory, which has enjoyed great pop-
ularity among Romance scholars. [55]

---

mare în timp care separă acest -*īs* arhaic latin de -*i* din italiană şi romînă
impune multă rezervă în acceptarea explicaţiei." ("the great distance in
time that separates this archaic Latin -*is* from the Italian and Rumanian -*i*
imposes great reservation in the acceptance of this explanation.)

[55] Cf. Sorin Stati, "Problemele," who, on discussing the analogical extension of second declension plural endings in -*i* to the third declension,
writes (p. 64) that "este explicaţia care se bucură azi de cel mai mult credit."
("it is the explanation that enjoys today the greatest repute.") The preference
for the analogical influence of the second declension plurals in -*i* on third
declension plurals in -*es* has likewise been expressed by Grandgent, p. 154;
Lausberg, II, 53; Rohlfs, *Grammatik*, II, 49; Densusianu, II, 166. We
are, of course, aware that -*i* for -*es* has been encountered in documentary
texts and glosses: cf. *successori* (in *Marculf*), *abbati* (*Capitul. de Pépin*,
A.D. 744), *sapienti* (*Gloss. Cassel*); *parenti* (Politzer, *Lombardic Documents*),
parti, *subcessori*, *homeni*, etc. (Politzers, *Romance Trends*; they attest 16
forms with 3rd decl. nouns ending in -*i* for the accusative and 7 for the
3rd decl. nom. plural in -*i*). Politzer in his *Lombardic Documents* mentions
(p. 86) that other than a final -*i* in two place names and one case in the
form *parenti* "the ending -*i* never occurs in the third declension plural" and
concludes (p. 87) that "as to the plural of third declension ... we believe
that the -*is* plural of our documents is the parent of the Italian plural in -*i*."
He goes on to mention that "whether the shift in pronunciation from -*es*
to -*is* was due to the closing influence of -*s* or to a possible fluctuation in
the pronunciation of -*e* in the final syllable generally speaking, both of
which possibilities are indicated in the documents, is a question we do not
endeavor to answer." It is surprising that he does not take the archaic
accusative and nominative -*is* ending into consideration. In *Romance Trends*
the Politzers conclude (p. 30) with respect to the -*i* plural in third declension
nouns that "with regard to the possibility of analogy with the second declension, the distinct gradation of the occurrence of the forms without -*s*
argues strongly against it, since if it were simply a matter of borrowing a
plural from another declension, one would expect to find less strict cor-
respondence with the phonetic fall of final -*s*." We thus see that documentary
evidence and inscriptional material are in general agreement as to the rejec-
tion of the analogical argument as the main factor in the formation of the
third declension plurals in -*i*. It should not be forgotten that a final -*i* could
very easily be the result of the -*is* ending with a loss of final -*s*. Even in
documentary texts of the eighth century, the -*i* ending is not always represented for third declension plurals. Pei in his *Texts* states (p. 147), with
respect to the -*es* and -*is* endings, that "there is a very strong tendency ...
to use -*is* in the place of -*es*, even in the nominative." It is noteworthy that
Pei does not find a single case of a third declension plural ending in -*i*,
although he gives (p. 380) 34 examples of -*is* compared to 51 examples of
-*es* in the nominative plural and 36 cases of -*is* as well as 36 cases of -*es*
in accusative plurals.

On the basis of our evidence we are in complete accord with Puşcariu who, in his *Études* states (pp. 294-95):

> Je crois qu'il faut voir dans cet -*i* des pluriels de la troi-sième décl. la terminaison latine -*is*, que nous trouvons souvent chez les écrivains latins (*omnis, civis, partis,* etc.) et que la grammaire latine désigne comme "archaïque." . . .
> Il y avait donc en latin une oscilation entre la désinence -*is* (à l'origine justifiée seulement pour les accusatifs des radi-caux en -*i*-) et -*es*. Cette oscillation apparait chez les écri-vains classiques, après même que la grammaire eut déclaré correcte la forme en -*es*. La même hésitation entre -*is* et -*es* s'aperçoit dans les inscriptions et elle continue jusque dans l'italien (*le vite* et *le viti*) et le roumain (*care, pace* à côté de *cari, paci*).
>
> Seule l'idée erronée suivant laquelle il y aurait un abîme infranchissable entre le latin archaïque et les langues ro-manes pourrait nous empêcher de voir une continuité entre les pluriels latins archaïques en -*is* et les pluriels italiens et roumains en -*i*.

Inscriptions, by showing a differentiation in the distribution of the -*is* ending in the various parts of Romania as well as its continuity in those areas where the plural -*i* was to develop, show themselves once again to be a valuable tool in a study of the dialectalization of Latin in the different regions of the Roman Empire. Inscriptions, by virtue of a comparative and quantitative study, also show that the -*es* ending was almost exclusively used in some parts of Romania, especially in the Latin of Africa, where final vowels faithfully main-tained their quality, a situation that is mirrored in the archaic vocalic system of Sardinian. Final -*es* is likewise overwhelmingly used in the Latin of pagan Britain, but this fact loses its pertinence since the Brit-tonic languages lose their final syllable in the evolution of both native words and Latin borrowings. [56]

---

[56] Jackson, *Language*, p. 618; Loth, pp. 112-13.

Latin /ĭ/, Represented by the Letter i

Initial

Africa	Century	Open Syllable		% Of Dev.	Closed Syllable		% Of Dev.	Totals		% Of Dev.
		/ĭ/ > i	/ĭ/ > e		/ĭ/ > i	/ĭ/ > e				
	3rd.	1	0		2	0		3	0	
	4th.	7	0		26	0		33	0	
	5th.	4	0		33	1	2.9	37	1	2.6
	6th.	8	0		17	0		25	0	
	7th.	0	0		2	0		2	0	
	n.d.	132	2	1.5	106	0		238	2	0.8
	Totals:	152	2	1.3	186	1	0.5	338	3	0.9

The three examples of deviation in this area are:

fedelis, D. 1402N, *CIL* VIII 25,135, Carthage, no date.
fedeli, D. 1406B, *CIL* VIII 25,302, Carthage, no date.
des(cessit), D. 3276A, *CIL* VIII 21,698, Albulae (Mauretania
Caesariensis), after A.D. 439. [57]

On the basis of the low percentage of deviation it appears that
initial /ĭ/ was stable in the Latin of Africa. Since the percentage of
deviation for initial /ē/ was 1.1 % (on the basis of 178 correct occurrences and 2 deviations: see *supra*, pp. 168-69), it would seem that
African Latin kept apart the two phonemes in initial syllables. Inasmuch as initial /ĕ/ showed a percentage of deviation of just 0.4 %
on the basis of 547 correct occurrences and two deviations (see *supra*,
pp. 144-45), it may be said that there was no merger of /ĭ/, /ē/, and
/ĕ/ in initial syllable, a characteristic of the Sardinian archaic vocalic
system, in contrast to the Italic qualitative vocalic system (and the
Balkan compromise system) where the merger of the three phonemes
is said to have taken place.

---

[57] The *des.* may possibly be an abbreviation for *d(isc)es* (*sit*), which
would decrease the percentage of deviation even more.

Britain	Century	Open Syllable		% Of Dev.	Closed Syllable		% Of Dev.	Totals		% Of Dev.
		/ĭ/ > i	/ĭ/ > e		/ĭ/ > i	/ĭ/ > e				
(Pagan)	1st.	5	0		2	0		7	0	
	2nd.	9	0		21	0		30	0	
	3rd.	26	0		66	0		92	0	
	4th.	2	0		17	0		19	0	
	n.d.	47	1	2.1	35	0		82	1	1.2
	Totals:	89	1	1.1	141	0		230	1	0.4

The single case of deviation in the Latin of pagan Britain is the deity *Menervae*, *RIB* 1200, *CIL* VII 313, Whitley Castle, no date. [58] This isolated case is probably the archaic spelling of the Greek goddess' name rather than a merger of /ĭ/ and /ē/, especially since this form was found in a pagan inscription of probably early date. [59] The initial phonemes /ĭ/, /ē/, and /ĕ/ are extremely stable in the Latin of the pagan inscriptions of Britain as evidenced by the negligible total percentage of deviation (0.3 %) calculated on the basis of 334 correct occurrences of /ĕ/ and no case of deviation (see *supra*, p. 145), 122 examples of correct /ē/ and one deviation to *i* (0.8 % deviation; see *supra*, p. 169) and the 230 examples of correct occurrences of /ĭ/ and one case of deviation (probably the archaic spelling in the word *Menervae*), the totals of the three phonemes coming to 686 cases of correct occurrences and just two examples of deviation (of which one is a probable archaism). This total percentage of deviation of 0.3 % on the basis of 686 correct occurrences and just two deviations for all three phonemes (/ĭ/, /ē/, /ĕ/) is ample proof that no merger of the front vowels took place in the Latin of pagan Britain. This would put the Latin of pagan Britain in the same category as the archaic vocalic system of the Latin of Africa,

---

[58] *Menerua* was the regular form in early inscriptions (e.g. *CIL* I, 191; I, 34). Lindsay mentions (p. 190) that "whether *Menerua* of early inscriptions ... became *Minerva* through loss of accent in the first syllable or by analogy of *minor* is uncertain." Sommer questions (p. 111) whether "*Minerua* für *Menerua*, wohl etruskischer Herkunft, durch volksetymologische Verknüpfung mit *minisci?*" Richter considers (p. 52) *Menerva* as the "noch archaische Stufe *Menerva*, Vorläuferin der Form *Minerva*."

[59] Besides the correct form *Minerua* found 3 times in undated pagan inscriptions, we find *Minervae*, *RIB* 91 in a first century inscription, and *Min(ervae)*, *RIB* 146 in a second century inscription.

in strong contrast to the Italic qualitative vocalic and Balkan compromise systems.

The Latin of Christian inscriptions of Britain has just a single correct occurrence of /ĭ/ and no deviations and no conclusion can, of course, be made.

Dalmatia Century	Open Syllable		% Of Dev.	Closed Syllable		% Of Dev.	Totals		% Of Dev.
	/ĭ/ > i	/ĭ/ > e		/ĭ/ > i	/ĭ/ > e				
4th.	1	0		3	0		4	0	
5th.	0	0		10	1	9.1	10	1	9.1
6th.	1	0		2	1	33.3	3	1	25.0
n.d.	9	0		30	0		39	0	
Totals:	11	0		45	2	4.3	56	2	3.4

The two examples of deviation, both in closed syllables, are:

cresteanor., D. 3870, CIL III 13,124, Salona, A.D. 426 or 430.
Sermenses (= Sirmiensis), D. 1653, CIL III 9551, Salona, A.D. 506 or 551.

Although the percentage of deviation of 3.4 % is high in comparison with the percentages of deviation of /ĭ/ for Africa (0.9 %) and pagan Britain (0.4 %), because of the limited cases where an initial /ĭ/ is found, it is hazardous to venture any remark concerning the merger of initial /ĭ/ and /ē/. When we compare, however, the figures for the front vowels /ĭ/, /ē/, and /ĕ/, we find a 4.3 % deviation for /ē/ calculated on the basis of 90 correct occurrences and four deviations (see supra, p. 169) and 1.5 % deviation for /ĕ/ on the basis of 133 correct occurrences and two deviations (see supra, p. 145), in addition to the 3.4 % of deviation for /ĭ/. The total percentage of deviation for the three phonemes is 2.8 %, calculated on 279 correct occurrences of /ĭ/, /ē/, /ĕ/ and eight examples of deviation. This figure is well above the figures derived for the percentages of deviation for African Latin (0.9 %) and British pagan Latin (0.4 %) and may well indicate that a merger was going on. We will give Gaeng's figures for his areas in our summary of the initial vowels and a more complete picture of the situation will be obtained at that time.

Balkans	Century	Open Syllable		% Of Dev.	Closed Syllable		% Of Dev.	Totals		% Of Dev.
		/ĭ/ > i	/ĭ/ > e		/ĭ/ > i	/ĭ/ > e				
Pagan)	1st.	1	0		1	0		2	0	
	2nd.	3	0		4	0		7	0	
	3rd.	3	0		9	0		12	0	
	4th.	1	0		1	0		2	0	
	n.d.	11	0		12	0		23	0	
	Totals:	19	0		27	0		46	0	
Christ.)	4th.	1	0		0	1	100.0	1	1	50.0
	n.d.	5	0		12	0		17	0	
	Totals:	6	0		12	1	7.7	18	1	5.3

The one case of deviation is found in *crestiana, D.* 1336, *CIL* III 13,529, Ovilava (Noricum), fourth century. Since our figures are too low for any conclusion to be drawn, it may be informative to glance at the total percentages of deviation for the front vowels /ĭ/, /ē/, /ĕ/, both in pagan and in Christian inscriptions. It is interesting to note that we found no examples of deviation in pagan inscriptions for the three phonemes under consideration, although there were 89 correct occurrences of /ĕ/, 26 cases of /ē/, and 46 examples of /ĭ/ (see *supra*, pp. 146, 170, 193), for a total of 161 correct occurrences. When we turn to Christian inscriptions, we see that there are fewer examples of correct occurrences, but a greater number of deviations. We encountered 55 correct occurrences of /ĕ/ and two deviations to *i*, 19 correct occurrences of /ē/ and two deviations to *i*, and 18 correct occurrences of /ĭ/ and one deviation to *e* (see *supra*, pp. 146, 170, 193), for a total percentage of deviation of 5.2 % on the basis of 92 correct occurrences and five deviations. This would seem to indicate that the Romance merger of the front phonemes /ĭ/, /ē/, /ĕ/ in the Balkans was evolving in the fourth century or thereabouts. [60]

---

[60] Our dating is only an approximation, but is in general agreement with the date given by Grandgent, p. 84: "The spelling *e* for *i* is common from the third century on: *frecare, legare*, etc." Since Grandgent does not give any statistics for his statement, the word "common" must be taken with caution. Pirson, on discussing the use of *e* for /ĭ/, states (p. 32) "qu'il constitue un des traits caractéristiques de la langue latine des Ve et VIe siècles." Väänänen, *Introduction*, considers (p. 36) the spelling *i* for *e* as "rare avant l'époque tardive."

PHONOLOGY

It is also noteworthy to mention that this incipient merger is seen through a comparative study of pagan and Christian inscriptions.

Summary of Correct Occurrences and Deviations in the Initial Front Vowels /ĭ/, /ē/, and /ĕ/ in the Various Parts of Romania

We will give below both the figures [61] obtained by Gaeng for his areas and the results of our findings for our areas, and then try to draw conclusions on the basis of a comparison between areas and percentages of deviation.

Area	Cent.	/ĕ/ e	i	% Of Dev.	/ē/ e	i	% Of Dev.	/ĭ/ i	e	% Of Dev.	Totals		% Of Dev.
Baetica	4-6	45	0		4	0		7	0		56	0	0.0
	7	36	1	2.7	17	0		10	1	9.1	63	2	3.1
	Totals	81	1	1.2	21	0	0.0	17	1	5.6	119	2	1.7
Lusitania	4-6	86	2	2.3	9	0		14	0		109	2	1.8
	7	10	0		5	0		1	1	50.0	16	1	5.9
	Totals	96	2	2.0	14	0	0.0	15	1	6.3	125	3	2.3
Tarraco-	4-6	48	0		8	0		11	0		67	0	0.0
nensis	7	9	1	10.0	1	0		3	0		13	1	7.1
	Totals	57	1	1.7	9	0	0.0	14	0	0.0	80	1	1.2
Narbo-	4-5	45	0		3	0		4	1	20.0	52	1	1.9
nensis	6-7	97	2	2.0	8	1	11.1	18	4	18.1	123	7	5.4
	Totals	142	2	1.4	11	1	8.3	22	5	18.5	175	8	4.4
Lugdu-	4-5	43	0		7	0		3	1	25.0	53	1	1.9
nensis	6-7	83	0		2	1	33.3	13	1	7.1	98	2	2.0
	Totals	126	0	0.0	9	1	10.0	16	2	11.1	151	3	1.9
Northern	4-5	129	0		29	1	3.3	25	3	10.7	183	4	2.1
Italy	6	69	0		14	0		15	1	6.3	98	1	1.0
	Totals	198	0	0.0	43	1	2.3	40	4	9.1	281	5	1.7

[61] We have taken the liberty of totaling the various categories and deriving the percentages of deviation for some operations, all of course on the basis of Gaeng's figures.

Area	Cent.	/ĕ/		% Of Dev.	/ē/		% Of Dev.	/ĭ/		% Of Dev.	Totals		% Of Dev.
		e	i		e	i		i	e				
Central	3-4	33	0		17	0		10	0		60	0	0.0
Italy	5	32	0		8	0		10	0		50	0	0.0
	6-7	54	0		22	0		17	0		93	0	0.0
	Totals	119	0	0.0	47	0	0.0	37	0	0.0	203	0	0.0
Southern	3-4	28	1	3.5	23	0		15	0		66	1	1.5
Italy	5	35	1	2.9	16	1	5.9	13	2	13.3	64	4	5.9
	6-7	99	2	2.0	53	0		15	0		167	2	1.2
	Totals	162	4	2.4	92	1	1.1	43	2	4.4	297	7	2.3
Rome	3-4	207	1	0.4	162	10	5.8	88	2	2.3	457	13	2.8
	5	131	1	0.7	95	10	9.4	38	6	13.6	264	17	6.0
	6-7	88	4	4.3	38	6	13.6	12	0		138	10	6.7
	Totals	426	6	1.4	295	26	8.1	138	8	5.5	859	40	4.4

Our findings for the corresponding correct occurrences and deviations for the areas of Africa, Britain, Dalmatia, and the Balkans are as follows:

Area	Cent.	/ĕ/		% Of Dev.	/ē/		% Of Dev.	/ĭ/		% Of Dev.	Totals		% Of Dev.
		e	i		e	i		i	e				
Africa	3rd.	11	0		4	0		3	0		18	0	0.0
	4th.	65	0		20	1	4.8	33	0		118	1	0.8
	5th.	86	0	2.1	19	0		37	1	2.6	142	1	0.7
	6th.	47	1		14	0		25	0		86	1	1.1
	7th.	1	0	0.3	5	0	0.9	2	0	0.4	8	0	0.0
	n.d.	337	1		116	1		238	1		691	3	0.4
	Totals	547	2	0.4	178	2	1.1	338	2	0.6	1063	6	0.6
Britain	1st.	19	0		5	0		7	0		31	0	0.0
	2nd.	48	0		21	0		30	0		99	0	0.0
(Pagan)	3rd.	64	0		43	0		92	0		199	0	0.0
	4th.	5	0		2	0		19	0		26	0	0.0
	n.d.	198	0		51	1	1.9	82	1	1.2	331	2	0.6
	Totals	334	0	0.0	122	1	0.8	230	1	0.4	686	2	0.3

Area	Cent.	/ĕ/ e	/ĕ/ i	% Of Dev.	/ē/ e	/ē/ i	% Of Dev.	/ĭ/ i	/ĭ/ e	% Of Dev.	Totals		% Of Dev.
(Christ.)	4th.	2	0		0	0		0	0		2	0	0.0
	5th.	3	0		0	0		0	0		3	0	0.0
	6th.	5	0		2	0		0	0		7	0	0.0
	7th.	1	0		2	0		0	0		3	0	0.0
	8th.	1	0		0	0		0	0		1	0	0.0
	n.d.	6	0		0	0		1	0		7	0	0.0
	Totals	18	0		4	0		1	0		23	0	0.0
Dalmatia	4th.	13	0		10	0		4	0		27	0	0.0
	5th.	20	0		19	1	5.0	10	1	9.1	49	2	3.9
	6th.	6	0		1	0		3	1	25.0	10	1	9.1
	n.d.	94	2	2.1	60	3	4.8	39	0		193	5	2.5
	Totals	133	2	1.5	90	4	4.3	56	2	3.4	279	8	2.8
Balkans	1st.	2	0		0	0		2	0		4	0	
	2nd.	3	0		4	0		7	0		14	0	
(Pagan)	3rd.	14	0		11	0		12	0		37	0	
	4th.	4	0		0	0		2	0		6	0	
	n.d.	66	0		11	0		23	0		100	0	
	Totals	89	0		26	0		46	0		161	0	0.0
(Christ.)	4th.	4	0		0	0		0	0		4	0	0.0
	5th.	1	0		1	0		1	1	50.0	3	1	25.0
	n.d.	50	2	3.8	18	2	10.0	17	0		85	4	4.5
	Totals	55	2	3.5	19	2	9.5	18	1	5.3	92	5	5.2

We will try to draw some conclusions on the basis of a comparative analysis of the quantitative data for the various regions of Romania.

An almost certain case for the stability of initial front vowels /ĕ/, /ē/, and /ĭ/, can be made for the Latin of Africa and pagan Britain. The total percentages of deviation for these two areas are so low that the conclusion must be drawn that a merger of the vowels did not take place. Both areas probably are representative of the Sardinian archaic vocalic system where /ĕ/ and /ē/ merge to give unstressed e, and /ĭ/ and /ī/ merge to form i. The Latin of Africa and Britain is extremely conservative and is in direct contrast to the Latin of those areas encompassed in the Italic quantitative vocalic system where a merger of the front vowels /ĕ/, /ē/, and /ĭ/ is posited.

The most striking linguistic change in the Latin of Italian inscriptions is the change of initial /ē/ to *i* in the area of Rome. In most of the other parts of Romania the change is sporadic, but in Rome there is a strong trend to represent /ē/ by *i*, starting from the third century and increasing in subsequent centuries. The marked tendency for Tuscan dialects to show *i* in initial position [62] is conspicuously absent in inscriptions of Central Italy, thus pointing to Rome as the center of irradiation of the change, with Central Italy receiving the innovation at a later date. It is also interesting to note that initial /ĕ/ also changes to *i* in Rome, but this change shows regularity only in the sixth century, thus indicating that there was a distinctiveness in the treatment of /ĕ/ and /ē/ in the area of Rome until a rather late date. The characteristic *i* of initial syllables in Italian thus began as a specific development from Latin /ē/ and only later was the reflex of Latin /ĕ/.

The stability of initial /ĕ/, /ē/, and /ĭ/ in Central Italy also requires comment. Gaeng found no deviation for these initial vowels in any dated inscription, and only two cases of /ē/ to *i* and one example of /ĭ/ to *e* in undated inscriptions (see Gaeng, pp. 131, 149). Since the total number of correct occurrences for these three vowels is 203 without any deviation, some explanation must be given for this anomalous situation. The immediate response is that the scribal tradition was more established there and that the stonemasons were more educated and conscious of their trade. The epigraphical material was therefore more Classical Latin oriented with the vulgar tendencies consciously submerged. This explanation, however, is too superficial when we consider that the Latin inscriptions of Rome are particularly decisive in our interpretation of the important change of initial /ē/ to *i* and yet it is unlikely that this particular change should be attributed to uneducated stonemasons in an area that was particularly well provided with schools and a relatively high level of education.

The inscriptions may be showing a general clarity of the vowels in Central Italy in comparison with other regions of Italy where unaccented vowels are weakened and syncopated to a greater degree than in Central Italy. Comparing the unaccented vowels of Tuscan and the Northern Italian dialects, Rohlfs states (*Grammatik*, I, 214) that

---

[62] See *supra*, p. 172, for references to the initial *i* in Italian.

"während im Toskanischen ... die unbetonten Vokale erhalten bleiben, erfolgt in den meisten Gebieten Oberitaliens mehr oder weniger
starke Abschwächung oder völliger Verlust." Continuing his comparison with Southern Italian dialects Rohlfs writes (Grammatik, I,
214) that "auch in Süditalian gibt es weite Gebiete, die zu einer
mehr oder weniger starken Reduktion der unbetonten Vokale neigen."
The merger of /ĭ/, /ē/, /ĕ/ that is posited for Tuscan vowels in
unaccented position (see supra, p. 136) may be a later development.

An explanation of the Central Italian stability of initial syllables
may also be given by the substratum theory. Meillet, a strong advocate of Etruscan influence on Tuscan development writes that
peculiarities inherent to Tuscan may suppose "une prononciation an-
ciennement différente." [63] Although he is primarily concerned with
the treatment of occlusives, he would probably include (p. 232) vocalic
phenomena in the "particularités de prononciation que révèle l'étude
des textes étrusques." The substratum theory is, of course, hotly
disputed and we are in no position to take sides in the debate on
Etruscan influence on Tuscan Italian, but the inscriptions of Central
Italy do seem to show that the Latin of this area was different from
other areas in the Italian Peninsula.

On the basis of Gaeng's figures, it appears that initial /ē/ and
/ĭ/ of Gaul were in the process of merging, this tendency being
particularly prevalent in Narbonensis. Of the regions in Italy, the
inscriptions of Northern Italy likewise show this trend of /ē/ and
/ĭ/ to merge, the Latin of Northern Italy possibly showing an early
indication of developing in a way similar to that of the Latin of Gaul.

An interesting case of pagan and Christian inscriptions showing
different linguistic habits is the Latin of the Balkans. Our corpus
does not show any deviation of initial /ĕ/, /ē/, and /ĭ/ in the pagan
inscriptions of the area, but Christian epigraphical material points to
a merger of these phonemes, which merger is posited for the compromise vocalic system of Rumanian. This distinct treatment of initial
vowels in Christian inscriptions may have an important chronological
implication for the development of Latin on Balkan soil.

The merger of initial vowels on the Dalmatian coast may be accepted on the basis of a total percentage of deviation of 2.8 % (279

---

[63] Antoine Meillet, Esquisse d'une histoire de la langue latine, Nouvelle
Edition (Paris: Klincksieck, 1966), p. 232.

correct occurrences to eight deviations). This figure of 2.8 % is definitely higher than the 0.6 % of Africa (1063 correct occurrences to six deviations) or the 0.3 % of pagan Britain (686 correct occurrences to two deviations), but one may question whether the findings of differentiation of Latin in the various parts of Romania are valid on the basis of just one or two percentage points.[64] It must be remembered, however, that deviations from the norm of Classical Latin must be small in number in comparison with the bulk of Latin inscriptions where a conscious attempt was made to conform to the standard orthography. It would be unreasonable to expect to find a distinct cleavage in the percentage of deviation of all linguistic phenomena in all parts of Romania.

Intertonic

Africa	Century	Open Syllable		% Of Dev.	Closed Syllable		% Of Dev.	Totals		% Of Dev.
		$/\breve{\imath}/ > i$	$/\breve{\imath}/ > e$		$/\breve{\imath}/ > i$	$/\breve{\imath}/ > e$				
	3rd.	1	0		0	0		1	0	
	4th.	15	0		1	0		16	0	
	5th.	14	0		1	0		15	0	
	6th.	25	0		4	0		29	0	
	7th.	1	0		0	0		1	0	
	n.d.	111	2	1.8	13	1	7.1	124	3	2.4
	Totals:	167	2	1.2	19	1	5.0	186	3	1.6

The examples of a change of /ĭ/ to e in this position are:[65]

lapide cesori (= *lapidicaesoris*, although given as two words in the inscriptions as recorded by Diehl), D. 655a, CIL VIII 8774, Thamalla (Mauretania Sitifensis), no date.

---

[64] The Politzers (*Romance Trends*), in their discussion of the loss of -s in Latin documents of Northern and Central Italy, write (p. 14) that "the distribution of the fall of -s is particularly striking..." and that "the distribution of this phenomenon is perfectly graded from south to north..." This important conclusion, however, was based on the following occurrences per 100 lines: Siena 3.3, Pisa 2.1, Lucca 1.6, Piacenza 0.9, North. Italy 0.4. These figures may seem far from decisive but do seem to portray the linguistic picture quite accurately.

[65] There is a proper name *Calbessanus*, D. 2651, Curubis (Proconsularis), no date, that may be a corruption of *Calvisianus*. In Diehl's index of proper names an asterisk is placed in front of the name (very rarely done) to show that it is one of those names that are "suspecta sive lectionis incertae."

arcediaco[*nu*]*s: D.* 1198, *CIL* VIII 58a, 11,117, Leptus
Minor, no date.
beates[*simorum*]: *D.* 2097, *CIL* VIII 27,545, Mascululitana,
no date.

Of the three examples recorded for this change, two may be more
morphological in nature than phonetic. The form *lapide cesori* is given
as one word in *Harper's Latin Dictionary*; the division of the word
into its component parts may show that the stonemason declined
both parts rather than just the final vowel of the single word. The *e*
in *arcediaco*[*nu*]*s* may likewise be morphological in nature rather than
a pure phonetic change. There are two Greek morphemes used in
word composition: ἀρχι - and ἀρχέ -. The analogical extension of
one to the detriment of the other would be a simple morphological
phenomenon and would not show a phonetic confusion of the intertonic vowels /ĭ/ and /ĕ/. It should be noted that both words are
not common Latin types and that only *beates*[*simorum*] is clearly a
phonetic change. The total percentage of deviation of 1.6 % (even
with two questionable changes of /ĭ/ to *e*) is low and it may be
stated that intertonic /ĭ/ was stable in the Latin of Africa.

Britain	*Century*	Open Syllable		% Of Dev.	Closed Syllable		% Of Dev.	Totals		% Of Dev.
		/ĭ/ > *i*	/ĭ/ > *e*		/ĭ/ > *i*	/ĭ/ > *e*				
(Pagan)										
	1st.	6	0		1	0		7	0	
	2nd.	21	0		5	0		26	0	
	3rd.	23	0		3	0		26	0	
	4th.	2	0		0	0		2	0	
	n.d.	39	2	4.9	1	0		40	2	4.8
	Totals:	91	2	2.2	10	0	0.0	101	2	1.9

The two examples of deviation in pagan Britain are:

significatur, RIB 221, Clothall, no date.
aureficinam, RIB 712, Malton (Derventio), no date.

The intertonic /ĭ/, on the basis of only two deviations compared
to 101 correct occurrences, seems stable in the Latin of pagan inscriptions of Britain. These two deviations are both popular in nature.
The form *significatur* is found in a *defixio* written in cursive script
and *aureficinam* is encountered on a building-stone, written without

too great care by the mason, the inscription itself being popular: *Feliciter sit / Genio loci / servule utere / felix tabern/am aurefi/ cinam.* Since the Latin of pagan Britain is, for the most part, Classical in nature, following the Sardinian archaic vocalic system shared by African Latin, these popular lapses may indicate that there was a definite difference between the Latin inscribed in inscriptions and borrowed by the Brittonic languages and the Latin used by the lower classes in their everyday intercourse. [66]

Britain	Century	Open Syllable		% Of Dev.	Closed Syllable		% Of Dev.	Totals		% Of Dev.
		/ĭ/ > i	/ĭ/ > e		/ĭ/ > i	/ĭ/ > e				
(Christ.)										
	5th.	0	0		1	0		1	0	
	6th.	1	0		0	0		1	0	
	7th.	2	0		0	0		2	0	
	n.d.	1	0		0	0		1	0	
	Totals:	4	0	0.0	0	0	0.0	5	0	0.0

[66] This difference between the usual conservative, archaic Latin found in inscriptions and borrowings in the Brittonic languages and a more popular, general Vulgar Latin is echoed by Jackson, *Language,* who writes (p. 88) that "loanwords [into Brittonic languages] show that the Classical quantity system was preserved, even with unstressed vowels, in the Latin of Roman Britain." He adds (p. 107) that "though it [British Vulgar Latin] agreed in a number of more or less important ways with the spoken Latin of the Continent under the Empire, there are several striking points in the phonology over which it differed very definitely; and the difference consists almost exclusively in this, that in these respects the sound-system of Latin in Britain was very archaic by ordinary Continental standards, still clinging in the fifth century to pronunciations which had gone out of colloquial use elsewhere as early in some cases as the first." Writing about the way Latin words were borrowed by the Brittonic languages, Jackson asks (p. 109): "What class of people would speak, or be anxious to learn, the semi-artificial Latin of the learned or upper classes and at the same time be in a position to transmit words in their pronunciation of the British language? Hardly the members of the army, nor the merchants, nor the middle and lower classes in the towns, all of whom no doubt spoke various types of the ordinary standard Vulgar Latin just as their counterparts did on the Continent. Surely it must have been the well-to-do landowners of the Lowland Zone, the native upper class of town and country, who owned the villas and had their town houses, too." We thus see that inscriptions generally reflect the conservative, archaic Latin, also found in Britonnic loanwords, but Vulgar Latin tendencies may occasionally be found, especially in inscriptions of a popular nature as would be expected from writings emanating from lower class masons.

Century	Open Syllable		% Of Dev.	Closed Syllable		% Of Dev.	Totals		% Of Dev.
	/ĭ/ > i	/ĭ/ > e		/ĭ/ > i	/ĭ/ > e				
Dalmatia 4th.	8	0		0	0		8	0	
5th.	5	1	16.7	3	0		8	1	11.1
6th.	0	0		1	0		1	0	
n.d.	15	5	25.0	13	0		28	5	15.2
Totals:	28	6	17.6	17	0	0.0	45	6	11.8

The examples of deviation in this area are:

calegario, D. 648, CIL III 2354, near Salona, no date.
opteneris (= obtineres, imperfect subjunctive), D. 2389, CIL III p. 961, Tragurium, no date.
calegario, D. 3791A, CIL III 14,305, Salona, no date.
nobelissimo, D. 3791C, near Tragurium, A.D. 425.
urdenaverunt (= ordinaverunt), D. 3835, CIL III 9585, Salona, no date.
[ur]denavimus (= ordinavimus), D. 3838N, CIL III 9695, Salona, no date.

The total percentage of deviation of intertonic /ĭ/ is considerably higher than that of the other areas studied by us. [67] This is particularly true for /ĭ/ in open syllables where we have a percentage of deviation of 17.6 % in strong contrast to 0.0 % for /ĭ/ in closed syllables. Although the figures are slight for intertonic /ĭ/ in both open and closed positions, it is tempting to interpret the marked difference in the percentage of deviation as an indication that intertonic /ĭ/ was treated differently according to the nature of the syllable. It can be safely stated, however, that Dalmatian Latin once again shows more deviation than that of our other areas under study, especially African and British Latin.

---

[67] The form opteneris may be morphological rather than phonetic in nature, the simple verb teneo possibly having intervened. Since the final vowel is also incorrect, the mason may have just confused the vowels in this particular verb.

[68] It must be remembered that there was a difference in the treatment of stressed vowels according to the nature of the syllable in Dalmatian. See Bàrtoli, Das Dalmatische, pp. 327-28; Lausberg, I, 217; Hadlich, pp. 72-73. Unaccented vowels in Vegliote have extremely complex reflexes depending on position in the word and type of syllable. Cf. Bàrtoli, Das Dalmatische, II, 343-49; Hadlich, p. 74.

Balkans	Century	Open Syllable		% Of Dev.	Closed Syllable		% Of Dev.	Totals		% Of Dev.
		/ĭ/ > i	/ĭ/ > e		/ĭ/ > i	/ĭ/ > e				
(Pagan)										
	1st.	1	0		0	0		1	0	
	2nd.	2	0		0	1	100.0	2	1	33.3
	3rd.	3	0		1	0		4	0	
	4th.	3	0		0	0		3	0	
	n.d.	10	0		1	0		11	0	
	Totals:	19	0	0.0	2	1	33.3	21	1	4.5

The single case of deviation in our corpus of pagan inscriptions in the Balkans is the word [p]u[g]ellares, Kalinka 226, CIL III 14,433, Silistra (Durostorum), Moesia Inferior, A.D. 226. There are too few examples for any conclusion to be drawn.

Balkans	Century	Open Syllable		% Of Dev.	Closed Syllable		% Of Dev.	Totals		% Of Dev.
		/ĭ/ > i	/ĭ/ > e		/ĭ/ > i	/ĭ/ > e				
(Christ.)										
	4th.	4	0		1	0		5	0	
	5th.	1	0		0	0		1	0	
	n.d.	17	0		1	0		18	0	
	Totals:	22	0	0.0	2	0	0.0	24	0	0.0

When we compare Gaeng's results for the areas of the Iberian Peninsula, Gaul, Italy, and Rome, and our findings for Africa, Britain, Dalmatia, and the Balkans, we see that there is a definite difference in treatment of intertonic /ĭ/ in some areas. We will give below a composite table of all areas under consideration and our conclusions. We are taking the liberty of totaling Gaeng's figures for purposes of comparison. It is noted that Gaeng does not distinguish the syllabic nature although our findings do give figures for both open and closed syllables. We have combined our figures for open and closed syllables so as to give a composite percentage of deviation for purposes of comparison. [69]

---

[69] The difference in the nature of the syllable may be important in the treatment of intertonic /ĭ/ in Dalmatian Latin. Cf. supra, p. 202, and footnote 68, p. 202.

Summary of Intertonic /ĭ/ in the Various Areas of Romania

Area	Century	/ĭ/ > i	/ĭ/ > e	% Of Dev.
Baetica	4th - 6th	5	0	
	7th	13	2	13.3
	Totals:	18	2	10.0
Lusitania	4th - 6th	7	1	12.5
	7th	2	0	
	Totals:	9	1	10.0
Tarraconensis	4th - 6th	10	1	9.1
	7th	3	0	
	Totals:	13	1	7.1
Narbonensis	4th - 5th	10	1	9.1
	6th - 7th	18	7	28.0
	Totals:	28	8	22.2
Lugdunensis	4th - 5th	7	1	12.5
	6th - 7th	10	8	44.4
	Totals:	17	9	34.6
Northern Italy	4th - 5th	36	5	12.2
	6th	10	0	
	Totals:	46	5	9.8
Central Italy	3rd - 4th	11	0	
	5th	10	0	
	6th - 7th	23	2	8.0
	Totals:	44	2	4.3
Southern Italy	3rd - 4th	13	0	
	5th	11	1	8.3
	6th - 7th	14	1	6.7
	Totals:	38	2	5.0
Rome	3rd - 4th	83	1	1.2
	5th	54	0	
	6th - 7th	12	1	7.7
	Totals:	149	2	1.3

Area	Century	/ĭ/ > i	/ĭ/ > e	% Of Dev.
Africa	3rd.	1	0	
	4th.	16	0	
	5th.	15	0	
	6th.	29	0	
	7th.	1	0	
	n.d.	124	3	2.4
	Totals:	186	3	1.6
Britain (Pagan)	1st.	7	0	
	2nd.	26	0	
	3rd.	26	0	
	4th.	2	0	
	n.d.	40	2	4.8
	Totals:	101	2	1.9
(Christ.)	5th.	1	0	
	6th.	1	0	
	7th.	2	0	
	n.d.	1	0	
	Totals:	5	0	0.0
Dalmatia	4th.	8	0	
	5th.	8	1	11.1
	6th.	1	0	
	n.d.	28	5	15.2
	Totals:	45	6	11.8
Balkans (Pagan)	1st.	1	0	
	2nd.	2	1	33.3
	3rd.	4	0	
	4th.	3	0	
	n.d.	11	0	
	Totals:	21	1	4.5
(Christ.)	4th.	5	0	
	5th.	1	0	
	n.d.	18	0	
	Totals:	24	0	0.0

We are immediately struck by the situation in the areas of Narbonensis and Lugdunensis where the substitution of *e* for intertonic /ĭ/ is extremely notable, especially for inscriptions of the sixth and seventh centuries. There can be no doubt that we are faced with a linguistic situation that is clearly mirrored in inscriptions. The change of intertonic /ĭ/ to *e* in Narbonensis in the sixth and seventh centuries (28 % deviation on the basis of 18 correct occurrences and 7 deviations) and Lugdunensis (44.4 % deviation on the basis of ten correct occurrences and eight deviations) is in marked contrast to the situation of Africa (total percentage of deviation of 1.6 % on the basis of 186 correct occurrences and 3 deviations) and pagan Britain (1.9 % total deviations in pagan inscriptions). Of the regions in Italy, Northern Italian shows the most deviation, especially in the fourth and fifth centuries, with a 12.2 % of deviation (36 correct occurrences and five deviations). It is difficult to account for the lack of deviation in the sixth century since Northern Italian seems drawn into the linguistic orbit of Gaul with respect to the weakening of intertonic /ĭ/ to *e,* but the low number of total correct occurrences (just ten cases) is not conclusive for the later centuries of Northern Italian development. Rome, with a total percentage of deviation of 1.3 % on the basis of 149 correct occurrences and two examples of deviation, shows itself to be against any weakening of the intertonic /ĭ/. The Balkans, although the figures are inconclusive (21 correct occurrences and one deviation in pagan inscriptions and 24 correct occurrences and no examples of deviation in Christian inscriptions) seems to be stable in the treatment of intertonic /ĭ/. Dalmatia, once again, deviates from the inner Balkans with 11.8 % of deviation (45 correct occurrences and six cases of deviation). The provinces of the Iberian Peninsula (Baetica, Lusitania, and Tarraconensis) do have deviations, but there is not sufficient material to make any valid judgment.

The interpretation of the different treatment of intertonic /ĭ/ in Gaul as compared to Africa, Britain, and Rome is best expressed by an understanding of the havoc wrought by the increased stress accent in various parts of Romania. Speaking about the intertonic vowels in general in various parts of the Romance world, Lausberg remarks (I, 305-06) that "en sar. e it. (especialmente en el centro de Italia) las vocales [intertónicas] se conservan casi todas. Son menos conservadores el rum., el port., el esp. (precisamente en el orden citado). En los restantes dominios (cat., prov., fr., retorrom., norteit.) se nota una fuerte tendencia a suprimir las vocales intertónicas, lo que está en relación con una intensificación de la gradación intensiva." Our findings in the inscriptions of the various areas of Romania agree to a remarkable degree with the Lausberg gradation of intervocalic treatment of vowels (especially /ĭ/, which shows a great tendency to weaken in the area of Gaul). It is seen that once again African Latin follows the Sardinian vocalic system very closely as does British Latin. Pei's findings for the treatment of unaccented short *i* in eighth-century texts of Northern France, namely, that "the change of short unaccented *i* to *e* is very frequent in our texts. In view of the fact that short unaccented *i* for the most part disappeared in French, this erroneous spelling probably indicates the weakening of the vowel sound into the *shva* that was the forerunner of total disappearance" (p. 46) thus seem clearly foreshadowed by inscriptional evidence. A contrary opinion is given by Pirson who writes (p. 36): "Faut-il y voir ... un affaiblissement de l'*i* atone et un acheminement vers la syncope? On peut en douter si l'on considère que cet *e* existait déjà à l'époque archaïque et qu'il a persisté dans plusieurs parlers romans, en espagnol, en catalan, en roumain et aussi en italien." It is precisely by a comparative, quantitative analysis that we can see that a linguistic change, apparently widespread over a large area, does show a distinctive trend in a specific region, in this case, a weakening of intertonic /ĭ/ to *e* in Gaul and the inscriptional evidence even points to the sixth or seventh century as the decisive chronological moment for the change.

It also appears that the sudden change in treatment of intertonic /ĭ/ in the sixth or seventh century gives credence to the Wartburg theory of a strong increase of the stress accent in Gaul caused by the Germanic invasions. The Germanic influence on the development of French can be summarized by Wartburg's own words: "... les transformations qui ont conduit à la différenciation du français en face des autres langues romanes et lui ont donné son caractère propre ont été provoqueés par l'irruption des Germains et la rencontre qui en est résultée de deux systèmes articulatoires entièrement distincts." [70] The relatively weak stress accent in Gaul in the period prior to the Germanic invasions is brought out by Herman who reports (p. 69) that at the end of the fifth century "l'accent d'intensité était ... plus énergique à Rome que dans les provinces, surtout en Gaule." We thus see by the comparative study of inscriptions in the following centuries that a great change had taken place in the Latin of Gaul, which was to evolve into languages radically different from other Romance lan-

---

[70] Wartburg, *Problèmes*, p. 177. Cf. also Politzers, *Romance Trends*, p. 42.

guages and dialects. It would thus appear that the sudden emergence of a strong stress accent was the main cause of the disturbance of the development of Latin on Gaulish territory and of the peculiar evolution of the Romance languages and dialects in Gaul. Richter is also a strong advocate of the importance of an increased stress accent in the development of the Romance forms when she writes (p. 7) that "das wichtigste Characteristikum der einzelnen romanischen Sprachen und der einscheidenste Unterschied zwischen ihren Entwicklungen liegt im stärkeren oder schwächeren Anwachsen des Hervorhebungsdruckes." [71]

It is interesting to note that the weakening of the intertonic vowel, especially in Gaul, is shown by epigraphical evidence in the form of an e for /ĭ/. The reverse change, that of i for /ĕ/, is also sporadically encountered (see *supra*, p. 147 ff.), but there is no such clear pattern as is seen for /ĭ/ changing to e. The probable explanation of this one-directional movement can be found in the fact that later Romance developments do show an intertonic e as a sign of this weakening of intertonic vowels in some areas, especially Gaul, prior to their fall. In inscriptions, the use of e for /ĭ/ presumably shows that the latter sound was opening.

We will now turn to the treatment of posttonic /ĭ/, another position where a strong stress accent is felt.

Posttonic

Area	Century	/ĭ/ > i	/ĭ/ > e	% Of Dev.
Africa	3rd.	11	0	
	4th.	48	0	
	5th.	34	0	
	6th.	40	0	
	7th.	3	0	
	n.d.	297	0	
	Totals:	433	0	0.0

Posttonic /ĭ/ is extremely stable on the basis of our corpus in the Latin of Africa. We are thus led to believe that the Latin of

---

[71] It must be remembered that although the weakening of intertonic vowels, especially in Gaul, is a direct result of the increased stress accent, there are other changes independent of the stress accent. The change of initial /ē/ > i, found in third century Roman inscriptions and characteristic of modern Tuscan does not depend on a stressed accent. (See *supra*, pp. 171-72.)

this area was very little affected by any increased stress accent. Intertonic /ĭ/, as we have already seen on page 199, was likewise very stable and corroborates the belief that African Latin was very conservative in its nature.

Britain	Century	/ĭ/ > i	/ĭ/ > e	% Of Dev.
(Pagan)	1st.	10	0	
	2nd.	21	0	
	3rd.	36	2	5.3
	4th.	3	0	
	n.d.	125	1	0.8
	Totals:	195	3	1.5

The examples of deviation are:

[c]ondedit: RIB 180, CIL VII 63, Camerton (Somerdale), about A.D. 235.
perdedit: RIB 306, CIL VII 140, Lydney Park, no date.
Felicessemus: (proper name): RIB 988, CIL VII 974, Bewcastle (Banna), Cumberland, 3rd century.

Of these three examples of deviation, two are probably verbal reconstructions based on the simple verb dedit (influencing the compound verbs condedit and perdedit) rather than a phonetic change, the very low percentage of deviation of 1.5 % becoming even more insignificant. Posttonic /ĭ/ in the Latin of pagan Britain is stable on the basis of our findings. This is in complete agreement with our results for intertonic /ĭ/ (see supra, p. 200) where there is only sporadic weakening of this vowel. The stress accent did not have any great effect on either posttonic /ĭ/ or intertonic /ĭ/ in British Latin, which is what is expected on the basis of the early date of pagan inscriptions (between the first and fourth centuries).

Britain	Century	/ĭ/ > i	/ĭ/ > e	% Of Dev.
(Christ.)	4th.	1	0	
	5th.	1	3	75.0
	6th.	4	0	
	7th.	2	0	
	8th.	4	0	
	9th.	4	1	20.0
	n.d.	7	0	
	Totals:	23	4	14.8

The deviations of posttonic /ĭ/ in Christian Britain inscriptions are:

R[o]stece (proper name), CIIC 421, Llanerfyl (Wales), fifth century.
emereto, CIIC 445, Nevern (Wales), fifth century.
nomena, CIIC 448, St. David's (Wales), fifth century.
speretus (= spiritus, gen. sing.), CIIC 1011, Llanwit (Wales), A.D. 870.

Although there are only limited examples of posttonic /ĭ/ in Christian inscriptions, there seems to be greater weakening of this vowel in this position than in the pagan inscriptions of Britain. Jackson explains away these deviations by saying (p. 191) that they are "probably spelling habits introduced from Gaul without having any real phonetic bearing on British Latin pronunciation."

Dalmatia	Century	/ĭ/ > i	/ĭ/ > e	% Of Dev.
	4th.	20	0	
	5th.	13	0	
	6th.	4	0	
	n.d.	121	11	8.3
	Totals:	158	11	5.9

The deviations for this area are:

Urvece (= Urbicae, proper name), D. 941, no date.
condedit, D. 2183, CIL III 9546, Salona, no date.
hominebus, D. 2389, CIL III p. 961, Tragurium (Trogir), no date.
grandene, D. 2389, CIL III p. 9661, Tragurium (Trogir), no date.
spirete, D. 2389, CIL III p. 9661, Tragurium (Trogir), no date.
caresseme, D. 3044A, Salona, no date.
parcetur, D. 3363, CIL III 9623, Salona, no date.
tradedet (= tradidit), D. 3791, CIL III 9601, Salona, no date.
vindedit (= vendidit), D. 3791A, CIL III 14,305, Salona, no date.
fabrece, D. 3836A, CIL III 9582, Salona, no date.
c[o]rporebus, D. 4735N, CIL III 9566, Salona, no date. [72]

---

[72] We are accepting the reading as given by Skok, Pojave, p. 30, although he does add the limitation "nesigurno." Diehl gives c[o]rporiebus, but adds "videtur voluisse corporebus" (p. 458).

We see that among the deviations given, three are probably verb reconstructions and therefore morphological rather than phonetic in nature. Nevertheless, there is a weakness in posttonic /ĭ/ just as there was a confusion in intertonic /ĭ/ in the Latin of Dalmatia (see *supra*, p. 202, for the treatment of intertonic /ĭ/). Writing about the change of posttonic /ĭ/ to *e*, Skok (*Pojave*, p. 30) states that "ali i u ovom položaju ima mnogo primjera za ĭ > e." [73]

Balkans	*Century*	/ĭ/ > *i*	/ĭ/ > *e*	% Of Dev.
(Pagan)	1st.	1	0	
	2nd.	9	0	
	3rd.	7	0	
	4th.	8	0	
	n.d.	27	0	
	Totals:	52	0	0.0

Posttonic /ĭ/ in pagan inscriptions of the Balkans appears stable.

Balkans	*Century*	/ĭ/ > *i*	/ĭ/ > *e*	% Of Dev.
(Christ.)	4th.	7	1	12.5
	5th.	2	0	
	n.d.	49	1	2.0
	Totals:	58	2	3.3

The two examples of deviation in Christian inscriptions of the Balkans are:

[ca]ndeda, D. 296, CIL III 4185, Savaria (Stein am Anger), Pannonia Superior, no date.

s[a]ntisse[mi..], D. 1856A, CIL III 11,206, Carnuntum (Petronell), Pannonia Superior, fourth century.

It would seem that on the basis of just two examples of deviation compare to 58 correct occurrences, the posttonic /ĭ/ in Christian inscriptions of the Balkans was relatively stable.

---

[73] Translation of the Serbian: "But there are also in this position many examples of ĭ > e."

A comparison of Gaeng's results for the areas of the Iberian Peninsula, Gaul, Italy, and Rome, with our findings for Africa, Britain, Dalmatia, and the Balkans points to a clear differentiation of the treatment of posttonic /ĭ/ in the various areas of Romania.

Summary of the Treatment of Posttonic /ĭ/ In the Various Areas of Romania

Area	Century	/ĭ/ > i	/ĭ/ > e	% Of Dev.
Baetica	4th - 6th	20	2	9.1
	7th	24	0	
	Totals:	44	2	4.3
Lusitania	4th - 6th	13	2	13.3
	7th	6	0	
	Totals:	19	2	9.5
Tarraconensis	4th - 6th	16	5	23.8
	7th	7	0	
	Totals:	23	5	17.9
Narbonensis	4th - 5th	16	1	6.2
	6th - 7th	17	15	46.8
	Totals:	33	16	32.7
Lugdunensis	4th - 5th	15	2	11.7
	6th - 7th	16	20	55.5
	Totals:	31	22	41.5
Northern Italy	4th - 5th	66	7	9.6
	6th	21	3	12.5
	Totals:	87	10	10.3
Central Italy	3rd - 4th	20	0	
	5th	16	0	
	6th - 7th	31	0	
	Totals:	67	0	0.0
Southern Italy	3rd - 4th	46	0	
	5th	20	0	
	6th - 7th	51	0	
	Totals:	117	0	0.0

Area	Century	/ĭ/ > i	/ĭ/ > e	% Of Dev.
Rome	3rd - 4th	249	0	
	5th	132	2	1.5
	6th - 7th	63	1	1.4
	Totals:	444	3	0.7
Africa	3rd.	11	0	
	4th.	48	0	
	5th.	34	0	
	6th.	40	0	
	7th.	3	0	
	n.d.	297	0	
	Totals:	433	0	0.0
Britain (Pagan)	1st.	10	0	
	2nd.	21	0	
	3rd.	36	2	5.3
	4th.	3	0	
	n.d.	125	1	0.8
	Totals:	195	3	1.5
Britain (Christ.)	4th.	1	0	
	5th.	1	3	75.0
	6th.	4	0	
	7th.	2	0	
	8th.	4	0	
	9th.	4	1	20.0
	n.d.	7	0	
	Totals:	23	4	14.8
Dalmatia	4th.	20	0	
	5th.	13	0	
	6th.	4	0	
	n.d.	121	11	8.3
	Totals:	158	11	5.9
Balkans (Pagan)	1st.	1	0	
	2nd.	9	0	
	3rd.	7	0	
	4th.	8	0	
	n.d.	27	0	
	Totals:	52	0	0.0
Balkans (Christ.)	4th.	7	1	12.5
	5th.	2	0	
	n.d.	49	1	2.0
	Totals:	58	2	3.3

From the preceding table it is evident that the area of greatest change of posttonic /ĭ/ to *e* is Gaul. It is also clear that the sixth and seventh centuries were the decisive chronological periods for the blurring of posttonic /ĭ/ in the provinces of Narbonensis and Lugdunensis. The percentages of deviation for Narbonensis (46.8 % on the basis of 17 correct occurrences and 15 deviations) and for Lugdunensis (55.5 % on the basis of 16 correct occurrences and 20 deviations) in the sixth and seventh centuries are so great that some external factor must have intervened to have caused such a discrepancy in the treatment of posttonic vowels, especially /ĭ/, in Gaul in comparison to the situation found in other areas. The most plausible explanation is once again the Germanic invasions of Gaul with the concomitant linguistic corollary of an increased stressed accent. It is also striking to find that a parallel situation is found in the treatment of intertonic /ĭ/ where the almost exact results are recorded: an obvious cleavage between the Latin of Gaul and that of other areas and the sixth and seventh centuries as the period of time where the greatest confusion is obtained (see *supra,* p. 212 ff.). Since an increased stress accent has serious repercussions in both intertonic and posttonic positions, it is remarkable to note that the weakening of /ĭ/ is clearly paralleled in the inscriptions of Gaul for both positions and during the same chronological period.

Of the regions in Italy, Northern Italy shows the greatest percentage of deviation, showing again as it did in intertonic position a tendency to follow in Gaul's footsteps although to a lesser degree. The areas of Central Italy, Southern Italy, and Rome show, however, a strong resistance to any weakening of posttonic /ĭ/. Africa shows overwhelming stability in posttonic /ĭ/, its percentage of deviation being zero on the basis of 433 correct occurrences without a single case of deviation. Pagan Britain is likewise stable with a percentage of deviation of 1.5 % calculated on 195 correct occurrences and three deviations. Dalmatia shows a slight tendency of posttonic weakness with a percentage of deviation of 5.9 % (the figure may be less because of several verbal reconstructions; see *supra,* p. 210 ff.). The provinces of the Iberian Peninsula show varying degrees of weakness of posttonic /ĭ/, the area of Tarraconensis being most prone to a weakness (17.9 % of deviation on the basis of 23 correct occurrences and five deviations), possibly influenced by its proximity to Gaul. The Latin of the Balkans shows little tendency to a weakening of post-

tonic /ĭ/. We thus see that there is a vast difference in the treatment
of posttonic /ĭ/ in the various areas of Romania. Grandgent's statement (p. 99) concerning posttonic /ĭ/, namely that "the treatment of
this vowels was apparently very inconsistent in Vulgar Latin, and
the conditions differed widely in different regions" is undoubtedly
true, but his explanation (p. 99) that the cause of this different treatment was probably due to a "conflict between cultivated and popular
pronunciation, both types often being preserved in the Romance
languages," must be questioned. Although cultured speech was probably the norm in Britain and Africa, this criterion certainly cannot
be applied to the Latin of the Balkans where there is little tendency
to weaken posttonic /ĭ/. [74] The Latin of Gaul, where we find the
greatest weakening of posttonic /ĭ/, is generally acknowledged as an
upper-class idiom. [75] We would prefer to explain the different treatment of posttonic /ĭ/ in the various regions of the Romance world
as the result of a stronger or weaker stress accent, especially in Gaul
where the Germanic invasions caused a very strong stress accent to
come into effect in the sixth and seventh centuries.

Inscriptions do seem to show, then, an important phonological
difference in the stability or weakening of posttonic /ĭ/ in some
areas of Romania. This differentiation is later encountered in the
generally proparoxytonic structure of standard Italian, Rumanian, Dalmatian, and Sardinian (African Latin is overwhelmingly conservative
in its treatment of posttonic /ĭ/, another indication of its archaic
vocalic nature), as compared to the essentially paroxytonic structure
of the languages of the Iberian Peninsula (Spanish, Portuguese, and
Catalan), Provençal, Northern Italian dialects, and French. (See *supra*,
p. 150.)

---

[74] Wartburg, *Problèmes*, specifically states (p. 28) that "en Dacie ... pays
dépeuplé par une longue guerre, on introduissait, de nombreux colons, autre-
ment dit, des gens appartenant aux classes sociales inférieures."

[75] Wartburg, *Problèmes*, on explaining the retention of final -s in France
and Spain against the loss of -s in Italy and the Balkans writes (p. 28) that
"le traitement de l' -s reflétait donc l'opposition entre les différentes couches
sociales. L'opposition sociale entre prononciation cultivée et prononciation
vulgaire s'est donc transformée en une opposition géographique." It is difficult to conciliate the retention of final -s in French, a cultured trait, and
the weakening of posttonic /ĭ/, a popular tendency, in the same area. A
paradoxical situation is also found in Italian, where we have a loss of -s, a
popular tendency, and a stable posttonic /ĭ/, a cultured mode of speech.

We have a few isolated cases of posttonic /ĭ/ written as *u* in our inscriptions. In pagan Britain we find *Maxsu(mi)*, *RIB* 1846, *CIL* VII 786, Hadrian's Wall (Carvoran to Birdoswald), no date, and *[Max]sumi*, *RIB* 249, *CIL* VII 187, Lincoln (Lindum), no date (although this latter reading has been questioned as *[Pos]tumi* could just as easily fit into the restoration), which are probably archaic orthographies. Three interesting forms found in Latin inscriptions of Africa are: *recumen* (= *regimen*), *D.* 190, *CIL* VIII 20,908, Tipasa, no date, in a poetical inscription; *[Do]minucus* (= *Dominicus*), *D.* 1402N, and *kres[s]ume* (= *carissimae*), *D.* 4192A, *CIL* VIII 21,305, Numerus Syrorum (Mauretania Caesariensis), A.D. 359. These three forms are likewise best explained as a confusion between the archaic and classical forms. [76] The normal orthography of superlatives is -*issimus* and *maximus* (both proper and common noun) as can be seen from the following table calculated on the basis of Christian inscriptions of Africa:

Century	Superlatives in -issimus (a, um, etc.)	Maximus (a, um, etc.)
3rd.	5	0
4th.	12	4
5th.	2	1
6th.	9	2
7th.	2	0
n.d.	27	7
Totals:	57	14

Christian inscriptions overwhelmingly show posttonic /ĭ/ rather than the archaic *u*, although the sporadic occurrence of *u* probably signifies that a faint memory of the vying posttonic vowels /ĭ/ and /ŭ/ still lingers in some areas of Romania; this confusion, however, is undoubtedly more orthographical in nature than a true phonetic phenomenon.

---

[76] Cf. Sommer, p. 106: "Wo u auf jüngeren Inschriften auftritt, liegt sicher vielfach Archaismus vor." See also Väänänen, *Introduction*, p. 37; Sturtevant, pp. 119-22; Niedermann, p. 24; Lindsay, pp. 25-29.

Hiatus

Area	Cent.	Initial		Pretonic		Posttonic		Totals		% Of Dev.
		/ĭ/ > i	/ĭ/ > e	/ĭ/ > i	/ĭ/ > e	/ĭ/ > i	/ĭ/ > e			
Africa	3rd.	1	0	3	0	12	0	16	0	
	4th.	3	0	24	0	81	0	108	0	
	5th.	1	0	17	0	100	0	118	1	0.8
	6th.	3	0	24	0	51	0	78	0	
	7th.	0	0	3	0	19	0	22	0	
	n.d.	31	0	174	0	449	0	654	0	
	Totals:	39	0	245	0	712	0	996	1	0.1

The only example of an /ĭ/ in hiatus becoming an *e* is in the posttonic position in the very common word *memorea*, D. 2053, *CIL* VIII 9865, Altava (Proconsularis), A.D. 419. As can be seen from the above table, there is for all practical purposes no confusion of /ĭ/ in hiatus. It is almost impossible to detect any confusion of /ĭ/ and /ĕ/ in hiatus, any indication of the semivocalic nature of the vowel in hiatus, and any loss of syllabic value. This is substantially the same conclusion for /ĕ/ in hiatus, although the figures (2.5 % of deviation on the basis of 77 correct occurrences and two deviations, one in pretonic position and one in posttonic position) are not as overwhelmingly conclusive (see *supra*, p. 152 for /ĕ/ in hiatus in African inscriptions). It appears that the confusion of /ĕ/ and /ĭ/ in hiatus, censured in the *Appendix Probi*, is not that apparent in inscriptions (see *supra*, p. 152 for references to confusion of /ĕ/ and /ĭ/ in hiatus in the *Appendix Probi*.

Britain	Cent.	Initial		Pretonic		Posttonic		Totals		% Of Dev.
		/ĭ/ > i	/ĭ/ > e	/ĭ/ > i	/ĭ/ > e	/ĭ/ > i	/ĭ/ > e			
(Pagan)	1st.	1	0	10	0	18	0	29	0	
	2nd.	3	0	22	0	46	0	71	0	
	3rd.	3	0	54	0	85	1	142	1	0.7
	4th.	2	0	3	0	10	0	15	0	
	n.d.	17	0	79	0	234	2	331	2	0.6
	Totals:	26	0	168	0	393	3	588	3	0.5

The cases of deviation in this area are:

Cocidei (a local Celtic deity), RIB 988, CIL VII 974, Bewcastle (Banna), Cumberland, 3rd century.

Exsupereus, RIB 154, Bath (Aquae Sulis), Somerset, no date.

palleum, RIB 323, Caerleon (Isca Silurum), Monmouth, no date.

We see that /ĭ/ in hiatus in pagan inscriptions of Britain is very stable.

Britain	Cent.	Initial		Pretonic		Posttonic		Totals		% Of Dev.
		/ĭ/ > i	/ĭ/ > e	/ĭ/ > i	/ĭ/ > e	/ĭ/ > i	/ĭ/ > e			
(Christ.)	4th.	0	0	0	0	1	0	1	0	
	5th.	0	0	1	0	4	0	5	0	
	6th.	2	0	3	0	16	0	21	0	
	7th.	0	0	1	0	5	0	6	0	
	n.d.	0	0	1	0	4	1	5	1	16.7
	Totals:	2	0	6	0	30	1	38	1	2.6

The example of /ĭ/ in hiatus changing to e in Christian inscriptions in Britain is in the proper name Laurenteus, D. 2192B, no date.

Dalmatia	Cent.	Initial		Pretonic		Posttonic		Totals		% Of Dev.
		/ĭ/ > i	/ĭ/ > e	/ĭ/ > i	/ĭ/ > e	/ĭ/ > i	/ĭ/ > e			
	4th.	1	0	11	0	28	0	40	0	
	5th.	2	0	12	1	34	0	48	1	2.0
	6th.	1	0	2	0	9	0	12	0	
	n.d.	8	0	58	1	175	0	241	1	0.4
	Totals:	12	0	83	2	246	0	341	2	0.6

The two examples of deviation, both in pretonic position, are:

usteari(us) (= ostiarius), D. 3791A, CIL III 14,305, Salona, no date.

cresteanor. (= christianorum), D. 3870, CIL III 13,124, Salona, A.D. 426 or A.D. 430.

The /ĭ/ in hiatus is likewise stable in Christian inscriptions of Dalmatia.

Balkans	Cent.	Initial		Pretonic		Posttonic		Totals		% Of Dev.
		/ĭ/ > i	/ĭ/ > e	/ĭ/ > i	/ĭ/ > e	/ĭ/ > i	/ĭ/ > e			
(Pagan)	1st.	0	0	0	0	3	0	3	0	
	2nd.	0	0	4	0	8	0	12	0	
	3rd.	1	1	6	0	15	0	22	1	4.3
	4th.	1	0	3	0	7	0	11	0	
	n.d.	11	1	19	0	86	0	116	1	0.9
	Totals:	13	2	32	0	119	0	164	2	1.2

The two examples of deviation, both in initial position, are:

Deanae, Kalinka 167, CIL III 14,414, Gigen (Moesia Inferior), no date.
Deana[e], Kalinka 169, CIL III 12,370, Ferdinandowo (Moesia Inferior), A.D. 200-01.

Balkans	Cent.	Initial		Pretonic		Posttonic		Totals		% Of Dev.
		/ĭ/ > i	/ĭ/ > e	/ĭ/ > i	/ĭ/ > e	/ĭ/ > i	/ĭ/ > e			
(Christ.)	4th.	1	0	3	0	11	0	15	0	
	5th.	0	0	1	0	4	0	5	0	
	6th.	0	0	0	0	1	0	1	0	
	n.d.	13	0	41	0	97	0	151	0	
	Totals:	14	0	45	0	113	0	172	0	0.0

We see that /ĭ/ in hiatus is very stable in all areas investigated by us and the change to e is recorded only very sporadically. Our findings agree with those of Gaeng who writes (p. 158) that "in the light of the generally admitted frequent orthographic confusion of e and i as an indication of the reduction of the vowel in hiatus to a semi-vocalic quality, it may be surprising to find an abundant sampling of Latin /ĭ/ appearing as i in spelling." It appears that epigraphic material for all of Romania does not corroborate Grandgent's statement (p. 94) that there arose "in late Latin spelling, a great confusion of e and i in hiatus."

Loss of /ĭ/ in Hiatus

Since two vowels in hiatus disturb the usual syllable norm in the sense that between two sounds of great aperture (vowels) an element of slight aperture (consonant) is missing, which usually divides two syllables, an attempt is made to do away with vowels in hiatus. [77] A common means is for one of the vowels in hiatus to be dropped. The Romance languages show that the Latin *quietus* evolved popularly with loss of /ĭ/ in hiatus: Fr. *coi*, Sp. Port. *quedo*, It. *cheto*, Rum. *cet*. This procedure is encountered in inscriptions although it is complicated by the problem of determining when a real loss of /ĭ/ in hiatus took place, and when we are faced with a simple abbreviation. We will give below a number of examples of loss of /ĭ/ in hiatus in initial, pretonic, and posttonic positions.

In initial position, we have:

> *quevit*, D. 388, *CIL* VIII 10,516, Ammaedara (Byzacena), A.D. 526.
> *quaevi<t>* (= *quievit*), D. 3104, *CIL* VIII 11,123, Lepti Minore, no date.
> *que(vit)*: D. 3106E, *CIL* VIII 5498, Calama (Proconsularis), no date.
> *quescunt*, D. 3476, *CIL* III 3551, Aquincum (Budapest), Pannonia Inferior, no date.
> *ceqquet* (= *quiescit*), D. 328, *CIL* VIII 21,428, Caesarea Maurorum, no date.
> *Quetus* (proper name), D. 3718, *CIL* VIII 20,304, Satafi (Mauretania Sitifensis), A.D. 349.
> *quevit*, D. 1892, Tigzirt, no date.

The loss of /ĭ/ in prettonic position is found in the following examples:

> *requet.* (= *requietionem* or *requievit*), D. 1470, Tingi (Mauretania Tingitana), A.D. 345.
> *exerun[t]*, D. 2774, *CIL* VIII 16,907, Madaura (Proconsularis), no date.
> *sunzaconus* (= *subdiaconus*), D. 1248, *CIL* VIII 21,588, Mauretania Caesariensis, A.D. 457.
> *promisonis* (= *promissionis*), D. 2068, *CIL* VIII 20,600, Tocqueville, A.D. 359.

---

[77] Väänänen, *Introduction*, p. 45.

cristan(um) (= *christianum*), *D.* 2093, *CIL* VIII 2334, near
Thamugadi (Numidia), no date.

The loss of /ĭ/ in posttonic position, complicated because of
the difficulty in determining whether the loss is a real dropping of the
vowel in hiatus, a simple abbreviation, or a change in suffix, is found
in the following cases:

> *tertu* (= *tertio*), *D.* 1383, *CIL* VIII 23,586, Maktar (Byza-
> cena), no date.
> *Atanasus* (= *Athanasius*), *D.* 2643, *CIL* VIII 13,469, Car-
> thage (Proconsularis), no date.
> *Marsas* (= *Martias*), *D.* 2863, *CIL* VIII 21,595, Mauretania
> Caesariensis, A.D. 488.
> *Evasse* (= *Evasiae*), *D.* 2866, *CIL* VIII 9804, Albulae (Mau-
> retania Caesariensis), A.D. 418.
> *Evasa*, *D.* 3095B, *CIL* VIII 21,476, Sufasar, no date.
> *Resus* (= *Resius?*), *D.* 3272C, *CIL* VIII 9815, Albulae
> (Mauretania Caesariensis), probably A.D. 444.
> *facunt* (= *faciunt*), *D.* 3476, *CIL* III 3551, Aquincum
> (Budapest), Pannonia Inferior, no date. The Rumanian
> verb form *fac* is posited on this form. [78]
> *Evassu* (= *Evasius*), *D.* 3610, *CIL* III 9578, Salona (Dal-
> matia), no date.
> *Ultima* (= *Voltinia*), *RIB* 1545, Hadrian's Wall (Carraw-
> burgh) (Brocolitia), Northumberland, A.D. 198-211.
> *provincae*, *D.* 189, *CIL* VIII 20,410, Sitifis (Mauretania
> Sitifensis), A.D. 454.
> *reque* (= *requie*), *D.* 2720, *CIL* VIII 25,411, Utica (Pro-
> consularis), no date.
> *memore* (= *memoriae*), *D.* 1100, *CIL* VIII 2009, Theveste
> (Proconsularis), no date.
> *Octava*, *D.* 2802, *CIL* III 8879, Salona, no date.
> *Cassus* (= *Cassius?*), *D.* 2849, *CIL* VIII 21,639, Arbal,
> A.D. 419.
> *deposito*, *D.* 3042, *CIL* III 9563, Salona, probably A.D.
> 344.
> *memore* (= *memoriae*), *D.* 3153, *CIL* VIII 27,918, Theveste
> (Proconsularis), no date.
> *mila* (= *milia*), *D.* 3854, Iader (Dalmatia), sixth century.
> This form is the base of the Italian *mila*. The Latin
> *milia* gives Old Rumanian *mie* as plural. The change of
> Rumanian *mie* to the singular brought about the analog-

---

[78] Rosetti, I, 130.

ical modern Rumanian plural *mii*. [79] The form *mila* is
an apparent example of an Italo-Romance influence on
Dalmatian soil rather than the Balkan Romance form.

A special case of the loss of /ĭ/ in hiatus is the contraction of
/ĭ/ followed by a /ī/ in morphological endings of second declension
genitive singulars, second declension nominative plurals, and first and
second declension dative and ablative plurals of i-stems. We will give
in tabular form below our findings for full and contracted endings in
our areas of Africa, Britain, Dalmatia, and the Balkans.

Area	*Century*	Genitive Sing.			Nominative Pl.			Dative & Abl. Plur.		
		-i	*-ii*	% of *-i*	*-i*	*-ii*	% of *-i*	*-is*	*-iis*	% of *-is*
Africa	3rd.	1	0		0	0		1	0	
	4th.	9	2		7	3		2	0	
	5th.	16	2		2	0		1	1	
	6th.	6	1		9	0		0	2	
	7th.	0	1		0	0		0	0	
	n.d.	50	4		5	0		6	4	
	Totals:	82	10	89.1	23	3	88.5	10	7	58.8
Britain	1st.	3	0		0	0		0	0	
	2nd.	6	0		0	0		0	1	
(Pagan)	3rd.	4	2		0	0		0	0	
	4th.	6	0		0	0		0	0	
	n.d.	35	1		3	0		8	3	
	Totals:	54	3	94.7	3	0	100.0	8	4	66.7
(Christ.)	5th.	4	0		0	0		0	0	
	6th.	8	1		0	1		0	0	
	7th.	3	0		0	0		0	0	
	n.d.	5	1		0	0		0	0	
	Totals:	20	2	90.9	0	1	0.0	0	0	0.0
Dalmatia	4th.	7	0							
	5th.	8	1							
	6th.	0	2							
	n.d.	7	2					1	0	
	Totals:	22	5	81.5				1	0	100.0

---

[79] Lausberg, II, 254.

Area	Century	Genitive Sing.			Nominative Pl.			Dative & Abl. Plur.		
		-i	-ii	% of -i	-i	-ii	% of -i	-is	-iis	% of -is
Balkans	1st.	1	0							
	3rd.	1	0							
(Pagan)	4th.	2	0							
	n.d.	6	0		0	1		2	2	
	Totals:	10	0	100.0	0	1	0.0	2	2	50.0
(Christ.)	6th.	0	1							
	n.d.	4	2		1	1		0	1	
	Totals:	4	3	57.1	1	1	50.0	0	1	0.0

From the above table we see that the contracted form is, for the most part, generally used in inscriptions of the areas of Africa, Britain, Dalmatia, and the Balkans. Speaking of the contraction of the endings of the nominative plural and dative and ablative plural (-ii to -i and -iis to -is), Väänänen mentions (*Introduction*, p. 45) that "la contraction des désinences -iī, -iīs, bien que rare dans la métrique ancienne et classique, devait cependant être courante dans la langue parlée, témoin les inscriptions d'allure populaire." Our findings show that the contracted form is more common than the full form in the nominative and dative and ablative plural endings. As for the genitive singular ending where -i is the primitive ending and -ii appears only after Virgil and Propertius, [80] our inscriptions show that the contracted form is definitely preferred.

Transitional i Between Vowels in Hiatus

If the vowels in hiatus are of too different timbres to be contracted, the most natural expedient, from a physiological point of view, is to insert between them a transitional consonant, *y* or *w*, according to the nature of the vowels in contact. [81] Although a transitional *y*, as in modern French *bayer* or in the pronunciation of modern French

---

[80] Väänänen, *Introduction*, p. 46; see also Ernout, *Morphologie*, pp. 28-29: "Les génitifs en -iī ne commencèrent à se répandre dans les substantifs que vers la fin du règne d'Auguste, et ne se généralisèrent que sous Domitien." Concerning the history of the dative and ablative plural of i-stems, Ernout says (p. 33) that "comme le nominatif en -ii, cette forme (-iis) demeure non contracte pendant toute la période républicaine... La contraction commence à l'époque impériale." Cf. Sommer, pp. 338-41, 347, 350.

[81] Väänänen, *Introduction*, p. 46; Niedermann, p. 104.

plier as *pli-y-er*, is not as common as transitional *w*, as in Italian *rovina* < *ruina*, *vettovaglia* < *victualia*, or French *pouvoir* < *potere*, Latin inscriptions and manuscripts have several examples of this transitional *i* in the words *eiius, cuiius, maiiorem, maiiestati, coiiux, Traiiani, aiiunt*, and *peiius*.[82] Ordinary Latin orthography usually presented these forms with a single *i*. Our inscriptions show several cases of *-ii* in the areas of Africa and Britain. In Africa, we have:

> *eiius*, D. 403, *CIL* VIII 21,634, Arbal (Mauretania Caesariensis), A.D. 372.
> *Maiias*, D. 2791, *CIL* VIII 21,479, Sufasar, A.D. 318.
> *Maiias*, D. 2858, *CIL* VIII 21,728, Altava (Mauretania Caesariensis), A.D. 361.
> *Maiias*, D. 3052A, *CIL* VIII 21,539, near Mina in Mauretania Maesariensis, no date.
> *ipsiius*, D. 3622N, *CIL* VIII 8640, Sitifis (Mauretania Sitifensis), no date.
> *Maiiorica*, D. 4360A, *CIL* VIII 21,644, Arbal (Mauretania Caesariensis), A.D. 366.

From Latin inscriptions of Britain, both pagan and Christian, we have:

> *eiius*, *RIB* 601, *CIL* VII 285, Lancaster, no date. (Pagan inscription.)
> *muliier*, *CIIC* 356, Cardigan (Wales), no date. (Christian inscription.)

The existence of this orthographic *i* between vowels in hiatus may be explained as a simple archaism to show this transitional sound. Attempting to explain the particular form *muliier*, Macalister writes (*CIIC*, I, 341) that "the reading *muliier* is certain; it is evidently a misspelling of *mulier*," or continuing in a footnote on the same page, he adds that it is "possibly an attempt to represent a word phonetically conceived as *muliyer*." Cicero used *-ii* quite often in an apparent attempt to distinguish cultured speech from popular speech.[83] This attempt to show careful speech, especially in British Latin, has been brought out by Jackson who considers hiatus-filling *u* the result of a "desire to preserve carefully the two syllables" in hiatus.[84] Since a

---

[82] Niedermann, p. 106; Sommer, p. 155; Grandgent, p. 114.
[83] Richter, p. 59.
[84] Jackson, *Language*, p. 87.

transitional *u* is also found in the Continental variety of Vulgar Latin, this innovation cannot be considered as particular to British Latin, but, as Jackson reminds us (p. 87), "its frequency in Britain implies careful speech." At any rate it is interesting to note that all our examples come from Africa and Britain where the vocalic systems are archaic in nature. (We will discuss transitional *u* in detail in its appropriate place.)

Final (Non-Morphological)

The results of Latin /ĭ/ in final syllable of non-morphological forms, mostly adverbs, are as follows:

Area	Century	/ĭ/ > i	/ĭ/ > e	% Of Dev.
Africa	6th.	1	0	
	n.d.	13	0	
	Totals:	14	0	0.0
Britain (Pagan)	1st.	1	0	
	n.d.	2	0	
	Totals:	3	0	0.0
(Christ.)	8th.	0	0	0.0
Dalmatia	4th.	1	0	
	n.d.	6	0	
	Totals:	7	0	0.0
Balkans (Pagan)		NO EXAMPLES		
(Christ.)	4th.	1	0	
	n.d.	1	1	50.0
	Totals:	2	1	33.3

The single example of deviation in Christian inscriptions of the Balkans is in the adverb *beni,* D. 4323N, *CIL* III 14,524, near Viminacium (Moesia Superior), no date.

Although the total number of occurrences of /ĭ/ in final syllable is relatively low, final /ĭ/ seems stable.

Morphological Endings: Declensional (Nouns and Adjectives)

The two most important categories where final /ĭ/ is found in inscriptions are the third declension nominative singular ending -*is* and the third declension genitive singular ending -*is*. We have already said (see *supra,* p. 154 ff.) that a relationship exists between the treatment of final vowels and a strong stress accent. We will first give our findings for final /ĭ/ in the areas of Africa, Britain, Dalmatia, and the Balkans and then compare them with those of Gaeng.

Area	Century	3rd Declen. Nomin. Sing.		% Of Dev.	3rd Declen. Genit. Sing.		% Of Dev.	Totals		% Of Dev.
		-*is*	-*es*		-*is*	-*es*				
Africa	3rd.	1	0		0	0		1	0	
	4th.	7	0		16	0		23	0	
	5th.	3	0		12	0		15	0	
	6th.	6	0		15	0		21	0	
	7th.	1	0		0	0		1	0	
	n.d.	111	5	4.3	92	0		203	5	2.9
	Totals:	129	5	3.9	135	0		264	5	1.9

The five examples of change in the nominative singular of third declension nouns from /ĭ/ to *e* are:

santimoniale (= *sanctimonialis*) D. 1683, *CIL* VIII 10,689, Theveste (Proconsularis), no date.
Apriles (proper name), D. 2648, Thabraca (Proconsularis), no date.
fidele, D. 1410, *CIL* VIII 25,313, Carthage (Proconsularis), no date.
dulce, D. 2543N, Thabraca (Proconsularis), no date.
Vitale (proper name), D. 2653, Hadrumetum (Byzacena), no date.

On the basis of the total percentage of deviation, we see that final /ĭ/ is stable in noun-adjective endings in the Latin of Africa. There is very little weakening of /ĭ/ in the final syllable and even those cases where we do find *e* for /ĭ/ it is probable that the change is more morphological than phonetic. Of the five cases of deviation in the third declension nominative singular endings, four examples show the same change, namely a final -*e* for -*is*. Although this change of /ĭ/ to *e* appears in these four cases with a loss of final -*s* and may be phonetic,[85] there is the possibility that we have a change of morphological endings, the neuter adjective ending *-e* (note that all the forms are adjectives) replacing the masculine and feminine ending *-is*. We may also have an incipient development of the one-form oblique case. The final deviation *Apriles* may be simply a confusion of the third declension nominative singular endings *-is* and *-es*, a morphological extension rather than a phonetic change. (See *supra*, p. 154 ff. for a discussion of the confusion of *-is* and *-es*.) It is significant that in the genitive singular of third declension nouns and adjectives, where there is little probability of a morphological substitution, there is no case of a change of /ĭ/ to *e*.

Area	Century	3rd Declen. Nomin. Sing.		% Of Dev.	3rd Declen. Genit. Sing.		% Of Dev.	Totals		% Of Dev.
		-is	-es		-is	-es				
Britain	1st.	5	1	16.7	1	0		6	1	14.3
	2nd.	6	0		5	0		11	0	
(Pagan)	3rd.	1	0		9	0		10	0	
	4th.	1	0		0	0		1	0	
	n.d.	22	5	18.5	28	0		50	5	9.1
	Totals:	35	6	14.6	43	0		78	6	7.1

All six examples of deviation are found in the noun *cives*:

cives, RIB 108, *CIL* VII 66, Cirencester, no date.
cives, RIB 149, Bath (Aquae Sulis), Somerset, no date.
cives, RIB 159, *CIL* VII 52, Bath (Aquae Sulis), first century.
cives, RIB 621, Templebrough (Yorkshire), no date.
cives, RIB 678, *CIL* VII 248, York (Eboracum), no date.
cives, RIB 2046, *CIL* VII 944, Hadrian's Wall, Burgh-by-Sands (Aballava), Cumberland, no date.

---

[85] Although there are cases of the loss of final *-s* in African inscriptions, it must be very seriously questioned whether this was a common occurrence in this area. The vocalism of the Latin of Africa is extremely similar to that of Sardinia as we have seen throughout the present work and although there is no certainty that the African Latin consonantal system follows the consonantal system of Sardinia, it would be surprising if African Latin did not follow the Sardinian pattern of preserving Latin final *-s*. A comparative and quantitative study of Latin final *-s* has yet to be carried out. Proskauer's *Das auslautende -s auf den lateinischen Inschriften* (Strassburg: Karl J. Trübner, 1909), although comparative, does not offer any statistical evidence for the loss or maintenance of final *-s* and must be considered inconclusive.

The correct form *civis* is found five times: *RIB* 109, 2nd century, *RIB* 103, 4th century, and three times in undated inscriptions: *RIB* 110, *RIB* 140, and *RIB* 684. We thus see that *cives* is more commonly used than the Classical Latin *civis* and we probably have a case of morphological confusion between *-is* and *-es*. This confusion of final vowels in a single word is very reminiscent of our findings for final *-e* in verb forms in Christian Britain, where the only deviation of /ĕ/ to *i* is found in the verb *iacit* (the correct *iacet* is found 5 times compared to the variant *iacit* found 33 times. See *supra*, p. 165). We thus conclude that final /ĭ/ in the pagan inscriptions of Britain is stable except for the single noun *cives* which, as a result of a morphological confusion, is preferred in this one case.

Britain	Century	3rd Declen. Nomin. Sing.		% Of Dev.	3rd Declen. Genit. Sing.		% Of Dev.	Totals		% Of Dev.
		-is	-es		-is	-es				
(Christ.)										
	4th.	1	0		0	0		1	0	
	5th.	0	1	100.0	1	0		1	1	50.0
	7th.	0	0		1	0		1	0	
	8th.	0	0		1	0		1	0	
	9th.	0	0		1	1	50.0	1	1	50.0
	n.d.	0	0		3	0		3	0	
	Totals:	1	1	50.0	7	1	12.5	8	2	20.0

The two examples of final /ĭ/ to *e* in Christian inscriptions are:

cive (= *civis*, nominative singular), D. 378a, *CIIC* 394, Penmachno (Carnarvon), Wales, fifth century.
pa[tr]es (= *patris*, genitive singular), *CIIC* 1011, Llantwit (Glamorgan), Wales, A.D. 870.

The figures are too scanty for any conclusion to be drawn with respect to the final /ĭ/ in Christian inscriptions of Britain.

Dalmatia	Century	3rd Declen. Nomin. Sing.		% Of Dev.	3rd Declen. Genit. Sing.		% Of Dev.	Totals		% Of Dev.
		-is	-es		-is	-es				
	4th.	2	0		6	0		8	0	
	5th.	1	0		4	1	20.0	5	1	16.7
	6th.	0	1	100.0	0	1	100.0	0	2	100.0
	n.d.	19	0		13	2	13.3	32	2	5.9
	Totals:	22	1	4.3	23	4	14.8	45	5	10.0

The following are the deviations in the Dalmatian inscriptions:

Domniones (=genitive of proper name *Domnio*), *D*. 1084, *CIL* III 14,897, Salona, no date.
martores (= *martyris*, gen. sing.), *D*. 1084, *CIL* III 14,897, Salona, no date.
Sermenses (= *Sirmiensis*, nom. sing.), *D*. 1653, *CIL* III 9551, Salona, A.D. 506 or 551.
Veneres (= *Veneris*, genit. sing.), *D*. 1653, *CIL* III 9551, Salona, A.D. 506 or 551.
Balentes (= *Valentis*, genit. sing.), *D*. 3870, *CIL* III 13,124, Salona, A.D. 426.

Although the change of final /ĭ/ to *e* in *Sermenses* is probably a morphological substitution, the other examples occur in the genitive singular where a phonetic change is undoubtedly the main cause. This is in marked contrast to our findings for final /ĭ/ in Africa and pagan Britain where we did not find any change to *e* in genitive singular forms although there were some changes in the nominative singular, where morphological extension is very probable.

Balkans	Century	3rd Declen. Nomin. Sing.		% Of Dev.	3rd Declen. Genit. Sing.		% Of Dev.	Totals		% Of Dev.
		-is	*-es*		*-is*	*-es*				
(Pagan)										
	1st.	0	0		2	0		2	0	
	2nd.	1	0		0	0		1	0	
	3rd.	0	0		2	0		2	0	
	n.d.	8	0		1	1	50.0	9	1	10.0
	Totals:	9	0		5	1	16.7	14	1	6.7

The single example of deviation in the pagan inscriptions of the Balkans is [*leg*]*ione* (= *legionis*, gen. sing.), *Kalinka* 387, *CIL* III 14,211, Aboba (Moesia Inferior), no date. There are not enough occurrences for any definite conclusion to be made.

Balkans	Century	3rd Declen. Nomin. Sing.		% Of Dev.	3rd Declen. Genit. Sing.		% Of Dev.	Totals		% Of Dev.
		-is	*-es*		*-is*	*-es*				
(Christ.)										
	4th.	2	0		0	0		2	0	
	n.d.	1	0		7	0		8	0	
	Totals:	3	0	0.0	7	0	0.0	10	0	0.0

The total number of occurrences is too low for any definite conclusion to be made.

We will now proceed to an analysis of verb forms ending in /ĭ/ to see whether there is anything distinctive in the treatment of /ĭ/ in the various areas of Romania. The verb terminations most often found in inscriptions are the -it of the present perfect indicative, the -it and -is of third and fourth conjugations in the present indicative, the -tis of the second person plural of all conjugations, the -it of both the future perfect indicative and the present perfect subjunctive, the -bit and -bis of first and second conjugations in the future indicative, and the -it, -itis, and -int of irregular present subjunctives.

Africa:

Cent.	Perf. Ind. 3rd Pers.		% Of Dev.	Pres. Ind. 3rd Pers.		% Of Dev.	Pres. Ind. 2nd Pers.		% Of Dev.	Pres. Ind. 2nd Plur.	
	-it	-et		-it	-et		-is	-es		-tis	-tes
3rd.	6	0		1	0		0	0			
4th.	44	0		1	0		2	0			
5th.	104	0		4	0		1	0			
6th.	24	0		0	0		2	1	33.3		
7th.	1	0		0	0		0	0			
n.d.	359	0		30	7		0	0		1	0
Totals:	538	0		36	7	18.9	5	1	16.7	1	0

Cent.	Future Perf. & Perf. Subj.		% Of Dev.	Future Ind.		% Of Dev.	Future Ind.		% Of Dev.
	-it	-et		-bit	-bet		-bis	-bes	
4th.	0	0		0	0		2	0	
5th.	2	0		0	0		0	0	
n.d.	7	0		3	0		1	0	
Totals:	9	0		3	0		3	0	

The examples of deviation in verb forms, found only for the second and third persons singular of third conjugation verbs in the present indicative, are:

> *lege* (= *legis*, 2nd pres. sing., pres. ind.), D. 1627, Hr.
> Zoura, sixth century.
> *quiescet*, D. 1697, *Carthage* (Proconsularis), no date.
> *tribuet*, D. 2031, *CIL* VIII 17,386, Thabraca (Proconsularis),
> no date.

cisquet (= *quiescit*), *D.* 3095B, *CIL* VIII 21,476, Sufasar, no date.
[r]*eddet*, *D.* 1618, *CIL* VIII 12,130, Chusira (Byzacena), no date.
ceqquet (= *quiescit*), *D.* 3628, *CIL* VIII 21,428, Caesarea Maurorum, no date.
requiescet, *D.* 4456A, *CIL* VIII 8190, Rusicade (Numidia), no date.
teget D. 4736, Madauros (Proconsularis), no date.

It is most significant to note that the only changes of /ĭ/ to *e* occur in the present indicative. The numerically superior endings of the present perfect indicative all end in -*it*.[86] It would appear that we are faced with a conjugational change of third conjugation verbs passing over to the second conjugation, which is, of course, a fairly common change in the development of the Romance languages.[87] The extreme stability of the other verb forms, especially the 538 cases of the perfect indicative ending in -*it* without any deviation, leads us to the conclusion that final /ĭ/ in African Latin was not phonetically confused with /ĕ/, although there are cases of conjugational confusion which is essentially morphological in nature. This stability of final /ĭ/ is an excellent indication of the conservative nature of the vocalism of African Latin, a situation which we have seen throughout our entire analysis of the Latin inscriptions of this area.

---

[86] We have a single deviation in the third person singular of the present perfect indicative in the verb form *feciit*, *D.* 3681, *CIL* VIII 9910, Pomaria (Mauretania Caesariensis), no date. It is difficult to ascertain, however, whether this form is written in cursive script with the -*iit* equivalent to an -*et*, the -*iit* is a morphological substitution (cf. *periit*), or is simply a scribal error.

[87] Lausberg, II, 259-61. It is significant that Sardinian also fuses forms of the second and third conjugations in verb paradigms. Compare the reflex of the second conjugation verb *videre* in the second and third persons singular present indicative: *bides, bidet/bidede* and the third conjugation verb *vendere* in the same persons of the present indicative: *béndet/béndede* (Lausberg, II, 329, 337).

Britain (Pagan)

Century	Perf. Ind. 3rd Pers.		% Of Dev.	Pres. Ind. 3rd Pers.		% Of Dev.	Pres. Ind. 2nd Plur.		% Of Dev.	Pres. Subj. 3rd Person	
	-it	*-et*		*-it*	*-et*		*-tis*	*-tes*		Sing. *-it*	Plur. *-int*
1st.	2	0					1	0			
2nd.	9	0					0	0			
3rd.	25	0					0	0			
n.d.	107	0		1	0		1	0		2	1
Totals:	143	0	0.0	1	0	0.0	2	0	0.0	2	1

On the basis of our findings, especially in the third person singular ending of the perfect indicative ending -*it,* the final /ĭ/ in the Latin inscriptions of pagan Britain is stable. This conservatism is in keeping with the general Classical Latin appearance of British Latin.

British	Century	Perf. Ind. 3rd Person		% Of Dev.
		-it	*-et*	
(Christ.)	4th.	2	0	
	5th.	3	0	
	6th.	1	0	
	7th.	1	0	
	8th.	1	0	
	9th.	4	0	
	n.d.	4	0	
	Totals:	16	0	0.0

We did not observe any deviation in final /ĭ/ in verb forms of the Latin of Christian Britain, although the total number of occurrences is low.

Dalmatia

Century	Perf. Ind. 3rd Pers.		% Of Dev.	Pres. Ind. 3rd Pers.		% Of Dev.	Pres. Ind. 2nd Pers.		Pres. Ind. 2nd Plur.	
	-it	*-et*		*-it*	*-et*		*-is*	*-es*	*-tis*	*-tes*
4th.	2	0		1	0					
5th.	14	0		3	1	25.0				
6th.	8	0		1	0					
n.d.	66	2	2.9	4	3	42.9	2	0	1	0
Totals:	90	2	2.2	9	4	30.8	2	0	1	0

Century	Fut. Perf. -it	Fut. Perf. -et	% Of Dev.	Fut. Perf. -it	Fut. Perf. -et	Fut. Perf. -int	Fut. Perf. -ent	Fut. Ind. -bit	Fut. Ind. -bet	Pres. Subj. -it	Pres. Subj. -et	% Of Dev.
4th.	4	1	20.0					1	0			
5th.	2	0						0	0			
6th.	1	0						1	0	0	1	100.0
n.d.	15	1	6.3	2	0	1	0	4	0	3	0	
Totals:	22	2	8.3	0	0	1	0	6	0	3	1	25.0

The deviations of final /ĭ/ in this area are:

(a) perfect indicative:

perquouset (= *percussit*), D. 2426, CIL III 10,190, Podgorica, no date.
tradedet (= *tradidit*), D. 3791, CIL III 9601, Salona, no date.

(b) present indicative:

requiiscet, D. 307, CIL III 2657, Salona, A.D. 435.
quiescet, D. 328A, CIL III 9532, Salona, no date,
solvet, D. 1940, CIL III 10,146, Island of Apsori, no date.
corret (= *currit*), D. 2389, CIL III p. 961, Tragurium, no date.

(c) future perfect indicative:

volueret, D. 507, Salona, no date.
volueret, D. 3835C, CIL III 9508, Salona, A.D. 382.

(d) present subjunctive:

vellet (= *velit*), D. 3854, Iader, 6th cent.

We thus see that the deviations are greater in this area than in the others which we have studied, although the problem is complicated because of the difficulty in determining which changes are primarily due to a real phonetic weakening of the final vowel and which are mainly morphological substitutions.

Balkans (Pagan)

Century	Perf. Ind. 3rd Pers.		% Of Dev.	Pres. Ind. 3rd Pers.		% Of Dev.	Fut. Perf.		% Of Dev.	Pres. Subj.	
	-it	*-et*		*-it*	*-et*		*-int*	*-ent*		*-itis*	*-ites*
1st.	1	0									
2nd.	1	0									
3rd.	1	0									
n.d.	38	0		0	1	100.0	1	0		1	0
Totals:	41	0	0.0	0	1	100.0	1	0	0.0	1	0

The single case of deviation in our corpus is the verb form *petet*, *Kalinka* 412, Nicopolis ad Istrum (Moesia Inferior), no date. On the basis of the 41 cases of the correct *-it* termination for the third person singular of the present perfect without any deviations, it seems that final /ĭ/ is stable in the Latin of the pagan inscriptions of the Balkans.

Balkans (Christian)

Century	Pres. Perf. 3rd Pers.		% Of Dev.	Pres. Ind. 3rd Pers.		% Of Dev.	Pres. Ind. 2nd Plur.		% Of Dev.	Fut. Ind.	
	-it	*-et*		*-it*	*-et*		*-tis*	*-tes*		*erit:*	*eret*
4th.	5	0		0	0					1	0
5th.	1	0		1	0					0	0
n.d.	40	1	2.4	4	2	33.3	1	0		2	0
Totals:	46	1	2.1	5	2	28.6	1	0	0.0	3	0

The following are the deviations in the Christian inscriptions of the Balkans:

(a)　present perfect:

　　vixcet (= *vixit*), D. 3659, Purbach (Pannonia), no date.

(b)　present indicative

　　r[e]quiescet, D. 215, *CIL* III 14,207, Serdica (Sofia), Thrace, no date.

　　requiescet, D. 1089, *CIL* III 14,207, Serdica (Sofia), Thrace, no date.

The final /ĭ/ in Christian inscriptions is apparently stable in the third person singular of the present perfect indicative, but modifications take place in the third person singular of the present indicative, but these may be more morphological than phonetic in nature.

We will now compare our results in both noun-adjective endings and verb terminations with those of Gaeng in these same categories. To simplify matters we will compare the nominative singular and genitive singular of nouns and adjectives of the third declension as representative of nouns and adjectives, and the third person singular of third and fourth conjugation verbs in the present indicative and the third person singular of the perfect indicative of all conjugations to see whether final /ĭ/ differs in its treatment throughout the various areas of Romania. We have excluded other substantive and verbal endings in -is or -it because of their low frequency of occurrence in epigraphical material. We will also try to determine whether the change of /ĭ/ to e in final position is due mainly to phonetic or morphological reasons or whether there is an admixture of both in a change that occurs in varying degrees in the later Romance languages and dialects.

Area	Century	3rd Decl. Nom. Sing.		% Of Dev.	3rd Decl. Gen. Sing.		% Of Dev.	Totals		% Of Dev.
		-is	-es		-is	-es				
Baetica	4th-6th	4	1	20.0	1	0		5	1	16.7
	7th	6	0		9	0		15	0	
	Totals:	10	1	9.1	10	0	0.0	20	1	4.8
Lusitania	4th-6th	1	0		1	0		2	0	
	7th	0	0		2	0		2	0	
	Totals:	1	0	0.0	3	0	0.0	4	0	0.0
Tarraco-	4th-6th	6	2	25.0	5	1	16.7	11	3	21.4
nensis	7th	0	0		2	0		2	0	
	Totals:	6	2	25.0	7	1	12.5	13	3	18.8
Narbo-	4th-5th	4	0		3	0		7	0	
nensis	6th-7th	3	2	40.0	12	5	29.4	15	7	31.8
	Totals:	7	2	22.2	15	5	25.0	22	7	24.1
Lugdu-	4th-5th	2	0		5	0		7	0	
nensis	6th-7th	6	1	14.3	8	2	20.0	14	3	17.6
	Totals:	8	1	11.1	13	2	13.3	21	3	12.5

Area	Century	3rd Decl. Nom. Sing.		% Of Dev.	3rd Decl. Gen. Sing.		% Of Dev.	Totals		% Of Dev.
		-is	*-es*		*-is*	*-es*				
Northern	4th-5th	13	1	7.1	12	0		25	1	3.8
Italy	6th	1	0		10	3	23.1	11	3	21.4
	Totals:	14	1	6.7	22	3	12.0	36	4	10.0
Central	3rd-4th	2	0		4	0		6	0	
Italy	5th	4	0		5	1	16.7	9	1	10.0
	6th-7th	1	0		16	0		17	0	
	Totals:	7	0	0.0	25	1	3.8	32	1	3.3
Southern	3rd-4th	3	1	25.0	3	0		6	1	14.3
Italy	5th	2	1	33.3	11	3	21.4	13	4	23.5
	6th-7th	3	1	25.0	31	2	6.1	34	3	8.1
	Totals:	8	3	27.3	45	5	10.0	53	8	13.1
Rome	3rd-4th	16	4	20.0	35	1	2.8	51	5	8.9
	5th	15	2	11.7	26	0		41	2	4.6
	6th-7th	9	0		12	1	7.6	21	1	4.5
	Totals:	40	6	13.0	73	2	2.7	113	8	6.6
Africa	3rd.	1	0		0	0		1	0	
	4th.	7	0		16	0		23	0	
	5th.	3	0		12	0		15	0	
	6th.	6	0		15	0		21	0	
	7th.	1	0		0	0		1	0	
	n.d.	111	5	4.3	92	0		203	5	2.9
	Totals:	129	5	3.9	135	0	0.0	264	5	1.9
Britain	1st.	5	1	16.7	1	0		6	1	14.3
(Pagan)	2nd.	6	0		5	0		11	0	
	3rd.	1	0		9	0		10	0	
	4th.	1	0		0	0		1	0	
	n.d.	22	5	18.5	28	0		50	5	9.1
	Totals:	35	6	14.6	43	0	0.0	78	6	7.1
Britain	4th.	1	0		0	0		1	0	
(Christ.)	5th.	0	1	100.0	1	0		1	1	50.0
	7th.	0	0		1	0		1	0	
	8th.	0	0		1	0		1	0	
	9th.	0	0		1	1	50.0	1	1	50.0
	n.d.	0	0		3	0		3	0	
	Totals:	1	1	50.0	7	1	12.5	8	2	20.0
Dalmatia	4th.	2	0		6	0		8	0	
	5th.	1	0		4	1	20.0	5	1	16.7
	6th.	0	1	100.0	0	1	100.0	0	2	100.0
	n.d.	19	0		13	2	13.3	32	2	5.9
	Totals:	22	1	4.3	23	4	14.8	45	5	10.0

Area	Century	3rd Decl. Nom. Sing. -is -es	% Of Dev.	3rd Decl. Gen. Sing. -is -es	% Of Dev.	Totals	% Of Dev.
Balkans	1st.	0 0		2 0		2 0	
(Pagan)	2nd.	1 0		0 0		1 0	
	3rd.	0 0		2 0		2 0	
	n.d.	8 0		1 1	50.0	9 1	10.0
	Totals:	9 0	0.0	5 1	16.7	14 1	6.7
Balkans	4th.	2 0		0 0		2 0	
(Christ.)	n.d.	1 0		7 0		8 0	
	Totals:	3 0	0.0	7 0	0.0	10 0	0.0

Before embarking on an analysis of the above table, we should like to bring out an important difference in the change of final /ï/ to *e* in the two categories examined. A change of the nominative singular -*is*, although possibly phonetic, is probably morphological because of the confusion with other nominative nouns of the third declension ending in -*es*. The change in the genitive singular -*is* to -*es* of third declension nouns is mainly phonetic because the possibility of morphological extension is largely lacking. Looking over the confusion between -*is* and -*es* throughout all of Romania, we find that the percentage of deviation for the nominative singular -*is* is 8.8 % on the basis of 300 correct occurrences and 29 deviations. The corresponding percentage of deviation for the genitive singular is 5.5 % on the basis of 433 correct occurrences and 25 deviations. The best examples of areas showing a deviation for the nominative singular but stability in the genitive singular are Africa with five deviations and 129 correct occurrences for a 3.9 % percent of deviation, but 135 correct occurrences of the genitive singular in -*is* without any case of deviation, and pagan Britain with six deviations and 35 correct occurrences in the nominative singular for a 14.6 % deviation, but 43 cases of correct occurrences and no deviations in the genitive singular. Rome also shows a significant percentage of deviation in the nominative singular with 13.0 % calculated on 40 correct occurrences and six deviations, but shows only sporadic deviations in the genitive singular with a 2.7 % deviation on the basis of 73 correct occurrences and two deviations. It is therefore striking to find some areas where there is a greater percentage of deviation in the genitive singular, a situation probably mirroring a

phonetic change, than in the nominative singular where either
a morphological substitution or in some cases a combination of both
morphological and phonetic reasons is the cause of the change of
/ĭ/ to *e*. An interesting picture is found in Narbonensis where in
the sixth/seventh centuries both the nominative singular and the
genitive singular show a definite trend to confusion of the final
vowel as evidenced by a percentage of deviation of 40.0 % for the
nominative singular (albeit the low frequency of occurrence: 3 correct occurrences and 2 deviations) and a percentage of deviation of
25.0 % for the genitive singular based on twelve correct occurrences
and five cases of deviation. A similar pattern holds true for the areas
of Lugdunensis and Northern Italy where there is a marked increase
in the percentage of deviation in the genitive singular in the sixth/
seventh centuries. An interesting possibility of explaining the confusion in the final vowel /ĭ/ in the areas of Narbonensis, Lugdunensis,
and Northern Italy, especially in the sixth/seventh centuries, is the
increase of the stress accent resulting from the Germanic invasions,
a blurring or weakening of an unaccented vowel which has already
been clearly seen in the treatment of intertonic /ĭ/ (see *supra*,
p. 204 ff.) and posttonic /ĭ/ (see *supra*, p. 212 ff.) in the same
areas. It must be remarked, however, that Dalmatia, where there was
little Germanic influence, likewise shows a higher percentage of deviation for the genitive singular (14.8 % calculated on 23 correct
occurrences and 4 deviations) than for the nominative singular (4.3 %
based on 22 correct occurrences and 1 case of deviation). The Latin
inscriptions of Southern Italy, while showing a high percentage of
deviation for the nominative singular (27.3 % based on 8 correct
occurrences and 3 cases of deviation, admittedly low frequencies of
occurrence), likewise offer a 10 % deviation for the genitive singular
(45 correct occurrences and 5 deviations). Cognizant of the linguistic
influence of Southern Romance on Dalmatian Romance, we are tempted to consider the situation of final /ĭ/ in Dalmatia as a result of
Southern Italian Latin influences on the east coast of the Adriatic.
Considering the noun-adjective endings in /ĭ/, we are finally led to
the overall conclusion that the change of final /ĭ/ to *e* is primarily
morphological in nature in some areas, especially in Africa, pagan
Britain, Rome, but phonetic and to a certain degree morphological in
Dalmatia, Southern Italy, Northern Italy, Narbonensis, and Lugdunensis. The Germanic invasions may very well have caused an increased

stress accent with the resultant blurring of the final vowel /ĭ/ in Narbonensis, Lugdunensis, and Northern Italy. This reasoning cannot account for the relatively high percentage of deviation in Southern Italy and Dalmatia.

We will now give the comparative figures for final /ĭ/ in verb endings for the third person singulars of the present indicative and present perfect indicative as other verb forms ending in final /ĭ/ are too sporadic for any valid comparison to be made. We will see whether the findings for verb forms collaborate the conclusions derived from noun-adjective endings.

Area	Century	Present Indic. 3rd Pers. Sing.		% Of Dev.	Perfect Indic. 3rd Pers. Sing.		% Of Dev.	Totals		% Of Dev.
		-it	-et		-it	-et				
Baetica	4th-6th	7	1	12.5	63	0		70	1	1.4
	7th	2	1	33.3	29	0		31	1	3.1
	Totals:	9	2	18.2	92	0	0.0	101	2	1.9
Lusitania	4th-6th	0	1	100.0	108	2	1.8	108	3	2.7
	7th	1	0		16	0		17	0	
	Totals:	1	1	50.0	124	2	1.6	125	3	2.3
Tarraco-nensis	4th-6th	11	11	50.0	41	2	4.8	52	13	20.0
	7th	0	0		6	0		6	0	
	Totals:	11	11	50.0	47	2	4.1	58	13	18.3
Narbo-nensis	4th-5th	8	2	20.0	23	6	20.6	31	8	20.5
	6th-7th	42	10	19.2	93	21	18.4	135	31	18.7
	Totals:	50	12	19.4	116	27	18.9	166	39	19.0
Lugdu-nensis	4th-5th	10	1	9.1	42	1	2.4	52	2	3.7
	6th-7th	23	9	28.1	64	14	16.6	87	23	20.1
	Totals:	33	10	23.3	106	15	12.4	139	25	15.2
Northern Italy	4th-5th	21	10	32.2	111	8	6.6	132	18	12.0
	6th	33	6	15.4	48	4	7.7	81	10	10.9
	Totals:	54	16	22.9	159	12	7.0	213	28	11.7
Central Italy	3rd-4th	3	2	40.0	29	1	3.3	32	3	8.6
	5th	8	2	20.0	23	0		31	2	6.1
	6th-7th	20	4	16.7	38	4	9.5	58	8	12.1
	Totals:	31	8	20.5	90	5	5.3	121	13	9.7

Area	Century	Present Indic. 3rd Pers. Sing.		% Of Dev.	Perfect Indic. 3rd Pers. Sing.		% Of Dev.	Totals		% Of Dev.
		-it	-et		-it	-et				
Southern	3rd-4th	2	1	33.3	39	1	2.5	41	2	4.7
Italy	5th	13	2	13.3	27	0		40	2	4.8
	6th-7th	52	1	1.9	57	1	1.7	109	2	1.8
	Totals:	67	4	5.6	123	1	1.6	190	6	3.1
Rome	3rd-4th	11	15	57.6	257	8	3.0	268	23	7.9
	5th	29	13	30.9	138	6	4.1	167	19	10.2
	6th-7th	49	4	7.5	64	3	4.3	113	7	5.8
	Totals:	89	32	26.4	459	17	3.6	548	49	8.2
Africa	3rd.	1	0		6	0		7	0	
	4th.	1	0		44	0		45	0	
	5th.	4	0		104	0		108	0	
	6th.	0	0		24	0		24	0	
	7th.	0	0		1	0		1	0	
	n.d.	36	7	18.9	359	0		389	7	1.8
	Totals:	36	7	16.3	538	0	0.0	574	7	1.1
Britain	1st.	0	0		2	0		2	0	
(Pagan)	2nd.	0	0		9	0		9	0	
	3rd.	0	0		25	0		25	0	
	n.d.	1	0		107	0		108	0	
	Totals:	1	0	0.0	143	0	0.0	144	0	0.0
Britain	4th.	0	0		2	0		2	0	
(Christ.)	5th.	0	0		3	0		3	0	
	6th.	0	0		1	0		1	0	
	7th.	0	0		1	0		1	0	
	8th.	0	0		1	0		1	0	
	9th.	0	0		4	0		4	0	
	n.d.	0	0		4	0		4	0	
	Totals:	0	0	0.0	16	0	0.0	16	0	0.0
Dalmatia	4th.	1	0		2	0		3	0	
	5th.	3	1	25.0	14	0		17	1	5.6
	6th.	1	0		8	0		9	0	
	n.d.	4	3	42.9	66	2	2.9	70	5	6.7
	Totals:	9	4	30.8	90	2	2.2	99	6	5.7
Balkans	1st.	0	0		1	0		1	0	
(Pagan)	2nd.	0	0		1	0		1	0	
	3rd.	0	0		1	0		1	0	
	n.d.	0	1	100.0	38	0		38	1	2.6
	Totals:	0	1	100.0	41	0	0.0	41	1	2.4

Area	Century	Present Indic. 3rd Pers. Sing.		% Of Dev.	Perfect Indic. 3rd Pers. Sing.		% Of Dev.	Totals		% Of Dev.
		-it	-et		-it	-et				
Balkans	4th.	0	0		5	0		5	0	
(Christ.)	5th.	1	0		1	0		2	0	
	n.d.	4	2	33.3	40	1	2.4	44	3	6.4
	Totals:	5	2	28.6	46	1	2.1	51	3	5.6

The problem of whether the change of final /ĭ/ to *e* is morphological or phonetic again looms important in the discussion of verb forms. Considering the percentage of deviation for the third person singular of present indicatives throughout the whole of Romania, we find a 21.7 percentage of deviation on the basis of 396 correct occurrences and 110 cases of deviation. This high percentage of deviation is in strong contrast to the 3.7 % of deviation for the third person singular of perfect indicatives, calculated on the basis of 2275 correct occurrences and 85 cases of deviation. Since the chance of morphological extension of verb conjugations is strong, witness the many examples of a change from second conjugation to the third and vice versa in the Romance languages, the change of final /ĭ/ to *e* in the third person singular of present indicatives is primarily a morphological change. This conclusion is corroborated by the change of final /ĭ/ to *e* in third person perfect indicative endings, where the change is mainly phonetic since the possibility of a morphological substitution is low, and where the 3.7 % of deviation shows that the change of /ĭ/ to *e* was sporadic. [88] We previously saw that in noun-adjective endings there was also a difference in the treatment of final /ĭ/ depending on whether the /ĭ/ was in the nominative singular -*is*, morphologically susceptible of change to *e*, or in the genitive singular -*is*, less open to a morphological change and therefore probably a phonetic change (see *supra*, p. 235 ff.). Our inscriptions thus show that in some cases of change in final position

---

[88] We are aware of the formulaic nature of inscriptional material and the inordinate use of a form like *vixit* where a mistake in the orthography is unlikely (but mistakes do occur in both consonants and vowels), but the difference in the percentages of deviation between the present indicative and perfect indicative is too great to affect the general conclusion that the change of /ĭ/ to *e* in present indicatives is primarily morphological while that of present perfects is sporadic and probably phonetic in nature.

the morphological element is undoubtedly the prime cause and the phonetic aspect is a subsidiary cause for change.

With respect to the individual areas of Romania, although it is true that every area shows a greater percentage of deviation for the present indicative than for the perfect indicative, Narbonensis once again shows a strong tendency to change final /ĭ/ to e in the primarily phonetic change of the perfect indicative ending -is as is evidenced by the 18.9 % of deviation based on 116 correct occurrences and 27 cases of deviation. Lugdunensis likewise shows a relatively large percentage of deviation for the perfect indicative ending -it with 12.4 %, based on 106 correct occurrences and fifteen cases of deviation. The third most important area for the change of /ĭ/ to e in perfect endings is Northern Italy, where we have a 7.0 % deviation on the basis of 159 correct occurrences and twelve deviations. This is essentially the same result which we obtained for the change of /ĭ/ to e in noun-adjective endings for the genitive singular -is, likewise primarily a phonetic change (see supra, p. 237 ff.). One important difference in the treatment of final /ĭ/ in perfect indicatives as compared to the change found in nominative singulars is the chronological element. We find a strong tendency in inscriptions of Narbonensis to change /ĭ/ to e in perfect indicatives in the fourth and fifth centuries (a 20.6 percentage of deviation based on 23 correct occurrences and 6 deviations), which would run counter to the theory of Germanic invasions as the main cause of a confusion of final vowels. The situation of Lugdunensis, however, does show a distinct cleavage between the fourth/fifth centuries and the sixth/seventh centuries (a 2.4 percentage of deviation based on 42 correct occurrences and 1 deviation for the early centuries and a 16.6 percentage of deviation based on 64 correct occurrences and 14 cases of deviation for the critical sixth and seventh centuries). Whatever the reason may be, it appears clear from epigraphic evidence that the final /ĭ/ in Narbonensis and Lugdunensis (and probably Northern Italy) is treated differently from other areas of Romania.

A striking contrast to the high percentage of deviation in the perfect indicative ending -it in Narbonensis and Lugdunensis is presented by the Latin of Africa. We found 538 cases of correct occurrences of -it in the perfect indicative without any case of a deviation. When we compare this 0.0 % for Africa to the 18.9 % for Narbonensis, the 12.4 % for Lugdunensis, and 7.0 % for Northern Italy, we have conclusive proof that the status of final /ĭ/ changes according to the various areas of Romania. The percentage of deviation of the present indicative for African Latin, however, shows 16.3 %, which indicates that a morphological change is probably responsible for the change of /ĭ/ to *e* in this verbal ending. Once again there is a dearth of examples of a phonetic change in certain verb forms, but there are morphological exchanges of /ĭ/ and *e* in some cases. The conservatism of African Latin is proved by the extreme stability of final /ĭ/ in the perfect indicative ending -*it*, but even in conservative areas there is room for a morphological change of final vowels, as is seen in the change of -*it* to -*et* in the third person singular of the perfect indicative. This extreme conservatism of African Latin is echoed by the marked stability in the genitive singular ending -*is* of third declension nouns and adjectives where we found 135 correct occurrences and no example of deviation. A 3.9 percentage of deviation in the nominative singular ending -*is* shows a parallel morphological change to -*es* (see *supra*, p. 236 ff.).

British pagan Latin shows a remarkable conservatism in the treatment of final /ĭ/ in the perfect indicative ending -*it*. We found 143 correct occurrences and no deviations. The present indicative ending -*it* was found only once in pagan inscriptions and cannot be used for comparative purposes. This conservative nature of British pagan Latin was also found in the genitive singular where we have 43 cases of correct occurrences without any deviation, although once again a morphological change is encountered in the nominative singular where we have a 14.6 % deviation based on 35 correct occurrences and six cases of deviation (although all six deviations are found in the same word *cives*; see *supra*, p. 227).

Of the Italian areas, Southern Italy is the most conservative in its treatment of final /ĭ/ in verb forms. Its percentage of deviation of 5.6 % in the present indicative (67 correct occurrences to 4 deviations) differs vastly from the 22.9 % for Northern Italy (54 correct occurrences and 16 deviations), the 20.5 % for Central Italy (31 correct occurrences and 8 deviations), and the 26.4 % for Rome (89 correct occurrences and 32 deviations). This same conservatism is also observed in the treatment of the perfect ending -*it*. Southern Italy shows a percentage of deviation of 1.6 % (123 correct occurrences to 2 deviations) compared to 7.0 % for Northern Italy (159 correct occurrences to 12 deviations), 5.3 % for Central Italy (90 correct occurrences to 5 deviations), and 3.6 % for Rome (459 correct occurrences and 17 deviations). Dalmatia shows only sporadic changes of /ĭ/ to e in the perfect endings (2.2 % of deviation based on 90 correct occurrences and 2 deviations) although the morphological change in the present indicative ending -it shows a 30.8 % deviation (9 correct occurrences and 4 deviations).

Of the Iberian Peninsula areas, Tarraconensis is most innovative, especially in the present indicative ending -it, where there is 50 % deviation (11 correct occurrences and 11 deviations). With respect to the perfect indicative ending -it, the three areas of Baetica, Lusitania, and Tarraconensis are all relatively stable: Baetica with 0.0 % based on 92 correct occurrences without any deviations; Lusitania with 1.6 % based on 124 correct occurrences and two deviations, and Tarraconensis with 4.1 % calculated on 47 correct occurrences and two deviations.

Concluding our treatment of unaccented /ĭ/ in all positions, initial, intertonic, posttonic, and final, we feel that we are in a position to state quite unequivocably that Latin inscriptions prove unquestionably that /ĭ/ was treated differently in the various areas of Romania, and that the tendencies evidenced in the different areas are corroborated by the reflexes in the Romance languages or by loanwords in peripheral areas, such as Latin borrowings by the Brittonic languages in Britain. The main cause of the change of /ĭ/ to e in initial, intertonic, and posttonic positions is phonetic, but in final position the morphological element seems more significant in some areas. The Latin of Gaul is by far the most innovative in the treatment of unaccented /ĭ/, the Latin of Africa and Britain the most conservative.

Latin /ī/, Represented by the Letter i

Latin /ī/ was found in our inscriptions in initial, intertonic, and final positions. It is especially in final syllables that Latin /ī/ deviated from the Classical Latin norm, although the problem is complicated because of morphological and syntactic considerations as well as phonetic change. In initial and intertonic positions, the Latin /ī/ was very stable although some sporadic changes did occur. [89]

---

[89] It should be noted that Gaeng (p. 175) did not find any deviations in initial or intertonic positions and consequently did not give any tables for /ī/ in these two positions.

Africa	Century	Open Syllable /ī/ > i	/ī/ > e	% Of Dev.	Closed Syllable /ī/ > i	/ī/ > e	% Of Dev.	Totals		% Of Dev.
	3rd.	0	0		1	0		1	0	
	4th.	11	0		10	0		21	0	
	5th.	2	0		7	0		9	0	
	6th.	3	0		5	0		8	0	
	n.d.	43	1	2.3	47	0		90	1	9.1
	Totals:	59	1	1.7	70	0	0.0	129	1	0.8

The single deviation in African inscriptions is in the proper noun *Hesidori* (= *Isidori*, gen. sing), *D.* 2070, Calama (Proconsularis), no date. We see from fairly numerous examples of initial /ī/ in the correct orthography (a percentage of deviation of 0.8 %) that initial /ī/ is very stable in African inscriptions.

Britain	Century	Open Syllable /ī/ > i	/ī/ > e	% Of Dev.	Closed Syllable /ī/ > i	/ī/ > e	Totals		% Of Dev.
(Pagan)	1st.	12	0		0	0	12	0	
	2nd.	11	1	8.3	10	0	21	1	4.5
	3rd.	10	0		17	0	27	0	
	n.d.	47	1	2.1	20	0	67	1	1.5
	Totals:	80	2	2.4	47	0	127	2	1.5

The two cases of deviation in pagan Britain are:

leb(ertus), *RIB* 143, *CIL* VII, Bath (Aquae Sulis), about A.D. 122.

demediam (= *dimidiam*), *RIB* 306, *CIL* VII 140, Lydney Park, no date.

The form *demediam* is particularly significant as the modern French *demi* shows that initial /ī/ did change to *e* under special circumstances. This particular word is found in a *defixio* where we would expect a more popular Latin to be used rather than the very Classical Latin that is so characteristic of pagan British inscriptions and Brittonic loanwords. [90]

---

[90] It is difficult to determine whether the form *demediam* shows a Gaulish influence or whether it is a parallel development. Pei records (*Texts*, p. 50)

We have a striking example of the difference in treatment of initial /ī/ in inscriptions as compared to what we find in the Latin loanwords in the Brittonic languages. We encountered six cases of initial /ī/ in the pagan inscriptions of Britain in *divinae*, *RIB* 91, 1st century; *divi[nae]*, *RIB* 707, 2nd century; *divin(a)*, *RIB* 897, 3rd century; *divine*, *RIB* 919, 3rd century; *divinae*, *RIB* 89, no date, and *divina*, *RIB* 1700, no date, without a single case of initial /ī/ changing to *e*. The dissimilation of initial /ī/ to *e* before an accented /ī/, well known[91] in the change of *vīcīnu* > *vecīnu* (Rum. *vecin*, Sp. *vecino*, Fr. *voisin*), *dīvīnat* > *devīnat* (Fr. *devine*, Prov. *devina*), *dīvīsa* > *devīsa* (Fr. *devise*), etc., is also found in the Welsh *dĕwin* < *devīnus < *dīvīnus*; compare also the Welsh *dĕwis* < *dĕvīso < *dīvīso*.[92] Besides the fact that Welsh shows that the original Latin initial /ī/ did change to *e*, it also shows that this *e* was open. The Latin inscriptions of pagan (or Christian) Britain do not show any case of this dissimilation of initial /ī/ to *e*.

Britain	Century	Open Syllable		% Of Dev.	Closed Syllable		% Of Dev.	Totals	
		/ī/ > i	/ī/ > e		/ī/ > i	/ī/ > e			
(Christ.)									
	5th.	1	0		0	0		1	0
	6th.	2	0		2	0		4	0
	Totals:	3	0	0.0	2	0	0.0	5	0

the form *demedium* in his work on Northern French texts of the 8th century, but our *demediam* is from a leaden *defixio* of pagan Latin origin about five centuries earlier. There are, of course, Gaulish and British Latin characteristics which are phonetically similar, but these similarities must not be exaggerated. See *supra*, p. 61 ff. for a discussion of the similarities and differences of the Latin of Gaul and Britain.

[91] Lausberg, I, 288; Meyer-Lübke, *Einführung*, pp. 158-59; Grandgent, p. 97.

[92] Jackson, *Language*, p. 305; Loth, p. 114.

The figures are too scanty for any conclusion to be drawn.

Dalmatia	Century	Open Syllable		% Of Dev.	Closed Syllable		% Of Dev.	Totals	
		/ī/ > i	/ī/ > e		/ī/ > i	/ī/ > e			
	4th.	0	0		2	0		2	0
	5th.	4	0		3	0		7	0
	6th.	1	0		0	0		1	0
	n.d.	14	0		20	0		34	0
	Totals:	19	0	0.0	25	0	0.0	44	0

On the basis of no deviations in the Latin inscriptions of Dalmatia, it appears that initial /ī/ was stable.

Balkans	Century	Open Syllable		% Of Dev.	Closed Syllable		% Of Dev.	Totals	% Of Dev.
		/ī/ > i	/ī/ > e		/ī/ > i	/ī/ > e			
(Pagan)	1st.	1	0		0	0		1 0	
	2nd.	0	0		0	0		0 0	
	3rd.	2	0		1	0		3 0	
	n.d.	15	0		2	1	33.3	17 1	5.6
	Totals:	18	0	0.0	3	1	25.0	21 1	4.5

The one example of deviation in pagan inscriptions of the Balkans is in the word *enfelicis* (nom. sing.), *Kalinka* 399, *CIL* III 7431, Gigen (Moesia Inferior), no date. It is difficult to draw conclusions on the basis of one deviation, but the form shows a popular change in making the Classical Latin *infelix* parisyllabic by assuming a more common third declension noun-type ending in -*is* used for both nominative and genitive singular, in addition to the change of initial /ī/ to *e*.

Balkans	Century	Open Syllable		% Of Dev.	Closed Syllable		% Of Dev.	Totals	
		/ī/ > i	/ī/ > e		/ī/ > i	/ī/ > e			
(Christ.)	n.d.	5	0		4	0		9	0
	Totals:	5	0	0.0	4	0	0.0	9	0

There are no deviations, but the total number of occurrences is too low for any conclusion to be made.

Although the incidence of initial /ī/ is low in some areas, it appears that this vowel is stable in the areas investigated by us, a conclusion which concurs with Gaeng's findings (p. 175) for the areas of the Iberian Peninsula, Gaul, Italy, and Rome. Our inscriptions do show that a sporadic dissimilation such as the form *demediam* does appear which foreshadows a Romance reality. This dissimilation of initial /ī/ to *e,* based on its being found in a pagan inscription of Britain, although undated, shows that the Romance dissimilation of initial /ī/ to *e* has its roots deep in Vulgar Latin speech. [93]

Intertonic

Africa	Century	Open Syllable		% Of Dev.	Closed Syllable		% Of Dev.	Totals	
		/ī/ > i	/ī/ > e		/ī/ > i	/ī/ > e			
	4th.	5	0		0	0		5	0
	5th.	2	0		0	0		2	0
	6th.	10	0		2	0		12	0
	n.d.	20	0		2	0		22	0
	Totals:	37	0	0.0	4	0	0.0	41	0

Intertonic /ī/ in African inscriptions does not show any deviation in our corpus and is apparently stable.

---

[93] In the leaden *defixio* where the form *demediam* is found, mention is made of the local Celtic deity, Nodens, whose worship, according to Blair, *Roman Britain and Early England,* p. 144, was confined to Lydney (Gloucestershire) where it was established not many years before the birth of St. Patrick. This would set the lower limit of the inscription in the middle of the fourth century, which is chronologically within the range given for most examples of the dissimilation of initial /ī/ to *e* in inscriptional material. Grandgent (p. 97) gives the fourth century for the epigraphic evidence of *divinus > devinus.* Richter considers (p. 131) vocalic dissimilation to be much later than assimilation, but does not give any date further back than A.D. 514 for the dissimilation of initial /ī/. See Collingwood-Myres, pp. 264-66, 273, for a discussion of the Celtic deity Nodens.

Britain	Century	Open Syllable		% Of Dev.	Closed Syllable		% Of Dev.	Totals	
		/ī/ > i	/ī/ > e		/ī/ > i	/ī/ > e			
(Pagan)	1st.	1	0		0	0		1	0
	2nd.	1	0		0	0		1	0
	3rd.	9	0		1	0		10	0
	n.d.	9	0		0	0		9	0
	Totals:	20	0	0.0	1	0	0.0	21	0
(Christ.)	7th.	1	0		0	0		1	0
	n.d.	0	0		0	0		0	0
	Totals:	1	0	0.0	0	0	0.0	1	0

There is no deviation in either pagan or Christian inscriptions of Britain, but the figures are too low, especially for Christian Britain, for any conclusion to be made.

Dalmatia	Century	Open Syllable		% Of Dev.	Closed Syllable		Totals		% Of Dev.
		/ī/ > i	/ī/ > e		/ī/ > i	/ī/ > e			
	4th.	2	0		1	0	3	0	
	5th.	3	0		0	0	3	0	
	6th.	1	0		0	0	1	0	
	n.d.	9	1	10.0	3	0	12	1	7.7
	Totals:	15	1	6.3	4	0	19	1	5.0

The single case of deviation is in [r]equesitus, D. 2389, CIL III, p. 961, Tragurium, no date. This form, however, is probably morphological rather than phonetic in nature, the simble verb quaero influencing the compounds through reconstruction. [94]

---

[94] Pei, in his Texts, pp. 50-51, mentions that all changes of /ī/ to e internally are compounds of quaero, a particularly favorite subject for etymological recomposition.

Balkans	Century	Open Syllable		% Of Dev.	Closed Syllable		Totals		% Of Dev.
		/ī/ > i	/ī/ > e		/ī/ > i	/ī/ > e			
(Pagan)									
	2nd.	1	0		0	0	1	0	
	3rd.	2	0		0	0	2	0	
	4th.	1	0		0	0	1	0	
	n.d.	1	0		0	0	1	0	
	Totals:	5	0	0.0	0	0	5	0	0.0
(Christ.)	n.d.	13	0		0	0	13	0	
	Totals:	13	0	0.0	0	0	13	0	0.0

There are no deviations in the Latin inscriptions of the Balkans, either pagan or Christian, but the figures are too low to permit any valid conclusion.

It appears that intertonic /ī/ is stable in our areas, although the number of occurrences is low. The one example of deviation was morphological in nature. Our conclusions agree with those of Gaeng who found intertonic /ī/ stable, since no deviation was recorded in the areas of the Iberian Peninsula, Gaul, Italy, and Rome.

Final (Non-Morphological)

Africa	Century	/ī/ > i	/ī/ > e	% Of Dev.
	4th.	1	0	
	5th.	1	0	
	n.d.	6	0	
	Totals:	8	0	0.0
Britain (Pagan)		NO EXAMPLES		
Britain (Christian)		NO EXAMPLES		
Dalmatia	n.d.	4	0	
	Totals:	0	0	0.0
Balkans (Pagan)		NO EXAMPLES		
Balkans (Christian)		NO EXAMPLES		

Final non-morphological /ī/, although rarely encountered in this position, is stable. Most of the forms of this category are numbers, especially the cardinal *viginti* (found six times in addition to the variants *biginti* and *vicinti*), and [*t*]*recenti*.

Morphological: Declensional (Noun-Adjective Terminations)

The most important declensional endings studied are the first declension dative and ablative plural in -ī, the second declension genitive singular -ī, the second declension nominative plural -ī, the second declension dative and ablative plural -īs, the third declension nominative singular -īx and the third declension dative singular -ī. [95] We will try to determine whether any change of final /ī/ to *e* or to any other vowel is phonetic or morphological in nature or possibly a combination of both factors. In some cases a syntactic cause may even be the predominant reason for a change.

Africa	Century	2nd Decl. Gen. Sing.		% Of Dev.	2nd Decl. Nom. Plur.		% Of Dev.	2nd Decl. Abl. Dat.		1st Decl. Abl. Plur.	
		-i	-e		-i	-e		-is	-es	-is	-es
	3rd.	0	0		1	0		2	0	0	0
	4th.	33	0		3	0		33	0	2	0
	5th.	21	0		1	0		46	0	0	0
	6th.	31	0		1	0		19	0	2	0
	7th.	0	0		0	0		2	0	0	0
	n.d.	182	1	0.5	29	0		199	0	8	0
	Totals:	271	1	0.4	35	0	0.0	301	0	12	0

Africa	Century	3rd Decl. Nom. Sing.		% Of Dev.	3rd Decl. Dat. Sing.		% Of Dev.
		-ix	-ex		-i	-e	
	3rd.	0	0		3	0	
	4th.	3	0		14	0	
	5th.	1	0		7	0	
	6th.	3	0		0	0	
	n.d.	10	0		28	2	6.7
	Totals:	17	0	0.0	52	2	3.7

[95] For a discussion of the confusion of the third declension ablative singular ending in -*i* and -*e* and the third declension nominative and accusative plurals ending in -*is* and -*es*, see *supra*, pp. 157-61, 175-80, and 182-89.

The deviations for final /ī/ in declensional endings are:

a) genitive singular of the second declension:

Pompone (= Pomponi or Pomponii, the genitive singular of Pomponius), D. 3232, CIL VIII 11,726, Thala (Byzacena), no date.

b) dative singular of the third declension:

Felice (proper name), D. 2443, CIL VIII 18,705, Numidia, no date.

inocente, D. 2547A, CIL VIII 25,289, Carthage (Proconsularis), no date.

On the basis of 688 correct occurrences for all the above declensional categories compared to three deviations for a total percentage of deviation of 0.4 %, we conclude that final /ī/ in declensional endings for the Latin of Africa is very stable. The single deviation of /ī/ to e in the genitive singular loses its impact when we consider that there are 271 correct occurrences of /ī/. We are not sure whether this is a mason's slip, the cursive script where an e and i are sometimes orthographically confused, or a true phonetic change. Gaeng records (p. 178) three sporadic cases of a genitive singular in -e in Latin inscriptions of Gaul and considers them, on the basis of their late date, as an indication of the general weakening of final vowels in this area. Carnoy mentions (p. 46) that "à partir du 8me siècle, on commence à trouver assez fréquemment e pour i final au génitif singulier" and asks whether "il faut voir dans cette orthographe la preuve du changement d'i final en e, en toute position, phénomène qui s'est produit certainement dans la préhistoire de l'espagnol." In the Latin inscriptions of Africa the genitive singular of second declension nouns and adjectives ends overwhelmingly in -i.

The dative singular of third declension forms sporadically ends in -e (2 deviations and 52 correct occurrences for a percentage of deviation of 3.7 %). When we consider that we found 35 cases of the second declension nominative plural in -i without any deviations, 301 cases of the second declension dative/ablative plural in -īs without any deviations, twelve cases of the first declension dative/ablative plural in -īs without any deviations, seventeen cases of the third declension nominative singular in -ī without any deviations, and only one deviation (possibly a scribal error) in the second declension genitive singular against 271 correct occurrences, it seems best to consider any change of final /ī/ to e as morphological in nature. The change of /ī/ to e in the dative singular of third declension nouns and adjectives has been recorded by other scholars who have investigated Latin inscriptions and documents.[96] The change of final /ī/ to e, however, is almost always limited to the dative singular of third declension nouns and to the ablative singular of third declension adjectives. In the latter case, the morphological substitution of the ablative in -e of third declension nouns is probably the best explanation.

We conclude that the final /ī/ in African inscriptions is extremely stable with those sporadic changes to e best explained as a morphological confusion of cases. It seems that an overall rule can be formulated for the explanation of the changes of final -i in particular and all final vowels in general for the Latin of inscriptions. When there is little or no chance for a morphological form to be substituted for the final syllable, the final vowel remains. When there is a possibility, however, of the morphological forms contending with the Classical Latin form, there are sporadic changes in the final vowel. This is not to deny any phonetic change in final vowels, but on the basis of our investigation of Latin inscriptions, it seems that the morphological influence is greater than the phonetic in the interpretation of change of final vowels. A change such as the intertonic and posttonic short /ĭ/ to e is overwhelmingly a phonetic phenomenon.

---

[96] Gaeng, p. 181; Carnoy, pp. 45-46; Grandgent, p. 103; Lindsay, p. 387; Pei, Texts, p. 51; it must be remembered that 3rd decl. datives in -e have been found in archaic inscriptions. The Latin 3rd decl. dative ending -i rests on a diphthong -ei attested in archaic Latin and Oscan inscriptions. This -ei before evolving into -i passed through an -e stage. The -e found in early Latin inscriptions may be therefore this intermediary stage or possibly a dialectalism. This final -e in datives of the 3rd declension of Christian inscriptions, however, is probably the result of a confusion of cases. See Sommer, p. 373; Ernout, Morphologie, p. 40; Kent, p. 40, for a historical discussion of the Latin third declension datives.

Britain	Century	2nd Decl. Gen. Sing.		2nd Decl. Nom. Plur.		% Of Dev.	2nd Decl. Dat./Abl.		% Of Dev.
		-i	-e	-i	-e		-is	-es	
(Pagan)									
	1st.	11	0	0	0		0	0	
	2nd.	21	0	2	0		3	0	
	3rd.	35	0	0	0		8	0	
	4th.	15	0	0	0		0	0	
	n.d.	61	0	9	0		41	0	
	Totals:	143	0	11	0	0.0	52	0	0.0

	3rd Decl. Nom. Sing.		3rd Decl. Dat. Sing.		% Of Dev.	1st Decl. Dat./Abl.		% Of Dev.
	-ix	-ex	-i	-e		-is	-es	
1st.	0	0	5	0		2	0	
2nd.	1	0	16	0		0	0	
3rd.	5	0	24	0		2	0	
4th.	0	0	2	0		0	0	
n.d.	6	0	73	4	5.2	15	0	
Totals:	12	0	120	4	3.2	19	0	0.0

The deviations for the pagan inscriptions of Britain are:

a) dative singular of the third declension:

   Nudente, RIB 307, *CIL* VII 139, Lydney Park (Gloucester), no date.

   Vitire, RIB 971, *CIL* VII 958, Netherby (Castra Exploratorum), Cumberland, no date.

   coniuge, RIB 1065, South Shields (Arbeia), no date. [97]

   Mar[t]e, RIB 1100, *CIL* VII 457, Ebchester (Vindomora), no date.

The final $/\bar{\imath}/$ in pagan Britain is stable on the basis of our findings for the second declension genitive singular, nominative plural, dative/ablative plural, the third declension nominative singular in *-ix*, and the first declension dative/ablative plural where we found no deviations. Once again the change of final $/\bar{\imath}/$ to *e* occurs in the dative singular of third declension nouns where the morphological factor remains predominant.

---

[97] This form is considered by the editor of the *Roman Inscriptions of Britain* to be in the ablative, although he admits (p. 356) that the dative is the normal case.

Britain	Century	2nd Decl. Gen. Sing.		2nd Decl. Nom. Plur.		2nd Decl. Dat./Abl.	
		-i	-e	-i	-e	-is	-es
(Christ.)							
	4th.	0	0	0	0	1	0
	5th.	9	0	0	0	1	0
	6th.	29	0	2	0	1	0
	7th.	8	0	0	0	0	0
	9th.	3	0	0	0	0	0
	n.d.	9	0	0	0	0	0
	Totals:	58	0	2	0	3	0

The final /ī/ is stable in Christian Britain although the only category where this is clearly shown is the genitive singular of second declension nouns and adjectives.

Dalmatia	Century	2nd Decl. Gen. Sing.		2nd Decl. Nom. Sing.		% Of Dev.	2nd Decl. Dat./Abl.		% Of Dev.
		-i	-e	-i	-e		-is	-es	
	4th.	12	0	1	0		3	0	
	5th.	19	0	0	0		1	0	
	6th.	4	0	0	0		1	0	
	n.d.	52	0	11	0	0.0	29	0	
	Totals:	87	0	12	0	0.0	34	0	0.0

		3rd Decl. Nom. Sing.		3rd Decl. Dat. Sing.		% Of Dev.	1st Decl. Abl. Plur.		% Of Dev.
		-ix	-ex	-i	-e		-is	-es	
	4th.	1	0	2	0		0	0	
	n.d.	2	0	44	1	2.2	6	1	14.3
	Totals:	3	0	46	1	2.1	6	1	14.3

The deviations in this area are:

a) dative plural of the second declension:

[c]onbives (= convivis), D. 835, CIL III 9672, Salona, no date.

b) dative singular of the third declension:

iugale, D. 675N, CIL III 14,904, Salona, no date.

The final /ī/ in Dalmatia is stable although the /ī/ to e in [c]onbives poses a problem as this change in the dative or ablative plural of first or second declension forms is extremely rare.

Balkans	Century	2nd Decl. Gen. Sing.		2nd Decl. Dat./Abl.		3rd Decl. Dat. Sing.		% Of Dev.	3rd Decl. Nom. Sing.	
		-i	-e	-is	-es	-i	-e		-ix	-ex
(Pagan)										
	1st.	2	0	0	0	0	0		0	0
	2nd.	7	0	0	0	6	1	14.3	0	0
	3rd.	2	0	1	0	7	0		1	0
	4th.	3	0	0	0	6	0		0	0
	n.d.	7	0	23	0	21	0		2	0
	Totals:	21	0	24	0	40	1	2.4	3	0

The single deviation in the pagan inscriptions of the Balkans is the dative singular *Caesare, Kalinka* 24, *CIL* III 762, Varna (Odessus), Moesia Inferior, A.D. 139-61. It is interesting to note that in the Greek portion of this bilingual inscription the dative is used: Αὐτοχράτορι χαίσαρι.

Balkans	Century	2nd Decl. Gen. Sing.		% Of Dev.	2nd Decl. Nom Plur.		2nd Decl. Dat./Abl.	
		-i	-e		-i	-e	-is	-es
(Christ.)								
	4th.	0	0		1	0	2	0
	n.d.	22	0		5	0	23	0
	Totals:	22	0	0.0	6	0	25	0

		3rd Decl. Dat. Sing.		% Of Dev.	3rd Decl. Nom. Sing.		1st Decl. Abl. Plur.	
		-i	-e		-ix	-ex	-is	-es
	4th.	1	0		0	0	1	0
	n.d.	18	1	5.3	1	0	0	0
	Totals:	19	1	5.0	1	0	1	0

The single deviation in the Christian inscriptions of the Balkans is *cumpare* (= *compari*), D. 3611, *CIL* III 10,237, Sirmium (Pannonia Inferior), no date. We see that once again the deviation is the dative singular where the final /ī/ to e is probably the result of a morphological substitution.

Morphological: Conjugational Endings

Verb endings having a final /ī/ are not common in our inscriptions. The following verb forms were found to have a final /ī/, but the total occurrences are too scanty to allow any conclusions to be drawn: the second person singular of fourth conjugation present indicative in -īs, the first person singular -i and the second person plural -sti of the perfect indicative, and the passive infinitive -i.

Area	Century	Perf. Ind. 1st Sing.		Perf. Ind. 2nd Plur.		4th Conj. 2nd Sing. Present		Passive Inf.	
		-i	-e	-sti	-ste	-is	-es	-i	-e
Africa	4th.	1	0	0	0	0	0	0	0
	5th.	0	0	1	0	0	0	0	0
	n.d.	8	0	2	0	1	0	2	0
	Totals:	9	0	3	0	1	0	2	0
Britain	1st.	1	0	0	0	0	0	0	0
(Pagan)	n.d.	6	0	0	0	0	0	5	0
	Totals:	7	0	0	0	0	0	5	0
(Christ.)	8th.	1	0	0	0	0	0	0	0
Dalmatia	4th.	3	0	0	0	0	0	1	0
	5th.	2	0	0	0	0	0	0	0
	n.d.	4	0	3	0	1	0	3	0
	Totals:	9	0	3	0	1	0	4	0
Balkans	1st.	0	0	0	0	0	0	1	0
(Pagan)	n.d.	0	0	0	0	0	0	2	0
	Totals:	0	0	0	0	0	0	3	0
(Christ.)	4th.	1	0	0	0	0	0	1	0
	n.d.	3	0	0	0	0	0	2	0
	Totals:	4	0	0	0	0	0	3	0

Although the total occurrences of final /ī/ in verbal forms are numerically low, we did not find any deviations. Summarizing the treatment of final /ī/ in both declensional and conjugational endings, we conclude that /ī/ is stable although we do have an occasional deviation, mainly the change of final /ī/ to e in the dative singular of third declension nouns and adjectives, a change that appears to be morphological in nature rather than a true phonetic change.

Genitive Singular Replaced Orthographically by -o

There are cases where a genitive is replaced by a dative or possibly an incipient oblique case ending in *-o*. Although Pei considers
(*Texts*, p. 218) that "the use of the oblique case for the genitive is
one of the most striking and frequent phenomena in the syntax" of
eighth-century texts in Northern France, it must be stated that the
genitive is firmly entrenched in inscriptions despite the sporadic appearance of forms ending in *-o*. The most plausible explanation for
the substitution of the genitive in *-i* by a form ending in *-o* is the
acceptance of the idea that the dative of possession replaces the genitive of possession. [98] Since both the dative of possession and the
genitive of possession have alternated from early Latin (the dative of
possession is attested in Plautus), and since the dative appears to be
more expressive than the genitive which establishes a closer grammatical dependency, [99] it is not surprising to find examples of the
dative of possession in rather popular Latin inscriptions. The opinion
that the oblique is not formed from the dative is strongly expressed
by Pei (*Texts*) who writes (p. 222) "that the case replacing the
genitive is the oblique, and not the classical dative, is abundantly
proved by the occurrence of instances in the plural, where the forms
of the oblique generally correspond to those of the accusative, and
by the occurrence of genitive and oblique forms in the same passage."
In our inscriptions, however, only the singular is encountered, so
that Pei's objections cannot apply to our findings. [100] Gaeng found
examples of the genitive singular appearing with the spelling *-o* which
he considered (p. 178) to be "the development of a single oblique
case." This statement is later modified by the comment (p. 180) that
"there is also the possibility of a confusion in the stonecutter's mind

---

[98] Väänänen, *Introduction*, writes (p. 122) that "la langue populaire fait
depuis l'époque ancienne [l'usage] du datif pour exprimer le rapport de possession." Norberg, *Syntaktische Forschungen auf dem Gebiete des Spätlateins und des frühen Mittellateins* (Uppsala: Lundequistska Bokhandeln,
1943), on explaining the use of the oblique for the genitive states (p. 43)
that "ohne Zweifel liegt in diesen Fällen ursprünglich ein Dativus sympa-
theticus vor."

[99] Ernout-Thomas, *Syntaxe*, p. 73.

[100] We have one example of a dative of possession in the plural, but the
form is in apposition with two proper names: *arca Viforini et Sextilite,
fratribus germanis*, D. 3639, CIL III 2603, near Salona (Dalmatia), no date.

of several stereotyped formulae, rather than the use of a single oblique case." Our examples of a genitive replaced by a dative mainly come from Dalmatia and the dative seems in most cases to be a dative of possession with the verb *esse* understood. The following are some examples of the replacement of the genitive by a dative or possibly the oblique:

> *hic iacit Theodoracis, filius* / *Eufrasio comiti*, D. 117, CIL III 9534, Salona (Dalmatia), no date. It is interesting to note that the Greek portion of the bilingual inscription does have the genitive: ἐνθάδε κατάκιτε/ θεοδωράκις, υἱὸς Εὐφρασίου/ κόμητος.
>
> *arca Saturnino militi Sālonitano*, D. 422, CIL III 9537, Salona (Dalmatia), no date.
>
> *arca I[o]hanni s/atori et I[ul]iae iuca/li eius*, D. 595, CIL III 14,903, Salona, no date.
>
> *arca Suro sarturi et Palumbe*, D. 646, CIL III 9614, Salona, no date.
>
> *arca Honorato calegario*, D. 648, CIL III 2354, near Salona, no date.
>
> [a]rca Pasc[asi]o *vitriario*, D. 667, CIL III 9542, Salona, no date.
>
> *arca Stephano pbr. et Martanae iugali eius*, D. 1172, CIL III 9552, Salona (Dalmatia), no date.
>
> *arca Iucundo puero* / *scae eccles. Sal.*, D. 1298, CIL III 13,147, Salona, no date.
>
> ar[c]a Filiciano [t]usuri et i[u]ga[l]i eius Pall[a]di, D. 3634A, CIL III 9062, Salona, no date.
>
> *arca Iuliano Pandurio*, D. 3635N, Salona, no date.
>
> *arca Messori cum coniuge sua Sevenuda*, D. 3638, CIL III 9603, Salona, no date.
>
> *arca Eclisio . . .* , D. 3638AN, CIL III 6402, Salona, no date.
>
> *arca Dalmatio fil[io . . .]*, D. 3635N, near Monastir, (Macedonia), no date.
>
> [a]rca Castorino ceri[olario?] / *et coniugi eius Dulcit[iae]*, D. 3637, Salona, no date.
>
> [arc]a Andreati et coniugi eiu[s], D. 3638A, CIL III 9561, Salona, no date.
>
> *arca Viforini et Sextilite,* / *fratribus germanis*, D, 3639, CIL III 2603, near Salona, no date.

It is obvious that most of the cases where a dative is used instead of a genitive occur with the formula *arca* plus the name of the person. It is also evident that a form of the verb *esse* (probably *est*) is understood. It appears in these examples that we are faced with the

dative of possession although we do have a genitive occasionally used
after *arca* in this formula: *arca Treioni coci, D.* 620a, *CIL* III 9552,
Salona (Dalmatia), no date.

What we do find in inscriptional material is a confusion of cases
caused by a lack of agreement between noun and the word in apposition, a mixing of two formulaic expressions, or even an apparent
dative but in reality a genitive with the loss of final *-s*. The power
of analogy and attraction is very strong in stonemasons lacking a
thorough knowledge of the niceties of the Latin language. The following cases of the dative or an apparent oblique for a genitive are
really oversights on the part of the stonemason rather than a true
indication of a one-case oblique morphological system:

> *arca Pascasii calegario, D.* 3791A, *CIL* III 14,305, Salona
> (Dalmatia), no date.
> *D.M.* / *Fl. Callimor/phi vix, ani XXXXII* / *et Serapioni
> vix.* / *ann. III m(ensibus) VI. Thesa/eus fratri et filio
> / f.c., RIB* 558, Chester (Deva), no date. [101]
> *pro salu[te] imperatoris* / *M. Antoni Gordiani ...* / *et
> Sab[in]iae Fur/iae Tranquil(lin)ae coniugi eius...*, *RIB*
> 897, *CIL* VII 344, Old Carlisle (Olerica), A.D. 242.
> *et memoriae Antistiae Firmine, coiugi rarissime, Kalinka*
> 386, *CIL* III 14,458, Varna (Odessus) Moesia Inferior,
> no date.
> *...felicissimis tempo/ribb. dd.mm. nostrorum Iustiniano et
> Theo/dora...*, *D,* 805, Thamugadum (Numidia), A.D.
> 539-540. [102]

Although a confusion of cases is common throughout the Romance world as indicated by the inscriptions, an interesting type of
confusion is found in Britain where the commonest confusion of
cases is the use of the nominative for the genitive, and vice versa,

---

[101] The editor of the *Roman Inscriptions of Britain* considers (p. 186)
"*Serapioni* attracted from genitive to dative, owing to *fratri et filio*" in the
same inscription, but it may well be the genitive with a loss of final *-s*.
Although this example and others are not datives or obliques ending in *-o*
for 2nd declension nouns or adjectives having an *-i* in the genitive singular,
we are giving them in order to show that this confusion between dative and
genitive is not limited to a single declension. It should also be pointed out
that the replacement of the genitive of 2nd or 3rd declension forms is made
by datives of the respective declensions and the oblique case seems to be
ruled out as an explanation of this confusion.

[102] *Iustiniano* is undoubtedly an ablative for the expected genitive.

but as stated by Jackson (*Language*, p. 193), "this question is complicated by other factors." We will first give examples of the use of the nominative for the genitive and then the reverse phenomenon, the genitive for the nominative, which seems to be even more common.

a) the nominative for the genitive:

> *Catacus hic iacit, filius Tegernacus*, CIIC 334, Brecon (Wales), no date.
> *Cnegumi fili Genaius*, CIIC 469, Mawgan (Cornwall), no date.
> *hic iacit Cantusus pater Paulinus*, CIIC 407, Glamorgan (Wales), 8th century. The importance of this inscription is brought out by Macalister who writes (p. 384) that "the syntax of the inscriptions in which, as in modern Welsh, genitive relationship is expressed by position only, is worthy of special notice."

b) the genitive for the nominative:

> *Barrivendi filius Vendubari hic iacit*, CIIC 368, Carmarthen (Wales), no date.
> *Latini ic iacit, filius Magari*, CIIC 470, Cornwall, no date.
> *Turpilli ic iacit, puueri Triluni Dunocati*, CIIC 327, Brecon (Wales), no date.
> *Cunocenni, filius Cunoceni, hic iacit*, CIIC 342, Brecon (Wales), no date.
> *Dervaci, filius Iusti, ic iacit*, CIIC 344, Brecon (Wales), no date.
> *Cantiori hic iacit...*, CIIC 394, Carnarvon (Wales), 6th or 7th century.
> *Culidori iacit et...*, CIIC 320, Anglesey (Wales), no date.
> *Brocagni ihc iacit Nodatti filius*, CIIC 478, Doydon (Cornwall), no date.
> *[A]nnicci filius [h]ic iacit Tecuri in hoc tumulo*, CIIC 331, Brecon (Wales), no date.
> *Vendumagli hic iacit*, CIIC 1028, Glamorgan (Wales), no date.
> *Bodvoci iacit...*, CIIC 408, Glamorgan (Wales), no date.

This rather characteristic confusion of cases found in Latin inscriptions of Christian Britain, namely the use of a nominative for a genitive and vice versa, is best explained, according to Macalister (p. xiv), by the fact that "as most of the external case-endings had already vanished from the spoken speech when these inscriptions came to be written, the I-termination had become a mere encumbrance. In fact, the genitive significance of the termination was itself forgotten, so that in the Latin inscriptions of Ogham type we often find a substantive, genitive in form, acting as the nominative of a verb or in apposition to a nominative. On the other hand, we sometimes, though very rarely, find a nominative when there should be a genitive." [103]

We have an isolated case of the dative of *unus* written as *uno*, D. 4318A, *CIL* III 14,292, Salona (Dalmatia), no date, on the analogy of regular datives of the second declension rather than the irregular *uni*. This final *-o* for final *-i* can in no way be considered phonetical; the use of final *-o*, whether a simple dative of possession or the oblique case, for the expected genitive ending *-i* is the result of syntactic factors rather than a phonetic change.

Latin /ŏ/, Represented by the Letter o

Initial

Area	Century	Open Syllable		% Of Dev.	Closed Syllable		% Of Dev.	Totals		% Of Dev.
		/ŏ/ > o	/ŏ/ > u		/ŏ/ > o	/ŏ/ > u				
Africa	3rd.	4	0		1	0		5	0	
	4th.	21	0		9	0		30	0	
	5th.	29	0		8	0		37	0	
	6th.	9	0		7	0		16	0	
	7th.	1	0		5	0		6	0	
	n.d.	103	1	1.0	104	1	1.0	207	2	1.0
	Totals:	167	1	0.6	134	1	0.7	301	2	0.7

The two examples of deviation in this area are:

Rutunda (proper name), D. 1393, *CIL* VIII 25,818, Furnitanus (Proconsularis), no date.

---

[103] Jackson, *Language,* substantially agrees with this explanation when he writes (p. 623) "It can certainly be said ... that once the meaning and existence of British cases was in fact forgotten the established custom of using the Latinising genitive termination would be apt to become wrongly applied, and to wrong British forms." In some cases, however, Jackson sees (p. 623) a simple anacolouthon, such as in the case — *(corpus) Domnici iacit* — rather than a real confusion of cases. When a confusion of cases does occur, Jackson sets (p. 623) the chronological beginning of the practice at the late 6th century.

Muntani (gen. of proper name), *D.* 1636, *CIL* VIII 2272, Mascula (Numidia), no date.

We see that on the basis of a total percentage of deviation of 0.7, initial /ŏ/ is stable in the Latin inscriptions of Africa.

itain	Century	Open Syllable		% Of Dev.	Closed Syllable		% Of Dev.	Totals		% Of Dev.
		/ŏ/ > o	/ŏ/ > u		/ŏ/ > o	/ŏ/ > u				
agan)	1st.	5	0		3	0		8	0	
	2nd.	14	0		13	0		27	0	
	3rd.	28	0		32	0		60	0	
	4th.	1	0		0	0		1	0	
	n.d.	49	0		49	0		98	0	
	Totals:	97	0	0.0	97	0	0.0	194	0	0.0
Christ.)	5th.	0	0		1	0		1	0	
	6th.	1	0		0	1	100.0	1	1	50.0
	7th.	1	0		2	0		3	0	
	9th.	1	0		0	0		1	0	
	n.d.	2	0		0	0		2	0	
	Totals:	5	0	0.0	3	1	25.0	8	1	11.1

The single deviation of initial /ŏ/ to *u* is in the proper name *Pumpeius, CIIC* 409, Glamorgan (Wales), sixth century. [104] The initial /ŏ/ of pagan inscriptions is stable since we did not find any deviation but 194 correct occurrences. Since there are only eight correct occurrences and one deviation in Christian inscriptions, we are not in a position to draw any firm conclusions.

almatia	Century	Open Syllable		% Of Dev.	Closed Syllable		% Of Dev.	Totals		% Of Dev.
		/ŏ/ > o	/ŏ/ > u		/ŏ/ > o	/ŏ/ > u				
	4th.	12	0		1	0		13	0	
	5th.	4	0		9	0		13	0	
	6th.	1	0		4	0		5	0	
	n.d.	44	2	4.4	41	3	6.8	85	5	5.6
	Totals:	61	2	3.2	55	3	5.2	116	5	4.1

---

[104] We do have a change of initial /ŏ/ to *u* in a Celtic name *Tunccetace, CIIC* 541, but we are not considering it in our tables since the change concerns only Welsh phonology. Jackson (*Language*) states (p. 272) that "British and Latin short o normally remain in WCB . . . The most important

The deviations from this area are:

putita, D. 3363, *CIL* III 9623, Salona, no date.
[f]usuri (= *fossori*), D. 3634A, *CIL* III 9062, Salona, no date. [105]
cunparabid (= *comparavit*), D. 838, *CIL* III 9567, Salona, no date.
cumpa[ravi], D. 3792A, Salona, no date.
cuncordiens, D. 3842N, *CIL* III 9541, Salona, no date.

Although some of the deviations can be explained by reconstruction with the prefix *cum-,*[106] it is interesting to note that most of the Latin borrowings into Albanian do show a *u* for unstressed /ŏ/.[107]

Balkans	Century	Open Syllable		% Of Dev.	Closed Syllable		% Of Dev.	Totals		% Of Dev.
		/ŏ/ > o	/ŏ/ > u		/ŏ/ > o	/ŏ/ > u				
(Pagan)	1st.	1	0		0	0		1	0	
	2nd.	5	0		2	0		7	0	
	3rd.	7	0		5	0		12	0	
	4th.	0	0		1	0		1	0	
	n.d.	16	0		14	0		30	0	
	Totals:	29	0	0.0	22	0	0.0	51	0	0.0

Balkans	Century	Open Syllable		% Of Dev.	Closed Syllable		% Of Dev.	Totals		% Of Dev.
		/ŏ/ > o	/ŏ/ > u		/ŏ/ > o	/ŏ/ > u				
(Christ.)	4th.	1	0		2	0		3	0	
	n.d.	16	1	5.9	13	0		29	1	3.3
	Totals:	17	1	5.6	15	0	0.0	32	1	3.0

exception to the preservation of *o* is that in Welsh before certain consonants or consonant groups, chiefly nasal plus stop, single nasal or liquid plus stop, the *o* was generally raised to *u*." Jackson dates (p. 273) the raising of *o* to *u* in *Tunccetace* to the first half of the sixth century.

[105] The restoration of this word could likewise be *[t]usuri* (= *tonsori*), which make the change initial /ō/ to *u*.

[106] Prinz, *De O et U,* p. 83.

[107] Gustav Meyer, "Die lateinischen Elemente im Albanesischen" in Gröber's *Grundriss der romanischen Philologie* (Strassburg: Karl J. Trübner, 1904-06), I, 1048.

The single deviation from this area is the proper name *Iuvi-nian[us]*, D. 2838N, *CIL* III 6446, Sirmium (Pannonia Inferior), no date. Inscriptions thus show that initial /ŏ/ in Balkan Latin was relatively stable since we found only one deviation and 32 correct occurrences for a total 3.0 % of deviation in Christian inscriptions and 51 correct occurrences and no deviations for pagan inscriptions. Inscriptions do not show, therefore, a characteristic of Balkan Latin that is apparent in modern Rumanian, namely, that unaccented /ŏ/ changes to *u*.[108] In fact, the change of /ŏ/ to *u* is relatively rare in inscriptions.[109] The most plausible explanation for the sporadic use of *u* in Balkan inscriptions and the general Rumanian use of u *in* unstressed vowels is that, although a *u* for an unstressed /ŏ/ did occasionally take place, this phonetic feature was generalized only after the Vulgar Latin period and could not therefore be depicted in epigraphic material. It should be remembered that Rumanian belongs to the compromise vocalic system according to which stressed /ō/ and /ū/ remain distinct. It would seem that this scheme also prevailed in unaccented syllables and only at a later date did all velar vowels become *u* in unaccented position.

Intertonic

Africa	Century	Open Syllable		% Of Dev.	Closed Syllable		% Of Dev.	Totals		% Of Dev.
		/ŏ/ > o	/ŏ/ > u		/ŏ/ > o	/ŏ/ > u				
	3rd.	1	0		0	0		1	0	
	4th.	7	0		0	0		7	0	
	5th.	4	0		0	0		4	0	
	6th.	9	0		0	0		9	0	
	n.d.	45	8	15.1	3	0		48	8	14.3
	Totals:	66	8	10.8	3	0	0.0	69	8	10.4

---

[108] Bourciez, p. 555; Lausberg, I, 287; H. Tiktin, "Die rumänische Sprache" in Gröber's *Grundiss der romanischen Philologie* (Strassburg, Karl J. Trübner, 1904-06), I, 573.

[109] Sturtevant, p. 117; Prinz, while admitting the use of *u* for /ŏ/ in pagan inscriptions to a wide extent, finds /ŏ/ the regular vowel in Christian inscriptions (*De O et U*, p. 88): "U vocalem ex dialectis Italicis in linguam Latinam invasisse et per totum imperium Romanum diffusam esse verisimile est. Sed cum in titulis christianis perpauca U vocalis exempla occurrant, temporibus recentibus iterum O prevaluisse videtur."

The examples of deviations, all similar in nature, are:

> *Adeud[at]a*, D. 1408A, *CIL* VIII 13,440, Carthage (Proconsularis), no date.
> *Theudotus*, D. 1413, *CIL* VIII 25,346, Carthage (Proconsularis), no date.
> *Adeudatus*, D. 1417, *CIL* VIII 13,784, Carthage (Proconsularis), no date.
> *Adeudatu(s)*, D. 1902, *CIL* VIII 10,714, near Theveste (Proconsularis), no date.
> *Deu<d>ati*, D. 2083, near Theveste (Proconsularis), no date.
> *Teudorae*, D. 794N, *CIL* VIII 14,547, between Bulla Regia and Simitthus (Proconsularis), no date.
> *Theudorae*, D. 794N, *CIL* VIII 1259, no date.
> *Adeudatus*, D. 1902N, near Theveste (Proconsularis), no date.

Since the *u* for /ŏ/ appears in the same phonetic environment, namely after *e* with both vowels in hiatus, it would appear that a single explanation should cover this particular type of deviation. Gaeng considers (p. 187) this change as a reflection of synaeresis, the semivocalization of the /ŏ/ in hiatus and its union with the preceding vowel into a diphthong. Since all cases of deviation take place in proper names with the elements *theu-* and *deu-*, the Greek and Latin morphemes meaning God, an additional explanation for this change may be the analogy with the Latin nominative *deus*, the *u* being carried over into positions where an *o* is expected. It would be very natural for a Latin mason writing a Greek (or even Germanic) name having the element *theo-* to relate it to the Latin term for God, *deus*, with the concomitant change of *o* to *u*. [110] While writing Latin names compounded with a form of *Deus*, the mason would most naturally extend the *u* to positions where an *o* was required. [111]

---

[110] Although we did not find any Germanic names with the change *Theo-* to *Theu-*, Gaeng records (p. 186) *Theudorici* and *Teudoberti*.

[111] It should be noted that Gaeng did not find any examples of the proper name *Adeodatus* or its variants, which is characteristic of African inscriptions.

Britain	Century	Open Syllable /ŏ/ > o	/ŏ/ > u	% Of Dev.	Closed Syllable /ŏ/ > o	/ŏ/ > u	% Of Dev.	Totals		% Of Dev.
Pagan)	1st.	0	0		0	0		0	0	
	2nd.	2	0		1	0		3	0	
	3rd.	3	0		2	0		5	0	
	4th.	2	0		0	0		2	0	
	n.d.	15	0		1	0		16	0	
	Totals:	22	0	0.0	4	0	0.0	26	0	0.0
Christ.)	4th.	2	0	0.0	0	0	0.0	2	0	0.0

Although the figures are scanty, intertonic /ŏ/ appears stable in the Latin inscriptions of Britain, especially in pagan inscriptions.

Dalmatia	Century	Open Syllable /ŏ/ > o	/ŏ/ > u	% Of Dev.	Closed Syllable /ŏ/ > o	/ŏ/ > u	% Of Dev.	Totals		% Of Dev.
	4th.	6	0		0	0		6	0	
	5th.	14	0		0	0		14	0	
	n.d.	27	0		3	0		30	0	
	Totals:	47	0	0.0	3	0	0.0	50	0	0.0

Intertonic /ŏ/ in the Latin inscriptions of Dalmatia is stable.

Balkans	Century	Open Syllable /ŏ/ > o	/ŏ/ > u	% Of Dev.	Closed Syllable /ŏ/ > o	/ŏ/ > u	% Of Dev.	Totals		% Of Dev.
Pagan)	4th.	1	0		0	0		1	0	
	n.d.	5	0		0	0		5	0	
	Totals:	6	0	0.0	0	0	0.0	6	0	0.0
Christ.)	n.d.	10	1	9.1	0	0	0.0	10	1	9.1

The single case of deviation in Balkan Christian inscriptions was the proper name *Theuprepius,* D. 1089, *CIL* III 14,207, Serdica (Sofia), Thrace, no date. This is the same change that was encountered in the Latin inscriptions of Africa, namely, the Greek form *Theo-* written as *Theu-* because of synaeresis (the *e* and *u* forming a diphthong from two vowels in separate syllables) or through the analogy of the Latin nominative *Deus.*

We thus see that intertonic /ŏ/ is stable in our inscriptions except for the special case of -eo- changing to -eu- in proper names formed from the Greek Theo- or the Latin Deo-.[112] The same situation was also found in the areas studied by Gaeng.

We have an isolated change of intertonic /ŏ/ to e in the proper name Xenephonte, RIB 2306, near Cawfields south of Hadrian's Wall, A.D. 222-229. The correct spelling X[e]noph(onte) is found in RIB 2299, near Vindolanda (Chesterholm), A.D. 222-229.

The intertonic /ŏ/ is lost in the proper name Dinysia, RIB 562, Chester (Deva), no date, although the editor of the RIB mentions (p. 187) that "Dinysia may be a mason's slip for Dionysia."

Posttonic

Africa	Century	/ŏ/ > o	/ŏ/ > u	% Of Dev.
	3rd.	1	0	
	4th.	4	0	
	5th.	5	0	
	6th.	4	0	
	n.d.	40	0	
	Totals:	54	0	0.0
Britain	1st.	0	0	
	2nd.	3	0	
	3rd.	2	0	
(Pagan)	4th.	1	0	
	n.d.	8	0	
	Totals:	14	0	0.0
(Christ.)	4th.	1	0	
	6th.	1	0	
	Totals:	2	0	0.0
Dalmatia	4th.	4	0	
	5th.	5	0	
	6th.	1	0	
	n.d.	11	1	8.5
	Totals:	21	1	4.5

---

[112] We have a single case of the Greek Theo- changing to They- in the proper name Theydoraci, D. 1349A, Africa, n.d. This is evidently a case of a reverse spelling of the Greek upsilon; the progression would be Theo- to Theu- to They-.

The single deviation in the Latin inscriptions of Dalmatia is the noun *corpura*, D. 838, *CIL* III 9567, Salona, no date. Since posttonic /ŏ/ to *u* is an isolated case,[113] it is best to consider this change as a case of analogy with the nominative singular *corpus*.[114]

Balkans	Century	/ŏ/ > o	/ŏ/ > u	% Of Dev.
(Pagan)	n.d.	3	0	0.0
(Christ.)	4th.	2	0	
	6th.	1	0	
	n.d.	8	0	
	Totals:	11	0	0.0

It appears therefore that posttonic /ŏ/ was stable in all of the areas which we studied. Gaeng records (p. 188) the Greek loanwords *diacunus* and *episcupo* as well as the Latin forms *pecture* and *curpure*, but they are all sporadic occurrences.

Final: Non-Morphological

There are very few examples of /ŏ/ in this position: Africa, no date, 6; Britain (pagan), no date, 1; Dalmatia, no date, 2; and Balkans (Christian), no date, 1. We found no deviations in our limited corpus. The only interesting deviation found by Gaeng was the reflex of the Classical Latin number *quattuor* in the area of Rome. He found (p. 188) three examples with a final *u: quatur*, D. 4400B, A.D. 399; *quatur*, D. 2612N, no date, and *quattur*, D. 2952N, no date, as well as two forms with a final *o: quator*, D. 2921, A.D. 431, and *quator*, D. 2810E, no date. In our African inscriptions we have five examples of this number, all with final *o: quattuo[r]*, D. 2046, no date; *quattor*, D. 2648A, no date; *quadtor*, D. 2670, no date; *quattuor*, D. 3085AN, no date, and *quatuor*, D. 3946, no date. Gaeng considers (pp. 188-89) the alternation of the *-or* and *-ur* spelling as a reflection of the weakening of the final vowel into a *shva* sound before metathesis took place: *quattro* in modern Italian is the result

---

[113] Skok in his *Pojave* gives (p. 30) *corpura* as the sole example of the change of posttonic /ŏ/ to *u* although his epigraphic material is extensive.

[114] See Prinz, *De O et U*, p. 78; Pei, *Texts*, p. 53; Gaeng, p. 188, for a similar interpretation.

of this process. The Logudorese form *battoro* would posit *quattor*. Gaeng's explanation, however, loses force when we consider that the French, Provençal, and Catalan *quatre*, the Spanish *cuatro*, and the Portuguese *quatro* all show metathesis, but inscriptional material does not show a final *u* for *o*, which is supposedly a sign of vowel weakening. The Rumanian *patru* shows both metathesis and a final *u* for /ŏ/, but our epigraphical evidence is too skimpy to be conclusive in the determination of the reflex of Latin *quattuor* in this area.

Final: Morphological

The only morphological endings that we are considering are the nominative singular endings of third declension nouns. The final /ŏ/ in conjugational endings, such as the first person singular of the present and future passives, is almost non-existent in our corpus.

	Century	Nom. Sing. 3rd Decl.		% Of Dev.	Nom. Sing. 3rd Decl.		Nom. Sing. 3rd Decl.	
		-or	*-ur*		*-ors*	*-urs*	*-ox*	*-ux*
Africa	4th.	3	0					
	5th.	9	0					
	6th.	4	0					
	n.d.	32	0		2	0	4	0
	Totals:	48	0	0.0	2	0	4	0
Britain	1st.	1	0					
	2nd.	0	0					
(Pagan)	3rd.	2	0					
	4th.	1	0					
	n.d.	14	0					
	Totals:	18	0	0.0	0	0	0	0
(Christ.)	6th.	4	1	20.0	0	0	0	0

The single deviation in Christian inscriptions of Britain is *servatur*, *CIIC* 360, Caermartenshire (Wales), before A.D. 569. It is interesting to note that the other third declension nominatives of the same inscription end in *-or*: *amato*[*r*] and *cul*[*t*]*or*.

Dalmatia	Century	Nom. Sing. 3rd Decl.		% Of Dev.
		-or	-ur	
	4th.	1	0	
	6th.	0	1	100.0
	n.d.	13	0	
	Totals:	14	1	6.7

The deviation in this area is *peccatur*, D. 79a, CIL III 9527, Salona, A.D. 599.

Balkans	Century	Nom. Sing. 3rd Decl.		% Of Dev.
		-or	-ur	
(Pagan)	n.d.	4	0	0.0
(Christ.)	4th.	1	0	
	n.d.	8	0	
	Totals:	9	0	0.0

We see that the -*or* ending of third declension nouns is stable in our areas, especially in Africa where we have 48 cases of correct occurrences and no deviations. This is somewhat in contrast with the findings of Gaeng who found for Narbonensis and Lugdunensis several examples of a -*ur* ending: *lectur, Bellatur, oxsur, Senatur, Vigur, amatur, doctur, inux* (= *innox*), *nuviliur* (= the comparative adjective *nobilior*). The deviations in the provinces of Gaul, however, do not occur before the sixth century,[115] a time when final vowels were especially obscure in Gaul.[116] Gaul is the only area given by Gaeng where there is a change of third declension nouns ending in -*or* to -*ur*.[117]

Although Prinz' explanation for the change of -*or* to -*ur* may be too inclusive, namely, that the noun ending was influenced by the analogy of the verbal termination,[118] our two deviations, *servatur* and

---

[115] Gaeng, p. 192; Prinz also states (*De O et U*, p. 77) that "apparet exempla ethnica paene plane deese. Etiam in titulis christianis -UR pro -OR nisi recentissimis linguae Latinae temporibus non obviam fit."

[116] Grandgent, p. 103.

[117] Cf. Prinz, p. 77: "Pleraque exempla in Gallia Transalpina exstant."

[118] *Ibid.*: "Mihi persuasum est in his vocabulis U ad analogiam terminationis verbalis ortam esse."

peccatur, do fit his theory perfectly. Whether one accepts Grand-gent's phonetic explanation of final vowel weakness or Prinz' analog-ical reasoning, it appears that there was a difference in the treatment of the third declension nominative singular ending *-or,* Gaul having deviated more than the other areas of Romania from the Classical Latin norm. Since final /ŏ/ is so rarely encountered in final syllables, however, the results for the nominative singular of third declension nouns may be too heavily weighted.

The final /ŏ/ of the cardinal number *duo* is twice changed to *a* on the analogy of regular neuter plural adjectives of the second declension; in both cases the neuter plural noun *corpora* is present: *at dua corpura deponenda,* D. 838, *CIL* III 9567, Salona (Dalmatia), no date, and [*si quis super*] *ea dua corpo*[*ra*], D. 821N, *CIL* III 9927, Burnum (Dalmatia), no date.

Latin /ō/, Represented by the Letter o

Initial

Africa	Century	Open Syllable		% Of Dev.	Closed Syllable		Totals		% Of Dev.
		/ō/ > o	/ō/ > u		/ō/ > o	/ō/ > u			
	3rd.	1	0		0	0	1	0	
	4th.	19	0		15	0	34	0	
	5th.	23	0		3	0	26	0	
	6th.	14	0		4	0	18	0	
	n.d.	54	0		20	0	74	0	
	Totals:	111	0	0.0	42	0	153	0	0.0

On the basis of the numerous correct occurrences of initial /ō/ without any deviations, it appears that initial /ō/ is stable in the Latin inscriptions of African.

Britain	Century	Open Syllable		% Of Dev.	Closed Syllable		Totals		% Of Dev.
		/ō/ > o	/ō/ > u		/ō/ > o	/ō/ > u			
(Pagan)	1st.	5	0		0	0	5	0	
	2nd.	4	0		1	0	5	4	
	3rd.	17	0		8	0	25	0	
	4th.	8	0		18	0	26	0	
	n.d.	22	1		7	0	29	1	3.3
	Totals:	56	1	0.0	34	0	90	1	1.1

The single deviation found in this area was the Celtic deity *Nudente*, *RIB* 307, Lydney Park, Gloucester, no date, although /ō/ is more prevalent: *Nodonti*, *RIB* 305, Lydney Park, Gloucester, no date; *Nodenti* (bis), *RIB* 306, Lydney Park, Gloucester, no date, and *Nodonti*, *RIB* 616, Cockersand Moss, Lancaster, no date.[119] On the basis of just a single deviation of a Celtic name in the Latin of the pagan inscriptions of Britain, it seems that initial /ō/ was stable.

Initial /ō/ in the Christian inscriptions of Britain was extremely rare, only one correct occurrence having been found in a closed syllable of a fifth century inscription. It is obviously impossible to draw any conclusions on the initial /ō/ of Christian inscriptions of Britain on such a limited corpus.

almatia Century	Open Syllable		% Of Dev.	Closed Syllable		% Of Dev.	Totals		% Of Dev.
	/ō/ > o	/ō/ > u		/ō/ > o	/ō/ > u				
4th.	5	0		14	0		19	0	
5th.	0	0		6	0		6	0	
6th.	3	0		1	0		4	0	
n.d.	17	1	5.6	12	4	25.0	29	5	14.7
Totals:	25	1	3.8	33	4	10.8	58	5	7.9

The examples of deviation in this area are:

ust[*iar*]*ius*, *D*. 1289, *CIL* III 13,142, Salona, n.d.[120]
pureremu (= *poneremus*), *D*. 838, *CIL* III 9567, Salona, n.d.
usteari(*us*), *D*. 3791A, *CIL* III 14,305, Salona, no date.

---

[119] The initial *o* as well as initial *u* came from the British diphthong *ou* in the etymon of this particular Celtic deity; cf. Jackson, *Language*, pp. 306-307, for a discussion of the *o* and *u* from British *ou*.

[120] The form *ustiarius* is likewise recorded by Gaeng for Lugdunensis. On the basis of the Romance languages (cf. Fr. *huis*, It. *uscio*, Rum. *uṣă*, Old Sp. *uzo*), it is most probable that Vulgar Latin had the form *ustium* as well as the Classical Latin *ostium*. Chronologically interesting is the date given to *ustium* by Meyer-Lübke, *Einführung*, p. 180: "Auch *ūstium*, im Lateinischen seit dem 6. Jahrh. bezeugt." It is noteworthy that in the *Appendix Probi* (No. 61) there is an item: *ostium non osteum*, without any mention of a Vulgar Latin pronunciation of the initial vowel. See Prinz, pp. 71-72, for a good summary of this word.

urdenaverunt (= *ordinaverunt*), *D.* 3835, *CIL* III 9585, Salona, no date.
u[rde]navi, *D.* 3838, *CIL* III 12,869, Salona, no date.

The total percentage of deviation of 7.9 % is substantially higher than the figures derived from the other areas studied (0.0 % for Africa and 1.1 % for pagan Britain) and seems to show that the treatment of initial /ō/ was different in the Latin spoken on the eastern coast of the Adriatic. Although the change of initial /ō/ to *u* in the word *ustiarius* (and its variants) was a general Romance phenomenon (see *supra*, footnote 120, p. 273), particular importance must be given to the *u* in the two perfect indicatives of the verb *ordino*. These two examples of initial /ō/ to *u* in these inscriptions from Salona, Dalmatia, cause Prinz to write (p. 67): "Verisimile est U vocalem in verbo Valachico 'urdina' referri posse ad eam U vocalem, quae iam in titulis Salonitanis bis occurrit." On discussing the form *pureremu*, Skok, *Pojave*, considers (p. 27) the change of initial /ō/ to *u* as a characteristic of Rumanian. [121]

Balkans	Century	Open Syllable		Closed Syllable		Totals	
		/ō/ > o	/ō/ > u	/ō/ > o	/ō/ > u		
(Pagan)	1st.	2	0	0	0	2	0
	2nd.	1	0	1	0	2	0
	3rd.	1	0	0	0	1	0
	4th.	1	0	4	0	5	0
	n.d.	2	0	1	0	3	0
	Totals:	7	0	6	0	13	0
(Christ.)	4th.	1	0	1	0	2	0
	5th.	0	0	0	0	0	0
	n.d.	5	0	2	0	7	0
	Totals:	6	0	3	0	9	0

The total number of occurrences is too scanty for any definite conclusion to be made concerning the treatment of initial /ō/ in the Balkans. Rumanian does show a *u* for unaccented *o*, a situation which may be foreshadowed by the treatment of initial /ō/ in Latin inscriptions of Dalmatia.

---

[121] "Mjesto o stoji u kao i u rumunskom jeziku." (Instead of o there is a u as in Rumanian too.)

Intertonic

Africa	Century	Open Syllable		% Of Dev.	Closed Syllable		Totals		% Of Dev.
		$/\bar{o}/ > o$	$/\bar{o}/ > u$		$/\bar{o}/ > o$	$/\bar{o}/ > u$			
	3rd.	2	0		0	0	2	0	
	4th.	1	0		0	0	1	0	
	5th.	2	0		0	0	2	0	
	6th.	3	0		0	0	3	0	
	n.d.	36	2	5.3	0	0	36	2	5.3
	Totals:	44	2	4.3	0	0	44	2	4.3

The two deviations in this area are:

Mesuleolus (= *Maesoleolus*), D. 3272C, *CIL* VIII 9815, Albulae (Mauretania Caesariensis), n.d.
musuleum (= *mausoleum*), D. 3680, *CIL* VIII 10,712, Hr.-Mabrek (Numidia), no date.

Since both deviations occur in words of Greek origin, it appears that intertonic /ō/ was stable in Africa. This conclusion is substantiated by the comparison of deviations showing an intertonic *u* which Gaeng found (p. 196) in the inscriptions of Gaul and Italy: *sanctemunialis, neguciatoris, octugenta, Victurinus, negutiator, octuginta, Victurina,* and *laburantibus.* The overall impression is that intertonic /ō/ is more stable in Africa than in Gaul and Italy, but Gaeng's figures are too scanty, unfortunately, for a more definite conclusion to be made. Although Gaeng qualifies his findings of *u* for intertonic /ō/ as sporadic (p. 196), in his tables (p. 195) both occurrences of intertonic /ō/ in Lugdunensis are deviations. In inscriptions of Northern Italy, Gaeng records (p. 195) ten correct occurrences and two deviations. It is unfortunate that the lack of epigraphical material precludes a quantitative analysis of the weakening of intertonic /ō/ in the various areas of Romania.

Britain	Century	Open Syllable		% Of Dev.	Closed Syllable		Totals		% Of Dev.
		/ō/ > o	/ō/ > u		/ō/ > o	/ō/ > u			
(Pagan)	1st.	1	0		0	0	1	0	
	2nd.	14	0		2	0	16	0	
	3rd.	19	1	5.0	0	0	19	1	5.0
	n.d.	15	0		0	0	15	0	
	Totals:	49	1	2.0	2	0	51	1	1.9

The single case of deviation in a Latin form is the proper name *Sebussian(ae)* (= assuming that it stands for *Sebosiane*), *RIB* 605, *CIL* VII 287, Lancaster, A.D. 262-266. [122] Intertonic /ō/ seems stable in the pagan inscriptions of Britain.

Intertonic /ō/ in Christian inscriptions of Britain is very rarely encountered, only two correct occurrences having been found in our corpus.

Dalmatia	Century	Open Syllable		Closed Syllable		Totals	
		/ō/ > o	/ō/ > u	/ō/ > o	/ō/ > u		
	4th.	1	0	0	0	1	0
	5th.	2	0	0	0	2	0
	n.d.	8	0	0	0	8	0
	Totals:	11	0	0	0	11	0

There are too few occurrences of intertonic /ō/ for any firm conclusion to be made.

Balkans	Century	Open Syllable		Closed Syllable		Totals	
		/ō/ > o	/ō/ > u	/ō/ > o	/ō/ > u		
(Pagan)	2nd.	2	0	0	0	2	0
	3rd.	3	0	0	0	3	0
	n.d.	5	0	0	0	5	0
	Totals:	10	0	0	0	10	0
(Christ.)	n.d.	5	0	0	0	5	0

There are too few occurrences of intertonic /ō/ in either pagan or Christian inscriptions for any conclusions to be made.

---

[122] We do have the proper name *Sebosiannae*, *RIB* 1041, Bollihope Common, Stanhope (Co. Durham), no date.

Final: Non-Morphological

Final /ō/ in non-morphological endings is very infrequent in our corpus and no deviations were found. We present the following table, however, to show the negative interest provided by non-morphological /ō/ in comparison to final /ō/ in morphological endings which do afford great comparative material.

Area	Century	/ō/ > o	/ō/ > u
Africa	n.d.	2	0
Britain (Pagan)	3rd.	1	0
Britain (Christian)	- -	0	0
Dalmatia	4th.	3	0
	n.d.	4	0
Totals:		7	0
Balkans (Pagan)	n.d.	1	0
Balkans (Christian)	4th.	2	0
	n.d.	1	0
Totals:		3	0

Final: Morphological

The declensional endings having a final /ō/ which we will investigate are the dative singular, ablative singular, and accusative plural of the second declension, and the nominative singulars -o and -os of the third declension. Although final /ō/ in conjugational endings is found in the first person singular of the present indicative, future indicative, future perfect indicative, and the second and third persons of the future imperative, these forms are virtually nonexistent in our corpus and will not be tabulated.

Area	Century	2nd Decl. Dat. Sing.		% Of Dev.	2nd Decl. Abl. Sing.		% Of Dev.	2nd Decl. Acc. Plur.	
		-o	-u		-o	-u		-os	-us
Africa	3rd.	7	0		1	0		0	0
	4th.	30	0		17	4	19.0	3	0
	5th.	8	0		25	4	13.8	10	0
	6th.	4	0		26	0		6	0
	7th.	0	0		3	0		0	0
	n.d.	51	0		106	27	20.3	65	0
Totals:		100	0	0.0	178	35	16.4	84	0

	3rd Decl. Nom. Sing.		% Of Dev.	3rd Decl. Nom. Sing.		% Of Dev.
	-o	*-u*		*-o*	*-u*	
3rd.	1	0		0	0	
4th.	4	0		0	0	
5th.	0	0		1	0	
6th.	2	0		0	0	
7th.	1	0		0	0	
n.d.	25	0		6	0	
Totals:	33	0	0.0	7	0	0.0

The only declensional ending showing a change of /ō/ to *u* in the Latin inscriptions of Africa in our corpus is the ablative singular *-o*. The percentage of deviation is also very high (35 deviations and 178 correct occurrences for a deviation of 16.4 %). When we consider that the vocalism of African Latin has been extremely conservative, with only a few sporadic deviations, we are struck by both the number of deviations and the high percentage of deviations in the final /ō/ of the ablative singular of the second declension. The question immediately arises whether this change of final /ō/ to *u* is primarily phonetic or morphological. The question is also complicated by the fact that in Sardinian Latin second declension nouns do end in *-u* in the singular, but *-os* in the plural. [123] The influence of African Latin on Sardinian has also been recognized. [124] Before entering into a discussion of this important change, we will give the categories in which the examples are found.

a)   In time expressions: [125]

> *tertiu kalendas Apriles indictione XIIII*, D, 234, Rusgunia, no date.
> *die undecimu*, D. 1105, CIL VIII 9707, Orléansville, A.D. 475.
> *sub die tertu decimu calendas Ianarias*, D. 1383, CIL VIII 23,586, Maktar, n.d.

---

[123] Lausberg, II, 32; Rohlfs, *Grammatik*, I, 243.

[124] See M. L. Wagner's discussion of the influence of African Latin on Sardinian in his *La lingua sarda: storia, spirito e forma* (Bern: A. Francke, 1951), p. 130.

[125] We are not considering cases where the accusative of time was the correct construction, such as: *Flabius ... bicxit annis XXX, mense unu, dies XXIIII*, D. 2646, CIL VIII 670, Maktar, no date. The form *unu* is probably the accusative with the loss of final *-m*.

deposita est sextu decimu k. Iunias, D. 1384, *CIL* VIII 23,230a, Sufetala, n.d.

sub die quintu kl. Apriles, D. 1387A, *CIL* VIII 5263, Hippo Regius, no date.

sub die quintu idus Februarias, D. 1388, *CIL* VIII 5264, Hippo Regius, no date.

septimu idus Sept(e)m(b)r(es), D. 2068, *CIL* VIII 20,600, Tocqueville, A.D. 359.

nonu idus Novembres, D. 2094, *CIL* VIII 5664, near Calama, no date.

tertiu idus Iunias, D. 2100, *CIL* VIII 6700, Mastari, no date.

sub die quartu kalendas Nobenbres, D. 2835, *CIL* VIII 2011, Theveste, no date.

die octabu kalendas Februarias, D. 3052B, *CIL* VIII 21,540, Mina, no date.

discess[i]t tersiu kal., D. 3272, *CIL* VIII 21,642, Arbal, A.D. 480.

die nonu kal. Ianuarias, D. 3276, *CIL* VIII 21,689, Albulae, A.D. 493.

deposita est qqartu decimu kaledas Decembres, D. 1349A, near El-Djem, no date.

decessit octau kal. Martias, D. 3718, *CIL* VIII 20,304, Satafi, A.D. 349.

decessit octau idus Apriles, D. 3954, *CIL* VIII 28,041, near Theveste, no date.

b) After prepositions: (non-time expressions)

de numeru, D. 495, *CIL* VIII 17,414, Hippo Regius, no date.

[in presby]teriu, D. 1186, *CIL* VIII 23,230c, Sufetala, no date.

a santu Crescituru e<p>iscu, D. 2061, near Sitifi, no date.

de lignu crucis, D. 2068, *CIL* VIII 20,600, Tocqueville, A.D. 359.

fide in deu, D. 2495, *CIL* VIII 2218a, near Theveste, no date.

in refrigeu (= *refrigerio*), D. 2722A, Thabraca, fourth century.

cum pace in deu, D. 3368, Hadrumetum, no date.

cum filiu suo Basso, D. 3402B, Carthage, n.d.

in bonu, D. 3409, *CIL* VIII 14,328, Utica, n.d.

in pace et paradissu, D. 3451, *CIL* VIII 13,603, Carthage, no date.

[i]n deu, D. 1346N, *CIL* VIII 13,977, Carthage, no date.

pro hunc lo(c)um san<ct>um, D. 2187, *CIL* VIII 11,134, Leptis Minor, no date.

c) In the ablative absolute construction:

infante peregrinu, D. 1475A, *CIL* VIII 23,017, Hadrumetum, no date.
Subitanu inocente in pace, D. 2547A, *CIL* VIII 25,289, Carthage, no date.

d) Miscellaneous:

gladiu percussus, D. 2054, *CIL* VIII 9866, Altava, not before A.D. 449.

From the foregoing categories, it is clear that the ablative in *u* is most often found in time expressions and after prepositions, both categories showing accusative structures under certain conditions. In time expressions it is very common to see an ablative expression followed by an accusative expression of time, such as *sub die quintu kl. Apriles,* or *deposita est qqartu decimu kaledas Decembres.* [126] The very common time expressions *vixit annis* and *vixit annos* also show that both the ablative and accusative of time were very easily confused in the mind of the Vulgar Latin speaker. It is also common for prepositions that govern the ablative case in Classical Latin to take the accusative case in Vulgar Latin inscriptions. We will give just a few African inscriptions to show the confusion of cases after prepositions:

cum titulum, D. 1571, *CIL* VIII 20,780, Auzia, A.D. 318.
in hoc signum semper vinces, D. 1621, *CIL* VIII 1767, Sicca Veneria, no date.

---

[126] Diehl in his study entitled *De M finali epigraphica* specifically mentions (p. 53) a time expression which we also recorded, *sub die quartu kalendas Nobenbres,* and expresses the difficulty in determining whether *quartu* should be ablative or accusative with the words: "decerni nequit, utrum 'quarto' an 'quartu(m)' interpretandum sit." Basing himself on the epigraphic material found in Leblant's *Inscriptions de la Gaule,* Diehl concludes (p. 54) that "unde patet casum ablativum longe praevaluisse, meros accusativos raros fuisse, locis igitur dubiis ablativum non accusativum casum interpretandum esse." Although the ablative was preferred in Gaul, Diehl admits that the situation may be different in other areas: "Concedo idem quadrare non debere ad ceteras provincias."

pro hunc lo(c)um san<ct>um, D. 2187, *CIL* VIII 11,134,
near Leptis Minor, no date.
in hunc s(e)culum, D. 2751, Hadrumetum, no date.
[*in h*]*oc signum, D.* 1622, *CIL* VIII 5346, Calama, no date.
in hoc signum, D. 1623, *CIL* VIII 1106, Carthage, no date.

It would appear that the use of a *u* for a final /ō/ in African
inscriptions is a morphological change, the accusative ending *-um*
dropping the final *-m*. If we were facing a phonetic change, the final
/ō/ in the dative singular of second declension forms should also
show this change of /ō/ to *u*, which is never the case in our corpus.
It is precisely those situations where an accusative case could be
substituted for an ablative (namely, in time expressions and after
prepositions) that we do have this change of final /ō/ to *u*.

The reality of the Sardinian case system must also be discussed.
As was previously mentioned, the Sardinian ending of second declension forms ends in *-u* in the singular. Since African Latin has
been acknowledged as an influence on Sardinian, an attempt can be
made to explain the Sardinian case system on the basis of our findings for final /ō/ in African inscriptions. An important key to the
problem is the treatment of final /ō/ in the dative singular ending
of second declension forms. The stability of final /ō/ in dative singular forms contrasts strongly with the change of /ō/ to *u* in ablative
constructions. This final *u* in ablative forms was seen to be mainly
morphological in nature since it appeared to be an accusative ending
with the loss of final *-m*. Our conclusion is that the accusative
ending *-u(m)* was the principal factor in determining the Sardinian
singular case ending *-u* without the merger of other cases as has been
proposed for other areas. [127]

---

[127] The problem of whether it was solely the Classical Latin accusative
case or a merger of the Classical Latin accusative, ablative, and dative that
brought about the various Romance language case systems has been reviewed
by Pei in his article "Accusative," pp. 241-67. Although Pei adheres to the
merger theory, he does admit that in the case of Sardinian, "the conflict was
apparently solved in favor of the accusative." He then remarks (p. 245):
". . . the triumph of the accusative in central Sardinia can be taken as proof
of only one fact: that in the sole instance where the phonetic fusion of the
oblique cases was not possible, the accusative proved stronger; and this in
a single region of Romance territory, very limited in extent and almost severed
from communication with the rest of the Latin-speaking world at the very
time when the all-important process of declensional change was beginning.

Another important finding of the Latin in African inscriptions is the stability of the second declension accusative plural ending -os. We found no deviations to -us and 84 correct occurrences. Since the Sardinian ending of second declension nouns in the plural is precisely -os, it is remarkable to note the parallel form in African inscriptions. The vocalic systems of Sardinian and African Latin are once again so similar that one must conclude that the Vulgar Latin archaic vocalic scheme was the same in both areas. The stability of the second declension plural ending -os in African inscriptions is almost diametrically opposed to the treatment of final -os in other areas of Romania. We will give below the figures for the areas studied by Gaeng so as to show the discrepancy in the stability or change of final -os in the various areas of the Empire.

Summary of the Treatment of Final -os, As Taken from Gaeng, pp. 199-200

	Century	-os	-us	% Of Dev.
Baetica	4th-6th	23	0	
	7th	13	0	
	Totals:	36	0	0.0
Tarraconensis	4th-6th	8	0	
	7th	3	0	
	Totals:	11	0	0.0
Lugdunensis	4th-5th	6	7	53.8
	6th-7th	13	26	66.6
	Totals:	19	33	63.5
Central Italy	3rd-4th	9	0	
	5th	5	3	37.5
	6th-7th	1	12	92.3
	Totals:	15	15	50.0
Northern Italy	4th-5th	30	8	21.0
	6th	14	6	30.0
	Totals:	44	14	24.1

Additional inferences derived from this fact seem arbitrary and unwarranted." Our findings of the accusative case as the basis of the Sardinian case system are, of course, limited to this area and should not be extended to all of Romania.

	Century	-os	-us	% Of Dev.
Southern Italy	3rd-4th	3	2	40.0
	5th	8	5	38.4
	6th-7th	17	16	48.4
	Totals:	28	23	45.1
Rome	3rd-4th	59	33	35.8
	5th	23	28	54.9
	6th-7th	8	19	70.3
	Totals:	90	80	47.1
Lusitania	4th-6th	36	1	2.7
	7th	4	0	
	Totals:	40	1	2.4
Narbonensis	4th-5th	4	3	42.8
	6th-7th	13	28	68.3
	Totals:	17	31	64.6

When we compare the above figures with our figures for African Latin, it is interesting to note that in addition to African Latin where final -os is stable, the Latin of Hispania also shows a stability in final -os. The areas of Baetica and Tarraconensis do not show any deviations, while Lusitania had one deviation and 40 correct occurrences for a total deviation of 2.4 %. The peripheral areas of Africa and Hispania are therefore very conservative when we compare the findings for final -os in the central areas of Gaul and Italy. Besides the very high total percentage of deviation in these areas (Narbonensis: 64.6 %, Lugdunensis: 63.5 %, Northern Italy: 24.1 %, Central Italy: 50.0 %, Southern Italy: 45.1 %, and Rome: 47.1 %), the chronological increase in deviations must also be brought out. Although the ending -us is encountered to a large degree in the fourth century (possibly the third), the percentage of deviation increases with the passage of time to the point where in some areas (Narbonensis, Lugdunensis, Central Italy, and Rome), the deviation becomes the regular form. Since the change of -os to -us occurs early in the areas of Gaul and Italy (the figures are just for Christian inscriptions and do not take into account pagan inscriptions), it does not appear that the initiation of the change was due to any Germanic influence which would, of necessity, be a factor in the later centuries. The predominance of the weakened ending -us in the sixth and seventh centuries may have been helped along by the strong stress accent caused by the Germanic incursions into Gaul, but the beginnings of the change can in no way be ascribed to an increased stress accent. The high percentage of deviation in Rome and Southern Italy would also militate against considering this change as the result of a strong stress accent brought on by the Germanic invasions.

The comparison of the treatment of the second declension accusative plural ending -os in Africa and in other areas as studied by Gaeng shows very clearly that there was a distinct differentiation of this ending in the various parts of Romania. Gaul and Italy are the two areas where -os changes to -us to the greatest extent. Sturtevant gives (p. 117) a substratum reasoning for this state of affairs: "The use of u for ō is most common in Southern Italy and Gaul, where the native languages, Oscan and Gaulish, lacked ō." Carnoy remarks (p. 48) that he found only one example of a -us ending for the second declension accusative plural in Spain and explains (p. 49) the change of -os to -us in the following terms: "Le succès de cette forme dépend sans doute de la phonétique, en ce que ō et ū finals se confondirent et de la morphologie, en ce qu'elle est le résultat d'une analogie. On aura fait la proportion:

$$\frac{\text{rosa(m)} \quad - \quad \text{annu(m)}}{\text{rosas} \quad - \quad \text{annus}}$$

Prinz likewise considers (De O et U, pp. 135-36) the analogical influence of the -u(m) in the accusative singular of second declension forms as the main reason for the -us ending in the accusative plurals of the second declension. [128] Grandgent stresses (p. 148) the idea that "one result of the intermediate confusion [between the fourth and second declensions] was an accusative plural spelling -us for -os." It is important to remember that whatever the reason or reasons may be for the interpretation of the change of -os to -us, especially in Gaul and Italy, they do not apply to the Latin of African inscriptions where the -os ending is stable. [129]

---

[128] "US terminationem vi analogiae ortam esse puto: U ex accusativo singulari in pluralem translata est, ut in declinatione altera eodem modo quo in ceteris declinationibus accusativi singularis et pluralis vocalis par redderetur."

[129] Pirson's comment (p. 42) that "dans les inscriptions chrétiennes, annus

Britain	Century	2nd Decl. Dat. Sing.		2nd Decl. Abl. Sing.		2nd Decl. Acc. Plur.	
		-o	*-u*	*-o*	*-u*	*-os*	*-us*
(Pagan)	1st.	3	0	5	0	0	0
	2nd.	32	0	24	0	1	0
	3rd.	99	0	55	0	2	0
	4th.	31	0	0	0	0	0
	n.d.	113	0	30	0	22	0
	Totals:	278	0	114	0	25	0

Britain	Century	3rd Decl. Nom. Sing.		3rd Decl. Nom. Sing.	
		-o	*-u*	*-os*	*-us*
(Pagan)	2nd.	5	0	0	0
	3rd.	3	0	1	0
	n.d.	10	0	2	0
	Totals:	18	0	3	0

From the above tables it is clear that final /ō/ is stable in declensional endings in the Latin of pagan inscriptions of Britain. It is even more conservative than the Latin of African inscriptions, both areas being the most classical in vocalic phenomena in Romania. The classical nature of the Latin of pagan inscriptions of Britain is also seen by the maintenance of both the *-u* and *-o* endings of the ablative singular of *domus*.

Britain	Century	Ablative of *domus*	
		-o	*-u*
(Pagan)	3rd.	4	2
	n.d.	3	2
	Totals:	7	4

Since we found no deviations in the ablative singular of second declension forms and 114 correct occurrences, it would appear that the final *u* in *domu* was the remnant of the fourth declension in a noun that had an intermixture of second declension endings in its inflection. [130] It should also be noted that the pagan inscriptions of

---

est pour ainsi dire devenu la forme régulière de l'accusatif pluriel," although correct for Gaul, is complètement inaccurate for Africa.

[130] Hale-Buck, p. 49; Allen and Greenough, p. 38.

Britain are the only ones where the ablative *domu* is found. In Christian inscriptions the form *domu* is not found. [131]

Britain	Century	2nd Decl. Abl. Sing.		2nd Decl. Acc. Plur.		3rd Decl. Nom. Sing.	
		-o	-u	-os	-us	-o	-u
(Christ.)	4th.	0	0	1	0	0	0
	5th.	2	0	1	0	0	0
	6th.	4	0	0	0	1	0
	7th.	2	0	0	0	1	0
	8th.	1	0	0	0	0	0
	n.d.	3	0	0	0	0	0
	Totals:	12	0	2	0	2	0

	3rd Decl. Nom. Sing.		% Of Dev.
	-os	-us	
9th.	1	0	
n.d.	0	2	100.0
Totals:	1	2	66.7

The two deviations in Christian inscriptions of Britain are:

nepus, *CIIC* 520, Wigtown (Scotland), no date.
pronepus, *CIIC* 408, Glamorgan (Wales), no date.

Dalmatia	Century	2nd Decl. Dat. Sing.		2nd Decl. Abl. Sing.		2nd Decl. Acc. Plur.		% Of Dev.
		-o	-u	-o	-u	-os	-us	
	4th.	0	0	10	0	4	0	
	5th.	0	0	39	0	3	0	
	6th.	0	0	9	0	1	0	
	n.d.	63	0	40	0	16	4	20.0
	Totals:	63	0	98	0	24	4	14.3

---

[131] This agrees substantially with Prinz' statement (p. 120) concerning the form *domu*: "Certae aetatis exempla inde ab Augusti temporibus usque ad saeculum tertium extant." Prinz also remarks (p. 120) that "etiam in codicibus U terminatio rara non est."

	3rd Decl. Nom. Sing.		3rd Decl. Nom. Sing.	
	-o	-u	-os	-us
4th.	5	0	0	0
5th.	5	0	1	0
n.d.	14	0	1	0
Totals:	24	0	2	0

The four deviations in this area, all in the accusative plural, are:

annus (bis), D. 405, *CIL* III 6399, near Salona, no date.
medianus, D. 2183, *CIL* III 9564, Salona, no date.
annus, D. 3835, *CIL* III 9585, Salona, no date.

Final /ō/ is stable in declensional endings in the Christian in-scriptions of Dalmatia, except for the accusative plural ending -*os* which changes to -*us* on occasion. Since this is the only declensional ending where there is a change of /ō/ to *u*, it is best to consider this change as morphological on the basis of analogy with the ac-cusative singular of second declension forms (see *supra*, p. 284).

Balkans	Century	2nd Decl. Dat. Sing.		2nd Decl. Abl. Sing.		2nd Decl. Acc. Plur.		% Of Dev.	3rd Decl. Nom. Sing.	
		-o	-u	-o	-u	-os	-us		-o	-u
(Pagan)	2nd.	10	0	7	0	0	0		0	0
	3rd.	10	0	10	0	1	0		0	0
	4th.	17	0	0	0	1	0		0	0
	n.d.	22	0	13	0	3	0		7	0
	Totals:	59	0	30	0	5	0	0.0	7	0
(Christ.)	4th.	1	0	7	0	1	0		0	0
	5th.	0	0	1	0	0	0		0	0
	n.d.	16	0	25	0	4	1	20.0	5	0
	Totals:	17	0	33	0	5	1	16.7	5	0

The single deviation in Christian inscriptions of the Balkans is:

annus, D. 3659, Purbach (Pannonia), no date.

We thus see that the Latin of both pagan and Christian in-scriptions of the Balkans maintained a stable final /ō/, especially in the dative and ablative singular forms of the second declension. Inscriptions do not foreshadow, therefore, the development in Rumanian of unaccented final /ō/ closing to *u*.

We have an isolated case of final /ō/ changing to *e* in the word *solides*, D. 829N, *CIL* III 12,841, Salona (Dalmatia), no date. Although it is tempting to consider this case as a weakening of final vowels, the uniqueness probably means that it is a simple error on the part of the stonemason. [132] We have already seen that final /ō/ is stable in Dalmatian inscriptions, except for the accusative plural ending -*os* that does have the tendency to change to -*us*.

Final /ō/ is changed to *a* in the numeral *amba*, D. 1505, *CIL* III 9505, Salona (Dalmatia), A.D. 359, on the basis of analogy with regular second declension neuter plural adjectives. We have already seen the same analogical influence on the final /ō/ of the cardinal number *duo* (see *supra*, p. 272), when it appears as *dua* as a modifier of the neuter plural noun *corpora*.

Accusative of Time vs. Ablative of Time: vixit annos *vs.* vixit annis

Although the accusative of duration of time was the classical structure, the ablative began to assume this function in the prose writers of the first century A.D. and was common in both pagan and Christian inscriptions. [133] In addition to figures for the accusative or ablative of duration of time for "*annos*" and "*annis*," we will also give a table for other divisions of time, such as months, days, and hours since the distribution of the accusative and ablative of time in the various parts of Romania may reveal morphological tendencies that may assume importance in the later development of the Romance languages.

---

[132] Cf. Skok, *Pojave*, pp. 32-33, who considers the possibility that final /ō/ could have weakened to *e* as in French and Polish, but is inclined to consider it as a mistake.

[133] See *supra*, pp. 38-41 of our "Introduction" for bibliographical sources and some conclusions drawn by scholars who have previously studied this problem.

Africa:

Century	annis	annos or annus	menses	mensis	mensibus	dies	diebus	horas	horis
3rd.	3	0	0	0	0	0	0	0	0
4th.	52	3	1	0	0	2	0	1	0
5th.	63	8	0	0	0	0	0	0	0
6th.	23	2	1	0	0	1	0	0	0
7th.	2	0	0	0	0	0	0	0	0
n.d.	214	54	36	1	1	30	3	12	1
Totals:	357	67	38	1	1	33	3	13	1

Britain: (Pagan)

	annis	annus	menses	mensis	mensibus	dies	diebus
3rd.	2	2	0	0	0	0	0
n.d.	28	20	6	0	3	3	3
Totals:	30	22	6	0	3	3	3

Britain: (Christian)

	annis	annus
4th.	1	1
5th.	0	1
Totals:	1	2

Dalmatia:

	annis	annus	menses	mensis	mensibus	dies	diebus
4th.	2	3	0	0	1	0	0
5th.	0	3	0	0	0	0	0
6th.	0	1	0	0	0	0	0
n.d.	9	12	3	2	0	6	0
Totals:	11	19	3	2	1	6	0

Balkans: (Pagan)

	annis	annus	menses	mensis	mensibus	dies	diebus
4th.	0	1	0	0	0	0	0
n.d.	13	2	0	1	0	0	1
Totals:	13	3	0	1	0	0	1

Balkans: (Christian)

	annis	annus	menses	mensis	mensibus	dies	diebus
n.d.	8	4	3	0	0	3	0

From the foregoing table it appears that the ablative of time is overwhelmingly used in African inscriptions with the expression *vixit annis,* but the accusative is used for the other divisions of time, i.e., *menses, dies,* and *horas.* In the pagan inscriptions of Britain the ablative of time with *annis* is the normal form, but the accusative is preferred with *menses.* It is interesting to note that the ablative with *annis* is the predominant form in pagan Britain in inscriptions that date from the first to fourth centuries, although pagan inscriptions of Britain are usually very classical in nature. These inscriptions thus show that the ablative of duration of time began early even in an area that is notoriously classical in its representation of Latin. Dalmatian Latin shows a preference for the accusative of time with *annos* as well as the other divisions of time (*menses, mensis,* and *dies*). Both pagan and Christian inscriptions of the Balkans prefer the ablative with *annis.*

Other scholars have tried to explain the paradoxical situation of the general use of the ablative with *annis,* but the accusative with the other divisions of time. Pirson, although not giving any figures to substantiate his conclusions, states (p. 183) that "dans les inscriptions de la Gaule, à quelque époque qu'elles appartiennent, l'ablatif se rencontre aussi souvent que l'accusatif." Since in many inscriptions the ablative and accusative of duration of time are juxtaposed in the same formula, Pirson concludes (p. 183) that "l'ablatif a été complètement assimilé à l'accusatif pour exprimer la durée, comme le prouve à l'évidence la présence simultanée de ces deux cas avec la même valeur dans la même proposition." As has been pointed out, [134] Pirson's own examples show that *annis* was preferred but *menses* and *dies* were prevalent in cases where various divisions of time are expressed in the Latin inscriptions of Gaul. Pirson's own examples thus negate his conclusion of assimilation of the ablative to the accusative when there is a series of time expressions.

Mihăescu evolved an important theory that supposedly sheds light on the morphological question of the plurals in -*i* in Rumanian and Italian on the basis of the use of *annis* in the inscriptions of Rome and the Danubian provinces. He mentions (*Limba,* p. 157) that in a study of approximately 31,000 inscriptions of Rome, there were 2,483 cases of the ablative *annis* and only 539 of the accusative of duration of time *annos.* He then adds that in the Danubian provinces (excluding Dalmatia) there were 84 cases of the ablative *annis* to 31 cases of the accusative *annos.* From these figures he makes the im-

---

[134] Löfstedt, *Syntactica,* II, 60-61.

portant conclusion ("Cîteva Observaţii," p. 89) that "această predilecţie pentru 'annis' în loc de 'annos' în Italia şi în provinciile
dunărene ne este intîmplătoare, ci arată că în limba vorbită pluralul
substantivelor masculine tendea spre forma unică în ī, din care a
rezultat în romîneste *ani*, în italiană *anni*." [135] Mihăescu's theory, a
significant step in the understanding of the plurals in Rumanian and
Italian, encounters obstacles that cannot be summarily dismissed. An
important objection to Mihăescu's figures for the breakdown of *annis*
and *annos* in Rome is his glossing over of the chronological element.
His gross figures of 2,483 cases of *annis* and just 539 for *annos* are
impressive evidence for his theory, but when one analyzes the distribution of these figures according to pagan and Christian inscriptions,
with the understanding that pagan inscriptions generally dry up
toward the third or fourth century, and that Christian inscriptions
generally assume greater proportions starting from the fourth century,
a serious problem arises. Although Gaeng did not investigate the
comparative figures for *annis* and *annos* in his study of the Christian
inscriptions of Gaul, Prinz breaks down the figures for various areas
of Romania with separate tables for pagan and Christian inscriptions.
We will reproduce his tables with the slight change of considering
the accusative *annus* under the same heading as the accusative *annos*.
From Prinz, *De O et U*, p. 134, we get the following figures:

A) Pagan Inscriptions:

	annis	annos (or annus)
Romae, in Latio	2,438	449
in Italia inferiore	807	122
in Italia superiore et in Gallia Cisalpina ...	333	230
in Gallia Transalpina et in Germania	158	77
in Hispania	48	5
in Africa	4,363	198
in Graecia	289	181
Totals:	8,436	1,262

---

[135] Translation of the Rumanian: "this predilection for 'annis' instead of
'annos' in Italy and in the Danubian provinces is not fortuitous, but shows
that in the spoken language the plural of masculine nouns tended to the
single form in -ī, the result of which was the Rumanian *ani*, the Italian *anni*.

B) Christian Inscriptions:

	annis	annos (or annus)
Romae, in Latio	638	655
in Italia inferiore	73	95
in Italia superiore et in Gallia Cisalpina ...	97	217
in Gallia Transalpina et in Germania	55	274
in Hispania	8	69
in Africa	367	70
in Graecia	15	20
Totals:	1,253	1,400

We thus see that although pagan inscriptions in those areas studied by Prinz are all predominantly proponents of the ablative of time, this tendency is reversed in Christian inscriptions where the accusative *annos* or *annus* is preferred, except in Africa where the ablative was always the dominant form. In dated Christian inscriptions from Rome, the preference for the accusative of time is even more pronounced, as is evidenced by Prinz' table. We will reproduce Prinz' figures just for the area of Rome although he shows the distribution for other areas as well.

C) In dated Christian Inscriptions from Rome:

	annis	annos (or annus)
ante a. 300	3	2
ab a. 301 ad a. 350	16	12
ab a. 351 ad a. 375	14	37
ab a. 376 ad a. 400	21	59
ab a. 401 ad a. 425	9	30
ab a. 426 ad a. 450	10	13
ab a. 451 ad a. 475	2	6
ab a. 476 ad a. 500	1	6
ab a. 501 ad a. 550	1	24
post a. 551	0	6
Totals:	77	195

We thus see that although Mihăescu's figures show a significant preference for the ablative of time, a more careful analysis brings out the paradoxical fact that the accusative was more common in later centuries in the Latin inscriptions of Rome. [136] Since it is precisely

---

[136] Prinz' study is mainly interested in the vowels *o* and *u* and the form *annus* assumes great interest for him. We have combined both *annos* and *annus* into one category for our purpose of investigating the relative frequency

late Vulgar Latin that should be the key to the incipient Romance languages, Mihăescu's theory loses its validity. Table C on the preceding page shows that the accusative of time (either *annos* or *annus*) was more common than the ablative *annis* in the late Vulgar Latin of Rome.

---

of the ablative and accusative of duration of time. It should be brought out that in pagan inscriptions *annus* was not very common (Prinz gives 8,436 cases of *annis*, 1,238 for *annos*, and just 24 cases of *annus* throughout those areas of Romania which he studied. This situation radically changes in Christian inscriptions where Prinz gives 1,253 cases of *annis*, 930 for *annos*, and 470 for *annus*). The dominance of *annis* and the low number of accusatives in *annus* of pagan inscriptions change in Christian inscriptions where the ablative of time loses its preeminence while the accusatives in *annus* greatly increase. We can only wonder whether there is any causal relationship between the decrease of *annis* and the increase of *annus*. A remarkable divergence in findings concerning the ablative and accusative of time in pagan and Christian inscriptions of Rome is found in *Sylloge Inscriptionum Christianarum Veterum Musei Vaticani*, edited by Henrico Zilliacus (Helsinki: Tilgmann, 1963), II, 30, as evidenced by the words: "La comparaison des pourcentages entre les documents païens et les documents chrétiens de la ville de Rome donne donc les résultats suivants:

	annis	*mensibus*	*diebus*
païens	92 %	21 %	15 %
chrétiens	95 %	24 %	18 %

	annos	*menses*	*dies*
païens	8 %	79 %	85 %
chrétiens	5 %	76 %	82 %

The editors thus conclude (p. 30) that "l'homogénéité à l'intérieur du groupe des inscriptions provenant de la ville de Rome est évidente et sans aucun rapport avec l'appartenance religieuse." It is almost unfathomable for Prinz and the editors of the *Sylloge* to come to directly opposite conclusions on the basis of pagan and Christian inscriptions of Rome. Concerning the form *annus*, usually taken as an accusative plural, the editors of the *Sylloge* have a very striking explanation: "Un passage de la désinence de l'accusatif *-os* à *-us* dans d'autres mots manque d'appuis épigraphiques ... il semble hautement probable que *annus* soit un nominatif singulier, qu'il constitue une dénomination stéréotypée de catégorie d' "années" dans les calculs de date et qu'il n'ait pas de forme de cas déterminée. Au total, il correspondrait assez à la formule: "année: tant et tant." (pp. 31-32). It is completely erroneous that the *-us* ending is found only with the single word *annus*. In our corpus we found the accusative plural *medianus* from Dalmatia (see *supra*, p. 287). Gaeng found (pp. 207-08) for Gaul the accusative plurals: *duus* (D. 3552), *duus* (D. 150), *livertus* (= *libertos*), (D. 1749), *ferus* (D. 1075), *denus* (D. 1218), *suus* (D. 2340); for Italy: *superus* (D. 4725), *iustus* (D. 3350); for Rome: *sanctus* (D. 2153), *santus* (D. 3358), *filius suus* (D. 4568), and *vivus* (D. 3757A). Pirson complements (p. 42) Gaeng's list with the following accusative plurals: *anemus, multus, orfanus, nudus, natus, emeritus, plenus*.

Another impediment to the acceptance of Mihăescu's reasoning is the situation of the Latin inscriptions of Dalmatia. Mihăescu deliberately left out the figures for *annis* and *annos* in Dalmatia when he spoke of the Danubian provinces preferring the ablative of time. It is very true that the Balkan provinces show the ablative of time as the preferred case (our figures agree with Mihăescu's findings: see *supra*, p. 289) and it is also true that Rumanian masculine plurals do end in *-i*, but it is also pertinent to remember that Vegliote also loses its final *-s* and although final vowels in unchecked position fall (except final *-a*), the masculine plural forms of second and third declension substantives posit a final *-i* because of its umlauting effect on a stressed *a*, causing it to change to *i*, or because of its affricating effect on a preceding velar or dental consonant, causing them to change to /č/. Compare the umlaut effect of final *i* on the pairs *kựonp* (< *campum*) and *kinp* (< *campi*), *suant* (< *san(c)tum*) and *sinč* (< *san(c)ti*), and the affricating influence of final *i* on the pairs *pựark* (< *porcum*) and *pựarč* (< *porci*), *cont* or *quont* (< *quantum*) and *kựinč* (< *quanti*). [137] The stressed *i* in *kin* 'dogs' and the final *č* in *dựanč* 'teeth' prove that the plural of these nouns could *not* have ended in an *-ēs*, but had an *-ī* or *-īs* ending. Although it has been advanced that the second declension *-i* ending was analogically extended to the third declension plurals in Italian and Rumanian, we did not find a single case of this substitution in our inscriptions of Dalmatia or in those of any other area of our corpus. The *-is* ending must have played an important role in the development of the plural in Vegliote. It is difficult, therefore, to conciliate the paradoxical situation of having to admit the importance of the ablative *annis* in the formation of Eastern Romance noun plurals in Italian and Rumanian, if Dalmatian, while positing a final *-i* or *-is* for its plurals, unaccountably prefers the accusative *annos*.

African Latin which follows the archaic vocalic system of Sardinian likewise prefers the ablative *annis*, both in pagan and Christian inscriptions (the only area except possibly for Britain where the ablative is the preferred case throughout its history) although Sardinian

---

[137] For a discussion of the loss of final *-s*, the loss of final vowels (except *a*) in unchecked position, and the umlauting and affricating effect of final *-i* in Dalmatian, see Bàrtoli, *Das Dalmatische*, II, 341-42, 346-47, 352, 373-74, 385-86, 412.

forms its masculine noun plurals in the Western Romance fashion with a final -s. There is no reason for African Latin to follow Sardinian blindly in its evolution, but up to now African Latin has been remarkably close to Sardinian in its development. A comparative and quantitative study of final -s in the various parts of Romania would be most welcome in an attempt to unlock the relationship of the ablative of time *annis* and the formation of Eastern Romance plurals. Mihăescu's theory, although most enticing, runs up against the serious objections of the chronology of pagan and Christian inscriptions, the situation in Dalmatian Latin where the accusative *annos* is preferred although Dalmatian follows the Eastern Romance pattern of noun plurals formed with the loss of final -s and with a final -i or -is posited, and possibly the problem of African Latin where the ablative *annis* has always been preferred although Sardinian, likewise following the archaic vocalic pattern, does form plurals with a final -s.

Löfstedt tries to unravel the problem of the confusion of cases in time expressions by bringing "harmony" into the picture. [138] Being aware of the preference of *annis* as well as the accusatives *menses* and *dies* (he does not give any comparative or quantitative analysis of the various regions of Romania, however), he offers the following solution:

> Wie ist diese eigentümliche Vorliebe für den Abl. *annis* neben den Akk. *menses* und *dies* in der Vulgärsprache — denn hier handelt es sich wirklich um vulgäres Latein — zu erklären? Da sowohl syntaktische wie logish-psychologische Gründe ausgeschlossen sind, muss die Erscheinung durch rein äusserliche, formale Momente bedingt sein. Offenbar hatte man ... das Gefühl, durch die Endungen -is, -es (-is), -es werde eine bessere äussere Harmonie gebildet als durch -is, -ibus, -ebus, sei es, dass man diese Harmonie vorzugsweise in der Zweisilbigkeit der Formen *annis, menses, dies* (im Gegensatz zu dem zweisilbigen *annis* neben den dreisilbigen *mensibus, diebus*) oder in der lautlichen und formalen Qualität der Endungen suchte.

The plausibility of the Löfstedt "harmony" theory is weakened by the one form that he neglects to mention in the division of time: *horas*. Although inscriptions regularly give the age of the deceased

---

[138] Löfstedt, *Syntactica*, II, 60-62.

in years, months, and days, they only occasionally resort to the fine distinction of hours. We have seen (see *supra*, p. 289) that of the areas studied by us, only the African inscriptions give any indication of the number of hours a person has lived. This fourth division of time, however, is very important as African inscriptions are very clear in the preference given to the accusative *horas* over the ablative *horis*. Our corpus shows that in African inscriptions *horas* was used thirteen times while *horis* appears only once. If, as Löfstedt claims, the ablative *annis* is preferred because of the formal ending *-is* which harmonizes with the accusative endings *-es* or *-is* and *-es* of *menses*, *mensis*, and *dies*, it is only reasonable to expect the ablative *horis* to be used rather than the accusative *horas* which breaks up the harmonious picture. The overwhelming preference of *horas* instead of *horis* seemingly negates the Löfstedt theory of "harmony."

Poukens in his study on the syntax of the Latin inscriptions of Africa likewise found that the ablative of time was greatly preferred to the accusative. He reports that "sous l'Empire il [the ablative] se multiplie si bien qu'il supplante presque complètement l'accusatif. Dans les 22,657 inscriptions africaines publiées jusqu'à ce jour, nous avons trouvé l'ablatif 2871 fois et l'accusatif 209 fois. Dans 142 exemples, les cas avaient été mêlés." [139] In cases where the ablative and accusative of time are mixed, he informs us (p. 76) that "presque toujours le premier substantif est à l'ablatif." Poukens explains the problem of expressions of time in a psychological vein: "La raison psychologique de ce fait n'est pas difficile à découvrir: nous sommes en présence d'un cas de contamination. Or l'ablatif étant de loin le cas le plus usité, il est naturel qu'il se soit le premier présenté à l'esprit." Unfortunately Poukens' reasoning is far from convincing. If a child under one year of age dies, the inscription will usually begin with *menses* or *mensis*, or *dies*, accusative forms; compare the following examples from African inscriptions:

> ... *fidelis in do. bicxit in pace menses qIII*, *D*, 1346, *CIL* VIII 11,106, Sullecthus (Byzacena), no date.
> *Euticianus innocens vixit in pacae dies numero triginta*, *D*. 2680, *CIL* VIII 16,351, near Cellas (Proconsular Province), no date.

---

[139] J. B. Poukens, *Syntaxe des inscriptions latines d'Afrique* (Louvain: Charles Peeters, 1912), p. 75.

Iulius Pascasi vix. in pace menses XXI, D. 2681, *CIL* VIII 23578, Maktar, no date.
Maximiano in pace. vixit minses III, zies III, D. 3263, *CIL* VIII 11,099, Thysdrum (Byzacena), no date.

Even in that extremely rare case where *annus* is replaced by *tempus*, we have the accusative case:

hic Honorata innocens, vixit in pace tempora III, D. 2125, Suffetula, no date.

It thus appears that the first element of time is in the ablative case when the formula begins with *annis*, but the accusative of time is usually preferred when the other divisions of time begin the time expressions.

Poukens' remark concerning the ablative case as the one most used and consequently the first to come to one's mind is so vague and unsubstantiated that it can be almost summarily dismissed. [140]

Our own feeling is that the use of the ablative *annis* but the accusatives *menses* (or *mensis*), *dies* and *horas* is not fortuitous or haphazard, but is the result of morphological factors, which may differ from region to region in anticipation of the incipient Romance languages which are to evolve in the particular area. The preference of *menses* or *mensis* over *mensibus* and *dies* over *diebus* is explained by the general loss of datives and ablatives ending in *-bus* with the contending accusative forms, although the simple fact that the accusatives are shorter and consequently offer the stonemason a time-saving device cannot be overlooked. [141] The accusative *horas* was preferred because of its importance in the declensional system where a tendency to equate the nominative and accusative plurals was taking

---

[140] It is interesting to see that Poukens considers the ablative as the most common Latin case since scholars have been arguing over whether it is the accusative or oblique that has been the prime determinant in the development of the various Romance language case systems. The reader is once again referred to Pei's article "Accusative or Oblique?", *The Romance Review*, XXVIII (1939), 141-67, for a summary of opinions on this problem.

[141] Löfstedt admits (*Syntactica*, II, 61) that the general loss of *-bus* may also be a factor in the preference of the accusatives over the ablatives: "Vielleicht ist ausserdem in der späteren Vulgärsprache überhaupt mit einer gewissen Abneigung gegen die im Romanischen ausgestorbene und also sicher nicht volkstümlich beliebte Endung *-bus* zu rechnen."

place. In those areas where feminine plurals were formed with a final -s, it would seem normal for the accusative *horas* to be uppermost in the minds of most speakers. Sardinian does form feminine plural nouns in -as.[142] The biggest drawback in a morphological solution to the problem of the mixing of cases is the ablative *annis*. Mihăescu's theory of the ablative *annis* being instrumental in the formation of Italian and Rumanian plurals has already been discussed (see *supra*, pp. 290-95). Theoretically, if *annis* is important in the formation of plurals in Eastern Romance, *annos* should be preferred in those areas where a later Romance language or dialect forms its plurals with final -s. On the basis of Prinz' figures (see *supra*, p. 292) for Christian inscriptions, the accusative *annos* or *annus* does prevail in the Iberian Peninsula and in Gaul. Our table (see *supra*, pp. 289-41) does indicate that *annis* was more common in the Balkan Peninsula. The areas of Italy, Dalmatia, and Africa offer, however, stumbling blocks for the acceptance of a morphological interpretation of the problem. According to Prinz' figures all of Italy shows a preference for the accusative *annos* or *annus* in Christian inscriptions (a complete reversal of the situation as seen in pagan inscriptions). Our figures (admittedly scanty) show that Dalmatia prefers the accusative *annos* although Dalmatian does form plurals without a final -s. African inscriptions have shown a preference for the ablative *annis* in both pagan as well as Christian inscriptions although they likewise indicate a strong tendency to use the accusative *horas*. As has been previously said, Sardinian, a follower of the archaic vocalic system as is African Latin, does form plurals with a final -s. More study, especially in the problem of final -s, is needed before the final word can be said on the intricate problem of the mixing of cases in time expressions in epigraphical material.

Ernout and Thomas consider the problem purely artificial when they remark (p. 112) that "sur les inscriptions funéraires d'époque impériale, pour indiquer l'âge du défunt, une alternance purement artificielle s'était établie entre l'accusatif et l'ablatif de durée. Dans le type le plus répandu, les années sont à l'ablatif, les mois et les jours à l'accusatif." This facile remark, although as valid as other interpretations at the present time, should be replaced with something more concrete after further study.

---

[142] Wagner, *La lingua sarda*, p. 322.

Latin /ŭ/, Represented by the Letter u

Initial

Africa	Century	Open Syllable		% Of Dev.	Closed Syllable		% Of Dev.	Totals		% Of Dev.
		/ŭ/ > u	/ŭ/ > o		/ŭ/ > u	/ŭ/ > o				
	3rd.	0	0		4	0		4	0	
	4th.	2	1	33.3	11	0		13	1	7.1
	5th.	0	0		2	0		2	0	
	6th.	0	0		5	0		5	0	
	n.d.	13	1		27	1	3.6	40	1	2.4
	Totals:	15	2	6.3	49	1	2.0	64	2	3.0

The two cases of deviation in this area are:

copientes, D. 779, Mauretania Sitifensis, 4th century.
Ostarricus, D. 1404, *CIL* VIII 20,909, Tipasa, no date.

On the basis of two deviations, one of which being an uncommon proper name, it appears that initial /ŭ/ in African inscriptions is stable.

Britain	Century	Open Syllable		% Of Dev.	Closed Syllable		% Of Dev.	Totals	
		/ŭ/ > u	/ŭ/ > o		/ŭ/ > u	/ŭ/ > o			
(Pagan)	1st.	1	0		0	0		1	0
	2nd.	2	0		2	0		4	0
	3rd.	3	0		5	0		8	0
	n.d.	13	0		23	0		36	0
	Totals:	19	0	0.0	30	0	0.0	49	0

The initial /ŭ/ in pagan inscriptions of Britain is stable.

Britain	Century	Open Syllable		% Of Dev.	Closed Syllable		Totals		% Of Dev.
		/ŭ/ > u	/ŭ/ > o		/ŭ/ > u	/ŭ/ > o			
(Christ.)	5th.	1	0		0	0	1	0	
	6th.	0	0		1	0	1	0	
	n.d.	0	1	100.0	0	0	0	1	100.0
	Totals:	0	1	50.0	1	0	2	1	33.3

The single deviation in Christian inscriptions of Britain is the proper name *Iovenali* (genitive), *CIIC* 389, Carnarvon, Wales, no date. Since the total number of occurrences of initial /ŭ/ is so limited, nothing concrete can be said about this vowel in this position.

Dalmatia	*Century*	Open Syllable		% Of Dev.	Closed Syllable		% Of Dev.	Totals	
		/ŭ/ > u	/ŭ/ > o		/ŭ/ > u	/ŭ/ > o			
	4th.	1	0		3	0		4	0
	5th.	0	0		3	0		3	0
	n.d.	16	0		17	0		33	0
	Totals:	17	0	0.0	23	0	0.0	40	0

No deviations were found in our corpus of Dalmatian inscriptions. Initial /ŭ/ appears stable in this area.

Balkans	*Century*	Open Syllable		% Of Dev.	Closed Syllable		% Of Dev.	Totals	
		/ŭ/ > u	/ŭ/ > o		/ŭ/ > u	/ŭ/ > o			
(Pagan)	3rd.	1	0		0	0		1	0
	n.d.	3	0		4	0		7	0
	Totals:	4	0	0.0	4	0	0.0	8	0
(Christ.)	4th.	3	0		0	0		3	0
	5th.	0	0		2	0		2	0
	n.d.	0	0		13	0		13	0
	Totals:	3	0	0.0	15	0	0.0	18	0

No deviations occurred although the total number of occurrences in both pagan and Christian inscriptions was low. Initial /ŭ/ is presumably stable in the Latin inscriptions of the Balkans.

Our findings show that initial /ŭ/ in those areas studied by us is stable, with only a few sporadic changes to *o*. Gaeng likewise found (p. 210) that initial /ŭ/ "is rarely spelled with *o*."

Intertonic

Africa	Century	Open Syllable		% Of Dev.	Closed Syllable		% Of Dev.	Totals		% Of Dev.
		/ŭ/ > u	/ŭ/ > o		/ŭ/ > u	/ŭ/ > o				
	3rd.	0	0		1	0		1	0	
	4th.	0	0		3	0		3	0	
	5th.	2	0		0	0		2	0	
	6th.	2	1	33.3	2	0		4	1	20.0
	n.d.	11	2	15.4	28	1	3.4	39	3	7.1
	Totals:	15	3	16.7	34	1	2.9	49	4	7.5

The four examples of deviation in African inscriptions are:

Thamogadiensis, D. 387, Thamugadi (Numidia), n.d.
Thamogadi, D. 335, CIL VIII 18,668, Thamugadi (Numidia), no date.
Tamogadiensis, D. 805, Thamugadi (Numidia), A.D. 539-540.
volontatis, D. 2464, CIL VIII 10,642, near Theveste (Proconsularis), no date.

Since three of the four examples refer to the root of a place name or the adjective based on it, it appears that intertonic /ŭ/ is stable in African inscriptions. Speaking generally of the treatment of /ŭ/ in African inscriptions, Prinz states (p. 36) that "... in Africa U bevis raro in O transiit." [143]

Britain	Century	Open Syllable		% Of Dev.	Closed Syllable		% Of Dev.	Totals		% Of Dev.
		/ŭ/ > u	/ŭ/ > o		/ŭ/ > u	/ŭ/ > o				
(Pagan)	1st.	0	0		0	0		0	0	
	2nd.	6	0		3	0		9	0	
	3rd.	11	0		7	0		18	0	
	n.d.	8	3	27.3	26	0		34	3	8.1
	Totals:	25	3	10.7	36	0	0.0	61	3	4.7

---

[143] It is interesting to note that Prinz in his very detailed analysis of Latin *o* and *u* does not record the changes of intertonic /ŭ/ to *o* in the cases of *Thamogadiensis, Thamogadi,* and *Tamogadiensis.* Diehl does give (III, 472) the above deviations in his *Indices.*

The deviations in pagan inscriptions of Britain are:

Viboleius, RIB 1052, South Shields (Arbeia), n.d. [144]
Belatocadro (= *Belatucadro,* from *Belatucadrus,* a Celtic deity), *RIB* 2039, *CIL* VII 935, Hadrian's Wall (Burgh-by-Sands: Aballava), Cumberland, no date.
Belatocairo (= *Belatucadro*), *RIB* 2056, *CIL* VII 333, Hadrian's Wall (Bowness-on-Solway: Maia), Cumberland, no date.

On the basis of three deviations, all proper names, it appears that intervocalic /ŭ/ was stable in pagan inscriptions of Britain. It should be remembered that stressed /ŭ/ likewise was stable, contrary to the general Vulgar Latin tendency of changing stressed /ŭ/ to *o*.

Britain	*Century*	Open Syllable		% Of Dev.	Closed Syllable		Totals		% Of Dev.
		/ŭ/ > *u*	/ŭ/ > *o*		/ŭ/ > *u*	/ŭ/ > *o*			
(Christ.)	6th.	0	0		1	0	1	0	
	7th.	0	0		1	0	1	0	
	8th.	1	0		0	0	1	0	
	n.d.	0	1	100.0	0	0	0	1	100.0
	Totals:	1	1	50.0	2	0	3	1	25.0

The single deviation in our corpus of Christian inscriptions of Britain is *monomenti, CIIC* 505, Stanton (Isle of Man), no date. The occurrence of an *o* for intertonic /ŭ/ in Christian inscriptions is a rarity since "monomentum semper fere occurrit in titulis ethnicis." [145] The total number of occurrences of intertonic /ŭ/ in Christian inscriptions of Britain is too insignificant for any generalization to be made.

[144] The editors of the *RIB* mention (p. 351) that "Vivoleius seems to be a variant of Vibuleius."
[145] Prinz, *De O et U,* p. 38. The same scholar maintains (p. 38) that "in inscriptionibus christianis unum exemplum obviam fit." (*D.* 3631, Vienna (Gaul), A.D. 517?) Our reading of *monomenti* is based on Macalister's interpretation. It is true that Hübner in his *Inscriptiones Britanniae Christianae,* inscr. no. 164, p. 60, gives *Aviti Noro/merti?,* but does acknowledge that others read *avit(um) monoment(um),* which he considers erroneous (*perperam sine dubio*). Prinz follows Diehl's readings throughout his work and since the latter used Hübner's corpus in the *ILCV,* Prinz had no inkling of the deviation *monomenti.* This shows the critical importance of epigraphical interpretation in a quantitative analysis of inscriptions.

Dalmatia	Century	Open Syllable		Closed Syllable		% Of Dev.	Totals		% Of Dev.
		/ŭ/ > u	/ŭ/ > o	/ŭ/ > u	/ŭ/ > o				
	4th.	2	0	2	0		4	0	
	5th.	3	0	0	0		3	0	
	n.d.	6	0	4	2	33.3	10	2	16.7
	Totals:	11	0	6	2	25.0	17	2	10.5

The two deviations, both found in the same inscription, are *inmondissime* (bis), D. 2389, *CIL* III p. 961, no date.

Balkans	Century	Open Syllable		Closed Syllable		Totals	
		/ŭ/ > u	/ŭ/ > o	/ŭ/ > u	/ŭ/ > o		
(Pagan)	4th.	1	0	1	0	2	0
	n.d.	4	0	2	0	6	0
	Totals:	5	0	3	0	8	0
(Christ.)	4th.	0	0	1	0	1	0
	n.d.	2	0	4	0	6	0
	Totals:	2	0	5	0	7	0

There are no deviations in either pagan or Christian inscriptions of the Balkans, but the total number of occurrences of intertonic /ŭ/ in this area is low.

Although the incidence of intervocalic /ŭ/ is slight in the areas investigated by us, one important insight can be gotten by a comparative analysis of the results gained by Gaeng for intertonic /ŭ/ of Narbonensis. For dated inscriptions of the sixth and seventh centuries, Gaeng reports (pp. 212-13) two correct occurrences and seven deviations (*Volosiano*, D. 2889, A.D. 503; *volontate*, D. 1432, A.D. 551-66; *secolares*, D. 1670, A.D. 557-602; *consolis . . . post consolato*, D. 1672, A.D. 540; *monomen[to]*, D. 3631, A.D. 517?; *adoliscens*, D. 2747, A.D. 524), for a percentage of deviation of 77.7 %. Gaeng concludes (p. 213) that "there is little doubt that in the Narbonensis the merger of /ŭ/ and /ō/ in this position is an accomplished fact by the sixth century." There is a striking similarity between the weakening of intertonic /ŭ/ and that of intertonic /ĭ/ (see *supra*, p. 204 ff. for figures and commentary) in Latin inscriptions of Gaul as compared to other areas of Romania. The Latin inscriptions of Gaul show a weakening of intertonic /ĭ/ to *e* and intertonic /ŭ/ to *o* that goes far beyond the sporadic deviations found for other areas of the Roman Empire. Epigraphical evidence shows conclusively that there was a differentiation in the treatment of intertonic /ŭ/ and /ĭ/ in Romania, with the Latin of Gaul deviating more from Classical Latin norms than any other region of the Empire. Since we are faced with a parallel development in the treatment of intertonic /ŭ/ and /ĭ/, we should expect to see the same pattern of weakness in posttonic /ŭ/ in Gaulish inscriptions as compared to a relative stability in the epigraphical material of other areas of Romania. We have already seen that posttonic /ĭ/ was weaker in the provinces of Narbonensis and Lugdunensis than in the other regions under investigation. (See *supra*, pp. 212-15, for figures and commentary concerning the treatment of posttonic /ĭ/ in the various areas of Romania.)

Before turning to the important topic of posttonic /ŭ/, we have a few cases of intertonic /ŭ/ changing to *i*. From pagan inscriptions of Britain, we find:

> *monime(ntum)*, *RIB* 375, *CIL* VII 133, Caerleon (Isca Silurum), no date.
> *monimentum*, *RIB* 620, Templebrough (Yorkshire), no date.
> *Belleticauro* (= *Belatucadro*), *RIB* 1521, *CIL* VII 620, Carrawburgh (Brocolitia), Northumberland (near Hadrian's Wall), no date.
> *Baliticauro* (= *Belatucadro*), *RIB* 1775, Hadrian's Wall: Carvoran (Magnis), Northumberland, n.d.

From an early Christian inscription of Africa we have:

> *monimentum*, *D*. 3631A, *CIL* VIII 8296, near Cuicul (Numidia), A.D. 212.

Besides the Classical Latin form *monumentum*, we thus have the deviations *monomentum* and *monimentum*. The popular development of this word in the Romance languages shows either an *i* or the loss of the intertonic vowel. [146]

---

[146] Prinz, *De O et U*, p. 38: "In 'monomentum' O vocalis syllabae alterius in linguis Romanensibus non occurrit, sed modo I extat, modo haec vocalis plane elisa est."

Posttonic

Africa	Century	/ŭ/ > u	/ŭ/ > o	% Of Dev.
	3rd.	5	0	
	4th.	5	0	
	5th.	4	0	
	6th.	4	0	
	n.d.	52	1	1.7
	Totals:	70	1	1.4

The single case of deviation in this area is the proper name *Istercolus* (= *Sterculus*), D. 2543N, Thabraca (Proconsularis), no date. We see that posttonic /ŭ/ is stable in African inscriptions, a situation that is paralleled in the treatment of posttonic /ĭ/ (see *supra*, p. 208), where we find in our inscriptional material 433 cases of correct occurrences of posttonic /ĭ/ without any deviations. From our findings derived from an analysis of both intertonic /ĭ/ and /ŭ/ and posttonic /ĭ/ and /ŭ/, we can conclude that the Latin of African inscriptions is very stable in these two positions, a situation that is starkly different from that of the inscriptions of Gaul. Once again we find a parallel conservatism in African inscriptions and Sardinian, the most conservative of the Romance languages. Writing about the archaic vocalism of Sardinian, Wagner (*Lingua sarda*) very neatly summarizes (p. 309) its vocalic system in the following words:

> Il Sardo, come ci si presenta nei documenti antichi e come tuttora suona nelle regioni centrali e soprattutto nel Bittese e nel Nuorese, si può considerare, anche foneticamente, il continuatore più schietto del latino. Il suo vocalismo si distingue per la chiarezza della pronuncia e non conosce vocali torbide o offuscate; anche le vocali pretoniche e posttoniche si conservano con una precisione meravigliosa, sicchè i dialetti centrali, continuando le condizioni del sardo antico, conservano le parole latine in una veste fonetica che non si scosta molto da quella latina.

Britain	Century	/ŭ/ > u	/ŭ/ > o	% Of Dev.
(Pagan)	1st.	2	0	
	2nd.	2	0	
	3rd.	16	1	5.9
	n.d.	40	1	2.4
	Totals:	60	2	3.2

The two deviations from the pagan inscriptions of Britain are:

Astor(um) (the gen. plural of the third declension), *RIB* 266, Lincoln (Lindum), no date.
Asto(rum), *RIB* 1337, *CIL* VII 513, Hadrian's Wall: Benwell (Condercum), Northumberland, A.D. 205-209.

Prinz considers (p. 34) the change of posttonic /ŭ/ to *o* in the above cases as the result of forms ending in -*tor*.[147] Posttonic /ŭ/ appears relatively stable in the pagan inscriptions of Britain.

Britain	Century	/ŭ/ > u	/ŭ/ > o	% Of Dev.
(Christ.)	5th.	2	0	
	6th.	3	0	
	n.d.	1	0	
	Totals:	6	0	0.0

There are no deviations in our corpus although the total number of occurrences is low.

Dalmatia	Century	/ŭ/ > u	/ŭ/ > o	% Of Dev.
	4th.	5	0	
	5th.	4	0	
	6th.	4	1	20.0
	n.d.	29	1	3.3
	Totals:	42	2	4.5

The two deviations, both common throughout Romania, are:

tumolum, D. 79b, *CIL* III 9527, Salona, A.D. 599.
coniogi, D. 3750, *CIL* III 14,309, Salona, no date.

---

[147] Prinz, *De O et U*, p. 34: "Cum in omnibus exemplis genetivus pluralis occurrat, O ad analogiam genetivi pluralis alterius declinationis et earum vocum, quae in TOR exeuntes tertiam declinationem sequebantur, ortam esse puto."

Balkans	Century	/ŭ/ > u	/ŭ/ > o	% Of Dev.
(Pagan)	3rd.	3	0	
	4th.	1	0	
	n.d.	11	0	
	Totals:	15	0	0.0
(Christ.)	4th.	2	0	
	n.d.	13	1	7.1
	Totals:	15	1	6.3

The only deviation in this region is the adjective *parvolas*, D. 3476, *CIL* III 3551, Aquincum (Budapest), Pannonia, no date. [148]

We now present in table form a summary of the treatment of posttonic /ŭ/ in the various areas of Romania to see whether there is a differentiation in the Latin of the various regions studied by Gaeng and this investigator.

Summary of the Treatment of Posttonic /ŭ/ in the Various Areas of Romania

Area	Century	/ŭ/ > u	/ŭ/ > o	% Of Dev.
Baetica	4th-6th	25	3	10.8
	7th	15	1	6.3
	Totals:	40	4	9.1
Lusitania	4th-6th	46	0	
	7th	20	0	
	Totals:	66	0	0.0
Tarraconensis	4th-6th	6	1	14.3
	7th	0	0	
	Totals:	6	1	14.3
Narbonensis	4th-5th	4	0	
	6th-7th	9	22	70.9
	Totals:	13	22	62.9

---

[148] Both *parvulus* and *parvolus* are given as Classical Latin forms in the *Harper's Latin Dictionary*, p. 1310.

Area	Century	/ŭ/ > u	/ŭ/ > o	% Of Dev.
Lugdunensis	4th-5th	11	3	21.4
	6th-7th	14	17	54.4
	Totals:	25	20	44.4
Northern Italy	4th-5th	35	4	10.2
	6th	34	5	12.8
	Totals:	69	9	11.5
Central Italy	3rd-4th	3	0	
	5th	8	0	
	6th-7th	5	2	28.6
	Totals:	16	2	11.1
Southern Italy	3rd-4th	7	0	
	5th	3	0	
	6th-7th	9	1	10.0
	Totals:	19	1	5.0
Rome	3rd-4th	38	0	
	5th	22	0	
	6th-7th	8	0	
	Totals:	68	0	0.0
Africa	3rd.	5	0	
	4th.	5	0	
	5th.	4	0	
	6th.	4	0	
	n.d.	52	1	1.7
	Totals:	70	1	1.4
Britain (Pagan)	1st.	2	0	
	2nd.	2	0	
	1rd.	16	1	5.9
	n.d.	40	1	2.4
	Totals:	60	2	3.2
Britain (Christ.)	5th.	2	0	
	6th.	3	0	
	n.d.	1	0	
	Totals:	6	0	0.0
Dalmatia	4th.	5	0	
	5th.	4	0	
	6th.	4	1	20.0
	n.d.	29	1	3.3
	Totals:	42	2	4.5

Area	Century	/ŭ/ > u	/ŭ/ > o	% Of Dev.
Balkans (Pagan)	3rd.	3	0	
	4th.	1	0	
	n.d.	11	0	
	Totals:	15	0	0.0
Balkans (Christ.)	4th.	2	0	
	n.d.	13	1	7.1
	Totals:	15	1	6.3

Scanning the above tables, we come to the inevitable conclusion that the provinces of Narbonensis and Lugdunensis are the most innovative in the weakening of posttonic /ŭ/. It is also pertinent to note that the sixth and seventh centuries are the period of greatest change, a situation that we have already encountered for posttonic /ĭ/ (see *supra*, p. 214). The most plausible reason for the increase in the number of deviations in the area of Gaul seems to be the increased stress accent caused by the Germanic invasions. As was the case with posttonic /ĭ/, Northern Italy shows a relatively high percentage of deviation for posttonic /ŭ/, probably pointing to its being influenced by the vocalic phenomena of its northern neighbor. Although our figures for some areas are too scanty for any firm conclusion to be drawn (such as the area of Tarraconensis where we have only six correct occurrences and one deviation for a percentage of deviation of 14.3 % or the area of Christian Britain where we have six correct occurrences and no deviations), our findings, when based on substantial figures, do seem to show a clear dichotomy between areas of relative stability and areas of weakening of posttonic /ŭ/. In contrast to the provinces of Narbonensis and Lugdunensis where there is a very strong tendency to weaken posttonic /ŭ/, we are faced with the stable areas of Lusitania (66 correct occurrences and no deviations for a 0.0 % of total deviation, Rome (68 correct occurrences and no deviations for a 0.0 % of deviation), Africa (70 correct occurrences and 1 deviation for a 1.4 % deviation), pagan Britain (60 correct occurrences and 2 deviations for 3.2 %), Dalmatia (42 correct occurrences and 2 deviations for 4.5 %), and the Balkans (15 correct occurrences and no deviations for pagan inscriptions and 15 correct occurrences and 1 deviation for Christian inscriptions for 6.3 %). The area of Baetica assumes an

intermediate position with a percentage of deviation of 9.1 % (40
correct occurrences and 4 deviations). Inscriptions thus show that there
is a gradation in the weakening or maintenance of posttonic /ŭ/ in
the various areas of Romania. This distinct treatment of posttonic
vowels as well as intertonic vowels according to area is closely allied
to the syncopation of these unaccented medial vowels which, in turn,
impinges on the paroxytonic or proparoxytonic nature of the syllabic structure which gives a different rhythmic balance to the various
Romance languages. We will postpone discussion of the important
phenomenon of syncope for our chapter on other vocalic phenomena.
It can be unequivocably stated, however, that the study of inscriptional material does show a systematic pattern of treatment of
both intertonic and posttonic /ĭ/ and /ŭ/ in the different areas of
Romania, namely a distinctive tendency of some parts to be innovative in the treatment of the vowels under consideration, especially
the Gaulish provinces of Narbonensis and Lugdunensis, and to a
lesser degree Northern Italy, whereas other regions show a decidedly
conservative nature in their treatment of the same vowels, especially
Africa and Britain. Inscriptions show that there was a differentiation
in the development of intertonic and posttonic /ĭ/ and /ŭ/ in the
Latin of the various areas of Romania.

Hiatus

We will study the deviations of /ŭ/ in hiatus according to its
initial, intertonic, and posttonic positions. We will also analyze the
transitional U that is occasionally found to show orthographically that
two vowels are kept in hiatus with an intervening consonantal glide,
a process already seen for transitional i.

It is interesting to note that we did not find any examples of
unaccented /ŭ/ in hiatus changing to o, although this change was
censured in the Appendix Probi[149] and occurs in inscriptional ma-

---

[149] Cf. No. 131: puella non poella. The reverse change of /ŏ/ in hiatus
is also found in the Appendix Probi: No. 86: cloaca non cluaca. The loss of
syllabication is seen in items 14 and 15 where we have: vacua non vaqua
and vacui non vaqui. Väänänen gives (p. 39) in his Pompéiennes examples
of /ŏ/ in hiatus changing to u (acruamatis = acroamatibus, from the Greek
ἀχρόαμα, and quactiliari = coactiliarii), but no examples of /ŭ/ in hiatus
changing to o. In our corpus we have a change of /ŭ/ in hiatus to o, but
this occurs in stressed position: soi (= suae, dative singular), D. 3659,
Purbach (Pannonia), no date.

terial, especially in Gaul. [150]

frica:

Century	Initial			Intertonic			Posttonic		
	/ŭ/ > u	u Lost	% Loss	/ŭ/ > u	u Lost	% Loss	/ŭ/ > u	u Lost	% Loss
3rd.	0	0		1	0		1	0	
4th.	0	0		5	2	28.6	4	0	
5th.	0	0		10	2	16.7	5	1	16.7
6th.	0	0		1	1	50.0	1	0	
n.d.	19	0		34	5	12.8	16	9	36.0
Totals:	19	0	0.0	51	10	16.4	27	10	27.0

Examples of loss of intertonic /ŭ/ in hiatus in African inscriptions are: [151]

Ianarias, D. 1383, *CIL* VIII 23,586, Maktar (Byzacena), no date.
Febrari[as], D. 1385, *CIL* VIII 2013, Theveste (Proconsularis), A.D. 508.
Febrarias, D. 1394, *CIL* VIII 23,061, near Hadrumetum (Byzacena), no date.
Febrarias, D. 2069, Kherbet-el-Ma-el-Abiod, A.D. 474.
septagita (= *septuaginta*), D. 2552E, Thabraca (Proconsularis), no date.
Ianari, D. 2860C, *CIL* VIII 21,736, Altava (Mauretania Caesariensis), A.D. 394.
Febrarias, D. 3324, *CIL* VIII 8766, Mauretania Sitifensis, no date.
Febrarias, D. 3687, *CIL* VIII 9975, Numerus Syrorum (Mauretania Caesariensis), A. D. 392.
Ianaris, D. 3619N, *CIL* VIII 21,737, Altava (Mauretania Caesariensis), A.D. 480?
Iannarius D. 2036, *CIL* VIII 23,141, Masclianis, no date.

---

[150] Gaeng, pp. 217-18, records *Febroarias* (D. 1808, A.D. 530), *Ienoarii* (D. 2222A, 5th/6th cent.), and *Genoarias* (D. 2891A, A.D. 530) from Narbonensis, *Febroari* (D. 2803, no date), and *foerunt* (D. 150, no date) from Lugdunensis, *actoarius* (D. 1311, no date) from Northern Italy, and *annoente* (D. 290, no date) from Rome.

[151] There is an interesting example of a loss of stressed *a* and the keeping of the /ŭ/ in hiatus: *Eanuria* (= *Ianuaria*), D. 4192, *CIL* VIII 21,804, Numerus Syrorum (Mauretania Caesariensis), no date.

Examples of loss of posttonic /ŭ/ in hiatus in African inscriptions are:

> *innoca*, D. 2549, Carthage (Proconsularis), no date.
> *qattor* (= *quattuor*), D. 2648A, *CIL* VIII 23,049a, Uppena, no date.
> *quadtor*, D. 2670, *CIL* VIII 14,125, Carthage (Proconsularis), no date.
> *innoca*, D. 2672, *CIL* VIII 25,339, Carthage, no date.
> *innoca*, D. 3231, *CIL* VIII 22,840, Taparura (Byzacena), no date.
> *ingenus*, D. 585, *CIL* VIII 25,817, Furnitanus (Proconsularis), no date.
> *mortus*, D. 1180, *CIL* VIII 8774, Thamalla, no date.
> *idum*, D. 1394A, *CIL* VIII 23,059, near Hadrumetum (Byzacena), no date.
> *innocus*, D. 2671, Thabraca (Proconsularis), no date.

We thus see that the loss of both intertonic and posttonic /ŭ/ is a common phenomenon in the Latin of African inscriptions. In Schuchardt's pioneering article entitled "Die romanischen Lehnwörter im Berberischen," we see that the Latin borrowings into Berber likewise show a loss of intertonic or posttonic /ŭ/: cf. Berber *gerdus* < *cardus* (from *carduus*); Berber *žebrari* or *šebrari* < *februarius*; Berber *tfaska* (with prefixed feminine definite article *t-* [or *te-*] < *pasca* [from *pascua*]). In Sardinian we likewise find a loss of intertonic and posttonic /ŭ/: *gennargu* (Campidanese) or *gannargu* (Bittese) < *ianariu* (from *ianuarius*); *friargu* (Campidanese) or *frearzu* (Logudorse) < *febrariu* (from *februarius*), and *ǧenna* (Campidanese) or *ǧanna* (Logudorese) < *ianua*. [152] The Latin of African inscriptions, although classical in nature, conforms closely to Sardinian even in its deviations.

---

[152] See Wagner, "Südsardischen," pp. 10, 19, 26.

ritain: (Pagan)

entury	Initial			Intertonic			Posttonic		
	/ŭ/ > *u*	*u* Lost	% Loss	/ŭ/ > *u*	*u* Lost	% Loss	/ŭ/ > *u*	*u* Lost	% Loss
1st.	0	0		1	0		0	0	
2nd.	3	0		2	0		5	0	
3rd.	4	0		3	0		13	0	
n.d.	4	0		14	0		25	3	10.7
otals:	11	0	0.0	20	0	0.0	43	3	6.5
	(Christian)								
6th.	0	0		0	0		2	0	
n.d.	0	0		0	0		1	0	
otals:	0	0	0.0	0	0	0.0	3	0	0.0

The three examples of loss of posttonic /ŭ/ in pagan inscriptions of Britain are:

posit (= *posuit*), *RIB* 621, Templebrough (Yorkshire), no date. [153]
posit, *RIB* 689, York (Eboracum), no date.
possit, *RIB* 1729, *CIL* VII 728, Hadrian's Wall: Great Chesters (Aesica), Northumberland, no date.

Although we did not find any examples of a loss of intertonic /ŭ/ in the pagan inscriptions of Britain, the loss of intertonic /ŭ/ must be posited for Latin loanwords into the Brittonic languages. [154]

---

[153] The verbal form *posit* has been explained as a contraction of *posiit* from *posivit*, a simple change in perfect indicative endings rather than a loss of posttonic /ŭ/, by Väänänen in his review of Mihăescu's *Limba latină în provinciile dunărene în imperiului roman* in *Neuphilologische Mitteilungen*, LXII (1961), 229. This same reasoning had already been put forth by Schuchardt in his *Vokalismus*, II, 469. A view contrary to the idea that *posit* < *posivit*, namely that we are faced with a loss of posttonic /ŭ/ is expressed by Richter, p. 67, who says: "Da die romanischen Sprachen alle die stammakzentuierte Form *posit* weiter entwickeln, ist diese Annahme nicht gefordert." We do have, however, in the pagan inscriptions of Britain the forms *posivit*, *RIB* 1529, Hadrian's Wall: Carrawburgh (Brocolitia), Northumberland, no date, and *possivit*, *RIB* 1592, *CIL* VII 656, Hadrian's Wall: Housesteads (Vercovicium), Northumberland, no date.

[154] Our corpus for pagan inscriptions of Britain gives 9 examples of the proper name *Ianuarius* or its variants with intertonic /ŭ/ present: *RIB* 600, 707, from the 2nd century; *RIB* 17 from the 3rd century, and *RIB* 506, 744, 780, 947, 1003, and 1459 from undated inscriptions. We did not find

Jackson (*Language*) gives (p. 274) the reflexes of *Ianarius, Febrarius* as *Ionor, Chwefror* in Modern Welsh, *Hwefral* in Modern Cornish, and *C'hwevrer* in Modern Breton. The loss of intertonic /ŭ/ in the Brittonic languages in the names of the months January and February shows that this change was an early and general Vulgar Latin phenomenon. [155] This is one of the few cases where an important Vulgar Latin deviation is seen in loanwords, but not in inscriptions.

Dalmatia:

Century	Initial			Intertonic			Posttonic		
	/ŭ/ > u	u Lost	% Loss	/ŭ/ > u	u Lost	% Loss	/ŭ/ > u	u Lost	% L₍
4th.	0	0		1	0		1	0	
5th.	1	0		2	0		1	0	
n.d.	10	0		13	0		17	0	
Totals:	11	0	0.0	16	0	0.0	19	0	0.

We did not find any example of a loss of intertonic or posttonic /ŭ/ in our corpus of Latin inscriptions of Dalmatia.

Balkans: (Pagan)

Century	Initial			Intertonic			Posttonic		
	/ŭ/ > u	u Lost	% Loss	/ŭ/ > u	u Lost	% Loss	/ŭ/ > u	u Lost	% L₍
3rd.	0	0		0	0		2	0	
4th.	0	0		0	0		0	2	100
n.d.	0	0		5	0		15	4	21
Totals:	0	0	0.0	5	0	0.0	17	6	26

Balkans: (Christian)

Century	Initial			Intertonic			Posttonic		
	/ŭ/ > u	u Lost	% Loss	/ŭ/ > u	u Lost	% Loss	/ŭ/ > u	u Lost	% I
4th.	0	0		2	0		3	0	
5th.	0	0		0	0		1	0	
n.d.	1	0		4	0		7	0	
Totals:	1	0	0.0	6	0	0.0	11	0	

any form of *Ianuarias* used in inscriptional dating, nor did we find any occurrence of *Februarius* or its variants in any pagan inscription of Britain.

[155] Cf. Jackson, *Language*, p. 274: "After a consonant, a VL *u* before stressed a, o, e, i was dropped, in the first to second century." For a similar comment, see Grandgent, p. 95.

The six deviations of posttonic /ŭ/ in pagan inscriptions of the Balkans are:

Ingenus (proper name), *Kal.* 376, *CIL* III 7471, Dewna (Marcianopolis), Moesia Inferior, no date.
possit (bis), *Kal.* 384, Tschekalewo (Thrace), 4th century.
Ingenus (proper name), *Kal.* 401, *CIL* III 12,436, Mekisch (Moesia Inferior), no date.
posit, *Kal.* 414, *CIL* III 12,334, Ormanliu (Thrace), no date.
Ingenus (proper name), *Kal.* 416, *CIL* III 14,211, Saradsche (Moesia Inferior), no date.

Hiatus-Filling u

In contrast to the general Vulgar Latin tendency to lose occasionally /ŭ/ in hiatus, we have several examples of a hiatus-filling *u* to avoid the contraction of two vowels in hiatus. Jackson (*Language*) considers (p. 365) this hiatus-filling *u* a distinctive element of the Latin of Britain as can be seen from his words: "It is remarkable that the Latin loanwords show the existence in British Latin of a peculiar hiatus-filling *u* when one of the vowels in a Latin hiatus is *u*; which is not found in native British nor, except to a very small extent, in Vulgar Latin. It seems, therefore, to have been a special feature of the Vulgar Latin of Roman Britain." [156] Jackson shows (p. 365) the development of stressed /ŭ/ in hiatus in Brittonic languages from Latin loanwords with the examples of Welsh *ystryw*, *distryw*, and Cornish *destrewy* which evolved from *struuo* and *destruuo* from the Latin *struo* and *destruo*. A different result ensues when the /ŭ/ in hiatus is not stressed as can be seen in the Welsh development *aw* which signifies that the *u* was reduced to *ə* and then became *a*. [157] Compare the examples: *construenda* > *constru-uenda* > *constrauenda* > W. *cystrawen*; *ruina* > *ruuina* > *rauina* > Pr. Welsh *rawin*, by vowel affection to Welsh *rhewin*. Jackson has found (p. 366) evidence of this change in a bilingual inscription where the Latin proper name *Ingenui* was rendered in

---

[156] In addition to epigraphical documentation such as *paevoniam*, *Glove* (= *Chloe*), *poveri* (= *pueri*), from Pompeian inscriptions (see Väänänen, *Pompéiennes*, p. 49), and others which we will give as examples from Africa and the Balkans; cf. also the Italian *rovina* < *ruina*, *vettovaglia* < *victualia*.
[157] Jackson, *Language*, pp. 365-66.

the Ogham inscription as *Igenavi,* an attempt by the engraver to spell in Ogham letters the sound of the British Latin. There is another development of hiatus-filling *u* which Jackson considers (p. 366) "even more remarkable, because it is entirely opposed to what happened in the VL. of the rest of the Empire. Yet it, too, cannot be of native origin, because it is not found in native words." This concerns the unstressed disyllabic terminations *-eus, -ea, -eum* which usually became monosyllabic *-i̯us, -i̯a,* and *-i̯um.* The regular Vulgar Latin tendency is, of course, seen in loanwords into the Brittonic languages: cf. *cuneus* > **cuni̯us* > Welsh *cyn.* This development represents the ordinary, standard everyday Vulgar Latin speech. There was, however, another treatment of this ending in British Latin, in which a glide *u̯* was inserted in the hiatus, giving *-eu̯us, -eu̯um* (there are no examples for *-ea*). [158] Jackson makes the important point (pp. 366-67) that "this happened only in the case of those words in which the terminations had not yet become *-i̯us, -i̯um* but were still disyllabic, very likely in the speech of a higher social level. These words then became stressed on the *e,* the penultimate syllable, under the influence of the British accent." Examples of this phenomenon in the unstressed endings *-eus* and *-eum* as well as a stressed *e* in hiatus are: *puteus* > **putéu̯us* > Welsh *pydew, oleum* > **oléu̯um* > Welsh *olew, leo* > **léu̯o* > Welsh *llew.*

Examples of this hiatus-filling *u,* found in both pagan and Christian inscriptions of Britain, are:

> *puueri, CIIC* 327, Brecon (Wales), 6th century. (A Christian inscription.)
> [*p*]*ossuu*[*it*], *RIB* 923, Old Penrith (Voreda), Cumberland, no date. [159]
> [*p*]*ossuuit, RIB* 1606, Hadrian's Wall: Housesteads (Vercovicium), Northumberland, n.d.
> *Devo* (= *Deo,* dat. sing. of *Deus*), *RIB* 306, *CIL* VII 140, Lydney Park (Gloucestershire), n.d.

This last example is interesting because it occurs in a *defixio,* which is a type of inscription that uses very popular Latin, contrary to Jackson's remark (p. 87) that "since it [the hiatus-filling *u*] must

---

[158] Jackson, *Language,* p. 366.
[159] The form *posuuit* was also found in a Christian inscription of Pannonia, *D.* 3659, Purbach (Pannonia), no date.

have arisen from a desire to preserve carefully the two syllables of the older Latin -e/us, etc., it would have come from the speech of an educated or conservative level of society."

This same phenomenon of a hiatus-filling u is also found in our corpus of Christian inscriptions of Africa:

> *Ianuuaria, D.* 3686, *CIL* VIII 21,803, Numerus Syrorum (Mauretania Caesariensis), A.D. 389.
> *instituuit* (= *instituit*), *D.* 3687, *CIL* VIII 9975, Numerus Syrorum, A.D. 392.
> *istituuerunt* (= *instituerunt*), *D.* 3691A, *CIL* VIII 9984, Numerus Syrorum, A.D. 429.

Although inscriptions do not prove that the hiatus-filling u was limited to pagan and Christian inscriptions of Britain, it should be remarked that a parallel situation was found for transitional i between vowels in hiatus (see *supra*, pp. 223-25), where inscriptions show that an inserted i was most often found in African and British Latin inscriptions. The fact that both hiatus-filling u and transitional i between vowels in hiatus are most often found in inscriptions of African and Britain would seem to indicate that we are dealing with two conservative areas, in which the Latin inscriptions are attempting to show orthographically a Classical Latin pronunciation of maintaining vowels in hiatus. We thus see that two conflicting tendencies are present in these areas, namely, the loss of vowels in hiatus versus the maintenance of vowels in hiatus, and although the loss of vowels is more prevalent in inscriptions, the conservative pronunciation is, nevertheless, still evident.

Final: Non-Morphological

Area	Century	/ŭ/ > u	/ŭ/ > o	% Of Dev.
Africa	5th.	9	0	
	6th.	5	0	
	n.d.	25	0	
	Totals:	39	0	0.0
Britain (Pagan)	2nd.	1	0	
	3rd.	1	0	
	n.d.	1	0	
	Totals:	3	0	0.0
(Christ.)	4th.	1	0	0.0

	Century	/ŭ/ > u	/ŭ/ > o	% Of Dev.
Dalmatia	4th.	5	0	
	5th.	1	0	
	6th.	2	0	
	n.d.	8	0	
	Totals:	16	0	0.0
Balkans (Pagan)	n.d.	1	0	0.0
(Christ.)	4th.	1	0	
	5th.	3	0	
	n.d.	3	0	
	Totals:	7	0	0.0

We found no examples of a final /ŭ/ in non-morphological endings changing to *o* in any of the areas studied by us. This stability of final /ŭ/ in our areas contrasts with the change to *o* in the adverb *menos*, [160] which Gaeng found four times in Narbonensis (*D.* 2831, *D.* 2896, *D.* 2898, and *D.* 4426), while the correct *minus* occurred twenty-three times (14.8 % of deviation). The adverb *iterum* changes once to *eterom* (*D.* 2889A, A.D. 524?) in the same area. In Northern Italy, Gaeng records (p. 220) the adverbs *menos* (*D.* 4179BN) and *secos* (*D.* 2287A) and concludes (p. 221) with the query as to whether there was a "neutralization of Latin /ŭ/ and /ŏ/ in the final syllable in both the areas of Gaul and Northern Italy." Prinz, while acknowledging that short *u* tended to *o* in Transalpine Gaul, considers the possibility of an analogical influence of the noun *annos* on the adverb *menos* since they are closely linked in the formula *vixit plus minus ... annos.* [161]

---

[160] Gaeng brings out the point (p. 221) that **minos* or **iterom* are never found in inscriptions, but always with the stressed /ĭ/ changed to *e* (*menos* and *eteron*, or *menus* and *eterum*) when deviations do occur, and concludes (p. 221) that the merger of final /ŭ/ and /ŏ/ must have been subsequent to that of Latin /ĭ/ and /ē/ in stressed syllable.

[161] Prinz, *De O et U*, p. 113: "In Gallia Transalpina O ita explicari potest, ut vulgo U brevis ad O inclinaverit. Cum in omnibus exemplis 'annos' praecedat vel subsequatur 'menos', etiam OS accusativi pluralis terminatio ad vocalis mutationem attribuisse potest." Prinz' analogy with *annos* may be questioned since the formula has *plus minus* and the /ū/ of *plus* and the /ŭ/ of *minus* would probably have changed the final /ō/ of *annos* to *annus*. It should also be remembered that *annis* was also used, probably to a greater extent than *annos*.

Final: Morphological

The main declensional and conjugational endings having a final /ŭ/ are the nominative singular (-us), accusative singular (and nominative singular of neuters) (-um), genitive plural (-rum) of the second declension, the dative and ablative plural of the third, fourth, and fifth declensions (-bus), the genitive plural (-um) of the third declension, several nominative singulars of the third declension (-ux, -us, etc.), the nominative and accusative singulars of the fourth declension (-us, -um), the third person plural of the present and perfect indicatives (-unt), the third person singular and plural of the present passive (-ur), and the first person plural of the present and perfect indicatives (-mus). We will analyze these various categories to see whether final /ŭ/ changes to o in all these endings, or just in a selected few, and whether any possible change in final /ŭ/ is motivated by phonetic or morphological considerations.

Declensional Endings

Africa:

Century	2nd Decl. Nom. Sing.			% Dev. For -o	2nd Decl. Sing. and Neut. Nom.			% Dev. For -o	2nd Declension Genit. Plural			% Dev. -oro
	-us	-u	-o		-um	-u	-o		-orum	-oru	-oro	
3rd.	4	0	0		1	0	0		2	0	0	
4th.	40	0	0		13	1	0		4	2	0	
5th.	57	2	0		7	1	0	40.0	2	0	0	
6th.	24	3	0		3	0	2		7	1	0	
7th.	8	8	1	5.9	0	0	0		1	0	0	
n.d.	370	6	1	0.3	60	7	0		28	3	0	
Totals:	503	19	2	0.4	84	9	2	2.1	44	6	0	0.0

Century	3rd/4th/5th. Dat./Abl. Plur.		% Of Dev.	3rd Decl. Gen. Plur.			% Of Dev.	3rd Declen. Nom. Sing.	% Of Dev.
	-bus	-bo		-um	-u	-o		-ux	
3rd.	1	0		1	0	0			
4th.	2	0		1	1	0			
5th.	1	0		2	0	0			
6th.	4	1	20.0	3	0	0			
7th.	1	0		0	0	0			
n.d.	35	0		24	8	0		3	
Totals:	44	1	2.2	31	9	0	0.0	3	0.0

	Nom. Sing. 3rd Decl.			For -o % Dev.	Nom. Sing. 4th Decl.			For -o % Dev.	Acc. Sing. 4th Decl.			For -o % Dev.
	-us	-u	-o		-us	-u	-o		-um	-u	-o	
3rd.	1	0	0		0	0	0		1	0	0	
4th.	1	0	0		1	0	0		2	0	0	
5th.	1	0	0		0	0	0		1	0	1	50.0
6th.	1	0	0		0	0	0		1	0	0	
7th.	0	0	0		1	0	0		0	0	0	
n.d.	7	1	0		11	2	0		7	1	1	11.1
Totals:	11	1	0	0.0	13	2	0	0.0	12	1	2	13.3

The deviations from African inscriptions in declensional endings are:

a)   2nd Declension Nominative Singular:

> *Fortunio epcs, D.* 931A, *CIL* VIII 22,656, Carthage (Proconsularis), A.D. 632-655.
> *Felix in pace. spiritu tuo in bonu, D.* 3409, *CIL* VIII 14,328, Utica (Proconsularis), no date. [162]

b)   2nd Declension Accusative Singular:

> *per Solomonem gloriosiss. et excell. magistro militum, . . . ac patricio, D.* 806, *CIL* VIII 1863, Theveste (Numidia), A.D. 527-549. [163]

c)   3rd Declension Ablative Plural:

> *. . . de suis pr(o)p(riis) laboribo . . .: D.* 28, *CIL* VIII 4354, near Casa Numidarum, A.D. 578-582. [164]

---

[162] The expression *spiritus tuus in bono* is quite common in inscriptions; cf. *D.* 2285A, 2285AN, 2316b, 2316bN, 2338, 3408-3410.

[163] Contrary to Gaeng (p. 228) and Prinz (p. 109), we are giving the change of final /ŭ/ to *o* after prepositions for the prime purpose of showing that this is quite rare in African inscriptions as compared to the reverse change of the use of the accusative for the ablative after prepositions as can be seen by the frequent change of this type under the heading of final /ō/ to *u* (see *supra*, pp. 278-80). This taking over of the accusative case after prepositions has been previously noted by B. Löfstedt, *Studien über die Sprache der Langobardischen Gesetze* (Uppsala: Almquist and Wiksells, 1961), p. 273: "Diese Rektionsfehler hängen wohl in der Regel mit dem allgemeinen Vordringen des Akkusativs als Universalkasus und analogischer Beeinflussung durch andere Präpositionem zusammen." Inscriptions definitely show that there was a one-directional flow to the accusative case after prepositions.

[164] Prinz explains (*De O et U*, p. 117) the form *laboribo* as an assimilation of the vowels (. . . de vocalium assimilatione cogitare licet). Speaking about the general change of the dative or ablative plural ending -bus to -bo

d) 4th Declension Accusative Singular:

Secundus maritus una cum suis domo aet. fec., D. 3678,
CIL VIII 21,793, Pomaria (Mauretania Caesariensis), no
date.
*Secundus frater carissi. et bene merenti salute domo Romula
istituerut . . . , D.* 3689, *CIL* VIII 9982, Numerus Syrorum (Mauretania Caesariensis), A.D. 416.[165]

From the very few deviations in declensional endings of African
inscriptions, it can be safely said that the final /ŭ/ was stable in
this area. This is particularly evident for the second declension
nominative singular where the correct ending -*us* is found 503 times
(in addition to -*u* with a loss of final -*s* found 19 times) against just
two deviations for an 0.4 % of deviation. It is also seen that when
final -*s* or *m*- is dropped, as is the case occasionally for the second
declension nominative singular, the second declension accusative
singular, the second declension genitive plural, the third declension
genitive plural, the third declension nominative singular in -*us*, the
fourth declension nominative singular, and the fourth declension accusative singular, the final /ŭ/ regularly remains.

Britain	Century	2nd Decl. Nom. Sing.			2nd Decl. Sing. and Neut. Nom.			2nd Declension Genit. Plural		
		-*us*	-*u*	-*o*	-*um*	-*u*	-*o*	-*orum*	-*oru*	-*oro*
(Pagan)	1st.	22	0	0	2	0	0	4	0	0
	2nd.	58	0	0	8	0	0	6	0	0
	3rd.	63	0	0	22	0	0	17	0	0
	4th.	5	0	0	1	0	0	0	0	0
	n.d.	275	0	0	41	1	0	30	1	0
	Totals:	423	0	0	74	1	0	57	1	0

throughout Romania, Prinz states (p. 116) that "in titulis recentioris aetatis
perpauca O vocalis exempla obviam fiunt."

[165] The expressions *domus aeterna* (or *aeternalis*) and *domus Romula* are
very common with Christian inscriptions: cf. *Diehl* 3650-3681 and *Diehl*
3682-3691D.

Britain	Century	3rd/4th/5th Dat./Abl. Plur.		3rd Decl. Gen. Plur.			3rd Decl. Nom. Sing.
		-bus	-bo	-um	-u	-o	-ux
(Pagan)	1st.	0	0	1	0	0	0
	2nd.	2	0	2	0	0	0
	3rd.	4	0	5	0	0	0
	n.d.	23	0	8	0	0	11
	Totals:	29	0	16	0	0	11

		3rd Decl. Nom. Sing.			3rd Decl. Nom. Sing.	4th Decl. Acc. Sing.		
		-us	-u	-o	-ur	-um	-u	-o
	1st.	1	0	0	0	0	0	0
	2nd.	0	0	0	0	0	0	0
	3rd.	0	0	0	0	0	1	0
	n.d.	2	0	0	2	0	0	0
	Totals:	3	0	0	2	0	1	0

We found no deviations in declensional endings for pagan inscriptions of Britain. The loss of final -s or -m was very rarely encountered in the above declensional endings.

Britain	Century	2nd Decl. Nom. Sing.			% Of Dev.	2nd Decl. Acc. Sing.			2nd Decl Gen. Plur	
		-us	-u	-o		-um	-u	-o	-orum	-oro
(Christ.)	4th.	1	0	0		1	0	0	0	0
	5th.	4	0	1	20.0	0	0	0	0	0
	6th.	24	0	0		2	0	0	1	0
	7th.	8	0	0		0	0	0	0	0
	n.d.	10	0	0		2	0	0	0	0
	Totals:	47	0	1	2.1	5	0	0	1	0

		3rd Decl. Abl. Plur.		% Of Dev.	3rd Decl. Gen. Plur.		3rd Decl. Nom. Sing.
		-bus	-bo		-um	-o	-ux
	5th.	0	0		1	0	0
	6th.	0	0		1	0	1
	7th.	0	0		2	0	0
	8th.	2	0		0	0	0
	Totals:	2	0	0.0	4	0	1

The single deviation found in the Christian inscriptions of Britain was [c]onsobrino, CIIC 394, Carnarvon (Wales), end of fifth century. [166] Fnal /ŭ/ in declensional endings, however, is stable as can be seen by the fact that only one deviation was recorded.

Dalmatia:

Century	2nd Declen. Nom. Singul.			% Dev. For -o	2nd Decl. Acc. Sing.		% Of Dev.	2nd Decl. Gen. Plur.		3rd Decl. Dat./Abl.	
	-us	-u	-o(s)		-um	-om		-orum	-oro	-bus	-bo
4th.	13	0	1		8	0		2	0	5	0
5th.	10	0	0	7.1	4	0		0	0	0	0
6th.	9	0	0		5	1	16.7	1	0	0	0
n.d.	95	1	3	3.0	33	4	10.8	10	0	15	0
Totals:	127	1	4	3.0	50	5	9.1	13	0	20	0

Century	3rd Declen. Gen. Plural		3rd Decl. Nom. Sing.		3rd Decl. Nom. Sing.	4th Decl. Acc. Sing.			% Of Dev.
	-um	-o	-us	-o	-ux	-um	-u	-o	
4th.	0	0	3	0	2	0	0	0	
5th.	0	0	1	0	0	0	0	0	
6th.	0	0	1	0	0	0	0	0	
n.d.	6	0	8	0	3	6	3	1	10.0
Totals:	6	0	13	0	5	6	3	1	10.0

The deviations in declensional endings in this area are:

a) Second Declension Nominative Singular:

tribunos, D. 1940, CIL III 10,146, Island of Apsori, no date.
deposito Ariver, filius..., D. 3042, CIL III 9563, Salona, A.D. 344. [167]
reventos, D. 3363, CIL III 9623, Salona, no date. [168]
domos, D. 2028N, CIL III 14,902, Salona, no date.

---

[166] In addition to the important deviation [c]onsobrino, the same inscription also contains the third declensional nominative form cive, showing a loss of final -s and a change of final /ĭ/ to e.

[167] We consider deposito as a nominative singular form for depositus, although Diehl writes (II, 121): "voluit depositio potius quam depositos." Skok, Pojave, likewise considers (p. 60) deposito as representing depositus ("deposito Ariver filius mjesto [instead of] depositus").

[168] This is a questionable case as Diehl considers (II, 186) that it should be "nemo revenit." Skok, Pojave, likewise says (p. 81): "reventos mjesto revenit."

b)   Second Declension Accusative Singular:

votom, D. 1940, *CIL* III 10,146, Island of Apsori, no date.
suom, D. 1940, *CIL* III 10,146, Island of Apsori, no date. [169]
[*ina*]*nte habias* [*I*]*ordani*[*s*] *fluvio*, D. 2389, *CIL* III p. 961, Tragurium, n.d.
per domino meum, D. 2389, *CIL* III p. 961, Tragurium, no date.
tertio post decimum, D. 79b, *CIL* III 9527, Salona, A.D. 599. [170]

c)   Fourth Declension Accusative Singular:

[*no*]*s obito* [*nostro*], D. 839N, *CIL* III 13,964, Salona, no date.

We see that the above examples of deviation, for the most part, occur after prepositions (admittedly examples of confusion of cases), appear in the same inscription, or are questionable interpretations. Final /ŭ/ in Dalmatian inscriptions is apparently quite stable.

Balkans: (Pagan)

Century	2nd Decl. Nom. Sing.			% Of Dev.	2nd Decl. Acc. Sing.			% Of Dev.	3rd/5th Dat./ Abl. Plural		3rd Decl. Gen. Plur.	
	-us	-u	-o		-um	-u	-o		-bus	-bo	-um	-o
1st.	0	0	0		2	0	0		0	0	0	0
2nd.	1	1	0		0	0	0		0	0	0	0
3rd.	11	0	0		0	1	0		0	0	0	0
4th.	1	0	0		0	0	0		0	0	0	0
n.d.	74	0	1	1.3	9	1	2	16.7	2	0	8	0
Totals:	87	1	1	1.1	11	2	2	13.3	2	0	8	0

Balkans: (Pagan)

Century	2nd Decl. Gen. Plur.		3rd Decl. Nom. Sing.		3rd Decl. Nom. Sing.	4th Decl. Acc. Sing.	
	-rum	-ro	-us	-o	-ux	-um	-o
2nd.	1	0	0	0	0	0	0
n.d.	4	0	2	0	4	1	0
Totals:	5	0	2	0	4	1	0

---

[169] Note that the accusatives *votom*, *suom* as well as the nominative singular *tribunos* come from the same inscription.

[170] The accusatives *domino* and *tertio* likewise occur in the same inscription, and both are governed by prepositions.

The deviations in the pagan inscriptions of this area are:

a) Second Declension Nominative Singular:

Crescentio, Kal. 398, CIL III 12,377, Ferdinandowo (Moesia Inferior), n.d. [171]

b) Second Declension Accusative Singular:

... voto libens posuit, Kal. 146, CIL III 6127, Gigen (Oescus), Moesia Inferior, no date. [172]
... titulo posuerunt, Kal. 398, CIL III 12,377, Ferdinandowo (Moesia Inferior), no date.

The figures show that final /ŭ/ in declensional endings in pagan inscriptions of the Balkans is stable.

Balkans: (Christian)

Century	2nd Decl. Nom. Sing.			% Of Dev.	2nd Decl. Acc. Sing.			% Of Dev.	2nd Declen. Gen. Plural			% Of Dev.
	-us	*-u*	*-o*		*-um*	*-u*	*-o*		*-rum*	*-ru*	*-ro*	
4th.	10	0	0		4	0	0		1	0	0	
5th.	4	0	0		2	0	0		1	0	0	
6th.	1	0	0		0	0	0		0	0	0	
n.d.	88	0	1	1.1	10	1	0		6	1	1	12.5
Totals:	103	0	1	1.0	16	1	0	0.0	8	1	1	10.0

---

[171] Although Kalinka equates Crescentio with Crescentius (*Kalinka*, p. 313), the juxtaposition of the names *Aurelius Crescentio ex prepositis* ... may seem to indicate that Crescentio was a third declension nominative singular. Diehl gives in his *Indices* references to both *Crescentius* and *Crescentio* as nominative forms. We do find the following examples of Crescentio in oblique cases in Christian inscriptions: *Crescentione*, D. 2358N, *Cr<e>scentioni*, D. 2576BN, *Crescentioni*, D. 2988N, *Crescentionis*, D. 3516D, *Crescentionis*, D. 3965h, *Crescentioni*, D. 4116E. The difficulty in determining whether a proper name is of the 2nd declension *-ius* type or the 3rd declension *-io* may also apply to the previously recorded *Fortunio* (see *supra*, p. 320) which was given as a change of final /ŭ/ to *o* in African inscriptions. Diehl gives in his *Indices* (III, 72) examples of both *Fortunius* and *Fortunio* used in nominative constructions and one example of *Fortunio* in the genitive case: *For[tun]ionis*, D. 1477A.

[172] Kalinka gives (p. 135) a syntactical explanation for *voto*: "voto statt des gewöhnlichen votum nicht so sehr infolge lautlicher Vermengung beider Formen, wofür diese Inschrift zu alt und zu sorgfältig geschrieben ist, als in syntaktischer Anlehnung an ex voto, voto suscepto u.dgl."

3rd Decl. Dat./Abl.		% Of Dev.	3rd Decl. Gen. Plur.		% Of Dev.	3rd Declen. Nom. Singul.		% Of Dev.
-bus	-bo		-um	-o		-us	-o	
4th. 1	0		1	0		1	0	
n.d. 1	0		3	0		3	0	
Totals: 2	0	0.0	4	0	0.0	4	0	0.0

3rd Decl. Nom. Sing.	% Of Dev.	4th Decl. Acc. Sing.		% Of Dev.	4th Declen. Nom. Singul.		% Of Dev.
-ux		-um	-o		-us	-o	
4th. 0		1	0		0	0	
n.d. 1		4	1	20.0	1	0	
Totals: 1	0.0	5	1	16.7	1	0	0.0

The deviations from the Christian inscriptions of the Balkans are:

a) Second Declension Nominative Singular:

domesticos, Kal. 428, D. 478, CIL III 14,207, Stara Sagora (Traiana), Moesia Inferior, no date. [173]

b) Second Declension Genitive Plural:

scutarioro, D. 564, CIL III 14,207, Perinthus (Thrace), no date. [174]

c) Fourth Declension Accusative Singular:

domo, Kal. 428, D. 478, CIL III 14,207, Stara Sagora (Traiana), Moesia Inferior, no date.

We thus see that there are sporadic deviations, but final /ŭ/ in declensional endings in the Christian inscriptions of the Balkans is generally stable.

---

[173] Prinz considers (De O et U, p. 111) this change as due to a Greek influence.

[174] Prinz considers (Ibid., p. 115) the final o of the ending -oro as due to the assimilation of the preceding -o-: "ORO(M) terminationem assimilatione ortam esse mihi persuasum est ita, ut ex O, quae praecedit, O altera orta sit..." Prinz also points out the fact that there is never the ending -ARO(M): "...in genetivo plurali primae declinationis nunquam ARO(M) terminatio obviam fit." We found a progressive assimilation of the first declension genitive plural -arum changing to -aram in ecclesiaram, D. 1826A, CIL VIII 2311, near Cedia, no date.

Considering all the declensional terminations in the various areas which we studied, we conclude that final /ŭ/ is stable, although sporadic deviations do occur. Gaeng's commentary (p. 227) concerning the change of -us to o can be applied to the other declensional endings for the areas studied by him: "... the occurrence of an o spelling for us in the nominative singular case ending, an apparent morphological extension..., is very sporadic and the overwhelming majority of instances of correct spelling would indicate that the -us ending in this grammatical function was quite stable throughout the period covered by our inscriptional material." We also consider the sporadic deviations as the result of morphological considerations (especially confusion of the ablative and accusative cases after prepositions and this confusion extended to the accusative as a direct object of the verb) and of phonetic assimilations (-orum to -oro as evidenced also by the change of -arum to -aram). An occasional foreign influence, such as Greek or Celtic, may also contribute to a change of final /ŭ/. [175]

Conjugational Endings

While final /ŭ/ was seen to be stable in declensional endings with only very sporadic changes to o, this stability is even better seen in conjugational endings where no deviations were found in our corpus. We will give the figures for correct occurrences to show the extent of final /ŭ/ in verbal endings.

---

[175] *Ibid.*, p. 112.

Africa:

Century	Present Indicat. 3rd Per. Plural	Perf. Indicative 3rd Pers. Plural [176]					Present Passive 3rd Per.	Perfect Indicat. 1st Per. Plural	Present Indicat. 1st Per. Plural
	-unt	-unt	-ut	-un	-um	-u	-ur	-mus	-mus
3rd.	0	1	0	0	0	0	1	2	
4th.	1	7	1	0	0	0	3	1	
5th.	0	13	1	0	0	0	2	0	
6th.	0	2	0	0	0	1	0	1	
n.d.	2	20	1	1	1	0	10	5	
Totals	3	43	3	1	1	1	16	9	

Britain: (Pagan)

	-unt	-unt	-ut	-un	-um	-u	-ur	-mus	-mus
1st.		1					0	0	
2nd.		3					0	0	
3rd.		5					0	1	
n.d.		9					2	0	
Totals:		18					2	1	

Britain: (Christian)

	-unt	-unt	-ut	-un	-um	-u	-ur	-mus	-mus
6th		1							1

Dalmatia:

Century	Present Indicat. 3rd Per. Plural	Perf. Indicative 3rd Pers. Plural					Present Passive 3rd Per.	Imperf. Subj. 1st Per. Plural	Pres. Sub. Of *posse* 1st Pers. Plural
	-unt	-unt	-ut	-un	-um	-u	-ur	-mus	
4th.	0	1					0	0	0
5th.	0	0					1	1 [177]	0
6th.	0	0					0	0	0
n.d.	1	14					7	0	1
Totals:	1	15					8	1	1

---

[176] It is interesting to note that although there are numerous consonantal changes, the final /ŭ/ in the third person plural of the perfect indicative remains stable: cf. *compleberut* (= *compleverunt*), D. 1917, no date; *istituerut*, D. 3688, fourth century; *istituerut*, D. 3689, fifth century; *fecerun*, D. 2667, no date; [e]*merum*, D. 3794, no date; *feceru*, D. 3670B, sixth century.

[177] The final -*s* is dropped in the imperfect subjunctive *pureremu* (= *poneremus*), D. 838, CIL III 9567, Salona (Dalmatia), no date. The change

Balkans: (Pagan)

Future Perf. Pass.

n.d.		1

	1

Balkans: (Christian)

Present Passive

4th.	0	1	0
5th.	0	1	0
n.d.	2	9	2
Totals:	2	11	2

On the basis of our study of both declensional and conjugational endings we conclude that final /ŭ/ was stable in those areas under investigation. We found no general trend of a merger of final /ŭ/ and /ō/, although sporadic changes of final /ŭ/ to *o* did occur. As to a regional differentiation of final /ŭ/, Gaeng considers (p. 234) that in the area of Gaul "a merger of Latin /ŭ/ and /ŏ̄/ in the final syllable does not seem unjustified" although he bases his opinion mainly on the fact that "the area of Gaul seems to be the only one where we found examples of the spelling of *or* for *ur* and vice versa in morphological endings." Although this conclusion is apparently supported by Grandgent's statement (p. 103) that "final vowels were especially obscure in Gaul in the sixth and seventh centuries," inscriptional material shows that there was no definite trend to a merger of final /ŭ/ and /ō/ in any area of Romania. In fact, Sardinian is especially characterized by its separation of final /ō/ and /ŭ/ as seen by the words of Wagner ("Lautlehre," p. 36): "In allen log[udore-sischen] Mda. [= Mundarten] sind die lat. Auslautvokale gut erhalten; insbesondere bleibt auch ausl. -o und -u streng geschieden: *káḍḍu*, Pl. *káḍḍos; kánto*, aber *kántămus*." Gaeng's own figures (pp. 223-24) indicate that final /ŭ/ was stable, although an occasional deviation did take place. To show that a phonetic merger of final /ŭ/ and /ō/ was developing, it would be necessary to have all or most of the declensional and conjugational endings in -*u* show a tendency to be confused with -*o*. This is not the case in inscriptional material where only a few declensional endings (and the single conjugational ending of the passives in -*ur*) show the change of /ŭ/ to

---

of *n* to *r* may foreshadow an important rhotasism that will be evident in future Rumanian dialects or the Albanian dialect of Tosk.

o, and even in these limited categories the percentage of deviation is low. The deviations themselves can likewise be explained by means other than a merger (confusion of cases after prepositions, assimilations, and foreign influences).

Other phenomena related to final /ŭ/ are the change of declension of the genitive plural *martyrum* found as *marturoru,* D. 1844, *CIL* VIII 27,332, Thugga (Africa), no date, and *marturorum,* D. 2099, *CIL* VIII 7924, near Constantine (Africa), no date, the ultracorrection of a Greek upsilon instead of *u* in [*S*]*erg*[*i*]*y,* D. 236, *CIL* VIII 22,656; *e*[*x*]*arcy,* D. 238, Carthage, of the Byzantine Age; *oratoriym,* D. 1836, *CIL* III 14,207, Serdica (Thrace), no date; [*pre*]*sbuterym,* D. 1836, *CIL* III 14,207, Serdica (Thrace), no date; *Stefanys,* D. 2042, *CIL* VIII 1392, Tichilla (Proconsularis), no date, the change of final /ŭ/ to *i* in the number *duobis,* D. 670, *CIL* III 42,222, Savaria (Pannonia Superior), no date, undoubtedly on the analogy of the dative and ablative plural forms of the third declension, and the change of declension (from second to third) of *zaconis* (= *diaconus*), D. 1223, *CIL* III 2654, Salona (Dalmatia), A.D. 358, and *zacon* (= *diaconus*), D. 1859, near Thamagadum (Numidia), A.D. 411. There are several cases of a neuter noun modified by a masculine adjective: ... *hunc* ... *sepulcrum* (acc.), D. 79b, *CIL* III 9527, Salona (Dalmatia), A.D. 599; ... *hunc sepulcrum* (acc.), D. 822N, *CIL* III 2632, Salona (Dalmatia), no date; *super hunc corpus alium corpus ponere volueret,* D. 3835C, *CIL* III 9508, Salona (Dalmatia), A.D. 382; ... *alium corpus ponere,* D. 3854, Iader (Dalmatia), sixth century. [178] We also have a few cases where there is an actual change of the neuter ending *-um* changing to the masculine *-us: posticius* (bis): D. 791, *CIL* VIII 5352, Calama (Proconsularis), no date; [179] *vexillus* (used as nominative), *RIB* 1154, Corbridge (Corstopitum), Northumberland, no date. [180]

---

[178] Other examples of the use of *alium* for *aliud* are found in D. 507, Salona (Dalmatia), n.d.; D. 3839A, *CIL* III 2635, near Salona (Dalmatia), n.d.; D. 839, *CIL* III 10,092, Vrnik (Dalmatian Island), no date.

[179] According to *Harper's Latin Dictionary,* p. 1406, the Classical Latin form is *posticum.*

[180] In the *RIB,* p. 382, the editor writes that "*vexillus* is a solecism for *vexillum.*"

Latin /ū/, Represented by the Letter u

The total number of occurrences of /ū/ in unstressed position is limited. The only cases of deviation are found in final position where the morphological factor of assimilation of fourth declension nouns to second declension forms is the overriding cause for the change. We will, however, give the overall figures for unaccented /ū/ in initial, intertonic, non-morphological final positions as well as for morphological final positions so as to give an idea of the extent of /ū/ in unaccented position in inscriptions.

Initial

Area	Century	Open Syllable /ū/ > u	Closed Syllable /ū/ > u	Totals
Africa	3rd.	1	0	1
	4th.	4	1	5
	5th.	4	1	5
	6th.	5	7	12
	n.d.	34	8	42
	Totals:	48	17	65
Britain	1st.	1	0	1
	2nd.	9	1	10
(Pagan)	3rd.	19	0	19
	4th.	0	1	1
	n.d.	43	1	44
	Totals:	72	3	75
Britain				
(Christ.)	n.d.	1	0	1

Area	Century	Open Syllable /ū/ > u	Closed Syllable /ū/ > u	Totals
Dalmatia	4th.	2	0	2
	5th.	2	1	3
	6th.	0	2	2
	n.d.	10	2	12
	Totals:	14	5	19

Balkans	2nd.	3		0		3
	3rd.	6		0		6
(Pagan)	4th.	2		0		2
	n.d.	7		0		7
	Totals:	18		0		18

Balkans	4th.	3		0		3
	n.d.	12		3		15
(Christ.)	Totals:	15		3		18

We see that initial /ū/ is extremely stable in all our areas, no deviations having been recorded.

Intertonic

Africa	Century	Open Syllable		Closed Syllable		Totals
		/ū/ > u		/ū/ > u		
	6th.	1		0		1
	n.d.	26		1		27
	Totals:	27		1		28

Britain	2nd.	1		0		1
	3rd.	1		0		1
(Pagan)	n.d.	6		1		7
	Totals:	8		1		9

Britain (Christian)		NO EXAMPLES				

Dalmatia	4th.	1		0		1
	5th.	2		0		2
	n.d.	1		1		2
	Totals:	4		1		5

Balkans	3rd.	1		0		1
(Pagan)	n.d.	1		0		1
	Totals:	2		0		2
(Christ.)	n.d.	2		0		2

Intertonic /ū/ is stable in our areas, once again no deviations having been found.

Final: Non-Morphological

Africa	Century	/ū/ > u	/ū/ > o
	6th.	1	0
	n.d.	2	0
	Totals:	3	0
Britain (Pagan)	NO EXAMPLES		
Britain (Christ.)	NO EXAMPLES		
Dalmatia	4th.	1	0
	n.d.	1	0
	Totals:	2	0
Balkans (Pagan)	NO EXAMPLES		
Balkans (Christ.)	NO EXAMPLES		

There are no deviations, but the total number of occurrences is extremely low and even nonexistent in some areas.

Final: Morphological

The declensional endings that were analyzed are the nominative singular of the third declension (-ūnx and -ūs), the genitive singular (-ūs), the ablative singular (-ū)[181] and the accusative plural (-ūs) of the fourth declension.

---

[181] There is a deviation of the final /ū/ to o of the dative singular of a fourth declension masculine noun from an African inscription (ispirito, D. 2311, Numidia, no date). In A Latin Grammar, by Hale and Buck, we see (p. 49) that "the dative singular in -u is regular in neuters, and, except in early Latin, is frequent in masculines and feminines." See also Allen and Greenough's New Latin Grammar (p. 37) where the dative singular in -ū as well as in -uī is given in the fourth declension paradigm.

Area	Century	3rd Decl. Nom. Sing.	4th Decl. Gen. Sing.		4th Decl. Abl. Sing.		% Of Dev.	4th Decl. Acc. Plur.	
		-us	-us	-o(s)	-u	-o		-us	-os
Africa	4th.	2	0	0	3	0		11	0
	5th.	0	0	0	1	0		10	0
	6th.	0	0	0	1	0		3	0
	n.d.	0	3	0	12	2	14.3	27	0
	Totals:	2	3	0	17	2	10.5	51	0

The two deviations from African inscriptions are:

> *Masticiana exunto* (= *ex sumptu*) *proprio fecit,* D. 802, *CIL*
> *VIII* 2079, near Theveste (Proconsularis), no date.
> *bono ispirito Mariani Deus refrigeret,* D. 2311, *CIL* VIII
> 8191, Rusicade (Numidia), n.d. [182]

This change of final /ū/ to *o* is undoubtedly the result of the assimilation of fourth declension nouns to the second declension, a morphological phenomenon.

Britain	Century	3rd Decl. Nom. Sing.	3rd Decl. Nom. Sing.	4th Decl. Gen. Sing.	4th Decl. Abl. Sing.	4th Decl. Acc. Plur.
		-us	-unx	-us	-u	-us
(Pagan)	2nd.	0	0	1	2	1
	3rd.	1	1	2	6	0
	n.d.	0	6	2	4	0
	Totals:	1	7	5	12	1

In the ablative singular of the fourth declension we have two examples of *domu* in the third century and two more examples in undated inscriptions. For a discussion of the variants *domu* and *domo* as ablative singulars of the noun *domus,* see *supra,* pp. 285-86.

---

[182] The final *o* in *ispirito* is for the dative singular ending *-ū,* an accepted variant of the more common ending *-ui* for masculine nouns. See the above footnote 181 for references for the *-u* ending for fourth declension nouns. The verb *refrigero* governs both the dative and accusative cases in inscriptions. We have calculated the final *-o* from /ū/ in the dative *ispirito* under the ablative singular since both have a final /ū/. This is the only example we have of a fourth declension noun ending in either *-u* or *-o* in the dative case.

Britain	Century	3rd Decl. Nom. Sing.	4th Decl. Gen. Sing.		% Of Dev.	4th Decl. Abl. Sing.		% Of Dev.	4th Decl. Acc. Sing.	
		-unx	-us	-o		-u	-o		-us	-os
(Christ.)	9th.		1	0						
	n.d		1	0						
	Totals:		2	0	0.0					
Dalmatia	4th.	0	0	0		1	0		3	0
	5th.	0	1	0		1	0		2	0
	6th.	0	0	0		0	0		1	0
	n.d.	1	0	1	100.0	3	1	25.0	12	0
	Totals:	1	1	1	50.0	5	1	16.7	18	0

The deviations in Dalmatian inscriptions are:

a) Genitive Singular:

in nom. dni Ieso Cri[s]ti, D. 2389, CIL III p. 961, Tragurium, no date. [183]

b) Ablative Singular:

Daniel de laco leonis, D. 2426, CIL III 10,190, Podgorica (near Doclea), n.d.

The change of final /ū/ to o in the above examples is once again the result of an assimilation of fourth declension nouns to the second declension, a morphological change that is widespread throughout the entire Romania. [184]

Balkans	Century	4th Decl. Gen. Sing.	3rd Decl. Nom. Sing.
		-us	-us
(Pagan)	n.d.	1	
(Christ.)	4th.		1

---

[183] The Latin Iesus, although originally derived from Hebrew, is declined like Greek masculine nouns and consequently the genitive singular is Iesu in Latin. The change of final /ū/ to o in Ieso may really be an intertonic change since the name Iesus Christus was probably considered as a single form. If this is so, it would be the only case of intertonic /ū/ changing to o in our corpus.

[184] Cf. Prinz, De O et U, p. 142; Grandgent, p. 148.

Thus, we see that final /ū/ in declensional endings is extremely stable as is unaccented /ū/ in all positions. The only deviations of final /ū/ to *o* were found in declensional endings where the morphological pull of the second declension is evident.

We have an example of a genitive singular fourth declension noun showing a final -*i* rather than the correct -*ūs* in *magistrati, CIIC* 394, Penmachno (Carnarvon), Wales, end of fifth century, another example of a declensional change.

Chapter III

GREEK UPSILON

Since Greek upsilon was first represented in Latin inscriptions by *y* in the middle of the first century B.C., we can expect to find in our inscriptions, both pagan and Christian, three main orthographic reflexes of this Greek sound: *y*, *u*, and *i*.[1] Various scholars have expressed the opinion that Greek upsilon was first represented by Latin *u*, then later by Latin *i*.[2] Disagreement must have arisen over the various ways to represent Greek Ʋ in Latin speech and writing.[3] An early indication of the vacillation of the symbols *y*, *u*,

---

[1] Stolz and Debrunner, p. 52: "In der Mitte des 1. Jh. v. Chr. wird nach dem Zeugnis der Inschriften griech. Ʋ nich mehr durch u (V), sondern durch modifiziertes V, d.h. Y (y) wiedergegeben. Vulgäre Inschriften ersetzen den neuen Laut durch *i*." Cf. Grandgent, p. 80.

[2] Cf. Väänänen, *Introduction*, p. 38; Grandgent, p. 80, points out the importance of Greek dialects when he states that "in the older borrowed words, perhaps taken mostly from Doric, Ʋ regularly was assimilated to Latin u." Chronologically speaking Grandgent mentions that "towards the end of the Republic, cultivated people adopted for Greek words the Ionic-Attic pronunciation, which is generally represented, in the case of Ʋ , by the spelling *y*." Commenting upon the social differentiation of this sound, he adds that "among the common people the unfamiliar *ü* was assimilated to *i*"; Pirson, in addition to the chronological information that "*u* . . . était seul en usage à l'époque archaïque," remarks (p. 39), with respect to the Latin inscriptions of Gaul, that "l'*i* de l'époque classique n'est pas moins en vogue, surtout s'il y a dans le corps du mot un *i* ou un jod posttoniques"; cf. also Lindsay, p. 4. This scholar writes (p. 11) that "before the introduction of the Greek letter (namely, *y*), Latin *u* was used in loanwords like *tumba*, etc., while at a later time *i* was employed, e.g., *cignus*; and the Romance forms of these earlier and later loanwords indicate that these spellings represented the pronunciation of the time."

[3] Sturtevant, p. 43: "When the Romans came into contact with Attic and Hellenistic Greek there was disagreement about representing Ʋ in

and *i* for Greek upsilon is encountered in the inscriptions of Pompei. [4] The situation is complicated by the fact that Greek upsilon was pronounced in various fashions in the Greek dialects themselves. [5] Proof of the different pronunciations of Greek upsilon is offered by Modern Greek where the upsilon is now pronounced /i/, except for Tsakonian where the original sound of /u/ has been preserved. [6] The change of /u/ to /i/ calls for the intermediate pronunciation of /y/, which is the classical Attic-Ionic pronunciation. [7] We will investigate the incidence of the *u* and *i* spellings in our inscriptions to see whether any area showed a particular proclivity to a certain orthography with the assumption that the spelling was a true indication of the actual pronunciation. [8] We will study Greek upsilon in the stressed, initial, intertonic, and posttonic positions, and then give a final tabulation to see whether there was a differentiation in Latin inscriptions with respect to the pronunciation of Greek upsilon.

Latin." Sturtevant adds that "the difficulty was finally overcome for educated Romans by the adoption of the foreign sound and the Greek letter," but this would certainly not solve the problem for the majority of unlettered Romans.

[4] Väänänen, *Pompéiennes*, pp. 32-33. Väänänen's conclusion (p. 33) that "les deux prononciations de Ʋ , *u* et *i*, ont existé à Pompéi concurremment, quel que soit le lieu d'articulation de la consonne qui suit" is intended to refute Graur's thesis, expressed in his work, *I et V en latin* (Paris, 1929), that the Latin use of *u* was confined to those cases where the Greek upsilon came before a labial consonant. Rosetti, I, 82, agrees in principle with his fellow countryman's theory " Ʋ grecesc, pronunțat ü, apare notat cu ajutorul literelor *y*, *u* și *i*; pronunțarea cu ü a persoanelor culte făcuse loc, în limba vorbită, pronunțării cu *u*, înaintea unei oclusive labiale, prin rotunjirea prematură a buzelor, și cu i, înaintea celorlalte consoane." ["Greek Ʋ , pronounced ü, appears annotated with the aid of the letters *y*, *u*, and *i*; the pronunciation of *ü* on the part of cultured speakers gave way in the spoken language to the pronunciation of *u*, before a labial occlusive, through a premature rounding of the lips, and of *i*, before the other consonants."] Rosetti does admit, however, that in practice, both graphies are mixed ("în practică, însă, cele două grafii sînt amestecate.")

[5] Sturtevant, p. 44; Hubert Pernot, *D'Homère à nos jours* (Paris: Librairie Garnier Frères, 1921), p. 138; A. Debrunner and A. Scherer, *Geschichte der griechischen Sprache*, 2nd ed. (Berlin: Walter de Gruyter, 1969), II, 48.

[6] Sturtevant, p. 42; Debrunner and Scherer, p. 48.

[7] Sturtevant, p. 44; Pernot, p. 141.

[8] It is unfortunate that Gaeng does not give any percentages for the use of *y*, *u*, and *i* in the inscriptions of Spain, Gaul, Italy, and Rome.

Accented Position

Area	Century	Open Syllable			Closed Syllable			Totals		
		y	*i*	*u*	*y*	*i*	*u*	*y*	*i*	*u*
Africa	3rd.	0	1	0	0	0	0	0	1	0
	4th.	0	1	0	0	0	0	0	1	0
	n.d.	3	3	3	1	2	0	4	5	3
	Totals:	3	5	3	1	2	0	4	7	3

The examples of an *i* spelling for Greek upsilon in African inscriptions are:

presbiteri (gen.), *D*. 1182, *CIL* VIII 20,300, Satafi (Mauretania Sitifensis), A.D. 363.
Eutitia (= *Eutychia*), *D*. 1697, Carthage (Proconsularis), no date.
Egiptii, *D*. 2099, *CIL* VIII 7924, near Constantine, no date.
presbitero, *D*. 2410, Thamallula, no date.
Egitia (= *Aegyptia*), *D*. 2532, Theveste (Proconsularis), no date.
Sirica, *D*. 2040, *CIL* VIII 25,037, Carthage, A.D. 203.
Eutichius, *D*. 2543, *CIL* VIII 25,224, Carthage, n.d.

We thus see that in accented position the *i* spelling is used in 50 % of the cases (seven *i* spellings out of a total number of fourteen occurrences of upsilon) for a predominant position in African inscription. [9]

Britain	Century	Open Syllable			Closed Syllable			Totals		
		y	*i*	*u*	*y*	*i*	*u*	*y*	*i*	*u*
(Pagan)	1st.	0	0	0	0	0	0	0	0	0
	2nd.	0	0	1	0	0	0	0	0	1
	3rd.	1	0	0	0	0	1	1	0	1
	n.d.	4	2	1	5	2	0	9	4	1
	Totals:	5	2	2	5	2	1	10	4	3

---

[9] Sardinian has both an *i* and a *u* according to the time when the Greek upsilon was borrowed. Cf. Wagner, "Lautlehre," p. 13: "Griech. y, das im volkstümlichen Latein *u* gesprochen wurde, ergab natürlich auch im Sardischen *u*: *túm(b)u* = *thymu*; *múrta* = *myrtha*; *bússa, búsa* = *byrsa*; in jüngeren Wörtern wie auf dem Festland auch *i*: log. *kíma*, camp. *címa* = *kyma*; log., camp. *armídda* = *serpyllu*."

The examples of an *i* spelling for Greek upsilon in pagan inscriptions of Britain are:

> *Dionisias*, RIB 147, Bath (Aquae Sulis), no date.
> *Tirintius* (= *Tirynthius*), RIB 291, CIL VII 158, Wroxeter (Viroconium), no date.
> *Dyonisius*, RIB 1175, CIL VII 477, Corbridge (Corstopitum), Northumberland, no date.
> *Nimfae*, RIB 1526, Hadrian's Wall: Carrawburgh (Brocolitia), Northumberland, no date.

The examples of a *u* spelling for upsilon in this area are:

> *Suriae*, RIB 726, CIL VII 272, Catterick (Cataractonium), Yorkshire, no date.
> *Tusdro* (= *Thysdro*), RIB 897, CIL VII 344, Old Carlisle (Olerica), Cumberland, A.D. 242.
> *Suriae*, RIB 1792, CIL VII 758, Hadrian's Wall: Carvoran (Magnis), Northumberland, A.D. 163-166.

Although the *i* spelling is just slightly more common than the *u* spelling (4 cases of *i* to 3 cases of *u*), what is surprising is the usual orthography with *y*, which supposes a higher level of education on the part of the stonemason.

Britain	Century	Open Syllable			Closed Syllable			Totals		
		y	*i*	*u*	*y*	*i*	*u*	*y*	*i*	*u*
(Christ.)	n.d.	0	0	0	0	0	0	0	0	0

There are no cases of Greek upsilon in our corpus of Christian inscriptions of Britain.

Dalmatia	Century	Open Syllable			Closed Syllable			Totals		
		y	*i*	*u*	*y*	*i*	*u*	*y*	*i*	*u*
	4th.	1	1	0	0	0	0	1	1	0
	5th.	2	0	0	0	0	0	2	0	0
	6th.	0	0	0	0	0	0	0	0	0
	n.d.	1	1	3	0	0	0	1	1	3
	Totals:	4	2	3	0	0	0	4	2	3

The examples of an *i* spelling in this area are:

martiribus, D. 78a, *CIL* III 9506, Salona, A.D. 375.
Olibrio, D. 660, *CIL* III 9524, Salona, no date.

The examples of a *u* spelling in stressed position in this area are:

Suro, D. 646, *CIL* III 9614, Salona, no date.
Putii (= gen. of *Pythius*), D. 4735N, *CIL* III 9566, Salona, no date.
Marturius, D. 3613, *CIL* III 1891, Narona, no date.

Although both *i* and *u* are found in stressed syllables, the popular nature of the *i* spelling can be seen from the form *presbeter*[*i*], D. 1172N, *CIL* III 9554, Salona, no date, which shows the change of *i* (< *y*) to *e*.

Balkans	Century	Open Syllable			Closed Syllable			Totals		
		y	*i*	*u*	*y*	*i*	*u*	*y*	*i*	*u*
(Pagan)	n.d.	3	0	1	0	0	0	3	0	1

The single example of Greek upsilon appearing as *u* in pagan inscriptions of the Balkans is *Su*[*r*]*a*, *Kal.* 413, Nikopol (Moesia Inferior), no date.

Balkans	Century	Open Syllable			Closed Syllable			Totals		
		y	*i*	*u*	*y*	*i*	*u*	*y*	*i*	*u*
(Christ.)	n.d.	3	3	1	0	0	0	3	3	1

The following are the examples of Greek upsilon written as *i* in the Christian inscriptions of the Balkans:

Sir(*us*), D. 1875, *CIL* III 14,368, Celeia (Noricum), no date.
martiribus, D. 2179, *CIL* III 5972, Castris Reginis, no date.
Dionisus, D. 935, *CIL* III 8080, Transilvania, no date.

The single example of a *u* spelling in this area is:

[*pre*]*sbuterym*, D. 1836, *CIL* III 14,207, Serdica (Sofia), Thrace, no date.

Initial Position

Area	Century	Open Syllable			Closed Syllable			Totals		
		y	i	u	y	i	u	y	i	u
Africa	3rd.	0	0	1	0	0	0	0	0	1
	4th.	0	1	0	0	0	0	0	1	0
	5th.	1	0	0	0	0	0	1	0	0
	6th.	0	0	0	0	1	0	0	1	0
	n.d.	1	3	0	1	1	0	2	4	0
	Totals:	2	4	1	1	2	0	3	6	1

The examples of an *i* spelling in initial syllables in African inscriptions are:

> *nimfarum*, D. 785, *CIL* VIII 23,673, near Maktar (Byzacena), sixth century.
> *Crisogoni* (bis), D. 1943, *CIL* VIII 21,511, Cartenna, no date.
> *Quiriaci* (= *Cyriaci*), D. 1979, *CIL* VIII 2519, near Cirta (Numidia), no date.
> *Cipriani*, D. 2068, *CIL* VIII 20,600, Tocqueville, A.D. 359.
> *Simposium*, D. 2330, *CIL* VIII 27,333, Thugga (Proconsularis), no date.
> *Dinamius*, D. 2937, *CIL* VIII 10,517, Ammaedara (Byzacena), no date.

The only example of a *u* spelling in our corpus for this area is:

> *[S]urorum*, D. 405, *CIL* VIII 9964, Numerus Syrorum (Mauretania Caesariensis), A.D. 272?

As was the case for stressed syllables, the *i* spelling is predominantly used for initial syllables in African inscriptions.

Britain	Century	Open Syllable			Closed Syllable			Totals		
		y	i	u	y	i	u	y	i	u
(Pagan)	n.d.	3	0	0	0	0	0	3	0	0

Although only three cases of Greek upsilon were found, all with the *y* spelling, it is interesting to note that this same situation was found for the stressed syllables, namely, that the y spelling was preferred, a probable indication of the better education of the stone-masons.

Britain	Century	Open Syllable			Closed Syllable			Totals		
		y	i	u	y	i	u	y	i	u
(Christ.)		0	0	0	0	0	0	0	0	0

No occurrences of Greek upsilon were found in our corpus of Christian inscriptions of Britain.

Dalmatia	Century	Open Syllable			Closed Syllable			Totals		
		y	i	u	y	i	u	y	i	u
	4th.	1	0	0	0	0	0	1	0	0
	5th.	0	0	0	1	0	0	1	0	0
	n.d.	0	2	0	1	0	0	1	2	0
	Totals:	1	2	0	2	0	0	3	2	0

The two examples of i spelling in initial syllables of this area are:

[Q]uiriace (= Cyriace), D. 3835D, CIL III 12,842, Salona, no date.
Quiriace, D. 3381, CIL III 14,306, Salona, no date.

Balkans	Century	Open Syllable			Closed Syllable			Totals		
		y	i	u	y	i	u	y	i	u
(Pagan)	n.d.	1	0	0	0	0	0	1	0	0
(Christ.)	n.d.	2	1	0	0	0	0	2	1	0

The single example of an i spelling in initial syllable in Christian inscriptions of the Balkans is Quirillus (= Cyrillus), D. 935, CIL III 8080, Transilvania, no date.

Intertonic Position

Africa	Century	Open Syllable			Closed Syllable			Totals		
		y	i	u	y	i	u	y	i	u
	n.d.	0	1	2	0	0	0	0	1	2

The example of *i* spelling in intertonic position in this area is:

> *Euticianus*, D. 2680, *CIL* VIII 16,351, near Cellas (Proconsularis), no date.

The examples of *u* spelling are:

> *marturoru*, D. 1844, *CIL* VIII 27,332, Thugga (Proconsularis), no date.
> *marturorum*, D. 2099, *CIL* VIII 7924, near Constantine, no date. [10]

Britain	Century	Open Syllable			Closed Syllable			Totals		
		y	*i*	*u*	*y*	*i*	*u*	*y*	*i*	*u*
(Pagan)	2nd.	1	0	0	0	0	0	1	0	0
	n.d.	1	0	0	0	0	0	1	0	0
	Totals:	2	0	0	0	0	0	2	0	0

Although there are no examples of a *u* spelling in intertonic position in our corpus of pagan inscriptions of Britain, we do have a case of an *o* spelling for an original Greek upsilon, thus showing the popular progression of *y* > *u* > *o*: *Palmorenus*, *RIB* 1171, Corbridge (Corstopitum), Northumberland, no date.

Britain	Century	Open Syllable			Closed Syllable			Totals		
		y	*i*	*u*	*y*	*i*	*u*	*y*	*i*	*u*
(Christ.)		0	0	0	0	0	0	0	0	0

No examples of Greek upsilon were found in our corpus in intertonic position for Christian inscriptions of Britain.

Dalmatia	Century	Open Syllable			Closed Syllable			Totals		
		y	*i*	*u*	*y*	*i*	*u*	*y*	*i*	*u*
	n.d.	1	2	0	0	0	0	1	2	0

---

[10] See *supra*, p. 330, for a discussion on the change of declension of the forms *marturoru* and *marturorum*.

The examples of an *i* spelling in intertonic position in Dalmatia are:

anaglifari(o), D. 660, *CIL* III 9524, Salona, no date.
conquiliarius (= *conchyliarius*), D. 3840B, *CIL* III 2115, near Salona, no date.

Balkans	*Century*	Open Syllable			Closed Syllable			Totals		
		y	*i*	*u*	*y*	*i*	*u*	*y*	*i*	*u*
(Pagan)	n.d.	0	0	0	1	0	0	1	0	0

Balkans	*Century*	Open Syllable			Closed Syllable			Totals		
		y	*i*	*u*	*y*	*i*	*u*	*y*	*i*	*u*
(Christ.)		0	0	0	0	0	0	0	0	0

There were no examples of Greek upsilon in our corpus of Christian inscriptions of the Balkans.

Posttonic Position

The number of occurrences of Greek upsilon is the highest in this position because of the great frequency of use of the oblique forms of the word *martyr*.

Area	*Century*	*y*	*i*	*u*
Africa	4th.	1	2	1
	5th.	0	5	0
	6th.	0	3	2
	n.d.	8	14	11
	Totals:	9	24	14

Examples of an *i* spelling in posttonic position in this area are:

martir(um), D. 791, *CIL* VIII 5352, Calama (Proconsularis), no date.
martir(es), D. 791, *CIL* VIII 5352, Calama (Proconsularis), no date.
Libiae (= *Libyae*), D. 806, *CIL* VIII 1836, Theveste (Proconsularis), A.D. 527-49. [11]

---

[11] We are including this form as a posttonic *i* spelling for Greek upsilon, although it is more accurately explained as a case of posttonic Greek upsilon in hiatus, which is rarely found in our corpus.

aelemosinae, D. 1103, *CIL* VIII 20,905, Tipasa, no date.
presviter, D. 1184D, *CIL* VIII 24,074, Proconsular Province, no date.
presbiter, D. 1185, Sufetula (Byzacena), no date.
presviter, D. 1590A, Madauros (Proconsularis), no date.
presviter, D. 1601B, Madauros (Proconsularis), no date.
martiri, D. 1829, *CIL* VIII 9271, Sidi-Ferruch, between A.D. 449-538.
martiris, D. 1830, *CIL* VIII 2220, near Mascula (Numidia), between A.D. 379-88.
martiri, D. 1842, near Theveste (Proconsularis), fourth century.
presbiter, D. 1859, near Thamugadi (Numidia), A.D. 411.
aelemosina, D. 2035, *CIL* VIII 20,906, Tipasa, no date.
martiris, D. 2043, *CIL* VIII 27,958, near Theveste (Proconsularis), sixth century.
martiri, D. 2052, Benian in Mauretania, A.D. 434.
martirum, D. 2069, Kherbet-el-Ma-el-Abiod, A.D. 474.
m[a]rtiru, D. 2095, *CIL* VIII 10,686, near Theveste (Proconsularis), no date.
martirum, D. 2096, *CIL* VIII 23,041, Uppena, no date.
presbiter, D. 2096, *CIL* VIII 23,041, Uppena, no date.
martiris, D. 2103, Tocqueville, no date.
martiris, D. 2104, *CIL* VIII 8630, Sitifis (Mauretania Sitifensis), A.D. 452.
martiris, D. 205N, Khenchela, no date.
martirum, D. 2073, *CIL* VIII 19,102, near Thibilis (Numidia), no date.

Examples of a *u* spelling are:

marturis, D. 1642, *CIL* VIII 23,127, Kairuan (Byzacena), no date.
marturis, D. 1917, *CIL* VIII 16,743, Aquis Caesaris near Theveste (Proconsularis), no date.
marturas, D. 2044, *CIL* VIII 9692, Cartenna, no date.
marture, D. 2049, *CIL* VIII 18,002, Bescera, no date.
marturu, D. 2068, *CIL* VIII 20,600, Tocqueville, A.D. 359.
marturis, D. 2086, near Thamalluma (Mauretania Sitifensis), no date.
marturu, D. 2087, near Sitifis (Mauretania Sitifensis), no date.
martures, D. 2091, Bordj Rdir, no date.
marturu, D. 2093, *CIL* VIII 2334, near Thamugadi (Numidia), no date.
marturum, D. 2094, *CIL* VIII 5664, near Calama (Proconsularis), no date.

marturum, D. 2096A, Sitifis (Mauretania Sitifensis), no date.
martur(um), D. 2098, Thabraca (Proconsularis), no date.
marturum, D. 2100, *CIL* VIII 6700, Mastari, no date.
marturi, D. 2060, *CIL* VIII 14,100, Carthage (Proconsularis), no date.

It is interesting to note that, although oblique forms of *martyr* with posttonic *i* and *u* are approximately equal in frequency of occurrence (15 cases of *martir-* and 14 cases of *martur-*), the form that prevailed in Logudorese was *márturu*. [12]

There is an example where Greek upsilon is written as *yi* in *martyiru, D.* 2066, *CIL* VIII 9716, Orléansville, no date, a spelling that may be an attempt to show the *i* orthography or possibly the Classical Greek pronunciation /y/.

On the basis of the overall figures for posttonic Greek upsilon, we see that the *i* spelling was preferred in the Latin inscriptions of Africa.

Area	Century	y	i	u
Britain	2nd.	0	0	1
(Pagan)	n.d.	1	0	0
	Totals:	1	0	1

The single example of a *u* spelling in posttonic position in pagan inscriptions of Britain is *Eutuches, RIB* 143, *CIL* VII 40, Aquae Sulis (Bath), Somerset, about A.D. 122.

Area	Century	y	i	u
Britain (Christ.)		0	0	0

There are no examples in our corpus of posttonic Greek upsilon in Christian inscriptions of Britain.

Area	Century	y	i	u
Dalmatia	4th.	0	1	0
	6th.	0	1	0
	n.d.	1	0	0
	Totals:	1	2	0

---

[12] Rosetti, I, 82.

The following are examples of *i* spelling in posttonic position in Dalmatia:

[*n*]*eofita*, D. 1505, *CIL* III 9505, Salona, A.D. 359.
presbiter, D. 79a, *CIL* III 9526, Salona, A.D. 599.

Although there are no examples of a *u* spelling in our corpus of Dalmatian inscriptions, we do have the popular development of *y* > *u* > *o* in *martores* (= *martyris*, genitive singular), D. 1084, *CIL* III 14,897, Salona, no date.

Area	Century	*y*	*i*	*u*
Balkans (Pagan)	n.d.	1	0	0
(Christ.)	4th.	0	1	0
	n.d.	2	1	1
	Totals:	2	2	1

The following are examples of *i* spelling in the Christian inscriptions of the Balkans:

neofitus, D. 1480, Vindobona (Pannonia), A.D. 385.
neofitus, D. 1506, Aquae (Moesia Superior), no date.

The example of the *u* spelling in this area is:

marture, D. 2182, *CIL* III 10,232, Sirmium (Pannonia Inferior), no date.

It should be noted that the Rumanian form is *martur*. Unfortunately, there are too few occurrences of Greek upsilon in Balkans inscriptions to determine what spelling was predominant in Vulgar Latin.

We will now summarize the *i* and *u* spelling in tabular form so as to see whether there was a distinct preference for one particular orthography in the various regions of Romania. The table below will include the *i* and *u* spellings in all positions studied and in open and closed syllable.

Summary of Spellings of Greek Upsilon

	Century	y	i	u
Africa	3rd.	0	1	1
	4th.	1	4	1
	5th.	1	5	0
	6th.	0	4	2
	n.d.	14	24	16
	Totals:	16	38	20
Britain	2nd.	1	0	2
	3rd.	1	0	1
(Pagan)	n.d.	14	4	1
	Totals:	16	4	4
(Christ.)	n.d.	0	1	0
Dalmatia	4th.	2	2	0
	5th.	3	0	0
	6th.	0	1	0
	n.d.	3	5	3
	Totals:	8	8	3
Balkans (Pagan)	n.d.	6	0	1
(Christ.)	n.d.	7	6	2

Although it is difficult to generalize for some areas because of the lack of sufficient data, it is clear that in African inscriptions, the *i* spelling is predominant. The *i* spelling is also preferred in the Latin inscriptions of Gaul on the basis of the reverse spelling of *y* for a correct *i*. Pirson concluded (p. 40) that "ces graphies fautives [the reverse spelling of *y* for *i*] prouvent que l'Y dans la langue des derniers siècles avait plutôt une tendance à passer à i." The Greek upsilon is also discussed in the *Appendix Probi*, and although both *i* and *u* are recorded, the *i* spelling is more common. The following items in the *Appendix Probi* refer to the Greek upsilon: *y* > *i*: *gyrus non girus* (28); *Byzacenus non Bizacinus* (48); *amycdala non amiddula* (140); *dys<entericus non disinte>ricus* (150); there are two items that call for the *i* spelling over the *u* spelling although the original form was a Greek upsilon: *porphireticum marmor non purpureticum marmur* [the Latin equivalent of the Greek πορφυρίτης λίθος] (1), and *Marsias non Marsuas* (17); there are three cases of reverse spelling of Greek upsilon for a correct Latin *i: vir non vyr* (120); *virgo non vyrgo* (121), *virga non vyrga* (122). The only items referring to a *u* spelling for the Greek upsilon are: *tymum non tumum* (191), and *myrta non murta* (195).[13] Dalmatian Latin also seems to prefer the *i* spelling as does the Latin of Christian inscriptions of the Balkans, although in both cases the limited number of occurrences makes any definite assertion hazardous. What is striking about the representation of the Greek upsilon in pagan inscriptions of Britain is the preference given to the *y* spelling, undoubtedly an indication of the high level of education, and therefore a consciousness of the Greek alphabet. An overzealousness on the part of the stonemasons in Britain to show their erudition caused them at times to use a reverse spelling of *y* for a correct *i*. Compare the following examples of a *y* spelling for a correct *i* in proper names of Greek origin or considered to be Greek in origin:

> *Dolychen*[o] (an epithet of Jupiter), *RIB* 1022, *CIL* VII 422, Piercebridge, A.D. 217.
> *Dyonisius*, *RIB* 1175, *CIL* VII 477, Corbridge (Corstopitum), Northumberland, no date.
> *Mytrae* (= *Mithrae*, the Persian God), *RIB* 1395, *CIL* VII 541, Rudchester (Vindovala), Northumberland, no date.
> *Mytrae*, *RIB* 1599, *CIL* VII 645, Hadrian's Wall: Housesteads (Vercovicium), Northumberland, third century.

In our corpus of pagan inscriptions of Britain we did not find any examples of a reverse spelling of *y* for a correct *u*. On the basis of our study, we conclude that the *i* spelling, and consequently its pronunciation, was well on its way to general acceptance as the reflex of Greek upsilon.

---

[13] We have already seen that the Sardinian words *túm(b)u* and *múrta* are derived precisely from a Vulgar Latin *u*. See *supra*, p. 339, footnote 9 for the reference.

CHAPTER IV

DIPHTHONGS

The Diphthong /aj/, *Represented By the Digraph* ae

The treatment of the diphthong *ae* has been extremely important to scholars in their interpretations of the development of Latin into the various Romance languages. Sittl considered [1] the monophthongization of *ae* to *e* as an Umbrian innovation which was one of a series of northern Italic phenomena leading to the dialectalization of Latin in the peninsula. Haudricourt and Juilland [2] believed that the breakdown of the Latin vocalic system based on quantitative differences was caused by the monophthongization of *ae* to a long open ē, a phoneme previously unknown in Latin and thus causing an asymmetrical arrangement of the phonological system. The collapse of the Latin quantitative system has been termed [3] as "eine der folgenschwersten Umgestaltungen des lateinischen Lautsystems zugleich

---

[1] Sittl, p. 4. On the basis of phonetic and morphological innovations emanating from north Latin dialects, this scholar concludes: "So sondern sich die nordlateinischen Mundarten ... durch verschiedene Eigentümlichkeiten der Aussprache und Deklination von der Masse der übrigen."

[2] A. G. Haudricourt and A. G. Juilland, *Essai pour une histoire structurale du phonétisme français* (Paris: Klincksieck, 1949), p. 23 ff. A strong criticism lodged against the Haudricourt-Juilland theory was made by Weinrich (p. 16) who said: "Ich kann mir nur schwer vorstellen, dass die Monophthongierung des Diphthongen *ae* so dringend war, dass dafür als Preis eine folgenschwere Revolution des ganzen Lautsystems hingenommen werden musste." For a critique of the various theories concerning the breakdown of the Latin quantitative system, see the article of N. C. W. Spence entitled "Quantity and Quality in the Vowel System of Vulgar Latin," *Word*, 21 (1965), 1-18.

[3] Weinrich, p. 16.

ein entscheidender Schritt auf dem Wege der Ausgliederung der romanischen Sprachräume." The virtual replacement of the first declension nominative plural ending -ae by -as in late Vulgar Latin texts, although the earliest attestation of this change comes from the Atellan farces of Pomponius in the first century B.C., has caused heated discussion as to the formation of first declension nouns in Italian and Rumanian. In our study of the diphthong ae, we will investigate the treatment of ae in stressed, initial, intertonic, and final positions (genitive and dative singulars and the nominative plural of the first declension) to see whether inscriptions can tell us anything about the intricacies of this most important diphthong.

Stressed Position

Africa	Century	Open Syllable		Closed Syllable		Totals		% of e
		$ae > ae$	$ae > e$	$ae > ae$	$ae > e$	ae	e	
	3rd	2	1	0	0	2	1	33.3
	4th.	2	1	0	0	2	1	33.3
	5th.	0	3	0	0	0	3	100.0
	6th.	2	0	1	0	3	0	0.0
	n.d.	10	14	0	0	10	14	58.3
	Totals:	16	19	1	0	17	19	52.8

Some examples of the monophthongization of the diphthong ae to e in stressed position in African inscriptions are:

> evum, D. 275, CIL VIII 9183, Auziensi, n.d.
> seculo, D. 331, Thena (Byzacena), no date.
> Elio, D. 387, Thamugadi (Numidia), no date.
> [p]redia, D. 780, CIL VIII 13,535, Carthage (Proconsularis), no date.
> primevum, D. 1593, Madauros (Proconsularis), fourth century.
> eclesiequae (= ecclesiaeque), D. 1697, Carthage, no date.
> predis, D. 1943, CIL VIII 21,511, Cartenna, no date.
> premia, D. 2031, CIL VIII 17,386, Thabracenses Afri, no date.
> cede (= caede), D. 2052, Benian (Mauretania), A.D. 434.
> querite, D. 2435, near Theveste (Proconsularis), no date.

On the basis of the percentage of use of e for ae (52.8 %) we see that monophthongization had definitely taken place in African inscriptions. It is interesting, however, to note the retention of the diphthong in a Latin loanword into Berber: *taida* from the Latin *taeda*, although monophthongization is also seen in the Berber loanword *iskir* or *tiskirt* from the Latin *aesculus*. [4]

We have an example of a stressed *ae* changing to *i* in *tidiat* (= *taedeat*), *D*. 2388A, Carthage (Proconsularis), no date. It is probable that the diphthong *ae* became a long, closed ę̄, verified by some Romance reflexes and reverse spellings in inscriptions, [5] rather than the usual long, open ē, with a subsequent closing because of the effect of the yod. This is an extremely isolated case of the closing effect of a yod on a preceding /ĕ/ or /ē/ since African inscriptions show a remarkable stability of stressed /ĕ/ and /ē/ in any phonetic environment. [6]

Monosyllables

We found seven examples of the demonstrative *haec* (either neuter accusative plural or feminine nominative singular), and seven examples of *hec*. It is seen that in both monosyllabic and polysyllabic words the monophthongization of *ae* took place. For the replacement of both *quae* and *que* as a feminine relative pronoun by the masculine *qui*, see *supra*, pp. 113-14.

---

[4] Schuchardt specifically mentions in his "Lehnwörter," p. 20, with respect to the word *taida* that "Das Wort ist ins Berberische mit dem altlateinischen Diphthongen aufgenommen worden." Unfortunately no chronological data are given as to the borrowing of the Latin *taeda*, the lack of references to time being a serious criticism of this pioneering article. It can be assumed that *taida* was an extremely early borrowing since the monophthongization of *ae* to *e* took place at the beginning of the second century B.C. (Niedermann, p. 59).

[5] Some examples of Romance words positing a closed /ē/ from the diphthong *ae* are: *saeta* > It. *sęta*, Fr. *soie*, Sp. *seda; blaesu* > Fr. *blois*, and *praeda* > Fr. *proie* (although compare It. *pręda* and Rum. *pradắ* which call for an open e). Pirson gives (p. 19) among others, the following examples of a stressed *ae* for a closed *e* in Latin inscriptions from Gaul: *requiaescit, quiaeti, faeminis, caeteris, muliaeri, diaebus*, etc., and concludes (p. 21) that "le roman a généralement traité le son *ae* comme *e* ouvert. Il y a pourtant certains mots où *ae* a été assimilé à *e* fermé et cette diversité paraît bien remonter à la double valeur de *ae* dans les documents de la décadence."

[6] See *supra*, pp. 78, 87, and 92 for percentages of deviation of the Latin vowels /ĕ/ and /ē/ to *i* in African inscriptions.

Britain	Century	Open Syllable		Closed Syllable		Totals		% Of *e*
		ae > *ae*	*ae* > *e*	*ae* > *ae*	*ae* > *e*	*ae*	*e*	
(Pagan)	1st.	2	0	0	0	2	0	0.0
	2nd.	22	0	0	0	22	0	0.0
	3rd.	35	3	0	0	35	3	7.9
	4th.	15	0	0	0	15	0	0.0
	n.d.	26	4	1	0	27	4	12.9
	Totals:	100	7	1	0	101	7	6.5

The examples of monophthongization in pagan inscriptions of Britain are:

> *Ces(aris)*, *RIB* 179, *CIL* VII 62, Combe Down (Somerset), A.D. 212-217.
> *Grecus*, *RIB* 251, *CIL* VII 190, Lincoln (Lindum), no date.
> *Mammeae* (= dative of *Mammaea*), *RIB* 919, *CIL* VII 319, Old Penrith (Voreda), Cumberland, A.D. 222-235.
> *let(us)*, *RIB* 923, Old Penrith (Voreda), Cumberland, no date.
> *Greca*, *RIB* 934, *CIL* VII 326, Old Penrith (Voreda), Cumberland, no date.
> *ed(em)* (= *aedem*), *RIB* 2148, *CIL* VII 1095, Scotland: Castlecary (Stirlingshire), in Falkirk Parish, no date.
> *Ces(ari)*, *RIB* 2257, a milestone about 1-1/2 miles south of Neath (Nidum), Glamorgan, A.D. 284-305.

Comparing the percentage of deviation of pagan inscriptions of Britain with that of African inscriptions, we find that, although monophthongization took place in British Latin, it was relatively low (6.5 % for *e*), especially when we compare it to the 52.8 % for African inscriptions. It must be remembered, however, that pagan inscriptions of Britain were, for the most part, very classical in nature. The maintenance of the diphthong *ae* must be orthographic and not phonetic since Latin loanwords into Brittonic appear as short /ĕ/; an example is *praecepta* > Welsh *prĕgeth*. [7] The only example of a

---

[7] Jackson, *Language*, p. 335, writes that "the Latin *ae* had become a short open ĕ already in the first to second centuries, and hence the Britons heard it as such and substituted it by their own medium-open short *e*." Loth (p. 112) says: "Cette diphthongue [*ae*] est devenue ę vers le IIe siècle après Jésus-Christ." H. Lewis and H. Pedersen, *A Concise Comparative Celtic Grammar* (Göttingen: Vandenhoeck & Ruprecht, 1961), p. 59, write that the diphthong *ae* "was treated in Celtic as a short e."

stressed *ae* remaining in loanwords is the Welsh *praidd* < *praeda*.[8] There are two examples of Latin *ae* changing into a Welsh *oe*, namely, *blaesus* > W. *bloesg* and *Graeca* > W. *Groeg*. The Welsh *oe* from Latin *ae* in these two examples apparently fell together with British *ai* and would imply a Latin pronunciation of /aj/, like that of the Republican period, but Jackson considers this as a remote possibility.[9] *Groeg* probably came from the Latin *Grāica*, the long *a* developing as a separate sound, with the subsequent contraction of both vowels. This explanation is also given by Loth on page 174 of his *Les Mots latins dans les langues brittoniques*. No satisfactory explanation is given for *bloesg* but Jackson says (p. 336) that "it is not at all probable that *blaesus* would behave in British as if it were /blaisus/, since in VL. the word was pronounced (exceptionally) with close ẹ̄." At any rate the appearance of *bloesg* from Latin *blaesus* contradicts Bourciez' remark (*Éléments*, p. 44) that "l'adj. *blaesus* qui ne paraît s'être conservé qu'en Gaule, y a donné *blēsus* (a. fr. *blois*, prov. *bles*)."

Stressed Diphthongs in Hiatus

In the pagan inscriptions of Britain, in addition to the monophthongization of *ae* to *e* in the verb form *praeest*, we also have a contraction of the diphthong *ae* plus *e* going to *ae* in *praest*. In the following table we will give the incidence of these three forms.

Century	praeest	preest	praest
2nd.	4	0	0
3rd.	1	0	1
n.d.	13	3	3
Totals:	18	3	4

The correct *praeest* is the predominant form as can be seen from the preceding table. The contraction of *ae* plus *e* to *ae* is probably due to an oversight of the stonemason who was unaccustomed to a succession of two *e*'s and omitted one.

---

[8] Loth, p. 112. This scholar also considers (p. 198) *praidd* as "un emprunt très ancien."

[9] Jackson, *Language*, p. 335.

Britain (Christian)

We have only a single example of monophthongization of *ae* to *e* in an undated inscription without any case of a correct occurrence. There is obviously too little material for any conclusion to be drawn.

Dalmatia	Century	Open Syllable		Closed Syllable		Totals		% Of *e*
		ae > ae	*ae > e*	*ae > ae*	*ae > e*	*ae*	*e*	
	4th.	4	0	0	0	4	0	0.0
	5th.	2	0	0	0	2	0	0.0
	6th.	1	0	0	0	1	0	0.0
	n.d.	7	5	1	0	8	5	38.5
	Totals:	14	5	1	1	15	5	25.0

The examples of monophthongization in stressed position in Dalmatia are:

> *Galilea* (= *Galilaeia*), D. 2389, *CIL* III p. 961, Tragurium, no date.
> *seculo*, D. 1934, *CIL* III 9635, Salona, n.d.
> *seculi*, D. 2436, *CIL* III 9625, Salona, n.d.
> [*p*]*restiti*, D. 2494, *CIL* III 9570, Salona, n.d.
> *mesto*, D. 3336, *CIL* III 9638, Salona, no date.

The percentage of monophthongization of 25.0 % shows that the change of *ae* to *e* was well established in Dalmatia. We have a single case of *ae > oe* in the proper name *Coelius*, D. 4110B, *CIL* III 9240, Salona, no date. Since *oe* develops in the Romance languages as a long closed ẹ̄, the use of *oe* for *ae* may indicate that the value of *ae* could be a closed ẹ as well as the more usual open ę. We have already seen that the dialectal long, closed ẹ̄ from *ae* did survive in several Romance forms (see *supra*, p. 353). Grandgent's comment (p. 90) that "in late Latin a bad spelling, *oe* for *ae* and *e*, became popular," is too noncommittal. Lindsay tries to explain (p. 44) the form through a confusion with the Greek: "... *coelum*, for *caelum*, confused with κοῖλος."

Balkans	Century	Open Syllable		Closed Syllable		Totals		% Of e
		$ae > ae$	$ae > e$	$ae > ae$	$ae > e$	ae	e	
(Pagan)	1st.	2	0	0	0	2	0	0.0
	2nd.	4	0	0	0	4	0	0.0
	3rd.	6	0	0	0	6	0	0.0
	4th.	2	0	0	0	2	0	0.0
	n.d.	4	0	0	0	4	0	0.0
	Totals:	18	0	0	0	18	0	0.0
(Christ.)	n.d.	3	3	0	0	3	3	50.0

Although we did not find any examples of monophthongization of *ae* in the stressed syllable of pagan inscriptions of the Balkans, an *e* for *ae* was encountered in initial and final positions.[10] The archaic spelling *ai* is found in the proper name *Ailio* (dative singular) in a pagan inscription recorded by *Kalinka* 384, Tschekalewo near Serdica (Sofia), Thrace, attributed to the fourth century. Kalinka considers (p. 302) the use of *ai* as due to Greek influence: "*Ailio* inmitten einer gräcisierten Bevölkerung minder auffällig." It is striking to find, however, the correct *Aelio* in the same inscription.

The examples of monophthongization in Christian inscriptions of the Balkans are:

> *quero, D.* 1336, *CIL* III 13,529, Ovilava (Noricum), no date.
> *celi, D.* 3419B, Serdica (Sofia), Thrace, no date.
> *Judeae, D.* 4918, *CIL* III 3688, Pannonia Inferior, no date.

Initial Position

Africa	Century	Open Syllable		Closed Syllable		Totals		% Of e
		$ae > ae$	$ae > e$	$ae > ae$	$ae > e$	ae	e	
	3rd.	1	0	0	0	1	0	0.0
	4th.	8	8	0	0	8	8	50.0
	5th.	0	17	0	0	0	17	100.0
	6th.	6	11	0	0	6	11	64.7
	7th.	0	1	0	0	0	1	0.0
	n.d.	15	27	0	0	15	27	64.3
	Totals:	30	64	0	0	30	64	68.1

---

[10] Stressed *ae* is treated like *e* in Rumanian. Cf. H. Tiktin, "Die rumänische Sprache," in Gröber's *Grundriss der romanischen Philologie* (Strassburg: Karl J. Trübner, 1904-06), I, 573.

A few examples of monophthongization in initial syllable in Africa are:

Cess. (= *Caesaribus*), D. 4, Sitifis (Mauretania Sitifensis), A.D. 326-33.
prefectus, D. 27, *CIL* VIII 1434, Tebursk (Proconsularis), A.D. 565-74.
edific(atum), D. 42, *CIL* VIII 9835, Altava (Mauretania Caesariensis), A.D. 508.
edificia, D. 234, Rusguniae (Mauretania Caesariensis), no date.
Mecenatia, D. 310, *CIL* VIII 12,260, Proconsularis, no date.
edilicius (bis), D. 310, as above.
presidali, D. 387, Thamugadi (Numidia), no date.
eternale, D. 423, *CIL* VIII 9870, Altava (Mauretania Caesariensis), A.D. 583.
precessit, D. 614, *CIL* VIII 9693, Cartenna, A.D. 357.
edifikbimus, D. 793, *CIL* VIII 12,035, Limasa (Byzacena), A.D. 582-602.
precelsi, D. 805, Thamugadi (Numidia), A.D. 539-40.
preconium, D. 1743, Thabraca (Proconsularis), n.d.
celorum, D. 1824, *CIL* VIII 20,914, Tipasis Maurorum, no date.
Emilius, D. 1859, near Thamugadi (Numidia), A.D. 411.
Ceselia, D. 2066, *CIL* VIII 9716, Orléansville, n.d.
Cecilius, D. 2096, *CIL* VIII 23,041, Uppena, n.d.
Egiptii, D. 2099, *CIL* VIII 7924, near Constantine, n.d.
letamini, D. 2410, Thamallula, no date.
Leto[r]ius, D. 2860D, *CIL* VIII 21,752, Altava (Mauretania Caesariensis), A.D. 398.

Monophthongization in initial syllable in African inscriptions is extremely common as can be seen by the very high percentage of forms written with *e* (68.1 %).

Britain	Century	Open Syllable		Closed Syllable		Totals		% Of *e*
		ae > *ae*	*ae* > *e*	*ae* > *ae*	*ae* > *e*	*ae*	*e*	
(Pagan)	2nd.	22	0	0	0	22	0	0.0
	3rd.	27	4	0	0	27	4	12.9
	n.d.	51	10	0	0	51	10	16.4
	Totals:	100	14	0	0	100	14	12.3

The examples of initial monophthongization in pagan inscriptions of Britain are:

pref(ectus), *RIB* 324, *CIL* VII 100, Caerleon (Isca Silurum), Monmouthshire, no date.

Cecilius, *RIB* 523, Chester (Deva), Cheshire, third century.

Fesonie (= *Faesoniae*), *RIB* 563, *CIL* VII 175, Chester (Deva), Cheshire, no date.

Emi(lia), *RIB* 677, *CIL* VII 253, York (Eboracum), no date.

prefe(ctus), *RIB* 829, Maryport (Cumberland), no date.

pref(ectus), *RIB* 897, *CIL* VII 344, Old Carlisle (Olerica), Cumberland, A.D. 242.

pre[to(re)], *RIB* 897, *CIL* VII 344, Old Carlisle (Olerica), Cumberland, A.D. 242.

pref(ecti), *RIB* 918, *CIL* VII 318, Old Penrith (Voreda), Cumberland, no date.

Esculap(io), *RIB* 1052, South Shields (Arbeia), Co. Durham, no date.

pref(ecto), *RIB* 1091, *CIL* VII 445, Lanchester (Longovicium), Co. Durham, no date.

pref(ectus), *RIB* 1546, Hadrian's Wall: Carrawburgh (Brocolitia), Northumberland, no date.

Retorum, *RIB* 1724, Hadrian's Wall: Great Chesters (Aesica), Northumberland, no date.

pref(ectus), *RIB* 1980, *CIL* 877, Hadrian's Wall: Castleheads (Uxellodunum), Cumberland, n.d.

Retorum, *RIB* 2117, Scotland, Cappuck (Roxburghshire), third century.

As was the case with stressed *ae*, there was monophthongization in pagan inscriptions of Britain, but it was not as extensive as in African inscriptions. It would appear that pagan inscriptions of Britain were even more classical in nature than African inscriptions.

There are isolated cases of the diphthong *ae* going to *a*, but this change occurs only in abbreviations and is therefore suspect: *praf.* (= *praefecto*), *RIB* 905, *CIL* VII 351, Old Carlisle (Olerica), Cumberland, A.D. 213, and *praf.* (= *praefectus*), *RIB* 1545, Hadrian's Wall: Carrawburgh (Brocolitia), Northumberland, A.D. 198-211. This change of *ae* to *a*, however, is also recorded by Pirson who gives (p. 21) the examples *sape* (= *saepe*), *CIL* XII 5695 (pagan inscription), no date, and *pradia* (= *praedia*), *CIL* XII 2117 (Christian inscription), no date. Pirson's remark (p. 21) that "du double son primitif *ai*, le son *e* seul a persisté dans les langues romanes" is erroneous since the change of *ae* to *a* did take place, although admittedly rarely.[11] Schuchardt gives in his *Vokalismus*, I, 221-23, a fairly long list of words showing an *a* for *ae* and mentions (p. 222) that although "manche dieser Schreibungen beruhen sicher auf einem sehr naheliegenden Schreibfehler, manche aber haben ebenso sicher ihren Grund in der vulgären Aussprache." He gives the following examples (p. 223) of *ae* > *a* in unstressed position: Sp. *arambre*; Port. *arame*; Prov. *aram*; Old Fr. *araim*; Walloon *arame*; Ladin *aram*, *arom* from the Latin *aeramen*;[12] Churwelsh *latezia* from Latin *laetitia*; Rum. *damuni* from *daemon*, and Münstertal *astà* from Latin *aestas*. The Latin *crapula* comes from the Greek χραιπάλη; the Italian *amatita* from αἱματίτης; the Italian *paggio* and the French *page* from παιδίον. It would appear that the monophthongization of *ae* to *a* assumes more importance than what is generally afforded this sporadic change.

Britain	Century	Open Syllable		Closed Syllable		Totals		% Of *e*
		ae > *ae*	*ae* > *e*	*ae* > *ae*	*ae* > *e*	*ae*	*e*	
(Christ.)	6th.	1	0	0	0	1	0	0.0
	n.d.	0	3	0	0	0	3	100.0
	Totals:	1	3	0	0	1	3	75.0

The examples, admittedly few, of monophthongization in Christian inscriptions of Britain are:

preparatus, CIIC 1023, Glamorgan (Wales), no date.
Eternali, CIIC 408, Glamorgan (Wales), no date.
Eterni, CIIC 389, Carnarvon (Wales), no date.

Monophthongization of *ae* to *e* is apparently a very common phenomenon in initial syllables in Christian inscriptions of Britain

---

[11] M. Jeanneret, *La Langue des tablettes d'exécration latine* (Paris: Attinger Frères, 1918), p. 26, gives the following examples of *ae* to *a*: *quastu* (= *quaestum*), from Mentana (Latium), 2nd-3rd centuries A.D., and *Adesicla* (= *Aedesicula*), from Carthage (Proconsularis), third century, A.D., but considers them due to "simples accidents graphiques, une évolution *ae* > *a* n'étant pas connue par ailleurs."

[12] Meyer-Lübke, on explaining the reflexes of the Latin *aeramen* with the change of *ae* to *a* in the Romance languages, writes (*Einführung*, p. 158) that "in ziemlich weitem Umfange findet dagegen Vokalassimilation statt, namentlich wird ein tonloser Vokal dem folgenden betonten angeglichen." This reasoning, although valid for *aeramen* and other forms, does not hold true for all of the words given by Schuchardt.

although the total number of occurrences of the diphthong and of its change is extremely slight in our corpus.

We have a change of the diphthong *ae* to *o*, which is probably a confusion of prefixes and not a phonetic change in the following words:

> *proparavit* (= *praeparavit*), *CIIC* 1022, Glamorgan (Wales), no date.
> *proparabit* (= *praeparavit*), *CIIC* 1015, Glamorgan (Wales), 8th or 9th century according to Hübner.
> *proparavit*, *CIIC* 1027, Glamorgan (Wales), 8th or 9th century, according to Hübner.

Since the change occurs in a single word, the change of *ae* to *o* is probably the confusion of the prefixes *prae-* and *pro-*. The dating of this confusion appears to be very late and is really beyond the chronological limits that are pertinent to a study of Vulgar Latin inscriptions.

Dalmatia	*Century*	Open Syllable		Closed Syllable		Totals		% Of *e*
		ae > *ae*	*ae* > *e*	*ae* > *ae*	*ae* > *e*	*ae*	*e*	
	4th.	1	0	0	0	1	0	0.0
	6th.	1	0	0	0	1	0	0.0
	n.d.	6	0	0	0	6	0	0.0
	Totals:	8	0	0	0	8	0	0.0

We found no examples of monophthongization of *ae* in initial syllables of Dalmatian inscriptions, but this is undoubtedly due to the low number of occurrences of *ae* in our corpus.

Balkans	*Century*	Open Syllable		Closed Syllable		Totals		% Of *e*
		ae > *ae*	*ae* > *e*	*ae* > *ae*	*ae* > *e*	*ae*	*e*	
(Pagan)	2nd.	2	1	0	0	2	1	33.3
	3rd.	2	0	0	0	2	0	0.0
	4th.	1	0	0	0	1	0	0.0
	n.d.	6	3	0	0	6	3	33.3
	Totals:	11	4	0	0	11	4	26.7

The examples of monophthongization in the pagan inscriptions of the Balkans are:

Present[*e*], *Kal.* 128, *CIL* III 7466, A.D. 153.
Emil(ianus), *Kal.* 394, *CIL* III 7421, Mikres, n.d.
pret(orianus), *Kal.* 394, *CIL* III 7421, Mikres, n.d.
prepositis, *Kal.* 398, *CIL* III 12,377, Ferdinandowo (Moesia Inferior), no date.

In addition to the cases of monophthongization of *ae* to *e* in initial syllable in the pagan inscriptions of the Balkans, we have an example of the *ae* changing to *oe* in *Coelia*[*nae*], *Kal.* 374, *CIL* III 14,207, no date. This same change of *ae* to *oe* has already been noted for accented syllables (see *supra*, p. 356).

Balkans	*Century*	Open Syllable		Closed Syllable		Totals		% Of *e*
		ae > ae	*ae > e*	*ae > ae*	*ae > e*	*ae*	*e*	
(Christ.)	4th.	1	2	0	0	1	2	66.7
	n.d.	2	1	0	0	2	1	33.3
	Totals:	3	3	0	0	3	3	50.0

The three examples of monophthongization in Christian inscriptions of this area are:

preteritorum, *D.* 11, Mursae (Eszek), Pannonia Inferior, A.D. 361-63.
eterna, *D.* 478, *CIL* III 14,207, Stara-Zagora (Moesia Inferior), no date.
pref(ectus), *D.* 1856A, *CIL* III 11,206, Carnuntum (Pannonia Superior), fourth century.

Besides the examples of monophthongization of *ae*, there is a single case of *ae* changing to *i* in *iterna*, *D.* 3659, Purbach (Pannonia), no date. [13] Although this is the only case of a change of *ae* to *i* in our corpus, Pirson does record (p. 20) the reverse spellings of *ae* for both /ĭ/ and /ī/ in Christian inscriptions of Gaul: *Epaefanius*, *CIL* XII 2089, A.D. 563, and *Aedibus* (= *Idibus*), *CIL* XII 2399c, no date. Pirson concludes (p. 20) that "dans certains cas, *ae* tient même lieu de l'*ĭ* et aussi de l'*ī*, ce qui prouve à l'évidence que dans les

---

[13] This particular inscription is extremely pregnant with deviations from Classical Latin. In addition to the change of *ae* to *i*, we have *mimoriae*, *Aurilia*, *Ciriscentina* (= *Crescentina*), *qui* (for *quae*, fem. rel. pronoun), *vixcet*, *annus* (acc. plur.), *Aurilius*, *sipurclu* (*sepulcrum*), *posuuit*, *cari* (= *carae*, dat. sing.), *cougi* (= *coniugi*), *soi* (= *suae*, dat. sing.), and *ert* (= *erit*).

textes vulgaires *ae* pouvait avoir la valeur d'un son fermé." Pei gives (*Texts*, p. 66) several examples of *ae* > *i* (*pristetirunt, pristamus, sancti baselici, basilici, pristetisse*), as well as the reverse spelling of *ae* for /ĭ/ and /ī/ (*emunaetas, iniquaetatis, mancaepammus, aemunitatis, adaepisci* and *paiaes, monastiriae, Dioninsiae, exquaesita*). Although this scholar explains away the use of *ae* for /ī/ because of its being found only in final syllables where all vowels except *a* had already weakened into a *shva*-sound and because of etymological reconstruction, he does come to the conclusion (p. 67) that "examples of the interchange of *ae* with long *e* and short *i*, in all positions . . . are too numerous and too clear to be explained away by reconstruction, analogy and other similar factors. The explanation rather appears to be that in the Eighth Century the combination *ae* was used indifferently to represent both the closed and the open sound of *e*." Thus, we see that the change of *ae* to *i* to show that the diphthong *ae* had the sound of a closed *e*, quite common in documentary evidence of later centuries, is mirrored sporadically in inscriptions at an earlier date.

Intertonic Position

The diphthong *ae* is extremely rare in this position and nothing definite can be said because of the paucity of both correct occurrences and deviations. We do have monophthongization in *lapide cesori* (= *lapidicaesoris*, gen. sing.), D. 655a, CIL VIII 8774, Thamalla (Africa), no date, but the stonemason seems to have considered this word as two, with the result that the change of *ae* to *e* is probably in initial position rather than intertonic.

Final: Morphological (Declensional)

We will consider the genitive and dative singular and the nominative plural of the first declension to see what inscriptions tell us about the development of *ae* in final position. We will combine the figures of the genitive and dative singular forms, but will keep the nominative plural separate so as to get an idea of the relative frequency of the *-ae* and *-as* endings for the first person nominative plural of first declension nouns and adjectives. [14]

---

[14] Gaeng combines the figures for the genitive and dative singular and the nominative plural of first declension forms in order to give one composite

Africa:

Century	Gen./Dat. Sing.		% Of *e*	Nomin. Plural		Nom. Plur.	% Of *ae(e)* in Nom. Plur.
	ae > ae	*ae > e*		*ae > ae*	*ae > e*	*-as*	
3rd.	9	2	18.2	1	0	0	100.0
4th.	19	16	45.7	2	1	1	75.0
5th.	17	16	48.5	2	2	0	100.0
6th.	12	6	33.3	0	5	0	100.0
7th.	1	0	0.0	0	0	0	0.0
n.d.	57	76	57.1	3	6	5	64.3
Totals:	115	116	50.0	8	14	6	78.6

Since there are too many examples of monophthongization in the genitive and dative singular endings, we will give only a few below:

a) Genitive Singular:

> *publice*, D. 8, Sertes (Mauretania Sitifensis), A.D. 343-50.
> *colonie, Marchiane, Traiane*, D. 387, Thamugada (Numidia), no date.
> *provincie*, D. 655b, *CIL* VIII 8774, Thamalla, A. D. 419.
> [*Ius*]*tiniane*, D. 794, *CIL* VIII 101, Capsa (Byzacena), before A.D. 543.
> *discipline*, D. 1189, Thabraca (Proconsularis), no date.
> *Surie* (= *Syriae*), D. 1346, *CIL* VIII 11,106, Sullecthus (Byzacena), no date.
> *nostre*, D. 1828, Hippo Regius (Proconsularis), fourth century.
> *ecresie*, D. 1844A, *CIL* VIII 839, Bou-Chad (Proconsularis), no date.
> *Matrone*, D. 1931, *CIL* VIII 5665, near Calama (Proconsularis), no date.
> *cause*, D. 1978, *CIL* VIII 10,701, Hr. Sid (Numidia), third century.
> *sacre*, D. 2052, Benian (Mauretania), A.D. 434.
> *Eufimie*, D. 2069, Kherbet-el-Ma-el-Abiod, A.D. 474.
> *sapientie*, D. 2417A, Cuicul (Numidia), no date.

---

percentage of deviation for the various areas under consideration. He reasons (p. 241) that "the *e* spelling for *ae* would seem to reflect the reduction of the diphthong to a monophthong, i.e. a phonological rather than morphological phenomenon." We feel that, although at times it is difficult to distinguish a genitive from a dative, the nominative plural *-ae* as differentiated from *-as* must be separate.

Evasse (= *Evasiae*), *D.* 2866, *CIL* VIII 9804, Albulae (Mauretania Caesariensis), A.D. 418.
Aurelie, *D.* 3267, *CIL* VIII 21,637, Arbal, A.D. 410.
Valentine, *D.* 3339, *CIL* VIII 20,303, Satafi (Mauretania Sitifensis), A.D. 352.

b) Dative Singular:

memorie, *D.* 394, *CIL* VIII 9909, Pomaria (Mauretania Caesariensis), no date.
Anastasie, *D.* 28, *CIL* VIII 4354, Ain-Ksar (Numidia), A.D. 578-82.
Quintille, Donatianille, honeste, femine, *D.* 331, Thena (Byzacena), no date.
pie, *D.* 883, *CIL* VIII 21,553, Mechera-Sfa (Mauretania Caesariensis), A.D. 434.
m[e]morie, *D.* 1182, *CIL* VIII 20,300, Satafi (Mauretania Sitifensis), A.D. 363.
venerande, *D.* 1842, near Theveste (Proconsularis), fourth century.
dulcissime, *D.* 2854B, *CIL* VIII 9856, Altava (Mauretania Caesariensis), A.D. 333.
carissime, *D.* 2857, *CIL* VIII 21,765, Altava, A.D. 350.
deposte, *D.* 1570, *CIL* VIII 20,277, Sitifis (Mauretania Sitifensis), A.D. 299.

c) Nominative Plural:

primitie, *D.* 1828, Hippo Regius (Proconsularis), fourth century.
memorie, deposite, *D.* 2069, Kherbet-el-Ma-el-Abiod, A.D. 474.
aque, *D.* 785, *CIL* VIII 23,673, near Maktar (Byzacena), sixth century.
posite, memorie, *D.* 2055, near Cirta (Numidia), A.D. 580.
deposite, *D.* 2057, Hr. Akhrib, A.D. 543.
memorie, *D.* 2062, *CIL* VIII 18,656, Lamasbam (Numidia), sixth century.
memorie, *D.* 2058, *CIL* VIII 10,515, Ammaedara (Byzacena), no date.
deposite, *D.* 2056b, Hr. Akhrib, no date.
posite, *D.* 2061, near Sitifis (Mauretania Sitifensis), no date.
deposite, *D.* 2083, Hr. Akhrib, no date.
benerande (= *venerandae*), *relyquie*, *D.* 2089, *CIL* VIII 23,921, Hr. Fallous, no date.

On the basis of our figures, we see that monophthongization of *ae* to *e* is a well-established change in final position as was the case for stressed and initial positions. The nominative plural of first declension nouns and adjectives is usually the expected *-ae* or *-e* ending, although there are cases of the *-as* termination (8 examples of *-ae*, 14 examples of *-e*, and 6 cases of *-as* for an 81.5 % incidence of the *-ae* or *-e* endings). We will discuss the significance of the figures for the nominative plural endings of the first declension more fully below.

Britain	Century	Gen./Dat. Sing.		% Of *e*
		ae > *ae*	*ae* > *e*	
(Pagan)	1st.	7	0	0.0
	2nd.	19	0	0.0
	3rd.	22	2	8.3
	4th.	3	4	57.1
	n.d.	85	44	34.1
	Totals:	136	50	26.9

Some examples of monophthongization in the genitive and dative singulars of first declension nouns and adjectives in pagan inscriptions of Britain are:

> [*pie*]*ntissime*, *RIB* 23, London, no date.
> *Victorie*, *RIB* 191, Colchester (Camulodunum), Essex, no date.
> *piissime*, *RIB* 373, *CIL* VII 124, Caerleon (Isca Silurum), Monmouth, no date.
> *centurie*, *RIB* 448, *CIL* VII 166, Chester (Deva), Cheshire, no date.
> *socaere* (= *socerae*, dative sing.), *RIB* 594, *CIL* VII 229, Ribchester (Bremetennacum), Lancaster, no date. [15]
> *Severe, honeste, femine*, *RIB* 683, *CIL* VII 249, York (Eboracum), no date.
> *Felicule*, *RIB* 710, *CIL* VII 263, Aldborough (Isurum Brigantium), Yorkshire, no date.
> *ale*, *RIB* 907, *CIL* VII 353, Old Carlisle (Olerica), Cumberland, no date.

---

[15] In addition to the monophthongization of final *ae* and the reverse spelling of the posttonic vowel, from short *e* to *ae*, the word itself is an analogical formation based on the masculine *socer*. The Italian *suocera* requires *socera*. The Classical Latin *socrus* was also replaced by *socra*. Cf *Appendix Probi* (170): *socrus non socra*. From *socra* we get Old Fr. *suire, suegre*; Prov. Cat. Port. *sogra*, Sp. *suegra*.

divine, *RIB* 919, *CIL* VII 319, Old Penrith (Voreda), Cumberland, A.D. 222-35.

carissime, *RIB* 959, *CIL* VII 931, Carlisle (Luguvalium), Cumberland, no date.

sancte, *RIB* 1056, South Shields (Arbeia), Co. Durham, no date.

pie, *RIB* 1102, *CIL* VII 476, Corbridge (Corstopitum), Northumberland, no date.

Fabie, *Honorate*, *filie*, *dulcissime*, *RIB* 1482, *CIL* VII 588, Hadrian's Wall: Chesters (Cilurnum), Northumberland, third century.

Coventine, *RIB* 1526, Hadrian's Wall: Carrawburgh (Brocolitia), Northumberland, no date.

die (= *deae*, dative sing. of *dea*, Goddess), *Coventine*, *RIB* 1525, Hadrian's Wall: Carrawburgh (Brocolitia), no date.

Covontine, *RIB* 1533, Hadrian's Wall: Carrawburgh (Brocolitia), Northumberland, no date.

Monophthongization of final *ae* to *e* was a common phenomenon in the pagan inscriptions of Britain. Unfortunately, we did not find any examples of the nominative plural of first declension nouns and adjectives, either the -*ae* or -*as* types.

Britain	*Century*	*Gen./Dat. Sing.*		% Of *e*
		ae > ae	*ae > e*	
(Christ.)	7th.	1	0	0.0
	8th.	0	1	100.0
	n.d.	0	2	100.0
	Totals:	1	3	75.0

The examples of monophthongization of final *ae*, few in number, of Christian inscriptions of Britain are:

Cuniovende (Celtic proper name), *CIIC* 454, Pembroke (Wales), no date.

Caune (Celtic proper name), *CIIC* 401, Denbigh (Wales), eighth century.

Adiune (Celtic proper name), *CIIC* 346, Brecon (Wales), no date.

Commenting on the terminations of feminine nouns, Jackson says (*Language*, p. 188) that "Celtic feminines are handled always in Latin as first-declension nouns, consequently with nominative in -*A* and genitive in -E." This generalizing of genitive names with a final -e would seem to prove that in Christian inscriptions of Britain the Latin ae had definitely monophthongized to e and the only ending available to the stonemason was, in fact, an e.

Dalmatia	Century	Gen./Dat. Sing.		% Of e	Nom. Plur.		Nom. Plur.
		ae > ae	ae > e		ae	-e	-as
	4th.	11	1	8.3	0	0	0
	5th.	5	2	28.6	0	0	0
	n.d.	55	40	42.1	0	1	0
	Totals:	71	43	37.7	0	1	0

Some examples of monophthongization in the genitive and dative singular forms of first declension nouns and adjectives in Dalmatian inscriptions are:

> Palumbe, D. 646, CIL III 9614, Salona, no date.
> Nate, D. 660, CIL III 9524, Salona, no date.
> Firmine, ree, D. 749, CIL III 9606, Salona, n.d.
> Claudie, D. 851, CIL III 8727, Salona, no date.
> bone, D. 1225a, CIL III 14,893, Salona, no date.
> Eufevie (= Eusebiae), D. 3042C, CIL III 9579, Salona, no date.
> Maxentie, caresseme, D. 3044A, Salona, no date.
> Quiriace (= Cyriacae), D. 3381, CIL III 14,306, Salona, no date.
> puelle, innocentissime, filie, D. 3633, CIL III 2233, Salona, no date.
> Marcelle, D. 3636, CIL III 14,906, Salona, n.d.
> Sabbatie, D. 3752, CIL III 9588, Salona, n.d.
> [virg]inie, D. 3835B, Salona, A.D. 375.
> fabrece (= fabricae), D. 3836A, CIL III 9582, Salona, no date.
> eclisie, catolice, D. 3870, CIL III 13,124, Salona, A.D. 426.
> Revocate, D. 4360, CIL III 3107, Brattia (Dalmatian Island), no date.
> Desidiene, D. 4502, CIL III 9028, Salona, no date.

We have a single case of the locative ending in -e in Ravenne, D. 455, CIL III 9518, Salona, A.D. 437. The only example of a nominative plural of a first declension noun in our corpus of Dalmatian inscriptions has the monophthong e: Parce, D. 3363, CIL III 9623, Salona, no date.

On the basis of our figures (37.7 % of the genitive and dative singulars have the ending -e) we see that monophthongization of final *ae* to *e* was a common phenomenon in Dalmatian inscriptions.

Balkans	*Century*	Gen./Dat. Sing.		% Of *e*
		ae > ae	*ae > e*	
(Pagan)	1st.	1	0	0.0
	2nd.	1	1	50.0
	3rd.	7	0	0.0
	n.d.	16	10	38.5
	Totals:	25	11	30.6

The examples of monophthongization of final *ae* in pagan inscriptions of the Balkans are: .

Diane, Kal. 168, *CIL* III 12,365, Swischtow (Moesia Inferior), no date.
[*re*]*gine, Kal.* 170, *CIL* III 12,373, Ferdinandowo (Moesia Inferior), A.D. 162.
Tyche (proper name), *Kal.* 370, *CIL* III 14,211, Gigen (Moesia Inferior), no date.
Alex(a)ndre, ale, piissime, Kal. 373, *CIL* III 12,452, Rjahowo (Moesia Inferior), n.d.
Firmine, rarissime, Kal. 386, *CIL* III 14,458, Varna (Moesia Inferior), no date.
Aurelie, Vericie, merite, Kal. 398, *CIL* III 12,377, Ferdinandowo (Moesia Inferior), n.d.

We found no examples of any form of the nominative plural of first declension nouns and adjectives in our corpus. The percentage of genitive and dative singular endings with the monophthongized *e* (30.6 %) shows that monophthongization was regular in pagan inscriptions of the Balkans.

Balkans	*Century*	Gen./Dat. Sing.		% Of *e*	Nom. Plur.		Nom. Plur.
		ae > ae	*ae > e*		*ae*	*-e*	*-as*
(Christ.)	4th.	1	0	0.0	0	0	0
	n.d.	31	12	27.9	0	0	6
	Totals:	32	12	27.3	0	0	6

The cases of monophthongization of final *ae* to *e* in Christian inscriptions of the Balkans are:

Done, D. 478, CIL III 14,207, Stara-Zagora (Moesia Inferior), no date. [16]

bone, D. 1376, CIL III 4217, Savaria (Pannonia Superior), no date.

memorie, Kalendine, D. 1376, CIL III 4217, Savaria (Pannonia Superior), no date.

bone, memorie, Celsine, D. 2201, CIL III 4220, Savaria (Pannonia Superior), no date.

bone, D. 2208, CIL III 4218, Savaria (Pannonia Superior), no date.

[Petro]nille, D. 3530, CIL III 14,340, Sirmium (Pannonia Inferior), no date.

dulcissime, D. 3611, CIL III 10,237, Sirmium (Pannonia Inferior), no date.

(ae)terne, D. 3659, Purbach (Pannonia), n.d.

Sarmann(i)ne, D. 2179, CIL III 5972, Castris Reginis, no date.

We found five examples of the nominative plural of first declension nouns and adjectives ending in -as, but all five cases were found in the same inscription, D. 3476, CIL III 3551, Aquincum (Budapest), no date. We did not encounter any -ae endings for the nominative plural in our corpus. The monophthongization of ae to e is common in the Christian inscriptions of the Balkans (27.3 % on the basis of 32 cases of ae and 12 cases of e for the genitive and dative singulars of first declension forms).

There are isolated cases of final ae changing to i in Christian inscriptions of the Balkans: Urbici (= Urbice for Urbicae, dative sing.), D. 3611, CIL III 10,237, Sirmium (Pannonia Inferior), no date; cari and soi (= suae), both datives, found in the same inscription, D. 3659, Purbach (Pannonia), no date, an inscription that has already been qualified as extremely unclassical in nature (see supra,

---

[16] Diehl considers the name Done (from Dona) a "nomen barbarum" (I, 101); Kalinka, however, writes (p. 331) that Done is the "lautliche Fortbildung aus Dom(i)nae (Dativ)." The development of m'n to n (dona < domina) would be extraordinary for Eastern Romance where the cluster mn usually remains (cf. Rumanian somn from somnum and domn from dom(i)-num). The Latin domina gives doamna in Rumanian. It appears that mn was a particularly favored development in Eastern Romance as evidenced by the fact that the consonant cluster gn likewise developed into mn: cf. the Rum. lemn < lignum and cumnat < cognatus. See Bourciez, Éléments, pp. 175-76 for the details of the evolution of mn and gn in the Romance languages.

p. 362, footnote 13). The two forms under consideration are found in the second sentence of a three-sentence inscription: ... *Aurilius Secumdinus sipurclu* (= *sepulcrum*) *posuuit cari* (= *carae*) *cougi* (= *coniugi*) *soi* (= *suae*)... It is difficult to interpret this change of *ae* to *i* in final position. We may be possibly faced with an orthography *i* to show that *ae* changed to a very closed $\bar{e}$; this same change is also found in later documents as evidenced by Pei (*Texts*, p. 66): *sancti baselici, basilici*; the final *i* may be used in the words *cari* and *soi* on the analogy of the third declension dative *cougi* (although this reasoning would not apply to *Urbici* where no third declension noun is juxtaposed; *Urbici* may possibly be considered a third declension noun rather than a first declension feminine form on the analogy of many third declension nouns or adjectives such as *Felici, Victrici, educatrici*, etc.). The *i*-ending may, of course, be a simple mistake on the part of the relatively unlettered stonemason.

To get an idea of the relative distribution of the monophthongization of *ae* to *e* in Romania, we offer below a summary of the figures as derived by Gaeng (see his pages 241, 249-50, 295-96) as well as our figures (see *supra*, pp. 352, 354, 356-58, 360-62, 364, 366-69), in stressed, initial, and final positions.

Even a cursory perusal of the preceding table shows that the monophthongization of *ae* to *e* was a very common phenomenon in all areas of Romania. In fact, of all the deviations collected from our corpus, the monophthongization of *ae* to *e* was by far the most common change found in our inscriptions. Various scholars have expressed their opinions as to the dating of the monophthongization of *ae*. Sturtevant makes the important distinction between the monophthongization of *ae* to close $\bar{e}$ in early dialectal and rustic Latin and the later monophthongization of *ae* to open $\breve{e}$ in standard Latin, concluding (p. 128) that "it is therefore unlikely that the two processes had any connection." Summarizing his views on the chronology of the monophthongization of *ae* to close $\bar{e}$ in dialectal Latin and to open $\breve{e}$ in standard Latin, this scholar writes (p. 129) that,

> ... in several dialects of Central Italy *ai* became $\bar{e}$ in prehistoric times, and this rustic $\bar{e}$ made its way into urban Latin in a few country words, such as *sēpes* and *fēnum*, and there it became close $\bar{e}$ like inherited $\bar{e}$. The monophthongization of genuine Latin *ae*, on the other hand, led to confusion between *ae* and open $\breve{e}$. It began in the popular

Area	Century	ae			e			Totals		% Of e
		Stress.	Init.	Final	Stress.	Init.	Final	ae	e	
Baetica	4th-6th	4	0	0	0	2	3	4	5	55.6
	7th	2	2	4	2	1	17	8	20	71.4
	Totals:	6	2	4	2	3	20	12	25	67.6
Lusitania	4th-6th	3	1	3	3	0	6	7	9	56.3
	7th	0	0	1	2	2	4	1	8	88.9
	Totals:	3	1	4	5	2	10	8	17	68.0
Tarraconensis	4th-6th	1	1	11	1	3	8	13	12	48.0
	7th	0	0	0	1	3	11	0	15	100.0
	Totals:	1	1	11	2	6	19	13	27	67.5
Narbonensis	4th-5th	0	0	18	2	1	4	18	7	28.0
	6th-7th	0	3	39	7	5	30	42	42	50.0
	Totals:	0	3	57	9	6	34	60	49	45.0
Lugdunensis	4th-5th	0	2	10	1	0	12	12	13	52.0
	6th-7th	1	1	34	2	5	21	36	28	43.8
	Totals:	1	3	44	3	5	33	48	41	46.1
Northern Italy	4th-5th	7	4	26	18	4	11	37	33	47.1
	6th	11	1	2	17	1	0	14	18	56.3
	Totals:	18	5	28	35	5	11	51	51	50.0
Central Italy	3rd-4th	1	3	13	1	2	11	17	14	45.2
	5th	0	3	3	2	0	0	6	2	25.0
	6th-7th	3	2	3	1	2	1	8	4	33.3
	Totals:	4	8	19	4	4	12	31	20	39.2

Area	Century	ae Stress.	ae Init.	ae Final	e Stress.	e Init.	e Final	Totals ae	Totals e	% Of e
Southern Italy	3rd-4th	0	4	11	0	1	12	15	13	46.4
	5th	2	3	10	2	1	2	15	5	25.0
	6th-7th	1	0	3	1	0	8	4	9	69.2
	Totals:	3	7	24	3	2	22	34	27	44.3
Rome	3rd-4th	8	18	93	6	13	65	119	84	41.4
	5th	4	7	18	3	2	6	29	11	27.5
	6th-7th	0	4	12	1	7	7	16	15	48.5
	Totals:	12	29	123	10	22	78	164	110	40.1
Africa	3rd.	2	1	9	1	0	2	12	3	20.0
	4th.	2	8	19	1	8	16	29	25	46.3
	5th.	0	0	17	3	17	16	17	36	67.9
	6th.	3	6	12	0	11	6	21	17	44.7
	n.d.	10	15	57	14	1	0	1	1	50.0
	7th.	0	0	1	0	27	76	82	117	59.4
	Totals:	17	30	115	19	64	116	162	199	55.1
Britain (Pagan)	1st.	2	0	7	0	0	0	9	0	0.0
	2nd.	22	22	19	0	0	0	63	0	0.0
	3rd.	35	27	22	3	4	2	84	9	9.7
	4th.	15	0	3	0	0	4	18	4	18.2
	n.d.	27	51	85	4	10	44	163	58	26.2
	Totals:	101	100	136	7	14	50	337	71	17.4
Britain (Christ.)	6th.	0	1	0	0	0	0	1	0	0.0
	7th.	0	0	1	0	0	0	1	0	0.0
	8th.	0	0	0	0	0	1	0	1	100.0
	n.d.	0	0	0	1	3	2	0	6	100.0
	Totals:	0	1	1	1	3	3	2	7	77.8

Area	Century	ae			e			Totals		% Of e
		Stress.	Init.	Final	Stress.	Init.	Final	ae	e	
Dalmatia	4th.	4	1	11	0	0	1	16	1	5.9
	5th.	2	0	5	0	0	2	7	2	22.2
	6th.	1	1	0	0	0	0	2	0	0.0
	n.d.	8	6	55	5	0	40	69	45	39.5
	Totals:	15	8	71	5	0	43	94	48	33.8
Balkans (Pagan)	1st.	2	0	1	0	0	0	3	0	0.0
	2nd.	4	2	1	0	1	1	7	2	22.2
	3rd.	6	2	7	0	0	0	15	0	0.0
	4th.	2	1	0	0	0	0	3	0	0.0
	n.d.	4	6	16	0	3	10	26	13	33.3
	Totals:	18	11	25	0	4	11	54	15	21.7
Balkans (Christ.)	4th.	0	1	1	0	2	0	2	2	50.0
	n.d.	3	2	31	3	1	12	36	16	30.8
	Totals:	3	3	32	3	3	12	38	18	32.1

speech of Southern Italy and of the city of Rome during the first century A.D., and made its way into standard Latin probably in the latter part of the second century A.D., certainly by the fourth century.

Bourciez considers (*Éléments*, p. 44) the monophthongization of *ae* to open ĕ as occurring "en général, depuis la fin de la République, et surtout au 1er siècle ap. J.-C." He acknowledges, however, the change of *ae* to close ē in some words as the result of "divergences locales remontant très haut." Lausberg arbitrarily sets (*Lingüistica*, I, 27) the monophthongization of *ae* to open ĕ in the first century A.D. Grandgent considered (p. 88) that "the regular change of *ae* to ĕ took place largely in Republican times in unaccented syllables; in stressed syllables in the first century of our era and later." He also mentions that the "spelling *e* for *ae* was usual in unaccented syllables before the third century, in stressed syllables from the fourth century on; it may be called regular by the fifth century."

When we consider the figures in our table for the monophthongization of *ae* to *e* in the various areas of Romania, we notice that there are no examples of this phenomenon in the pagan inscriptions of Britain for the first and second centuries although there are nine examples of *e* for *ae* (9.7 % of *e*) in the third century. In the pagan inscriptions of the Balkans, however, we did encounter two examples of monophthongization in the second century in unaccented syllables, the earliest dated inscription coming from A.D. 153. Christian inscriptions dated in the third century show many examples of monophthongization, while from the fourth century on, the *e* spelling is extremely common. We are inclined to consider the third century as a period when serious inroads were made in the use of *e* for *ae* and the fourth century as the time when the *e* orthography was definitely established. It must be forcefully brought out that our figures show that inscriptions show a very high percentage of monophthongization for every area of Romania under consideration without exception. We conclude that the epigraphical evidence accurately describes the linguistic situation throughout all of Romania: monophthongization had taken place in probably all of the Latin-speaking territories of the Roman Empire in the third or fourth centuries. The fact that the inscriptions of Africa and pagan Britain, two extremely conservative areas of Latin vocalism, show monophthongization is a highly eloquent testimonial for the importance of epigraphical material in linguistic research. It must be assumed, for example, that African stonemasons, who portrayed the development of monophthongization of *ae* to *e*, likewise gave a reliable account of other linguistic phenomena, in the case of the Latin of African inscriptions, the proof of an archaic vocalic system. The theoretical implications are clear: inscriptions can show that a linguistic change took root throughout all of Romania as well as corroborate our contention that epigraphical material can point to a differentiation of Latin in some areas. Inscriptions thus indicate that with respect to some vocalic phenomena the Latin in the various areas was developing in a unified manner, but epigraphic evidence can also show that there was a divergence in the development of Latin in other regions of Romania. Inscriptions consequently prove a linguistic reality in the evolution of the Romance languages: Latin was evolving into the Romance tongues throughout the Empire, at times showing similarities in its development, at times showing differences in the individual regions of Romania.

We will now discuss various problems on the basis of our findings for *ae*.

The Nominative Plural of First Declension Nouns and Adjectives

Although Classical Latin calls for the ending -*ae* in the nominative plural of first declension nouns and adjectives, the termination -*as* has also been attested in this function from its earliest appearance in the Atellan farces of Pomponius in the first century B.C. to late Latin texts. Grandgent, while acknowledging the substitution of an -*as* for -*ae* in the nominative plural, also remarks (p. 149) that "it probably was not common until late Vulgar Latin or early Romance times." The early use of -*as* as a nominative plural is generally considered as an influence from the Italic dialects. [17] Väänänen (*Pom-*

---

[17] Cf. Mohl, p. 207: "Le vieux nominatif en -as, protégé ou même rétabli sous l'action assimilatrice des dialectes indigènes de l'Italie, s'est ainsi maintenu tout d'abord dans la plus grande partie tout au moins de la péninsule comme il s'est constamment maintenu dans le parler des provinces extrapéninsulaires." Väänänen, *Introduction*, p. 116: "...un provincialisme qui a fait tache d'huile, sorti du contact avec des parlers italiques, qui avaient conservé le nom. pl. indoeuropéen en -ās." Lausberg, *Lingüística*, II, 26: "Probablemente se trata de un temprano osco-umbrismo del latín hablado."

péiennes, p. 84) offers the oft-quoted example of *C. Lollium Fuscum II vir(um) Vaspp Asellinas rogant nec sine Zmyrina* with *Asellinas* as an example of a nominative plural in *-as* in Pompeian inscriptions. [18] It is most remarkable that Pirson in his thorough study of the Latin inscriptions of Gaul did not find a single example of the *-as* ending used as a nominative plural. This fact has not escaped the attention of scholars who have delved into the problem of the use of *-as* as a nominative plural ending. Commenting on the distribution of *-as* for *-ae* in the Latin inscriptions of the Empire, Norberg remarks (*Syntaktische*, p. 28) that "die meisten Belege sind aus Rom oder Italien, aber auch in Spanien, Afrika und den Balkanprovinzen hat man den Nom. auf *-as* benutzt. Dagegen fehlt diese Form auffälligerweise in den Inschriften Galliens." This complete absence of an *-as* ending for the nominative plural in the inscriptions of Gaul is in strong contrast with later documents from the same area. Pei concludes (*Texts*, p. 140) "that by the eighth century the reduction ... of the plural to a single form in *-as* was fairly under way." With respect to Italy, inscriptions do offer examples of *-as* used as a nominative plural, as is evidenced by the cases adduced by Gaeng (pp. 253-54), although his assumption (p. 255) that "by the fifth century the formal

---

E. Löfstedt, *Syntactica*, II, 332: "... in dem Einfluss der italischen Dialekte." Norberg, *Syntaktische*, p. 30: "Es dürfte somit keinem Zweifel unterliegen, dass man den Ursprung dieser Spracherscheinung in den italischen Dialekten zu suchen hat, in denen die idg. Endung *-as* sich im Nom. Plur. der l. Dekl. erhalten hatte. Mit oskisch-umbrischen Einwanderern hat sich dieser Provinzialismus ... in den untersten Schichten der römischen Bevölkerung verbreitet. Mit der Ausbreitung der lat. Sprache über das Imperium folgte auch die Nominativendung *-as*." See also Sommer, p. 329; Ernout, *Morphologie*, pp. 21-22; Kent, p. 26.

[18] It is not generally pointed out that this is the sole example of a nominative plural in *-as* in Pompeian inscriptions. Väänänen also gives (*Pompéiennes*, p. 24) examples of an *-ae* or *-e* ending for the nominative plural: *nule* (= *nullae*) *aliae, dulcisime et pissimae* (1261) and *tabule* (2465). Although there are examples of *-as* throughout the Pompeian inscriptions, Väänänen notes (p. 117) that "quant aux noms en *-as*, nous croyons devoir les ranger parmi les accusatifs faisant fonction de phrases monorèmes, plutôt que les ramener au nom. pl. *-ās*." The form *nugas*, also considered by some (Norberg, *Syntaktische*, p. 28) as an example of *-as* as a nominative plural in Pompeian inscriptions, found in the inscription *tu mortus es, tu nugas es* (5279) is explained by Väänänen himself (p. 116) in the following way: "L'accusatif *nugas* s'est glissé à la place du nominatif attribut (plutôt que *nūgās* pour *nugāx*) grâce aux tours fréquents tel que *nūgās agere*, d'où aussi l'exclamation."

opposition between the Cl. Latin nominative and accusative plural had been obliterated ... and that the -as ending had taken over both the subject and direct object functions" seems extremely hazardous on the basis of the relatively scarce material offered as proof. A more acceptable statement concerning the outcome of nominative plurals in later Italian documents, however, is made by Politzer in his *A Study of the Language of Eighth Century Lombardic Documents*, when he writes (p. 70) that "the striking feature is the almost complete absence of the ending -ae (-e)." [19] In an important article entitled "On the Origin of the Italian Plurals," *The Romanic Review*, XLIII (1952), 271-81, Politzer also writes (p. 276) that "the conclusion which is suggested is that at the beginning of the eighth century the nominative in -ae was quite dead also in the central Italian area, and could thus not possibly have furnished the Italian plural form." [20] In his attempt to reconcile the documentary evidence of a predominance of -as endings in the eighth century with the Italian endings -e of the first declension of plural nouns and adjectives, Norberg (*Syntaktische*, p. 30) emphasizes the importance of the loss of final -s in Italian: "Aber als in Italien s finalis verstummte, wodurch man den Sing. -a vom Plur. -a(s) nicht unterscheiden konnte, kam der echtlateinische Nom. auf -ae, der niemals ganz verdrängt worden war, wieder zu Ehren und lebt noch im Italienischen fort." Politzer also insists on the loss of final -s as the deciding factor in the formation of Italian plurals. [21] We are of the opinion that a quantitative and comparative study of the final -s in epigraphical

----

[19] Politzer's conclusion was based, as he says (p. 70) on the fact that "in the thirty-one instances in which the nominative plural occurs, the ending -as appears twenty-three times, -a (with fall of -s) five times, and -e only three times."

[20] In a footnote in the same article, Politzer writes (p. 276) that "the fact seems to be that inscriptional evidence also indicates that the popular language throughout all the Romance world generalized -as at a very early date and that at the beginning of the eighth century -as was the only plural form still in popular use." It is unfortunate that Politzer is not more specific as to the dating of the "generalizing" of the -as ending in inscriptions. We can admit the sporadic use of the -as ending in inscriptions at an early date, but we are sceptical about a generalized use of -as without more concrete evidence.

[21] Politzer "Origin," p. 274: "For effacement of the -s obviously necessitated plural forms different from the ones to which the eighth-century texts seem to point."

material would go a long way toward the solution of this problem, termed by B. Löfstedt (p. 129) as one of the "schwierigsten, aber zugleich wichtigsten Problemen der lateinisch-romanischen Lautgeschichte." Proskauer's conclusion of the loss of final -s in Italian and Rumanian as being independent of the Archaic Latin situation, derived from her study of Latin inscriptions, has been seriously questioned. [22]

In our corpus the only area that shows enough examples of the nominative plural in any form is Africa. We have already seen (see *supra*, p. 364) that African inscriptions offer eight examples of an -ae ending, fourteen examples of monophthongized -e, and six examples of -as. Combining the number of cases of the -ae and -e endings for the nominative plural (22 examples) versus the six examples of -as, we see that the -ae (-e) ending was used 78.6 % of the time compared with the 21.4 % for -as. We will give below the inscriptions in which the -as was used:

a)   African Inscriptions:

> *una et bis senas turres crescebant in ordine totas*, D. 791, *CIL* VIII 5352, Calama (Proconsularis), no date. [23]
> *santas tres Maxima et Donatilla, Secunda, bona puella*, D. 2042, *CIL* VIII 1392, Tichilla (Proconsularis), no date.

---

[22] Proskauer, p. 99: "Diese Befestigung [of final -s] war vollständig und durchgehend, derart, dass das Vulgärlatein ein schwaches oder geschwundenes -s nicht aufweist, und der Schwund des -s im Italienischen und Rumänischen mit dem im Altlateinischen in keinem Zusammenhang steht." Commenting on Proskauer's conclusion, B. Löfstedt writes (p. 130) that "Proskauer ist aber, wie das u.a. Sommer 305 und Baehrens, Komm. 93 hervorheben, in der Leugnung des -s Schwundes zu weit gegangen." Although agreeing with Proskauer that many cases of loss of final -s can be explained by the use of abbreviations, lack of space, damage to the inscription, confusion of case and declination, Löfstedt pointedly remarks (p. 130) that "es bleiben aber nicht gerade wenige Belege übrig, die sich so nicht erklären lassen. Es scheint mir gewagt, hier ohne weiteres eine phonetische Erklärung abzuweisen, und diese Belege legen auch die Vermutung nahe, dass Proskauer bisweilen zu Unrecht für die anderen Fälle eine andere — epigraphische, mechanische, morphologische etc. — Erklärung statt eine phonetischen in Anspruch genommen hat." This scholar summarizes the opinion of other researchers when he writes (p. 131) that "zwischen dem altlat. und dem rom. -s Wegfall ein Zusammenhang besteht, indem die niederen Klassen das -s nie völlig restituiert haben."
[23] This inscription is dated A.D. 539 by Sommer (p. 329) although Diehl considers it undated.

Egusa, Sat[urnina? . . .]ta marturas Chr[isti . . .], D. 2044, *CIL* VIII 9692, Cartenna, no date. [24]

hic abetur (= *habentur*) *reliquias martiris Bincenti, D.* 2103 Tocqueville, no date.

[fil]ias patri dulcissimo fecerunt pr. CCLXXXIIII, D. 2854A, *CIL* VIII 9855, Altava (Mauretania Caesariensis), A.D. 323.

In addition to the above six forms ending in *-as* (*senas, totas, santas, marturas, reliquias, [fil]ias*) for the nominative plural of the first declension, there is a sporadic use of the accusative case for a nominative plural of second declension nouns:

> *cui filios et nepotes obitum fecerunt in pacem, D.* 3052B, *CIL* VIII 21,540, near Mina (Mauretania Caesariensis), no date.
>
> *cui filios fec. dm. eter, a.p. CCCCXQIII, D.* 3676, *CIL* VIII 21,792, Pomaria (Mauretania Caesariensis), A.D. 458.

When we consider, however, that the usual forms of the nominative plural of *filius* is *fili* in African inscriptions with an occasional example of *filii*, as can be seen by the following table:

Century	fili	filii
4th.	7	2
5th.	2	0
6th.	9	0
n.d.	5	0
Totals:	23	2

and the fact that there were thirty-five examples of final *-i* for other nouns and adjectives (see *supra*, p. 251), it is best to consider these two examples as cases of the general trend of the accusative taking over the function of the nominative. [25] We thus see that although

---

[24] The form *marturas* is probably the analogical feminine based on first declension nouns so as to differentiate gender, rather than a phonetic change of final /ĕ/ to *a*. The nominative singular *martura* is also found in *D.* 1996N in an undated inscription from Rome.

[25] This use of the accusative plural used as a nominative in African inscriptions may indicate that the final *-s* was retained in African Latin, a situation that is found in the languages of Western Romance, including Sardinian.

the use of -as as a nominative plural is much more prevalent than the corresponding use of -os for -i in the nominative plural function, the latter can be found in inscriptions. [26] In attempting to explain the use of -as as a nominative plural, Norberg, while considering the prime cause as dialectal, looks for favorable circumstances for the spread of -as throughout the Romance world and concludes (*Syntaktische*, p. 31) that "diese [Umständen] waren m.E. rein formalen Charakters. Man pflegt das Verhältnis im Sing., wo der Nom. *rosa* und der Akk. *rosam* in der Volkssprache zusammengefallen waren, als analogisch wirkend anzuführen. Doch scheint mir dies eine ziemlich abgelegene Analogie zu sein. Kräftiger dürfte die oft vorkommende Zusammenstellung mit Substantiven oder Adjectiven der 3. Dekl. gewirkt haben." Norberg's reasoning holds true for some examples of the use of -as (as well as of -os) (*senas turres, filios et nepotes*), but it cannot explain most of our attestations.

The only other areas where the use of -as (not that of -os) is documented in our corpus is the Balkans. Compare the following examples:

b) Inscriptions of the Balkans:

> *fecerunt collegas f[. . .]*, D. 670, *CIL* III 4222, Savaria (Pannonia Superior), n.d.
>
> *hic quescunt duas matres, duas filias - numero tres facunt - et advenas II parvolas*, D. 3476, *CIL* III 3551, Aquincum (Pannonia Inferior), no date.

It is quite strange to find six examples (*collegas, duas, duas, filias, advenas,* and *parvolas*) of -as as nominative plurals without a single case of the expected -ae or -e ending, although five forms do come from the same inscription. It is therefore too hazardous to venture any sweeping statement as to the form of the nominative plural in Latin inscriptions of the Balkans, although the occurrences of the

---

[26] Comparing the numerical superiority of the cases of -as over -os as nominative plurals, E. Löfstedt (*Syntactica*, II, 331) remarks: "Wie man sieht, handelt es sich in der überwiegenden Mehrzahl der Fälle nicht ohne weiteres um einen Acc. pro nom., sendern vielmehr um eine bestimmte und auffällige Vorliebe für die Endung -as." With respect to Spanish inscriptions, Carnoy found several examples of -as (*filias, amicas, viduas*) as nominative plurals, but not a single case of -os in this function. This scholar writes (p. 228): "L'on ne constate jamais un barbarisme analogue au masculin."

-*as* ending in epigraphical material must be taken into account in any discussion of the plural formation of Rumanian feminine nouns. [27]

We have already seen that the only occurrence of a nominative plural in the inscriptions of Dalmatia is the proper noun *Parce, D. 3363, CIL* III 9623, Salona, no date. When we consider, however, that African inscriptions show a 21.4 % use of -*as* as nominative plural (8 examples of -*ae*, 14 of -*e*, and 6 of -*as*), that the Balkan inscriptions all show the -*as* ending (admittedly not conclusive because of only two inscriptions showing 6 examples of -*as*), that Italian and Roman inscriptions do have numerous cases of -*as*, [28] that the Spanish inscriptions have an occasional example of -*as*, while Gaul shows a conspicuous absence (see *supra*, p. 377) of -*as* in inscriptional material, it is possible to posit a differentiation in the distribution of the -*as* ending in the various parts of Romania.

Genitive Singular of First Declension Nouns

In addition to the usual genitive singular endings -*ae* and -*e* of first declension nouns and adjectives (see *supra*, p. 364), we found other endings for the genitive singular of first declension nouns, namely, -*aes*, -*es*, -*ai*, -*ais*, and -*as*. [29] It is of particular importance to bring out that these latter genitive endings are almost exclusively found in African inscriptions, only one form in our corpus coming from outside of this area, that one deviation originating in Dalmatia. We did not find a single example of a genitive ending in any form other than -*ae* or -*e* in the pagan inscriptions of Britain although the total number of genitives is high in this region (see *supra*, p. 366).

---

[27] Väänänen writes (*Introduction*, p. 115) that "la forme en -ās, plutôt que celle en -*ae*, semble être à la base du pl. it. en -*e*, et sans doute aussi de celui du roumain." Lausberg is more cautious in his attempt to explain the feminine plurals in Italian and Rumanian: "en italiano y rumano no resulta nada fácil señalar de manera inequívoca la base latino-vulgar (-*ae*, o bien -*as*) de la terminación -*e*." (*Lingüística*, II, 27.)

[28] See Gaeng, pp. 253-54.

[29] It is interesting to note that all our examples of genitives ending in -*aes*, -*es*, -*ai*, -*ais*, and -*as* were found in nouns, never in adjectives. Jeanneret's examples of genitives ending in -*aes*, -*es*, and -*as* (p. 70) are all nouns. E. Pieske, *De Titulorum Africae Latinorum Sermone Quaestiones Morphologicae* (Trebnitizia: Maretzke and Maertin, 1913), p. 11, does give examples of adjectives ending in -*ai*, but those ending in -*aes*, -*es*, -*ais*, -*as* are all nouns.

The genitive of first declension nouns and adjectives is likewise -*ae* and -*e* in both pagan and Christian inscriptions of the Balkans (see *supra*, p. 369). In addition to African inscriptions, the genitive endings -*aes* and especially -*es* are found in inscriptions emanating from Rome.[30] It appears that Africa and Rome are the two areas where the genitive endings in -*aes*, -*es*, -*ais*, and -*as* (the ending -*ai* is an archaic spelling and is abundant in other areas) are most often found.[31] From our corpus we found the following examples of the above genitive endings of the first declension:

a)   The Genitive Ending -*ai*:

Crementiai (= Clementiae), D. 2113, CIL VIII 19,643, Constantine (Africa), no date.

Since the genitive and dative singulars of the first declension have the same form, it is not surprising to find the ending -*ai* also used for datives:

---

[30] It is surprising that Gaeng does not mention the genitive endings -*es* and -*aes* in his dissertation, especially since they are quite common in Roman inscriptions. Some of the examples of -*es* as given by Diehl in his *Inscriptiones Latinae Christianae Veteres* for Rome and occasionally from other parts of Italy are: from Rome: *Stefanes*, D. 3002B, A.D. 373; *Hilares*, D. 3003, A.D. 384; *Amanties*, D. 3003A, A.D. 396; *Fructuoses*, D. 3006B, no date; *Annes* and *Sususannes* (sic), D. 3007B, no date; *Eraclies*, D. 3008A, no date; *Secundes*, D. 3009C, no date; *Eusebies*, D. 3009D, no date; *Matronilles*, D. 3009E, no date; *Iustes*, D. 3009F, no date; *Marcianes*, D. 3013B, no date; *Fautines*, D. 3013F, no date; *Vincenties*, D. 3016A, no date; *Cat[a]fronies*, D. 3016B, no date; *Leonties*, D. 3016E, no date; *Discolies*, D. 3017, no date; *Matrones*, D. 3017C, no date; *Stercores*, D. 3023A, no date; *Castes*, D. 3051C, no date. From other parts of Italy we have: *Cepasies*, D. 3021, Pisaurum (Umbria), no date; *Aselies*, D. 3029, Stabiae (near Pompeii, in Campania), no date; *Vervices*, D. 3036, near Rignanum, A.D. 395. Examples of the genitive ending in -*aes* are all from Rome: *Iustinaes*, D. 3009B, no date; *Nunnosaes*, D. 3011, no date; *Sapriciaes*, D. 3016, no date. The forms in -*es* are much more common than those in -*aes*.

[31] Pirson gives (p. 18) examples of genitives (and datives) ending in -*ai*, but not a single form ending in -*aes*, -*es*, -*ais*, or *as* in his exhaustive study of Latin inscriptions of Gaul. In Diehl, however, we have a single case of an -*es* genitive ending in the proper name *Selentioses* (= *Silentiosae*), D. 3039, Lugudunum (Lyon), dated A.D. 334. Carnoy mentions (p. 81) several cases of a genitive in -*ai*, but only two genitives ending in -*aes*: *Staiaes*, *Ampliataes*, CIL II 4975, both in the same inscription.

maritai, D. 2864, *CIL* VIII 9842, Altava (Mauretania Caesariensis), A.D. 489.
dulcissimai, D. 2865, *CIL* VIII 9882, Altava, no date.

It is generally assumed that the spelling -*ai* for -*ae* is a remnant
of an archaic Latin orthography. [32] Since the change of -*ai* to -*ae* took
place in the second or third century B.C., and inscriptional material
has shown it to be evident at least as late as the end of the fifth
century A.D. (cf. *maritai*, dated to A.D. 489), we can see the powerful
influence exerted by an archaic orthographic system. [33]

b) The Genitive Endings -*aes* and -*es*

Castulaes, D. 3323, *CIL* VIII 11,111, Sullecthum (Africa),
no date.
Reguliaes, D. 3752, *CIL* III 9588, Salona (Dalmatia), no
date. [34]
alogies (= *cena funeraticia*), D. 1573, *CIL* VIII 20,334, near
Satafi (Mauretania Sitifensis), no date.

Scholars usually attribute the genitive endings -*aes* and -*es* to a
compromise between the Latin genitive -*ae* and the Greek -*ης*, or to

---

[32] Sommer considers (p. 71) the use of -*ai* in inscriptions dating from
Imperial times as a "künstlichen Archaisierungssucht." Carnoy finds (p. 81)
the spelling -*ai* in Late Latin inscriptions as "une affectation d'archaïsme."
Pirson offers (p. 17) the explanation of -*ai* as one of "les tendances archaï-
santes de l'époque impériale." E. Hoffmann, *De Titulis Africae Latinis Quaestiones Phoneticae* (Breslau: Robert Noske, 1907), p. 73, however, prefers to
explain the use of -*ai* as an influence of Greek writing: "Rectius fortasse
coniciemus subesse imitationem scripturae graecae."

[33] For the dating of the change of *ai* to *ae* in general, see Niedermann,
p. 59 (3rd cent. B.C.); Sommer, p. 70 (2nd cent. B.C.); Lindsay, p. 43
(2nd cent. B.C.). This affectation of archaic spelling is best seen in the
attitude of Emperor Claudius (A.D. 41-54) who insisted that his title be
written *Caisar*. The importance of this conscious effort on the part of
Claudius to create an aura of archaism is well expressed by Niedermann
who writes (p. 60): "L'on se mit même alors à prononcer Caisar, et c'est
sous cette forme que le mot parvint chez les Germains sur le Rhin, et, plus
tard, chez les Gots sur le cours inférieur du Danube. De là *kaisar* dans la
traduction gotique de la bible par Wulfila, évêque des Wisigots, établis en
Mésie. Dans ce même texte, on trouve Krēks "Grec," qui repose sur le
latin *Graecus*, prononcé *Grēcus*, et qui montre que la prononciation factice
ai était restée limitée au seul *Caisar*, auquel on voulait sans doute conférer
ainsi un aspect solennel."

[34] For other examples of the genitive endings in -*aes* and -*es* in Dalmatian
inscriptions, see Skok, *Pojave*, p. 63.

a contamination of the Osco-Umbrian genitive -as with the Latin genitive -ae.[35] Although our limited examples seem to point to the use of -aes with Latin names, and -es with Greek, a theory already expressed, this distinction is found to be faulty when we consider the long list of proper names from Roman inscriptions (see *supra*, p. 383).[36] It is probably best to consider the e of the ending -es as a more popular spelling for the monophthongized -ae of earlier times. We have already seen, for example, that the ending of the nominative plural of first declension nouns and adjectives regularly terminated in -e (see *supra*, pp. 372-74 for the table on the monophthongization of ae).

   c) The Genitive Ending -ais

   Dativais, Saguntinais, D. 1684, *CIL* VIII 20,301, Satafi (Mauretania Sitifensis), between A.D. 349 and 436.
   Victo[r]ia[i]s, D. 2068, *CIL* VIII 20,600, Tocqueville (Africa), A.D. 359.
   dulcisimais, filiais, D. 3629, *CIL* VIII 28,045, near Theveste (Proconsularis), no date.
   Donatais, D. 3708, *CIL* VIII 20,476, near Sitifis (Mauretania Sitifensis), n.d.

---

[35] Ernout, *Morphologie*, pp. 20-21, in addition to the Greek or Oscan-Umbrian influence, also mentions that the analogy of third declension nouns with an -s in the genitive also helped in the formation of the -aes ending; Sommer considers (p. 327) the -aes as a result of the Greek genitive; Kent writes (p. 25) that "the ending -aes ... has taken on -s in imitation of the corresponding Gr. gen. in -ης; Lindsay writes (p. 381) that the -aes is "probably a feature of the Italian-Greek patois, for it is practically confined to epitaphs of the uneducated (from the last century of the Republic)." Väänänen (*Pompéiennes*) favors (p. 83) the compromise between the -ae of the Latin and the -ης of the Greek inasmuch as "cette explication rend compte du fait que ce barbarisme n'apparaît guère en dehors des *cognomina* d'esclaves, dans lesquels l'influence du grec peut le plus facilement se faire valoir, en raison de la provenance étrangère de ceux-ci." This scholar also adds (p. 83) that "la théorie d'une contamination du gén. osque en -as avec le gén. lat. en -ae est caduque" although he accepts the theory that "l'analogie de la 3e déclinaison a pu favoriser cette formation en -aes." Pieske, however, favors (p. 12) an Italic origin of the -aes ending, accepting a theory brought forth by Elias Lattes in his work entitled *Le iscrizioni paleolatine* (Milan, 1892): Pieske writes (p. 12) that the "genetivos in -aes (-es, -ais, -as) desinentes non e genetivis Graecis sumptos, sed, cum iam antiquissima aetate in usu fuerint, vi linguae Graecae servatos esse."

[36] Cf. Sommer, p. 327: "Dass -aes vorwiegend bei lateinischen -ēs bei griechischen Namen steht, erklärt sich als Anlehnung an die Schulorthographie beider Sprachen." The popular nature of these inscriptions would seem to preclude, however, the learned influence of schools.

Adeotais (= Adeodatais), D. 3708A, CIL VIII 19,211, Saf-
far (Numidia), no date.
Sabinais, D. 3710, CIL VIII 8292, between Milev and Cuicul
(Numidia), no date.
Urbanais, D. 3711, CIL VIII 8706, near Sitifis (Mauretania
Sitifensis), n.d.

This genitive ending, apparently not as widespread as the others,
has been explained as a barbarism, a formation based on the analogy
of the genitive -is of the third declension, and as a Greek spelling
for -aes. [37] Basing himself on the fact that almost all of the inscriptions having this -ais genitive ending are found in eastern Mauretania
or western Numidia, Pieske explains (p. 13) this particular termination
as the imitation of Greek speech or rather writing on the part of a
single stonemason. [38] Since Pieske studied the morphology of African
inscriptions, his reasoning may be satisfactory (although doubtful) for
the examples he adduced, but our examples of dulcisimais and filiais,
both from inscription D. 3629, CIL VIII 28,045, are from Aquae
Caesaria near Theveste in the province of Africa Proconsularis and
thus show that the genitive ending in -ais was not limited to the
provinces of Mauretania Sitifensis and Numidia, even in Africa. Diehl
records an example of a genitive in -ais from an inscription from
Umbria, which also militates against Pieske's theory of a single stonemason being responsible for the -ais genitive. [39] We are inclined to
consider this particular genitive as the result of an -s being added
on the analogy of Greek genitives to the genitive ending in ai- likewise probably of Greek origin or of an archaic nature. The distribution
of this ending, however, seems to be mainly limited to inscriptions
from Africa. [40]

---

[37] Sommer, p. 327; Pieske, p. 12.
[38] Pieske, pp. 12-13: "Tamen, si omnes inscriptiones supra citatas eius-
dem regionis esse viderimus, Mauretaniae orientalis vel Numidiae occidentalis,
— excepta paenultima, quae cum sit in lucerna insculpta, origo statui non
potest, — imitationem esse sermonis vel potius scripturae Graecae ab uno
lapicida adhibitam sumere malemus."
[39] Diehl, Vulgärlateinische Inschriften (Bonn: Marcus u. Weber, 1910),
p. 73, inscription no. 834 found in the CIL XI 6727 from Umbria gives
the proper name Paoniais.
[40] It is interesting to note that although Väänänen records (Pompéiennes,
pp. 23, 83) the genitive endings -ai, -aes, and -es in Pompeian inscriptions,
he does not give a single example of the -ais genitive.

d) The Genitive Ending -as

Saturas, D. 3108A, *CIL* VIII 21,427, Caesarea Maurorum (Mauretania), n.d.

Fortunatas, D. 3403B, Thabraca (Proconsularis), no date.

familias, D. 3666, *CIL* VIII 9869, Altava (Mauretania Caesariensis), A.D. 536.

Quintas, D. 3709, near Orléansville (Mauretania Caesariensis), no date.

vitas, D. 4736, Madauros (Proconsularis), n.d.

The Italic genitive in -as was still used in the oldest Latin documents (Ennius, *vias*; Livius Andronicus, *escas, Latonas, Monetas*; Naevius, *terras, Fortunas*), but was generally replaced at an early date by -ai and -ae. [41] The -as genitive ending remained only in phrases with *familias* as an archaic legal term. [42] From the above examples, we see that in addition to the archaism *familias* used in the phrase *pater familias*, found in an inscription dated A.D. 536, other forms also show this -as genitive ending. The use of the genitive -as at this late time is attributed to a Greek influence. [43]

We see that, other than the genitive ending in -ai, the forms -aes, -es, -ais, and -as are not evenly distributed in Latin inscriptions from all areas of Romania. The two areas where these non-classical forms are most often found are Africa and Rome, both areas profoundly influenced by a dense Greek populace. It would seem that the main reason for the appearance of the genitives ending in -aes, -es, -as, and -ais in these areas is therefore a Greek influence. The complete lack of these forms in pagan inscriptions of Britain and the conspicuous absence of any mention of them by Pirson in his thorough study of the Latin inscriptions of Gaul (see *supra*, footnote 31, p. 383 for

---

[41] Ernout, *Morphologie*, p. 19; Kent, p. 25; Sommer, p. 325.

[42] Ernout, *Morphologie*, p. 19; Kent, p. 25; Sommer, p. 325.

[43] Sommer, p. 325, simply mentions that the -as in late Latin "zeigt griechischen Einfluss." Pieske is more specific in his explanation of the forms he found, saying (p. 13): "Quod in his vocibus, quamquam nisi post ε, ι, ρ exitus -as locum non esse constat, tamen semper -as adhibetur, dubitationem non habet, cum et lingua Graeca occidentalis ad illas formas valere potuerit et hodierna lingua Graeca in femininis in -α desinentibus ubique -ας substituerit terminationi -ης." Jeanneret explains the single form *Rufas Pulica(s)* found in his *defixiones* as an "influence dialectale plutôt qu'un dernier vestige du gen. lat. archaïque en -ās." The genitive in -as is found on a *defixio* from Mentana (Latium) dated the 2nd or 3rd century A.D.

a single example of the genitive in -es in a Christian inscription from Lugudunum, A.D. 334) are eloquent testimonies of a differentiation of the genitive endings in the various areas of Romania. The two examples of a genitive ending in -aes from the same inscription from Spain (the -ai ending is more common), and the lack of any example in either pagan or Christian inscriptions from the Balkans (our corpus admittedly being scanty) would seem to indicate that the non-classical genitive endings were of little importance in these areas. Dalmatia holds an intermediate position since, in addition to our example of *Reguliaes,* Skok gives several other cases of genitive endings in -aes and -es.

An interesting observation can be made concerning African inscriptions. Although, as we have already seen, the vocalism of African Latin is extremely conservative in nature, very few deviations from Classical Latin having been noted, this situation apparently does not hold true for morphological endings where a plethora of terminations deviating from the classical norm can be seen.

The Dative and Genitive Singular of First Declension Forms Ending in -a

Sittl, in his attempt to show the differences in Latin throughout Romania, believed that the Latin of Rome was strongly influenced by the other Italic languages. To substantiate his contention of a dialectalization of Latin, he stressed the importance of a "munizipalen Latein," which differed in some respects from the Latin of Rome. One of the points which he stressed in his assertion of an Italic influence on the Latin of Rome was precisely the dative singular of first declension nouns and adjectives. He noted the distribution of datives ending in -a and remarked (p. 2) that "hier treffen wir sowohl im Norden als im Süden Beispiele, während sie, Präneste ausgenommen, das in Sprache und Kultur immer eine Sonderstellung einnahm, in Latium gänzlich fehlen." Studying more closely this particular phenomenon, the same scholar writes (p. 3) that "dies Dative scheinen also von Nordumbrien (Pisaurum) ausgegangen und zunächst in die benachbarten Länder eingedrungen zu sein, worauf sie später auch nach Süditalien kamen während sie im Norden allmällig verschwanden." Sommer acknowledges (p. 327) the "vulgäres -ā" for archaic inscriptions and considers it as "die Pausaform -ā̆ des alten -āī ge-

genüber ursprünglich antekonsonantischem -ae sein." [44] When the datives in -a are found in later inscriptions, however, this author considers them (p. 328) as examples of a "vulgärer Kasusvertauschung." It must be brought out that in our corpus examples of both dative and genitive forms of nouns and adjectives ending in -a were found. We will give below some examples from our corpus of a dative or genitive ending in -a rather than the expected -ae or e.

I. From African Inscriptions:

memoria Aureliae Felicia (gen.), *D.* 2833, *CIL* VIII 21,543, near Tiaret (Mauretania Caesariensis), A.D. 476.

memoriae Aureliae Lorida (gen.), *D.* 2867, *CIL* VIII 21,682, Albulae (Mauretania Caesariensis), A.D. 475.

salvis dominis nostris xristianissimis et invictissimis imperatoribus Iustino et Sofia (dat.) *Augustis, D.* 27, *CIL* VIII 1434, Tebursk (Thibursicu Bure), Proconsularis, A.D. 565-74.

... fecerunt mesa Peregrini patri et Aulurula (dat.) *coniugi pie matrique pi<e>, D.* 883, *CIL* VIII 21,553, Mechera-Sfa (Mauretania Caesariensis), A.D. 434.

mem. Robbe, sacre dei, germana (gen.) *Honor[ati], D.* 2052, Benian (Mauretania), A.D. 434.

memoria Iuli Sapida (gen. masc.), *D.* 2862B, *CIL* VIII 21,747, Altava (Mauretania Caesariensis), A.D. 430.

... annis provincia (gen.), *D.* 3276, *CIL* VIII 21,689, Albulae (Mauretania Caesariensis), A.D. 493.

memoria Ponponi Feva (gen. masc.), *D.* 3276A, *CIL* VIII 21698, Albulae (Mauretania Caesariensis), after A.D. 439.

memoria dulcisimais filiais mea Flabana (gen.) *D.* 3629, *CIL* VIII 28,045, Aquae Caesaris near Theveste (Numidia), no date. [45]

---

[44] Lindsay shows (p. 386) scepticism concerning both the examples and the importance of datives in -a: "Of the 'Datives in -a,' only found on very old inscriptions, most of the apparent examples come from Pisaurum (*CIL* i. 167-180), where -e was the Dat. suffix of Ā-stems, and may be Genitives in -as with omission of the final -s, or else a mere dialectal variety, which would prove nothing for the Latin dative." For a historic explanation of the Latin dative, see Ernout, *Morphologie*, p. 21; Kent, p. 26; Palmer, p. 241.

[45] Note the juxtaposition of the genitives in -ais with the genitives in apposition, *mea Flabana* (probably for *Flaviana*). It seems difficult to imagine a stonemason writing four consecutive feminine genitive singulars of the first declension without a single correct ending.

II. From Pagan Inscriptions of Britain:

Dea (dat.) Diana (dat.) sacratissima (dat.) votum solvit Vet-
tius . . . , RIB 138, CIL VII 46, Bath (Aquae Sulis), Somerset, no date. [46]

Peregrinus Secundi fil(ius) civis Trever Loucetio Marti et
Nemetona (dat.) v.s.l.m., RIB 140, CIL VII 36, Bath
(Aquae Sulis), Somerset, no date. [47]

Titia (dat.) Pinta (dat.) vixit ann. XXXVIII et Val. Audiutori
vixit ann. XX et Varialo vixit ann. XV Val. Vindicia-
nus . . . , RIB 720, CIL VII 266, Eastness (Yorkshire), no
date.

. . . libertus Numeriani [e]qitis ala (gen.) I Asturum . . . , RIB
1064, Arbeia (South Shields), Co. Durham, no date.

. . . Catuallauna D.M. Regina (dat.) liberta (dat.) et coniuge . . . Catuallauna (dat.), RIB 1065, Arbeia (South
Shields), Co. Durham, no date. [48]

D.M. Hermagora (dat.) alumno Honoratus trib(unus), RIB
1291, CIL VII 1056, Bremenium (High Rochester), Northumberland, no date. [49]

coh(ortis) I Dacor(um) c(enturia) Ael(i) Dida (gen. masc.),
RIB 1365, Hadrian's Wall: Benwell to Rudchester, no
date. [50]

Coventina (dat.) Agusta (dat.) votu manibus suis Saturninus
fecit Gabinius, RIB 1531, Hadrian's Wall: Carrawburgh
(Brocolitia), Northumberland, no date.

III. From Dalmatian Inscriptions:

hunc [or nunc] illi dismisit duo anxia (dat.) natos, D. 3363,
CIL III 9623, Salona, n.d. [51]

---

[46] Sittl gives the example of sacratissima (not Dea or Diana, however) as
a dative ending in -a found during Imperial times: (footnote on p. 3):
"Interessant ist, dass in der Kaiserzeit die lateinisch sprechenden Britannier
dieselben Formen [dative ending in -a] gebrauchten, vgl. Nemetona, C.I.L.
VII 36 und sacratissima 46."

[47] See footnote 45 for the importance of the dative Nemetona for Sittl.

[48] The editor of Roman Inscriptions of Britain writes (p. 356): "Regina,
liberta, coniuge, Catuallauna: in ablative, instead of the normal dative case."
We are considering them as datives (in the case of coniuge, with a final
-i to e) since after the formula D.M., the dative, genitive, and nominative
cases are used, the ablative case, for practical purposes never being used with
this particular formula.

[49] The editor of R.I.B. writes (p. 427): "Hermagora, a Greek form of
dative."

[50] The drawing of this inscription, RIB 1365, on p. 449, shows that the
a of Dida is squeezed under the righthand side of the d and the omission
of the e may just be because of lack of space.

[51] In his notes to this inscription, Diehl writes (II, 186): "anxia aut pro

ego Thaeodosius emi a F<l> Vita[li], prb. [presbytero]
sanc(tae) Matrona (gen.), *D.* 3791C, near Tragurium,
A.D. 425.
... post ovitum eorum, Ursa (gen.), *Vernantilla* (gen.)...,
D. 3835A, Salona, no date.
arca Firmine ree ex iure [cum pa?]tre De[n?]tiano, nata
dat. or gen.) *Delo, D.* 749, *CIL* III 9606, Salona, no
date.

IV. From Balkan Inscriptions:

A. *Pagan*

Septimus [Cl]a[r]us vetra(n)us legion(is) V Ph(ilippianae)
M(acedonicae) pia (gen.) *fidel[is]...*, *Kal.* 125, *CIL* III
14,207, Ichtiman (Thrace), A.D. 246-47. [52]
M(arcus) Aur(elius) Maxim[u]s ... mem(oriam) bruti Amica
(dat.) *posuit, ...*, *Kal.* 412, Nicopolis ad Istrum (Moesia
Inferior, no date). [53]

B. *Christian*

Aurelia (dat.) *Urbici Fla. Martiniano, ... mater piissima*
dolies <f>ratri et <f>iliae maemoriam posuit, D. 3611,
CIL III 10,237, Sirmium (Pannonia Inferior), no date.
in pace Au[l. Quinti]llae vir., q. [vixit an.] XII, et Aul.
Ma[...], q. vixit an. q, et A[ul. Quin]tina (dat.) *Soror,*
q. [vixit an...], D. 3611N, *CIL* III 10,236, Sirmium
(Pannonia Inferior), no date.
bonae memoriae Aureliae Marcellinae Oesc(o), pientissimae
f(eminae), habens ius liberorum, filia (gen.) *qd. Marce-*
llini..., D. 393, *CIL* III 755, Nicopolis (Moesia Inferior),
no date.
de donis di et sci Cosma (gent.), *D.* 1941, *Kal.* 233, *CIL*
III 14,207, Kawarna (Moesia Inferior), probably 4th to
6th centuries. [54]
[i]n nomine domin[i] [m]emoria domna (gen.) *[..]lna, ucsor*
In[no]centi, D. 2445, *CIL* III 597, Beroea (Macedonia),
no date.

---

anxiae est aut abl. nominis angores significantis." Skok omits the form *anxia*
in his *Pojave,* probably considering it a correct ablative.

[52] Kalinka writes (p. 119): "pia Grundform statt des Genetivs."

[53] Note the use of *bruti* (= *nurui*) of Germanic origin, meaning 'daughter-in-law,' the etymon for the French 'bru,' found in a pagan inscription of the Balkans.

[54] According to Kalinka, p. 196, "Cosma griechischer Genetiv."

When we analyze the above examples of a change of final *ae* to *a* in the dative and genitive singulars of the first declension, we see that most examples are clear cases of "Kasusvertauschung" (see *supra*, p. 389). The word is either in apposition, at a distance from the form it modifies, or the first word in the sentence where the nominative case looms strong in the mind of the stonemason. Most examples simply show a lack of agreement, an indication of the low educational level of the stonemason who just cannot master the intricacies of Classical Latin concord. Other times, the use of a final *-a* for *-ae* in the genitive singular may be a Greek genitive, especially if the word is Greek in origin. At times an exotic name may have the ending of the nominative case, the proper name being indeclinable in the mind of the stonemason. The lack of space, the need to abbreviate, or a downright oversight may likewise result in a change of final *ae* to *a*. As can be seen from the examples listed herein on page 391, the mistakes (especially the lack of agreement, the most significant reason for a change of final *ae* to *a*) are found in all areas of Romania and seem to show the difficulty of maintaining Classical Latin standards in popular speech. Once again inscriptions demonstrate that lack of agreement was a widespread fault and was not limited to a certain area.

This breakdown of case distinctions can also be seen in the occasional use of an *ae* or *e* for *a*, although this change is not as common. Compare the examples which follow, where we are dealing with confusion of the nominative singular, ablative singular, and genitive singular cases.

> *Crementia, ancillae* (nom.) *vix. an. XXXVII,* ..., D. 1471, *CIL* VIII 21,816, Tingi (Mauretania Tingitana), no date.
> *Ipsa, q(uae) nutri(i)t, iaces et sobriae* (nom.) *semper,* D. 1570, *CIL* VIII 20,277, Satafi (Mauretania Sitifensis), A.D. 299.
> ...*pro animae* (abl.)..., *CIIC* 427, Caldey Island, Pembroke (Wales), no date.
> ...*pro Flavia Ingenuae* (abl.)..., *Kal.* 389, *CIL* III 14,213, Dewna (Marcianopolis), Moesia Inferior, no date. [55]
> ...*cum Peregrine* (abl.)..., D. 883, *CIL* VIII 21,553, Mechera-Sfa (Mauretania Caesariensis), A.D. 434.

---

[55] According to Kalinka (p. 306): "*Ingenuae* wohl Schreibfehler."

Cunaide (nom.) *hic in tumulo iacit, CIIC* 479, Hayle (Cornwall), Britain, 5th century.
Brohomagli Iatti ic iacit et uxor eius Caune (nom.) *CIIC* 401, Pentrefoelas (Wales), sixth century.
Tunccetace (nom.) *uxsor Daari hic iacit, CIIC* 451, Pembroke (Wales), sixth century.
Evali fili Dencui Cuniovende (nom.) *mater eius, CIIC* 454, Pembroke (Wales), fifth century. [56]

Although we had previously seen the change of final *ae* to *a* in the dative and genitive cases of the first declension, this confusion is not limited to just these two cases. We have sporadic examples of the nominative plural of the first declension ending in -*a* rather than in the expected -*ae*:

> *m[e]morie depositionis presbiteri Securi posita* (nom. pl.) *a fratres Fatale et Flora...*, D. 1182, *CIL* VIII 20,300, Satafi (Mauretania Sitifensis), A.D. 363.
> *hic meria* (= *memoriae*, nom. pl.) *sti* (= *sancti*) *Pastoris deposite sunt in pace*, D. 2083b, Hr. Akhrib (Mauretania Sitifensis), no date.

We thus see that the change of final -*ae* to -*a* and the reverse change of -*a* to -*ae* occurred in the nominative, genitive, dative, and ablative singulars, and the nominative plural of the first declension, and were definitely not limited to the dative singular, as postulated by Sittl (see *supra*, p. 388) in his attempt to show an Italic influence on the Latin of Rome.

Reverse Spellings of ae for /ĕ/ and /ē/

The importance of the reverse spelling of *ae* for /ĕ/ as well as the change of *ae* to *e* was brought out by Väänänen in his study of Pompeian inscriptions. He considers this confusion of *ae* and /ĕ/

---

[56] The genitive forms *Cunaide, Caune, Tunccetace*, and *Cuniovende* (listed in the last four inscriptions above), for the nominative singular of these proper Celtic names are examples of Celtic feminines being treated always in Latin as first declension nouns ending in -*e* in the genitive. The use of the genitive in -*e* for the nominatives in -*a* of Celtic nouns is the feminine counterpart of second declension masculine nouns with a genitive in -*i* being used as a nominative. See *supra*, pp. 261-62, for examples of the genitive of second declension masculine nouns used as nominatives. For Celtic nouns with Latin endings, see Jackson, *Language*, p. 188.

as proof of the breakdown of the Latin quantitative system as can be seen from his words (p. 18):

> En effet, nos matériaux pompéiens déjà renferment des particularités phonétiques qui dénoncent l'état périmé du rythme quantitatif. Cette preuve capitale, croyons-nous, est livrée notamment par nombre d'exemples attestant la confusion entre *ae* et *e* ... Le Pompéien qui écrit *ADVAENTU* pour *Adventu* ou *VICINAE* pour *vicine* [vocative], montre par là indirectement que dans sa prononciation les sons de *ae* et *ĕ* se confondaient. Ces graphies nous permettent de déduire non seulement que l'ancien *ae* était dès lors une monophthongue ou quasi-monophthongue dont le timbre était ouvert (les contrépels *AE* pour *ē* étant très peu nombreux), [57] mais encore que l'opposition de timbre commençait déjà à l'emporter sur l'opposition de quantité des voyelles, puisque cette monophthongue issue de *ae*, et qui par origine était une voyelle longue, se confond, comme nous venons de le voir, plutôt avec *ĕ* (bref et ouvert) qu'avec *ē* (longue et fermé).

We will study the reverse spelling of *ae* for both /ĕ/ and /ē/ in stressed, initial, intertonic, posttonic, and final positions to see whether there was any local variation in the representation of the reverse spelling.

I. Reverse Spelling of *ae* for /ĕ/

A. Stressed Syllable

(1) In African Inscriptions:

Aennia (= *Ennia,* proper name), *D.* 3272B, *CIL* VIII 21,675, Albulae (Mauretania Caesariensis), A.D. 519.

(2) In Pagan Inscriptions of Britain:

aeques (= *eques,* 'trooper'), *RIB* 356, *CIL* VII 118, Caerleon (Isca Silurum), Monmouthshire, no date. [58]

---

[57] Väänänen emphasizes (*Pompéiennes,* p. 25) the rarity of the reverse spelling of *ae* for /ē/ compared to the relative frequency of *ae* for /ĕ/: "Nous voyons que des contrépels *ae* pour *ē,* seul *AEGISSE* est un exemple sûr de la confusion de *ae* et *ē,* les autres exemples de *ae* pour *ē* étant des mots grecs ... ou des formations barbares. Par contre la graphie *ae* pour *ĕ* est assez bien représentée."

[58] The editor of *Roman Inscriptions of Britain* writes (p. 121) that "*aeques* is a solecism for *eques.*"

(3) In Christian Inscriptions of the Balkans:

praesbyter, D. 393, *CIL* III 755, Nicopolis (Moesia Inferior), no date.

B. Initial Syllable

(1) In African Inscriptions:

aeclesia, D. 1103, *CIL* VIII 20,905, Tipasa, no date.
aelemosinae, D. 1103, *CIL* VIII 20,905, Tipasa, no date.
baeatiss[i]mi, D. 2039, *CIL* VIII 25,036, Carthage (Proconsularis), n.d.
aelemosina, D. 2035, *CIL* VIII 20,906, Tipasa, no date.
baeatissimi, D. 2330, *CIL* VIII 27,333, Thugga (Proconsularis), no date.
aecle[si]ae, D. 2422, near Theveste (Proconsularis), no date.

(2) In Pagan Inscriptions of Britain:

Daeab[u]us, *RIB* 1047, Chester-le-Street (Co. Durham), no date.
Aesuio (= *Exuvio*, proper name), *RIB* 2226, CIL VII 1150, milestone at Bitterne (Clausentum), A.D. 270-73.

(3) In Dalmatian Inscriptions:

aeclesiae, D. 1223, *CIL* III 2654, Salona, no date.
Thaeodosio, D. 3791C, near Tragurium (Troghir), A.D. 425.
Thaeodosius, D. 3791C, near Tragurium (Troghir), A.D. 425.
aec[l]esiae, D. 3834, *CIL* III 2704, Tragurium (Troghir), no date.
aeclesiae, D. 3837C, near Heraclea Lyncestis, no date.

(4) In Christian Inscriptions of the Balkans:

maemoriam, D. 3611, *CIL* III 10,237, Sirmium (Pannonia Inferior), no date.

C. Intertonic Position

We found no example of a reverse spelling of *ae* for /ĕ/ in any area under investigation. [59]

---

[59] We found, in fact, only one example of an *ae* in intertonic position in all of our areas: *[aq]uaeductium*, *RIB* 430, Caernarvon (Segontium), Carnarvonshire, A.D. 198-209. Gaeng likewise mentions (pp. 250-51) no examples of the reverse spelling of *ae* for /ĕ/ although he gives numerous examples of an *ae* for /ĕ/ in both initial and final positions. Pirson, however, does record (p. 19) *vetaeranus*, his only example of a reverse spelling of *ae* for /ĕ/ in intertonic position. For several examples of an *ae* for /ĕ/ in Dalmatian in-

D. Posttonic Position

(1) In Pagan Inscriptions of Britain:

Thesaeus, RIB 556, Chester (Deva), Cheshire, no date.
socaere (= *socerae*), RIB 594, CIL VII 229, Ribchester
(Bremetenacum), Lancastershire, no date. [60]

(2) In Christian Inscriptions of Britain:

fidaei, CIIC 360, Caermartenshire (Cambria), before A.D.
569.

E. Final Position

(1) Non-Morphological

a) In African Inscriptions:

eclesiequae, D. 1695, Carthage (Proconsularis), no date.

b) In Christian Inscriptions of the Balkans:

benae, D. 393, CIL III 755, Nicopolis (Moesia Inferior), no
date.

(2) Morphological

a) In African Inscriptions:

in pacae, D. 1582, Thabraca (Numidia), n.d.
in pacae, D. 2297, Hadrumetum (Sousse), Byzacena, no date.
in pacae, D. 2297K, Hadrumetum (Sousse), Byzacena, no
date.
in pacae, D. 2680, CIL VIII 16,351, near Cellas (Proconsularis), no date.
in pacae, D. 2682, CIL VIII 23,570, Maktar (Byzacena), no
date.
in pacae, D. 3233B, CIL VIII 11,120, Leptis Minor (Byzacena), no date.
in pacae, D. 3325, CIL VIII 16,806, near Theveste (Proconsularis), no date.

b) In Christian Inscriptions of the Balkans:

in <p>acae, D. 3611, CIL III 10,237, Sirmium (Pannonia
Inferior), no date.

---

scriptions, see Skok, *Pojave,* pp. 22-23. For an occasional change of *ae* for
/ĕ/ in pagan inscriptions of Africa, see Hoffmann, pp. 54-55. The only
example of a reverse spelling in Spanish inscriptions as recorded by Carnoy
is the word *piaentissima* in a pagan inscription (p. 74).

[60] See *supra,* footnote 15 on p. 366, for a discussion of this word.

II. Reverse Spelling of *ae* for /ē/

A. Stressed Syllable

(1) In African Inscriptions:

quaevi<*t*> (= *quievit*), *D*. 3104, *CIL* VIII 11,123, Leptis Minor (Byzacena), n.d.

(2) In Pagan Inscriptions of Britain:

Horta[*e*]*s*[*i*] (= *Hortensius*) *RIB* 1477, *CIL* VII 608, Hadrian's Wall: Chesters (Cilurnum), Northumberland, no date.

B. Initial Syllable

(1) In African Inscriptions:

aeminentissimi, *D*. 806, *CIL* VIII 1863, Theveste (Proconsularis), A.D. 527-49.
aeducatrici, *D*. 2038, *CIL* VIII 20,913, Tipasa, no date.

(2) In Dalmatian Inscriptions:

Haeraclia, *D*. 2769, *CIL* III 2663, Salona, no date.

C. Final Syllable

(1) Non-Morphological

a) In African Inscriptions:

devotae, *D*. 1720, *CIL* VIII 21,738, Altava (Mauretania Caesariensis), A.D. 530. [61]

b) In Dalmatian Inscriptions:

inlibatae (adverb), *D*. 821, *CIL* III 9507, Salona, A.D. 378.

(2) Morphological

a) In African Inscriptions:

diae (abl. sing.), *D*. 2791, *CIL* VIII 21,479, Sufasar, A.D. 318.

b) In Pagan Inscriptions of Britain:

Hermionae (nom. sing. of a Greek proper name), *RIB* 845, *CIL* VII 397, Maryport, Cumberland, no date. [62]

---

[61] Rather than a reverse spelling for the adverb *devote*, Diehl admits (I, 335) the possibility that *devotae* stands for *devota f(emina)*.

[62] The correct nominative singular of this particular Greek proper name, *Hermione*, is found in *RIB* 813, Maryport, Cumberland, no date.

c)   In Dalmatian Inscriptions:

diae (abl. sing.), *D.* 543, *CIL* III 9538, Salona, no date.

We will summarize our findings in tabular form for the purpose of convenience:

SUMMARY OF REVERSE SPELLING OF *ae* FOR /ĕ/

Area	Stressed Syllable	Initial Syllable	Posttonic Syllable	Final Syllable		Totals
				Non-Mor.	Morph.	
Africa	1	6	0	1	7	15
Britain:						
(Pagan)	1	2	2	0	0	5
(Christ.)	0	0	1	0	0	1
Dalmatia	0	5	0	0	0	5
Balkans:						
(Pagan)	0	0	0	0	0	0
(Christ.)	1	1	0	1	1	4

SUMMARY OF REVERSE SPELLING OF *ae* FOR /ē/

Area	Stressed Syllable	Initial Syllable	Final Syllable		Totals
			Non-Mor.	Morph.	
Africa	1	2	1	1	5
Britain:					
(Pagan)	1	0	0	1	2
(Christ.)	0	0	0	0	0
Dalmatia	0	1	1	1	3
Balkans:					
(Pagan)	0	0	0	0	0
(Christ.)	0	0	0	0	0

From the above tables we can see that there were thirty examples of reverse spelling of *ae* for /ĕ/ as compared to ten examples of reverse spelling for /ē/. This predominant confusion of *ae* and /ĕ/ is reflected in the Romance languages where the *e* monophthongized from the diphthong *ae* is treated like the regular Latin /ĕ/.[63] The

---

[63] Sommer, p. 72; Sturtevant, pp. 127-28; Väänänen, *Introduction*, p. 39; Niedermann, p. 61.

several cases of reverse spelling of *ae* for /ē/, especially in accented syllable, however, do show that a close pronunciation of the *e* from *ae* was possible, and the Romance languages do posit a close /ē/ for some words. [64] Speaking of the reverse spelling of *ae* for /ē/ in inscriptions, Sommer considers (p. 72) it as either a simple slip or possibly a local variation of the Latin: "Wo *ae* inschriftl. auch für altes ē auftritt, können blosse orthographische Entgleisungen vorliegen; denkbar sind jedoch auch (lokal begrenzte?) Artikulationsschwankungen (entweder engere Aussprach des aus *ae* entstandenen Lautes oder offnere des alten ē)." Carnoy studied the reverse spellings of *ae* and came to several important conclusions with respect to the Latin as spoken in Spain. He writes (p. 74) that "c'est toujours un ĕ qui est remplacé par *ae*" and continues (p. 75): "On ne trouve *ae* pour ē qu'à la finale; mais ces exemples sont précisément parmi les moins sûrs ... Chose remarquable, même à l'époque chrétienne, on ne rencontre *ae* que pour ĕ ..., sauf à la finale dans les adverbes *pridiae, religiosae* et à l'ablatif *diae*." Carnoy then considers (pp. 75-76) that "cette distinction soigneuse entre l'ẹ et l'ę est loin d'être observée dans toutes les provinces ... C'est donc une particularité très intéressante des inscriptions de l'Espagne que cette barrière infranchissable entre l'*e* ouvert et l'*e* fermé. Nous pouvons en inférer que le vocalisme latin a été scrupuleusement respecté en ce point particulier dans notre péninsule." He then compares (p. 76) the situation of Spain with that of other areas and writes that "aucune évolution populaire, aucune réaction de la langue livresque ne sont venus troubler ici l'état primitif contrairement à ce qui semble s'être passé dans l'Italie du Sud et les deux Gaules." This picture for Spain is in strong contrast with the findings of Pirson in his study of the Latin inscriptions of Gaul. Although the reverse spelling of *ae* for /ĕ/ is encountered quite often in this area, Pirson adds (p. 19) the important remark that "mais il arrive presque aussi souvent que l'*ae* représente un ē." As we have already seen, we do find cases of the reverse spelling *ae* for /ē/ in inscriptions from Africa, pagan Britain, and Dalmatia, but most cases of reverse spelling are for /ĕ/. In the inscriptions from Africa, the only area where we have a sufficient number of occurrences of a reverse spelling *ae* for both /ĕ/

---

[64] See *supra,* footnote 5, p. 353, for examples in the Romance languages of a close *e* from a Latin *ae*.

and /ē/, we see that there are fifteen cases of reverse spelling for /ĕ/ and five examples for /ē/, a percentage of 75 % for /ĕ/ and 25 % for /ē/. [65] Thus, we conclude that in our corpus of inscriptions from the area of Africa, and probably pagan Britain and Dalmatia, the reverse spelling for both /ĕ/ and /ē/ occurred, but the change of /ĕ/ to *ae* predominated. There may have been a local variation of Latin in this respect, as evidenced by the findings of Carnoy and Pirson, but our results are based on too few occurrences for us to be bold in our assertions. Since we did not find a single example of a reverse spelling of *ae* for /ĭ/ in our corpus and only two cases of a change of *ae* to *i* (*tidiat*, D. 2388A, Carthage, no date, and *iterna*, D. 3659, Purbach (Pannonia), no date; see *supra*, pp. 353, 362-63, for a discussion of *ae* to *i*), Pei's remark, based on his study of eighth-century texts of Northern France, that "examples of the interchange of *ae* with long *e* and short *i*, in all positions ... are too numerous and too clear to be explained away by reconstruction, analogy and other similar factors. The explanation rather appears to be that in the Eighth Century the combination *ae* was used indifferently to represent both the closed and the open sound of *e*." probably does not hold true for our inscriptions.

The Diphthong /oj/, *Represented by the Digraph* oe

Since the primitive *oi* changed to *oe* which in turn generally evolved into a *ū* in the second century B.C., the intermediate stage *oe* remaining only after an initial occlusive or labial fricative when no *i* followed (cf. *poena* but *punire*, *Poenus* but *Pūnicus*, *foedus*), we find only a limited number of words in Classical Latin with the diphthong *oe*. [66] The diphthong *oe* monophthongized to *ę* probably in the first century B.C., although the change of *oe* to *e* is first encountered in Pompeian inscriptions of the first century A.D. [67] The

---

[65] It is interesting to note that Hoffmann in his *De Titulis Africae Latinis Quaestiones Phoneticae*, a detailed study of both pagan and Christian inscriptions of Africa, found (pp. 54-56) 82 examples of a reverse spelling *ae* for /ĕ/ and 36 examples of /ē/ for the respective percentage of 69.5 % and 31.5 %, figures which are close to our 75 % and 25 %.

[66] For the historical discussion of *oi* developing to *u* or remaining as *oe*, see Sommer, p. 74 ff.; Lindsay, pp. 246-48; Niedermann, pp. 61-63.

[67] Lausberg, I, 276; Sturtevant, p. 133; Niedermann, p. 63; Väänänen, *Introduction*, p. 39.

Romance languages posit a long *e* for Fr. *peine,* Sp. *pena,* It. *pena,* from Latin *poena,* Sp. *feo* from Lat. *foedu(m),* etc. It is therefore not surprising to find examples of the change of the diphthong *oe* to *e* in our corpus of inscriptions. There are, of course, only a few examples of the correct orthography *oe* in our epigraphic evidence: from Africa we have: *coeptis, D.* 1891, no date; *foedera, D.* 779, 4th century; *moen[ia], D.* 795, 6th century;[68] *coeperat, D.* 1641, no date; *Moen[ae], D.* 2089, no date, and *coemeterum, D.* 3681A, no date; from pagan inscriptions of Britain we have: *coeptam, RIB* 978, 3rd century; from Dalmatia we have: *poene, D.* 3834, no date; *poenae, D.* 3834N, no date; from the Christian inscriptions of the Balkans we have: *Oesc(o)* (a place-name in Moesia), *D.* 393, no date and *moenia, D.* 790, no date. We will give below a list of those examples where the diphthong *oe* is represented by *e* in our inscriptions, although we will not give percentages because of the paucity of the total occurrences of this phoneme.

a) The Change of *oe* to *e*:

   penam, D. 814, *CIL* III 10,016, Iader (Dalmatia), no date.
   pena, D. 835, *CIL* III 9672, Salona (Dalmatia), no date.
   quepit (= *coepit*), *D.* 1943, *CIL* VIII 21,511, Cartenna (Africa), no date.

In addition to these sporadic examples of a change of *oe* to *e* we have a single case of a change of *oe* to *i* in an initial syllable.

b) The Change of *oe* to *i*:

   ciperunt, D. 2426, Podgorica near Doclea (Dalmatia), no date.

Since the diphthong *oe* had monophthongized to a long *e* by this time, this change to *i* probably means that the *e* had a very close sound, approaching that of *i.* We have already seen (*supra,* p. 170) that initial long *e* did sporadically change to *i* in Dalmatian inscrip-

---

[68] The diphthong *oe* in the word *moenia* is an exception to the rule. Niedermann writes (p. 63) that "l'*oe* de *moenia* 'remparts' en face de *murus* 'mur' n'est pas phonétique. Peut-être ce *moenia* est-il une innovation analogique d'après la formule proportionelle *punire: poena = munire: moenia* qui aurait été favorisée par le désir de différencier les homonymes **munia* 'remparts' et *munia* 'obligations.'"

tions. This example assumes greater importance, however, when we consider the words of Sittl who, in his attempt to show the distinctiveness of the Latin of Gaul, wrote (p. 60): "Dennoch glaube ich vorläufig folgende Resultate mit einiger Sicherheit aufstellen zu können: nur gallische Inschriften und Urkunden ziehen in lateinischen Wörten OE zu I zusammen, wodurch Formen wie *cipit* ... und *opidiencia* (= *oboedientia*) ... entstehen." Obviously the change of *oe* to *i* was not limited to the Latin inscriptions of Gaul. [69]

There is a single case of the change of *oe* to *ae* in our corpus of inscriptions.

c) The Change of *oe* to *ae*:

    paenam, D. 405, *CIL* III 6399, near Salona (Dalmatia), no date.

Since both *oe* and *ae* had monophthongized to *e*, the former a long *e*, the latter usually a short *e*, the confusion of these two diphthongs orthographically may show that the *e* evolving from *ae* was occasionally similar to that of the *e* from *oe*, or it may be that the stonemason simply used the more common diphthong *ae* to represent the sound of /ē/ inasmuch as, of the two possible orthographic devices to show a sound of *e* (whether long or short), the *ae* was a much more common symbol. [70]

We have already seen the use of *oe* for *ae* in *Coelius* and *Coelia[nae]* (see *supra*, pp. 356, 362).

The Diphthong /aw/, Represented by the Digraph au

Although the Latin diphthong *au* remained during the Vulgar Latin period and the monophthongization of *au* to ǭ was a particular

---

[69] Gaeng gives (p. 258) the following examples of a change of *oe* to *i*: *Misacorum* (= *Moesiacorum*), D. 557, Northern Italy, no date; *cimiterium*, D. 2000, Ostia (Central Italy), 7th cent.; *cimiterium*, D. 2163, Tarracina (Central Italy), no date; *cimitero*, D. 2119, Rome, no date, and *cymiterium*, D. 2149, Rome, no date.

[70] For the possibility of a local variation of an *ae* developing to long *e*, see Sommer, pp. 72, 77; Pei writes (pp. 73-74), with respect to the problem of *ae* signifying a long *e* that "if this closed *e* could be represented by *ae* ... it is fairly evident that the symbol *ae* could represent the closed as well as the open sound of *e*. The replacement of *oe* by *ae* could not have taken place if *ae* had only the sound of open *e*." Grandgent simply states (p. 90) that "in late Latin a bad spelling, *oe* for *ae* and *e*, became popular."

development of the individual Romance languages, the dialectal change of *au* to ǫ, mainly an Umbrian phenomenon, and the simplification of *au* to *a* in initial position warrant an investigation into this phoneme. [71] Carnoy, on viewing the various changes that he recorded for the diphthong *au*, was forced to comment (p. 87) that "il suffit de jeter un coup d'œil [on the forms attested] pour se rendre compte de la complication qui règne dans l'histoire de la diphthongue *au*. Ce problème n'a pas encore reçu de solution bien satisfaisante." We will devote our attention to the treatment of *au* in accented and initial syllables since *au* was only rarely encountered in intertonic position. [72]

---

[71] For the stability of the diphthong *au* throughout the Vulgar Latin period, see Grandgent, p. 89; Väänänen, *Introduction*, p. 39; Lindsay, p. 38; Niedermann, p. 66; Sommer, p. 78; Lausberg, I, 277; Bourciez, p. 44. With respect to the treatment of *au* in the Romance languages, Lausberg, I, 277, writes: "Dentro de la Romania se encuentra todavía como *au* diptongal en el sur de Italia, en grisón (excepto el engad., en que monoptongó en *o*), en rum., en prov. ant. y, en parte, todavía en prov. mod. (por ej., en gascón). Como diptongo *ou* aparece en la mayoría de los dialectos del prov. mod., así como en port., donde la grafía *ou*, que antes se pronunciaba como verdadero diptongo, suena hoy corrientemente *o* (dialectalmente todavía se pronuncia *ou* o con su disimilación *oi*). En el resto de la Romania (norte de la Galia, España [excepto Portugal, pero incluyendo Cataluña, que en esto se opone al prov.], norte y centro de Italia) *au* monoptonga en ǫ. En sardo *au* dio *a*." The late development of a monophthongization to ǫ is indicated by the palatalization of initial /k-/ and /g-/ in the French *chose* from *causa* and *joie* from *gaudia,* where the *au* must be posited rather than the vowel /ŏ/ and in the lack of sonorization of intervocalic consonants in the Spanish *poco* from *paucu* and *coto* from *cautu.* It must be emphasized that the early dialectal monophthongization of *au* gave a long close *o* while the Romance development shows an open quality.

[72] We found only two examples of an *au* in intertonic position: *restauravit,* D. 234, Rusguniae (Mauretania Caesariensis), 6th cent., and *Arausione* (modern Orange), *RIB* 3, London, no date. We are recording the place-names *Pisauro, RIB* 260, Lincoln (Lindum), no date, and *Nemauso, RIB* 814, Maryport (Alauna), no date, as examples of stressed *au* although the corresponding modern forms *Pésaro,* the Umbrian city, and *Nîmes,* the capital of the Department of Gard in Southern France, posit a stressed initial syllable, the *au* thus being posttonic, which is, of course, contrary to the Latin "Paenultima Law," according to which the accent falls on the antepenult if the paenultima is short, on the paenultima, if it is long. Writing about the latter word, Niedermann reminds us (p. 67) that it is "Némausus avec l'accent initial gaulois, prononcé Némasus par les colons romains, qui est, sous cette dernière forme, à la base de Nemze, l'ancienne dénomination régionale de Nîmes." Carnoy considers (p. 90) these examples of posttonic *au* as the result of "une accentuation préromaine spéciale à certains noms de lieux."

The Diphthong au in Stressed Syllable

Area	Century	Open Syllable		Closed Syllable		Totals		% Of o
		au > au	au > o	au > au	au > o	ae	o	
Africa	3rd.	1	0	0	0	1	0	
	4th.	6	0	0	0	6	0	
	5th.	0	1	1	0	1	1	50.0
	6th.	4	0	0	0	4	0	
	7th.	1	0	0	0	1	0	
	n.d.	38	0	3	0	41	0	
	Totals:	50	1	4	0	54	1	1.8

The single example of a monophthongization of au to o in our corpus of African inscriptions occurs in the proper name Oria (= Auria for Aurea), D. 2966, CIL VIII 8708a, near Sitifis (Mauretania Sitifensis), A.D. 448. The correct Aurea is found in an undated African inscription of Tunis, D. 1401. The rustic use of o for au in the Latin aurum and its derivatives is well illustrated by the anecdote attributed to Festus, as quoted by Sturtevant, p. 130: "Orata, genus piscis, appellatur a colore auri, quod rustici orum dicebant, ut auriculas oriculas. Itaque Sergium quoque praedivitem, quod et duobus anulis aureis et grandibus uteretur, Oratam dicunt esse appellatum." Although a specific rustic pronunciation did enter the Latin of Rome in several words, not later than the early part of the first century B.C., stressed au is almost universally maintained. [73]

Britain	Century	Open Syllable		Closed Syllable			Totals		
		au > au	au > o	au > au	au > o	au > a	au	o	a
(Pagan)	1st.	2	0	0	0	0	2	0	0
	2nd.	3	0	0	0	0	3	0	0
	3rd.	3	0	0	0	1	3	0	1
	n.d.	19	1	1	0	0	20	1	0
	Totals:	27	1	1	0	1	28	1	1

[73] Sturtevant, writing about rustic o getting into urban Latin, mentions (p. 131) that "among the best authenticated forms are ōlla, cōda, cōdex, cōlis, cōpō, lōtus, plōdere, plōstrum. When these words are preserved in Romance their ō gives the same result as inherited ō." To give an idea of the extention of the distribution of this rustic ō for Classical Latin au, it is enlightening to take the example of cōda (= cauda). Besides the Rumanian coadă, the Provençal coza, the French queue, and the Italian coda, all positing the vowe! ō, the Sardinian kŏa likewise requires the Latin coda.

The one case of monophthongization of *au* to *o* is in the proper name *Clodius*, *RIB* 635, *CIL* VII 208, Ilkley (Yorkshire), no date. The plebeian form *Clodius* rather than the Classical Latin *Claudius* is well known from the story concerning Cicero's rival who changed his name precisely to *Clodius* for political purposes so as to curry favor with the mob.[74] The spelling of this name or its feminine form with *au* (*Claudius* and *Claudia*) is found eight times.

We have a single case of accented *au* becoming *a* in *Fas[t]us*, *RIB* 1875, *CIL* VII 808, Hadrian's Wall: Birdoswald (Camboglanna), Cumberland, A.D. 237. Although this is the only example found in our corpus of a stressed *au* simplifying to *a* because of a *u* in the following simple, other examples such as *Cladius*, *Scarus*, *Glacus*, etc., have been recorded, mostly for pagan inscriptions, by other scholars.[75] It would appear that the change of *au* to *a* in accented syllables was more widespread in earlier times than is generally assumed, especially when we consider that this change is regular in Sardinian[76] (regardless of following vowel) and in the Latin loanwords in Albanian[77] (before a *u* in the next syllable). After having studied this problem thoroughly, Carnoy evolved his solution to this change with the statement (p. 91) that "il semble donc se dessiner assez clairement que *au* tonique comme *au* atonique ne devient phonétiquement *a* que devant un *u* ou un *o*." For exceptions to this general rule, Carnoy writes (p. 89) that "on admettrait, en outre, que plus tard, *a* pour *au* aurait pu s'étendre accidentellement en dehors de son domaine

---

[74] See Lindsay, p. 41, and Sturtevant, p. 131, for references to this particular story.

[75] See Pirson, p. 26; Carnoy, pp. 86-87. Other investigators, having found the change of *au* to *a* when a *u* did not follow, deny the theory of dissimulation first set forth by Meyer-Lübke in his article "Die lateinische Sprache in den romanischen Ländern," in the first edition of Gröber's *Grundriss der romanischen Philologie* (Strassburg: Karl J. Trübner, 1888), I, 362. Writing about the change of *au* to *a*, Pirson strongly opposes Meyer-Lübke's theory with the words (p. 26): "Mais ce phénomène n'est nullement conditionné au voisinage d'un *u*, comme le pense Meyer-Lübke." For a similar point of view, see Hoffmann, p. 71. Proponents of Meyer-Lübke's theory of dissimulation are, among others, Sommer, p. 110; Niedermann, p. 67; Lindsay, p. 38; Grandgent, p. 89; Väänänen, *Introduction*, p. 40; Bourciez, p. 44.

[76] Wagner, "Lautlehre," p. 14: "Heute haben wir in allen echtsard. Wörtern immer *a*." Compare *paku* < *paucu*, *kama* < *cauma*, *pabaru* < *pauperu*, *a* < *aut*, *pasu* < *pausu*.

[77] Gustav Meyer, p. 1047: "*ar* < *aurum*, *a* < *aut*, *gaszi* < *gaudium*, *lar* < *laurus*, *pak* < *paucus*."

primitif." To show that the treatment of *au* evolved differently when other vowels followed, Carnoy adduces the examples of Sardinian and the Latin loanwords into Albanian. This scholar states (p. 92) that "en albanais, on a *ar, gaszi, lar, pak* (de *aurum, gaudium, laurum, paucum*), tandis que *causa, laudem,* donnent *kafše, láft.*" For Sardinian he writes (p. 92) that "en sarde, *au* accentué ou non devient *o* dans *gosare, orija, orire, osare, cosa, foga,* mais devant *u* on trouve *a* aussi bien à la tonique qu'à l'atone: *ascultare, attunziu, atorgare, austa, pagu, laru, pasu, trau* (= *taru*)." The importance which Carnoy attaches to Sardinian and the Latin element of Albanian is very great, as can be seen by his words (p. 92): "Il est donc fort possible qu'en ce point comme en beaucoup d'autres, ces dialectes aient per- pétué un état de chose ancien qui a péri dans les autres parlers romans sous des influences plus récentes, par exemple, celle de la langue écrite." Carnoy, unfortunately, apparently went too far in his insistence on a distinctive development of the *au* according to whether a *u* (or *o*) or another vowel followed with respect to Sardinian. Max Leopold Wagner, probably the greatest expert on Sardinian, wrote ("Lautlehre," pp. 15-16) that "der bedingunglose Übergang von bet. *au* zu *a* ist... vollständig erwiesen." [78] It appears that Carnoy did not take into consideration the question of borrowings from Vulgar Latin or other Romance languages into Sardinian. Forms such as *gosare, orija, cosa,* etc., are either Romance borrowings or show the dialectal Latin change of *au* to *o,* a general change for several Latin words of rustic origin which, of course, is completely unrelated to the development of Sardinian. [79] It would appear that the change of *au* to *a* in accented syllables was more prevalent in earlier Latin as intimated by Carnoy, but this change was not necessarily conditioned by a following *u* as shown by Wagner in his works on Sardinian.

---

[78] It is interesting to note that Meyer-Lübke changed his opinion on this question of the treatment of *au* to *a* in Sardinian. Although first admitting the theory of the dissimulation of the *au* to *a* because of a following *u,* he later changed his opinion and considered the change "bedingungslos." See Wagner, "Lautlehre," p. 13, for a discussion of this problem.

[79] Wagner in his "Südsardischen" writes (p. 57) that "*gosái,* log. *gōsare* 'sich freuen' ... ist sicher = Span. *gozar,* wie schon die Behandlung des *au* zeigt." In the same work Wagner states (p. 21) that "*orija* geht auf schon vgl. *oricla* zurück." Concerning the Sardinian *cosa,* Wagner in his "Lautlehre" writes (p. 16) that "das alte *casa* = *causa* ist verschwunden; heutiges *kósa* ist Italianismus."

Grandgent, on attempting to explain the attestations of a stressed *a* for *au*, writes (p. 89) that "perhaps they represent a provincial pronunciation, or possibly they are only orthographic." Sardinian and the Latin loanwords in Albanian would undoubtedly discredit any attempt to consider this change as merely "orthographic." There are too few examples of this change to warrant any firm conclusion as to the "provincial" nature of this phenomenon. We can only state that on the basis of our findings (only 1 example of the simplification of *au* to *a* in a pagan inscription and none in Christian inscriptions) this change had ceased to be of any significant importance in the Latin of inscriptions, especially after the fourth century.

Britain	*Century*	Open Syllable		Closed Syllable		Totals	
		au > *au*	*au* > *o*	*au* > *au*	*au* > *o*	*au*	*o*
(Christ.)	5th.	1	0	0	0	1	0
	6th.	1	0	0	0	1	0
	7th.	1	0	0	0	1	0
	Totals:	3	0	0	0	3	0
Dalmatia	4th.	0	0	0	0	0	0
	5th.	3	0	2	0	5	0
	6th.	0	0	0	0	0	0
	n.d.	18	0	1	0	19	0
	Totals:	21	0	3	0	24	0

On the basis of the twenty-four examples of *au* without any deviation, this diphthong appears stable in this area. [80] Dalmatian likewise maintained this diphthong unchanged. [81]

---

[80] Skok in his *Pojave*, a thorough study of both pagan and Christian inscriptions, gives (p. 23) the examples of *au* to *o* in the proper names *Clodius, Plotia*, and *Polio*. He does not give any examples of a change of *au* to *a*.

[81] Bàrtoli, *Das Dalmatische*, II, 338, gives the Vegliote examples of *pauk, jaur* (= *aurum*), *kausa, pauper*, and even the Germanic *rauba*. See also Hadlich, p. 74.

Balkans	Century	Open Syllable		Closed Syllable		Totals	
		$au > au$	$au > o$	$au > au$	$au > o$	au	o
(Pagan)	1st.	1	0	0	0	1	0
	2nd.	0	0	0	1	0	1
	n.d.	4	1	0	0	4	1
	Totals:	5	1	0	1	5	2

The two examples of this change of *au* to *o* are found in the proper names *Plotius, Kal.* 147, *CIL* III 14,411, Lom (Moesia Inferior), no date, and *Pollio, Kal.* 32, *CIL* III 7418, Radomir (Thracia), A.D. 196. Both names, especially the original forms and their variants, *Plautus, Plotus,* and *Paullus* or *Paulus, Polo, Pollus,* etc., are often found in inscriptions with both spellings. [82] Carnoy writes (p. 85) that "*Polla* est la forme ordinaire en Italie." Sturtevant stresses (p. 130) the antiquity of the proper name *Polia*, considering this form, first found in Praeneste, to be from as early as the seventh century B.C. The Umbrian name *Plautus* was written *Plotus* at an early date also. [83] On the basis of the proper names *Plotius* and *Pollio*, found in the Balkans, and *Clodius*, found in a pagan inscription of Britain, we see that the dialectal or rustic change of *au* to *o* in certain words was widespread in general Vulgar Latin and even reached the periphery of Romania.

Balkans	Century	Open Syllable		Closed Syllable		Totals	
		$au > au$	$au > o$	$au > au$	$au > o$	au	o
(Christ.)	4th.	1	0	0	0	1	0
	5th.	0	0	0	0	0	0
	6th.	0	0	0	0	0	0
	n.d.	2	0	0	0	2	0
	Totals:	3	0	0	0	3	0

Summarizing the treatment of *au* in accented position in our inscriptions, we conclude that this dipththong generally remained except for those cases, usually proper names, where an originally dialectal or rustic monophthongization to *o* occasionally took place.

---

[82] Pirson, p. 27; Carnoy, p. 85.
[83] Carnoy, p. 85; Sturtevant, pp. 130-31.

The Diphthong au in Initial Syllable

In initial syllables the diphthong *au* generally remains although in the particular form *Augustus* and its variants a simplification to *a* takes place quite regularly. [84] There is also a sporadic change of *au* to *o* under certain conditions. In our tables for the treatment of *au* in initial syllables, we will give separate figures for the individual word *Augustus* and its variants (both proper names and the name of the month) and for all other words. Although the monophthongization of *au* to *a* occurs only in the word *Augustus* and its variants, we will give the figures for all forms so as to give an idea of the general stability of *au* in the initial syllable of regular words.

Area	Century	August-		Other Words			% Of *a* in August-
		au	*a*	*au*	*a*	*o*	
Africa	3rd.	0	0	3	0	0	
	4th.	9	0	7	0	0	0.0
	5th.	5	2	13	0	0	28.6
	6th.	5	1	10	0	0	16.7
	7th.	0	1	0	0	0	100.0
	n.d.	8	5	27	0	2	38.5
	Totals:	27	9	60	0	2	25.0

The examples of the monophthongization of *au* to *a* in initial syllable in African inscriptions are:

Agust[a], D. 32, *CIL* VIII 10,681, Theveste (Proconsularis), A.D. 610-41.

Agustas, D. 214, *CIL* VIII 451, Ammaedara (Byzacena), no date.

Agusta, D. 332B, *CIL* VIII 20,644, Mauretania Sitifensis, A.D. 467.

Agus[t]as, D. 1408, *CIL* VIII 25,331, Carthage (Proconsularis), no date.

---

[84] In our corpus we did not find any examples of the monophthongization of *au* to *a* in *auscultare* and *augurium*, although the Romance languages generally posit an initial *a* through dissimilation because of a *u* in the following syllable: It. *ascoltare*, Old Sp. *ascuchar* (modern *escuchar*), Old Fr. *ascouter*, Sard. *askurtare*, from *ascultare*, and Sp. *agüero*, Port. *agoiro*, Raetian *agur*, Old French *ëur* (modern *bonheur*, *malheur*), Sard. *aguriu*, from *agurium*.

Agustas, D. 2096, *CIL* VIII 23,041, Uppena, n.d.
Acustas, D. 3272C, *CIL* VIII 9815, Albulae (Mauretania Caesariensis), possibly A.D. 444.
Agustas, D. 4548, *CIL* VIII 458, Ammaedara (Byzacena), no date.
Ag., D. 28, *CIL* VIII 4354, Ain-Ksar near Casas Numidiarum, A.D. 578-82.
Ags., D. 1399, *CIL* VIII 23,049, Uppena, n.d.

On the basis of a percentage of 25 % for forms with initial *a-* instead of *au-* in *Augustus* and its variants, we see that *Agust-* was a common root in the Latin of African inscriptions. Sardinian also posits a Latin *Agustu* for the name of the month. [85]

The two examples of monophthongization of initial *au* to *o* are:

Oriclo (= *Auriculo*, proper name), *D.* 2522, *CIL* VIII 13,821, Carthage (Proconsularis), n.d.
Clotoianus (= *Claudianus*), *D.* 2657, *CIL* VIII 27,813a, Altiburos, no date.

The change of initial *au* to *o* in *Oriclo* is general Vulgar Latin, the rustic pronunciation of *ō* for *au* having infiltrated into the Latin of Rome. [86] The monophthongization of *au* to *o* in *Clotoianus* is probably due to the stressed *o* of the proper name *Clodius*, a dialectal form that entered the Latin of Rome at an early date (see *supra*, p. 405).

---

[85] Cf. Wagner, "Lautlehre," p. 23: "heute bitt.- nuor. *agústu*; log. camp. *aústu.*"

[86] Väänänen, *Introduction*, p. 39, writing about the word *oricula* says that "aussi la prononciation *ō* pour *au* passait-elle à Rome à la fois pour provinciale et, dans certains mots à valeur affective, pour familière. Cicéron, dans une lettre à son frère Quintus, insère, pour indiquer son attitude politique, la locution proverbiale *oricula infima polliorem* 'plus souple que le lobe de l'oreille." Although the Sp. *oreja,* Cat. *orella,* Fr. *oreille,* It. *orecchio* cannot prove the monophthongization of *au* to *o* because of their similar treatment of initial *au* and *o,* the Portuguese *orelha,* Rumanian *ureche,* and the Sardinian *orija* do require the Latin *oricla.* Cf. also in the *Appendix Probi* (83) "auris non oricla."

Britain	Century	August-		Other Words			% Of *a* in August-
		au	*a*	*au*	*a*	*o*	
(Pagan)	1st.	1	0	2	0	0	0.0
	2nd.	34	0	5	0	0	0.0
	3rd.	65	1	35	0	0	1.5
	4th.	11	1	0	0	0	8.3
	n.d.	30	3	30	0	0	9.1
	Totals:	141	5	72	0	0	3.4

The five examples of monophthongization of initial *au* to *a* are:

Agustalis, RIB 154, Bath (Aquae Sulis), Somerset, no date. [87]
Agustinus, RIB 310, Caerwent (Venta Silurum), Monmouth-shire, no date.
Agusta, RIB 1531, Hadrian's Wall: Carrawburgh (Brocoli-tia), Northumberland, no date.
Ag., RIB 2225, *CIL* VII 1151, milestone: Bitterne (Clausen-tum), Hants, A.D. 270-73.
Ag., RIB 2267, milestone, about four miles west of Caerhun Fort (Kanovium), Wales, A.D. 307-37.

Although the percentage of *a* in *August-* is apparently low, the figure of 3.4 % may be deceiving. [88] At any rate, the Welsh name of the month *awst*, and the Welsh proper name *Awstin* do posit the Latin forms *agustus* and *Agustinus*. [89]

Britain	Century	August-		Other Words			% Of *a* in August-
		au	*a*	*au*	*a*	*o*	
(Christ.)	6th.	0	0	3	0	0	
	7th.	0	0	1	0	0	
	Totals:	0	0	4	0	0	0.0

---

[87] This inscription is dated in the 2nd or 3rd century A.D., by Jeanneret, p. 25.

[88] The percentage of initial *a* in *August-* may be unusually low because of the surprisingly high number of abbreviations in pagan inscriptions of Britain. Of the 141 examples of initial *au* in the root *August-*, 127 are of the type *Aug.* or *Augg.*, only 14 examples written out completely.

[89] Loth, p. 136.

Without any examples of initial *au* in *August-* it is, of course, impossible to determine the treatment of this diphthong in the Latin of Christian inscriptions of Britain.

Dalmatia	*Century*	August-		Other Words			% Of *a* in August-
		au	*a*	*au*	*a*	*o*	
	4th.	8	0	3	0	0	0.0
	5th.	6	1	3	0	0	14.3
	6th.	2	0	0	0	0	0.0
	n.d.	5	1	31	0	0	16.7
	Totals:	21	2	37	0	0	8.7

The examples of monophthongization of initial *au* to *a* in this area are:

Agustas, D. 3418, *CIL* III 9610, Salona, n.d.
Ag., D. 3870, *CIL* III 13,124, Salona, A.D. 426.

The root apparently seems to be *Agust-*, a conclusion bolstered by the Vegliote word for the name of the month, *aguást*. [90]

Balkans	*Century*	August-		Other Words			% Of *a* in August-
		au	*a*	*au*	*a*	*o*	
(Pagan)	1st.	3	0	0	0	0	0.0
	2nd.	4	0	0	0	0	0.0
	3rd.	13	1	5	0	0	7.1
	4th.	3	0	0	0	0	0.0
	n.d.	3	0	13	0	0	0.0
	Totals:	26	1	18	0	0	3.7

The single example of monophthongization of initial *au* to *a* in pagan inscriptions of the Balkans is found in the word *Agust[i]*, *Kal.* 125, *CIL* III 14,207, Ichtiman (Thrace), A.D. 246-47. The percentage of 3.7 % of initial *a* in this word may be deceiving since, of the twenty-six occurrences of *au*, twenty-four are abbreviations of the type *Aug.* or *Augg.* Although modern Rumanian does preserve initial *au* in the name of the month *August*, this is probably a learned word since the monophthongization of *au* to *a* takes place in *asculto* and

---

[90] Bàrtoli, *Das Dalmatische*, II, 169.

the Rumanian *toamnă* would require an initial *a-* for apheresis to have taken place. [91] The Albanian *gŭst* also comes from Latin *agustus* and the Albanian *uroj* as well as the Rumanian *ura* both posit a Latin *agurare* rather than the Classical Latin *augurare*. [92]

Balkans	Century	August-		Other Words			% Of *a* in August-
		au	*a*	*au*	*a*	*o*	
(Christ.)	4th.	1	0	1	0	0	
	5th.	0	0	0	0	0	
	n.d.	0	0	27	0	0	
	Totals:	1	0	28	0	0	0.0

There are too few occurrences of any form of *Augustus* to warrant any discussion of the treatment of *au* in this particular word.

To get an idea of the distribution of the monophthongization of initial *au* to *a* in the root *August-* throughout Romania we will summarize in tabular form Gaeng's findings as well as our own.

Area	Century	August-	Agust-	% of *a* in *Agust-*
Baetica	4th-6th	4	2	33.3
	7th	3	0	0.0
	Totals:	7	2	22.2
Lusitania	4th-6th	3	3	50.0
	7th	0	2	100.0
	Totals:	3	5	62.5
Tarraconensis	4th-6th	4	2	33.3
	7th	0	0	0.0
	Totals:	4	2	33.3
Narbonensis	4th-5th	2	0	0.0
	6th-7th	9	4	30.7
	Totals:	11	4	26.7

[91] For the use of *agust* in Rumanian dialects and in Old Rumanian, see Rosetti, I, 86.

[92] Gustav Meyer, p. 1049.

Area	Century	August-	Agust-	% of *a* in *Agust-*
Lugdunensis	4th-5th	3	0	0.0
	6th-7th	2	2	50.0
	Totals:	5	2	28.6
Northern Italy	4th-5th	16	3	15.8
	6th	20	3	13.0
	Totals:	36	6	14.3
Central Italy	3rd-4th	12	0	0.0
	5th	4	0	0.0
	6th-7th	6	0	0.0
	Totals:	22	0	0.0
Southern Italy	3rd-4th	6	0	0.0
	5th	5	4	46.6
	6th-7th	9	1	10.0
	Totals:	20	5	20.0
Rome	3rd-4th	39	1	2.1
	5th	25	3	10.7
	6th-7th	15	5	25.0
	Totals:	79	9	10.2
Africa	4th.	9	0	0.0
	5th.	5	2	28.6
	6th.	5	1	16.7
	7th.	0	1	100.0
	n.d.	8	5	38.5
	Totals:	27	9	25.0
Britain	1st.	1	0	0.0
	2nd.	34	0	0.0
(Pagan)	3rd.	65	1	1.5
	4th.	11	1	8.3
	n.d.	30	3	9.1
	Totals:	141	5	3.4

Britain (Christian)   N O   E X A M P L E S

Area	Century	August-	Agust-	% of *a* in *Agust-*
Dalmatia	4th.	8	0	0.0
	5th.	6	1	14.3
	6th.	2	0	0.0
	n.d.	5	1	16.7
	Totals:	21	2	8.7

Area	Century	August-	Agust-	% of *a* in *Agust-*
Balkans	1st.	3	0	0.0
	2nd.	4	0	0.0
(Pagan)	3rd.	13	1	7.1
	4th.	3	0	0.0
	n.d.	3	0	0.0
	Totals:	26	1	3.7
Balkans (Christ.)	4th.	1	0	0.0

Although the percentages of monophthongization of initial *au* to *a* in the above table differ greatly acording to the area considered, it should be remembered that almost all regions of Romania do have at least one example of this change in the root *August-*. This is all the more significant since both Gaeng and this researcher record the monophthongization of *au* to *a* only in the particular root *August-*, no other word in our corpus being affected. [93] It is also important to realize that the monophthongization of initial *au* to *a* in the root *August-* is corroborated by loanwords into the Brittonic languages and Albanian as well as the Romance languages, including Sardinian and Vegliote. This particular linguistic phenomenon is extremely well verified by a collaboration of inscriptions, loanwords, and Romance reconstruction. We thus see in this case of initial monophthongization that inscriptions give an inkling of the linguistic change, but the definitive proof must be bolstered by other means, such as loanwords and reconstruction.

Summarizing our findings for the diphthong *au* in both stressed and unstressed positions, we see that inscriptions show that stressed *au* was stable in all areas studied, but a dialectal or rustic monophthongization to *o* is still evidenced by sporadic occurrences, especially in proper names, even in the late Vulgar Latin period of the fifth century. The simplification of stressed *au* to *a*, more common in early Latin, is encountered only once in a pagan inscription of Britain,

---

[93] Gaeng writes (p. 260) that "our inscriptional material seems to offer ample evidence of the apparent reduction of the diphthong /aw/ to /a/ before a stressed /u/ in the following syllable, although this phenomenon is exclusively limited to the proper names *Augustus/Augusta* and the name of the corresponding month."

dated A.D. 237, but this phenomenon, found in Sardinian and the Latin element in Albanian, has practically disappeared in epigraphical material. Unstressed initial *au* is likewise stable in inscriptions, but the monophthongization to *a* is a common occurrence in the single root *August-*. The sporadic monophthongization of initial *au* to *o* is found, but this change has its origin in a rustic pronunciation (*Oriclo* as a proper name for *Auriculo*) or is influenced by a dialectal *o* in the stressed syllable (*Clotoianus* for *Claudianus*, derived from *Clodius*).

In addition to the general conclusions given above, there are several changes that merit only slight attention. We have a case of initial *au* written as *ao* in *Faostina*, D. 2543N, Thabraca (Proconsularis), no date. This is probably a variant spelling for the diphthongal sound of /aw/. [94] This orthographic vacillation of *au* and *ao* is seen in Rumanian where *adăuga* and *adăoga* (= 'to add' from Latin *adaugēre* with change of conjugation) are both permissible.

There is a peculiar change of initial *au* monophthongizing to *e* and *u* in the words *Mesuleolus* (proper name), D. 3272C, *CIL* VIII 9815, Albulae (Mauretania Caesariensis), A.D. 444, and *musuleum*, D. 3680, *CIL* VIII 10,712, Hr.-Mabrek (Numidia), no date. Carnoy, in attempting to explain the form *maesoleum* (he also records *mesoleus* and *misolio*) writes (p. 101) that "*mausoleum* devait se réduire phonétiquement à *masoleum*, et il se pourrait donc aussi que *maesoleum* soit le résultat de quelque méprise commise ultérieurement par les demi-lettrés qui s'efforçaient de rétablir la diphtongue." Although this explanation may be satisfactory for the change of initial *au* to *ae* (or the vulgar *e*), it cannot, of course, explain the multiple forms that are found throughout Romania, such as, for example, our *musu-*

---

[94] Hoffmann, p. 72, gives the example of *Paoli* (= *Pauli*) from an African inscription, *CIL* VIII 10,479. He also gives (p. 72) the reverse phenomenon of *ao* spelled *au* to represent the diphthong, although of the three examples two cases result from the loss of an intervocalic consonant: *Brauniaco* (= *Bravoniaco*, *v* = *b*), *CIL* VIII 4800; *Fausa* (= *Favosa*), *CIL* VIII 6938, and *Laudicia* (= λαοδίχεια), *CIL* VIII 3151. Writing about the sound equivalency of the spellings *ao* and *au* on the basis of these examples, Hoffmann says (p. 72) that "sonum vocalium continuarum *ao* diphthongum *au* aequavisse efficitur ex his scripturis." It is interesting to note that we have in our corpus *Faosa*, D. 2862C, *CIL* VIII 21,745, Altava (Mauretania Caesariensis), A.D. 432. There is in our inscriptions an example of the monophthongization of initial *ao* to *a* in *Ladic(ena)*, D. 2201, *CIL* III 4220, Savaria (Pannonia Superior), no date.

leum, and *Musolus, masoleum,* adduced by Hoffman, from Africa; other forms are *moesoleum, masoleum, mansoleum, menseleum, musolu, muslie.* [95] It is true, however, that most of the changes of initial *au* in *mausoleum* do occur as *ae* or *e.* Since many examples of contamination with other words may come to the mind of the ingenious thinker, it seems best to follow Hoffman's advice (p. 72) and permit these exotic forms "linguarum Asiaticarum peritis explicandas."

---

[95] See Schuchardt, II, 321, for a complete listing.

CHAPTER V

SOME VOCALIC PHENOMENA

Prothesis

The prefixing of a vowel, usually *i*, more rarely *e*, before a word beginning with an *s* followed by a consonant (the impure *s*) is generally attributed to the second century A.D., although the first example of a prothetic vowel found in Latin inscriptions is the proper name *Ismurna*, recorded by Väänänen (p. 48) in his *Le Latin vulgaire des inscriptions pompéiennes*. [1] It is interesting to note that the

---

[1] For the dating of prothesis to the second century A.D., see Lindsay, p. 105; Bourciez, p. 48; Meyer-Lübke, *Einführung*, p. 157; Jackson, *Language*, p. 88; Grandgent, p. 98; Carnoy, p. 115; Lausberg, I, 343; Sommer, p. 293. Since *Ismurna* and *Izmaragdus*, the two oldest datable examples of prothesis, are both Greek proper names beginning with the consonant cluster *sm-*, Prinz, in his important article entitled "Zur Entstehung der Prothese vor s-impurum im Lateinischen," *Glotta*, XXVI (1938), questions (p. 113) whether "überhaupt die Prothese vor *sm* mit den übrigen Beispielen [s plus Tenuis] auf die gleiche Stufe gestellt werden kann." According to this scholar (pp. 113-14): "Zwischen den beiden Gruppen besteht zunächst der Unterschied, dass die Spirans in der Verbindung *sm* stimmhaft, bei *s* + Tenuis stimmlos war. Ferner war dem Lateinischen der Anlaut *sm* fremd, hingegen *s* + Tenuis ganz geläufig. So kann vor *sm* die Prothese unter anderen Voraussetzungen eingetreten sein als andersowo, was auch aus einigen Inschriften hervorzugehen scheint (cf. *CIL* VI 156 *Izmaragdus: Storax*; 13,413 *Ismyrnae: Scurrae*; 26,010 *Izmaragdis: Scirtia, Stabilio*). Die Ursache für das Entstehen der Prothese vor *sm* mag einerseits in der Erleichterung des ungewöhnlichen Anlautes, andererseits in analoger Einwirkung von Name, die mit ursprünglichem *Ism-* anlauteten (*Ismarus, Ismene* u.ä.), zu suchen sein. Unter diesen Umständen wird man diese Gruppe von den übrigen Fällen trennen müssen." Sommer also mentions (p. 293) that "in echtlat. Wörtern kommen nur *sc-, sp-, st-* vor."

Latin grammarians fail to take cognizance of the phenomenon of prothesis until St. Isidore of Spain in the seventh century A.D., nor is there any mention of it in the *Appendix Probi*. The cause of prothesis is usually considered a foreign influence or a spontaneous phonetic development. Two of the strongest proponents of an outside influence to account for the prothetic vowel are Schuchardt, who wrote (*Vokalismus*, II, 348):

> Vielleicht übten fremde Sprachen einen Einfluss auf das Vulgärlatein aus. Wenigstens darf man, wenn irgendwo, so hier einen solchen annehmen, da diese Lauteigenthümlichkeit nicht, wie fast alle anderen, durch allgemein-lateinische Analogieen vorbereitet erscheint. Wurde sie etwa mit dem Christenthum aus dem Orient nach Italien verpflanzt? Die Zeit, zu welcher sie aufkam, würde hiermit stimmen. Oder war sie — da die frühesten Belege zum grössten Theil Afrika angehören — aus einem einheimischen Dialekte . . . in die lingua rustica Afrikas übergegangen und hatte sich von hier aus weiter verbreitet?

and Prinz who, commenting on the most numerous occurrences of prothesis found at Rome as compared to other areas of Romania, wrote ("Entstehung," p. 114):

> Bekanntlich sind in der Haupstadt Leute aus allen Gegenden des weiten Reiches zusammengeströmt, die bei der Aussprache des Lateins schwerlich die Eigenart ihrer Muttersprache haben verleugnen können. So ist es möglich, dass beispielsweise die zahlreichen nach Rom gekommenen Semiten vor dem in ihrer Sprache ungewöhnlichen s- impurum einen prothetischen Vokal sprachen, wie ja auch die lateinischen mit s- impurum anlautenden Lehnwörter in den semitischen Sprachen einen solchen erhielten. [2]

---

[2] Although a Semitic influence appeared possible for Prinz, he also considered (p. 114) that "auch können Bewohner der Gegenden, in denen griechisches s- impurum mit Prothese gesprochen wurde, bei Übersiedlung nach dem Westen die Verbreitung der Prothese gefördert haben." Prinz, although admitting a strong Greek cultural and religious influence on Latin, warns (p. 107), however, that "das Griechische hat jedoch im allgemeinen keine Abneigung gegen anlautendes s-impurum gehabt, so auch noch die heutige griechische Volkssprache. Im Altertum findet sich im griechischen Sprachgebiet nur auf einem fest begrenzten Raume Prothese vor s-impurum und zwar in Kleinasien, von Phrygien südostwärts bis nach Syrien." Although this scholar considered a Punic influence from Northwest Africa also a

Most investigators, however, believe that prothesis arose as a spontaneous phonetic development, especially after a word ending in a consonant. [3] Lausberg wrote (I, 343), nevertheless, that "la prótesis de la vocal se produjo, como era de esperar, por razones de fonética sintáctica dentro del ritmo elocutivo después de consonante, así como al comienzo del ritmo elocutivo." Väänänen goes further and maintains (*Introduction*, p. 48) that "la prothèse, au lieu d'obéir à un principe d'euphonie (comme plus tard en italien), se produit aussi bien après une finale vocalique et au début de l'énoncé qu'après consonne finale." B. Löfstedt, after sifting the various points of view as to whether the prothetic vowel was utilized only after a word ending in a consonant or whether it also occurred after a word ending in a vowel or in initial position, concluded (p. 110):

> dass es nicht möglich ist, an Hand der Inschriften nach-zuweisen, dass die Prothese von Anfang an nur nach Kons. im Satzinlaut vorkam: sie begegnet in allen Provinzen schon früh sowohl am Satzanfang als auch (etwas seltener) nach Vokal. Dies scheint darauf hinzudeuten, dass diejenigen recht haben, die meinen, die Prothese komme von Anfang an sowohl im Satzanlaut als im Satzinlaut nach Kons. vor. [4]

We will give below a listing of the examples of prothesis found in our corpus of inscriptions and the conclusions that can be drawn from them.

From Dalmatia:

> *in hoc iseplucrum volveret super hoc corpus alium ponere,*
> ... D. 507, Salona, no date. [5]

---

strong possibility for the origin of the prothetic vowel, he concluded (p. 114) "dass nur Afrikaner die Prothese nach Rom verpflanzt haben, ist nich nachweisbar und auch kaum wahrscheinlich."

[3] Bourciez, p. 48; Sommer, p. 293; Carnoy, pp. 116-17.

[4] For a general synthesis of the problems inherent in prothesis, see B. Löfstedt, *Studien über die Sprache der Langobardische Gesetze* (Uppsala: Almquist und Wiksells, 1961), pp. 107-12.

[5] The prothetic *i* in *iseplucrum* is suspect; in addition to the fact that it precedes a single *s*, the sentence itself is lacking the conditional particle *si*. The stonemason may very well have confused the writing of this inscription. Skok does include this example in his *Pojave*, considering (p. 25) this as a case of prothesis before other consonants.

ancilla Balentes (= *Valentis*), *esponsa Dextri*, ... *D*. 3870,
CIL III 13,124, Salona, A.D. 426 or A.D. 430.
[*de*]*positio Superi ixtabu*[*l*]*a*[*ri*], *D*. 376, Rider, no date. [6]

We thus see that prothesis is existent but rare in the Latin inscriptions of Dalmatia. This is the conclusion also reached by Skok
in his more detailed study of Dalmatian inscriptions. [7] Bàrtoli in his
Das Dalmatische, however, considers (II, 349) prothesis as an important phenomenon in Vegliote: "Umgekehrt findet man im Veglio-
tischen manche wichtige Spur der vulgärlat. Prosthesis vor s +
Konson.: *espojur* '*spogliare*,' *istala* '*stalla*.' " When we look over
Bàrtoli's Index of Vegliote words, nevertheless, most words are found
with the impure *s* intact without any prothetic vowel: *skáina* '*schie-
na*,' *skirp* '*scarpa*,' *scrivru* '*scrivere*,' *skual*' '*scoglio*,' *spaica* '*spica*,'
spangro '*spingere*,' *sperájo* '*spero*,' *spiách* '*specchio*,' *spiaz* '*specie*,'
spusuot '*sposato*,' *stáign* '*stagno*,' *stajáun* '*stagione*,' *stiass* '*stesso*,'
strúota '*strada*,' *stur* '*stare*,' etc. Even in the transcription of Udina-
Burbur's (the last speaker of Vegliote) discourse, Bàrtoli does not
write any prothetic vowel, regardless of the surrounding environment.
Compare just a few examples taken at random of connected speech
where there is no prothetic vowel whether the preceding word ends
in a consonant or a vowel: (II, 27): "...*la traviérsa striáta* '*il
grembiule stretto*'; (p. 29): ...*per stur alégri* '*per stare allegri*'; *fenta
le skirp* '*fino alle scarpe*'; ...*el spuás* '*lo sposo*'; (p. 35): ...*le stal
del zíl* '*le stelle del cielo*'; (p. 43): ...*per fúr el spág per le skirp
'per fare lo spago per le scarpe*.' " Although, as we have seen, Dalmatian Latin inscriptions do show a sporadic case of a prothetic
vowel and the Romance language Vegliote likewise shows some vestiges

---

[6] The form *ixtabulari* may very well be *stabulari* with a prothetic *i* or
possibly stand for *ex stabulari*, or *ex tabulari*. Skok omits the word entirely
in his *Pojave*. Prinz gives it (p. 101) as an example of prothesis in his
"Entstehung." In his Indices to *Inscriptiones Latinae Christianae Veteres*,
Diehl gives this particular word as a variant of *stabulari*, but this is the only
example of this relatively low occupation found in his Christian inscriptions.
The form *tabularius* or a declined form, however, is found three times in
the Indices, one occurrence being precisely *Atilius Crescens*, *v.p.*, *ex tabulario
Palati*, ..., *D*. 285, *CIL* V 6182, Milan, no date. It appears that the form
in question, *ixtabulari*, is best taken as a variation of *ex tabulari*. See *supra*,
p. 83, for the change of short *e* to *i* in monosyllables.

[7] Skok, *Pojave*, p. 25: "I za protezu *e* i imamo dosta malo primjera."
("And with respect to prothesis of *e* and *i* we have rather few examples.")

of prothesis, it is noteworthy to point out that the Latin loanwords in Albanian do not show any indication of prothesis. [8] In fact, it appears that prothesis did not get a foothold beyond the Dalmatian coast, since Rumanian does not have this vocalic phenomenon nor do the inscriptions of the other Balkan provinces offer examples of prothesis. Mihăescu emphasized the regional nature of the distribution of prothesis when he wrote (p. 273) in his *Limba latină in provinciile dunărene ale imperiului român*: "Fenomenul [e plus s plus cons.] a ajuns pînă în Dalmația, dar n-a pătruns mai departe și a rămas necunoscut izvoarelor scrise din celelalte provincii dunărene." [9]

From Africa:

> ... *edifikberunt III ff. Maximianus, Istfanus et Mellosus*, D. 793, *CIL* VIII 12,035, Limasa (Byzacena), between A.D. 582-602. [10]
>
> *Istefanus fidelis bixit in pace ...*, D. 1593A, Sufetula (Byzacena), no date.
>
> *sancs Istefanus*, D. 2040d, *CIL* VIII 25,037, Carthage (Proconsularis), possibly A.D. 203.
>
> *isues* (= *spes*) *in deo*, D. 2236, *CIL* VIII 253, in the Plain of Sufetula (Byzacena), no date.
>
> *in ispe dei*, D. 2240, near Hammam-Sif in Tunisia, no date.
>
> *bono ispirito Mariniani deus refrigeret*, D. 2311, *CIL* VIII 8191, Rusicade (Numidia), no date.
>
> *bono qui iscribsit*, D. 2410c, Thamallula (Mauretania Sitifensis), no date.
>
> *m(emoria) Istefani*, D. 2843, *CIL* VIII 20,921, Tipasa, no date.
>
> *memoria Istefanie*, D. 2922A, *CIL* VIII 20,922, Tipasa, no date.
>
> *ispiritu* [sole word after pause], D. 3402B, Carthage (Proconsularis), no date.

---

[8] Gustav Meyer (p. 1049): "Prothetische Vokale gibt es im Albanesischen nicht."

[9] Translation: "The phenomenon [e plus s plus cons.] reached as far as Dalmatia, but did not penetrate further and remained unknown to the written sources of the other Danubian provinces." For other references to the lack of prothesis in Rumanian, see Densusianu, I, 93, and Rosetti, I, 110.

[10] The spelling *Istfanus* is probably the result of an omission of the stressed vowel through lack of space. In the same inscription we have *patrco* for the full form *patricio*.

ispiritu Cal[en]dionis in pa[ce]. ispiritu Fortunatas in pace, D. 3403B, Thabraca (Proconsularis), no date.
Istercolus senex, D. 2543N, Thabraca (Proconsularis), no date.
Ispensina vixit in pace . . . , D. 2675N, *CIL* VIII 150, Capsa (Byzacena), no date.
memoria innocentium Istablici, D. 3622N, *CIL* VIII 8640, Sitifis (Mauretania Sitifensis), no date.
. . . cui ispon[s]us fec. dom. [ete]rna p. CCCCLXXXIII, D. 3662, *CIL* VIII 21,788, Pomaria (Mauretania Caesariensis), A.D. 529.
d.m.s. Valerius Istefanus vit annis LV, D. 3762, *CIL* VIII 21,791, Pomaria (Mauretania Caesariensis), A.D. 589.
memoria Ispiaci Cerialis, D. 2054, *CIL* VIII 9866, Altava (Mauretania Caesariensis), not before A.D. 449.
Isttoracius, D. 1402N, *CIL* VIII 25,345, Africa, no date.

From the preceding examples, we see that the prothetic vowel *i-* is used seven times initially, six times after a vowel, four times after a consonant (one of the preceding words ending in an *m*), and two times after a pause. It is obvious that in African inscriptions the prothetic vowel *i-* does not occur solely after a word ending in a consonant, but is used in all environments. It is also important to note that once again the Latin of African inscriptions agrees with the vocalic system of Sardinian, which also has a prothetic vowel and which is also *i-*. [11]

What is striking in our investigation of prothesis is the complete lack of any example in the Latin inscriptions of Britain and the Balkans. Since there was not a single case of prothesis in our source book, *Roman Inscriptions of Britain,* a collection of 2,314 pagan inscriptions, we are faced with a serious regional differentiation when we compare the situation of the Latin of Britain with respect to prothesis with that of Africa. [12] Although both areas are classical in

---

[11] Wagner, "Lautlehre," pp. 55-56 "Wie schon im Lateinischen der späteren Kaiserzeit wird im Altsardischen vor s plus Kon. ein *i-* vorgeschlagen; . . . Heute ist die i-Prothese auf dem grössten Teile des Gebietes die Regel, vor allem in allen log. und nuor. Mundarten; nur im Camp. ist der i-Vorschlag nicht üblich. Man wird nicht fehlgehen, wenn man darin den Einfluss des Italienischen sieht und dann wieder des Gebrauchs der Hauptstadt auf die übrigen camp. Mda."

[12] The *Roman Inscriptions of Britain* by Collingwood and Wright contains practically all pagan inscriptions found on stone in this particular area; it is much more a complete collection of inscriptions than volume VII of the

nature, the Latin of Britain maintains its purity even more so than that of Africa, a linguistic reality that has been repeatedly observed throughout this work. Contrasting the existence of a prothetic vowel in other areas of Romania, Jackson writes (p. 88) that "the Latin loanwords in British show no sign of it." Modern Welsh has a prothetic vowel, namely y-, but this is a later development and is independent of the Vulgar Latin prothesis, since it appears only in Welsh and is absent in Cornish and Breton. [13] The Latin pagan inscriptions and loanwords into Brittonic corroborate each other in the conclusion that prothesis was absent in the Latin of Britain.

Although we did not find any examples of a prothetic vowel in the pagan or Christian inscriptions of the Balkans, our conclusion cannot be considered as conclusive since our corpus contains only 99 pagan inscriptions and 83 Christian inscriptions from this area (see *supra*, p. 47, for the respective number of inscriptions for each area studied). Prinz in his study of prothesis gives, however, figures for the occurrence of a prothetic vowel for the various areas taken from an extensive corpus of inscriptions. [14] We will give below Prinz' figures (p. 106) for examples of prothesis from the various areas of Romania to see whether a regional differentiation can be posited.

Area	No. of Examples of Prothesis From Pagan Inscrip.	No. of Examples of Prothesis From Christ. Inscrip.	Totals
Rome and Latium	34	73	107
Southern Italy and Sicily	7	4	11
Northern Italy and Gallia Cisalpina	3	4	7

Corpus Inscriptionum Latinarum devoted to *inscriptiones Britanniae* which contains only 1,355 inscriptions.

[13] Jackson, *Language*, p. 528.

[14] Prinz' figures are all taken from inscriptions, not from documents, since he says (p. 97) "eine solche [Untersuchung] muss vornehmlich auf den Inschriften fussen, denn aus dieser Quelle schöpfen wir das zuverlässigste Material für die lateinische Lautentwicklung in den ersten nachchristlichen Jahrhunderten."

Area	No. of Examples of Prothesis From Pagan Inscrip.	No. of Examples of Prothesis From Christ. Inscrip.	Totals
Gallia Transalpina and German Provinces	1	4	5
Spain	2	5	7
Northwest Africa	34	18	52
Dalmatia	0	2	2
Asia	22	0	22
Egypt	0	1	1

From the preceding table, we see that prothesis is conspicuously absent in the inscriptions from Britain and the Balkans (other than Dalmatia). [15] When we consider the lack of occurrences of a prothetic vowel in the inscriptions of Britain and the Balkans in addition to the absence of any prothetic vowel in the Latin loanwords in the Brittonic languages and Albanian, and the antipathy of Rumanian to a prothetic vowel, it appears that prothesis was not a general linguistic phenomenon throughout all of Romania.

It may be objected that the number of inscriptions varies greatly from region to region, that a certain word may appear more often in one area than another (such as *spes* or *spiritus* or the proper name *Stephanus*), or that the educational level of stonemasons may vary greatly throughout the Roman Empire with a resultant fluctuation

---

[15] Since final consonants fell in Italian and most words consequently ended in a vowel, a prothetic vowel is not generally used in Italian except after the prepositions *con, in, per,* and after *non* (*per iscritto, in iscuola* but *lo scritto, la scuola*), Lausberg is right in maintaining (II, 344) that "se generalizó la forma aprotética" in Italian; on the basis of the absence of a prothetic vowel in the Latin inscriptions of the inner Balkans, however, we must question this scholar's insistence that the aprothetic form was likewise generalized in Rumanian. It appears that a prothetic vowel never really took a foothold in the inner Balkans.

in the appearance of a prothetic vowel in epigraphical material. [16] Although it is undoubtedly true that there are more inscriptions from Rome and Africa (the *CIL* gives 39,340 for Rome up to the year 1933 and 28,085 for Africa up to 1916) than from the other provinces, the two examples of prothesis in all of the Balkans (both coming from Dalmatia) cannot be explained by a paucity of material since the *CIL* gives 15,220 inscriptions for all of the Balkans up to the year 1902. Since there are no examples of a prothetic vowel in inscriptions from Britain (the *CIL* gives 1,355 inscriptions while our *Roman Inscriptions of Britain* gives the higher number of 2,314 up to December 31, 1954), the complete absence of a prothetic vowel stands in strong contrast with the 107 occurrences found by Prinz for Rome and Latium, regardless of the numerical comparison.

The relative frequency of particular words beginning with an impure *s-* may be different according to the various regions of Romania, but this will have to be studied in detail before this factor assumes any importance in any investigation of prothesis.

The educational level of the populations and consequently of the stonemasons undoubtedly also differed according to the importance of schools and the social stratum of the inhabitants of the different regions. Although the lack of prothesis may be attributed to the classical nature of the Latin spoken in Britain, this theory breaks down for the numerous examples of a prothetic vowel found in the Latin inscriptions of Africa, an area also known for its educational centers of learning. [17] This reliance on a high educational level and a high social stratum of the inhabitants and stonemasons for the interpretation of the orthographic accuracy of epigraphic material is

---

[16] After mentioning these objections to an absolute acceptance of the figures for the occurrence of a prothetic vowel in inscriptions, Prinz concludes (p. 107) nevertheless, that "selbst unter Berücksichtigung dieser Faktoren bleibt das häufige Vorkommen der Prothese in Rom und besonders auf den heidnischen inschriften Nordwestafrikas auffällig." B. Löfstedt criticizes Prinz' figures because of a lack of comparative statistics for the various regions where prothesis is found. He writes (p. 107) that "zunächst muss betont werden, dass die von Prinz gegebenen Zahlen über die geographische Verbreitung der Prothese in Inschriften vom statistischen Gesichspunkt aus nicht ganz zuverlässig sind, da sie nich zu der Anzahl der auf uns gekommenen Inschriften in den verschiedenen Provinzen in Relation gesetzt worden sind."

[17] See *supra*, footnote 70, p. 55, for references to the intellectual climate of Africa in general and Carthage in particular.

completely demolished when we consider the problem of prothesis in the Balkans. Dacia, for example, was romanized by a lower social class and the lack of schools and literary centers for this area is well known. [18] In this particular Roman province where we should expect to find deviations from the Classical Latin norm precisely because of the educational and social factors, we see that in the case of prothesis inscriptional evidence points to the exact opposite of our expectations: the prothetic vowel is absent from the Latin of the Balkans. We can only conclude that the inscriptions are portraying an accurate picture of the spoken language of the area.

On the basis of the numerical disparity of the occurrences of a prothetic vowel in the various parts of Romania, a differentiation corroborated in many cases by the treatment of Latin loanwords into non-Latin languages, we conclude that prothesis was not a general phonetic phenomenon throughout the Latin lands, but that it differed according to the region where Latin was spoken or introduced. In some cases a prothetic vowel was prefixed to the impure *s* at an early date, in certain areas it evolved at a later date, probably in post-Latin times, and in other regions it can be said that it never gained a foothold. Prothesis is a phonetic phenomenon that is not limited to some of the Romance languages, but is very widespread throughout the most disparate languages of the world. [19] The results of our findings culled from the Latin inscriptions of various parts of Romania show that prothesis did not develop equally nor was its distribution the same in all of Romania, a conclusion that is at variance with statements of other investigators of this interesting problem. [20]

---

[18] See *supra*, p. 71, and footnotes 116 and 117 on p. 71, for references to the low social stratum of the speakers of Dacian Latin and the general lack of schools and literary centers of this region.

[19] For references to studies of prothesis in Prakrit, Greek, Armenian, Persian, the Semitic languages, Hungarian, Turkish, etc., see B. Löfstedt, p. 108.

[20] Compare the conclusion of Jeanneret (p. 29): "C'est sans doute par un hasard que cette voyelle prothétique n'est attestée que dans des *defixiones* de provenance africaine. Les inscriptions des autres provinces et les langues romanes sont là pour prouver qu'elle était également répandue dans toute la Romania." Schuchardt wrote (*Vokalismus*, II, 348): "Die Prosthese war allen Dialekten des Vulgärlateins gemein, da wir sie in den Denkmälern aller Gegenden ausgedrückt finden." Meyer-Lübke in his *Einführung* maintained (p. 157) that "seit dem 2. Jahrh. begegnet auf Inschriften aller Gegenden *is* plus Konsonant statt *s* plus Konsonant." It is very curious and even contradictory to see that Prinz, who in his "Entstehung" gave figures

Apheresis

The loss of an initial vowel generally before an impure *s*, a
phenomenon which is the opposite of prothesis, has been termed
a reverse spelling when it occurs in inscriptions. [21] Commenting on
the occurrence of apheresis in Late Latin texts, B. Löfstedt stresses
(p. 114) the non-spoken aspect of this phonetic change when he
writes: "Sie [Aphärese] ist sicher nicht als Reflex einer gesprochenen
Form zu betrachten, sondern als eine Hyperkorrektur: man war sich
dessen bewusst, dass man bisweilen vor *s* plus Kons. ein *i* oder *e*
zu Unrecht aussprache (und schrieb), und bei dem Bestreben, diesen
Fehler zu vermeiden, ist man gelegentlich zu weit gegangen." Attempting to explain apheresis in the Romance languages (Italian,
Rumanian, and Rheto-Romance), however, Lausberg subordinates the
loss of an initial vowel to the disappearance of the prothetic vowel
in these languages on the basis of analogy, a theory that would account for apheresis as a late development in the Romance languages
and only remotely connected to the Vulgar Latin situation. [22] It seems

---

for the occurrences of a prothetic vowel in the various parts of Romania,
figures that differed greatly from area to area (even the complete absence of
examples in some regions), could conclude (p. 115) "dass diese Prothese sich
über das ganze römische Reich verbreitet hat, zeigen auch die romanischen
Sprachen." Gaeng mentions the use of a prothetic vowel in his inscriptional
material, stating (p. 264) that "it appears most frequently in inscriptions
from Italy, particularly the area of Rome. On the other hand, this phenomenon is not particularly frequent in inscriptions from the Iberian area,
whereas in the area of Gaul only a single trustworthy example was found."
He does not generalize, however, on the differentiation of prothesis in all
of Romania.

[21] Prinz, "Entstehung," p. 104, writes: "Bisweilen findet man Inschriften,
auf denen ein ursprünglich anlautender Vokal vor *s* plus Konsonant ausge-
lassen ist. Gewöhnlich liegt in diesen Fällen umgekehrte Schreibung vor."

[22] Lausberg, II, 345: "La desaparición de la *i* protética en rumano, italiano y retorromano acarrea como consecuencia la desaparición analógica de
una *e* (*i*) originaria ante *s* plus consonante: *aestimare* italiano *stimare*, sobreselvano *stimar*; *excadere* rumano *scădeá*, italiano *scadere*, sobreselvano
scader; *excernere* italiano *scernere*; *Hispania* italiano *Spagna*." It must be
questioned, however, whether the prothetic vowel was in reality lost in
Rumanian since, on the basis of the complete omission of a prothetic vowel
in inscriptions of Dacia, it appears that the prothetic vowel never took root
in this part of Romania. See *supra*, p. 425 and footnote 15 for a discussion
of the prothetic vowel in Balkan inscriptions and prothesis in modern
Rumanian. Schuchardt had previously expressed the idea in his *Vokalismus*,
II, 372, that apheresis took place in Italian, Rumanian, and Rheto-Romance

difficult to conciliate the merely written hypercorrection of apheresis in inscriptions with the linguistic reality of a loss of an initial vowel in Italian, Rumanian, and Rheto-Romance. A more thorough study of this phenomenon throughout the whole Vulgar Latin period and in early Romance would be most welcome.[23] Examples of apheresis in inscriptional material are, unfortunately, far from extensive, a situation that renders the problem even more difficult. In our corpus of inscriptions we found only two occurrences of apheresis.

Compare the following examples of apheresis and the environment in which they are found:

> *suc* (= *sub*) [*cu*]*ius stantia* (= *instantia*)..., *D.* 2410,
> Thamalluma (Mauretania Sitifensis), no date,
> ...*ex prov. Span.* (= *Hispaniae*), *D.* 3842N, *CIL* III 9541,
> Salona (Dalmatia), no date.

Although the examples of apheresis are very scanty, they occur, nevertheless, in areas where we have already noted cases of a prothetic vowel prefixed to an impure *s-*. In fact, the spelling *Spania* for *Hispania* has been considered indirect proof of the existence of prothesis.[24] Taking Africa as an example of an area where prothesis was strongly evidenced, we can account for the numerical disparity between the relatively high number of examples of prothesis (19 examples of a prothetic *i* before impure *s*: see *supra*, pp. 422-23, for

---

after the loss of the prothetic vowel: "Diese Aphärese kömmt nur bei den Italienern, Walachen und Rhätoromanen vor, also bei denjenigen Nationen, welche die Prosthese verschmähen."

[23] Bourciez' conclusion (*Éléments*, p. 156) that "la tendance qui favorisait à l'initiale *s* plus cons. a été de bonne heure très forte en Italie," a conclusion based on very few examples, was strongly criticized by B. Löfstedt, who felt (p. 113) that "wenn man wahrscheinlich machen will, dass eine für das Italienische charakteristische Lautentwicklung sich bereits im späten Latein Italiens (wenigstens also eine Tendenz) nachweisen lässt, genügt es nicht, ein oder zwei herausgegriffene Beispiele aus spätlat. Texten aus Italien anzuführen, sondern man muss ein möglichst umfangreiches Material sowohl aus Italien wie aus einer anderen Provinz, z.B. Gallien, darauf hin untersuchen, ob die betreffende Erscheinung häufiger in Italien als anderswo vorkommt; nur wenn dem so ist, kann man mit einiger Sicherheit von einer im späten Latein Italiens vorhandenen Tendenz zu einer bestimmten Lautentwicklung sprechen."

[24] Prinz, "Entstehung," p. 104: "Wenn *Hispania, Hispanus* u.ä. bisweilen mit anlautendem *s* begegnen, so dürfen wir diese Fälle nicht ohne weiteres als indirekte Zeugnisse für die Prothese ansehen."

the inscriptional evidence) and the single case of apheresis by concluding that the prothetic vowel was a linguistic reality and the loss of a
correct initial vowel was a sporadic phenomenon that only rarely
occurred to the purist consciousness of a small number of overzealous
stonemasons. This would be the linguistic situation in those areas
where prothesis occurred during the Vulgar Latin period. In an
area, such as Britain, where prothesis did not take place, we would
not expect to find cases of apheresis. It is interesting to note that
in the pagan inscriptions of Britain, we find many examples of *Hispanus* or *Hispania* or even one example of *Ispani*, but no examples
of a *Span-* spelling in the collection *Roman Inscriptions of Britain:
Hisp(anus)*, *RIB* 159, first century, A.D.; *Ispani* (gen.), *RIB* 256, no
date; *His(panae)*, *RIB* 659, before A.D. 120; *His(anorum)*, *RIB* 814,
no date; *Hispa(norum)*, *RIB* 815, no date; *His(panorum)*, *RIB*
816, no date; *Hispano(rum)*, *RIB* 817, no date; *Hispa(norum)*,
RIB 822, no date; *His(panorum)*, *RIB* 823, either A.D. 123-26 or
133-37; *His(panorum)*, *RIB* 827, no date; *Hispano(rum)*, *RIB* 828,
no date; *His(panorum)*, *RIB* 829, no date; *Hispanorum*, *RIB* 968, no
date; *Hispanorum*, *RIB* 978, A.D. 222; *Hispanorum*, *RIB* 1334,
A.D. 238; *Hispanorum*, *RIB* 2213, probably first century A.D.

   The occurrence of an example of apheresis in the Latin inscriptions of Dalmatia calls for comment. The toponymic *Span.* (= *His-
paniae*) is the only example which we encountered and may be an
isolated case. [25] We have already seen that the examples of prothesis
in the Latin inscriptions of Dalmatia are very limited and very late
(only two examples of prothesis in Christian inscriptions according
to Prinz: see *supra*, p. 425) and since our theory is based on the
contention that apheresis can only take place as a purist reaction to
the linguistic reality of prothesis during the period of Vulgar Latin,
we conclude that Dalmatian Latin was a non-apheretic variant of
Latin. [26] Our theory is also bolstered by the fact that Vegliote does

---

[25] In his detailed study of Dalmatian inscriptions, Skok gives not even
a single example of apheresis, not even the form *Span.* which we have
recorded.

[26] We have already seen (*supra*, pp. 420-22) that prothesis was a very
sporadic phenomenon in the Latin inscriptions of Dalmatia and that Vegliote
belongs to those languages not having a prothetic vowel although a rare
example may have slipped in. It should be pointed out again that Bàrtoli's
statement (*Das Dalmatische*, II, 349): "Umgekehrt findet man im Veglioti-
schen manche wichtige Spur der vulgärlat. Prosthesis vor *s* + Konson.:

not partake in apheresis in native words. [27] The problem of apheresis in Dalmatian Latin may thus be elucidated by the quantitative-comparative method.

The Balkans pose a problem for the interpretation of apheresis. The Latin inscriptions of the Balkans, as has been pointed out, do not offer any examples of prothesis; our epigraphical material does not show any case of apheresis, which would follow our contention that apheresis is conditioned by the appearance of prothesis. In modern Rumanian, however, we do have many examples of apheresis, especially the loss of the vowel *e* from the Latin prefix *ex-* giving the morpheme *s-*, but prothesis caused by an impure *s-* is not present. Although Lausberg's explanation that the loss of the prothetic *i* brought about the analogical loss of an original *i* or *e* before *s* plus consonant holds true for Italian, an area where prothetic *i* is abundantly attested in inscriptions, this line of reasoning seems to be faulty when applied to Rumanian since the prothetic *i* appears to be completely absent in Latin inscriptions of the areas as well as in the modern language. The prime condition for the loss of the prothetic *i* in Italian was, according to Lausberg, the disappearance of the final consonants. [28] In Rumanian, however, although final Latin consonants were generally lost, this tendency for final consonants to fall was not as strong and presumably not as early as it was in Italian. [29] The conditions that prevailed for apheresis in Italian apparently were not duplicated for Rumanian. Although it is possible to account for some cases of apheresis in Rumanian through borrowings, onomatopoeia, and contamination with words of Slavic origin, there are too many popular words of Latin origin to overlook the obvious fact that apheresis is a common phenomenon in modern

---

espojur 'spogliare', istala 'stalla' " is completely contradicted by his own examples given in his glossary and the transcription of the discourse of Udina-Burbur, the last speaker of Vegliote.

[27] Bàrtoli, *Das Dalmatische*, II, 349: "Wichtig ist eher ein negatives Ergebnis: kein einheimisches Zeugnis bietet das Dalm. für die Aphäresis."

[28] Lausberg, I, 344: "En italiano, la desaparición de las consonantes finales desembocó asimismo en un desmoronamiento de las condiciones de la prótesis."

[29] *Ibid.*, p. 423: "Esta tendencia [for Vulgar Latin to avoid final consonants] se afianzó más que en ningún otro sitio en italiano, algo menos en español y portugués, menos todavía en rumano, provenzal y catalán y muy poco en el norte de la Romania occidental (francés, italiano del noroeste, retorromano)."

Rumanian. [30] We are inclined to view apheresis in Rumanian as a late development although its evolution can only be conjectured because of the paucity of material between the Vulgar Latin Balkan inscriptions generally ending in the sixth century and the emergence of Rumanian in documents of the sixteenth century.

In conclusion, we would like to emphasize the fact gleaned from our inscriptions that apheresis was a less common phenomenon than prothesis and to express the opinion that apheresis was conditioned by the prefixing of the prothetic vowel before an impure *s*. We consider the prothetic vowel as the linguistic reality and the prime cause for the loss of an initial vowel through a hypercorrection, for the most part written, but to a certain degree also in the spoken language. Without prothesis, however, apheresis would be improbable in Vulgar Latin. The opinion expressed by scholars that apheresis evolved in the Romance languages (namely, Italian, Rumanian, and Rheto-Romance) as the result of a loss of the prothetic vowel because of the dropping of final consonants and the analogical loss of the original vowel before impure *s* appears well established for Italian, but is not convincing for the other two, especially Rumanian. [31]

---

[30] Many modern Rumanian words showing apheresis, such as *straordinar*, come from the Italian, since as Puşcariu writes in his *Die rumänische Sprache* (p. 481): "Auch der italienische Einfluss ist ziemlich mächtig gewesen, besonders am Hofe des Brancoveanu und gegen Ende des 18. Jahrhunderts." Puşcariu even speaks of a prothetic *s-* rather than the apheresis of a vowel in his *Études* (p. 339): "De telles racines onomatopéiques peuvent s'adjoindre un s- prothétique. A côté de la racine *far-*, avec la variante *for-*, nous avons les variantes *sfar* et *sfor-*." In addition to the immense influence of the Slavic languages on Rumanian vocabulary, there are cases where a contamination of a Slavic word with the Latin produces the initial cluster *s* plus consonant, an initial sound formation that is common in both Slavonic and Rumanian. Puşcariu writes (*Die rumänische Sprache*, p. 351): "Manchmal hat sich das slawische Wort über das lateinische gelegt weil dieses eine ähnliche Gestalt hatte. So hat *sfânt* (slaw. *sventu*) das alte *sân* (lat. *sanctus*) ersetzt."

[31] We are, of course, not discussing the cases of apheresis caused by a false separation of the definite article, a phenomenon that is frequent in Italian and Rumanian. Compare, for example, the Italian *guglia* < *acucula*, *bottega* < *apotheca*, etc. It must be remembered, however, that the definite article is postpositive in Rumanian, which complicates the problem. Some forms are quite general in Romance, as evidenced by the Romance developments of the originally Greek *apotheca*: in addition to the Italian *bottega*, we have the French *boutique* and the Spanish *bodega*. Schuchardt generalizes (*Vokalismus*, II, 378) the apheresis of a vowel before consonants other than the impure *s* as "gemeinromanisch." For a general discussion of all types

Syncope

Syncope, the loss of an unaccented vowel, is a linguistic phenomenon that has occurred throughout the history of Latin from its prehistoric stage to its modern counterparts in the Romance languages. [32] The main reason for this vocalic loss is strongly expressed by Sturtevant when he writes (p. 177) that "such loss of vowels is known to occur in the unaccented syllables in languages that have a strong stress accent, and it is not known to occur under any other circumstances. [33] Since both the syncopated and unsyncopated forms occur simultaneously on occasion, the rate of speech must also be a factor in the loss or maintenance of the unaccented vowel. [34] An interesting facet of the problem of syncope is the fact that only posttonic syncope was possible in preliterary Latin since the accent was on the initial syllable, a situation that was probably inherited from Primitive Italic. [35] It was not until the Latin accent changed from an initial stress accent to the penultimate accentuation that both a pretonic as well as posttonic syncope could be possible. [36]

of apheresis with abundant examples, see Schuchardt, *Vokalismus*, II, 365-84. For apheresis in Romance other than before impure *s*, see Lausberg, I, 293. For apheresis in Italian, see Pei, *Italian Language*, pp. 39-40.

[32] Lindsay, p. 172; Väänänen, *Introduction*, p. 41.

[33] This same idea is emphasized by Lindsay who states (p. 107): "The syncope or suppression of an unaccented vowel is a common feature of languages which have a stress accent, and is carried to the greatest length by the languages whose stress accent is most powerful." See also Väänänen, *Pompéiennes*, p. 42.

[34] Niedermann, p. 32; Sommer, p. 136; Väänänen, *Pompéiennes*, p. 42; Puşcariu, *Études*, p. 234. Rapid speech is best illustrated in the popular, familiar style, characteristic of the lower social classes, while slower, more careful pronunciation would be the appanage of the more cultured, higher social classes. A slow, overly deliberate speech can also be considered affected as seen by the anecdote attributed to Emperor Augustus concerning the unsyncopated word "calidus" as recorded in Quintilian (Inst. I, 6, 19): "sed Augustus quoque in epistulis ad C. Caesarem scriptis emendat, quod is 'calidum' dicere quam 'caldum' malit, non quia id non sit Latinum, sed quia sit otiosum." (Quoted from Niedermann, p. 32.)

[35] Sturtevant, p. 178; Lindsay, p. 172; Niedermann, p. 13.

[36] Lindsay, p. 172. It is interesting to note that of the multiple cases of syncope recorded in the *Appendix Probi*, only one pertains to pretonic syncope, the others all dealing with posttonic syncope, a situation that has been completely ignored by scholars. Compare, for example, the one case of pretonic syncope in the *Appendix Probi*, (202) *constabilitus non constablitus*, with the following examples of posttonic syncope: (3) *speclum*, (4)

Since syncope was probably dialectal in ancient Italy and with the passing of time syncope increased to the point where the modern Romance languages show a distinct cleavage in their preference for a proparoxytonic or a paroxytonic rhythm, scholars have wondered whether this differentiation in the Romance languages, Eastern Romance (Rumanian, Italian, eastern Rheto-Romance) and Sardinian called "proparoxytonic" and Western Romance (French, Spanish, Provençal, Catalan, Portuguese, and western Rheto-Romance) characterized as "paroxytonic," had its origins in the Latin period. [37] The question was already enunciated by Pirson who comments (p. 48) that,

> ... le provençal et le français se différencient surtout des autres langues romanes en ce qu'ils ont généralement supprimé toutes les voyelles posttoniques ou protoniques non initiales. On est, par conséquent, en droit de se demander si une certaine prédilection pour les formes syncopées ne distinguait pas déjà le latin de la Gaule du latin des autres provinces.

Although this scholar prefers to wait for a comparative study of syncope in all parts of Romania before coming to a definite conclusion, he considers the possibility of "une différence locale," especially since, as he reminds us (p. 48) "l'accent celtique aurait eu une force

---

masclus, (5) vetulus non veclus, (6) vitulus non viclus, (7) vernaclus, (8) articlus, (9) baculus non vaclus, (10) anglus, (11) iuglus, (35) iuvencus non iuvenclus, (53) calda, (54) frigida non fricda, (83) auris non oricla, (111) oclus, (130) tabla, (133) fax non facla, (142) stablum, (167) capitulum non capiclum, (171) neptis non nepticla, (172) anus non anucla, (200) tribla, (201) virdis, (215) vapulo non baplo. The conclusion can be drawn that posttonic syncope at the time of writing of the Appendix Probi, the third or fourth centuries A.D., was undoubtedly more common and usual than pretonic syncope, a situation that may be significant in any discussion of syncope in the Romance languages.

[37] For syncope as a dialectal manifestation in ancient Italy, see Lindsay, p. 170; Väänänen, Introduction, p. 41. It is also well known that Oscan and Umbrian had even more syncope than Latin. For a summary of syncope in the various Romance languages, see Lausberg, I, 301-07. See also Elcock, pp. 41-42, for the division of Eastern and Western Romance on the basis of proparoxyton and paroxyton tendencies. Bourciez, pp. 143-44, also insists on the opposition of East and West Romance as the result of the loss or maintenance of the posttonic vowel.

exspiratoire beaucoup plus considérable que l'accent latin." [38] An attempt to investigate syncope throughout all of Romania on the basis of a comparative study of the epigraphical material available was made by Cross in his work entitled *Syncope and Kindred Phenomena in Latin Inscriptions.* He came to the important conclusion (p. 93) that "not only are the various regions very much in agreement, but the occurrence of syncopation or short forms seems to clash with the stated classification of the Romance languages." From his study, Cross also arrived at the conclusion (p. 99) that "in general, throughout the whole of the Roman world..., there is a surprising lack of syncope." [39] Since Cross' study was a first attempt at a comparative analysis of syncope, it does not seem presumptuous for us to investigate the same phenomenon so as to see whether we arrive at the same conclusions as he. [40] We will direct our attention mainly to pretonic and posttonic syncope as found in our corpus of inscriptions. The problem is compounded by the inability, at times, to decide whether a loss of a vowel is really due to syncope or whether it is a simple case of an abbreviated form. The Romance languages and the Latin loanwords into non-Romance languages are a great help in our discussion of syncope in the various regions of the Romance Empire.

Posttonic Syncope

Africa

> *domni*, D. 234, Rusguniae (Mauretania Caesariensis), no date.

---

[38] Note that Pirson is willing to ascribe Celtic linguistic habits to the Latin of Gaul if syncope should be found to be more prevalent in this area than others of Romania. Compare also the explanation of Elcock for the maintenance of the posttonic vowel in Eastern Romance (p. 41): "In a large part of Romania, particularly to the east, the process [of syncope] continued no farther, the consonantal groupings which would have resulted being presumably repudiated through local habits of articulation."

[39] A strong criticism of Cross' work was lodged by Väänänen in his *Le Latin vulgaire des inscriptions pompéiennes*, p. 42, footnote 2: "...la chronologie est négligée; qui pis est, comme l'auteur ne définit point son sujet, il lui arrive de rassembler des matériaux qui reflètent des phénomènes linguistiques disparates."

[40] Cross writes (p. 8): "The comparison which I have undertaken here does not seem to have been seriously attempted before. The standard works cited in the bibliography and the works of other scholars and investigators lack systematic and comparative tables of syncope. Further, works like those of Pirson and Carnoy deal with the Latin of one region only."

Veglus (assuming it to be from *Vetulus*), *D.* 311, *CIL* VIII 8346, Cuicul (Numidia), no date. [41]

domni, D. 807, *CIL* VIII 8805, Zabi (Mauretania Sitifensis), no date.

deposte, D. 1570, *CIL* VIII 20,277, Satafi (Mauretania Sitifensis), A.D. 299.

domno, D. 1835, *CIL* VIII 8429, near Sitifis (Mauretania Sitifensis), no date.

domnus, D. 2036, Masclianis, no date.

domni, D. 2065, *CIL* VIII 10,693, near Theveste (Proconsularis), no date.

Maricl(u)s, D. 2092, *CIL* VIII 16,396, Aubuzza (Proconsularis), no date. [42]

domni, D. 2117a, Cuicul (Numidia), no date.

domni, D. 2117b, Cuicul (Numidia), no date.

Oriclo (= *Auriculo*), *D.* 2522, *CIL* VIII, 13,821, Carthage (Proconsularis), no date. [43]

copre (= *corpore*), *D.* 2773, *CIL* VIII 16,740, near Theveste (Proconsularis), no date. [44]

Domn(i)c(us), D. 28, *CIL* VIII 4354, near Casas Numidarum, A.D. 578-82. [45]

Repostus, D. 2543N, Thabraca (Proconsularis), no date.

Vernacla, D. 2862N, *CIL* VIII 23,053r, Uppena, no date. [46]

From the above examples, excluding *copre* which is probably an abbreviation, we see that posttonic syncope generally took place with the vowels *i, u*. To give an idea of the extent to which syncope took place in the Latin of African inscriptions, we offer the following tables.

---

[41] Cf. *Appendix Probi*, (5) *vetulus non veclus.*

[42] Although the form *Maricl(u)s* may very well be a case of the diminutive ending -*culus* syncopated to -*clus*, it is suspect. The inscription in which it is found consists mainly of a list of proper names, many of which are written in an abbreviated form. There is also a line over the *cl*, normally used to indicate that the word in question is an abbreviation.

[43] Cf. *Appendix Probi*, (83) *auris non oricla.*

[44] The form *copre* for *corpore* is very unlikely. It is found in the phrase *exibit de copres.* Diehl writes in his notes to this inscription that the phrase probably stands for *de corpore suo*, probably a case of an abbreviation. He also writes (II, 50) that it may also stand for *exib. id. Decembres* or *Octobres.*

[45] *Domn(i)c(us)* is probably derived from the syncopated form *Domnus.* If we started with the unsyncopated *dominicus*, the form *domnicus* would show loss of an accented vowel, a phonetic impossibility.

[46] Cf. *Appendix Probi*, (7) *vernaculus non vernaclus.*

Syncope of Posttonic i

Africa	Century	Unsyncopated Form	Syncopated Form	% Of Sync.
	3rd.	11	1	8.3
	4th.	48	0	0.0
	5th.	34	0	0.0
	6th.	42	1	2.3
	7th.	3	0	0.0
	n.d.	298	8	2.6
	Totals:	436	10	2.2

When we take into consideration the total number of unsyncopated forms, we conclude that posttonic *i* generally remained. The single word *domnus* (and its derivative *Domn(i)c(us)*) exceptionally show the loss of posttonic *i* as seen by the following table:

Century	domin-	domn-	% Syncope
4th.	2	0	0.0
6th.	2	1	33.3
n.d.	25	7	21.9
Totals:	29	8	21.6

A surprising fact about the word *domnus* (and its various derivatives) is that it is not mentioned in the *Appendix Probi*, a document, as we have seen, that criticized many posttonic syncopes, most of which having reflexes in the Romance languages. This same situation holds true for the derivatives of *postus* which we recorded: *deposte* and *Repostus*. The best explanation to give for this omission of such common forms in the *Appendix Probi* is to consider that they were so widespread and common that they were considered regular and unworthy of any particular mention. [47] The other posttonic syncopes in the *Appendix Probi*, although common as evidenced by the Romance languages, had not acquired, however, the aura of respectability, at least in the mind of a critical Latin grammarian.

---

[47] The forms *domnus* and *domna* are attested in Plautus and Terence, as well as in Pompeian inscriptions; see Väänänen, *Pompéiennes*, p. 43, and Bourciez, p. 36.

Syncope of Posttonic u

Africa	Century	Unsyncopated Form	Syncopated Form	% Of Syn.
	3rd.	5	0	0.0
	4th.	5	0	0.0
	5th.	4	0	0.0
	6th.	4	0	0.0
	n.d.	52	4	7.1
	Totals:	70	4	5.4

Of the four examples of posttonic syncope of short *u*, three pertain to the loss of the *u* in the diminutive ending -*clus: Maricl(u)s* (possibly only an abbreviation), *Oriclo*, and *Vernacla*. The other example is the change of the ending -*tulus* to -*clus* (or -*glus*) in *Veglus* from *Vetulus*. Although the original Indo-European *-tlo-* was really instrumental, the termination -*clu*, derived from the full form -*culu* through an epenthetic *u*, was confused with the diminutive -*clu*. [48] We thus see that posttonic *u* in the Latin inscriptions of Africa is generally maintained, although the diminutive ending -*clu* and the instrumental -*clu* arising from an original *-tlo* > -*culu* are seen in the syncopated forms, a situation of general Vulgar Latin as evidenced by the numerous cases of the syncopated form of the diminutive ending -*clu* and the change of -*tulu* to -*clu* in the *Appendix Probi*: (4) *masculus non masclus*, (7) *vernaculus non vernaclus*, (8) *articulus non articlus*, (35) *iuvencus non iuvenclus*, (83) *auris non oricla*, (133) *fax non facla*, (171) *neptis non nepticla*, (172) *anus non anucla*, and (5) *vetulus non veclus*, (6) *vitulus non viclus*, (167) *capitulum non capiclum*.

Britain (Pagan)

Decmus, RIB 240, Wood Eaton, Islip (Oxon.), no date. [49]
Domna, RIB 323, Caerleon (Isca Silurum), Monmouthshire, no date.

---

[48] In Plautus, the instrumental -*clus* is distinguished from the diminutive -*culus* as we are reminded by Lindsay, p. 175, and Väänänen, *Introduction*, p. 43.

[49] Although *Decmus* may be a simple abbreviation of the proper name *Decimus*, the syncopated numerical adjectives *decmus* and *decmo* are both found in the same pagan inscription from Rome, *CIL* 12 1014.

piissma, *RIB* 369, *CIL* VII 126, Caerleon (Isca Silurum), Monmouthshire, second century.

mintla (= *mentula*), *RIB* 631, *CIL* VII 204, Adel (Yorkshire), no date.[50]

Decmus, *RIB* 1396, *CIL* VII 542, Hadrian's Wall: Rudchester (Vindovala), Northumberland, n.d.

Procli, *RIB* 1570, *CIL* VII 625, Hadrian's Wall: Carrawburgh to Housesteads, Northumberland, no date.[51]

Ercl[i] (= *Hercli* from *Herculi*), *RIB* 1781, *CIL* VII 751, Hadrian's Wall: Carvoran (Magnis), Northumberland, no date.

Hercl(i), *RIB* 2177, *CIL* VII 1114, Auchendavy (Scotland), no date.

There are several examples of the Celtic deity *Vitiris* spelled with a loss of the posttonic vowel:[52]

Vetri, *RIB* 1335, *CIL* VII 511, Hadrian's Wall: Benwell (Condercum), Northumberland, no date.

Vitirbus, *RIB* 1336, *CIL* 512, Hadrian's Wall: Benwell (Condercum), Northumberland, no date.

Votri, *RIB* 1458, *CIL* VII 583, Hadrian's Wall: Chesters (Cilurnum), Northumberland, no date.

Hvitri, *RIB* 1603, Housesteads (Vercovicium), Northumberland, no date.

We did find, however, forty-two examples where the posttonic vowel was kept in this particular name.

---

[50] The syncopated form *mentla* is also found in the Pompeian inscriptions (Väänänen, *Pompéiennes*, p. 44). Cf. also Italian *minchia*, Logudorese *minkra*.

[51] Väänänen (*Pompéiennes*, p. 44) records 9 examples of syncopated *Procl-* and 28 cases of the unsyncopated *Procul-*. The probability that this syncope was a characteristic of general Vulgar Latin can be seen by the statement made by Lewis and Pedersen in their *A Concise Comparative Celtic Grammar* pertaining to the Latin of Britain. They state (p. 56) that "The Vulgar Latin known to the Celts did not vary considerably from Class. Latin." Among the deviations from Latin, however, they mention that "the ending *-ulus* after a cons. became *-lus*."

[52] For a discussion of this rather mysterious Celtic deity, see Collingwood-Myres, pp. 268-69. The name seems to have been confused in the minds of its humble worshippers with the Latin *veter*, the dedication *deo veteri* 'to the old god' thus being used instead of *deo Vitiri*. The worship of this particular Celtic god became popular in the third century A.D. Blair considers the spelling of this deity as *Veteres* in his *Roman Britain and Early England* (New York: Norton and Company, 1963), p. 139.

When we consider the relationship between the number of examples of loss of posttonic i and u in the pagan inscriptions of Britain, we find that syncope was not a common phenomenon. Compare the following tables:

Syncope of Posttonic i

Britain	Century	Unsyncopated Form	Syncopated Form	% Of Syn.
(Pagan)	1st.	10	0	0.0
	2nd.	21	1	4.8
	3rd.	36	0	0.0
	4th.	3	0	0.0
	n.d.	125	7	5.3
	Totals:	195	8	3.9

Syncope of Posttonic u

Britain	Century	Unsyncopated Form	Syncopated Form	% Of Syn.
(Pagan)	1st.	2	0	0.0
	2nd.	2	0	0.0
	3rd.	16	0	0.0
	4th.	0	0	0.0
	n.d.	40	4	9.1
	Totals:	60	4	6.3

When we take into consideration the fact that of the cases of syncope recorded some are of foreign names, others may possibly be abbreviations, it is clear that syncope was not a general practice in the Latin of the pagan inscriptions of Britain. Those clear cases of syncope belong to general Vulgar Latin.

It is interesting to note that the doublets *balineum* and *balneum* exist in the pagan inscriptions of Britain. [53] Although the full form *balineum,* borrowed from the Greek βαλανεῖον, is exclusively found

---

[53] We found three examples of the unsyncopated form: *balineum*, *RIB* 605, *CIL* VII 287, Lancaster (Lancs.), A.D. 262-66; *balineum*, *RIB* 730, *CIL* VII 273, Bowes (Lavatrae), Yorkshire, prior to A.D. 198, and *balineo*, *RIB* 1212, *CIL* VII 984, Risingham (Habitancum), Northumberland, no date, and two examples of the syncopated form: *balneum*, *RIB* 791, Cliburn (Westm.), no date, and *balneum*, *RIB* 1091, *CIL* VII 445, Lanchester (Longovicium), Co. Durham, A.D. 238-44.

in Plautus and Terence, the syncopated *balneum* becomes common from the time of Varro and Cicero (the first century B.C.).[54] It would appear that the full form in pagan inscriptions of the second and third centuries A.D. should be considered an archaic spelling. Väänänen's remark (*Introduction*, p. 43) that "le succès de la forme syncopée [balneum], où il y a à noter que la voyelle atteinte était porteuse de l'accent, est sans doute dû à l'usage fréquent du mot dans la langue de tous les jours, pour désigner une institution populaire entre toutes, ainsi qu'au fait qu'il s'agit d'un mot d'emprunt" is vitiated by his insistence on the syncope of the stressed vowel. This Greek borrowing entered Latin at an early date when the Latin accent was still on the initial syllable and the syncope that took place was the result of the loss of a posttonic vowel.

We have an interesting example of the loss of posttonic *i* in a Christian inscription of Britain in the noun *multitudnem*, *CIIC* 391, Penllech (County of Carnarvon), Wales, attributed to the sixth century.[55] We present below a summary of the treatment of posttonic *i* and *u* in Christian inscriptions to give a fuller picture of syncope or rather the lack of syncope in later inscriptions of Britain.

Syncope of Posttonic i

Britain	Century	Unsyncopated Form	Syncopated Form	% Of Syn.
(Christ.)	4th.	1	0	0.0
	5th.	1	0	0.0
	6th.	4	1	20.0
	7th.	3	0	0.0
	n.d.	7	0	0.0
	Totals:	16	1	5.9

---

[54] For a discussion of the accentuation and attestations of both *balineum* and *balneum*, see Lindsay, pp. 173-74.

[55] Although the loss of posttonic *i* in *multitudnem* may be due simply to the omission of a ligatured *i* in the form of an extended arm of the *n* or to an oversight on the part of the stonemason, it should be noted that the change of -*túdine* to -*túdne* is recorded twice in Diehl's *Altlateinische Inschriften: Valetudne* in inscriptions 206 and 207 of his collection, p. 21, corresponding to *CIL* 12 390 and *CIL* 12 391.

Syncope of Posttonic u

Britain	Century	Unsyncopated Form	Syncopated Form	% Of Syn.
(Christ.)	5th.	2	0	0.0
	6th.	3	0	0.0
	n.d.	1	0	0.0
	Totals:	6	0	0.0

We thus see that our one example of syncope of posttonic *i* is an isolated case, but since the total number of occurrences of posttonic *i* and *u* is not very great, it is difficult to generalize on the treatment of posttonic *i* and *u* in Christian inscriptions of Britain.

Dalmatia

> *domnus, D.* 2426, *CIL* III 10,190, Podgorica near Doclea, no date. [56]
> *post(a), D.* 2934, Salona, no date.
> *Ursicli* (bis), *D.* 3834, *CIL* III 2704, Tragurium (Troghir), no date.
> *tumlum, D.* 3363, *CIL* III 9623, Salona, no date.
> [*Do*]*mnicae, D.* 4455, *CIL* II 9567, Salona, n.d.
> *depostio* (= *depositio,* nom. sing.), *D.* 3835C, *CIL* III 9508, Salona, A.D. 382. [57]

To get a complete picture of posttonic syncope in this area we are giving the following tables:

---

[56] This seems to be an example of the syncopated form used to designate God rather than the more usual full form *Dominus,* the shortened *domnus* reserved as a title of respect for persons of high birth other than God or the Lord. Väänänen wrote (*Introduction,* p. 43) that "les inscriptions chrétiennes restituent la forme originale *dominus* pour désigner Dieu." The reference to the Lord is clearly seen in context: *domnus Laiarum* (= *Lazarum*) *resuscitat.*

[57] A posttonic syncope would have had to occur in the root *pos(i)tus* before the derivative *depostio* was formed. A loss of the *i* in the full form *depositio* would mean the loss of a stressed vowel, a phonetic impossibility.

Syncope of Posttonic i

Dalmatia	Century	Unsyncopated Form	Syncopated Form	% Of Syn.
	4th.	20	1	4.8
	5th.	13	0	0.0
	6th.	4	0	0.0
	n.d.	121	3	2.4
	Totals:	158	4	2.5

Syncope of Posttonic u

Dalmatia	Century	Unsyncopated Form	Syncopated Form	% Of Syn.
	4th.	5	0	0.0
	5th.	4	0	0.0
	6th.	4	0	0.0
	n.d.	29	3	9.4
	Totals:	42	3	6.7

Analyzing the above tables, we concludes that syncope was not a strong tendency in the Latin inscriptions of Dalmatia. Those examples of posttonic syncope of *i, u,* the only vowels syncopated, are either the same examples found in other areas or exhibit the same consonantal environment in which the vowel is lost. The posttonic syncope found in Dalmatian inscriptions is of the general Vulgar Latin variety.

Balkans (Pagan)

Valdio, Kal. 380, *CIL* III 14,434, Silistra (Durosturum), Moesia Inferior, no date. [58]

---

[58] We are assuming that *Valdio* is the dative singular of the proper name *Valdius,* a derivation from *Validius* already syncopated, the latter derived from the adjective *validus.* The adverb *valde* can be seen in Plautus. The form *Valdio* must be from the syncopated *Valdius* since the loss of the *i* from the full form *Validius* would have been a syncope of a stressed vowel, a phonetic impossibility. For a similar process in the formation of the proper names *Domn(i)c(us)* and *[Do]mnicae,* see *supra,* p. 436 (footnote 45), and p. 442. It is surprising that Diehl does not give the proper names *Validius, Valdius, Validus,* or *Valdus* in his Indices in Vol. III of his *Inscriptiones Latinae Christianae Veteres.*

titlum, Kal. 421, *CIL* III 14,413, Tetewen, Moesia Inferior, no date.

The following tables will give an overall picture of posttonic syncope in the pagan inscriptions of the Balkans:

Syncope of Posttonic i

Balkans	Century	Unsyncopated Form	Syncopated Form	% Of Syn.
(Pagan)	1st.	1	0	0.0
	2nd.	9	0	0.0
	3rd.	7	0	0.0
	4th.	8	0	0.0
	n.d.	27	1	3.6
	Totals:	52	1	1.9

Syncope of Posttonic u

Balkans	Century	Unsyncopated Form	Syncopated Form	% Of Syn.
(Pagan)	1st.	0	0	0.0
	2nd.	0	0	0.0
	3rd.	3	0	0.0
	4th.	1	0	0.0
	n.d.	11	1	8.3
	Totals:	15	1	6.3

From the above tables we see that posttonic syncope was not a regular change in the pagan inscriptions of the Balkans.

Balkans (Christian)

> *domnum, D.* 2181, *CIL* III 10,233, Sirmium (Pannonia Inferior), no date.
> *domna, D.* 2445, *CIL* III 597, Beroea (Macedonia), no date.
> *Domna, D.* 3314, *CIL* III 7584, Tomi (Thrace), no date.
> *Done* (= *dominae*), *D.* 478, *CIL* III 14,207, Stara Sagora (Thrace), no date. [59]

---

[59] According to Kalinka, *Antike Denkmäler in Bulgarien*, p. 332, *Done* is the "lautliche Fortbildung aus *Dom(i)nae* (Dativ)." Diehl considers it (I, 101) a "nomen barbarum." The change of *-m'n* to *-n-* is more an Italian development than Rumanian, where the *-mn-* remains.

Compare the following tables for posttonic syncope in the Christian inscriptions of the Balkans:

Syncope of Posttonic i

Balkans	Century	Unsyncopated Form	Syncopated Form	% Of Syn.
(Christ.)	4th.	7	0	0.0
	5th.	2	0	0.0
	6th.	0	0	0.0
	n.d.	49	4	7.5
	Totals:	58	4	6.5

Syncope of Posttonic u

Balkans	Century	Unsyncopated Form	Syncopated Form	% Of Syn.
(Christ.)	4th.	2	0	0.0
	n.d.	13	0	0.0
	Totals:	15	0	0.0

We see that posttonic syncope is not a strong tendency in the Christian inscriptions of the Balkans, and the only example of a loss of a posttonic *i* occurs in the word *dom(i)nus*, once again a syncope belonging to the general Vulgar Latin type.

Pretonic Syncope

Although pretonic syncope is usually thought of as the loss of an intertonic vowel, the vowel found between the primary and secondary accents, we do have several examples of the loss of a pretonic initial vowel that merit our attention. Very often, of course, it is simply an orthographic loss as the result of an abbreviation. This is probably the case of the noun *dsciplinae*, D. 746, *CIL* VIII 20,162, Cuicul (Numidia), no date, since the resulting initial consonant cluster does not fit into the overall phonological system of Latin. [60]

---

[60] For a study investigating the relationship between the consonantal distribution of environments in which syncope is found to the phonological system of consonantal distribution in Vulgar Latin, see James M. Anderson, "A Study of Syncope in Vulgar Latin," *Word*, XXI (1965), 70-85.

Compare, however, the following examples of loss of an initial
vowel in which a real phonetic loss may be a possibility:

From Britain:

> *Vleriani* (= *Valeriani*), *RIB* 1711, *CIL* VII 720, Hadrian's
> Wall: Chesterholm (Vindolanda), Northumberland, no
> date.
> *Vle(rio)* (= *Valerio*), *RIB* 2237, *CIL* VII 1154, milestone
> about 3 miles north of Cambridge beside the road to
> Huntingdon, A.D. 306-07.
> *Blatucairo* (= *Belatucadro*), *RIB* 774, *CIL* VII 295, Brougham
> (Brocavum), Westmorland, no date. [61]
> *Blatucadro*, *RIB* 1776, *CIL* VII 745, Hadrian's Wall: Car-
> voran (Magnis), Northumberland, n.d.

From Africa:

> *Klendas*, *D.* 189, *CIL* VIII 20,410, Sitifis (Mauretania Si-
> tifensis), A.D. 454.
> *krissimo* (= *carissimo*), *D.* 3687, *CIL* VIII 9975, Numerus
> Syrorum (Mauretania Caesariensis), A.D. 392.
> *klendas*, *D.* 3688, *CIL* VIII 9977, Numerus Syrorum, A.D.
> 398.
> *klendas*, *D.* 3689, *CIL* VIII 9982, Numerus Syrorum, A.D.
> 416.
> *klenda*, *D.* 4192, *CIL* VIII 21,804, Numerus Syrorum, no
> date.
> *kres[s]ume* (= *carissimae*) *D.* 4192A, *CIL* VIII 21,805, Nu-
> merus Syrorum, A.D. 359.
> *klendas*, *D.* 4427AN, *CIL* VIII 27,335, Thugga (Procon-
> sularis), no date.
> *hdelis* (= *fidelis*), *D.* 4737, Hadrumetum (Byzacena), no
> date. [62]

---

[61] Commenting on the form of the Celtic deity *Blatucairo* rather than
the usual orthography *Belatucadro*, Jackson writes (*Language*, p. 267, footnote 2) that "syncope of the first syllable is unexpected in Brittonic but
not unparalleled."

[62] The form *hdelis* is suspect; in addition to the fact that the loss of
initial *i* is accompanied by a change of initial *f* to *h*, a most unusual change
in Latin inscriptions of Africa, the form *fidelis* itself is extremely common
in Christian inscriptions. We found 106 examples of *fidel-* in African inscriptions.

Pirson in his study of the Latin inscriptions of Gaul explains (pp. 53-54) the loss of initial *a* in *Krissimo* found in an undated pagan inscription (*CIL* XII 1131) as the result of the use of a syllabic system of writing, the *k* being used for both the consonant and the following vowel *a*. A Latin grammarian of the second century A.D., Terentius Scaurus, did mention the practice of an earlier date of using a syllabic alphabet in parts of Italy. The possibility of the use of a syllabic alphabet has been offered as an explanation of syncope in the Praenestine dialect of Latin where forms such as *Dcumius* (for *Decumius*), *CIL* I 1133; *Gminia* (for *Geminia*), *Eph. Epigr.* I, 72; *Ptronio* (for *Petronio*), *Eph. Epigr.* I, 92, and *Mgolnia* (for *Magolnia*), *CIL* I 118, are striking. The peculiar Praenestine pronunciation (*conea* for *ciconia*, 'stork') was commented upon, however, by Plautus in his *Truculentus*.[63] Although the use of a syllabic alphabet may be an adequate explanation for early syncope in pagan inscriptions, this reasoning loses its force when applied to Christian inscriptions of Africa of the fifth century A.D. The simplest answer seems to be that our examples are abbreviations although the particular words *klendas* and *krissimo* (and their variants) may be actual pronunciations influenced by an analogical similarity with other forms beginning with *cl-* and *cr-*, two initial consonant clusters that are common in the Latin phonological system.

We will now give examples of the usual cases of pretonic syncope, the loss of an unstressed vowel between the primary and secondary accents.

Africa

> *vetranus*, D. 435, *CIL* VIII 16,655, Theveste (Proconsularis), no date.[64]
> *edifikberunt* (= *aedificaverunt*), D. 793, *CIL* VIII 12,035, Limasa (Byzacena), between A.D. 582 and A.D. 602.

---

[63] For a discussion of the problem of a real pronunciation or the use of a syllabic alphabet in the syncope of Praenestine and the remarks of Terentius Scaurus, see Lindsay, p. 177. Cf. also Sittl, pp. 21-25, for a full listing of syncope in Praenestine and a discussion of the same problems.

[64] The loss of pretonic short *e* in *vet(e)ranus* is attested from the first century A.D., according to Väänänen (*Introduction*, p. 41). Compare Rum. *batrîn*, Vegliote *vetrun*, Friul. *vedran*, dialectal Ital. *vetrano*, Old Logudor. *betranu*.

Bictrian(u)s (= *Victorianus*), D. 2092, *CIL* VIII 16,396, Aubuzza (Proconsularis), n.d.

Herclanius, D. 2513d, *CIL* VIII 25,243, Carthage (Proconsularis), no date.

edifcabimus, D. 800, *CIL* VIII 28,000, between Theveste (Proconsularis) and Thelepte (Byzacena), no date.

It is interesting to note that while posttonic syncope dealt almost exclusively with the short vowels *i* and *u*, pretonic syncope can also take place, as seen above, with short *e*, *a*, and long *o*, as well as with short *i* and *u*. Pretonic syncope is not a regular occurrence in the Latin inscriptions of Africa as we see from the following table. Since we have only one sporadic example of pretonic syncope for the vowels short *e*, *ă*, long *o*, short *i*, and short *u*, we will give only the number of correct occurrences.

Century	ĕ	ă	ō	ĭ	ŭ
3rd.	2	0	2	1	0
4th.	10	11	1	15	0
5th.	5	13	2	14	3
6th.	1	12	3	25	2
7th.	0	0	0	1	0
n.d.	44	78	36	111	11
Totals:	62	114	44	167	16

When we consider the total number of correct occurrences (403) and the total number of examples of pretonic syncope (5), we see that the total percentage of pretonic syncope for these five vowels is 1.2 %, a very low percentage, especially when we consider that only five vowels were taken into account, all in open syllables. There is also the possibility that in some cases we do not have a true case of pretonic syncope, but a derivation from a form having undergone posttonic syncope (cf. *Herclanius*, either showing pretonic syncope of the form *Herculanius*, or derived from the form *Hercles* which already had lost the posttonic vowel of the proper name *Hercules*; we have already recorded in pagan inscriptions of Britain the forms *Ercl*[i] from *Herculi* (dative), *RIB* 1781, *CIL* VII 751, Hadrian's Wall: Carvoran (Magnis), Northumberland, no date, and *Hercl(i)*, *RIB* 2177, *CIL* VII 1114, Auchendavy (Scotland), no date.

Britain (Pagan)

> *vetrano, RIB* 478, Chester (Deva), Cheshire, no date.
> *vetr(anus), RIB* 495, Chester (Deva), Cheshire, no date.
> *Augstinus, RIB* 685, *CIL* VII 245, York (Eboracum) York-
> shire, no date. [65]

We thus see that the Latin of the pagan inscriptions of Britain is not prone to a loss of a pretonic vowel. The loss of pretonic short *e* in *vetrano* is an example of general Vulgar Latin syncope.

We see the doublets *Lugudunen(sis), RIB* 311, Caerwent (Venta Silurum), Monmouthshire, no date, and *Lugduni* (locative), *RIB* 365, *CIL* VII 125, Caerleon (Isca Silurum), Monmouthshire, no date, although Pirson gives only the syncopated forms in his study on the Latin inscriptions of Gaul. [66]

No examples of pretonic syncope were found in the Christian inscriptions of Britain although our corpus is admittedly poor in total occurrences.

Dalmatia

> *abtissa, D.* 1653, *CIL* III 9551, Salona, A.D. 506 or A.D.
> 551.
> *Domn[ionis], D.* 1083, *CIL* III 9575, Salona, no date. [67]
> *Domni[onis], D.* 1083N, *CIL* III 2662, Salona, n.d.
> *Domniones, D.* 1084, *CIL* III 14,897, Salona, n.d.
> *Domnionis, D.* 3835C, *CIL* III 9508, Salona, n.d.
> *Vetranio, D.* 2964, *CIL* III 9509b, Salona, no date.
> *Salont[anae]* (= *Salonitanae*), *D.* 3837, *CIL* III 9535, Salona,
> no date. [68]

---

[65] The full form *Augustinae* is found in the same inscription. Loth gives in his *Les Mots latins dans les langues brittoniques,* p. 130, the proper name *Awstin* derived from the Latin *Agustinus.* Our form *Augstinus* is apparently either an abbreviation or an oversight on the part of the stonemason.

[66] Cf. Pirson, p. 52.

[67] It is impossible to determine whether *Domn[ionis]* and the following examples are true examples of pretonic syncope from the full form *Dominionis* or whether they are derivatives from the already syncopated form *Domnus.*

[68] Although Skok in his *Pojave* records *abtissa,* the various forms of *Domnionis, Vetranio,* and others as examples of pretonic syncope, he does not mention *Salont[anae].* The omission of pretonic *i* may very well be due to a desire to save space in a very long place name or to a forgotten ligature.

We see that examples of pretonic syncope in the Latin inscriptions of Dalmatia are sporadic and, for the most part, are derivations of syncopated forms of the general Vulgar Latin type (*domnus, vetranus*).

Balkans (Pagan)

> *vetra(n)us*, *Kal.* 125, *CIL* III 14,207, Ichtiman (Thrace), A.D. 246-47.
> *vetr(anus)*, *Kal.* 405, *CIL* III 12,348, Beschli (Moesia Inferior), no date.

Pretonic syncope in pagan inscriptions of the Balkans is apparently not common and once again those forms found belonged to the category of general Vulgar Latin.

We did not find any examples of pretonic syncope in the Christian inscriptions of the Balkans.

When we consider the overall picture of both pretonic and posttonic syncope in the areas studied, we conclude that syncope was not a very common phenomenon in the Latin of Africa, Britain, Dalmatia, and the Balkans, and that those examples of a loss of a pretonic or posttonic vowel are remarkably similar in all areas investigated. We are therefore in agreement with Cross when he writes (p. 93) that "not only are the various regions very much in agreement, but the occurrence of syncopated or short forms seems to clash with the stated classification of the Romance languages" and with another conclusion which he expressed with the words (p. 99) that "in general, throughout the whole of the Roman world . . . , there is a surprising lack of syncope." Gaeng came to inherently the same conclusion which we reached, when he wrote (p. 267) that "instances of syncopation found in our material are not much different from those given by Cross." Although we are in general agreement with the remarks made by both Cross and Gaeng, a refinement must be made in the interpretation of the phenomenon of syncope and its place in the development of the Romance languages from Vulgar Latin. The division of the Romance-speaking world into an East and West Romance on the basis of syncope or the maintenance of unstressed vowels must also be elaborated.

We have already seen that syncope in the Latin inscriptions of Africa is not a regular phenomenon, although examples do occur. It

is pertinent to remember, however, that the cases of syncope in the
Latin inscriptions of Africa are, for the most part, precisely those
forms found in early Latin writers or censured by the *Appendix
Probi*. The examples of syncope recorded for African inscriptions are
therefore of the general Vulgar Latin type, words such as *domnus,
depostus, Oriclo, Vernacla, vetranus,* etc., having been accepted early
by the average speaker of Vulgar Latin. The vocalism of the Latin
of African inscriptions, as has been repeatedly maintained throughout
this work, is remarkably close to that of Sardinian and a survey of
syncope in Sardinian, generally regarded as a language belonging to
the proparoxytonic variety and therefore not normally partaking of
syncope, should be informative. Wagner is most explicit when he
writes:

> Konservativ ist der schwachtonige Vokalismus auch insofern,
> als ihm die Synkopierung widerstrebt. Die Fälle, in welchen
> eine solche vorzuliegen scheint, betreffen entweder schon für
> das Lateinische bezeugte Fälle oder Lehnwörter.
>
> Als schon vulgärlateinisch ist die Synkope belegt oder an-
> zusehen in folgenden Fällen: *kaldu* 'heiss'; *lardu* 'Speck';
> *birde, -i* 'grün'; *donnu, -a* 'Herr(in)'; log. *sogru,* camp.
> *sorgu* 'Schweigervater'; *frittu* 'kalt'; *postu* 'gesetzt'; ... alt-
> log. *betranu = vetranu* für *veteranu*..., heute nicht mehr
> erhalten.
>
> Schon lateinisch ist die Synkope, ebenso im Suffix *c'lu,* sowie
> in den Gruppen *-g'l-, -b'l-.* (cf. nuor. *orikra < oric'la*; nuor.
> *okru < o'clu.*) [69]

Sardinian is therefore a conservative language in which syncope
is not an important factor, although examples of both posttonic and
pretonic syncope do occur in those words which were already syncopated in general Vulgar Latin. This seems to be the same situation
for the Latin inscriptions of Africa, another example of close similarity between Sardinian and the Latin of Africa.

Looking over the cases of syncope in the pagan inscriptions of
Britain, one of the most conservative areas with respect to Latin
vocalism, we see that syncope was not an important factor in the
Latin of this area, although there are cases of syncope in certain

---

[69] Wagner, "Lautlehre," pp. 19-20, 31, 167.

words or types of formation (*domna, mintla, Procli, vetrano,* etc.), losses of unstressed vowels that belong to general Vulgar Latin. An analysis of the Latin loanwords into the Brittonic languages helps immeasurably in the determination of the treatment of posttonic and pretonic vowels in the Latin spoken in Britain. Posttonic syncope of early Vulgar Latin is clearly seen in British loanwords. [70] Jackson gives (p. 268) a few examples: *discip'lus* > W. *disgybl; pop'lus* > W. *pobl; sol'dus* > W. *swllt; vir'dis* > W. *gwyrdd.* To these can be added others given by Loth in his Index: *artic'lus* > W. *erthygl; bac'lus* > W. *bagl; carrica* > W. *carg; cing'la* > W. *cengl; colpus* > W. *cwlff; fac'la* > W. *fagl; lam'na* > W. *lafn; musc'lus* > W. *musgl; peric'lum* > W. *perigl; stab'lum* > W. *staul; ung'la* > W. *ongl,* etc. [71] Since the Late British accent fell on the penultimate syllable, those Latin words borrowed between the first and fifth century and not undergoing a posttonic syncope maintain the posttonic vowel in Brittonic with the stress falling on this posttonic vowel. [72] Examples of the posttonic vowel maintained in Brittonic languages from Latin loanwords are both numerous and important, since many of these Latin words show syncope in some of the Romance languages. We will give some cases where the Latin posttonic vowel was kept in Welsh, the Celtic language most permeated by a Latin influence. The following examples are taken from Loth (pp. 233-43): *asinus* > *asyn; calamus* > *calaf; cubitus* > *cufydd; culcita* > *colched; cupidus* > *cybydd; de subito* > *disfyd; humilis* > *ufyll; manica* > *maneg; masculus* > *mascul; medicus* > *meddyg; opera* > *ober; litterae* > *llythyr; pectinem* > *peithyn; placitum* > *plegyd; tabula* > *tafol; tegula* > *teol; tempero* > *tymheraf; tenerum* > *tyner; veneris (dies)* > *gwener; vesperus* > *gosper,* etc. On the basis of our investigation of epigraphic material and the treatment of posttonic vowels in Latin loanwords into the Brittonic languages, we concur with Loth's conclusion (p. 72): "Toutes les pénultièmes latines, même atones, sont conservées, excepté, naturellement dans le cas où la pénultième atone avait déjà disparu en latin vulgaire." The Latin of Britain, although conservative, had shared, nevertheless, in

---

[70] Jackson, *Language,* p. 268.
[71] See the Index of Loth's *Les Mots latins dans les langues brittoniques,* pp. 233-43, for a very complete list of Latin words borrowed by the Brittonic languages.
[72] Jackson, *Language,* pp. 265, 268; Loth, p. 113.

the posttonic syncope of general Vulgar Latin, but otherwise was adverse to posttonic syncope.

Examples of pretonic syncope in Latin loanwords borrowed into the Brittonic languages can be found, but it is difficult to determine whether the syncope took place as a result of the Latin development or whether it was due to a British syncope which evolved in the mid- or late sixth century. [73] Cases of pretonic syncope where there is doubt as to the origin are, for example: W. *benffyg* < *ben'ficium*; W. *elfen* < *el'menta*; W. *mynwent* < *mon'menta*; W. *taflod* < *tab'latum*. [74] There are occasions, as Jackson points out (p. 268), where the syncope is definitely British: "W. *awdurdod* < *auctoritatem*, *cardod* < *caritatem*, *pylgaint* < *pullicantio*, *trindod* < *trinitatem*, *melltith* < *maledictio*, since if these Latin words had come into British without the intertonic vowel, the results would have been * *awdurthod*, * *carthod*, * *pylchaint*, * *trinod*, and * *mellith*." Summarizing the treatment of pretonic vowels in the Latin loanwords in British, Jackson concludes (p. 269) that "the absence of this syncope in loanwords in British seems to be commoner than its presence."

Taking into consideration both posttonic and pretonic syncopes in the Latin loanwords in the Brittonic languages, we would imagine that since posttonic syncope was generally limited to those words encountered in general Vulgar Latin, it would seem plausible that pretonic syncope was likewise a phenomenon of general Vulgar Latin and that those examples of pretonic syncope found in loanwords in the Brittonic languages occurred mostly after the Vulgar Latin period and should be considered a development of the British period.

Syncope in Dalmatian is a topic that has been conveniently overlooked by Romance scholars in the division of the Romance world into the supposedly proparoxyton Eastern Romance and the paroxyton Western Romance. Although Lausberg groups Dalmatian with Eastern

---

[73] For the dating of British pretonic syncope in the mid- or late sixth century, see Jackson, *Language*, p. 656.

[74] *Ibid.*, p. 268. Lewis and Pedersen in their *A Concise Comparative Celtic Grammar* are more definite in their denial of any pretonic (or posttonic) syncope in Celtic when they write (p. 63), with respect to the evidence of Latin borrowings for the chronology of the Celtic sound changes that "Loss and reduction of vowels in medial syllables due to the accent had not yet taken place."

Romance, [75] in his discussion of posttonic and intertonic vowels he unaccountably omits any reference to Dalmatian. Note his remarks on the treatment of posttonic vowels of proparoxytons in the Romance languages (p. 302):

> El sar. y el román. oriental (it. y rum.) conservan los proparoxítonos en gran escala. En cambio, en la Romania occidental sucumben las más veces a la reducción, siendo el port. el más conservador dentro de la Romania occidental. En esp. la reducción alcanza ya proporciones considerables; el cat., el galorrom., el retorrom. y el norteit. muestran fenómenos de reducción creciente.

The same disregard for the position of Dalmatian in his survey of the treatment of the intertonic vowels can likewise be seen in his comments pertaining to this topic. Note, for example, the following statement (pp. 305-06) on the development of intertonic vowels in the Romance languages:

> En sar. e it. (especialmente en el centro de Italia) las vocales se conservan casi todas. Son menos conservadores el rum., el port., el esp. (precisamente en el orden citado). En los restantes dominios (cat., prov., fr., retorrom., norteit.) se nota una fuerte tendencia a suprimir las vocales intertónicas, lo que está en relación con una intensificación de la gradación intensiva.

It may be argued that since Dalmatian died out toward the end of the nineteenth century, Lausberg simply gave examples of living Romance languages. Throughout his book, however, references to Dalmatian vocalic developments are continuously given. It seems more probable that Lausberg preferred to gloss over a contradiction in the position of Dalmatian among languages of Eastern Romance and the treatment of posttonic and pretonic vowels in Dalmatian. Although Dalmatian presumably belongs to Eastern Romance, syncope is a very prevalent factor in the development of this language. Since stressed vowels show a marked development, unstressed vowels tend to dis-

---

[75] Lausberg, I, 97: "La Romania oriental abarca, pues, el centro y sur de Italia, así como también los Balcanes (dálmata, rumano)."

appear. [76] Posttonic syncope is common although a distinction is made between early and later losses of posttonic vowels. [77] Bàrtoli gives many examples of posttonic syncope (p. 345), the following being only a sampling: *kuald* [< *cal(i)du*]; *suald* [< *sol(i)du*]; *pepro* [< *pipere*]; *pretro* [< *pre(s)bitero*]; *vindre* [< *veneris*]; *gonbro* [< *vomere*]; *jamna* [< *anima*]; *jomno* [< *homine*]; *basalka* [< *basilica*]; *piakno* [< *pectine*]; *surko* [< *sorice*]; *dotko* [< *duodecim*]; *medko* [< *medicu*]; *rakla* [< *auricula*]; *uaklo* [< *oculu*]; *lipro* [< *lepore*]; *pira* [< *pecora*], etc. With respect to pretonic syncope the problem is complicated because of the problem of determining again which cases took place in Vulgar Latin and which resulted from a later Dalmatian development. [78] Note some of the examples of pretonic syncope given by Bàrtoli (II, 348): *vetrún* (< *veteranu*); *karviale* (< *cerebellu*); *blasmúr* (< *blasphemare*); *mončál* (< *monticellu*); *karkút* (< *carricatu*); *sansóika* (< *sanguisuga*); *santút* (< *sanitate*), etc.

We thus see that syncope is an important characteristic of Dalmatian and consequently necessitates putting Dalmatian in the group of Western Romance languages, contrary to the usual scheme of considering it a member of Balkan Romance. It has already been pointed out, however, that Bàrtoli's conclusion that Dalmatian is a member of the Apennino-Balkan (or East) Romance group requires refinement. Hadlich in his *The Phonological History of Vegliote* admits (p. 87) that on the basis of the consonantal development of Dalmatian, it is an East Romance language, but he states (p. 87) that, "if a division

---

[76] Cf. Bàrtoli, *Das Dalmatische*, II, 341: "Wie aus der reichen Entwicklung der betonten Vokale zu erwarten war, neigen die unbetonten dem Schwund zu."

[77] Cf. Bàrtoli, *Ibid.*, II, 345: "Hier tritt zwar die Synkope unter allen Umständen ein, doch ist sie bei den Klanglauten früher als zwischen Geräuschlauten geschehen, wie die Behandlung des Tonvokals zeigt." Posttonic syncope seems to be more prevalent than pretonic according to Tagliavini in his article "Dalmatica, Lingua," *Enciclopedia Italiana* (Rome: Istituto Giovanni Treccani, 1931), p. 244: "... nel vocalismo, la postonica del proparossitono scompare mentre la finale resta; al contrario, nei parossitoni, tutte le vocali finali cadono e solo -a resta ... Le protoniche in generale si conservano abbastanza bene." It has already been pointed out that posttonic syncope of many Vulgar Latin forms was severely criticized in the *Appendix Probi*, but only one example of pretonic syncope was mentioned (see *supra*, p. 433, footnote 36).

[78] Bàrtoli, *Ibid.*, p. 348: "Auch ist hier nicht zu entscheiden, welche Fälle der Synkope schon vulgärlat., welche erst dalm. sind."

of Romance languages were to be made on the basis of vowel development, Vegliote would have to be considered a West Romance language." It would appear that syncope would also place Dalmatian in the West Romance group, another corroboration of the duality of this neglected Romance language.

Although syncope in Dalmatian is therefore an established characteristic, its chronology is problematical. Bàrtoli himself distinguished between proparoxytons that became paroxytons early in the language and those that were a later development. He writes (II, 356) that "die Proparoxytona, die früh zu Paroxytona geworden sint, werden wie die alten, primären Paroxytona behandelt: *miarla mer(u)la* wie *miarda merda*. Nicht so die jüngeren: *medko medico*." Wartburg, who was instrumental in proposing the Germanic invasions as the main cause of the differentiation of Gallo-Romance from the other Romance languages because of the extreme development of its phonology, acknowledges (*Ausgliederung*, p. 152) the unusually advanced state of development of the vocalic system of Vegliote without the benefit of any increased stress accent due to the Germanic invasions, but accounts for it in a different way. For Wartburg it is the Serbo-Croatian influence that is the root cause for the extreme development of the Dalmatian vocalic system. [79] It would appear then that Dalmatian likewise partook of the general Vulgar Latin syncope, but the more advanced syncope took place during the Dalmatian period as a result of a Slavic influence that could not have taken root before the sixth or seventh century.

Rumanian, as has already been indicated, is generally considered a proparoxytonic language, the posttonic vowel usually being maintained. Pușcariu, however, maintains (*Études*, p. 233) that "la syncope apparaît de façon irrégulière déjà dans le latin vulgaire ainsi que dans les langues romanes." The syncopated forms of Rumanian he adduces, nevertheless, are very revealing: *încarca* (*carricare*); *culca* (*collocare*); *batrân* (*veteranus*); *domn* (*dom(i)nus*); *veghia* (*vig(i)lare*), *cald* (*cal(i)dus*); *verde* (*vir(i)dis*); *lard* (*lar(i)dus*); *solzi* (*sol(i)di*); *ridica* (**rig(i)dicare*), *adăpost* (*pos(i)tus*), etc. They are, for the most

---

[79] Wartburg, *Ausgliederung*, p. 152: "Ausserdem weisen die benachbarten serbo-kroatischen Mundarten ganz ähnliche Verhaltnisse auf wie Veglia.... Diese dalmatischen Vokalverhältnisse sind daher nur im Zusammenhang mit dem Serbo-Kroatischen zu verstehen und scheiden aus unserer Betrachtung aus."

part, precisely those syncopated forms found in inscriptions and which belong to general Vulgar Latin. When we consider some unsyncopated forms in Rumanian, such as *lingură, singur, bunătate, oameni, deget, neted, frasin* (< *fraximum*), *pieptene* (< *pectinem*), *purece* (< *pulicem*), *piedică, pulbere, iederă, iepure* (< *leporem*), *lacrimă, tînăr* (< *tenerum*), *cumpăra, biserică, grindină*, etc., forms that are, for the most part, syncopated in Western Romance, it appears reasonable to group Rumanian with the proparoxytonic languages of Eastern Romance.

On the basis of our inscriptional material and our study of both pretonic and posttonic syncope in the Romance languages as well as the Latin loanwords in non-Romance languages, we conclude that syncope was not a common phenomenon in Vulgar Latin inscriptions other than those that permeated the general speech of the Latin speakers throughout all of Romania and that no region can be differentiated from another because of its special affinity for pretonic or posttonic syncope. The syncope that differentiates the Romance languages is a later development that cannot be traced to a local variety of Latin in a particular area of Romania. We therefore agree with Cross' conclusion (p. 93) that "the various regions [are] very much in agreement [with respect to syncope]," but his further remark (p. 93) that "the occurrence of syncopated or short forms seems to clash with the stated classification of the Romance languages" is overstated since the Romance languages agree to a remarkably close degree as to those syncopated forms found in general Vulgar Latin, forms encountered in Plautus, Terence, Cicero, Varro, the Pompeian inscriptions, etc., and criticized in the *Appendix Probi*. Inscriptions dated up to the sixth century cannot be expected to show differences in syncope which are apparent only during a later Romance development. Cross himself wrote (p. 104) that "the differences cognizable to us must be due to occurrences that took place in the separate development of the Romance languages, not in the parent speech." Cross, however, is completely illogical when he writes (p. 104) that "as far as the evidence of the inscriptions bears on the phenomena treated comparatively in this work, the following conclusion is appropriate: The divarication of the Romance languages is not due to essential differences between the Latin of one region and the Latin of another region." To conclude that the Romance languages do not differ because of a lack of differentiation in the Latin of various regions of Romania on the basis of an extrapolation of data limited to a study of syncope is completely erroneous. Inscriptions show that syncope of forms common to all Romance languages was a general feature of early Vulgar Latin, but the syncope that differentiates the Romance languages is a later development and is not mirrored in inscriptions. Instead of condemning inscriptions for failing to show illusory differences in the problem of syncope, we should praise inscriptions for their remarkable accuracy in portraying a linguistic reality. The corroboration of epigraphic evidence by the study of Latin loanwords in the Brittonic languages is, for example, an outstanding example of the usefulness of inscriptions. The Latin of Britain, as has been repeatedly stated in this work, is one of the most conservative variants of the Latin language, and yet both inscriptions and loanwords show that the Latin spoken in this peripheral area underwent syncope of the general Vulgar Latin variety.

Since the weakening of pretonic and posttonic vowels, especially the change of /ĭ/ and /ŭ/ to e and o respectively, is closely allied to the questions of pretonic and posttonic syncope, it is well that we consider the interrelationship of both phenomena to see whether we can drawn any pertinent conclusions. We have already seen in our tables concerning the treatment of intertonic /ĭ/ (see *supra*, pp. 204-205) and posttonic /ĭ/ (see *supra*, 212-13) that the Latin of Gaul stands out from the Latin of all other areas of Romania with respect to the weakening of this vowel to an e, but only in inscriptions dated in the sixth or seventh. An analogous situation was also seen with respect to the weakening of intertonic and posttonic /ŭ/ to o (see *supra*, pp. 307-309) in the Latin inscriptions emanating from Gaul dated in the sixth and seventh centuries, a parallelism that cannot be overlooked. Since the weakening of pretonic and posttonic vowels is the first step toward syncope, inscriptions apparently show that the Latin of Gaul was different from that of other areas of Romania in this very important respect, but only starting in the sixth century. The increased stress accent brought in by the Germanic-speaking peoples accounts very nicely for the weakening of unstressed vowels in the Latin of Gaul at a time when the Germanic influence began to make itself felt. Inscriptions, therefore, may once again portray a linguistic reality, namely, that a weakening of the unstressed medial vowels /ĭ/ and /ŭ/ in the Latin of Gaul of the sixth century was the forerunner of the complete loss of these vowels in a language that was to become the most extreme variant of Latin among the Romance languages.

Haplology

Closely linked to syncope is the phenomenon of haplology, the loss of an entire syllable because of its similarity to an adjacent syllable. Although haplology is more characteristic of the transition from Latin to Old French, we do have several sporadic examples of this phenomenon in Latin inscriptions, but they are too rare to permit any importance to be attached to them.[80] Haplology is limited to two forms in our corpus:

> *Restuto* (= *Restituto*), D. 581, *CIL* III 9840, Altava (Mauretania Caesariensis), A.D. 335.
> *Restuius* (stonemason's mistake for *Restutus*), D. 2513, *CIL* VIII 25,282, near Carthage, n.d.
> *Restuta*, D. 2536, *CIL* VIII 24,511, Djebel-Dhellud (Proconsularis), no date.
> *Restuta*, D. 3264, *CIL* VIII 23,053, Sidi-Habich, no date.

Although the proper names *Restuta* and *Restutus* were found in our corpus solely in Africa, other scholars have recorded the same example of haplology in the inscriptions coming from Pompei, Gaul, and Spain.[81]

> *depossio* (= *depositio*), D. 479, *CIL* III 2656, Split (Spalatum), Dalmatia, possibly A.D. 415.
> *depossionis* (gen.), D. 1684, *CIL* VIII 20,301, Satafi (Mauretania Sitifensis), between A.D. 349 and A.D. 436.
> *depossio*, D. 3044, *CIL* III 14,915, Salona (Dalmatia), no date.

To account for the loss of a syllable in *depossio* from *deposito* through haplology, scholars have resorted to the expediency of considering that the *-tio* was pronounced *-sio* by means of assibilation, the resulting form *depositsio* or *deposisio* (or the oblique *deposision-*)

---

[80] For a discussion of haplology in Latin texts of the 8th century from Northern France and its relationship to the development of Old French, see Pei, *The Language of the Eighth-Century Texts in Northern France,* pp. 126-27.

[81] See Väänänen, *Pompéiennes,* p. 46; Pirson, p. 54, Carnoy, p. 118.

then losing one of the -*si*- syllables. [82] The form *depossio* or its variants can also be considered as coming directly from the syncopated *depostio* with a later assibilation. We have already seen (*supra*, p. 442) that *depostio* was attested in a Dalmatian inscription dated to A.D. 382.

It is interesting to note that although we did not find any examples of the word *matutinus* or *matutina* or with haplology *mattinus* (or *mattina*), the base form for the French *matin*, Prov. *mati*, Ital. *mattino*, Cat. *matí*, the Latin loanwords in the Brittonic languages posit *mattina* or *matina*: cf. the Irish *maiden* < *matina*, or the Middle Cornish *mettin*, *myttyn*, Middle and Modern Breton *mintin*, and the Welsh *meityn*, coming from the Latin *mattina*. [83]

Anaptyxis (Epenthesis)

The insertion of a "parasitic" vowel (called a "svarabhaktic" vowel in the terminology of the Sanskrit grammarians) to facilitate pronunciation of difficult consonant clusters was a process often used to accommodate Greek loanwords into archaic Latin when the consonant combination was not common to the Latin phonemic system. [84] The I.E. instrumental *-tlo- entered archaic Latin as -clo-, later lengthened to -culo- through an epenthetic vowel and subsequently reduced in some cases to -clo- again through syncope. [85] As for the quality of the epenthetic vowel, Lindsay defines it in careful terms when he writes (p. 147) that "the inserted vowel takes the quality of the vowel in the syllable containing the liquid." [86]

The following are the examples of anaptyxis in our corpus, although they are too few in number to allow any definitive conclusions to be drawn:

---

[82] This line of reasoning was put forth by Pirson, p. 54, and Hoffman, p. 14. The latter considered the loss of the syllable, however, as an example of syllabic dissimulation.

[83] For the use of the Latin forms with haplology in the Brittonic languages, see Jackson, *Language*, pp. 135-36, and Loth, p. 187.

[84] For the archaic Latin forms *techina*, *drachuma*, *Tecumessa*, *Alcumena*, *mina*, etc., taken from the Greek with an epenthetic vowel, see Lindsay, p. 146, and Sommer, p. 139.

[85] See Lindsay, p. 93. Plautus still wrote the instrumental -*clo*- without the epenthetic *u* almost exclusively except at the end of a line for purposes of meter.

[86] For a similar account of the quality of the inserted vowel, see Sommer, p. 139.

Africa:

offeret, D. 1832, *CIL* VIII 2389, Thamugadi (Numidia), no date. [87]

Apirius, D. 3273, *CIL* VIII 9794, Arbal, n.d. [88]

---

[87] Rather than a case of anaptyxis, the *e* of *offeret* is probably an example of analogy with the third pers. sing. of the present indicative of regular thematic verbs. Carnoy found (p. 112) five examples of *offeret* in Spanish inscriptions dated from A.D. 621 to A.D. 631. He likewise considered the form an analogous third pers. sing. indicative of thematic verbs.

[88] Assuming the proper name was originally *Aprius,* it would seem strange that the epenthetic vowel would assume the accent in *Apirius.* A transfer of the stress is found, however, although not onto the epenthetic vowel, in the important type of words such as *integrum, cólubra, ténebrae, tónitrus,* etc. (words having a mute plus liquid), where the stress is changed from the antepenult to the penult: *intégrum, colúbra, tenébrae, tonítrus,* etc. An explanation of this displacement of the accent, a hallmark of Vulgar Latin pronunciation, as the result of the insertion of an epenthetic vowel is offered by Niedermann, who writes (pp. 16-17): "Dans les mots du type *integrum, cólubra, ténebrae, tónitrus,* l'accent s'est porté sur la pénultième brève, d'où *intégrum, colúbra, tenébrae, tonítrus.* Cette dernière accentuation, supposée par les langues romanes (fr. *entier;* ital. *intero;* fr. *couleuvre;* esp. *tinieblas;* v. fr. *toneire, tonoire*) était considérée comme normale au temps d'Isidore de Séville; ... On pourrait être tenté de rapprocher le contraste entre l'accentuation du latin littéraire *integrum, cólubra,* et celle du latin vulgaire *intégrum, colúbra* du fait que, chez les poètes de l'âge classique, la pénultième de ces mots et de tous les autres de même structure comptait tantôt pour une brève et tantôt pour une longue. Mais un tel rapprochement ne tiendrait pas devant la critique. En effet, la double prosodie en question s'explique par la coupe syllabique, le groupe occlusive plus *r* pouvant ou bien être rattaché tout entier à la syllabe suivante, de sorte que la syllabe précédente était ouverte et, par conséquent, brève (*inte-grum, colu-bra*), ou bien être partagée entre la syllabe précédente et la syllabe suivante, auquel cas celle-là était fermée et, partant, longue (*integ-rum, colub-ra*). Or, le traitement roman de la syllabe accentuée de *intégrum,* par example, indique qu'elle était ouverte; comp. fr. *entier* de *inté-grum* comme *pied* de *pé-dem* par opposition à fr. *sept* de *sép-tem, enfer* de *infér-num.* La place de l'accent dans les prononciations vulgaires *intégrum, colúbra,* etc. n'a donc rien à voir avec la scansion longue de la syllabe pénultième de ces mots dans la poésie classique des Romains. Au surplus, il est universellement reconnu, aujourd'hui, que cet alongement 'par position' reposait sur l'imitation savante de la métrique grecque, en d'autres termes qu'il était artificiel et ne correspondait point à une prononciation courante. La cause véritable du déplacement de l'accent, survenu dans *integrum, colubra* et autres cas semblables, paraît devoir être recherchée ou bien dans l'influence analogique de *aurícla, fundíblum,* doublets vulgaires de *aurícula, fundíbulum,* ou bien dans la tendance de la prononciation vulgaire à insérer un élément vocalique dans le groupe occlusive plus *r* qui avait pour conséquence forcée de faire avancer l'accent d'une syllabe." For a briefer mention of the displacement of the accent in words like *colú-bra,* etc., with the accented vowel, see Meyer-Lübke, *Einführung,* pp. 138, 142.

Cipirianus (= *Cyprianus*), D. 3138N, *CIL* VIII 11,648, Ammaedara (Byzacena), no date.
Posorica, D. 3709, Mauretania Caesariensis, no date. [89]

Britain: (Pagan)

Discipulinae, RIB 1127, Corbridge (Corstopitum), Northumberland, probably in the 3rd century. [90]
Discipu[l]inae, RIB 1978, *CIL* VII 896, Hadrian's Wall: Castlesteads (Uxellodunum), Cumberland, A.D. 209 to A.D. 217.
Imilico, RIB 193, *CIL* VII 87, Colchester (Camulodunum), Essex, no date. [91]

Dalmatia:

dulcisis[imo], D. 3842, Salona, no date. [92]
Acame (< Ἀχμή), D. 4115, *CIL* III 9605, Salona, no date.

Balkans: (Pagan)

Ziepyr(um) (= *Zephyrum*), Kal. 109, *CIL* III 12,389, Gabare (Moesia Inferior), n.d. [93]
ar[g]enito, Kal. 226, *CIL* III 14,433, Silistra (Durostorum), A.D. 226. [94]

---

[89] It is presumed that *Posorica* is the Latin proper name derived from the Greek Ψωρικός, with an epenthetic *o* to avoid the non-Latin initial consonant cluster *ps-*. See *Diehl,* II, 261.

[90] *Discipulinae* is probably an analogical form based on the noun *discipulus* rather than a true case of anaptyxis.

[91] Cf. the editor's comment in *The Roman Inscriptions of Britain* concerning the spelling of this proper name (p. 64): "*Imilico* seems to be a variant of *Imilco,* see *CIL* VIII 1249, 1562, 23,834 (Africa, Proconsularis)."

[92] The spelling *dulcisis[imo]* may very well be a simple mistake on the part of the stonemason, the superlative ending *-issim-* more likely to be syncopated than to show an epenthetic vowel. This form is not given in Skok's *Pojave* under anaptyxis although this scholar does record several cases of anaptyxis in Dalmatian inscriptions.

[93] According to Kalinga, p. 104: "das *i* nach Z anaptyktisch."

[94] Although the epenthetic *i* in this word may be a simple mistake on the part of the stonemason, it is interesting to note that the Oscan *aragetud* (= *Lat. argento*) does show anaptyxis (albeit pretonic). It is well known, of course, that Oscan was more disposed to anaptyxis than Latin and that it occurred under different circumstances. Väänänen writes (*Pompéiennes,* p. 47): "La diffusion considérable de ce phénomène [anaptyxis] dans les dialectes de l'Italie méridionale serait une habitude physiologique héritée de

Balkans: (Christian)

interantem, D. 2181, *CIL* III 10,223, Sirmium (Pannonia Inferior), no date.[95]

Ciriscentina (= *Crescentina*), D. 3659, Purbach (Pannonia), no date.[96]

patir(i), D. 4896, *CIL* III 10,599, Gran (Pannonia Inferior), no date.[97]

On the basis of our examples we conclude that anaptyxis was not a common phenomenon in Latin inscriptions, many examples being probably a mistake on the part of the stonemason or analogous forms, although we do have examples of epenthesis in Latin loanwords borrowed from the Greek as well as in occasional native Latin forms, usually to break up the combination of an unvoiced occlusive (*p*, *c*, *t*) and *r*.

---

la population osque qui avait autrefois occupé cette région. En effet, l'osque a donné à l'anaptyxe une extension considérable, mais dans des conditions assez différentes de celles que montre le latin." See also Lindsay, p. 147, and Sommer, p. 141, for anaptyxis in Oscan.

[95] The parasitic *e* in *interantem* is probably caused by analogy with the preposition *inter* rather than a true case of anaptyxis. The preposition *inter* is found in the same inscription.

[96] It is interesting to note that the epenthetic vowel is *i*, having assumed the same quality as the initial vowel *i*, which itself had changed from *e* before the consonant cluster -*sc*-.

[97] Cf. Lindsay, p. 93: "The development in Romance of a word like *patrem*, suggests that it must in Vulgar Latin have sounded almost like a trisyllable, **paterem*."

CHAPTER VI

CONCLUSIONS

Although it would be too lengthy to give all the intricacies of
the results recorded in the foregoing pages, we will present the principal conclusions that pertain to the question of a differentiation of
Latin in the various areas of Romania and the role played by inscriptions in the determination of the unity or breakdown of Latin.

As a result of the present quantitative and comparative study of
Latin inscriptions from Christian Africa, pagan and Christian Britain,
Christian Dalmatia, and the pagan and Christian Balkans, in conjunction with the investigation of Paul Gaeng on the Christian inscriptions
of the Iberian Peninsula, Gaul, and the various parts of Italy, including Rome, it can be stated definitely that there was a differentiation
in the vocalic systems of the Latin spoken throughout Romania.

The Latin of Gaul is undoubtedly the most innovative variant of
Latin in all of the areas investigated, and differs fundamentally from
the Latin of Africa and Britain. On the basis of our methodology
of determining the percentage of deviation from the Classical Latin
norm, it is seen that the Latin of Gaul evolved tendencies in its
vocalic development that place it in strong contrast with the conservative Latin of Africa and Britain. In accordance with the Lausberg
division of the Romance languages, the vocalism of the Latin of Gaul
belongs to the Italic qualitative system, whereas the Latin of Africa
and Britain belongs to the Sardinian archaic vocalic system. We will
substantiate these assertions with a few figures taken from our study
of the stressed and unstressed vowels of the various areas of Romania.

The mergers of stressed /ē/ and /ĭ/ and of stressed /ō/ and
/ŭ/ are the prime requirements for the Italic qualitative vocalic system, sometimes erroneously called the "Vulgar Latin" vocalic system.

In the Sardinian archaic system, the above phonemes are kept separate. From the figures appearing on the table in page 104, we have the following tabulation: Gaul shows a percentage of deviation of /ē/ to *i* in open syllables of 17.5 % (52 examples of /ē/ and 11 examples of *i*) and of 33.3 % in closed syllables (96 examples of /ē/ and 48 examples of *i*), for a total deviation of 28.5 % (148 examples of /ē/ and 59 examples of *i*). Africa, on the other hand, shows 0.9 % of deviation of /ē/ to *i* in open syllables (429 examples of /ē/ and 4 examples of *i*) and 2.0 % deviation in closed syllables (97 examples of /ē/ and 2 examples of *i*) for a total of 1.1 % deviation (526 examples of /ē/ and 6 examples of *i*). Britain is even more conservative in its vocalic structure with pagan Britain showing 0.0 % deviation of /ē/ in open syllables (184 examples of /ē/ and no examples of *i*) and 8.0 % in closed syllables (23 examples of /ē/ and 2 examples of *i*, although both examples are of a questionable nature and could bring down the figure even more) for a total percentage of deviation of 1.0 % (207 examples of /ē/ and 2 [questionable] examples of *i*). The Latin of Christian Britain does not have any deviations of /ē/, but the total number of correct occurrences is very low (13 examples of /ē/ in open syllables and 1 example of /ē/ in closed syllables).

The Latin of Gaul likewise deviates more than that of any other region of Romania with respect to the change of /ĭ/ to *e*. Gaul shows a 35.8 % deviation in open syllables (61 examples of /ĭ/ and 34 examples of *e*) and 19 % in closed syllables (34 examples of /ĭ/ and 8 examples of *e*) for a total deviation of 30.7 % (95 examples of /ĭ/ and 42 examples of *e*). This percentage of deviation of /ĭ/ to *e* contrasts sharply with that of African Latin where we have a 0.5 % deviation in open syllables (207 examples of /ĭ/ and 1 example of *e*) and 1.2 % in closed syllables (242 examples of /ĭ/ and 3 examples of *e*) for a total 0.9 % of deviation (449 examples of /ĭ/ and 4 examples of *e*). The Latin of pagan Britain is also strongly conservative in this problem of the deviation of /ĭ/ to *e*: it shows a 1.5 % deviation in open syllables (132 examples of /ĭ/ and 2 examples of *e*) and 2.3 % in closed syllables (85 examples of /ĭ/ and 2 examples of *e*) for a total of 1.8 % deviation (217 examples of /ĭ/ and 4 examples of *e*).

This same pattern holds true in the discussion of the merger of /ō/ and /ŭ/ or the stability of these phonemes. From the tables on pages 128 and 130, we observe that Gaul deviates from the Classical Latin norm more than any region of Romania. The Latin of Gaul shows a 6.8 % deviation of /ō/ to *u* in open syllables (123 examples of /ō/ and 9 examples of *u*) and 0.0 % in closed syllables (12 examples of /ō/ and no examples of *u*) for a total deviation of 6.3 % (135 examples of /ō/ and 9 examples of *u*). The percentage of deviation of /ŭ/ to *o* is very high at 38.3 % in Gaul in open syllables (37 examples of /ŭ/ and 23 examples of *o*) and 3.2 % in closed syllables (28 examples of /ŭ/ and 1 example of *o*) for a total percentage of deviation at 27.0 % (65 examples of /ŭ/ and 24 examples of *o*).

These percentages of 6.3 % for the deviation of /ō/ to *u,* and especially 27.0 % for the deviation of /ŭ/ to *o* in the Latin of Gaul, are strongly contrasted by the figures for the Latin of Africa and pagan Britain. In the Latin of Africa we have a 0.2 % deviation of /ō/ to *u* in open syllables (451 examples of /ō/ and 1 example of *u*) and 0.0 % in closed syllables (11 examples of /ō/ and no examples of *u*) for a total deviation of 0.2 % (462 examples of /ō/ and 1 example of *u*). The figures for the deviation of /ŭ/ to *o* are likewise conservative in the Latin of Africa. We have 2.9 % of deviation in open syllables (33 examples of /ŭ/ and 1 example of *o*) and 0.7 % in closed syllables (145 examples of /ŭ/ and 1 example of *o*) for a total deviation of 1.1 % (178 examples of /ŭ/ and 2 examples of *o*).

The figures are even more conservative for the Latin of pagan Britain. We did not find a single case of deviation of either /ō/ to *u* or /ŭ/ to *o,* although the total number of occurrences was relatively high (233 examples of /ō/ in open syllables and 7 examples in closed, and 31 examples of /ŭ/ in open syllables and 80 examples in closed syllables).

Thus, we see that in stressed syllables the mergers of /ē/ and /ĭ/ as well as that of /ō/ and /ŭ/ are clearly evident in the Latin of Gaul, a situation that contrasts sharply with the separation of these phonemes in the Latin of Africa and Britain.

It must be emphasized that the changes in the stressed vowels of the Latin inscriptions of Gaul are not haphazard, but conform to a neat pattern. They show that the vocalism of the Latin of Gaul belongs to a system, the Italic qualitative system, the most important vocalic base of the Romance languages, but certainly not the only one in all of Romania. The Latin inscriptions of Christian Africa and pagan Britain, on the other hand, clearly indicate that the Latin of these areas belongs to the Sardinian archaic vocalic system with its emphasis on the stability of the /ē/, /ĭ/, /ō/, and /ŭ/ phonemes. These two distinct vocalic systems would seem to indicate that there was a differentiation in the Latin spoken throughout Romania, and that the theory of the "unity" of Latin is consequently inadmissible.

The most important deviation of the Latin of Gaul in unstressed syllables is the weakening of both intertonic and posttonic vowels, especially /ĭ/ and /ŭ/. Although figures (pp. 204-205) for some areas are too low for any significant comparison, Narbonensis shows a 22.2 % deviation of intertonic /ĭ/ on the basis of twenty-eight examples of /ĭ/ and eight examples of e; Lugdunensis has a 34.6 % deviation of /ĭ/ with seventeen examples of /ĭ/ and nine examples of e. If the figures for both parts of Gaul were combined, we would arrive at a total of 27.4 % for the weakening of intertonic /ĭ/ to e on the basis of 45 examples of /ĭ/ and seventeen examples of e. This high percentage of deviation of intertonic /ĭ/ for the Latin of Gaul is highlighted by a comparison with the figures for Africa where we have a deviation of 1.6 % on the basis of 186 examples of /ĭ/ and three examples of e. The Latin of pagan Britain is likewise conservative in its treatment of intertonic /ĭ/. Here we have a deviation of 1.9 % with 101 examples of /ĭ/ and two examples of e. Rome is also a conservative area in the preservation of intertonic /ĭ/, showing a deviation of 1.3 % on the basis of 149 examples of /ĭ/ and two examples of e.

A similar picture emerges for the treatment of posttonic /ĭ/ in the areas of Gaul and Africa, pagan Britain, and Rome. The area of Narbonensis shows a weakening of posttonic /ĭ/ to e of 32.7 % (33 examples of /ĭ/ and 16 examples of e), and Lugdunensis offers a weakening of 41.5 % (31 examples of /ĭ/ and 22 examples of e) for a total of 37.3 % of deviation of posttonic /ĭ/ in Gaul. In contrast to the considerable weakening of posttonic /ĭ/ in Gaul, we see a strong conservatism in the treatment of posttonic /ĭ/ in the Latin of Africa, where we have no examples of weakening and 433 correct occurrences of a posttonic /ĭ/. The Latin of Britain shows a stability in posttonic /ĭ/ with a deviation of 1.5 % (195 examples of /ĭ/ and 3 examples of e). Rome, too, is very conservative in the question of the weakening of posttonic /ĭ/, having a deviation of 0.7 % (444 examples of /ĭ/ and 3 examples of e). The chronological element is also illustrated by the sudden increase of deviation in the sixth century for the figures of Narbonensis and Lugdunensis. In Narbonensis the percentage of deviation for the weakening of posttonic /ĭ/ to e is 46.8 % (17 examples of /ĭ/ and 15 examples of e) while that of Lugdunensis is 55.5 % (16 examples of /ĭ/ and 20 examples of e). This sudden increase in the weakening of posttonic /ĭ/ could very well be the result of an increased stress accent brought about by the Germanic invaders. The Latin of Northern Italy shows a deviation of 10.3 % (87 examples of /ĭ/ and 10 examples of e), which might indicate that the Latin of this area was being drawn into the orbit of the Latin of Gaul.

The figures for the weakening of pretonic /ŭ/ to o are not sufficient to allow a firm comparison, but on the basis of a deviation of 77.7 % in the Latin of Narbonensis (2 examples of /ŭ/ and 7 examples of o), Gaeng did write (p. 213) that "there is little doubt that in the Narbonensis the merger of /ŭ/ and /ō/ in this position is an accomplished fact by the sixth century." The Latin of Africa shows a 7.5 % deviation (49 examples of /ŭ/ and 4 examples of o, but of these four examples, three show the change of /ŭ/ to o in the root Thamogad-, which would probably show that pretonic /ŭ/ was more stable than the percentage of deviation indicates. The Latin of pagan Britain presents a 4.7 % deviation of pretonic /ŭ/ (61 examples of /ŭ/ and 3 examples of o, but all three examples are proper names, Viboleius, Belatocadro, and Belatocairo, the latter two being variant forms of the same Celtic deity). It would appear that the pretonic /ŭ/ in the Latin of Africa and pagan Britain was unquestionably more stable than that of Gaul.

The contrast between the Latin of Gaul and that of Africa and pagan Britain is clearly shown by the figures for posttonic /ŭ/. Once again Narbonensis shows a high percentage of deviation with a figure of 62.9 % (13 examples of /ŭ/ and 22 examples of o) and Lugdunensis yields 44.4 % (25 examples of /ŭ/ and 20 examples of o) for a total percentage of deviation of 52.5 % (38 examples of /ŭ/ and 42 examples of o) for the area of Gaul. Africa, on the other hand, shows a stability of posttonic /ŭ/ with 1.4 % deviation (70 examples of /ŭ/ and 1 example of o). Pagan Britain shows a weakening of posttonic /ŭ/ to o with 3.2 % (60 examples of /ŭ/ and 2 examples of o, both examples of o appearing in the form Astor(um), a fact which would probably lower the figure for the percentage of deviation). Rome had no examples of deviation of posttonic /ŭ/, with

sixty-eight examples of correct occurrence. Once again the chronological element appears with the striking increase of this weakening
in Gaul taking place in the sixth century. Narbonensis shows 70.9 %
deviation (9 examples of /ŭ/ and 22 examples of *o*) and Lugdunensis has a percentage of 54.4 % deviation (14 examples of /ŭ/
and 17 examples of *o*). The impact of the Germanic invasions, with
the concomitant increase in the stress accent, could very well be the
external cause for this distinctive trait of the Latin of Gaul. Northern
Italy yields a 11.5 % of deviation (69 examples of /ŭ/ and 9 examples of *o*), which might indicate that the Latin of this area tended
to follow in the wake of the Latin of Gaul.

As was the case for a systematic merger of stressed /ĭ/ and /ē/,
/ō/ and /ŭ/ in the Latin of Gaul, we see a systematic pattern
emerging for the weakening of intertonic and posttonic /ĭ/ and /ŭ/
in the same Latin of Gaul, although probably at a later date. While
the merger of the above stressed vowels is chronologically estimated
to be of the fourth century, the weakening of the intertonic and posttonic /ĭ/ and /ŭ/ seems dateable to the sixth century. The systematic change in the weakening of the unstressed medial vowels must
be emphasized, since a pattern, not a haphazard, sporadic deviation
is noted. The Latin of Gaul apparently tends to be assuming an
incipient paroxytonic rhythm rather than to be maintaining the proparoxytonic structure of the Latin of Africa, pagan Britain, and Rome.
This distinctive vocalic weakening of intertonic and posttonic /ĭ/
and /ŭ/ in the Latin of Gaul, in contrast to the Latin of the more
conservative areas of Africa, Britain, and Rome, is another indication
of the differentiation of Latin vocalism in the various parts of
Romania.

Another case of a differentiation of the Latin of Gaul with respect
to other areas of Romania is the treatment of final vowels, especially
final /ĭ/. Although the problem is complicated by the possibility of
morphological considerations, we have devised a methodology of sep-
arating morphological and phonetic factors to a surprising degree. In
the terminations of noun-adjective endings of third declension forms,
for example, the nominative singular ending -*ĭs* changes very often
to -*es*, but the reason in many cases is analogy with other third declension nominative endings, especially -*ĕs* and -*ēs*, but also -*ĕx*,
-*ĕr*, -*ĕn*, and -*ĕ*, and possibly with the second declension ending -*ĕr*,
and the fifth declension nominative ending -*ēs*. Although it is possible

that the change is phonetic, it is more probable that it is a morphological change due to analogy with other nominative endings. The change of the genitive singular ending -*is* to -*es* of third declension nouns and adjectives, however, is undoubtedly primarily phonetic since the possibility of a confusion with another genitive singular ending in -*es* is morphologically remote. This same reasoning holds true for conjugational endings. The change of -*it* to -*et* in the third person singular of the present indicative could very well be a change from one conjugation to another, a well known fact attested in the Romance languages. Although it may be a phonetic change, it is more likely to be a morphological substitution. The same change of -*it* to -*et* in the third person singular of the present perfect indicative, however, is presumably a phonetic change since there is little chance for a morphological ending to intercede. Applying these theoretical assumptions to the study of the change of final vowels, we come to several startling conclusions. Although most areas in Romania show the morphological change of final -*is* to -*es* in the nominative singular of third declension forms, the area of Narbonensis stands out in the phonetic change of -*is* to -*es* in the genitive singular of the third declension. Narbonensis shows a 25.0 % deviation (15 examples of -*is* and 5 examples of -*es*). Lugdunensis shows a 13.3 % deviation (13 examples of -*is* and 2 examples of -*es*, although unfortunately the total number of occurrences is small). Africa, on the other hand, while showing a morphological change of 3.9 % in the nominative singular (129 examples of -*is* and 5 examples of -*es*), does not have any phonetic change to -*es* in the genitive singular, although there are 135 examples of -*is*. The Latin of pagan Britain, in a similar vein, while showing a 14.6 % deviation in the morphological change of the nominative singular (35 examples of -*is* and 6 examples of -*es*, all in the particular noun *cives*), does not show any phonetic change in the genitive singular although it does have 43 examples of -*is*. It is clear that the Latin of Gaul does tend to a phonetic change of final /ĭ/ to *e*, while the Latin of Africa and pagan Britain maintains final /ĭ/ intact.

This weakening of final /ĭ/ in the Latin of Gaul is even more clearly seen in the conjugational endings. While most areas under consideration show a change of final -*it* to -*et* in the present indicative, a morphological rather than a strictly phonetic change, Narbonensis shows in the perfect indicative a percentage of 18.9 %

deviation (116 examples of -*it* and 27 examples of -*et*) and Lugdunensis has a 12.4 % weakening (106 examples of -*it* and 15 examples of -*et*). Northern Italy, apparently drawn again into the influence of Gaulish Latin, shows 7.0 % (159 examples of -*it* and 12 examples of -*et*). The situation for the Latin of Africa and pagan Britain is remarkably different. While showing a morphological change in the endings of the present indicative (16.3 % on the basis of 36 examples of -*it* and 7 examples of -*et*), Africa is most conservative in the treatment of final /ĭ/ in the perfect indicative. We did not find any examples of a change of final -*it* to -*et* in the perfect indicative, an indication of the phonetic stability of final /ĭ/,[1] although African inscriptions show 538 examples of -*it* in the perfect indicative. The Latin of pagan Britain is likewise very conservative in the treatment of final /ĭ/. Once again there is no example of a change of -*it* in the perfect indicative, although there are 143 examples of the correct termination. The comparison of the extreme areas of Gaul on the one hand, and Africa and pagan Britain on the other, in the treatment of final /ĭ/, shows that the Latin of Gaul tended to weaken the final vowel, whereas that of Africa and pagan Britain maintained it to a remarkable degree. This weakening of the final vowel in Gaul, and its stability in Africa and Britain, is another indication of the differentiation of the Latin spoken throughout Romania. The selection of the genitive singular of third declension forms rather than the nominative singular, and the option for the third person singular of the perfect indicative rather than that of the present indicative show that it is possible to distinguish between a phonetic and morphological change to a remarkable degree.

Another important result of our investigation of epigraphical material is the delineation of the characteristics of the Latin of Africa. Many scholars, as we have seen in our Introduction, have attempted to study the phenomenon of "Africitas" from various points of view, some investigators convinced of the peculiarity of the Latin spoken in this part of the Roman Empire, others equally convinced that African Latin was not basically different from the general Latin

---

[1] We did find the verb form *feciit* in an African inscription, *D.* 3681, *CIL* VIII 9910, Pomaria (Mauretania Caesariensis), no date, which may be the cursive writing for *e*, but as Diehl does not give any photographs or drawings of the inscriptions included in this collection, we have no way of determining the exact significance of this spelling.

of Romania. Scholars have also discussed the mutual relationships between Africa and Sardinia, the Iberian Peninsula, and Southern Italy, those areas that were most important in the development of the Latin of Africa. On the basis of our findings in African inscriptions we come to the conclusion that the Latin of Africa can be characterized by the extreme conservatism of its vocalism. It belongs to the Sardinian archaic vocalic system and the similarities which it shares with Sardinian are so numerous that they cannot be accounted for as merely fortuitous developments. Both the Latin of Africa and Sardinia evolved in close unison. In addition to the stability of stressed /ĭ/ and /ē/, /ō/ and /ŭ/, phonemes that remain separate in the Sardinian archaic vocalic system in contrast to their merger in the Italic qualitative system, both the Latin of Africa and Sardinian share the conservative tendency of maintaining the quality of unstressed medial vowels, and maintain the final vowels, even distinguishing final /ō/ and /ŭ/. Both show the ending -os in the accusative plural of second declension forms, in contrast to those areas where the ending -us is common, the loss of /ŭ/ in hiatus in words of general Vulgar Latin such as *Ianarias, Febrarias, mortus, qattor*, etc., the use of prothetic *i-* in words like *ispiritu, Istefanu*, etc., the monophthongization of initial *au-* to *a-* in such words as *Agustus*, etc., the monophthongization of *ae* to *e* in all positions, the general Vulgar Latin syncope of words such as *domnus, Oriclo, postus*, etc., although they both maintain a proparoxytonic structure to a great degree; the Latin of Africa even has examples of -*as* used as the nominative plural of first declension forms, the form -*as* being the regular feminine plural ending in Sardinian. Our conclusion of the classification of African Latin vocalism as a conservative variant of spoken Latin belonging to the Sardinian archaic system conflicts with and complements Wartburg's statement in his *Ausgliederung* (p. 63): "Das Latein Afrikas näherte sich wohl dem Iberiens; aber in Ermangelung moderner romanischer Idiome geben die Zeugnisse zu wenig Aufschluss, um es in eine strenge Klassifikation auf Lautlicher Grunlage einzureihen." It appears that a quantitative and comparative analysis of Latin inscriptions throughout Romania can help to classify the Latin of an individual area, in this case the very important Latin of Africa.

Our research has also shown that the Latin of pagan Britain is extremely conservative, even more so than that of Africa. This conclusion is almost diametrically opposed to the theory proposed by some scholars that the Latin of Britain is simply an extension of the Latin of Gaul. As we have already seen, the Latin of Gaul is the most innovative variant of spoken Latin of Romania and its vocalic changes have little repercussion in the Latin of Britain, one of the most conservative idioms of the Roman Empire. The Latin of pagan Britain maintains the separation of stressed /ĭ/ and /ē/, /ō/ and /ŭ/, shows great stability in intertonic and posttonic /ĭ/ and /ŭ/, and does not merge final vowels. The Latin of pagan Britain shows the peculiar change of a noun termination in the word *cives* for *civis*, and Christian inscriptions of Britain show a conjugational change in *iacit* for Classical Latin *iacet*, but these are isolated, morphological changes and are contrary to the general conservatism of the language. The Latin of pagan Britain does partake in the general syncope of early Vulgar Latin, but this syncope is common to all areas of Romania and is a characteristic of Latin, even in those areas which are considered proparoxytonic. The Latin of Britain does not offer examples of a prothetic *i-*, contrary to the situation of the Latin of other areas, even of the conservative Latin of Africa. The prothetic *y-* of modern Welsh is a later development as evidenced by its exclusion from the other Brittonic languages of Cornish and Breton. The Latin of Britain does present the monophthongization of *ae* to *e*, but this is a general characteristic of Vulgar Latin and is found in all areas of Romania. Changes not found in our corpus of Latin inscriptions of Britain have been revealed, however, by a comparison with loanwords into the Brittonic languages. The monophthongization of initial *au-* to *a-* through dissimilation with a following *u* is assured by the Welsh *awst* for *agustus* and *Awstin* from *Agustinus*. This change is common to most of the Romance languages as is the loss of /ŭ/ in hiatus in words like *Ianarius*, *Febrarius*, etc., a loss not encountered in inscriptions but surmised from Latin loanwords into the Brittonic languages. Loanwords also show that initial /ī/ was dissimilated to *e* before a stressed /ī/ in words such as *divinus* to *devinus*, although this change is not found in inscriptions of Britain. An indication of the extremely conservative status of the Latin in pagan Britain is its maintenance of the Classical Latin quantitative system instead of its replacement by a qualitative system, a feature of the Vulgar Latin period. Jackson remarks (*Language*, p. 270) that "There are no certain traces in British Latin of this whole important feature, even with unstressed vowels."

There are other examples where inscriptions show a differentiation of Latin in several vocalic points which impinge on later Romance development. Initial /ē/ tends to change to *i* in the Latin inscriptions of Rome much more than in other areas of Romania, as witnessed by an 8.1 % deviation (295 examples of /ē/ and 26 examples of *i*) compared to a 1.1 % deviation in the Latin of Africa (178 examples of /ē/ and 2 examples of *i*), an 0.8 % deviation in the Latin of pagan Britain (122 examples of /ē/ and 1 example of *i*), and even to the other parts of Italy: Northern Italy has a 2.3 % deviation (43 examples of /ē/ and 1 example of *i*); Central Italy has no examples of deviation but 47 examples of a correct occurrence, and Southern Italy has a 1.1 % deviation (92 examples of /ē/ and 1 example of *i*). The Italian tendency to have an initial *i* where other Romance languages prefer an *e* would seem to emanate from Rome, a center of irradiation that can be dated as early as the third century A.D. on the basis of inscriptions.

The use of *-as* as a nominative plural ending of first declension nouns and adjectives offers another example of differentiation of Latin according to the individual areas of Romania. In this case it is Gaul that stands out because of the conspicuous absence of any *-as* endings in the nominative plural in inscriptions of this area, although most of the other regions do have examples of this termination, an ending that assumes importance in the understanding of the plural formation of feminine nouns and adjectives in those Romance languages that keep the final *-s*. The situation of inscriptional evidence with its complete lack of examples of a nominative *-as* contrasts sharply with later documentary evidence where the termination *-as* has almost universally taken over the nominative plural of feminine forms. The treatment of final *-s* seems to be instrumental in any discussion of the plural of feminine forms, a problem that goes beyond the scope of this work.

An important example of differentiation in the Latin of the various areas of Romania is the distribution of the accusative plural ending *-is* of third declension nouns and adjectives and its more common rival *-es*. Comparing the percentages of use for the *-is* ending, we find that Narbonensis with 40.0 % (9 examples of *-es* and 6 examples of *-is*), Lugdunensis with 54.5 % (5 examples of *-es* and 6 examples of

-*is*), North Italy with 33.3 % (10 examples of -*es* and 5 examples of -*is*), Central Italy with 11.5 % (23 examples of -*es* and 3 examples of -*is*), Southern Italy with 33.3 % (12 examples of -*es* and 6 examples of -*is*), Rome with 28.9 % (59 examples of -*es* and 24 examples of -*is*), and Dalmatia with 26.9 % (19 examples of -*es* and 7 examples of -*is*), are the regions where an -*is* ending tends to assume considerable importance as the accusative ending of third declension forms. These areas differ sharply from Africa where we have a 4.6 % figure for the use of -*is* (104 examples of -*es* and 5 examples of -*is*) and Baetica which does not have any examples of an -*is* termination and fifteen examples of -*es*. The Latin of the pagan Balkans does have an example of an -*is* in a nominative plural function and an -*is* ending in an accusative plural of a Christian inscription, but the figures are too scanty to allow a more definite conclusion to be drawn for the Latin of the Balkans. What we do observe, however, is the pertinent fact that in those areas where we do have an -*i* ending for the formation of the masculine plural, an -*is* ending appears as a rather common termination in Latin inscriptions of the area. This is particularly true for Italian, Dalmatian where a final -*i* is posited for an umlaut effect although final Latin vowels generally drop, and Rumanian although the picture for this area is incomplete because of a paucity of examples. African Latin shows a marked tendency to maintain the -*es* ending and this situation is reflected in Sardinian where once again there is a marked similarity between it and the Latin of Africa. The linguistic picture of French cannot prove the importance of the -*is* ending since all final vowels, except *a*, were lost. The Spanish plural ending of nouns ending in a consonant is also -*es*, which appears to be the preferred ending in inscriptions although there are few examples. Contrary to scholars who believe that the -*is* ending was an archaic form and consequently not used in later Latin, we see that inscriptions show that there was no break in the continuity of the use of -*is* accusative plurals in those areas where the plural formation in -*i*, with a loss of final -*s*, is posited. Inscriptions also show that the analogical plural formation taken from the second declension ending -*i*, a theory proposed by many scholars, was not evident in epigraphical material. Third declension nouns and adjectives have either an -*es* or -*is* plural ending, not an analogical -*i* nor an -*i* with a loss of final -*s*. The distribution of these endings in the various parts of the Roman Empire would seem to indicate that the Latin differed in this important aspect and the Romance languages corroborate the findings of inscriptional evidence.

An interesting case of differentiation is the tendency for the Latin of some areas of Romania to prefer the ending -us rather than the Classical Latin -os for the accusative plural forms of the second declension. Although the Latin of Africa, with its stability of final vowels, has no examples of a -us ending and 84 examples of the regular -os, the Latin of pagan Britain is likewise conservative in its treatment of final vowels showing no examples of -us and 25 examples of -os, the Latin of the Iberian Peninsula also overwhelming in its preference for -os with Baetica having thirty-six examples of -os and no examples of -us, Tarraconensis having eleven examples of -os without any examples of -us, and Lusitania offering only one example of -us but forty examples of -os, it is interesting to note that other areas show a striking preference for the -us ending: the Latin of Lugdunensis shows a 63.5 % use of the -us ending (19 examples of -os and 33 examples of -us), Narbonensis has a 64.6 % figure of use (17 examples of -os and 31 examples of -us), Northern Italy has 24.1 % (44 examples of -os and 14 examples of -us), Central Italy shows 50.0 % (15 examples of -os and 15 examples of -us), Southern Italy offers 45.1 % (28 examples of -os and 23 examples of -us), and Rome has 47.1 % (90 examples of -os and 80 examples of -us). Dalmatia, as is so often the case, holds an intermediate position with 14.3 % with twenty-four examples of -os and four examples of -us. The Balkans offer too few examples for any comparison to be made. That a differentiation existed in the Latin of the various regions of Romania, with respect to the form of the accusative plural of the second declension is clear; what is more difficult is to account for this distinction in the Latin of the various areas. Sturtevant was convinced of the influence of the substratum since, as he writes (p. 117) "The use of u for ō is most common in Southern Italy and Gaul, where the native languages, Oscan and Gaulish, lacked ō." Carnoy and Prinz both considered the analogy of the second declension accusative singular ending -u(m) as the prime reason for the accusative plural -us. Grandgent offers the questionable view that the accusative plural of the fourth declension influenced the more numerous forms of the second declension. To these explanations must be added the possibility of a weakening of final vowels in those areas where final -os is closed to -us. Whatever the explanation may be, the fact remains that there was an apparent differentiation in the distribution of the accusative plural endings -*os* and -*us* in Romania.

The question of a prothetic vowel before an impure -*s* is another case of a differentiation of Latin throughout the individual areas of Romania. The Latin of Africa, although conservative, offers many examples of a prothetic *i*-, as does the Latin of Rome. The areas of Gaul, the Iberian Peninsula, Southern Italy, and Northern Italy show an occasional example of a prothetic vowel, while Dalmatia offers only a sporadic sampling of prothesis. Conspicuous in their absence of a prothetic vowel are the Latin of Britain, the Balkans, and the Latin loanwords in Albanian. It appears that the Latin of Dalmatia was the outer eastern limit for prothesis, since Rumanian and the Latin element of Albanian do not offer this phenomenon. The lack of prothesis in the Latin of Britain is interesting since Welsh does have a prothetic *y*- before an impure *s*-, but this must be a later development since other Brittonic languages do not have prothesis. The Latin of Africa, with its numerous examples of prothetic *i*-, once again shows the same development as Sardinian, which also has a prothetic *i*-. Although no cogent explanation can be offered for the different treatment of prothesis in the various areas of Romania, the distribution of this phenomenon shows that a differentiation evidently was present.

While inscriptions have been used to show that Latin was differentiated in various areas of Romania with respect to several basic vocalic phenomena, it is also true that inscriptions prove that Latin developed homogeneously in many respects throughout the vast Roman Empire. The Latin of the individual areas at times developed differently from other regions, but in other vocalic features there was at times a general development of the language that can be seen in the similarities evident in the Romance languages. Our epigraphical evidence shows that all areas under consideration treated both stressed and unstressed /ī/ and /ū/ in a similar vein, without any area evolving markedly from any other region. There is no certain case of diphthongization or at least no clear trend to diphthongize that can be detected in any area of Romania. The monophthongization of *ae* to *e* is clearly established in all positions, in all areas studied, although the pagan inscriptions show a lower but still substantial percentage of deviation as compared to Christian inscriptions. Monophthongization of *ae* to *e* is by far the most common vocalic change observed in inscriptions and it can definitely be stated that the monophthongization of *ae* was a general characteristic of Christian inscriptions throughout all areas of Romania. An excellent indication of the general acceptance of the monophthongized *e* is the fact that the Latin of Africa, repeatedly mentioned as a conservative area and belonging to the Sardinian archaic system, prefers the vowel *e* rather than the diphthong *ae* in all positions as is evidenced by the 55.1 % of deviation calculated for this area (162 examples of *ae* and 199 examples of *e*). Since all stonemasons, regardless of their competence, aspired to write Classical Latin, the high percentages of deviation for this particular change is eloquent testimony to the contention that the monophthongization of *ae* had already taken place. The Latin of pagan Britain shows the lowest percentage of deviation for the monophthongization of *ae*, a substantial 17.4 % (337 examples of *ae* and 71 examples of *e*), a percentage which would be considered innovative in other respects for this extremely conservative area of Romania. The possibility of a chronological analysis of this phenomenon may be surmised from the fact that in the Latin inscriptions of pagan Britain there were no examples of monophthongization in the first and second centuries A.D., but a gradual increase in subsequent centuries did take place. Although nothing definite can be stated as to the precise origin of the monophthongization of *ae* on the basis of our corpus of inscriptions, it is clear that this was a general vocalic feature of Vulgar Latin in the third or fourth centuries A.D.

Another example of a general vocalic change throughout all of Romania is the extension of the masculine forms *qui* and *quem* at the expense of the feminine *quae* and *quam*. Inscriptions show this important evolution in all areas under consideration with abundant examples. The contracted forms of the genitive singular ending in *-i*, the nominative plural in *-i*, and the dative and ablative plurals in *-is*, are generally preferred to the full forms *-ii*, *-ii*, and *-iis*. This preference is best seen in the fairly numerous examples of the Latin of Africa where we have an 89.1 % use of the contracted form of the genitive singular (82 examples of *-i* and 10 examples of *-ii*) and 88.5 % for the nominative plural (23 examples of *-i* and 3 examples of *-ii*). The occurrences for the genitive singular are more numerous than those of the nominative plural or dative and ablative plural. The percentage of use of the contracted forms of the genitive singular is relatively constant as, in addition to the 89.1 % for the Latin of

Africa, we have 94.7 % for pagan Britain (54 examples of -*i* and 3 examples of -*ii*), 90.9 % for Christian Britain (20 examples of -*i* and 2 examples of -*ii*), and 81.5 % for Dalmatia (22 examples of -*i* and 5 examples of -*ii*). The monophthongization of initial *au* to *a* before a stressed *u* in the root *august*- is also an example of a general Vulgar Latin tendency commonly encountered in epigraphical material. Inscriptions show that Greek upsilon, although evolving into both *i* and *u*, tended to develop into the *i*-sound in general Vulgar Latin. The only area in our corpus which shows a relatively extensive portrayal of the development of the Greek upsilon is Africa, where we have 38 examples of *i* and twenty examples of *u*. There was no period of time in the Latin of Africa from the third century on, when the *u*-sound was dominant. Dalmatian Latin has eight examples of *i* and three examples of *u*, while the Latin of the Christian Balkans has six examples of *i* and three examples of *u*, but the figures for these two areas are too low to permit any firm conclusion to be drawn.

An extremely important example of a general Vulgar Latin tendency found throughout all areas of Romania is the relative lack of syncope encountered and those cases of syncope which are found are, for the most part, common to all parts of the Roman Empire. No area stands out for its syncopating tendencies. Those syncopated forms which acquired acceptance in the Vulgar Latin speech of early times as evidenced by their being attested in the writings of Plautus, Terence, Cicero, Varro, the Pompeian inscriptions, and criticized in the *Appendix Probi*, are found in the Latin of all areas, even the most conservative variants such as the Latin of Africa and pagan Britain, proof that early syncope had taken place and had been accepted by the general populace. This early, general Vulgar Latin syncope, however, must be carefully distinguished from the later syncope that was to differentiate the paroxytonic members of the Romance languages from the more conservative proparoxytonic languages. Sardinian, considered one of the most archaic Romance languages in the whole of Romania, is most conservative in its treatment of pretonic and posttonic vowels, but it, too, offers precisely those examples of general Vulgar Latin syncope which are found in the more innovative languages. Inscriptions prove to an exceptionally high degree that early syncope was a common vocalic phenomenon throughout Romania, but they also intimate through the lack of any distinctiveness in the treatment of syncope that those areas later distinguished by their paroxytonic rhythm developed this feature during Romance times and not earlier in the Vulgar Latin period. In the Latin of Gaul, the most innovative idiom of Late Latin, there was a differentiation in the treatment of the pretonic and posttonic vowels /ĭ/ and /ŭ/, but this weakening of the medial vowels, the forerunners of their complete loss, appears from epigraphic evidence to have assumed importance only in the sixth century. It would appear that modern French and Provençal, notable for their syncopation, began to differ with respect to medial vowels in their sixth century Latin from the Latin of other areas and continued this trend in their Romance period. The immediate cause for the weakening of pretonic and posttonic vowels may possibly be ascribed to the increased stress accent brought in by the invading Germanic peoples.

Inscriptions, on the basis of our investigation, show that the Latin of some parts of the Empire was evolving differently from other areas of Romania, both in systematic vocalic patterns and individual phenomena. Inscriptions also indicate that, in some respects, the Latin of all areas was developing in the same way. This is precisely the linguistic situation of the Romance languages where basic similarities underlie a common heritage, but whose differences are too often emphasized in an attempt to highlight the more scintillating aspects of the individual Romance languages. The Romance languages are a composite of both similarities and differences, and this situation is mirrored most definitely in the Latin inscriptions of the various areas of Romania. We therefore consider the Latin of inscriptions as a relatively faithful portrayal of the general speech of the region under investigation, with the understanding that this Latin must be judged on the basis of an extensive corpus of inscriptions and not on limited, isolated, and fragmentary epigraphical evidence.

One of the most important results of this entire work is the reliability of the methodology utilized. Our method of a quantitative-comparative analysis, based on the number of correct occurrences as well as the deviations, and the comparisons made among the various areas of Romania, differs greatly from the usual work dealing with the problems of Vulgar Latin of a single area, without any mention of the frequency of occurrence of deviations. It is precisely the laborious, uninspiring, and time-consuming collation of correct occurrences that lends a solid base to our investigation. A simple enumeration of deviations from the Classical Latin norm, while worthwhile in itself, too often leads scholars to draw superficial conclusions which are later parroted by succeeding generations of Romance researchers. This criticism can be leveled at the conclusions of Maurice Jeanneret in his oft-quoted *La Langue des tablettes d'exécration latines,* a work that has had considerable influence on the thinking of Romance scholars. This investigator concluded (p. 157) his work with the following comments:

> Bref, nous constatons dans les tablettes d'exécration latines de nombreux vulgarismes, des dialectismes italiques, quelques archaïsmes. Les différenciations provinciales sont nulles, ou d'intérêt tout à fait secondaires; dans les tablettes africaines, si incohérentes de style, si emphatiques et violentes, on serait tenté de reconnaître des manifestations du *tumor africus,* si la plupart de celles d'Europe ne présentaient sensiblement les mêmes caractères, qui sont ceux de notre genre d'écrits.

> Ces conclusions, enfin, corroborent en de nombreux points nos connaissances en latin vulgaire, parfois y ajoutent et, pour quelques cas, elles confirment des hypothèses de romanistes.

Although Jeanneret admitted finding vulgarisms, dialectalisms, and archaisms, he concluded that the differentiations from Classical Latin as found in the Latin of the Roman provinces were of no consequence or at best of secondary importance. In no part of his work, however, does he give any numerical evidence to bolster his strong views. His attempts at comparison must be considered presumptuous, especially when we read in his Introduction (p. 5) that "Nos observations porteront ainsi sur le total assez restreint de 125 inscriptions." A more careful scrutiny of the breakdown of his inscriptions shows (p. 6) that the 54 inscriptions found in Europe are distributed in the following manner: 2 from Austria; 16 from Germany; 2 from England; 2 from France; 1 from Spain, and 31 from all of Italy. Of the 71 African inscriptions, thirty-one came from Carthage, thirty-nine from Souza, and one from Constantine. Any comparative study based on the extremely low figures offered as evidence must of necessity be of questionable value. Jeanneret himself was aware of the limitations of his investigation, inasmuch as he wrote (p. 12) that "Il est regrettable seulement que des textes du genre des tablettes d'exécration ne soient ni plus nombreux, ni plus étendus." Here, too, we see the overwhelming importance of finding a deviation in one area that is likewise found in another part of Romania without any consideration given to the frequency of occurrence. We have seen throughout our work that at times a deviation can be detected in various areas, but the percentage of deviation may be so marked in the individual areas as to force one to admit that the particular tendency is so great in certain areas that a differentiation must be posited to explain the discrepancy. The need for a complete lack of any deviation in an area under study, coupled with the utter disregard of any notion of a frequency of occurrence, is one of the greatest defects encountered in the reasoning of too many Romance linguists who can think only in absolute terms. Until a particular form has established itself in a language or dialect, various contending forms may be striving for supremacy. In the development of Latin into the Romance languages, it is unreasonable and un-scientific to expect a unanimity of evolution. In many cases abortive tendencies, although having disappeared in the modern Romance language or dialect, may very well have been present in an earlier stage. This insistence on tendencies and not exclusiveness is an important result of our investigation. Densusianu's remark (p. 53) that "Il serait chimérique de chercher dans les inscriptions d'une province quelconque, du moins jusqu'à une certaine époque, des faits linguistiques propres à cette province et qui n'auraient jamais existé dans les autres pays de l'Empire" is too restricting and completely ignores the factor of tendencies. We disagree with Pirson's conclusion with regard to local differences, when he writes (p. 324) that,

> ...les résultats obtenus en ce point sont peu importants. L'existence de différences locales dans le latin de l'Empire est incontestable et incontestée, mais on peut se demander si les documents latins que nous possédons nous permettront jamais d'approfondir cette question. On peut en douter lorsqu'on les compare entre eux; on constate qu'une foule de particularités qu'on serait tout d'abord tenté de considérer comme spéciales à une province, se retrouvent dans les textes provenant d'autres régions.

It is precisely Pirson's area of study, the Latin of Gaul, that shows a distinctiveness in the vocalism of its inscriptions. Pulgram's statement (*Tongues*, p. 407) with respect to the uniformity of written Latin is likewise not completely accurate:

No wonder, then, that those who consider only what is written marvel at the uniformity and the lack of dialectalization of the language throughout the Empire down to the eighth century — a uniformity which contradicts all sensible expectations and all that we know of the ways of human speech, whose outstanding quality is change, notably that of disintegration of an idiom through the agencies of longevity, expansion, and superimposition upon multiple linguistic substrata.

Our study shows that even the written language, in this case inscriptions, offers examples of a differentiation of Latin in various parts of the Empire, the Latin of Gaul being most innovative in contrast to the Latin of Africa and of Britain, variants that are the most conservative; epigraphical evidence proves that variations took place before the eighth century, in some cases the sixth century being crucial, and occasionally the fourth century assuming importance in the problem of differentiation. A correct use of written material shows that the unity of Latin throughout Romania is a fiction. We, of course, deny Väänänen's statement (*Introduction*, p. 26) that: "L'unité du latin postclassique et tardif dans ses grandes lignes, du moins dans sa forme écrite, est un fait indéniable, puisque démontré par l'analyse des textes."

The methodology used, inspired by the previous works of Pei, Politzer, and Gaeng, although primarily used to investigate vocalic phenomena in the present work, can be used advantageously in the study of consonantal changes, morphological and syntactical considerations, and lexical problems. The use of a quantitative and comparative format is practically unlimited. If this methodology, in addition to the results attained in our investigation, can stimulate other scholars to study outstanding problems in the field of Romance linguistics, our painstaking efforts will have been more than compensated.

A SELECTED BIBLIOGRAPHY

PRIMARY SOURCES WITH ABBREVIATIONS

CIL = Corpus Inscriptionum Latinarum, consilio et auctoritate Academiae Litterarum Borussicae editum. Berlin, 1863-1943.

Collingwood, *RIB* = Collingwood, R. G., and Wright, R. P. *The Roman Inscriptions of Britain*. Vol. I. Oxford: Clarendon Press, 1965.

Diehl, *AI* = *Altlateinische Inschriften*. 4th ed. Ed. Ernst Diehl. Berlin: Walter de Gruyter, 1959.

Diehl, *ICLV* = *Inscriptiones Latinae Christianae Veteres*. 3 vols. Ed. Ernst Diehl. Berlin: Weidman, 1925-31. Vol. IV is the Supplement to *Inscriptiones Latinae Christianae Veteres*, edited by J. Moreau and H. I. Marrou. Berlin: Weidman, 1967.

Diehl, *VI* = *Vulgärlateinische Inschriften*. Ed. Ernst Diehl. Bonn: Marcus u. Weber, 1910.

Hübner, *IBC* = *Inscriptiones Britanniae Christianae*. Ed. Emil Hübner. Berlin: Georg Reimer, 1876.

Kalinka, *Kal.* = *Antike Denkmäler in Bulgarien*. Ed. Ernst Kalinka. Schriften der Balkankommission. Vol. IV. Vienna: Alfred Hölder, 1906.

Macalister, *CIIC* = Macalister, R.A.S. *Corpus Inscriptionum Insularum Celticarum*. Vol. I. Dublin: Stationery Office, 1945.

CHIEF WORKS USED WITH ABBREVIATIONS

Anderson = Anderson, James. "A Study of Syncope in Vulgar Latin." *Word*, 21 (1965), 70-85.

Bàrtoli, *Das Dalmatische* = Bàrtoli, Matteo G. *Das Dalmatische: Altromanische Sprachreste von Veglia bis Ragusa und ihre Stellung in der apennino-balkanischen Romania*. 2 vols. Schriften der Balkancommission, Nos. IV, V. Vienna: Alfred Hölder, 1906.

Bàrtoli, *Neolinguistica* = Bàrtoli, Matteo G. *Introduzione alla neolinguistica*. Biblioteca dell' "Archivum Romanicum," Serie II, Linguistica, Vol. 12. Geneva: Olschki, 1925.

Blaise = Blaise, Albert. *Manuel du latin chrétien*. Strasbourg: Le Latin Chrétien, 1955.

Bloch = Bloch, Raymond. *L'Epigraphie latine*. 4th ed. Paris: Presses Universitaires de France, 1969.

Bourciez = Bourciez, Edouard. *Eléments de linguistique romane*. 5th ed. Paris: Klincksieck, 1967.

Brüch = Brüch, Josef. Review of "A Chronology of Vulgar Latin," by H. F. Muller. *Zeitschrift für französische Sprache und Literatur*, 54 (1931), 357-82.

Budinszky = Budinszky, Alexander. *Die Ausbreitung der lateinische Sprache.* Berlin: Hertz, 1881.

Burn = Burn, A. R. *The Romans in Britain: An Anthology of Inscriptions.* 2nd ed. Columbia, S.C.: University of South Carolina Press, 1969.

Carnoy = Carnoy, Albert J. *Le Latin d'Espagne d'après les inscriptions.* 2nd ed. Louvain: J. B. Istas, 1906.

Collart = Collart, Jean. *Histoire de la langue latine.* Paris: Presses Universitaires, 1967.

Collingwood-Myres = Collingwood, R. G., and Myres, J. N. L. *Roman Britain and the English Settlements.* 2nd ed. The Oxford History of England. Oxford: Clarendon Press, 1963.

Colombis = Colombis, Antonio. "Elementi veglioti nell'isola di Cherso-Ossero." *Archivum Romanicum*, XXI (1911), 75-116.

Cross = Cross, Ephraim. *Syncope and Kindred Phenomena in Latin Inscriptions.* New York: Institute of French Studies, 1930.

Densusianu = Densusianu, Ovide. *Histoire de la langue roumaine.* Vol. I. Paris: Ernest Leroux, 1901.

Devoto = Devoto, Giacomo. *Storia della lingua di Roma.* Istituto di studi romani, Vol. XXIII. Bologna: Licinio Cappelli, 1940.

Díaz = Díaz y Díaz, Manuel C. *Antología del latín vulgar.* 2nd ed. Biblioteca Románica Hispánica. Madrid: Editorial Gredos, 1962.

Diehl, *De m Finali* = Diehl, Ernst. *De m Finali Epigraphica.* Leipzig: B. G. Teubner, 1899.

Elcock = Elcock, W. D. *The Romance Languages.* London: Faber and Faber, 1960.

Ernout, *Morphologie* = Ernout, Alfred. *Morphologie historique du latin.* 3rd ed. Paris: Klincksieck, 1953.

Ernout-Thomas, *Syntaxe* = Ernout, Alfred, and Thomas, François. *Syntaxe latine.* 2nd ed. Paris: Klincksieck, 1964.

Friedwagner = Friedwagner, Matthias. "Über die Sprache und Heimat der Rumänen." *Zeitschrift für romanische Philologie*, 54 (1934), 641-715.

Gaeng = Gaeng, Paul A. *An Inquiry into Local Variations in Vulgar Latin as Reflected in the Vocalism of Christian Inscriptions.* University of North Carolina Studies in the Romance Languages and Literatures, No. 77. Chapel Hill: University of North Carolina Press, 1968.

Grandgent = Grandgent, C. H. *An Introduction to Vulgar Latin.* 1907; rpt. New York: Hafner, 1962.

Guiraud = Guiraud, Pierre. *Problèmes et méthodes de la statistique linguistique.* Paris: Presses Universitaires de France, 1960.

Hadlich = Hadlich, Roger L. *The Phonological History of Vegliote.* University of North Carolina Studies in the Romance Languages and Literatures, No. 52. Chapel Hill: University of North Carolina Press, 1965.

Hall = Hall, Robert A., Jr. "The Reconstruction of Proto-Romance." *Language*, 26 (1950), 6-27.

Hanslik = Hanslik, Rudolf, Review of *Limba latină în provinciile dunărene ale imperiului român*, by H. Mihăescu. *Kratylos*, 10 (1965), 211-13.

Herman = Herman, J. "Aspects de la différenciation territoriale du latin sous l'Empire." *Bulletin de la Société de la Linguistique de Paris*, 60 (1965), 53-70.

Hoffmann = Hoffmann, Ernst. *De Titulis Africae Latinis Quaestiones Phoneticae.* Diss. Breslau, 1907. Breslau: Robert Noske, 1907.

Hofmann = Hofmann, J. B. *Lateinische Umgangssprache.* 3rd ed. Indogermanische Bibliothek. Heidelberg: Carl Winter, 1951.

Iordan = Iordan, Iorgu. *Lingüística románica.* Trans. Manuel Alvar. Madrid: Ediciones Alcalá, 1967.

Jackson, *Language* = Jackson, Kenneth. *Language and History in Early Britain.* Edinburgh: Edinburgh University Press, 1953.

Jackson, "Vulgar Latin" = Jackson, Kenneth. "On the Vulgar Latin of Roman Britain," in *Mediaeval Studies in honor of Jeremiah Denis Matthias Ford,* ed. Urban T. Holmes, Jr., and Alex J. Denomy, C. S. B. Cambridge, Mass.: Harvard University Press, 1948, pp. 83-103.

Jeanneret = Jeanneret, Maurice. *La Langue des tablettes d'exécration latines.* Diss. Neuchatel, 1916. Paris: Attinger Frères, 1918.

Kent = Kent, Roland G. *The Forms of Latin.* Baltimore: Linguistic Society of America, 1946.

Knott = Knott, Betty. "The Christian 'Special Language' in the Inscriptions." *Vigiliae Christianae,* X (1956), 65-79.

Kroll = Kroll, W. "Das afrikanische Latein." *Rheinisches Museum für Philologie,* 52 (1897), 569-90.

Kübler = Kübler, Bernhard. "Die lateinische Sprache auf afrikanischen Inschriften." *Archiv für lateinische Lexikographie und Grammatik,* 8 (1893), 161-202.

Kuhn = Kuhn, Alwin. *Die romanischen Sprachen.* Vol. I. Bern: A. Francke, 1951.

Lausberg, *Lingüística* = Lausberg, Heinrich. *Lingüística románica.* 2 vols. Trans. J. Pérez Riesco and E. Pascual Rodríguez. Biblioteca Románica Hispánica. Madrid: Editorial Gredos, 1966.

Lausberg, "Südlukaniens" = Lausberg, Heinrich. "Die Mundarten Südlukaniens." *Zeitschrift für romanische Philologie,* Beiheft 90. Halle: Max Niemeyer, 1939.

LeBlant = LeBlant, Edmond. *L'Epigraphie chrétienne en Gaule et dans l'Afrique romane.* Paris: Ernest Leroux, 1890.

Lewis-Pedersen = Lewis, Henry, and Pedersen, Holger. *A Concise Comparative Celtic Grammar.* Göttingen: Vandenhoeck & Ruprecht, 1961.

Lindsay = Lindsay, W. M. *The Latin Language.* Oxford: Clarendon Press, 1894.

B. Löfstedt = Löfstedt, Bengt. *Studien über die Sprache der langobardischen Gesetze.* Uppsala: Almquist & Wiksells, 1961.

Löfstedt, *Late Latin* = Löfstedt, Einar. *Late Latin.* Oslo: Aschehoug, 1959.

Löfstedt, *Syntactica* = Löfstedt, Einar. *Syntactica.* Vol I: *Über einige Grundfragen der lateinischen Nominalsyntax.* Lund: C. W. K. Gleerup, 1928. Vol. II: *Syntaktisch-stilistische Gesichtspunkte und Probleme.* Lund: C. W. K. Gleerup, 1933.

Lot = Lot, F. "A quelle époque a-t-on cessé de parler latin?" *Archivum Latinitatis Medii Aevi,* VI (1931), 97-159.

Loth = Loth, J. *Les Mots latins dans les langues brittoniques.* Paris: Emile Bouillon, 1892.

Maccarrone = Maccarrone, Nunzio. "Il latino delle iscrizioni di Sicilia." *Studi romanzi,* 7 (1911), 75-116.

Martin = Martin, Henry. *Notes on the Syntax of the Latin Inscriptions found in Spain.* Diss. Hopkins. Baltimore: J. H. Furst, 1901.

Maurer = Maurer, Theodoro. *O problema do latim vulgar.* Biblioteca Brasileira de Filologia, No. 17. Rio de Janeiro: Livraria Acadêmica, 1961.

Meillet, *Esquisse* = Meillet, Antoine. *Esquisse d'une histoire de la langue latine.* Nouvelle Edition. Paris: Klincksieck, 1966.

Meyer = Meyer, Gustav. "Die lateinischen Elemente im Albanischen." *Grundriss der romanischen Philologie.* 2nd ed. Ed. Gustav Gröber. Strassburg: Karl J. Trübner, 1904-06. I, 1038-57.

Meyer-Lübke, *Einführung* = Meyer-Lübke, W. *Einführung in das Studium der romanischen Sprachwissenschaft.* 3rd ed. Heidelberg: Carl Winter, 1920.

Meyer-Lübke, *Grammaire* = Meyer-Lübke, W. *Grammaire des langues romanes.* 4 vols. Trans. Eugène Rabiet. Paris: Stechert, 1890-1906.

Migliorini = Migliorini, Bruno. *The Italian Language,* abridged and recast by T. Gwynfor Griffith. London: Faber and Faber, 1966.

Mihăescu, "Cîteva observaţii" = Mihăescu, H. "Cîteva observaţii asupra limbii latine din provinciile dunărene ale imperiului român." *Studii şi Cercetări Lingvistice,* 10 (1959), 77-99.

Mihăescu, *Limba* = Mihăescu, H. *Limba latină în provinciile dunărene ale imperiului român.* Comisia pentru studiul formării limbii şi poporului romîn, Vol. III. Bucharest: Editura Academiei Republica Populare Romîne, 1960.

Mohl = Mohl, Friedrich G. *Introduction à la chronologie du latin vulgaire.* Bibliothèque de l'École des Hautes Études. Sciences philologiques et historiques, Fasc. 122. Paris: E. Bouillon, 1899.

Mohrmann, *Études* = Mohrmann, Christine. *Études sur le latin des chrétiens.* 3 vols. Rome: Edizioni di Storia e Letteratura, 1961-65.

Mohrmann, *Latin vulgaire* = Mohrmann, Christine. *Latin vulgaire, latin des chrétiens, latin médieval.* Paris: Klincksieck, 1955.

Muller = Muller, Henri F. "A Chronology of Vulgar Latin." *Zeitschrift für romanische Philologie,* Beiheft 78. Halle: Max Niemeyer, 1929.

Niedermann = Niedermann, Max. *Précis de phonétique historique du latin.* 4th ed. Paris: Klincksieck, 1953.

Norberg, *Beiträge* = Norberg, Dag. *Beiträge zur spätlateinischen Syntax.* Uppsala: Almquist and Wiksells, 1944.

Norberg, *Syntaktische* = Norberg, Dag. *Syntaktische Forschungen auf dem Gebiete des Spätlateins und des frühen Mittellateins.* Uppsala Universitets Arsskrift, 9. Uppsala: Lundequistska Bokhandeln, 1943.

Palmer = Palmer, L. R. *The Latin Language.* London: Faber and Faber, 1954.

Pei, "Accusative" = Pei, Mario A. "Accusative or Oblique?" *The Romanic Review,* XXVIII (1937), 241-67.

Pei, "Intervocalic Occlusives" = Pei, Mario A. "Intervocalic Occlusives in 'East' and 'West' Romance." *The Romanic Review,* XXXIV (1943), 235-47.

Pei, *Italian Language* = Pei, Mario A. *The Italian Language.* 2nd ed. New York: S. F. Vanni, 1954.

Pei, *Texts* = Pei, Mario A. *The Language of the Eighth-Century Texts in Northern France.* New York: Carranza, 1932.

Pieske = Pieske, Erik. *De Titulorum Africae Latinorum Sermone Quaestiones Morphologicae.* Frederick William of Silesia, 1913. Trebnitzia: Maretzke and Maertin, 1913.

Pirson = Pirson, Jules. *La Langue des inscriptions latines de la Gaule.*

Bibliothèque de la Faculté de Philosophie & Lettres de l'Université de Liège, Fascicule XI. Bruxelles, 1901.

Pogatscher = Pogatscher, Alois. *Zur Lautlehre der griechischen, lateinischen, romanischen Lehnworte im Altenglischen.* Quellen und Forschungen zur Sprache- und Culturgeschichte der germanischen Völker, Vol. LXIV. Strassburg: Karl J. Trübner, 1888.

Politzer, "Final -s" = Politzer, Robert. "Final -s in the Romania." *The Romanic Review,* XXXVIII (1947), 159-66.

Politzer, "Origin" = Politzer, Robert. "On the Origin of the Italian Plurals." *The Romanic Review,* XLIII (1952), 272-81.

Politzer, *Lombardic Documents* = Politzer, Robert L. *A Study of the Language of Eighth Century Lombardic Documents.* New York: privately printed, 1949.

Politzers, *Romance Trends* = Politzer, Frieda N., and Politzer, Robert L. *Romance Trends in 7th and 8th Century Latin Documents.* University of North Carolina Studies in the Romance Languages and Literatures, No. 21. Chapel Hill: University of North Carolina Press, 1953.

Posner = Posner, Rebecca. *The Romance Languages: A Linguistic Introduction.* Anchor Books. New York: Doubleday, 1966.

Poukens = Poukens, J.-B. *Syntaxe des inscriptions latines d'Afrique.* Louvain: Charles Peeters, 1912.

Prinz, *De O et U* = Prinz, Otto. *De O et U vocalibus inter se Permutatis in Lingua Latina.* Halle: Eduard Klinz, 1932.

Prinz, "Prothese" = Prinz, Otto. "Zur Entstehung der Prothese vor s-impurum im Lateinischen." *Glotta,* XXVI (1938), 97-115.

Proskauer = Proskauer, Carola. *Das auslautende -s auf den lateinischen Inschriften.* Strassburg: Karl J. Trübner, 1909.

Pulgram, "Spoken and Written" = Pulgram, Ernst. "Spoken and Written Latin." *Language,* 26 (1950), 458-66.

Pulgram, *Tongues* = Pulgram, Ernst. *The Tongues of Italy.* Cambridge, Mass.: Harvard University Press, 1958.

Puşcariu, *Études* = Puşcariu, Sextil. *Études de linguistique roumaine.* Cluj-Bucharest: Imprimeria Naţională, 1937.

Puşcariu, *Rumänische Sprache* = Puşcariu, Sextil. *Die rumänische Sprache: Ihr Wesen und ihre volkliche Prägung.* Trans. Heinrich Kuen. Rumänische Bibliothek, No. 1. Leipzig: Otto Harrassowitz, 1943.

Richter = Richter, Elise. "Beiträge zur Geschichte der Romanismen: Chronologische Phonetik des Französischen bis zum Ende des 8. Jahrhunderts." *Zeitschrift für romanische Philologie,* Beiheft 82. Halle: Max Niemeyer, 1934.

Rohlfs, *Grammatik* = Rohlfs, Gerhard. *Historische Grammatik der italienischen Sprache und ihrer Mundarten.* 3 vols. Bibliotheca Romanica, Series prima: Manualia et Commentationes, V-VII. Bern: A. Francke, 1949-54.

Rohlfs, *Romanische* = Rohlfs, Gerhard. *Romanische Philologie.* I. 2nd ed. Heidelberg: Carl Winter, 1966. II. Heidelberg: Carl Winter, 1952.

Rohlfs, *Vulgärlatein* = Rohlfs, Gerhard. *Vom Vulgärlatein zum Altfranzösischen.* Sammlung kurzer Lehrbücher der romanischen Sprachen und Literaturen, No. 15. Tübingen: Max Niemeyer, 1960.

Rosenkranz = Rosenkranz, Bernhard. "Die Gliederung des Dalmatischen." *Zeitschrift für romanische Philologie,* 71 (1955), 269-79.

Rosetti = Rosetti, Al. *Istoria limbii romîne.* 3 vols. 4th ed. Bucharest: Editura Ştiinţifică, 1964.

Russu = Russu, I. I. Review of *Limba latină in provinciile dunărene ale imperiului român*, by H. Mihăescu. *Cercetări de Lingvistică*, 6 (1961), 209-18.

Sandfeld = Sandfeld, Kristian. *Linguistique balkanique*. La Société de Linguistique de Paris, XXXI. Paris. E. Champion, 1930.

Sas = Sas, Louis Furman. *The Noun Declension System in Merovingian Latin*. Paris: Pierre André, 1937.

Schmeck = Schmeck, Helmut. *Aufgaben und Methoden der modernen vulgärlateinischen Forschung*. Heidelberg: Carl Winter, 1955.

Schrijnen = Schrijnen, Jos. *Charakteristik des altchristlichen Latein*. Latinitas Christianorum Primaeva, Fasciculus Primus. Nijmegen: Dekker and van de Vegt, 1932.

Schuchardt, "Lehnwörter" = Schuchardt, Hugo. "Die romanischen Lehnwörter im Berberischen." *Kaiserliche Akademie der Wissenschaften in Wien*, Sitzungsberichte, 188 (1918), 1-82.

Schuchardt, *Vokalismus* = Schuchardt, Hugo. *Der Vokalismus des Vulgärlateins*. 3 vols. Leipzig: B. G. Teubner, 1866-68.

Şiadbei, "Albanais" = Şiadbei, I. "Sur l'élément latin de l'Albanais," in *Mélanges Linguistiques*, publiés à l'occasion du VIIIe Congrès international des linguistes à Oslo, du 5 au 9 août 1957. Bucharest: Academia Republicii Populare Romîni, 1957, pp. 63-69.

Şiadbei, "Contribuţii" = Şiadbei, I. "Contribuţii la studiul latinei orientale." *Studii şi Cercetări Lingvistice*, IX (1958), 71-91, 175-197.

Silva Neto = Da Silva Neto, Serafim. *História do latim vulgar*. Biblioteca Brasileira de Filologia, No. 13. Rio de Janeiro: Livraria Acadêmica, 1957.

Sittl = Sittl, Karl. *Die lokalen Verschiedenheiten der lateinischen Sprache mit besonderer Berücksichtingung des afrikanischen Lateins*. Erlangen: Andreas Deichert, 1882.

Skok, *Pojave* = Skok, Petar. *Pojave vulgarno-latinskoga jezika na natpisima rimse provincije Dalmacije*. Jugoslavenska Akademija Znanosti i Umjetnosti, Vol. XXV. Zagreb: Hartman, 1915.

Skok, "Balkanlatein" = Skok, Petar. "Zum Balkanlatein." *Zeitschrift für romanische Philologie*, 48 (1928), 398-403; 50 (1930), 484-532; 54 (1934), 175-215, 424-99.

Söderström = Söderström, Gunnar. *Epigraphica Latina Africana*. Diss. Uppsala, 1924. Uppsala: Appelbergs Boktryckeri, 1924.

Sofer, "Differenzierung" = Sofer, Johann. "Die Differenzierung der romanischen Sprachen." *Die Sprache*, II (1950-52), 23-28.

Sofer, *Problematik* = Sofer, Johann. *Zur Problematik des Vulgärlateins: Ergebnisse und Anregungen*. Vienna: Gerold, 1963.

Sommer = Sommer, Ferdinand. *Handbuch der lateinischen Lautund Formenlehre*. 2nd and 3rd eds. Heidelberg: Carl Winter, 1948.

Spence = Spence, N. C. W. "Quantity and Quality in the Vowel System of Vulgar Latin." *Word*, 21 (1965), 1-18.

Stati, "Declinării romînesti" = Stati, Sorin. "Din problemele istoriei declinării romîneste." *Studii şi Cercetări Lingvistice*, 10 (1959), 63-75.

Stati, *Review* = Stati, Sorin. Review of *Limba latină în provinciile dunărene ale imperiului român*, by H. Mihăescu. *Studii şi Cercetări Lingvistice*, 4 (1960), 957-63.

Stolz-Debrunner = Stolz, Friedrich, and Debrunner, Albert. *Geschichte der lateinischen Sprache.* 4th ed., revised by Wolfgang P. Schmid. Sammlung Göschen, Band 492/492a. Berlin: Walter de Gruyter, 1966.

Straka "Dislocation" = Straka, Georges. "La Dislocation linguistique de la Romania et la formation des langues romanes à la lumière de la chronologie relative des changements phonétiques." *Revue de Linguistique Romane,* XX (1956), 249-57.

Straka, *Review* = Straka, Georges. Review of *Limba latină în provinciile dunărene ale imperiului român,* by H. Mihăescu. *Revue de Linguistique Romane,* XXIV (1960), 403-6.

Strecker = Strecker, Karl. *Introduction à l'étude du latin médiéval.* 3rd ed. Trans. Paul van de Woestijne. Société de Publications Romanes et Françaises, XXVI. Geneva: Librairie Droz, 1939.

Sturtevant = Sturtevant, Edgar H. *The Pronunciation of Greek and Latin.* 2nd ed. Philadelphia: Linguistic Society of America, 1940.

Sylloge = Sylloge Inscriptionum Christianarum Veterum Musei Vaticani, edited by Henrico Zilliacus. 2 vols. Acta Instituti Romani Finlandiae. Helsinki: Tilgmann, 1963.

Tagliavini, "Dalmatica" = Tagliavini, Carlo. "Dalmatica, Lingua." *Enciclopedia Italiana.* Rome: Istituto Giovanni Treccani, 1931.

Tagliavini, *Origini* = Tagliavini, Carlo. *Le origini delle lingue neolatine.* 3rd ed. Bologna: Patròn, 1962.

Tiktin = Tiktin, H. "Die rumänische Sprache." *Grundriss der romanischen Philologie.* Ed. Gustav Gröber. Strassburg: Karl J. Trübner, 1904-06. I, 564-607.

Tovar = Tovar, Antonio. "A Research Report on Vulgar Latin and Its Local Variations." *Kratylos,* 9 (1964), 113-34.

Väänänen, *Pompéiennes* = Väänänen, Veikko. *Le Latin vulgaire des inscriptions pompéiennes.* 2nd ed. Abhandlungen der deutschen Akademie der Wissenschaften zu Berlin, No. 3. Berlin: Akademie-Verlag, 1959.

Väänänen, *Introduction* = Väänänen, Veikko. *Introduction au latin vulgaire.* Bibliothèque Française et Romane, Série A: Manuels et Études Linguistiques, 6. Paris: Klincksieck, 1967.

Väänänen, *Review* = Väänänen, Veikko. Review of *Die Sprache der longobardischen Gesetze,* by B. Löfstedt. *Neuphilologische Mitteilungen,* LXII (1961), 221-26.

Vidos = Vidos, B. E. *Manuale di linguistica romanza.* Trans. G. Francescato. Biblioteca dell' "Archivum Romanicum." Serie II. Linguistica, Vol. 28. Geneva: Olschki, 1959.

Vossler = Vossler, Karl. *Einführung ins Vulgärlatein.* Herausgegeben und bearbeitet von Helmut Schmeck. Munich: Max Hueber, 1953.

Wagner, "Lautlehre" = Wagner, Max Leopold. "Historische Lautlehre des Sardischen." *Zeitschrift für romanische Philologie,* Beiheft 90. Halle: Max Niemeyer, 1941.

Wagner, *Lingua sarda* = Wagner, Max Leopold. *La lingua sarda: storia, spirito e forma.* Bibliotheca Romanica, Series prima, Manualia et Commentationes, III. Bern: A. Francke, 1951.

Wagner, "Südsardischen" = Wagner, Max Leopold. "Lautlehre der südsardischen Mundarten." *Zeitschrift für romanische Philologie,* Beiheft 12. Halle: Max Niemeyer, 1907.

Wartburg, *Ausgliederung* = von Wartburg, Walther. *Die Ausgliederung der romanischen Sprachräume.* Bibliotheca Romanica, Series prima, Manualia et Commentationes, VIII. Bern: A. Francke, 1950.

Wartburg, *Origines* = von Wartburg, Walther. *Les Origines des peuples romans.* Trans. Claude Cuénot de Maupassant. Paris: Presses Universitaires de France, 1941.

Wartburg, *Problèmes* = von Wartburg, Walther. *Problèmes et méthodes de la linguistique.* 2nd ed. Trans. Pierre Maillard. Paris: Presses Universitaires de France, 1963.

Weinrich = Weinrich, Harald. *Phonologische Studien zur romanischen Sprachgeschichte.* Forschungen zur romanischen Philologie, Heft 6. Münster, Westfalen: Aschendorffsche, 1958.

REFERENCE GRAMMARS AND DICTIONARIES

Allen and Greenough = Allen and Greenough's *New Latin Grammar*, ed. J. B. Greenough, G. L. Kettredge, A. A. Howard, and Benj. L. D'Ooge. Revised edition. Boston: Ginn and Company, 1916.

Bailly = Bailly, Anatole. *Dictionnaire grec-français*, rédigé avec le concour de E. Egger. 11th ed. Paris: Librairie Hachette, first published in 1894.

DuCange = DuCange, D. D. *Glossarium Mediae et Infinae Latinitatis.* 8 vols. 1883-87; reprint. Graz: Akademische Druck- u. Verlagsanstalt, 1954.

Hale-Buck = Hale, William Gardner, and Buck, Carl Darling. *A Latin Grammar.* Alabama Linguistic and Philological Series, No. 8. 1903; reprint. Alabama: University of Alabama Press, 1966.

Harper's = *Harper's Latin Dictionary: A New Latin Dictionary Founded on the Translation of Freund's Latin-German Lexicon.* Ed. E. A. Andres. Revised, enlarged, and in great part rewritten by Charles T. Lewis and Charles Short. New York: American Book Company, 1907.

Meyer-Lübke, *REW* = Meyer-Lübke, W. *Romanisches etymologisches Wörterbuch.* 3rd ed. Heidelberg: Carl Winter, 1935.

Thesaurus = *Thesaurus Linguae Latinae.* Leipzig: B. G. Teubner, since 1900.

NORTH CAROLINA STUDIES IN THE
ROMANCE LANGUAGES AND LITERATURES

I.S.B.N. Prefix 0-88438

Recent Titles

THE FOUR INTERPOLATED STORIES IN THE "ROMAN COMIQUE": THEIR SOURCES AND UNIFYING FUNCTION, by Frederick Alfred De Armas. 1971. (No. 100). -900-6.

LE CHASTOIEMENT D'UN PERE A SON FILS, A CRITICAL EDITION, edited by Edward D. Montgomery, Jr. 1971. (No. 101). -901-4.

LE ROMMANT DE "GUY DE WARWIK" ET DE "HEROLT D'ARDENNE," edited by D. J. Conlon. 1971. (No. 102). -902-2.

THE OLD PORTUGUESE "VIDA DE SAM BERNARDO," EDITED FROM ALCOBAÇA MANUSCRIPT ccxci/200, WITH INTRODUCTION, LINGUISTIC STUDY, NOTES, TABLE OF PROPER NAMES, AND GLOSSARY, by Lawrence A. Sharpe. 1971. (No. 103). -903-0.

A CRITICAL AND ANNOTATED EDITION OF LOPE DE VEGA'S "LAS ALMENAS DE TORO," by Thomas E. Case. 1971. (No. 104). -904-9.

LOPE DE VEGA'S "LO QUE PASA EN UNA TARDE," A CRITICAL, ANNOTATED EDITION OF THE AUTOGRAPH MANUSCRIPT, by Richard Angelo Picerno. 1971. (No. 105). -905-7.

OBJECTIVE METHODS FOR TESTING AUTHENTICITY AND THE STUDY OF TEN DOUBTFUL "COMEDIAS" ATTRIBUTED TO LOPE DE VEGA, by Fred M. Clark. 1971. (No. 106). -906-5.

THE ITALIAN VERB. A MORPHOLOGICAL STUDY, by Frede Jensen. 1971. (No. 107). -907-3.

A CRITICAL EDITION OF THE OLD PROVENÇAL EPIC "DAUREL ET BETON," WITH NOTES AND PROLEGOMENA, by Arthur S. Kimmel. 1971. (No. 108). -908-1.

FRANCISCO RODRIGUES LOBO: DIALOGUE AND COURTLY LORE IN RENAISSANCE PORTUGAL, by Richard A. Preto-Rodas. 1971. (No. 109). 909-X.

RAIMOND VIDAL: POETRY AND PROSE, edited by W. H. W. Field. 1971. (No. 110). -910-3.

RELIGIOUS ELEMENTS IN THE SECULAR LYRICS OF THE TROUBADOURS, by Raymond Gay-Crosier. 1971. (No. 111). -911-1.

THE SIGNIFICANCE OF DIDEROT'S "ESSAI SUR LE MERITE ET LA VERTU," by Gordon B. Walters. 1971. (No. 112). -912-X.

PROPER NAMES IN THE LYRICS OF THE TROUBADOURS, by Frank M. Chambers. 1971. (No. 113). -913-8.

STUDIES IN HONOR OF MARIO A. PEI, edited by John Fisher and Paul A. Gaeng. 1971. (No. 114). -914-6.

DON MANUEL CAÑETE, CRONISTA LITERARIO DEL ROMANTICISMO Y DEL POSROMANTICISMO EN ESPAÑA, por Donald Allen Randolph. 1972. (No. 115). -915-4.

THE TEACHINGS OF SAINT LOUIS. A CRITICAL TEXT, by David O'Connell. 1972. (No. 116). -916-2.

HIGHER, HIDDEN ORDER: DESIGN AND MEANING IN THE ODES OF MALHERBE, by David Lee Rubin. 1972. (No. 117). -917-0.

JEAN DE LE MOTE "LE PARFAIT DU PAON," édition critique par Richard J. Carey. 1972. (No. 118). -918-9.

CAMUS' HELLENIC SOURCES, by Paul Archambault. 1972. (No. 119). -919-7.

FROM VULGAR LATIN TO OLD PROVENÇAL, by Frede Jensen. 1972. (No. 120). -920-0.

When ordering please cite the *ISBN Prefix* plus the last four digits for each title.

Send orders to: University of North Carolina Press
Chapel Hill
North Carolina 27514
U. S. A.

NORTH CAROLINA STUDIES IN THE ROMANCE LANGUAGES AND LITERATURES

I.S.B.N. Prefix 0-88438

Recent Titles

GOLDEN AGE DRAMA IN SPAIN: GENERAL CONSIDERATION AND UNUSUAL FEATURES, by Sturgis E. Leavitt. 1972. (No. 121). *-921-9.*

THE LEGEND OF THE "SIETE INFANTES DE LARA" (*Refundición toledana de la crónica de 1344* versión), study and edition by Thomas A. Lathrop. 1972. (No. 122). *-922-7.*

STRUCTURE AND IDEOLOGY IN BOIARDO'S "ORLANDO INNAMORATO," by Andrea di Tommaso. 1972. (No. 123). *-923-5.*

STUDIES IN HONOR OF ALFRED G. ENGSTROM, edited by Robert T. Cargo and Emmanuel J. Mickel, Jr. 1972. (No. 124). *-924-3.*

A CRITICAL EDITION WITH INTRODUCTION AND NOTES OF GIL VICENTE'S "FLORESTA DE ENGANOS," by Constantine Christopher Stathatos. 1972. (No. 125). *-925-1.*

LI ROMANS DE WITASSE LE MOINE. *Roman du treizième siècle.* Édité d'après le manuscrit, fonds français 1553, de la Bibliothèque Nationale, Paris, par Denis Joseph Conlon. 1972. (No. 126). *-926-X.*

EL CRONISTA PEDRO DE ESCAVIAS. *Una vida del Siglo XV,* por Juan Bautista Avalle-Arce. 1972. (No. 127). *-927-8.*

AN EDITION OF THE FIRST ITALIAN TRANSLATION OF THE "CELESTINA," by Kathleen V. Kish. 1973. (No. 128). *-928-6.*

MOLIÈRE MOCKED. THREE CONTEMPORARY HOSTILE COMEDIES: *Zélinde, Le portrait du peintre, Élomire Hypocondre,* by Frederick Wright Vogler. 1973. (No. 129). *-929-4.*

C.-A. SAINTE-BEUVE. *Chateaubriand et son groupe littéraire sous l'empire.* Index alphabétique et analytique établi par Lorin A. Uffenbeck. 1973. (No. 130). *-930-8.*

THE ORIGINS OF THE BAROQUE CONCEPT OF "PEREGRINATIO," by Juergen Hahn. 1973. (No. 131). *-931-6.*

THE "AUTO SACRAMENTAL" AND THE PARABLE IN SPANISH GOLDEN AGE LITERATURE, by Donald Thaddeus Dietz. 1973. (No. 132). *-932-4.*

FRANCISCO DE OSUNA AND THE SPIRIT OF THE LETTER, by Laura Calvert. 1973. (No. 133). *-933-2.*

ITINERARIO DI AMORE: DIALETTICA DI AMORE E MORTE NELLA VITA NUOVA, by Margherita de Bonfils Templer. 1973. (No. 134). *-934-0.*

L'IMAGINATION POÉTIQUE CHEZ DU BARTAS: ELEMENTS DE SENSIBILITE BAROQUE DANS LA "CREATION DU MONDE," by Bruno Braunrot. 1973. (No. 135). *-934-0.*

ARTUS DESIRE: PRIEST AND PAMPHLETEER OF THE SIXTEENTH CENTURY, by Frank S. Giese. 1973. (No. 136). *-936-7.*

JARDIN DE NOBLES DONZELLAS, FRAY MARTIN DE CORDOBA, by Harriet Goldberg. 1974. (No. 137). *-937-5.*

MYTHE ET PSYCHOLOGIE CHEZ MARIE DE FRANCE DANS "GUIGEMAR", par Antoinette Knapton. 1975. (No. 142). *-942-1.*

THE LYRIC POEMS OF JEHAN FROISSART: A CRITICAL EDITION, by Rob Roy McGregor, Jr. 1975. (No. 143). *-943-X.*

THE HISPANO-PORTUGUESE CANCIONERO OF THE HISPANIC SOCIETY OF AMERICA, by Arthur Askins. 1974. (No. 144). *-944-8.*

HISTORIA Y BIBLIOGRAFÍA DE LA CRÍTICA SOBRE EL "POEMA DE MÍO CID" (1750-1971), por Miguel Magnotta. 1976. (No. 145). *-945-6.*

When ordering please cite the *ISBN Prefix* plus the last four digits for each title.

Send orders to: University of North Carolina Press
Chapel Hill
North Carolina 27514
U. S. A.

NORTH CAROLINA STUDIES IN THE ROMANCE LANGUAGES AND LITERATURES

I.S.B.N. Prefix 0-88438

Recent Titles

THE DRAMATIC WORKS OF ÁLVARO CUBILLO DE ARAGÓN, by Shirley B. Whitaker. 1975. (No. 149). *-949-9.*

A CONCORDANCE TO THE "ROMAN DE LA ROSE" OF GUILLAUME DE LORRIS, by Joseph R. Danos. 1976. (No. 156). *0-88438-403-9.*

POETRY AND ANTIPOETRY: A STUDY OF SELECTED ASPECTS OF MAX JACOB'S POETIC STYLE, by Annette Thau. 1976. (No. 158). *-005-X.*

STYLE AND STRUCTURE IN GRACIÁN'S "EL CRITICÓN", by Marcia L. Welles, 1976. (No. 160). *-007-6.*

MOLIERE: TRADITIONS IN CRITICISM, by Laurence Romero. 1974 (Essays, No. 1). *-001-7.*

CHRÉTIEN'S JEWISH GRAIL. A NEW INVESTIGATION OF THE IMAGERY AND SIGNIFICANCE OF CHRÉTIEN DE TROYES'S GRAIL EPISODE BASED UPON MEDIEVAL HEBRAIC SOURCES, by Eugene J. Weinraub. 1976. (Essays, No. 2). *-002-5.*

STUDIES IN TIRSO, I, by Ruth Lee Kennedy. 1974. (Essays, No. 3). *-003-3.*

VOLTAIRE AND THE FRENCH ACADEMY, by Karlis Racevskis. 1975. (Essays, No. 4). *-004-1.*

THE NOVELS OF MME RICCOBONI, by Joan Hinde Stewart. 1976. (Essays, No. 8). *-008-4.*

FIRE AND ICE: THE POETRY OF XAVIER VILLAURRUTIA, by Merlin H. Forster. 1976. (Essays, No. 11). *-011-4.*

THE THEATER OF ARTHUR ADAMOV, by John J. McCann. 1975. (Essays, No. 13). *-013-0.*

AN ANATOMY OF POESIS: THE PROSE POEMS OF STÉPHANE MALLARMÉ, by Ursula Franklin. 1976. (Essays, No. 16). *-016-5.*

LAS MEMORIAS DE GONZALO FERNÁNDEZ DE OVIEDO, Vols. I and II, by Juan Bautista Avalle-Arce. 1974. (Texts, Textual Studies, and Translations, Nos. 1 and 2). *-401-2; 402-0.*

GIACOMO LEOPARDI: THE WAR OF THE MICE AND THE CRABS, translated, introduced and annotated by Ernesto G. Caserta. 1976. (Texts, Textual Studies, and Translations, No. 4). *-404-7.*

LUIS VÉLEZ DE GUEVARA: A CRITICAL BIBLIOGRAPHY, by Mary G. Hauer. 1975. (Texts, Textual Studies, and Translations, No. 5). *-405-5.*

UN TRÍPTICO DEL PERÚ VIRREINAL: "EL VIRREY AMAT, EL MARQUÉS DE SOTO FLORIDO Y LA PERRICHOLI". EL "DRAMA DE DOS PALANGANAS" Y SU CIRCUNSTANCIA, estudio preliminar, reedición y notas por Guillermo Lohmann Villena. 1976. (Texts, Textual Studies, and Translation, No. 15). *-415-2.*

LOS NARRADORES HISPANOAMERICANOS DE HOY, edited by Juan Bautista Avalle-Arce. 1973. (Symposia, No. 1). *-951-0.*

ESTUDIOS DE LITERATURA HISPANOAMERICANA EN HONOR A JOSÉ J. ARROM, edited by Andrew P. Debicki and Enrique Pupo-Walker. 1975. (Symposia, No. 2). *-952-9.*

MEDIEVAL MANUSCRIPTS AND TEXTUAL CRITICISM, edited by Christopher Kleinhenz. 1976. (Symposia, No. 4). *-954-5.*

SAMUEL BECKETT. THE ART OF RHETORIC, edited by Edouard Morot-Sir, Howard Harper, and Dougald McMillan III. 1976. (Symposia, No. 5). *-955-3.*

FIGURES OF REPETITION IN THE OLD PROVENÇAL LYRIC: A STUDY IN THE STYLE OF THE TROUBADOURS, by Nathaniel B. Smith. 1976. (No. 176). *0-8078-9176-2.*

THE DRAMA OF SELF IN GUILLAUME APOLLINAIRE'S "ALCOOLS", by Richard Howard Stamelman. 1976. (No. 178). *0-8078-9178-9.*

When ordering please cite the *ISBN Prefix* plus the last four digits for each title.

Send orders to: University of North Carolina Press
Chapel Hill
North Carolina 27514
U. S. A.